MOROCCO

THE ROUGH GUIDE

£1

D1386086

THE ROUGH GUIDES

ROUGH GUIDE CREDITS

Series Editor: Mark Ellingham
Editorial: Martin Dunford, John Fisher, Jack Holland, Jon Buckley,
        Greg Ward and Richard Trillo
Production: Susanne Hillen, Kate Berens, Gail Jammy and Andy Hilliard
Typesetting: Greg Ward and Mark Ellingham

Thanks

This **third edition** of the *Rough Guide to Morocco* owes a great deal to previous **readers and users** who took the trouble to write in with news and information, changes and additions. Thanks to all. In particular: Hamish Brown and Dan Eitzen for their contributions towards the hiking sections; Margaret Hubbard for the piece "From a Woman's Perspective"; Jon Marks for updating the history/politics; Chris Overington for the wildlife section; Jonathan Charteris-Black for his article on *moussems*; Andrew Gilchrist for filling in the gaps in the south; Martin Spafford for his efforts on the Figuig map; David Cocovini for the Telouet–Aït Benhaddou walk; Don Grisbrook, Lee Marshall and Chris Scott for their frequent and generous correspondence; Manuel Dominguez and David Muddyman for the section on music; Nicky Lund, Matthew Tostevin, Julie Jones and Peter Obrenshaw, Martin Humphrey, Peter Tucker, Fransje de Waard, David Poolton and Karin Dreissig, and Mike Easterbrook for spot-on contributions; Dave Driscoll for late-night and last-minute checking; and – above all – Natania Jansz, who helped get the original edition into shape.

Thanks also to the many **Moroccan friends**, acquaintances, guides – everyone – who showed us around and shared knowledge and ideas. We hope this guide reflects a shared enthusiasm.

On the **production** front, thanks, as ever, to Susanne Hillen for keeping everything rolling, to Greg Ward for setting and to Kate Berens for patient and creative proofreading and subediting.

The "Basics" and "Contexts" page illustrations are by Henry Iles; the small illustrations in Part One and Part Three by Ed Briant.

Grateful **acknowledgements** to Paul Bowles for the "Moroccan Fictions"; and to Marion Boyars and Peter Owen, respectively, for permission to reprint the pieces by Paul Bowles and Elias Canetti in the "Writers on Morocco" section.

Published by Harrap Columbus, Chelsea House, Market Square, Bromley, Kent BR1 1NA .

Typeset in Linotron Univers and Century Old Style to an original design by Andrew Oliver.
Printed by Cox & Wyman Ltd, Reading.

© Mark Ellingham and Shaun McVeigh 1990
512p, includes index
Rev. ed. of Morocco: The Rough Guide (1985, 1987, 1988)

British Library Cataloguing-in-Publication

Ellingham, Mark
1. Morocco: the rough guide
I. Title II. McVeigh, Shaun
916. 4'045

ISBN 0–7471–0152–3

MOROCCO
THE ROUGH GUIDE

WRITTEN AND RESEARCHED BY

MARK ELLINGHAM and SHAUN McVEIGH

CONTRIBUTORS

Hamish Brown, Jon Marks, Andrew Gilchrist, Margaret Hubbard,
Peter Morris, Dan Richardson, Dan Eitzen, Manuel Dominguez,
Chris Overington, Dave Driscoll and David Muddyman

EDITED BY

MARK ELLINGHAM

HARRAP-COLUMBUS ■ LONDON

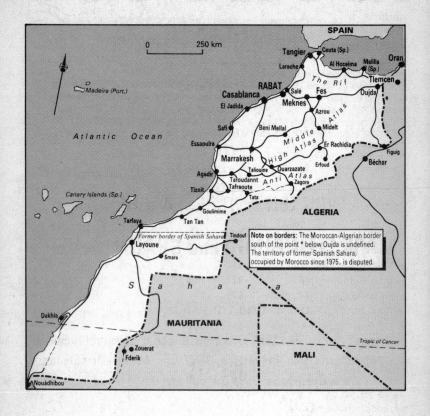

Note on borders: The Moroccan-Algerian border south of the point * below Oujda is undefined. The territory of former Spanish Sahara, occupied by Morocco since 1975, is disputed.

CONTENTS

Introduction viii

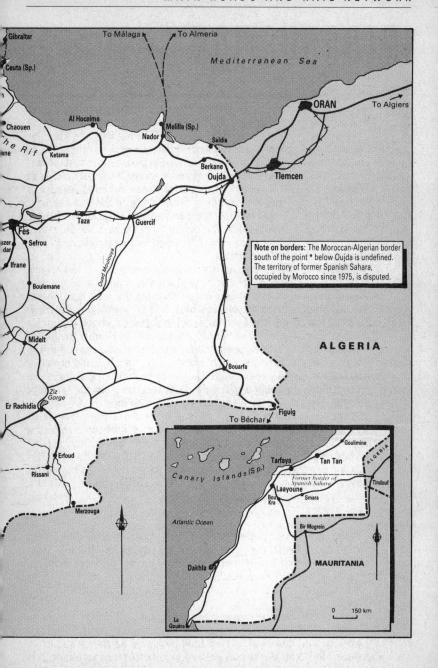

Gibraltar

Ceuta (Sp.)

To Málaga   To Almeria

Mediterranean Sea

Chaouen

Al Hoceima

Melilla (Sp.)

ORAN

To Algiers

Nador

Saidia

he Rif

Ketama

Berkane

Oujda

Tlemcen

Fès

Taza

Guercif

zer
dar

Sefrou

Ifrane

Note on borders: The Moroccan-Algerian border
south of the point * below Oujda is undefined.
The territory of former Spanish Sahara,
occupied by Morocco since 1975, is disputed.

Boulemane

Oued Moulouya

Midelt

ALGERIA

Bouarfa

Ziz
Gorge

Er Rachidia

Figuig

To Béchar

Erfoud

Goulimine

Tarfaya

Tan Tan

ALGERIA

Rissani

Canary Islands (Sp.)

Former border of
Spanish Sahara

Laayoune

Tindouf

Bou
Kra

Smara

Merzouga

Atlantic Ocean

Bir Mogrein

Dakhla

MAURITANIA

0   150 km

La
Gouéra

INTRODUCTION

For Westerners, **Morocco** holds an immediate and enduring fascination. Though just an hour's ride on the ferry from Spain, it seems at once very far from Europe, with a culture – Islamic and deeply traditional – that is almost wholly unfamiliar. Throughout the country, despite the years of French and Spanish colonial rule and the presence of modern and cosmopolitan cities like Rabat or Casablanca, a more distant past constantly makes its presence felt. **Fes**, perhaps the most beautiful of all Arab cities, maintains a life still rooted in medieval times, when a Moroccan empire stretched from Senegal to northern Spain; while in the mountains of the **Atlas** and the **Rif**, it is still possible to draw up tribal maps of the Berber population. As a backdrop to all this, the country's physical make-up is also extraordinary: from a Mediterranean coast, through four mountain ranges, to the empty sand and scrub of the Sahara.

All of which makes **travel** here an intense and rewarding – if not always easy – experience. Certainly, there can be problems in coming to terms with your privileged position as tourist in a nation that, for the most part, would regard such activities as those of another world. And the northern cities especially have a reputation for hustlers: self-appointed guides whose eagerness to offer their services – and whose attitude to tourists as being a justifiable source of income (and to women as something much worse) – can be hard to deal with. If you find this to be too much of a struggle, then it would probably be better to keep to low-key resorts like Essaouira or Asilah, or to the more cosmopolitan holiday destination of Agadir, built very much in the image of its Spanish counterparts, or even a packaged sightseeing tour.

But you'd miss a lot that way. Morocco is at its best well away from such trappings. A week's hiking in the Atlas; a journey through the southern oases or into the pre-Sahara; or leisured strolls around Tangier, Fes or Marrakesh – once you adapt to a different way of life, all your time will be well spent. And it is difficult for any traveller to go for long without running into Morocco's equally powerful tradition of hospitality, generosity and openness. This is a country people return to again and again.

Regions

Geographically, the country divides into five basic zones: the **coast**, Mediterranean and Atlantic; the great cities of the **plains**; the **Rif** and **Atlas** mountains; and the oases and desert of the **pre-** and fully-fledged **Sahara**. With two or three weeks – even two or three months – you can't expect to cover all of this, though it's easy enough (and highly recommended) to take in something of each aspect.

You are unlikely to miss the **mountains**, in any case. The three ranges of the Atlas, with the Rif a kind of extension in the north, cut right across the interior – physical and historical barriers, and inhabited for the most part by the indigenous Moroccan **Berbers**. Contrary to general preconceptions, it is actually the Berbers who make up most of the population; only around ten percent of Moroccans are "pure" Arabs, although with the shift to the industrialised cities, such distinctions are becoming less and less significant.

A more current distinction, perhaps, is the legacy of Morocco's colonial occupation over the fifty-odd years before it reasserted its independence in 1956. The colonised country was divided into **Spanish** and **French** zones – the former contained Tetouan and the Rif, the Mediterranean and the northern Atlantic coasts, and parts of the (now disputed) Western Sahara; the latter comprised the plains and the main cities (Fes, Marrakesh, Casablanca and Rabat), as well as the Atlas. It was the French, who ruled their "protectorate" more closely, who had the most lasting effect on Moroccan culture, Europeanising the cities to a strong degree and firmly imposing their language, which is spoken today by all educated Moroccans (after Moroccan Arabic or the local Berber languages).

Highlights

The attractions of the individual regions are discussed in the chapter introductions. Broadly speaking, **the coast** is best enjoyed in the north at **Tangier**, beautiful and still shaped by its old "international" port status; at **Larache**; or at **Saïdia**, below the Rif; in the south at **El Jadida**; at **Essaouira**, perhaps the most easy-going resort; or at remote **Sidi Ifni**. **Agadir**, the main package tour resort, is less worthwhile – but a functional enough base for exploration.

Inland, where the real interest of Morocco lies, the outstanding cities are **Fes** and **Marrakesh**. The great imperial capitals of the country's various dynasties, they are almost unique in the Arab world for the chance they offer to witness some city life that, in patterns and appearance, remains in large part medieval. For monuments, Fes is the highlight, though Marrakesh, the "beginning of the south", is for most visitors the more enjoyable and exciting.

Travel in the **south** – roughly beyond a line drawn between Casablanca and Meknes – is, on the whole, easier and more relaxing than in the sometimes frenetic north. This is certainly true of the **mountain ranges**. The **Rif**, which can feel disturbingly anarchic, is really for hardened travellers; only **Chaouen**, on its periphery, could be counted a "holiday spot". But the **Atlas ranges** (Middle, High and Anti-) are beautiful and accessible.

Hiking in the **High Atlas**, especially around North Africa's highest peak, **Djebel Toubkal**, is in fact something of a growth industry. Even if you are no more than a casual walker, it is worth considering, with summer treks possible at all levels of experience and altitude. And, despite inroads made by commercialisation, it remains essentially "undiscovered" – like the Alps must have been in the last century.

Equally exploratory in mood are the great **southern routes** beyond – and across – the Atlas, amid the **oases** of the pre-Sahara. Major routes here can be travelled by bus; minor ones by rented car or local taxi; the really remote

Morocco's **area** of 710,000 square kilometres is as great as that of France, Spain or Italy. The **population**, over half of which is under 20 years of age, is around 23 million – a dramatic increase compared with just 8 million at independence in 1956.

ones by four-wheel drive vehicles or by getting lifts on local *camions* (lorries), sharing space with the market produce and livestock.

The oases, around **Tinerhir**, **Zagora** and **Erfoud**, or (for the committed) **Tata** or **Figuig**, are classic images of the Arab world, vast palmeries stretching into desert horizons. Equally memorable is the architecture that they share with the Atlas – bizarre and fabulous mud (or *pisé*) **kasbahs** and **ksour**, with Gothic-looking turrets and multi-patterned walls.

Climate

As far as the **climate** goes, it would be better to visit the south – or at least the desert routes – outside **midsummer**, when for most of the day it's far too hot for casual exploration, especially if you're dependent on public transport. But July and August, the hottest months, can be wonderful on the coast and in the mountains; there are no set rules.

Spring, which comes late by European standards (around April to May), is perhaps the best overall time, with a summer climate in the south and in the mountains, and water warm enough to swim in on both the Mediterranean and Atlantic coasts. **Winter** can be perfect by day in the south, though be warned that desert nights can get very cold – a major consideration if you're staying in the cheaper hotels, which rarely have heating. If you're planning to **hike** in the **mountains**, it's best to keep to the months from April to October unless you have some experience of snow conditions.

Weather conditions apart, the **Islamic religious calendar**, and its related festivals, will have the most seasonal effect on your travel. The most important factor is **Ramadan**, the month of daytime fasting; this can be a problem for transport, and especially hiking, though the festive evenings do much to compensate. See "Festivals" in the *Basics* section following for details of its timing, as well as that of other festivals.

MOROCCO'S CLIMATE

Average Temperatures (°F)

	JAN	FEB	MAR	APR	MAY	JUN	JUL	AUG	SEP	OCT	NOV	DEC
AGADIR	69	70	72	75	76	78	80	79	79	78	76	69
AL HOCEIMA	61	62	65	67	72	78	83	85	81	74	69	63
CASABLANCA	63	63	66	68	72	75	81	81	80	77	68	64
ESSAOUIRA	64	64	64	66	68	68	72	70	70	70	68	66
FES	61	63	66	72	79	88	97	97	90	81	66	61
MARRAKESH	66	66	73	79	84	91	102	101	91	82	70	66
MEKNES	59	61	64	70	74	84	93	93	86	79	66	61
OUARZAZATE	63	67	73	80	86	96	102	100	91	80	70	62
RABAT	63	64	66	70	73	77	82	82	81	77	68	64
TANGIER	59	61	62	66	72	77	80	82	79	73	64	61
TAROUDANNT	72	73	79	81	86	90	99	100	95	90	77	72
ZAGORA	69	73	78	86	93	102	108	106	97	86	78	70

Note these are all very much average temperatures: Zagora often hits 120°F at midday in midsummer, whilst in the Rif and High Atlas mountains, winters can be literally freezing.

PART ONE

THE

BASICS

You tell me you are going to Fes.
Now, if you say you are going to Fes,
that means you are not going.
But I happen to know that you are going to Fes.
Why have you lied to me, you who are my friend?

Moroccan saying quoted in Paul Bowles' *The Spider's House.*

GETTING THERE

The simplest way to get to Morocco is, of course, to fly. There are flights to Tangier, Agadir, Casablanca and Ouarzazate direct from Britain and to other Moroccan airports via Paris. Alternatively, you can travel overland (or fly) to France, Spain or Gibraltar and pick up a ferry from there. All-in package deals are worth considering, too, either for specialist holidays or off-season bargains.

FLIGHTS FROM BRITAIN

Flying to Morocco from Britain, you have the choice between **direct flights** – scheduled or on charters – or, for the cost-conscious, **flying to Spain** and making your way on from there (see the "Ferries" box, following). The main problem with charters is time limitation – most are valid for just one or two weeks. With a scheduled *APEX* flight you can stay for up to three months and fly to one airport and return from another.

DIRECT SCHEDULED FLIGHTS

Direct scheduled flights from London to Morocco are offered by *Royal Air Maroc* (from Heathrow, Terminal 2) and *Gibair* (from Gatwick).

Royal Air Maroc (205 Regent St, London WI; ☎071/439 4361) flies several times a week direct to Tangier, Casablanca, Marrakesh and Agadir, and on Fridays to Ouarzazate. *APEX* fares, booked two weeks in advance, cost around £150–200 to Tangier or Casablanca, £185–220 for Agadir or Marrakesh; flight times are around three hours (five hours for Marrakesh flights via Casablanca).

Gibair, handled by *British Airways* (75 Regent St, London WI; ☎071/439 9584), has flights to Casablanca on Tuesdays and Fridays and to Tangier on Fridays only. Return fares are comparable to those of *RAM*.

SCHEDULED FLIGHTS VIA PARIS

Paris is extremely well connected with Morocco, *Air France* and *Royal Air Maroc* sharing services on routes to Casablanca (4–6 flights daily), Marrakesh (1–2 daily), Agadir (daily), Tangier (daily), Oujda and Fes (3–4 weekly).

For tickets and details of services, including an add-on flight from various destinations in the UK or Europe, contact *Air France* (158 New Bond St, London WI; ☎071/499 9511) or *Royal Air Maroc* (see above).

CHARTER FLIGHTS

The main Moroccan destinations for British charter flights are **Tangier** in the north and **Agadir** in the south, although a few operators also offer **Marrakesh**. The cheapest flights are invariably from London. From here, outside peak periods (July & Aug, Christmas/New Year and Easter), you might find return flights to Tangier or Agadir for as low as £70–100 return. In peak season periods you should expect to pay £180–200 return and may have problems finding a seat.

Looking for a charter fare, it is worth keeping an eye out for full **package holidays**. At certain times of the year major operators like *Thomson* sell off holidays, including accommodation, at prices no greater than the cost of a flight. Lists of tour operators are given on p.8.

FLIGHTS TO SPAIN AND GIBRALTAR

Flights are usually easier to come by to **Spain** than to Morocco, especially if you want to travel from one of the smaller regional British airports. Fares drop as low as £60–80 return to Málaga or Almería (the best destinations for travelling on to Morocco) if you are flexible and strike lucky.

Gibraltar, with low-season scheduled flights on *Gibair* (see above for address) at around £95 return (high season about £130), is a good standby. *Gibraltar Travel Ltd* (24 New Broadway, London W5; ☎081/579 0307) is a specialist agent and useful, too, for information on travel on from Gibraltar to Morocco.

TRAVELLING ON FROM GIBRALTAR

Travelling on from Gibraltar, *Gibair* operate a daily flight to Tangier (Mon–Fri; £40–70 return), a Tuesday flight to Casablanca (£50–110 return), and in winter twice weekly (Mon & Fri) flights to Marrakesh (£80–120 return). Bookings can be made in the UK through *British Airways* or in Gibraltar through *Bland Ltd*, Cloister Building, Irish Town, Gibraltar 79200.

You can also cross over to Tangier on the daily **catamaran** service, again handled in Gibraltar by *Bland Ltd*. For details and frequency of services, see the "Ferries" box.

TRAVELLING ON FROM MÁLAGA

If you get a flight to Málaga, you've a choice of onward travel to Morocco: a ferry direct to **Melilla** (most leave at 2pm: see "Ferries" box) or a bus journey down to Algeciras and the more convenient crossings to **Ceuta or Tangier** (again see "Ferries" box).

Heading for Algeciras, it's a simple journey by bus (there's no direct train route). From Málaga airport, take the train into Málaga (every 20–30min; follow the *Ferrocarril* signs across the car park from the terminal building), and get off at the city's main *RENFE* train station. The bus station is directly across the esplanade as you emerge from the *RENFE* station.

The bus journey from Málaga to Algeciras takes three to five hours depending on traffic. Buses arrive in Algeciras on the seafront, 500m or so east of the ferry terminal, though on the return trip to Málaga most leave from opposite the ferry terminal.

FLIGHT SOURCES AND AGENTS

The best **sources for finding a flight** are the classified advertisements in the travel section of *The Sunday Times* newspaper or (for London) *Time Out*. High street travel agents are also worth a look for reductions on package holidays and charter flights.

Among specialised travel **agents**, *STA Travel* (86 Old Brompton Rd, London SW7; ☎071/937 9921) and *Campus Travel* (52 Grosvenor Gardens, London SW1; ☎071/730 6525) cater for **student/youth** needs, but have a range of fares open to all. And **Morocco specialists** like *CLM*, *Morocco Bound*, and *Moroccan Travel Bureau* will all book flight-only holidays, too. See p.8 for addresses and phone numbers.

FLIGHTS FROM IRELAND

Ireland has no direct flights to Morocco, so the cheapest access is either to pay a tag-on fare for a **transit via London or Paris**, or to travel **via Spain** – Málaga (see above) being the obvious airport choice.

Among agents worth contacting are *Joe Walsh Tours* (8–11 Lower Baggot St, Dublin; ☎789 555), who are usually good for budget fares, and *USIT* (7 Angelsea St, Dublin; ☎778 117), who specialise in student/youth deals.

FLIGHTS FROM AUSTRALASIA

There are no direct flights between Australia or New Zealand and North Africa. The most "direct" route is via **Singapore**, where you can get a *Royal Jordanian* flight to Casablanca. Most Australasian travellers, however, make their way to Morocco **via Britain** – and a flight to London, with tag-on flight or overland transport to Tangier or Agadir, usually works out cheapest.

Reliable **agents** to try for flights to London (and connections on to Morocco) are *STA Travel*, who have offices throughout Australia and New Zealand. Their principal offices are:

AUCKLAND: 10 High St (☎9/399-995)
SYDNEY: 1a Lee St, Sydney (☎02/212-1255)
MELBOURNE: 256 Flinders St (☎03/347-6911).

BY TRAIN

London to Morocco by **train and ferry** takes the best part of three days, but it's a great trip if you have the time to stop en route and take in something of France and Spain. Paris, the Pyrenees, Madrid, Córdoba and Granada all lie pretty much on the route.

Unless you are under 26 (the age qualification for discount *BIGE* tickets or rail passes), however, you will probably end up paying rather more than for a flight.

Train departures are from London's **Victoria Railway Station** (Victoria tube).

REGULAR TICKETS

Standard rail tickets to Tangier, inclusive of the ferries en route, cost just under £200 return. They are available from any *British Rail* travel office, or from *Thomas Cook* and other major travel agents.

For schedules contact the **British Railways** International Information Line (☎071/ 834 2345).

YOUTH TICKETS

BIGE **youth tickets** discount standard rail prices by 20–35 percent. They are marketed in Britain through *Eurotrain* (whose main office is *London Student Travel*, 52 Grosvenor Gardens, London SW1; ☎01/730 3402) and are available from any youth/student travel agency.

The tickets allow any number of stopovers along a pre-specified route and are valid on most European trains (some express services have a surcharge). They are valid for two months if within Europe, but with a Moroccan destination have a six-month validity. Return **fares** from London, inclusive of ferries, are around £175 to Tangier, £180 to Casablanca.

THE INTERRAIL PASS

Morocco is covered by the European **InterRail pass** (currently £155). This buys one month's unlimited travel on trains in Europe and Morocco, along with half-price fares on most ferries (including those from Algeciras to Tangier).

Hidden costs are supplements on express trains and fifty percent of the fares on the channel ferries and between the British station you set out from/return to. The pass is available through youth/student travel agencies or from any major *British Rail* station or travel office.

BY COACH

There are regular **coach services from London to Algeciras**, where you can catch the ferry across to Tangier or Ceuta. However, the 48-hour journey is quite an endurance test and recommended only if you can find no alternative means of reaching Morocco.

The coaches are operated jointly by the British and Spanish companies, *Eurolines* and *Iberbus*. Departures are four times a week from April to September, two a week for the rest of the year.

London to Algeciras costs £125 return, £70 one way; there is a ten percent reduction for students or anyone under 26. For details contact *Eurolines* (52 Grosvenor Gardens, London SW1; ☎071/730 0202) or any *National Express* office in Britain.

Bus departures are from London's **Victoria Coach Station** (Victoria tube).

DRIVING OR HITCHING

If you plan to **drive down to Morocco through Spain and France**, you'll want to set aside a minimum of four days for the journey. The buses detailed above cover the route in 48 hours but they are more or less non-stop, with two drivers and just a few short meal breaks.

There are **car ferries** across to Morocco from Spain at **Almería and Málaga** (to Melilla) and at **Algeciras** (to Ceuta or Tangier). Ferries also sail to Tangier (and to Nador from June to Sept) from **Sète** in France (these tend to be booked far in advance: see the "Ferries" box), and to Tangier from **Faro** on the Portuguese Algarve.

For the Spanish ferries the most direct **route** to drive is:

   London – Dover/Folkestone (channel ferry to Calais/Boulogne); Calais/Boulogne – Paris – Tours – Poitiers – Bordeaux – Bayonne; San Sebastian – Madrid – Jaen/Córdoba; then Jaen – **Almeria**, Córdoba – **Malaga**, or Córdoba – **Algeciras**.

However, there is much to be said for getting off at least some of the main routes in France.

Alternatively, if you are not interested in (or don't have the time for) the French section of the route, it is possible to travel by **car ferry from Plymouth** in England to **Santander** in northern Spain. This ferry runs twice weekly most of the year (no sailings in January); for details and prices phone *Brittany Ferries* in Plymouth (☎0752/21321).

VEHICLE RED TAPE

Driving to Morocco you must take out **Green Card Insurance** (available from insurance companies, or the AA/RAC motoring clubs) for the trip down through Europe. Once in Morocco you will need to take out additional "Frontier Insurance", see p.21.

Entering Morocco, you will need to present your vehicle registration document, which must be in your name or accompanied by a letter from the registered owner. Caravans need temporary importation documents, which are obtainable at the frontier for no charge. Some visitors choose to tip at the frontier, leaving a note in their passport, or engage the services of a tout to get through quickly: a matter of taste. Entering Morocco through the Spanish enclaves of Ceuta or Melilla (the most economic crossings for vehicles), try to avoid, if possible, arriving at the weekend. If there are any problems, you may well be sent back to Ceuta or Melilla to wait until the Monday to sort them out.

European, Australasian and North American **driving licences** are recognised and valid in Morocco, though an International Driving Licence, with its French translations (available from the AA or equivalent motoring organisations) is a worthwhile investment, with its French translations. The **minimum age** for driving in Morocco is 21 years.

See also "Driving in Morocco", p.21.

HITCHING

Hitching down to Morocco through France and Spain, it's worth buying a bus ticket to cover the first part of the journey. You will, in any case, have to pay for a channel ferry ticket, and buses from London to French cities such as Rouen or Tours don't add significantly to that cost, at around £50 return. You could easily spend a lot of time (and money on food and accommodation) hitching out of London or the channel ports.

The worst place of all to hitch is Paris; people can wait days on the roads out of the city – don't try it! Once south of Paris, getting rides becomes a little easier but the position deteriorates again as you cross the border into Spain – and Madrid is another terrible city for hitchers. In fact, once at Madrid, you'll probably save money cutting your losses and saving on accommodation by taking the night train down to Algeciras (about 2000ptas, £12). Harassment is also especially overt in southern Spain and hitching there is not recommended for women travelling alone.

Hitching back from Morocco, starting at the car ferry in **Ceuta** is by far your best bet. It's quite possible you'll get a lift the whole way back to Britain from there. Other useful points to ask around are the **campsites** at **Fes**, **Meknes** and **Martil** (near Tetouan), all traditional last stops.

See "Driving" above, for routes.

THE FERRIES

Crossing to Morocco by ferry – sailing from Europe to Africa – is the most satisfying (and apt) way to arrive in the country. From Spain the trip is just a couple of hours by ferry – or under an hour on the (passenger-only) hydrofoil to Ceuta.

Your main choice is in deciding **which port** to head for.

● Most overland travellers cross from Algeciras to either Ceuta (a Spanish enclave) or Tangier. **Ceuta** is a cheaper crossing – with considerable savings for cars – but for pedestrians it is time-consuming, as you need to get a bus to the Moroccan border and another from there to the somewhat daunting town of Tetouan. **Tangier** is more straightforward, as well as being better placed for public transport, at the beginning of the railway line.

● The longer crossings from Málaga and Almería to **Melilla** (another Spanish enclave) can be useful for drivers, cutting out part of the journey through Spain. So too, if you can get tickets, are the crossings from **Sète** in France to Tangier and Nador.

● The new ferry crossing from **Faro** (Portugal) is a useful route, though there is some uncertainty about its long-term status. Phone ahead for details if you are planning a trip around it.

● After a very shaky start, the pedestrian-only **catamaran** service from **Gibraltar** to Tangier now seems as reliable as the ferries.

● The pedestrian-only **hydrofoil** services from **Algeciras** save time and hassle, but are often block-reserved for tour groups, so at all times of year advance bookings are advisable. At present, the hydrofoil from Tarifa to Tangier (formerly the quickest of all crossings) seems to be permanently suspended.

And it's **important to note**:

● On all the ferries you must complete a **disembarkation form** and have your passport stamped – *before arrival* – at the purser's office. Announcements to this effect are not always made in English. If you don't have a stamp, you'll have to wait until everyone else has cleared frontier and customs controls before being attended to.

● The **ferries to Ceuta, Tangier, and Melilla** are booked solid for three to five days from the beginning of August, and **from those ports to Spain** during the last three to five days of August. This is the holiday month for Moroccans working in France, Belgium and Holland and travelling back to Morocco by car.

SPAIN

● **Algeciras–Tangier** 3–4 crossings daily in summer, 1–2 daily in winter. Passenger £15.50, small car £35; 2hr 30min.

● **Algeciras–Ceuta** 12 crossings daily in summer; 6–8 out. Passenger £7.50, small car £25; 1hr 20min.

*Tickets for Tangier and Ceuta ferries can be bought from any of the **agents** in Algeciras (there are dozens along the front and the road into the city from Málaga) or from the ferry terminal building. It is generally easier to buy from an agent (prices are standard at all outlets), and you can use plastic; the ferry terminal ticket office accepts cash only.*

● **Málaga–Melilla, Almería–Melilla** 1–3 crossings daily, except Sun, from each port from April to early Sept, dropping to 2–3 a week in winter. Passenger £11, small car £33; 6–7hr.

*Both of these Melilla ferries are operated by **Transmediterranea**; tickets are available through Spanish travel agencies, at embarkation points, or in Britain through **Melia Travel** (12 Dover St, London W1; ☎071/499 6731).*

● **Hydrofoils**

Algeciras–Ceuta Mon–Sat 4–5 crossings daily, all year round 9am–8pm, no service on Sun. Passenger £12; 30min.

Algeciras–Tangier 1 crossing daily, except Sun; mid-March to mid-Sept only. Passenger £16; 1hr.

*Hydrofoils are operated by **Transtour** (☎956/ 665200) and do not run in rough weather. Tickets can be bought either at points of embarkation or in advance from Spanish travel agencies.*

PORTUGAL

● **Faro–Tangier** Leaves Faro at 11am on Mon/ Thurs/Sat, arriving Tangier 9pm; passenger £42, small car £80.

*There are plans to start this route further west along the Algarve at Portimão. Book through local agents on the Algarve or **ACP Viages**, Rua Rosa Araugo 49a, 1200 Lisboa (01/527-858 or 01/560-382). Handled by **COMANAV** in Morocco.*

GIBRALTAR

● **Gibraltar–Tangier** Daily **catamaran** service (except Thurs and Sat) in season; 3–4 a week out of season; service usually suspended in February. Passenger £18 one-way, £30 *Seapex* return; 2hr.

● **Gibraltar–M'diq Catamaran service** every Thursday, mid-March to mid-Sept. Passenger £16 one-way; 1hr 30min.

Details from Seagle Ltd, 9b George's Lane, Gibraltar; (☎71415 or ☎76763).

FRANCE

● **Sète–Tangier** 2 crossings weekly in summer, 1 weekly in winter; 36hr.

● **Sète–Nador** 1 crossing weekly, June–Sept only; 38hr.

*Bookings well in advance are essential for Sète ferries. UK agent: **Continental Shipping and Travel Ltd**, 179 Piccadilly, London W1V 0BA (☎071/491 4968). In Morocco, book tickets through **COMANAV** offices in Tangier, Casablanca, Marrakesh or Agadir (see local "Listings" sections in the main guide).*

HIKING, SPECIALIST AND PACKAGE OPERATORS

Morocco is covered by many of the **mainstream tour operators**, whose package deals can be excellent value if you are looking for a flight and resort base. In addition, however, there are a number of **specialist companies** offering a range of small group **hiking** and **overland tours**, or specialist, **tailor-made holidays**.

HIKING TOURS

Sherpa Expeditions, 131a Heston Rd, Hounslow, Middlesex, TW5 0RD (☎01/577 2717). Choice of four fifteen-day tours in the High Atlas (Toubkal area and little-explored Mgoun Massif) and Djebel Sahro. Most treks are fine for any fit walker, though there is also a strenuous Atlas High Peaks tour for the experienced only.

Exodus Expeditions, 9 Weir Rd, London SW12 0LT (☎01/675 5550). Fifteen-day High Atlas and Djebel Sahro treks.

Explore Worldwide, 1 Frederick St, Aldershot, Hants (☎0252/344161). Fifteen-day High Atlas treks, Anti-Atlas trekking tour, desert truck tours.

Waymark Holidays, 295 Lillie Road, London SW6 7LL (☎071/385 5015). Unusual sixteen-day tour of the Western High Atlas/Djebel Sirwa (trekking out from Taroudannt/Taliouine), and fourteen-day tour including some hiking in the Todra Gorge.

Note: High Atlas tours are offered in spring, summer and autumn. In winter these are areas for experienced hikers only; south-facing areas such as the Djebel Sahro, Anti-Atlas (Tafraoute region) and Djebel Sirwa are offered instead.

OVERLAND EXPEDITION TOURS

Guerba, 101 Eden Vale Rd, Westbury, Wilts (☎0373/826611). Two-week tours in customised trucks of the "Moroccan Deserts and Mountains", and "Deep South" (Anti-Atlas region).

Encounter Overland, 267 Old Brompton Rd, London SW5 (☎071/370 6845). Fifteen-day tour of Morocco including a trip up the Todra Gorge and on southern pistes, again in customised trucks.

Top Deck, 64–65 Kenway Rd, London SW5 (☎071/ 373 5095). Tours of Morocco and southern Spain in converted London double-decker buses. Younger clientele than the companies above, and a perennial favourite with Australians in Europe.

Discover, Timbers, Oxted Rd, Godstone, Surrey RA9 8AD (☎0883/744392). Three or four tours each year, taking in some Atlas trekking and overland transit down to Zagora and the desert.

MOROCCAN SPECIALISTS

CLM ("Morocco Made to Measure"), 4a William St, London SW1 (☎071/235 2110). Highly flexible and reliable agency, who will arrange flights and personally planned holidays. These range from out of the way 2* auberges to luxury hotels. Upmarket but value for money.

Best of Morocco, Seend Park, Seend, Wiltshire SN12 6NZ (☎0380/828533). A similar service to *CLM*, with accommodation in quality hotels. They print a specialist brochure on golfing holidays.

Moroccan Sun, Suite 202, Triumph House, 189 Regent St, London W1 (☎071/437 3968).

Morocco Bound, Suite 603, Triumph House, 189 Regent St, London W1 (☎071/734 5307).

Moroccan Travel Bureau, 304 Old Brompton Rd, London SW5 (☎071/373 4411).

These three companies offer tailor-made holidays, though they concentrate more on budget priced flight and accommodation packages in the main cities and resorts. Note that Moroccan Sun *and* Morocco Bound *are entirely separate companies, despite sharing the same address.*

MAINSTREAM PACKAGE OPERATORS

The advantage of mainstream operators rests in getting a good value deal on flight plus resort accommodation; some can offer excellent rates, too, on stays at the country's top hotels, like the Mamounia in Marrakesh, El Minzah in Tangier or Palais Jamai in Fes. Phone around the following – or check travel agents – for brochures and prices.

Cadogan ☎0703/332551.

Horizon ☎021/632 6282.

Redwing ☎0293/560777.

Martin Rooks ☎071/730 0808.

Sovereign ☎0293/517866.

Thomson ☎071/387-8484.

Wings ☎021/632-6282.

RED TAPE AND EXTENDED STAYS

If you hold a full passport from Britain, Ireland, Australia, New Zealand, the Scandinavian countries or North America, you require no visa to enter Morocco for up to ninety days. Among European nations, only Dutch and Belgian citizens need visas – imposed in response to restrictions placed on visiting Moroccans. In theory (though not, it seems, in practice), entry to Morocco is refused to anyone with an Israeli or South African stamp in their passport. If this applies to you, a replacement passport might be worth obtaining. Note that British Visitor's Passports are not valid for entering Morocco.

When **entering the country**, formalities are fairly straightforward, though you will have to fill in a form stating personal details, purpose of visit and your **profession**. In recent years, Moroccan authorities have shown an occasional reluctance to allow in those who categorise themselves as "journalist"; an alternative profession on the form might be wise. Hippies, too, engender official disfavour; very long hair is best discreetly tied.

Note that items such as **electronic equipment and video cameras** are entered on your passport. If you lose them during your visit, they will be assumed "sold" when you come to leave and (unless you have police documentation of theft) you will have to pay 100 percent duty. All goods on your passport should be "cleared" when leaving to prevent problems on future trips.

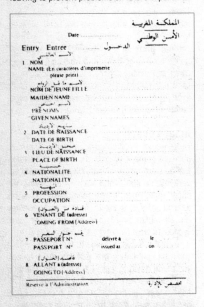

VISA EXTENSIONS

To **extend your stay** in Morocco you should – officially – apply to the *Bureau des Etrangers* in the nearest main town for a residence permit (see below). This is, however, a very complicated procedure and it is usually possible to get around the bureaucracy by simply leaving the country for a brief time when your three months is up. If you decide to try this – and it is not foolproof – it is best to make a trip of at least a few days outside Morocco, to Algeria or Spain. Some people just go to the enclave of Ceuta; the more cautious re-enter the country at a different post.

OFFICIAL BUSINESS

Extending a stay officially involves opening a bank account in Morocco (a couple of days' procedure in itself) and obtaining an *Attestation de Residence* from your hotel, campsite, or landlord. You will need a minimum of 14,000dh (£1100) deposited in your bank account before making an application.

Once you have got through these two stages, you need to go to the **Bureau des Etrangers** equipped with: your passport; seven passport photos; two copies of the *Attestation de Residence*; two copies of your bank statement (*Compte de Banque*); and a 60dh stamp (available from any *Tabac*). If the police are not too busy they'll give you a form to fill out in duplicate and, some weeks later, you should receive a plastic-coated permit with your photo laminated in.

For anyone contemplating this labyrinthine operation, the *Bureau des Etrangers* in **Agadir** is perhaps the simplest place to approach, since a number of expatriates live in the city and banking facilities there (try the *Banque Populaire)* are fairly efficient. The *Bureau is* located behind the fire station on Rue du 18 Novembre.

MOROCCAN CONSULATES ABROAD

Britain: 49 Queens Gate Gardens, London SW7 (☎071/581 5001).

Australia: 2 Phillis Lane, North Curl Curl, Sydney NSW (☎649.6019).

USA: *Embassy.* 1601 21st St NW, Washington DC (☎462-7979). *Consulate:* 597 5th Av., New York (☎758-2625).

Canada: 38 Range Rd, Ottawa (☎236-7391).

Netherlands: Oranje Nassaulaan 1-1075, Amsterdam (☎736-215).

Denmark: Oregarrds Allé 19, 2900 Hellerup, Copenhagen (☎62.45.11).

Sweden: Kungsholmstorg 16, Stockholm (☎54.43.83).

Spain: *Embassy.* Serrano 179, Madrid (☎458.0950). *Consulates:* Rambla de Catalunya 78, Barcelona (☎32.99.66); Av. de Andalucia 63, Málaga (☎952/329962); Av. de Francisco 4, Algeciras (☎67.36.98).

COSTS AND MONEY

Once you've arrived, Morocco is an inexpensive and excellent value destination. Costs for food, accommodation and travel are all low by European standards, and the pound is at its highest level for some years against the Moroccan dirham. If you stay in the cheaper hotels (or camp out), eat local food, and share expenses and rooms with another person, £50 a week would be enough to survive on. On £80 to £100 you could actually live pretty well, and with £250 to £350 a week between two people, you would be approaching luxury.

SOME BASIC COSTS

Accommodation costs range from about £2–5 a night for a double room in a basic, unclassified hotel to a cool £160–200 a night in the country's half-dozen luxury palaces. On a limited budget, you can expect to get a decent double room in a one- or two-star hotel for around £5–8. The occasional splurge in a four-star hotel, with a pool, will cost around £20–30 for a double room off season, £30–45 at peak periods.

The price of a **meal** reflects a similar span, but the basic Moroccan staple of soup (usually the bean-based *harira*), brochettes or *tajine* (casserole) can be had in a local café for around £1–1.50. More substantial Moroccan meals can be had for £2.50–3.50 and European-style meals in restaurants from around £4. **Drinks** are really the only things that compare unfavourably with European prices: a bottle of Moroccan wine costs

upwards of £3 and a small glass of beer about 60p – a lot more in the fancy hotels, which are sometimes a city's only outlets serving alcohol.

Beyond accommodation and food, your major outlay will be for **transport** – expensive if you're hiring a car (£200 a week plus petrol), but reasonable if you use the local trains, buses, and collective taxis. The 475km trip from Fes to Marrakesh, for instance, costs around £10 by bus, or perhaps £14 if you use the faster collective taxis.

REGIONAL VARIATIONS

To some extent, all of these costs are affected by **where you are and when**. Inevitably, the big **cities** and **resorts** (Agadir especially) prove more expensive, with bottom-line hotel prices up to around £7 a night for a double. In more **remote parts** of the country, too, where all goods have to be brought in from some distance away and where transport (often only lorries or Land Rovers) has to be negotiated, prices can be even steeper; this is particularly true of the popular hiking region of Djebel Toubkal.

HIDDEN COSTS

Hidden costs in Morocco are twofold. The most obvious, perhaps, is that you'll almost certainly end up buying a few things. Moroccan **crafts** are very much a part of the fabric of the towns and cities, with their labyrinthine areas of *souks* (markets). Rugs, blankets, leather and jewellery are all outstanding – and few travellers leave without at least one of these items.

A harder aspect to come to terms with is that you'll be confronting real **poverty**. As a tourist, you're not going to solve any problems, but with a labourer's wages at around 3 dirhams (20p) an hour, and an unemployment rate in excess of 25 percent, even a small tip to a guide can make a lot of difference to individual family life. For Moroccans, giving money and goods is a natural function – and a requirement of Islam. For tourists, rich by definition, local poverty demands at least some response.

CURRENCY

Morocco's basic unit of **currency** is the **dirham** (dh). The dirham is not quoted on international money markets, a rate being set instead by the

Moroccan government. Recently, £1 sterling has hovered between 14 and 15 dirhams – almost 40 percent more than its value in the mid-1980s.

The dirham is divided into 100 **centimes** (5-, 10-, and 20-centime coins are in circulation), and in markets you may well find prices written or expressed in centimes rather than dirhams. Confusingly, centimes may also be referred to as *francs* or, in former Spanish zones of the country, as *pesetas*. And you may also hear prices quoted in **rials**, or *reales*. In most parts of the country a dirham is considered to be 20 *rials*, though in Tangier and the Rif there are just 2 *rials* to the dirham. These are forms of expression only, however. There are no actual physical Moroccan *rials*, *francs*, or *pesetas*.

It is possible to buy a small amount of dirhams at the bank exchange desks in the Algeciras ferry terminus, but the currency is basically **not exchangeable outside Morocco**, and there are, in any case, regulations against taking dirhams out of the country. When you're nearing the end of your stay, it's best to get down to as little Moroccan money as possible. To change money back from dirhams, you will be asked to produce exchange receipts – and you can change back only fifty percent of sums detailed on these.

CARRYING YOUR MONEY

Arriving in Morocco it is useful to have at least two days' survival money in **cash**. English pounds, US dollars, French francs or Spanish pesetas are easy to exchange. If you are coming from Britain, beware that **Scottish currency** is not accepted in any Moroccan banks.

The rest of your money should, ideally, be spread around different forms – Eurocheques, travellers' cheques or Girocheques and plastic – for the sake of security.

Travellers' cheques and cash are easily exchanged at most Moroccan banks, and at some hotels, travel agencies and tourist shops. **Eurocheques** are widely accepted at banks, too, with a limit on each of 1500dh (about £115). In the UK they are available from all major banks, in bundles of ten cheques each. **International Girocheques** (available through European post offices) can be changed at any sizeable Moroccan post office.

VISA and **Access** (*Mastercard*) can also be used to obtain cash at some banks (see below), as well as in payment at a few upmarket hotels,

restaurants and tourist shops, and for car hire. Using credit cards you may be asked to pay the card's six percent commission: it's worth bargaining – a compromise can usually be arrived at.

BANKS AND EXCHANGE

For exchange purposes, by far the most useful and efficient chain of banks is the **BMCE** (*Banque Marocaine du Commerce Exterieur*). There is at least one *BMCE* in all major cities and they are dotted about in smaller towns (see listings in the text of the guide). Their *bureaux de change* are open every day, including weekends, from 8am to 8pm. They handle travellers' cheques (2dh commission) and Eurocheques (no commission), and give cash advances on *VISA* and *Access*, as well as currency exchange.

The **Banque Credit du Maroc** also handle *VISA*. Most other banks don't often have facilities for credit-card transactions, despite the stickers in their windows, though most will exchange cash, Eurocheques and travellers' cheques. If you are travelling in the south, where often the **Banque Populaire** alone is represented, don't expect to be able to use credit cards outside the few principal cities.

HOURS, COMMISSION AND EXCHANGE
Hours for banks other than the *BMCE* are normally Monday to Friday, 8.30am to 11.30am and 3pm to 4.30pm in winter; in summer and during Ramadan (see "Festivals") from 8.30am to 2pm. In major resorts there is usually one or more bank that keeps flexible hours on *bureau de change* to meet tourist demand.

Commission is not generally charged on exchange, though some branches of the *Banque Populaire* seem to make a charge of 40dh per transaction (irrespective of the amount exchanged).

Banks tend to take quite a while to **exchange money**, with customers generally filling in forms at one desk, then joining a second queue for the cashier. **Allow an hour** for a transaction in most banks, more if you need to draw cash on a credit card. Cashing travellers' cheques, you may be asked to produce the receipts for purchase.

AMERICAN EXPRESS

American Express is represented by the *Voyages Schwartz* agencies in Tangier, Casablanca, Marrakesh and Agadir. Their agency in Rabat is at present closed, though it is scheduled to reopen in the *Hyatt Regency* hotel. At all these offices, not every *American Express* service is available. *Voyages Schwartz* can cash and issue *AmEx* travellers' cheques, and hold clients' mail, but they cannot cash personal cheques or receive wired money.

Addresses are:

TANGIER: *Voyages Schwartz*, 54 Bd. Pasteur (☎334.59).

CASABLANCA *Voyages Schwartz*, 112 Av. du Prince Moulay Abdallah (☎27.80.54).

MARRAKESH *Voyages Schwartz*, Rue Mauritania (☎328.31).

AGADIR: *Voyages Schwartz*, Av. Hassan II (☎228.94).

Most **offices are open** Monday to Friday 8.30am to 12.30pm and 3pm to 6pm, though banking services are sometimes mornings only.

EMERGENCY CASH

Despite the number of travellers' tales, very few people lose (or are conned out of) all their money in Morocco – but it does happen. Access to an **emergency source** of money – whether it be a credit card or an arrangement with your bank or family to wire you money after a phone call – is reassuring and may prove invaluable.

As a last resort, your **consulate** is duty-bound to offer some assistance – though this will rarely go as far as lending you the money to continue a holiday, or even to fly home unless you accept "repatriation". For addresses, see p.17.

HEALTH AND INSURANCE

For most minor health complaints, a visit to a *pharmacie* is likely to be sufficient. Moroccan pharmacists are well trained and dispense a wide range of drugs, including many normally on prescription in Europe. If they feel you need a full diagnosis, they can usually recommend a doctor – sometimes working on the premises. A list of English- and French-speaking doctors in major cities can also be obtained from consulates, large hotels and some tourist offices.

If you need **hospital treatment**, contact your consulate at once and follow their advice. If you are near a major city, reasonable treatment may be available locally. Morocco, however, is no country in which to fall seriously ill.

INOCULATIONS

There are no **inoculations** officially required of travellers, although you should always be up-to-date with polio and tetanus. Typhoid and cholera are widespread, so a shot against these is worthwhile, too – although some doctors doubt the effectiveness of the cholera shot. **Malaria pills** (preferably *Chloroquine* taken weekly) are also advisable if you're travelling in the south, and **Gamma-globulin** is advised by some doctors as protection against hepatitis.

If you haven't had a typhoid shot then buy some *Intétrix* capsules (available from any pharmacy in Morocco). These are excellent antibacterial medication – useful for diarrhoea as well as typhoid prevention – and some doctors consider them more effective than inoculation. They are certainly valuable if you are travelling for any length of time in the South.

WATER AND HEALTH HAZARDS

The **tap water** in northern Morocco is generally safe to drink (in Chaouen, for example, it is pumped straight from a well), though in the south it's best to stick to bottled mineral water.

A more serious problem in the south is that many of the **river valleys and oases** are said to be infected with **bilharzia**, so avoidance of all contact with oasis water is a wise precaution. Care should be taken, too, in drinking water from **mountain streams**. In areas where there is livestock upstream **giardiasis** is prevalent. Using water purification tablets and boiling any drinking or cooking water would be sensible.

DIARRHOEA

At some stage in your Moroccan travels, it is likely that you will get **diarrhoea**. As a first stage of treatment it's best simply to adapt your diet. Yoghurt is an effective stomach settler and cactus fruit (widely available in summer) are good, too. Steer clear of other fruit and keep up your body fluids by drinking quantities of bottled water and tea.

If this course doesn't shake it off in a couple of days, you could obtain **carbosylate capsules** (eg *Carbosylane*) from a chemist, or, if you have an "enteric" type attack (with cramps, for example), ***Imodium***. It is important, especially for children, not to exceed the suggested doses; *Imodium* is a morphine-related drug.

OTHER HAZARDS

There are few natural hazards in northern Morocco, whose wildlife is not far different to that of Mediterranean Europe. If you venture into the Sahara, however, be aware of the very real dangers of a bite from a **snake**, **palm rat** or **scorpion**. Several of the Saharan snakes are deadly, as is the palm rat. Bites should be treated as medical emergencies.

A much more common problem for travellers is **heatstroke**. Make sure you are adequately protected against the sun, or you will be extremely vulnerable to attacks – resulting, most commonly, in headaches and nausea.

AIDS

Moroccan cities such as Tangier and Marrakesh have a reputation as gay resorts – diminished these days, but still evident. There is very little awareness of AIDS (or *SIDA*, as it is called in French), although the Moroccan Health Ministry has been represented at recent AIDS conferences. At present, official statistics of AIDS sufferers in Morocco are only just in double figures, but if the European experience is anything to go by, they are likely to rise quickly.

As throughout the world, the need for extreme caution, and safe sex, cannot be overstressed.

INSURANCE

Travel insurance can buy you peace of mind as well as save you money. Before you purchase any insurance, however, check what you have already. North Americans, in particular, may find themselves covered for medical expenses and loss, and possibly loss of or damage to valuables, while abroad, as part of a family or student policy. Some credit cards, too, now offer insurance benefits if you use them to pay for tickets.

If you are travelling for any real length of time, however, you are likely to find additional or **specific travel insurance** reassuring. Most policies on offer – which can be bought through virtually any bank or travel agent – are quite comprehensive, anticipating everything from charter companies going bankrupt to delayed (as well as lost) baggage, by way of sundry illnesses and accidents.

Premiums are what vary. At the budget end there are good policies for under £20 a month; at the other, there are those so expensive that the cost for two or three months of coverage will approach the cost of the worst possible combination of disasters. It pays to shop around. *ISIS*, formerly a "student" policy but now open to everyone, is reliable and fairly good value; operated by *Endsleigh*, it is available through any student/youth travel agency.

REIMBURSEMENT

All insurance policies work by **reimbursing you** once you return home, so be sure to keep all your receipts from doctors and pharmacists. Any thefts should be reported immediately to the nearest police station and a police report obtained; no report, no refund.

If you have had to undergo serious medical treatment, with major hospital bills, contact your consulate. They can normally arrange for an insurance company, or possibly relatives, to cover the fees, pending a claim.

INFORMATION, MAPS AND HIKING BOOKS

Besides this book, the most readily available (and obvious) sources of information on Morocco are the country's tourist board (the ONMT), its offices and Syndicats d'Initiatives located throughout Morocco, and local, often self-appointed, guides (see the section following).

TOURIST OFFICES

The **ONMT** maintains general information offices in several European capitals (see box below), where you can pick up a limited range of pamphlets and lists. The most useful of these – indeed, the one thing really worth a phone call to acquire – is the complete **list of officially rated hotels**. We've included numerous small hotels in this book that aren't classified in the ONMT book, and many more that are, but there might be times when you'll find it useful as a backup or to check on facilities or booking agents.

It is also worth picking up the ONMT's series of **pamphlets** on **Tangier**, **Rabat-Salé**, **Casablanca**, **Fes**, **Marrakesh**, and **Agadir**. Each has large and colourful maps printed on the reverse; the maps in this guide are more functional, but these are bigger and often cover a wider area, so they are vaguely useful complements.

In Morocco itself, there's either a **Syndicat** or **ONMT** office in all towns of any size or interest – often both; their addresses are detailed in the relevant sections of the guide. Occasionally, these offices can supply you with particular local information sheets and they can of course try to help you out with specific questions. Their main use, though, is to get you in touch with an officially recognised guide.

ROADMAPS

Maps of Moroccan **cities**, beyond those we've printed and the ones you can get for free from the ONMT, are not particularly worthwhile. The most authoritative local series, the **Plan-Guides** published by *Editions Gauthey*, look impressive but are next to useless once you're trying to find your way around the lanes of a medina.

What you will probably want, though, is a good **road map**. The best are those published by *Michelin* (1:1,000,000; sheet 169; generally the most accurate), *Kummerley & Frey* (1:1,000,000), and *Hildebrand* (1:900,000; new and very clear).

Note that maps (or guidebooks) which do not show the **former Spanish Sahara (Western Sahara)** as Moroccan territory are liable to confiscation. Even maps showing a reduced scale version of the territory can be confiscated. The previous edition of this guide was withdrawn from sale in Morocco due to its maps (this one should be acceptable) as was the old edition of the *Michelin* guide.

ONMT OFFICES ABROAD

Australia
c/o Moroccan Consulate, 11 West St, Sydney NSW 2060 (☎9576.717).

Britain
205 Regent St, London W1(☎071/437 0073).

Netherlands
150 Roking Le, Amsterdam 1012 (☎240025/239089).

Spain
C/Quintana 2 (2°e), Madrid (☎5427431).

Sweden
Sturegatan 16, Stockholm 11436 (☎66099/66013).

There are no Moroccan tourist offices in the other Scandinavian nations, nor in Ireland.

HIKING MAPS AND GUIDES

The Moroccan government periodically clamps down on distribution of **topographic maps** – which are, of course, invaluable to hikers. At present, the policy is that no such maps are available, even the 1:50,000 sheet covering Djebel Toubkal, the country's major hiking destination.

If you have plans to hike, it is therefore well worth contacting **specialist map outlets** before you leave, in case they have old stock. *Stanfords* (12–14 Long Acre, London WC2E 9LP; ☎071/836 1321) and *McCarta* (122 Kings Cross Rd, London WC1X 9DS; ☎071/278 8276) are worth trying, as are the mail order *Atlas Maps* (21 Carlin Craig, Kinghorn, Fife, KY3 9RX, Scotland; sae with all correspondence) and *West Col* (Goring, Reading, Berks, RG8 9AA). In Morocco you may be able to pick up a map of Toubkal on the spot in Imlil, the trailhead for hikes in the area.

In addition to the official Moroccan survey maps, you may be able to find a French satellite-generated 1:100,000 map of *Toubkal/Sirwa* (Editions Astrolabe), while *Atlas Maps* (see above) produce very useful, photocopied map-guides to the Asni-Toubkal, Western High Atlas (Taroudannt) and Sirwa (Taliouine) areas. Written by our High Atlas contributor, Hamish Brown, these are useful complements to our coverage – and constantly updated.

Other, more **detailed hiking guides** are also available in both English and French. The most useful are Michael Peyron's *Grand Atlas Traverse* (West Col; 2 vols; £11.95 each), Robin Collomb's *Atlas Mountains* (West Col; £10.95) and Karl Smith's *Atlas Mountains: A Walker's Guide* (Cicerone Press; £9.95). The two Moroccan walks detailed in Hamish Brown's *Great Walking Adventure* (Oxford Illustrated Press; £12.95) are also well worth a read.

If you can get to London en route, you might also want to consult some of the Expedition Reports at the **Royal Geographical Society** (1 Kensington Gore, London SW7); the RGS's ***Expeditionary Advisory Centre*** (☎071/581 2057) will help locate relevant material, maps and reports.

GUIDES AND HUSTLERS

The question of whether to employ a guide will be one of your first (and most frequent) decisions in Morocco. With tourism so important a part of the economy, guiding has become quite a business – especially in the major cities of Fes and Marrakesh. In addition to the guides trained by the government, there are scores of young Moroccans offering their services to show you around the *souks* **(markets) and sights. The "unofficial guides" are not, strictly, legal, and there are occasional crackdowns by the police on offenders. However, they remain very much a factor of tourist life.**

With all guides, it is important to establish what you want to see. You may well find it useful to agree an itinerary in advance – perhaps showing your guide the points you want to visit on the maps in this book. Do not be pushed into a tour of the craft stores – where your guide will be looking for commission on purchases – or you will see nothing else. If you do want to visit shops, make it clear what kind of goods you are interested in seeing, and equally clear that you do not want to purchase on an initial visit.

OFFICIAL GUIDES

Official guides, engaged through tourist offices (or some of the larger hotels), are paid at a fixed rate for either a half or a full day – respectively 30dh (£2.10) and 50dh (£3.50). The rate is for the guide's time, and can be shared by a group of people – though obviously the latter would be expected to make some additional tip.

Taking an introductory tour of a new city with an official guide can be a useful exercise in orientation – especially in the vast *medinas* (old quarters) of Fes and Marrakesh. Your guide may well be an interesting and entertaining presence, too. Some are highly knowledgeable. There is an advantage also in that, if you are accompanied by an official guide, you won't be approached or hassled by any of their (sometimes less than reputable) unauthorised equivalents.

Official guides can identify themselves by a large, brass "sheriff's badge".

UNOFFICIAL GUIDES AND HUSTLERS

Unofficial guides will approach you in the streets of any sizeable town, offering to find you a hotel, show you the sights, or perhaps, if you look a likely customer, sell you some *kif* (hashish). You will need to develop a strategy to deal with these approaches, otherwise you are unlikely to enjoy urban Morocco.

The most important point to realise is that there are **good and bad guides**. Some are genuine students, who may want to earn a small fee, but may equally be interested (as so many claim) in practising their English. Others are out-and-out hustlers, preying on first-visit innocence and paranoia. Your task is to distinguish between offers, to accept (perhaps limited) services from those who seem friendly and enjoyable company, and to deal as humanly as possible with approaches you wish to decline. There is rarely any harm in agreeing to let a guide show you to a hotel, though it is best to know which you want to go to – check our listings before arrival.

At other times, when you are approached for a tour of the town, you may well want to avoid the offer. To do so, it is a golden rule to look as if you know where you are going. Never admit to this being your first visit to Morocco. If you feel confident enough, say that you have visited the town before and that you are glad to be back. You will be on your way to setting the parameters of discussion. The most exploitative guides will probably drop you to look elsewhere. If you are unsure of a guide, suggest taking a mint tea together in a café. Don't make any agreement to employ him prior to this, or any suggestion of an agreement. Never allow yourself to be bullied into going with someone with whom you don't feel at ease. There is no shortage of candidates.

If you do decide to hire an unofficial guide, be sure to fix the rate, as well as the itinerary, in advance. You should make it clear that you know the official rates for guides and should agree on these as a maximum. Many unofficial guides will attempt to charge a rate per person.

Finally, forewarned is forearmed, so **a few notes on the most common scams**:

● As stressed in the introduction, all guides have an interest in getting you into craft shops. Even if you say you're not interested, they may suggest taking tea with a cousin who owns a shop. Don't be afraid to keep to your agreed itinerary.

● A favourite line is that there is a Berber market taking place – and this is the only day of the week to see it. This is rarely true. You will probably visit everyday shops and *souks*.

● Some of the more exploitative hustlers will guide you into the *medinas*, then, when you have no idea where you are, charge a large fee to take you back out and to your hotel. If this happens to you, don't be afraid to appeal to people in the street; your hustler may not enjoy attention.

● A few tales are told each year of people approaching visitors with a letter or package to mail to the USA or Europe when you leave Morocco. Never agree to this; you may be involving yourself in a drugs plant.

ATTITUDES AND BEHAVIOUR

If you want to get the most from a trip to Morocco, it is vital not to start assuming anyone who approaches or talks to you is a hustler. Too many tourists do, and end up making little contact with what must be one of the most hospitable peoples in the world.

Behaviour and attitude are equally important on your part. If some Moroccans treat tourists with contempt, and exploit them as a simple resource, it has much to do with the way the latter behave. It helps everyone if you can avoid **rudeness** or aggressive behaviour in response to insistent offers from guides. And be aware, too, of the importance of **dress**: shorts are acceptable only on the beach, in resorts; shirts (for both sexes) should cover your arms.

Photography needs to be undertaken with care. If you are obviously taking a photograph of someone, ask their permission – especially in the more remote, rural regions where you can cause genuine offence. On a more positive front, taking a photograph of (and sending it to later to) someone you've struck up a friendship with, or exchanging photographs, is often – in the towns at least – greatly appreciated.

When **invited to a home**, you normally take your shoes off before entering the reception rooms. It is customary to take a gift: sweet pastries or tea and sugar are always acceptable, and you might even take meat (perhaps by arrangement) to a poorer home. At a meal never use the left hand when in the company of Moroccans.

● Many more hustlers will simply use the excuse of a letter ("Could you help translate or write one?") as a means of attaching themselves to you; it's best to decline assistance.

● Beware of offers to meet "Blue Men" (desert nomads) in the south. They are almost invariably rogues.

● Don't trust anyone who begins their routine with "Where have I seen you before . . . ".

DEALING WITH KIDS

In the countryside, and especially along the major southern routes, you will find fewer hustlers and guides, but many more kids, eager for a dirham or a *cadeau* (present). A Dutch correspondent writes: "Dealing with small children is a lot easier than hustlers. All of us have our own odd tricks, like being able to roll one's eyes, imitate bird calls, or wiggle one's earlobes. Ours is to put one finger in our mouth and produce spectacular plopping noises. As soon as a child had asked for a dirham, we performed our trick and the child was usually flabbergasted. Most of the time we ended up teaching the entire villlage youth the trick. Dirhams were a thing of the past, and giggling the universal language."

Working out your own strategy is all part of the game . . .

SECURITY, THE POLICE AND CONSULATES

Keeping your luggage and money secure is an important consideration in Morocco. Even though, for all the tales, the situation is probably no worse than in Spain or Italy, it is obviously wise not to carry large sums of cash or valuables on your person – especially in the main tourist cities like Fes, Marrakesh and Tangier.

Hotels, generally, are secure and useful for depositing money before setting out to explore; larger ones will keep valuables at reception. **Campsites** are considerably less secure, and many campers advise using a **money belt** – to be worn even while sleeping. If you do decide on a money belt (and many people spend time quite happily without!), leather or cotton materials are preferable to nylon, which can irritate in the heat.

If you are **driving**, it almost goes without saying, you should not leave anything you cannot afford to lose visible or accessible in your car.

THE POLICE

There are two main types of **police**: the *Gendarmerie* (who dress in khaki and green berets) and the *Sûreté* (who wear grey uniforms).

The *Sûreté* are the people to approach if you need to report any kind of crime, or if you want assistance; they are based in towns and cities, but also patrol roads. The *Gendarmerie* are more of a military force, running security from their network of barracks in both urban and rural areas, and operating the checkpoints that you come across in the south and in the Rif (see the "Getting Around" section).

The **police emergency number** is ☎19.

FOREIGN CONSULATES IN MOROCCO

United Kingdom *Embassy*: 17 Bd. de la Tour Hassan, Rabat (☎07/20.905). *Consulates*: 9 Rue Amerique du Sud, Tangier (☎09/358.95 or 358.97); 60 Bd. d'Anfa, Casablanca (☎0/2216.53).

USA *Embassy*: 2 Av. de Marrakech, Rabat (☎07/62.265). *Consulates*: 8 Bd. Moulay Youssef, Casablanca (☎0/22.41.49).

Canada *Embassy*: 13 bis Rue Joafar Assadik, Agdal, Rabat (☎07/714.76 or 713.75).

Netherlands *Embassy*: 40 Rue de Tunis (☎07/335.12). *Consulates*: Immeuble Miramonte, 47 Av. Hassan II, Tangier (☎09/93.12.45).

Denmark *Embassy*: 4 Rue de Khemisset, Rabat (☎07/326.84). *Consulates*: 150 Bd. Rahal el Meskini, Casablanca (☎0/31.44.91); 3 Rue Henri Regnault (4th floor), Tangier (☎09/381.83).

Sweden *Embassy*: 159 Av. Pres. Kennedy, Souissi, Rabat (☎07/547.40). *Consulates*: 3 Rue du Lt. Sylvestre, Casablanca (☎0/30.46.48); 3 Rue de l'Entraide, Agadir (☎08/230.48).

Norway *Embassy*: 22 Charia as-Souira, Rabat-Chellah (☎07/76.10.96). *Consulates*: 3 Rue Henri Regnault, Tangier (☎09/93.36.33); Sogep-ONP, Immeuble A, Agadir (☎08/82.17.01).

Irish, **Australian** and **New Zealand** citizens should use UK consular facilities in Morocco.

GETTING AROUND

Moroccan public transport is, on the whole, pretty good. There is an efficient rail network linking the main towns of the north, the coast and Marrakesh, and elsewhere you can travel easily enough by bus or collective taxi. In the mountains and over the more remote desert routes, where roads are often just dirt tracks or *pistes*, locals maintain a network of market-day lorries – uncomfortable but fun. And for hikers, the Atlas mountains, in particular, are crossed by a series of beautiful trails, some easy enough to follow by yourself, others best trekked with a guide and mule.

Hiring a car can be a good idea, at least for a part of your trip, opening up routes that are time-consuming or difficult on local transport. Most companies allow you to hire a car in one city and return it to another.

TRAINS

Trains cover a limited network of routes, but for travel between the major cities they are the best option – comfortable, efficient, and fairly fast.

The **communications map** at the beginning of this book shows all the train routes in the country, and schedules are listed in the "Travel Details" at the end of each chapter. These change very little from year to year, but it's wise to check times in advance at stations. **Timetables**, printed by *ONCF*, the national railway company, are available for a couple of dirhams at major train stations.

There are three **classes** of tickets – confusingly, first, second and fourth (*economique*). Fourth-class is used only by poorer Moroccans

and some railway officials won't sell such tickets to foreigners. **Costs** for a second-class ticket are comparable to what you'd pay for buses; on certain "express" services, which are first- and second-class only, they are around thirty percent higher. In addition, there are **couchettes** (50dh extra) available on the Tangier–Marrakesh and Tangier–Oujda night trains; these are worth the money for the sake of security, as passengers are locked into a carriage with a guard.

Most of the **stations** are located reasonably close to the modern city centres, in the French-built quarters – the *villes nouvelles*. They generally have **luggage consignment** depots, though these accept only luggage that can be locked (effectively excluding rucksacks). An alternative is usually provided by nearby cafés, who will look after your luggage for a small tip.

GRANDS TAXIS

Collective **grands taxis** are one of the best features of Moroccan transport. They operate on a wide variety of routes, are much quicker than the buses (often quicker than trains, too), and fares are very reasonable. They are also a good way of meeting people and having impromptu Arabic lessons.

The taxis are usually big Peugeot or Mercedes cars carrying six passengers (four in the back, two in the front). Most business is along specific routes, and the most popular routes have more or less continuous departures throughout the day. Consequently, you don't have to worry about time-

---

FARES

Fares for train, bus and *grand taxi* journeys follow a reasonably consistent pattern.

For **train** or **bus** journeys, reckon on around 1.5dh for each 10km – 2–2.5dh for an express service.

Grands taxis charge around 2dh per person for each 10km, if travelling a regular route. Chartering a taxi for yourself or for a group, reckon on 12–15dh per 10km.

Sample fares
Train Tangier–Rabat, 2nd class: 50dh.
Bus Meknes–Fes: 8.5dh.

tables. You just show up at the terminal (locations are detailed, city by city, in the guide) and ask for a *place* to a specific destination. As soon as six (or, if you're willing to pay extra, four or five) people are assembled, the taxi sets off.

Most of the *grands taxis* run over a fairly short route, from one large town to the next. If you want to travel further, you will have to change taxis from time to time. Some routes are covered routinely in **stages** (eg Agadir–Taroudannt, or Agadir–Taliouine) and on others taxi drivers will generally assist you in finding a connecting taxi and in settling the fare with the driver.

On established routes *grands taxis* keep to fixed **fares** for each passenger. Before leaving, ask at your hotel (or around the terminal) what that price is – or, as a general guideline, consult the "Fares" box on the facing page.

If you want to take a **non-standard route**, or an excursion, it is possible to pay for a whole *grand taxi (une course)* for yourself or a group. But you'll often have to bargain hard before you get down to a realistic price.

BUSES

Bus travel is marginally cheaper than taking a *grand taxi*, and there are far more **regular routes**. Travelling on public transport for any length of time in Morocco, you are likely to make considerable use of the various networks.

Where you can take a *grand taxi* rather than a bus, however, do so. The difference in **fare** is small, and all except the express buses are very much slower and less comfortable than *grands taxis*. Bus legroom is extremely limited and long journeys can be torture for anyone approaching six feet or more in height. In summer, it can be worthwhile taking **night buses** on the longer journeys. Though still not very comfortable, many long-distance buses run at night and they are both quicker and cooler.

CTM AND PRIVATE LINES

There are a variety of different bus services and companies. In all sizeable towns, you will generally find both *CTM* (the national company) and a number of other companies, privately owned and operated.

The *CTM* **buses** are usually the more reliable, with numbered seats and fixed departure schedules. Some of the larger **private company** buses, such as *SATAS* (which operates widely in the south) are of a similar standard. However,

many other of the private companies are tiny outfits, with a single bus which leaves only when the driver considers it sufficiently full.

In some of the larger cities – Rabat and Marrakesh, for example – *CTM* and the private companies share a single **terminal**, often positioned on the edge of town. You can find out the most useful departure times and routes by asking around at the various windows. In other cities, there might be two or more separate termini (these are detailed in the guide) and possibly no choice of companies on a particular route.

On the more popular trips, such as those around the oasis valleys in the south, it is worth trying to buy **tickets in advance**; this may not always be possible, but it's always worth enquiring. You can sometimes experience problems getting tickets at **small towns** along major routes, where buses often arrive and leave already full. It's usually possible to get around this problem by taking a local bus or a *grand taxi* for the next section of the trip (until the bus you want empties a little), or by waiting for a bus that actually starts from the town you're in. Overall, the best policy is simply to arrive early in the day (ideally 5.30–6am) at a bus station.

On private line buses, you generally have to pay for your **baggage** to be loaded onto the roof (and taken off). Moroccans pay just a small tip for this but tourists are expected to pay 2–3dh (some

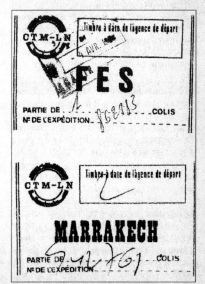

porters ask as much as 10dh for a rucksack!). If you are asked for more than 2–3dh, try to resist. On *CTM* buses your luggage is weighed and you are issued with a receipt (again about 3dh).

ONCF BUSES

An additional service, on certain major routes, are the express buses run by the train company, **ONCF**. These are fast and very comfortable, connecting Tetouan, Nador, Beni Mellal, Agadir and Laayoune to the main railway lines from, respectively, Tnine Sidi Lyamani (near Asilah), Taourite and Marrakesh (Agadir/Laayoune). They are, however, fifty percent more expensive than the regular buses, and compare, both in terms of time and cost, with the *grands taxis*.

TRUCKS AND HITCHING

In the countryside, where buses may be sporadic or even nonexistent, it is a standard practice for **vans** and **lorries** (*camions*) and **pick-up trucks** (*camionettes*) to carry and charge passengers. You may be asked to pay a little more than the locals, and you may be expected to bargain over this price – but it's straightforward enough.

In parts of the Atlas, the Berbers run more or less scheduled truck services, generally to coincide with the pattern of local *souks*. If you plan on traversing any of the more ambitious Atlas *pistes*, you'll probably be dependent on these vehicles, unless you hike. For some general guidelines – above all, about paying at the end – see Dan Richardson's account on p.344–47.

HITCHING

Hitching is not very big in Morocco. Most people, if they own any form of transport at all, have mopeds – which are said to outnumber cars by something like five hundred to one. However, it is often easy to get rides from other **tourists**, particularly if you ask around at the campsites, and for **women travellers** this can be an effective and positive option for getting around – or at least a useful respite from the generally male preserves of buses and *grands taxis*.

Out on the road, it's inevitably a different matter – and hitching is definitely not advisable for women travelling alone. Hitchers should not be surprised to be asked to **pay for a ride** if picked up by country Moroccans. Local rides can operate in much the same way as truck taxis (see above).

POLICE CHECKS ON TRAVEL

Police checks take place on travellers throughout the country. They come in three forms. One is a check on local transport; European cars, or hire cars, are waved through. The second is a routine but simple passport check – usually polite and friendly, with the only delay due to a desire to relieve boredom with a chat.

The third is more prolonged and involves being stopped by police stationed at more or less permanent points on the roads, who will conduct a fairly detailed inquisition into all non-resident travellers. There is a considerable amount of form-filling and delay. In the Deep South these checks may be conducted by the military rather than by the police.

In the **Rif mountains**, especially in the kif (hashish) producing region near Ketama, you may also come across police checks – concerned, obviously enough, with just the one substance.

CAR HIRE

Car hire is expensive at £140–200 a week, depending on season, but pays obvious dividends if you are pushed for time. Having a car will allow you to explore unusual routes and take in much more in a lot less time. This is especially true in the **south**, where getting around and getting to see anything can be quite an effort if you have to rely on local buses.

Many visitors choose to hire a car in Casablanca, Marrakesh or Agadir, expressly for the southern routes. If you're organised, however, it usually pays to **arrange car hire in Britain**, through the travel agent who arranges your flight. If you have problems, try one of the Morocco specialists detailed on p.8.

Details of **car hire companies in Morocco** are given where relevant in city listings in the guide. The best value places are mostly in Casablanca and Agadir. Deals to go for are unlimited mileage and daily/weekly rates; paying by the kilometre invariably works out more expensive than you expect. The cheapest car on offer is usually a **Renault 4** – well designed for travel on unsurfaced piste roads, with its high suspension and sturdy frame. If you can't or don't want to drive, car hire companies can usually arrange a **driver** for around 100–150dh (£8–12) a day.

Before making a booking, be sure to find out if you can pick the car up in one city and return it to another – freeing yourself for the most interesting routes. Most companies will allow this. Check also, if booking in Morocco, whether you will be charged extra for payment with a credit card; there is often a (negotiable) six percent fee for this. Before setting out, make sure the car comes with spare tyre, tool kit and full documentation – including insurance cover, which is compulsory issue with all rentals.

DRIVING IN MOROCCO

There are few real problems driving in Morocco, but keep in mind that the experience is often very different from that of Europe. Accident rates are high – in large part because much of the population is not yet tuned in to looking out for motorised vehicles. You should treat all pedestrians with the suspicion that they will cross in front of you, and all cyclists with the idea that they may well swerve into the middle of the road.

Daytime driving can, with the caveats stated above, be as good as anywhere. Good road surfaces, long straight roads, very little traffic and fairly long distances between inhabited areas allow for high average speeds. The official **speed limit** outside towns is 100km per hour, which is difficult to keep down to in desert areas, where concepts of speed change. On certain roads the speed limit can be as low as 40km per hour. There is an on-the-spot fine of 30dh for each offence.

Be very wary about driving **after dark**. It is legal to drive without lights at up to 20 kilometres per hour, which allows all cyclists and mopeds to wander at will; donkeys, goats and sheep do not carry lights, either. Obstructions, sand drifts, rocks and potholes are additional hazards, and in spring even main roads can ford, when dried-up river beds are flooded by mountain snow streams.

PISTE DRIVING

On the **pistes** (rough, unpaved tracks in the mountains or desert), there are special problems. Here you do need a good deal of driving and mechanical confidence – and if you don't feel your car's up to it, don't drive on these routes. On **mountain roads**, beware of gravel, which can be a real danger on the frequent hairpin bends.

EQUIPMENT

Whether you rent a car or drive your own, always make sure you're carrying a **spare tyre** in good condition (plus a jack and tools). Flat tyres occur very frequently, even on fairly major roads, and you can often be in for a long wait until someone drives along with a possible replacement.

Carrying an emergency windscreen is also useful, especially if you are driving your own car for a long period of time. There are lots of loose stones on the hard shoulders of single lane roads and they can fly all over the place.

If you're not mechanically minded, make sure to bring a car **maintenance manual** with you – a useful item, too, for anyone planning to hire.

PETROL AND BREAKDOWNS

Petrol stations are plentiful in larger towns but can be few and far between in rural areas. Always fill your tank to the limit. *Premium* is the standard brand for cars.

Moroccan **mechanics** are usually excellent at coping with breakdowns and all medium-sized towns have garages (most with an extensive range of spare parts for Renaults and other French cars). But be aware that if you break down miles from anywhere you'll probably end up paying a fortune to get a lorry to tow you back.

If you are driving your own vehicle, there is also the problem of having to re-export any car that you bring into the country (even a wreck). You can't just write off a car: you'll have to take it out of Morocco with you.

VEHICLE INSURANCE

Insurance must by law be sold along with all hire agreements.

Driving your own vehicle, you will need to take out *Assurance Frontière* insurance. (The green card is not accepted here, as it is in Algeria or Spain). *Assurance Frontière* costs around £22 a month, £48 for ninety days. As the name suggests, it can normally be issued at the frontier on your arrival in the country. It is not, however, available at Figuig, the southern entry point from Algeria.

For insurance renewal, the main office is at 197 Av. Hassan II, Casablanca (☎276.142).

PARKING: *GARDIENS* AND HOTELS

In almost every town of at least moderate size, you will find a **gardien de voitures** makes an appearance. *Gardiens* are often licensed by local authorities to look after cars, claiming a few dirhams by way of parking fees.

Most of the larger **hotels** in the *ville nouvelle* quarters of cities have parking space (and occasionally garaging) available.

*Important note: the **minimum age** for driving in Morocco is 21 years.*

FLIGHTS

Royal Air Maroc (*RAM*) operates **domestic flights** between all the major cities. If you're very pressed for time, you might want to use the service between **Tangier** and **Marrakesh** (via Casa); this would cost around £44, well above the bus and train fares but – at two, as opposed to nearly thirteen hours – saves considerable effort. For anyone intrepid enough to explore the **Deep South** of the country, flights can also be worthwhile – for example, returning from the southernmost visitable towns of Ad Dakhla or Laayoune.

Details of *RAM* flights, and addresses of the company's local offices, are given in the main part of the guide and the "Travel Details" at the end of chapters. Remember that you must always confirm flights at a *RAM* office 72 hours before departure.

Student and under-26 youth **discounts** of 25 percent are available on all *RAM* domestic flights but only if the ticket is bought in advance from one of their offices.

TRAVELLING BY BIKE

Biking – and particularly **mountain biking** – is becoming an increasingly popular pursuit for western travellers to Morocco. The country's network of *pistes* – dirt tracks – makes for exciting mountain bike terrain, leading you into areas otherwise accessible only to hikers or four-wheel drive expeditions. Some of the more intrepid mountain bikers cover footpaths in the High Atlas, too, though for the less than super-fit this can be extremely heavy going. Better, on the whole, to stick to established *pistes* – many of which are covered by local trucks, which you can pay for a ride if your legs (or your bike) give out.

However you intend to cycle, you will need to go with your eyes wide open. The heat and the long stretches of dead straight road across arid, featureless plains – the main routes to (or beyond) the mountain ranges – can all too easily drain your energy. And a constant backdrop of water-sculpted ·slopes, all very picturesque by car, is quite another matter if you are cycling through them all day. Even in the mountains, public **water** is very rare – there are very few roadside watering places such as are found in Europe – and **population is sparse**, with towns and villages often a long way apart.

Regular roads are generally well-surfaced but narrow and you will often have to get off the

CITY TAXIS

Most Moroccan towns are small enough to cover on foot, especially if you stay in a hotel in or near the Medina – where you'll want to spend most of your time. In larger cities, however, local buses can be useful, as can *petits taxis* – usually Fiats or Simcas – which take up to three passengers.

Petits taxis, as opposed to *grands taxis*, are limited to trips within city limits. Officially, all of them should have meters, but in practice you're unlikely to find one that works (at least for tourists) except in Rabat. It is then a matter of bargaining for a price – either before you get in (wise to start off with) or by simply presenting the right sum when you get out.

Fares vary enormously (in Marrakesh and Agadir, for example, they can often be excessive), though everywhere it depends to a large extent on what you look like, how you act, and where you're going. Don't be afraid to use *petits taxis* or to argue with the driver if you feel you're being unreasonably overcharged.

tarmac to make way for traffic. Cycling on the *pistes*, mountain bikes come into their own with their "tractor" tyres and wide, stabilising handlebars. There are few *pistes* that could be recommended on a regular tourer.

ROUTES
Rewarding areas for biking must include:

● **Tizi n'Test** (High Atlas): **Asni to Ijoukak**, and an excursion to Tin Mal.

● **Asni to Setti Fatma** (High Atlas: Ourika Valley) and beyond if you have a mountain bike.

● **Western** (well-watered) **side of the Middle Atlas.**

In summer, at least, it wouldn't be a good idea to go much **beyond the Atlas**, though given cooler, winter temperatures **southern oasis routes** – like **Ouarzazate to Zagora** or **Ouarzazate to Tinerhir** – could be rewarding.

REPAIRS
Most towns reveal a wealth of **general repair shops** in their *medina* quarters, well used to servicing local bikes and mopeds. Though they are most unlikely to have the correct spare parts for your make of bike, they can usually sort out some kind of temporary solution.

USING LOCAL TRANSPORT

Cycles are carried on **trains** for a small handling fee. However, they must be registered in advance as baggage and won't necessarily travel on the same train as you. Expect up to a day's delay.

Buses will generally carry cycles on the roof. *CTM* usually charge around 10dh per bike; on other lines it's very much up to you to negotiate with the driver and/or baggage porter (who will expect at least another 5dh for himself). Some **grands taxis** also agree to carry cycles, if they have space on a rack. The fare will be about the same as for a place in the taxi: again, you may well have to bargain!

In mountain/desert areas, as mentioned, you can have your bike carried with you on **truck services**. Prices for this are highly negotiable, but should not exceed your own passenger fare.

FURTHER INFORMATION

For a fact sheet on conditions for cyclists in Morocco and some suggested routes, it's worth contacting the **Cycle Touring Club**, Cotterell House, 69 Meadrow, Godalming, Surrey, GU7 3HS (☎04868/7217). The club also arranges good value insurance, etc, for members.

HIKING

Hiking is one of the very best things Morocco has to offer. In the High Atlas, the country boasts one of the most rewarding mountain ranges in the world – and one of the least spoilt. If you are used to the Pyrenees or Alps, here you will feel you are moving a century or so back in time.

A number of **long-distance Atlas routes** can be followed – even the Grand Traverse, as described in Michael Peyron's guides. Most hikers, however, limit themselves to **shorter trails** around the **Toubkal** area (best in spring or autumn – serious climbers only in winter). Other promising areas include the **Djebel Sirwa** (Western High Atlas), or in winter the **Djebel Sahro** and **Tafraoute** regions of the **Anti-Atlas**.

Each of these regions is featured in some detail in this guide. For further information, check the **hiking books** detailed on p.15. And if you haven't had much experience or feel a little daunted by the lack of organised facilities, try one of the **specialist hiking companies** offering Moroccan trips (see box on p.7).

For general practicalities on hiking, see the High Atlas hiking details in the relevant chapter.

SLEEPING

Hotels in Morocco are cheap, good value, and usually pretty easy to find. The only times you might have a problem getting a room are in the peak seasons (August, Christmas or Easter), and then only in a handful of main cities and resorts – Fes, Agadir, Tangier and sometimes Tetouan.

There is a basic distinction between **classified hotels** (which are given star-ratings by the tourist board and start at around £6 a double) and **unclassified hotels** (both unrated and unlisted by the ONMT, which charge about £2–5 for a double).

UNCLASSIFIED HOTELS

Unclassified hotels are mainly to be found in the older, Arab-built parts of cities – the *medinas* – and are almost always the cheapest options. They offer the additional advantage of being at the heart of things: where you'll want to spend most of your time, and where all the sights and markets are concentrated.

The disadvantages are that the *medinas* can at first appear daunting – with their mazes of narrow lanes and blind alleys – and that the hotels themselves can be, at worst, dirty flea traps with tiny, windowless cells and half-washed sheets. At best, however, they're far different – beautiful, traditional houses with whitewashed rooms grouped around a central patio.

On the down side, unclassified *medina* hotels do regularly have a problem with **water**. Most of the *medinas* remain substantially unmodernised, and in the hotels hot showers are a rarity and the squat toilets sometimes pretty disgusting.

Expect unclassified **rates** to fluctuate widely, according to place, season and demand. The best value rooms are, for some reason, in Chaouen, where hotels charge from around 25dh (£2) a double; in Fes, by contrast, where the quality is a lot worse but rooms in short supply, you would do well to find a double at under 60dh (£5).

CLASSIFIED HOTELS

Rated hotels are almost always in a town's ***ville nouvelle*** – the "new" or administrative quarters, built by the French and usually set slightly apart from the *medina*.

The **star-ratings** are fairly self-explanatory: starting at the bottom with 1*B, 1*A, 2*B, etc, and going up to 4*B, 4*A, and finally 5*Luxury. **Prices** are reasonable for all except the 5* categories (see table below). At the **lower end**, there's often little difference between a 1*B and 1*A, either of which will offer you a basic double room with a washbasin for £6–7, with a private shower and wc for an additional £1–1.50. Going up to 2* and 3*, there's a definite progression in comfort, and you can find a few elegant, old hotels in these categories which used once to be very grand but have since slipped in competition with the new, purpose-built tourist complexes.

However, if you want **a bit of luxury**, you'll most likely be looking for a room with access to a swimming pool – which means, on the whole, four stars. This will set you back around £15–30 for a double. If you can afford the upper end of this scale (4*A hotels), you'll be moving into real style, with rooms looking out onto palm-shaded pools and gardens, in buildings that have sometimes been converted from old palace residences.

Bookings for the four- or five-star hotels are best made through the central reservations office of the chain owning the hotel. Details of these are to be found in the ONMT hotels guide. Turning up at an individual hotel, or even phoning ahead, you may find reluctance to book you in, with staff perhaps claiming the hotel is full. Many rely on tour groups for their business and are not very interested in individual travellers.

A SUGGESTED BUDGET COURSE . . .

Ideally, the best course for anyone on a limited budget is to **alternate between the extremes**, spending most nights in basic *medina* hotels but going for the occasional blast of grandeur.

At any rate don't limit yourself to the middle categories – these are mostly dull, and staying all the time in the *villes nouvelles* will cut you off from the most interesting aspects of traditional Moroccan life.

YOUTH HOSTELS AND *REFUGES*

At the lower price levels – though at 15dh (£1) per person often no cheaper than a shared room in the *medina* – there are six **youth hostels**, or ***Auberges de Jeunesse***. One, in Asni in the High Atlas, is a hiking base – useful and recom-

OFFICIAL HOTEL RATES

Hotels graded by the Moroccan tourist authorities are obliged to levy official rates, which have **maximum charges** for rooms with and without bathrooms in 1*B to 4*A categories; luxury (5*) hotels can set their own rates. Inevitably, you will come upon various legitimate (17–19 percent tax) or not so legitimate supplements but, at the time of writing, the rates below should be more or less the maximum charged.

Category	Single	Single (w/bath & wc)	Double	Double (w/bath & wc)
1*B	58dh	67dh	70dh	86dh
1*A	66dh	85dh	85dh	98dh
2*B	75dh	92dh	92dh	112dh
2*A	94dh	119dh	110dh	138dh
3*B	119dh	151dh	151dh	186dh
3*A	138dh	175dh	174dh	212dh
4*B	191dh	231dh	235dh	292dh
4*A	230dh	280dh	300dh	358dh

HAMMAMS

The absence of hot showers in some of the cheaper *medina* hotels is not such a disaster. Throughout all the medina quarters, you'll find local **hammams** – steam baths where you can go in and sweat for as long as you like, get scrubbed down and rigourously massaged, and douse yourself with endless buckets of hot and cold water.

Several *hammams* are detailed in the text, but the best way of finding one is always to ask at the hotel where you're staying. You will often, in fact, need to be led to a *hammam*, since they are usually unmarked and very hard to find.

In some towns, you find separate *hammams* for women and men; at others there are different hours for each sex – usually 9am–7pm for women, 7pm–1am (and sometimes 5–9am) for men. Those for women seem particularly welcoming. For men, there's a strange element of modesty: you undress facing the wall, and bathe in your underpants or swimsuit.

As part of the Islamic tradition of cleanliness and ablutions, *hammams* sometimes have a religious element, and you may not be welcome (or allowed in) to those built alongside mosques, particularly on Thursday evenings, before the main weekly service on Friday. On the whole, though, there are no restrictions against *Nisara* ("Nazerenes", or Christians).

---

mended. The others are all in major cities. Those in Fes, Casablanca and Marrakesh are good fallbacks, close to the train stations; the one in Meknes is all right but a little far from everything; Rabat's has a reputation for being pretty squalid. Addresses and details are given for all of these in the relevant sections of the guide. One general attraction is the opportunity for meeting other travellers, including Moroccans on holiday who sometimes visit them for just this purpose.

REFUGES

In the High Atlas mountains, you will also find a number of huts, or **refuges**, equipped for hikers. These provide dormitory beds and sometimes meals and/or cooking facilities. They are detailed in the relevant sections.

CAMPSITES

Campsites, too, are good meeting places, and even if you're staying elsewhere can be worth visiting in order to find a lift or people to share car costs. Most sites are very cheap, at around 5dh (40p) per person and per tent; the fancier places, in Meknes, Fes or Marrakesh, for example, charge around double this, but offer swimming pools and better facilities. Details and addresses are given in relevant sections of the guide.

Note that campsites don't provide total **security**, and you should never leave valuables unattended. When camping outside official sites, this applies even more; however, if you're hiking in the Atlas, it is usually possible to set up a tent and pay someone to act as a *gardien*.

EATING AND DRINKING

Like accommodation, food in Morocco falls into two basic categories: ordinary Moroccan meals served in the *medina* cafés (or bought from stalls), and French-influenced tourist menus in most of the hotels and *ville nouvelle* restaurants. There are exceptions – cheap local cafés in the new cities and occasional "palace"-style places in the *medina* – but, in general, this still holds true. Once again, it's best to stick largely to the *medina* places (most are cleaner than they look), with an occasional splurge in the best restaurants you can find.

BASIC CAFÉ FOOD

Basic Moroccan meals generally centre on a thick, very filling soup – most often the spicy, bean-based **harira** (which is a meal in itself, and eaten as such to break the Ramadan fast). To this you might add a plateful of **kebabs** (either *brochettes*, shish kebabs, or *kefta*, made from minced meat) and perhaps a **salad** (which is often very finely chopped, vaguely similar to the Spanish *gazpacho*), together with **dates** bought at a market stall.

Alternatively, you could go for a **tajine** – essentially a stew, cooked slowly in an earthen-ware pot over a charcoal fire. Mopped up with bread, it can be unbelievably delicious.

Either alternative will set you back about £1.50 for a hearty meal at one of the hole-in-the-wall places in the *medina*, each with about two or three tables. You are not expected to bargain for cooked food, but prices can be lower at café-restaurants without menus if you enquire how much things cost before you start eating.

Vegetarians can get by quite happily on most of the soups (though some use lamb for stock) and usually on the *tajines* (which you can anyway ask to be served without meat).

GLOSSARY OF MOROCCAN FOOD

*Note that where food/dishes are commonly available in all kinds of restaurants, both **French** and **Arabic** words are given; in Arabic words, the letters printed in **bold italics** should be stressed.*

BASICS

Pain	l-**hobs**	Bread	Sel	l-me**lha**	Salt
Oeufs	l-**bed**	Eggs	Sauce	l-**merga**	Sauce
Poissons	l-**hout**	Fish	Sucre	zoukar	Sugar
Viande	l-**hem**	Meat		(*Zanida* is granulated sugar;	
Huile	zit	Oil		zoukar, lump sugar)	
Poivre	leb**zar**	Pepper	Légumes	l-**khoudra**	Vegetables
Salade	shal**ada**	Salad	Vinaigre	l-**khel**	Vinegar

SOUPS, SALADS AND VEGETABLES

—	**Har**ira	Spicy bean soup	Frites	l'**batata**	Fried potatoes
Potage	—	Thick soup	Tomates	**matecha**	Tomatoes
Bouillon	—	Thin soup	Epinards	salk	Spinach
Salade Marocaine	—	Mixed salad	Oignons	l-ba**sla**	Onions

MAIN DISHES

Tajine de viande	l-**hem**	Meat stew
Tajine des poissons	l-**hout**	Fish stew
Couscous (aux sept légumes)	Couscous bidaoui	Couscous (with seven vegetables)
Poulet aux olives et citron		Chicken with olives and lemon
—	Djaja mahamara	Chicken stuffed with almonds, semolina and raisins
Boulettes de viande	**kef**ta	Meatballs
Bifteck	l-habra	Steak
Agneau	Mechoui	Roast lamb
Pastilla	B'stilla	Pigeon pie

MEATS, POULTRY AND FISH

Poulet	djaj	Chicken	Sardines	sardile	Sardines
Pigeon	leh**mama**	Pigeon	Merlan	l-**mirla**	Whiting
Lapin	qniya	Rabbit	Crevettes	—	Shrimps
Mouton	l-**houli**	Mutton	Langouste	—	Lobster

For **breakfast or a snack**, you can buy a half *baguette* – plus butter and jam, cheese or eggs, if you want – from many bread or grocery stores, and take it into a café to order a drink.

RESTAURANT MEALS

More expensive dishes, available in some of the *medina* cafés as well as in the dearer restaurants, include **fish**, particularly on the coast, and **chicken** *(poulet)*, either spit-roasted *(rôti)* or with lemon and olives *(poulet aux olives et citron)*.

You will sometimes find **pastilla**, too, a succulent pigeon pie, prepared with phyllo pastry coated with sugar and cinnamon; it is a particular speciality of Fes. And, of course, there is **couscous**, the most famous Moroccan dish, based on a huge bowl of steamed semolina piled high with vegetables and mutton, chicken, or occasionally fish. *Couscous*, however, tends to be disappointing. There is no real tradition of going out to eat in Morocco, and this is a dish that's traditionally prepared at home for a special occasion (on Friday, the holy day, in richer households; perhaps for a festival in poorer ones). At festivals, which are always good for interesting food, and at the most expensive tourist restaurants,

SWEETS AND FRUITS

Cornes de gazelles	kab l-ghzal	Marzipan-filled pastry horns	Amandes	louze	Almonds
—	m'hencha	Coiled, almond-filled pastry	Bananes	banane	Bananas
			Fraises	l-fraise	Strawberries
Briouats au miel	—	Similar – but covered in honey	Cerises	hblmluk	Cherries
			Pêches	l-khoukh	Peaches
—	fekkas	Sweet aniseed biscuits	Oranges	limoune	Oranges
			Melon	l-battikh	Melon
Fromage	formage	Cheese	Pasteque	dellah	Watermelon
—	ejben	Camel cheese	Raisins	la'anb	Grapes
			Pommes	tufaah	Apples
Dattes	tmer	Dates	Abricots	mishmash	Apricots
Figues	chriha	Figs	Figues de Bsarbarie	Kermus d'ensarrah (or Takanareete)	Cactus fruit (prickly pear)

DRINKS

Eau (Minerale)	agua, l-ma (mazdini)	Water (Mineral)	Bière	birra	Beer
			Vin	sh-rab	Wine
Thé (à la menthe)	atay (dial neznaz)	Tea (Mint)	Café (au lait)	qahwa (bi lahlib)	Coffee (with milk)

SOME ARABIC PHRASES

What do you have …	**Ash**noo **kane** …
to eat?	… f'l-**mak**la?
to drink?	… f'l-much**a**roubat?
What is this?	Shnoo **had**a?
Can you give me	A**tee**nee …
… a knife/fork/spoon?	… moos/for**shet**a/**mal**ka?
… a plate/glass/napkin?	… **t'b**-sil/**kess**/l-**fo**ta?
Less/without sugar	**Shwee**ya/ble azouk**a**r
Without meat	Ble l-**hem**
This is not what I asked for!	**He**dee mushee **hee**a **lit** lubt!
This is not fresh/clean!	**He**dee mushee **tree**a/n'**kee**a!
This is good!	**He**dee mushee mu**zyen**a!
The bill, please.	L'h'**seb** minfad**lik**.
Please write it down.	Minfad**lik**, k'**tib**'h.

you may also come across **mechoui** – a whole sheep roasted on a spit.

To supplement these standard offerings, most tourist restaurants add a few **French dishes** – steak, liver, various fish and fowl, etc – and the ubiquitous *salade marocaine*, actually very different from the Moroccan idea of salad, since it's based on a few tomatoes, cucumbers and other greens. Together with a dessert consisting either of fruit or pastry, these meals usually come to around £4–6 a head.

CAKES, DESSERTS AND FRUIT

Cakes and desserts are also available in some Moroccan cafés, though you'll find them more often at pastry shops or street stalls. They can be excellent. The most common are *cornes de gazelles*, sugar-coated pastries filled with a kind of marzipan, but there are infinite variations, like *m'hencha* – almond-filled pastry coils which sometimes appear covered in honey.

Yoghurt (*yaourt*) is also delicious, and Morocco is surprisingly rich in seasonal **fruits**. In addition to the various kinds of **dates** – sold all year but at their best fresh from the October harvests – there are grapes, melons, strawberries, peaches and figs, all advisably washed before eaten. Or for a real thirst-quencher (and a good cure for a bad stomach), you can have quantities of **prickly pear**, cactus fruit, peeled for you in the street for a couple of dirhams.

TEA AND OTHER DRINKS

The national drink is *thé à la menthe* – green tea ("Whisky Marocain" or "Whisky Berber") flavoured with sprigs of mint and a minimum of four cubes of sugar per cup. It tastes a little sickly at first but is worth getting used to – perfect in the summer heat and a ritual if you're invited into anyone's home (you leave after the third glass) or if you're doing any serious bargaining in a shop.

EAU MINERALE NATURELLE
sidi harazem

In cafés, it is usually cheaper to ask for a pot (*une théière*) for two or three people. You can also occasionally get red or amber tea – more expensive and rarely available, but delicious when you can find it. Wonderful, too, and easily found at cafés or street stalls, are the fresh-squeezed **juices**: *jus d'orange, jus d'amande* (almond), *jus des bananes*, and *jus de pomme* (apple), the last three all milk-based and served chilled. *Leben* – yoghurt and water – is often sold at train and bus stations, and can do wonders for an upset stomach.

Other **soft drinks** inevitably include Coke, along with Fanta and other fizzy lemonades – all pretty inexpensive and sold in large bottles. **Mineral water**, which is a worthwhile investment throughout the country, is usually referred to by brand name, ubiquitously *Sidi Harazem* or *Sidi Ali*, or the naturally sparkling *Oulmès*.

Coffee (*café*) is best in French-style cafés – either *noir* (black), *cassé* (with a drop of milk), or *au lait* (white).

WINE AND BEER

As an Islamic nation, Morocco gives **drinking alcohol** a low profile. It is, in fact, not generally possible to buy any alcohol at all in the *medinas*, and for beer or wine you always have to go to a tourist restaurant or hotel, or a bar in the *ville nouvelle*.

Moroccan **wines**, however, can be very good, if a little heavy for drinking without a meal. Among varieties worth trying are the strong red *Cabernet*, the rosé *Gris de Boulaoune* and the dry, white *Spécial Coquillages*. These brands apart, reds are most reliable. Those Moroccans who drink in **bars** – a growing number in the industrial cities – tend to stick to **beer**, usually the local *Stork, Flag Pils*, or, preferably, *Flag Special*. Beers cost around 12dh a bottle in ordinary bars.

KIF (HASHISH)

The smoking of *kif* (hashish, *chocolaté*) has for a long time been a regular pastime of Moroccans and tourists alike. Indeed, in the 1960s and 1970s (or further back, in the 1930s), its ready availability, good quality and low cost made kif a major tourist attraction. It is, however, illegal, or, as the ONMT puts it:

> Tourists coming to Morocco are warned that the first article in the Dahir of April 24th 1954 prohibits the POSSESSION, the OFFER, the DISTRIBUTION, the PURCHASE, the SALE and the TRANSPORTATION as well as the EXPORTATION of CANNABIS IN WHATEVER FORM. The Dahir allows for a penalty of IMPRISONMENT from three months to five years and a fine of 2400 to 240,000 dirhams, or only one of these. Moreover the law court may ordain the SEIZURE of the means of transport and the things used to cover up the smuggling as well as the toxic products themselves.

What this means in practice is slightly different. There is no real effort to stop Moroccans from using kif, but as a tourist you are peculiarly vulnerable. Not so much because of the **police**, as because of the **dealers**. Many have developed aggressive tactics, selling people hash (or, occasionally, even planting it) and then returning or sending friends to threaten to turn you in to the police; or occasionally they themselves may even be actual informers, and turn you in to the police. Either way, it can all become pretty paranoiac and unpleasant – and large fines (plus prison sentences for substantial amounts) do get levied.

What can you do to avoid all this? Most obviously, keep well clear – above all, of the kif-growing areas of the **Rif mountains** and the processing centre in **Ketama** – and always reply to hustlers by saying you don't smoke. If you *are* coming to Morocco to indulge, don't buy anything in the first few days (definitely not in Tangier and Tetouan), and only smoke* where you feel thoroughly confident and in control.

Above all, **do not try to take any out** by air (*Midnight Express* could equally have been about Morocco), or bring any out of the Rif area. And don't even think of taking any into Algeria or over to Spain. Penalties in **Algeria** are amazingly harsh (a life sentence is theoretically possible), and there's nearly always a prison sentence in **Spain**, too, for anyone caught importing.

If you do find yourself in trouble there are **consulates** for most nationalities in Rabat/Casablanca and, to a lesser extent, in Tangier (see lists on p.17). All of the consulates are notoriously unsympathetic to drug offenders – the British one in Rabat has an old French poster on the wall, "*Le kif détruit l'esprit*" – but they can help with technical problems and find you legal representation.

---

*Kif is not necessarily what's smoked in Morocco – a traditional speciality is *majoun*, a kind of fudge made with the pounded flowers and seeds of the plant. As James Jackson wrote in his *An Account of the Empire of Morocco, 1814*, "a piece of this as big as a walnut will for a time entirely deprive a man of all reason and intellect". It is also reputed to be good for settling your stomach.

COMMUNICATIONS – POST, PHONES, AND MEDIA

MAIL AND POSTE RESTANTE

Letters between Western Europe and Morocco generally take around a week to ten days, around two weeks to North America or Australasia. **Stamps** can often be bought alongside postcards or at a PTT (post office); **sending letters**, always post them at a PTT. To send a **parcel**, take the goods unopened to a post office and queue at the parcels counter, where you will have to pay a small fee for the goods – after examination – to be wrapped.

Post office hours are Monday to Friday, 8am to noon and 3 to 6pm in winter, 8am to 3pm in summer; closed Saturday and Sunday.

POSTE RESTANTE

Receiving letters **poste restante** can be a bit of a lottery, as Moroccan post office workers don't always file letters under the name you might expect. Ask for all your initials to be checked (including *M* for Ms, etc), and, if you're half-expecting anything, suggest other letters as well.

To pick up your mail you need your passport. To have mail sent to you, it should be addressed (preferably with your surname underlined) to *Poste Restante* at the *PTT Centrale* of any major city (Marrakesh is notoriously inefficient).

Alternatives to sending *poste restante* to post offices are to pick a big **hotel** (anything with three or more stars should be reliable) or have things sent **c/o American Express** – represented in Morocco by *Voyages Schwartz* in Tangier, Fes, Casablanca, Agadir and Marrakesh (see the section in "Costs and Money" for addresses).

PHONES

The **public telephone section** is usually housed in a city's main post office (*PTT Centrale*), though it often has a separate entrance and stays open longer hours – 24 hours a day in some of the main cities. Since **international direct dialling** reached Morocco it's been possible to place calls with little problem (two-hour delays are almost a thing of the past . . .). In most major towns you can also make international calls from centrally placed **phone boxes** (*cabines*). Alternatively, you can **make calls through a hotel**. Even fairly small places will normally do this, however be sure to ask in advance both of possible surcharges and the chargeable rate.

To **make a call from a phone box** you put your money into the slot at the top of the phone-set and then dial. A few dirhams are enough for a call within Morocco (pay phones accept ten-, twenty-, fifty-centime, or one-dirham and five-dirham coins) but for international calls you need at least three 5dh coins for Europe and six or more for North America or Australia.

DIALLING

To call a **number within Morocco**, simply dial the area code and individual number. **Local** codes are displayed near the phone in *cabines* and *PTTs* – and are listed at the end of each chapter in this guide. The **ringing tone** consists of one-and-a-half-second bursts of tone, separated by a three-and-a-half-second silence. The

engaged tone is similar to the one used in Britain. A series of rapid pips may also be heard, indicating that your call is being connected.

For an **international call**, dial 00 and wait for a musical-sounding dialling tone, which is the signal that you can put in an international call. Then dial the country code:

Australia (161)	*Canada/USA (1)*
Britain (44)	*Netherlands (31)*
Spain (34)	

and finally the individual number, leaving out the initial 0 of its local code. If you are successfully connected you will hear the local tones for your number. If not, you will hear either a busy signal, a recording in Arabic and then French informing that lines are "saturated", or silence. Persevere: it may take three or four attempts to get through.

The **rate for international calls** is currently around 15dh (£1) a minute to Britain and Western Europe, 50dh (£3.75) a minute to the US and Canada. A good policy is to phone someone briefly and get them to ring you back. Actual reverse charge calls are hard to arrange.

CALLING MOROCCO FROM ABROAD

Phoning Morocco from abroad, dial the international code (010 from Britain), then the country code (212), area code (see boxes at end of each chapter) and finally the individual number.

See note on dialling tones above.

THE MEDIA

As for other means of staying in touch, various British and French **newspapers** and the *International Herald Tribune* are available in all the main cities. *Le Monde* is the most common.

If you take a short-wave radio, you can pick up the **BBC World Service**, which is broadcast on various frequencies through the day, from 6am to midnight local time. The most consistent evening reception is generally on 9.41 and 5.975 mHz (31.88m and 50.21m bands); full programme listings are available from the BBC or the British Council in Rabat.

Some of the pricier hotels these days can receive **satellite TV** – occasionally *Sky* and more commonly the French *TV5* channel. In the north of the country you can also receive Spanish stations and, in Tangier, the English-language Gibraltar broadcasts. **Morocco's own two TV channels** broadcast in Arabic, but include some French programmes – and French-language news.

THE MOROCCAN PRESS

The **Moroccan press** encompasses a reasonable range of papers, published in French and Arabic. Of the **French-language** papers, the most accessible is the official – and somewhat rigorously pro-government – French-language daily, *Le Matin du Sahara* (circulation 70,000).

Others include *L'Opinion* (conservative opposition) and *Al-Bayannne* (communist).

In **Arabic**, there are *Al Alam* (circ. 50,000), which is supportive of the Istiqlal party, and *Al Muharnir* (circ. 17,000), which supports the socialist USFP party. There is also a fundamentalist paper, *Al Djemaa* (circ. 3000).

FESTIVALS: RAMADAN, HOLIDAYS AND *MOUSSEMS*

If the popular image of Islam is somewhat puritanical and ascetic, Morocco's festivals – the *moussems* and *amouggars* – do their best to contradict it. The country abounds in holidays and festivals of all kinds, both national and local, and coming across one can be the most enjoyable experience of travel in Morocco – with the chance to witness music and dance, as well as special regional foods and market *souks*.

Perhaps surprisingly, there are rewards, too, in coinciding with one of the major Islamic celebrations – above all *Ramadan*, when all Muslims (which in effect means all Moroccans) observe a total fast from sunrise to sunset for a month. This can pose some problems for travelling but the celebratory evenings are again good times to hear music and to share in hospitality.

RAMADAN

Ramadan, in a sense, parallels the Christian Lent. The ninth month of the Islamic calendar, it commemorates the time in which the Koran was revealed to Muhammad. In contrast to the Christian West, though, the Muslim world observes the fast extremely rigorously – indeed Moroccans are forbidden by law from "public disrespect" of the fast, and a few are jailed for this each year.

What the fast involves is abstention from food, drink and smoking during daylight hours, and abstinence from sex throughout the month. Strict Muslim men will often sit up all night at the cafés, so that everyone knows they have abstained from sex.

With most local cafés and restaurants closing during the day, and people getting on edge toward the month's end, Ramadan is in some respects a disastrous time to travel. It is certainly no time to try and hire a guide in the mountains – nobody will undertake the work – and it is probably safer to travel by bus during the mornings only, as drivers wil be fasting, too. (Airline pilots are forbidden from observing the fast).

But there is a compensation in witnessing and becoming absorbed into the pattern of the fast. At sunset, signalled by the sounding of a siren and the lighting of lamps on the minarets, an amazing calm and sense of wellbeing fall on the streets, as everyone drinks a bowl of *harira* and, in the cities at least, gets down to a night of celebration and entertainment.

The **entertainment** takes different forms. If you can spend some time in Marrakesh during the month, you'll find the Djemaa el Fna square there at its most active, with troupes of musicians, dancers and acrobats coming into the city for the occasion. In Rabat and Fes, there seem to be continuous promenades, with cafés and stalls all open up to 3am. Urban cafés provide venues for live music and singing, too, and in the southern towns and Berber villages, you will often come across the ritualised *ahouaches* and *haidus* – circular, trance-like dances often involving whole communities.

If you are a **non-Muslim** outsider you are not expected to observe Ramadan, but it is good to be sensitive about not breaking the fast (particularly smoking) in public. In fact, the best way to experience Ramadan – and to benefit from its naturally purifying rhythms – is to enter into it. You may not be able to last without an occasional glass of water, and you'll probably have breakfast later than sunrise, but it is worth an attempt.

OTHER ISLAMIC HOLIDAYS

At the end of Ramadan comes the feast of **Aïd es Seghir**, a climax to the festivities in Marrakesh, though observed more privately in the villages. Extremely important as well to the Muslim calendar is **Aïd el Kebir**, which celebrates the willingness of Abraham to obey God and to sacrifice Isaac. The Aïd el Kebir is followed, about three weeks later, by **Moharem**, the Muslim new year.

Both *aïds* are traditional family gatherings. At the Aïd el Kebir every household that can afford it will slaughter a sheep. You see them tethered everywhere, often on rooftops, for weeks prior to the event; after the feast, their skins are to be seen, being cured on the streets.

The fourth main religious holiday is the **Mouloud**, the Prophet's birthday. This is widely observed, with a large number of *moussems* (see next page) timed to take place in the weeks around it.

PUBLIC HOLIDAYS

Nowadays each of the big **religious feasts** are usually marked by **two days off**. These are announced or ratified by the king, each time, on TV and radio the preceding day.

On these public holidays, and on the secular *Fêtes Nationales* (see box below), all **banks**, **post offices** and most **shops** are closed; **transport** is reduced, too, but never stops completely.

MOUSSEMS AND AMMOUGARS

Moussems – or *amouggars* – are held in honour of saints or marabouts. They are basically local, and predominantly rural, affairs. Besides the Aïd es Seghir and Aïd el Kebir, however, they form the main religious and social celebrations of the year for most Moroccans, especially for the country Berbers.

Some of the smaller *moussems* amount to little more than a market day with religious overtones; others are essentially harvest festivals, celebrating a pause in agricultural labour after a crop has been successfully brought in. Quite a number, however, have developed into substan-

---

RAMADAN AND ISLAMIC HOLIDAYS

Islamic religious holidays are calculated on the **lunar calendar**, so their dates rotate throughout the seasons (as does Ramadan's). Exact dates in the lunar calendar are impossible to predict – they are set by the Islamic authorities in Fes – but approximate dates for the next three years are:

	1991	**1992**	**1993**
Ramadan	March 18	March 7	Feb 24
Aïd es Seghir	April 17	April 6	March 26
Aïd el Kebir	June 26	June 15	June 4
Moharem	July 9	June 29	July 18
Mouloud	Oct 3	Sept 23	Sept 12

FETES NATIONALES

Fêtes Nationales, all celebrated to some extent, are tied to Western calendar dates:

January 1	New Year's Day	August 14	Allegiance Day
March 3	Feast of the Throne	November 6	Green March
May 1	Labour Day	November 18	Independence Day
July 9	King's Birthday		

The **Feast of the Throne** is the largest secular holiday, a very colourful affair, celebrated throughout Morocco with flags and lights, processions, dancing and music.

tial occasions – similar in some respects to Spanish fiestas – and a few have acquired national significance. If you are lucky enough to be here for one of the major events, you'll get the chance to witness Moroccan popular culture at its richest, with horse-riding, music, singing and dancing, and of course eating and drinking.

AIMS AND FUNCTIONS

The ostensible aim of the *moussem* is religious: to obtain blessing, or *baraka*, from the saint and/ or to thank God for the harvest. But the social and cultural dimensions are equally important. *Moussems* provide an opportunity for country people to escape the monotony of their hard working lives in several days of festivities. They may provide the year's single opportunity for friends or families from different villages to meet. Harvest and farming problems are discussed, as well as family matters – marriage in particular – as people get the chance to sing, dance, eat and pray together.

Music and singing are always major components of a *moussem* and locals will often bring tape recorders to provide sounds for the rest of the year. The different religious brotherhoods, some of whom may be present at larger *moussems*, each have their own distinct styles of music, dancing and dress.

Moussems also operate as **fairs**, or markets, with artisans offering their produce to a wider market than is available at the weekly *souk*. Buyers in turn can inform themselves about new products and regional price differences, as the *moussem* attracts people from a much wider area than the *souk*. There is a welcome injection of cash into the local economy, too, with traders and entertainers doing good business, and house-holders renting out rooms.

At the **spiritual level**, people seek to improve their standing with God through prayer, as well as the less orthodox channels of popular belief. Central to this is *baraka*, good fortune, which can be obtained by intercession of the saint. Financial contributions are made and these are used to buy a gift, or *hedia*, usually a large carpet, which is then taken in procession to the saint's tomb; it is deposited there for the local *shereefian* families, the descendants of the saint, to dispose of as they wish. Country people may seek to obtain *baraka* by attaching a garment or tissue to the saint's tomb and leaving it overnight to take home after the festival.

The procession which takes the gift to the tomb is the high point of the more **religious moussems**, such as that of **Moulay Idriss**, where an enormous carpet is carried above the heads of the religious **brotherhoods**. Each of these brotherhoods will be playing its own music, hypnotic in its rhythms; spectators and participants may go into trance, giving themselves up to the music. If you witness such events, it is best to keep a low profile (and certainly don't take photographs); the presence of foreigners or non-Muslims at these times is sometimes considered to impede trance.

Release through trance probably has a therapeutic aspect, and indeed some *moussems* are specifically concerned with **cures** of physical and psychiatric disorders. The saint's tomb is usually located near a freshwater spring, and the cure can simply be bathing in and drinking the water. Those suffering from physical ailments may also be treated at the *moussem* with herbal remedies, or by recitation of verses from the Koran. Koranic verses may also be written and placed in tiny receptacles placed next to the ailment. The whole is reminiscent of the popular remedies found at European pilgrimage centres like Lourdes.

PRACTICALITIES

There are enormous numbers of *moussems*. An idea of quite how many can be gathered from the frequency that, travelling about the countryside, you see *koubbas* – the square, white-domed buildings covering a saint's tomb. Each of these is a potential focal point of a *moussem*, and any one region or town may have twenty to thirty separate annual *moussems*. Establishing when they take place, however, can be difficult for outsiders; most local people find out by word of mouth at the weekly *souks*.

Many *moussems* are held around religious occasions such as the **Mouloud**, which change date each year according to the lunar calendar (see box opposite). Others, concerned with celebrating the **harvest**, have their date decided at a local level according to when the harvest is ready. *Moussems* of this type are obviously more difficult to plan a visit around than those which occur at points of the Islamic year. **August** and **September** are the most promising months overall, with dozens of *moussems* held after the grain harvest when there is a lull in the agricultural year before sowing starts prior to the first rains in October or November.

The **lists** below give an approximate idea (sometimes an exact one) of when the *moussems* are, but you will generally need to ask at a local level for information. Sometimes tourist offices may be able to help, though often not.

The **accommodation** situation will depend on whether the *moussem* is in the town or countryside. In the country, the simplest solution is to take a tent and camp – there is no real objection to anyone camping wherever they please during a *moussem*. In small towns there may be hotels – and locals will rent out rooms in their houses. **Food** is never a problem, with dozens of traders setting up stalls, though it is perhaps best to stick to the grills, as stalls may not have access to running water for cleaning.

MOULOUD *MOUSSEMS*

Meknes: Ben Aissa *Moussem*

The largest of all the *moussems*, this includes a spectacular **fantasia** (a charge of horses with riders firing guns at full gallop) if weather conditions permit, held near Place El Hedim. With this, the enormous conical tents, and crowds of country people in white djellabahs, beneath the city walls, it has the appearance of a medieval tournament. At least, that is, until you see the adjoining fairground, which is itself fun, with its illusionists and riders of death.

In the past, this *moussem* was the principal gathering of the **Aissoua** brotherhood, and the occasion for them to display their extraordinary powers of endurance under trance – cutting themselves with daggers, swallowing glass, and the like. Their activities today are more subdued, though they still include going into trance, and of course playing music. Their focus is the marabout tomb of Ben Aissa, near the road in from Rabat.

Accommodation in Meknes is a problem at this time unless you arrive two or three days in advance. However, you could quite easily visit on a day trip from Fes.

Salé: Wax Candle *Moussem*

As the name suggests, this festival centres on a procession of wax candles – enormous lantern-like creations, carried from Bab El Rih to the Grand Mosque on the eve of the Mouloud. The candle bearers (a hereditary position) are followed by various brotherhoods, dancing and playing music.

The **procession** starts about 3pm and goes on for three or four hours; the best place to see it is at Bab Bou Hadja, where the candles are presented to local dignitaries.

OTHER POPULAR *MOUSSEMS*

May	**Moulay Bousselham**. *Moussem of Sidi Ahmed Ben Mansour*.
June	**Goulimine**. Traditionally a camel traders' fair, elements of which remain.
	Tan Tan. *Moussem of Sidi Mohammed Ma el Ainin*. Large-scale religious and commercial *moussem*. Saharan "Guedra" dance may be seen performed.
July	**Tetouan**. *Moussem of Moulay Abdessalem*. A very religious, traditional occasion with a big turnout of local tribesmen. Impressive location on a flat mountain top south of the town.
	Setti Fatma. Large and popular *moussem* in the Ourika valley, southeast of Marrakesh.
August	**El Jadida**. *Moussem of Moulay Abdallah*. Located about 9km west of the city at a village named after the saint. Features displays of horse-riding, or *fantasias*.
	Tiznit. *Moussem of Sidi Ahmed ou Noussa*. Primarily religious.
	Chaouen. *Moussem of Sidi Allal Al Hadh*. Located in the hills out of the town.
September	**Moulay Idriss Zerhoun**. *Moussem of Moulay Idriss*. The largest religious *moussem*, but visitable only for the day as a non-Muslim. Impressive display by brotherhoods, and a highly charged procession of gifts to the saint's tomb. Also a large *fantasia* above the town.
	Imilchil. *Marriage Moussem*. Set in the heart of the Atlas mountains, this is the most celebrated Berber *moussem* – traditionally the occasion of all marriages in the region, though today also a tourist event. In fact there now seem to be two *moussems*, with one laid on specifically for package tours from Marrakesh and Agadir; the real event is held in the last week in September or the first in October.
	Fes. *Moussem of Moulay Idriss II*. The largest of the *moussems* held inside a major city, and involving a long procession to the saint's tomb. The *medina* is packed out, however, and you will need to line the route early in order to see anything.

HARVEST *MOUSSEMS*

February	Tafraoute (almonds)
March	Beni Mellal (cotton)
April	Immouzer des Ida Outanane (honey)
May	Berkane (clementines)
	El Kelâa des Mgouna (roses)
June	Sefrou (cherries)
July	Al Hoceima (sea produce)
August	Immouzer du Kandar (apples/pears)
November	Erfoud (dates)
	Rhafsaï (olives)

CULTURAL FESTIVALS

The big cultural highlights are the **Marrakesh Festival** (1st and 2nd week of August), which brings together musicians and dancers from throughout the country, and the **Asilah International Festival** (August). The latter features a mixed bag of the arts, with exhibitions of Moroccan and Egyptian artworks and whole sequence of concerts from performances by Egyptian and Lebanese singing stars to American college enembles. For more details, see, respectively, p.284 and p.70.

SPORTS AND ACTIVITIES

Morocco is doing much to keep up with the increasing interest in activity and sporting holidays. In addition to its magnificent hiking opportunities (for information on which see p.23), the country offers impressive golf and tennis facilities, a couple of ski resorts (plus some adventurous off-piste skiing) and excellent fishing. The national sporting obsession, however, is football, and you can join in any number of beach kick-about games, or watch in the developing national league and cup matches.

FOOTBALL

Football is important in Morocco. When the national team gained a place in the 1986 World Cup quarter finals (their finest hour to date), the squad were rewarded with villas, cars and small businesses. On their return, they were taken to a massive victory celebration in Casablanca, parading through the streets on a float with a giant football – out of whose hatch stepped King Hassan to shake hands with each player.

Although Morocco failed to qualify for the 1990 championships and its bid to host the 1994 championship was narrowly (many would say unjustly) defeated by the USA, enthusiasm remains high, with teams competing at the top level in the various **African Cup** club and country championships.

Domestically, there is an annual **league** and a knock-out competition, the **Throne Cup**. For a long time there was just one full-time professional team, **FAR** (the army), but recent seasons have seen the introduction of sponsorship and other semi-professional sides, the best of which are **WIDAD** and **RAJA**, the two big Casablanca teams, **MAS** from Fes and **KAC** from Kenitra.

The league games have a tendency towards defensive play – the points system gives two points for a draw and three for a win – but there is always the potential for displays of individual dynamism and inspiration, a parallel, so Moroccans would have it, with the Brazilian style of play. Brazilian comparisons could certainly be made with the social background of Moroccan football, players developing their game in unstructured kick-arounds on the beach, street or patches of wasteland. The lack of a team strip in these games (and hence easy recognition of team mates) discourages long balls and intricate passing, and encourages individual possession and quick one-twos. The same conditions produced Pelé and Maradona.

SKIING

The country's main ski resorts are at **Oukaïmeden** in the High Atlas, an hour's drive from Marrakesh, and **Mischliffen** in the Middle Atlas (near Ifrane). Oukaïmeden (Dec–April) has seven piste runs, a ski lift, local instructors, equipment for hire and plenty of accommodation. Mischliffen – a volcanic crater – has rather more limited facilities, with three lifts, a shorter season (perhaps five weeks on average) and sporadic equipment hire. A third prospective ski resort is **Ketama** and its adjoining **Djebel Tighidine**, in the Rif Mountains, though as the centre of the Moroccan drug industry this remains some way, still, from holiday resort status. So too does the high altitude resort of **Bou Iblane** in the Anti-Atlas, which offers little more than an approach road (not always covered by the snowplough) and a single ski lift.

Off-piste skiing is increasingly popular in the High Atlas, in particular around the famed Toubkal massif. The pursuit has become increasingly popular in recent years with French and British groups, many of whom combine skiing with mountaineering to the summits. At present, in the absence of organised facilities, this is an area of the sport best limited to those with considerable experience and expertise.

RIDING

The established base for **riding holidays** is *La Roseraie* hotel at **Ouirgane** on the Tizi n'Test road. The hotel runs trekking tours into the **High Atlas**, offering anything from one-day excursions to extended trips staying at villages en route. In addition, it has tennis courts, a swimming pool and is developing a health centre – all at quite reasonable cost.

Stays or packages at *La Roseraie* can be arranged through most of the Moroccan specialist agents detailed on p.9.

FISHING

French visitors to Morocco have long appreciated the possibilities for fishing. The country offers an immense Atlantic (and small Mediterranean) **coastline**, with opportunities to arrange boat trips at Safi, Essaouira, Moulay Bousselham (near Asilah) and elsewhere.

Inland, the **Middle Atlas** shelters beautiful **lakes** and **rivers**, many of them well stocked with trout. Good bases could include **Azrou** (near the Aghmas lakes), **Ifrane** (near Zerrrouka), **Khenifra** (the Oum er Rbia river) and **Ouirgane** (the Nfis river). Pike are also to be found in some Middle Atlas lakes (such as Aguelmame Azizgza, near Khenifra), and a few of the huge artificial **barrages**, like **Bin el Ouidaine** (near Beni Mellal), are said to contain huge bass.

For the really determined and adventurous, the most exciting Moroccan fishing is reputed to be along the coast of the **Western Sahara**, where catches weigh in regularly at 20–30 kilos. The regional capital of Laayoune is the only feasible base at present, unless you're totally self-reliant.

For all fishing in the country, you need to take your own **equipment**. For coarse or fly fishing you need a **permit** from the *Administration des Eaux et Fôrets* (11 rue Revoil, Rabat). For trout fishing, you are limited to the hours between 6am and noon; the season starts on March 31.

WATER SPORTS AND SWIMMING

Agadir has **sailing**, **yachting**, **windsurfing** and **diving** on offer, with **Tarhazoute**, just north of the resort, developing a growing reputation among **windsurfers**. The biggest windsurfing destination, however, is **Essaouira**, more or less west of Marrakesh, which draws European devotees of the sport year-round. Anywhere on the Atlantic coast, be aware of strong undertows.

Inland, most towns of any size have a municipal **swimming pool** – they're always very cheap and addresses are given in the guide. In the south, you'll be dependent on campsite pools or on those at the luxury hotels (who often allow outsiders to swim, either for a charge or if you buy drinks or a meal).

GOLF AND TENNIS

The British opened a golf course in Tangier as far back as 1917 – a rather more refined alternative to their then favoured sport of pig-sticking in the hills. Today the country has an international level course at **Rabat** (*Royal Dar-es-Salam*), further 18-hole courses at **Mohammedia** (*Royal Golf*), **Marrakesh** (*Royal Golf*) and **Tangier** (*Royal Country Club*), and nine-hole courses at **Casablanca** (*Royal Anfa*), **Agadir** (*Royal Golf*), **Cabo Negro** (*Royal Golf*) and **Meknes** (*Royal Golf* – actually within the Royal Palace gardens).

For a **golf-centred holiday** package, or details (and photos) of the courses, consult the golf brochure issued by *Best of Morocco* (100 Week St, Maidstone, Kent ME14 1RG; ☎0622/692278). *CLM* (4a William St, London SW1; ☎071/235 2110) also arrange golfing holidays.

Tennis courts are now to be found at virtually all of Morocco's 4* and 5* hotels, especially those in Agadir (which now has a total of over 120 courts) and Marrakesh. To check on the presence or otherwise of courts consult the ONMT's *Guide des Hôtels*.

Equipment can often be loaned from hotels but it is rarely of a quality to satisfy serious enthusiasts: it's best to take rackets and balls.

SOUKS AND MOROCCAN CRAFTS

Souks – markets – are a major feature of Moroccan life, and one of its great attractions. They are to be found everywhere: every town has its special quarter, large cities like Fes and Marrakesh have labyrinths of individual *souks* (each filling a street or square and devoted to one particular craft), and in the countryside there is a moveable network, shifting between the various villages of a region.

SOUK DAYS

Some of the villages, or areas between villages, are in fact named after **their market days**, so it's easy to see when they're held.

The *souk* days are:

Souk el Had – Sunday (literally, "first market")

Souk el Tnine – Monday market

Souk el Tleta – Tuesday market

Souk el Arba – Wednesday market

Souk el Khamees – Thursday market

Souk es Sebt – Saturday market

There are no village markets on Friday (*el Djemaa* – the "assembly", when the main prayers are held in the mosques), and even in the cities, *souks* are largely closed on Friday mornings and very subdued for the rest of the day.

CRAFT TRADITIONS

Moroccan **craft**, or *artesanie*, traditions are still highly active, and even goods mass-produced for tourists are surprisingly untacky. To find pieces of real quality, however, is not that easy – some crafts have become dulled by centuries of repetition and others have been corrupted by modern techniques and chemical dyes.

In general, if you're planning on buying anything, it's always worth getting as close to the source of the goods as possible, and to steer clear of the main tourist centres. **Fes** might have the richest traditions, but you can often find better work at much cheaper prices elsewhere; **Tangier** and **Agadir**, neither of which have imaginative workshops of their own, are certainly best avoided. As stressed throughout the guide, the best way to get an idea of standards and quality is to visit the various **traditional crafts museums** spread around the country: there are good ones in Fes, Meknes, Tangier, Rabat and Marrakesh.

CARPETS, RUGS AND BLANKETS

Moroccan carpets are not cheap – you can pay £1000 and more for Arab designs in Fes or Rabat – but it is possible to find **rugs** at fairly reasonable prices, from £20 to £35 for a strong, well-designed weave.

Most of these will be of Berber origin and the most interesting ones usually come from the High and Middle Atlas; if you're looking seriously, try to get to the town *souk* in **Midelt** or the weekly markets in **Azrou** and other villages around **Marrakesh**. The chain of *Maison Berbère* shops in Ouarzazate, Tinerhir and Rissani are good hunting grounds, too.

On a simpler and cheaper level, the **Berber blankets** (*foutahs*, or *couvertures*) are imaginative, and often very striking with bands of reds and blacks; for these, **Tetouan** and **Chaouen**, on the edge of the Rif, are promising.

JEWELLERY

Silver jewellery went into decline with the loss to Israel of Morocco's Jewish population, the country's traditional workers in precious metals and crafts in general; in the **south**, however, you can pick up some fabulous Berber necklaces and bracelets, always very chunky, with bold combinations of semiprecious (and sometimes plastic) stones and beads. There's a particularly good jewellery *souk* in Essaouira.

SEMI PRECIOUS STONES

You'll see a variety of semi precious stones on sale throughout Morocco, and in the High Atlas they are often aggressively hawked on the roadsides. If you're lucky enough to be offered genuine **amethyst** or **quartz**, prices can be bargained to very tempting levels. Be warned, however, that all that glitters is not necessarily the real thing. Too often, if you wet the stone and rub, you'll find telltale traces of dye on your fingers . . .

WOOD AND POTTERY

Marquetry is one of the few crafts where you'll see genuinely old pieces – inlaid tables and shelves – though the most easily exportable objects are boxes and chess sets, beautifully inlaid in *thuya* and cedar woods in **Essaouira**.

Pottery on the whole is disappointing, but tourist produce though it is, the blue-and-white designs of **Fes** and the multicoloured pots of **Chaouen** are highly attractive. The essentially domestic pottery of **Safi** – Morocco's major pottery centre – is worth a look, too, with its crude but effective plates and garden pots.

CLOTHING AND LEATHER

Moroccan clothes are easy to purchase and though Westerners – men at least – who try to imitate Moroccan styles by wearing the cotton or wool *djellaba* (a kind of cloak) tend to look a little silly, there are some highly desirable items. Some of the cloth is exquisite in itself, and walking down the dyers' *souks* is an inspiration.

Leather is also excellent, and here you can buy and wear goods with perhaps greater confidence. The classic Moroccan shoes are *babouches*, open at the heel, immensely comfortable, and produced in yellow (the usual colour), white, tan and occasionally grey or (for the truly fetishistic) black; a good pair – and quality varies enormously – can cost £8–15.

BARGAINING

Whatever you buy, and wherever you buy it, you will want (and be expected) to **bargain**. There are no hard and fast rules – it is really a question of paying what something is worth to you – but there are a few general points to keep in mind.

First, **bargaining is entirely natural** in Morocco. If you ask the price in a market, the answer, as likely as not, will come in one breath – "Twenty; how much will you pay?"

Second, don't pay any attention to **initial prices**. These are simply a device to test the limits of a particular deal or situation. Don't think, for example, in terms of paying one-third of the asking price (as some guides suggest) – it might well turn out to be a tenth or even a twentieth. Equally, though, it might not – some sellers actually start near the price they have in mind and will bustle you out of their shop for offering an "insulting" price. Don't feel intimidated by either tactic; if you return the following day for some coveted item, you will most likely be welcomed as an old friend. Take your chances!

Third, **don't ever let a figure pass your lips** that you aren't prepared to pay – nor start bargaining for something you have absolutely no intention of buying – there's no better way to create bad feelings.

Fourth, take your time. If the deal is a serious one (for a rug, say), you'll probably want to sit down over tea with the vendor, and for two cups you'll talk about anything but the rug and the price. If negotiations do not seem to be going well, it often helps to have a friend on hand who seems a little less interested in the purchase than you – as they may well become, given the protracted experiences involved . . .

The final and most golden rule of them all is never to go shopping with a **guide** or a hustler, even "just to look" – the pressures will be either too great or it'll be too boring, depending on how long you've been in the country and how you've learned to cope with these people.

In the main city *souks* – and particularly in Marrakesh – you might find **bartering goods** to be more satisfactory than bargaining over a price. This way you know the value of what you're offering better than your partner (though he'll have a pretty good idea, too), and in a sense you're giving a fairer exchange. Items particularly sought after are training shoes (even if they're well worn), printed T-shirts (rock designs – especially Prince – are favourites) or football shirts, brand-name jeans, basic medicines (in country areas), and Western department-store clothes (Mark & Spencer, for some reason, has particularly good currency).

An approximate idea of what you should be paying for handicrafts can be gained from checking the **fixed prices** in the state-run *Centres Artisanals*. Even here, though, there is sometimes room for bargaining as prices are set slightly higher than you could expect to pay elsewhere.

MOSQUES AND MONUMENTS

Without a doubt, the major disappointment of travelling in Morocco is not being allowed into its mosques: all non-Muslims are excluded and the rule is strictly observed. However, there is much architecture to be admired in the form of *medersas* – medieval "colleges" attached as teaching institutions to urban mosques – and in the numerous, elaborately decorated gateways (*babs*) to be found in any well preserved city walls. Cities also reveal some beautiful *fondouks* – caravanersais – and the occasional palace. There is a scattering of remains, too, from Morocco's ancient civilisations under Roman and even Phoenician rule. Most public monuments, including *medersas*, museums and archaeological sites levy a standard 10dh admission fee.

MOSQUES AND KOUBBAS

The only "mosques" that non-Muslims *are* allowed to visit are the ruined Almohad structure of **Tin Mal** in the High Atlas, the courtyard of the sanctuary-mosque of Moulay Ismail in **Meknes**, the sanctuary of Mohammed V in **Rabat**, and the Bou Inania *medersa* in **Fes**. Elsewhere, you'll have to be content with an occasional glimpse through open doors, and even in this you should be sensitive: people don't seem to mind tourists peering into the Kairaouine Mosque in Fes (the country's most important religious building), but in the country you should never approach a shrine too closely.

This rule applies equally to the numerous domed and whitewashed **koubbas** – the tombs of marabouts, or local saints – and the "monastic" **zaouias** of the various Sufi brotherhoods. It is a good idea, too, to avoid walking through **graveyards**, as these also are regarded as sacred places.

OTHER ISLAMIC MONUMENTS

As some compensation, many of the most beautiful and architecturally interesting of Morocco's monuments are open to public view – the great imperial gateways, or **babs**, of the main cities, for example, and, of course, the **minarets** (towers from which the call to prayer is made) attached to the mosques.

Of buildings that can be visited, highlights must include the **Berber kasbahs** (fortified castle residences) of the south; a series of city **palaces** and **mansions** – many of them converted into hotels, restaurants or craft shops – in Fes and Marrakesh; and the intricate **medersas** of Fes, Meknes, Salé, and Marrakesh.

The **medersas**, many of them dating from the thirteenth and fourteenth centuries, are perhaps the most startling – and certainly the most "monumental" – of all Moroccan buildings, each displaying elaborate decoration and designs in stucco (gypsum or plaster), cedar, and tile mosaics (known in Morocco as *zellij*). Originally, these buildings served as religious universities or student residences for a neighbouring mosque school, but by the turn of the century they had largely fallen into decay and disuse. Today, they have almost all become secularised. Their role is discussed in the chapter on **Fes**, which is where you'll find the richest and most varied examples.

ANCIENT REMAINS

Unlike Tunisia and Algeria, Morocco never saw extensive **Roman** colonisation – and indeed, the south of the country remained unconquered by any outside force until the French invasion of the 1920s. Ancient sites are, therefore, limited. The most interesting, and really the only one worth going out of your way to visit, is **Volubilis**, close to Meknes. For enthusiasts, **Lixus** (near Larache) is worthwhile, and there are good bronze collections and statuary at **Rabat**.

Prehistoric sites, with well preserved **rock paintings**, are to be found in the south of the country, though most are extremely difficult to gain access to, including the most significant one at **Foum El Hassan**. The most rewarding ones you can get to without very much difficulty are around **Oukaïmeden**, near Marrakesh.

FROM A WOMAN'S PERSPECTIVE

● **Margaret Hubbard spent one month travelling on her own around Morocco:**

I knew that there were likely to be difficulties in travelling as a woman alone around Morocco. I'd been warned by numerous sources (this book's previous edition included) about hustling and harassment and I was already well aware of the constraints imposed on women travellers within Islamic cultures. But above and beyond this, I knew I'd be fascinated by the country. I had picked up a smattering of Arabic and the impetus to study Islamic religion and culture during trips to Damascus and Amman (both times with a male companion). Also, I already had enough experience of travelling alone to know that I could live with myself should I meet up with no one else.

So, a little apprehensive, but very much more determined and excited, I arrived in Tangier, took the first train out to Casablanca, and found a room for the night. It was not until I emerged the next morning into the bright daylight of Casablanca that I experienced my first reaction to Morocco.

BEGINNINGS
Nothing could have prepared me for it. Almost instantly, I was assailed by a barrage of: "*Voulez-vous coucher avec moi?*" "*Avez-vous jamais fait l'amour au Maroc?*" "*Venez avec moi, madame*" "*Viens, m'selle*". Whatever I had to say was ignored at will, and wherever I went, I felt that I was being constantly scrutinised by men.

Fighting off the panic, I headed for the bus station, where, after a lot of frantic rushing to and fro (I couldn't decipher the Arabic signs), I climbed onto a bus for Marrakesh.

Marrakesh proved to me that I was right in coming to Morocco. It wasn't that the harassment was any less – in fact, it was almost as constant as in Tangier. But wandering through the Djemaa el Fna (the main square and centre of all life in Marrakesh), among the snake charmers, kebab vendors, blanket weavers, water sellers, monkey trainers, and merchants of everything from false teeth to handwoven rugs, I became ensnared to such an extent that my response to the men who approached me was no longer one of fear but rather a feeling of irrelevance.

There was too much to be learned to shut out contact with people, and I heard myself utter, as if it were the most normal reply in the world: "*Non, monsieur, je ne veux pas coucher avec vous, mais pouvez-vous me dire pourquoi ils vendent false teeth/combien d'années il faut pour faire des tapis à main/pourquoi les singes* (monkeys). . . ?" That first night, I returned to my room at 2am more alive than I had felt for months.

STRATEGIES
I'd also stumbled upon a possible strategy for pre-empting, perhaps even preventing, harassment. Moroccan hustlers know a lot about tourists and have reason to expect one of two reactions from them: fear or a sort of resigned acceptance.

What they don't expect is for you to move quickly through the opening gambits and launch into a serious conversation about Moroccan life. Using a mixture of French and Arabic, I developed the persona of a "serious woman" and, from Marrakesh to Figuig, discussed the politics of the Maghreb, maternity rights, housing costs, or the Koran with almost anyone who wanted my attention.

It became exhausting, but any attempt at more desultory chat was treated as an open invitation and seemed to make any harassment more determined. That isn't to say that it's impossible to have a more relaxed relationship with Moroccan men – I made good friends on two occasions with Arab men and I'm still corresponding with one of them. But I think this was made easier by my defining the terms of our friendship fairly early on in the conversation. (As a general rule, whenever I arranged to meet up with someone I didn't know very well, I chose well-lit public places. I was also careful about my clothes – I found it really did help to look as inconspicuous as possible, and I almost always wore loose-fitting blouses, longish skirts, and, occasionally, also a head scarf.)

CONTACT: THE *HAMMAM*

After exploring Marrakesh for five days, I took a bus out over the Atlas mountain range to Zagora. The journey took twelve hours and the bus was hot and cramped, but wedged between a group of Moroccan mothers, jostling their babies on my lap and sharing whatever food and drink was going around, I felt reassured, more a participant than an outsider.

This was also one of the few occasions that I'd had any sort of meaningful contact with Moroccan women. For the most part, women tend to have a low profile in public, moving in very separate spheres from the tourists. There are some women's cafés but they're well hidden and not for foreigners.

For me, the most likely meeting place was the *hammam*, or steam bath, which I habitually sought out in each stopping place. Apart from the undoubted pleasures of plentiful hot water, these became a place of refuge for me. It was a relief to be surrounded by women, and to be an object of curiosity without any element of threat. Any ideas about Western status I might have had were lost in the face of explaining in French, Arabic, and sign language to an old Moroccan woman with 24 grandchildren the sexual practices and methods of contraception used in the West. "Is it true that women are opened up by machine?" is a question that worries me still.

FESTIVITIES

I arrived in Zagora on the last night of the festival of the king's birthday. It was pure chance. The town was packed with Moroccans who had travelled in from nearby oases. Oddly, though, I met just one other tourist – a German man. We were both swept along, as insignificant as any other single people in the crowd, dancing and singing in time to the echoing African sounds.

At the main event of the night, the crowd was divided by a long rope with women on one side and men on the other, with only the German and I standing side by side. I felt overwhelmed with a feeling of excitement and wellbeing, simply because I was there.

INTO THE DESERT

From Zagora I headed for Figuig and the desert, stopping overnight en route in Tinerhir. It's possible that I chose a bad hotel for that stop, but it was about the worst night that I had spent in the entire trip. The men in and around the hotel jeered, even spat, at me when I politely refused to accompany them, and throughout the night I had men banging on the door shutters of my room. For twelve hours I stood guard, tense, afraid, and stifled by the locked-in heat of that dismal hotel room. I escaped on the first bus out.

Further south I met up with a Danish man in a Land Rover and travelled on with him to spend four days in the desert. It was a simple business arrangement – he wanted someone to look after the van while he slept and I wanted someone to look out for me while I slept. I can find no terms that will sufficiently describe the effect the desert had on me. It was awesome and inspiring and it silenced me. I also found that the more recent preoccupations that I had about my life, work, and relationships had entirely slipped from my mind. Yet strangely, I could recall with absolute clarity images from over ten years ago. I

remain convinced that the desert, with its simplicity, its expansiveness, and its power changed me in some way.

At Figuig I parted company with the Dane and made it in various stages to Fes. I tended to find myself becoming dissatisfied after travelling for a while with a male companion. This was not because I didn't enjoy the company, which was, more often than not, a luxury for me, but I used to feel cheated that I was no longer at the forefront and that any contact with Moroccans would have to be made through him. This is often the case in Islamic countries, where any approaches or offers of hospitality are proffered man to man, with the woman treated more or less as an appendage. I was prepared to go on alone however uncomfortable it might become, so long as I was treated as a person in my own right.

JOGGING

In Fes I discovered yet another, perhaps even more effective, strategy for changing my status with Moroccan men. I am a runner and compete regularly in marathons, and I'm used to keeping up with my training in almost any conditions. Up until Fes, I'd held back, uncertain as to the effect of dashing out of a hotel in only a tracksuit bottom and a T-shirt. My usual outfit, the long skirt and blouse, was hardly suitable for the exercise I had in mind. After seriously considering confining myself to laps around the hotel bedroom, I recovered my sanity and my sense of adventure, changed my clothes, and set off.

The harassment and the hustling all melted away. I found that the Moroccans have such a high regard for sport that the very men who had hassled me in the morning were looking on with a respectful interest, offering encouragement and advice as I hurtled by in the cool of the evening. From then on, I became known as "the runner" and was left more or less in peace for the rest of my stay.

After this, I made it a rule to train in all the villages and towns I stayed in on my way back to Tangier. Now when I run, I conjure up the image of pacing out of Chaouen towards the shrine on the hillside, keeping time with the chants of the *muezzin* at dawn.

RETURN TO TANGIER

Returning to Tangier, I felt as far removed as it is possible to feel from the apprehensive new arrival of the month before. I felt less intimidated and more stoic about my status as an inferior and an outsider, and I had long since come to accept that I was a source of income to many people whose options for earning money are severely limited.

Walking out of the bus station, I was surrounded by a group of hustlers. I listened in silence and then said, in the fairly decent Arabic that I had picked up along the journey from Figuig to Fes, that I had been in the Sahara and hadn't got lost so I didn't think I needed a guide in Tangier, and furthermore, that I had talked with some Touaregs in Zagora who told me that it is a lie that Moroccans buy their women with camels; would they please excuse me, I had arrangements?

I spent the next few days wandering freely around the town, totally immersed in plotting how to return.

■ OTHER READERS' ADVICE ■

Don't be afraid to express outrage. Public harassment of women is never something that would be accepted within the community. If you are harassed in the street, or a public place, a loud expression of outrage, or an attempt to involve passers by, should immediately result in public anger against the man and a very uncomfortable situation for him. This works in Morocco in a way that it wouldn't, for example, in Spain or Italy, where macho male attitudes mean that public harassment is a fact of life for Spanish or Italian women.

DIRECTORY

ADDRESSES Arabic names – *Derb, Zankat*, etc – are gradually replacing French ones. The main street or square of any town, though, is still invariably *Avenue* or *Place* Hassan II (the present king) or Mohammed V (his father). Street signs are usually in French and Arabic lettering.

BRITISH MOROCCAN SOCIETY The society publishes a quarterly newsletter and organises various Moroccan-oriented events and discussions, usually in London. For details contact: Mrs Alcha Alaoui, c/o Embassy of Morocco, 49 Queens Gate Gdns, London SW7 5NE (☎071/581 5801).

CONSULATES AND EMBASSIES are in Rabat, Tangier and Casablanca; see p.17 for lists.

CONTRACEPTIVES Somewhat poor quality and unreliable condoms can be bought in most chemists, and so can the pill (officially by prescription, but this isn't essential). If you're suffering from diarrhoea, the pill (or any other drug) may not be in your system long enough to be absorbed, and consequently may become ineffective.

CUSTOMS You're allowed to bring a litre of spirits into Morocco, which is well worth doing.

ELECTRICAL VOLTAGE Most of the country runs on 220v but some towns still have 110v sockets and it's not uncommon to have both in the same building. Always check.

GAY ATTITUDES Male homosexuality is common in Morocco, although attitudes towards it are a little schizophrenic. No Moroccan will declare himself gay – which has connotations of femininity and weakness; the idea of being a passive partner is virtually taboo, while a dominant partner may well not consider himself to be indulging in a homosexual act. Private realities, however, are rather different from public show.

If you are visiting Morocco specifically as a "gay destination" be warned that the legendary Joe Orton days of Tangier – and Marrakesh – as gay resorts are over, the Moroccan government having instituted a major crackdown (and wholesale closure of brothels) following independence. Gay sex is, of course, still available, and men travelling alone or together will certainly be propositioned. But attitudes are tending increasingly toward hustling and exploitation on all sides. It is, in addition, officially illegal under Moroccan law. Article 489 of the Moroccan penal code prohibits any "shameless or unnatural act" with a person of the same sex and allows for imprisonment of six months to three years, plus a fine. There are also various provisions in the penal code for more serious offences, with correspondingly higher penalties in cases involving, for example, corruption of minors.

As emphasised under "Health", AIDS is a real threat in Morocco, despite a lack of reported cases. There is some awareness of AIDS among Moroccans but most are steadfast in seeing it as a "disease for foreigners" and the concept, let alone practice, of "safe sex" is yet to emerge.

There is no public perception of lesbianism.

HOSPITAL EMERGENCIES ☎15.

LAUNDRIES in the larger towns will take in clothes and wash them overnight, but you'll usually find it easier to ask at hotels – even basic places will be able to offer the service.

RELATIONSHIPS Following clampdowns on "unofficial guides", there are laws in effect that can make relationships with Moroccans problematic. In theory, any Moroccan – without a guide's permit – seen accompanying a tourist can be arrested and imprisoned. In practice this is rarely enforced. However, friendships, especially in tourist cities like Tangier, Agadir or Marrakesh, should be discreet.

TAMPONS can be bought at general stores, not chemists, in most Moroccan cities. Don't expect to find them in country or mountain areas.

TIME Morocco keeps Greenwich Mean Time the whole year. It is therefore one hour (two hours in summertime) behind Spain – something to keep in mind when catching ferries.

TIPPING You're expected to tip – amongst others – waiters in cafés (1dh per person) and restaurants (5dh or so); museum and monument curators (3dh); *gardiens de voitures* (4–5dh; see "Driving"); petrol pump attendants (2–3dh); and bus porters (3–4dh; see "Buses").

WORK Your only chance of paid work in Morocco is teaching English. The *Centre for British Teachers* (Quality House, Quality Court, Chancery Lane, London WC2; ☎071/242 2982) regularly advertise posts. Or you could contact the *British Council* (6 Av. Moulay Youssef, Rabat; or 10 Spring Gdns, London SW1; ☎071/930 8466), the *American Language Centre* (1 Place de la Fraternité, Casablanca; also in Rabat, Kenitra, Tangier, Tetouan, Meknes, Fes and Marrakesh) or the *American School* (Rue Al Amir Abdelkader, Agdal, Rabat; also in Casablanca and Tangier). Reasonable spoken French is normally required by all of these.

WORK CAMPS If you are interested in taking part in a work camp, a number of possibilities exist. The *United Nations Association* (UK head office: 3 Whitehall Court, London SW1; ☎071/930 2931) recruit international teams to work on manual and community projects for two or three weeks in the summer; applicants pay their own travel costs but are provided with accommodation. Alternatively, there are three Moroccan organisations: *Les Amis des Chantiers Internationaux de Meknes* (PO Box 8, Meknes), whose projects generally involve agricultural or construction work around Meknes – three weeks in July and August, accommodation and food provided; *Chanteuse Jeunesse Maroc* (PO Box 566, Rabat), who offer some inspired work camps – recently, creating green spaces at Asilah, and constructing lanes and alleyways in shanty towns near Mohammedia; or *Pensés et Chantiers* (26 Rue de Pakistan, BP 1423, Rabat), involving community schemes – painting, restoration and gardening. Most of the work camps are open to all-comers over 17 years of age; travel costs have to be paid by the participant, but you generally receive free accommodation (take a sleeping bag) and meals.

USEFUL THINGS TO BRING

● **Alarm clock**. Vital for early-morning buses.

● **Bags** should be lockable. Left-luggage depots at train stations will only accept locked bags.

● **Bartering gifts**. If you want to bargain for handicrafts, bring things to barter with (see "Bargaining"); hiking in the Atlas, spare gear is always appreciated by local guides.

● **Camping gear**. If you are planning on a lot of camping, a sleeping bag and foam pad are invaluable, but it is worth considering whether you will make enough use of campsites to justify the weight. Hotels are remarkably cheap. A good compromise is to pack a sheet sleeping bag – reassuring in those hotels that don't relentlessly pursue cleanliness awards.

● **Clothes**. Keep both practicality and sensitivity in mind. As emphasised in the piece "From a Woman's Perspective", Morocco is a deeply conservative nation: the more modest your dress the less hassle you will attract.

On the practicalities front, keep in mind that the mountain areas and Sahara alike can get distinctly **chilly** at night, even in spring and autumn. A warm sweater is invaluable. So too, in winter and

spring, is some kind of waterproof clothing and a solid pair of shoes: storms (and resulting flash floods) are commonplace and wandering around a muddy *medina* in sodden sandals is a miserable experience. For advice on **hiking gear**, see p.292.

● **Film**. Kodak and Fuji film is available in most towns and major resorts, but it's relatively expensive and may well be pretty old stock. It's best to bring adequate supplies. For photography in the *medinàs* – all dark alleyways and hidden corners – fast film (400–800 ASA) is useful. If you're looking for good landscape photographs, especially in the south, slow film (and/or early rising) is a must. See notes on behaviour.

● **Medicines**. Salt tablets, some insect repellent, water purifying tablets, anti-diarrhoea tablets and aspirin are all useful.

● **Plug**. If you like your water to fill a basin, it is worth packing an omnisize plug: few hotels (even relatively upmarket ones) supply such equipment.

● **Toiletries and toilet paper** are easy enough to obtain in all but the most remote parts of the country.

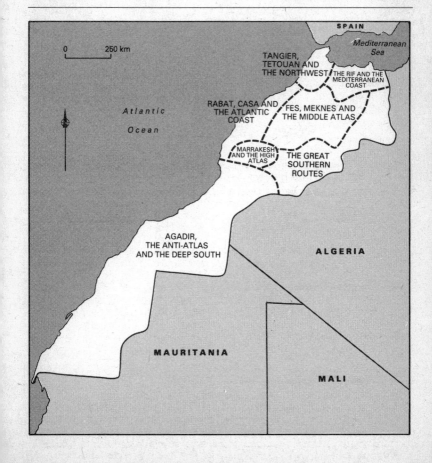

SPAIN

*Mediterranean
Sea*

0   250 km

TANGIER,
TETOUAN AND
THE NORTHWEST   THE RIF AND THE
MEDITERRANEAN
COAST

Atlantic

RABAT, CASA AND
THE ATLANTIC
COAST   FES, MEKNES AND
THE MIDDLE ATLAS

Ocean

MARRAKESH
AND THE HIGH
ATLAS   THE GREAT
SOUTHERN
ROUTES

AGADIR,
THE ANTI-ATLAS
AND THE DEEP SOUTH   ALGERIA

MAURITANIA

MALI

CHAPTER ONE

TANGIER, TETOUAN AND THE NORTHWEST

T**he northwest** can be an intense introduction to Morocco. Its two chief cities, Tangier and Tetouan, are by reputation difficult, with guides and hustlers preying on first-time travellers. However, once clear of the points of arrival, and having set your bags down in a hotel, it doesn't take long to get the measure of them – and to enjoy the experience. **Tangier**, hybridised and slightly seedy from its long European contact, has a setting and skyline the equal of any Mediterranean resort, and is immediately compelling in its role as meeting point of Europe and Africa. **Tetouan**, in the shadow of the wild Rif mountains, feels more Moroccan – its Medina a glorious labyrinth, dotted with squares, *souks* and buildings from its seventeenth-century founding by refugees from Spanish Andalusia.

Moving on from either city, the most popular destination is the mountain town of **Chaouen** – a small-scale and enjoyably laid-back place to come to terms with being in Morocco. It is most easily reached via Tetouan. Heading south from Tangier – which stands at the beginning of the railway lines to Fes, Rabat, Casablanca and Marrakesh – the best places to get acclimatised are the seaside resorts of Asilah and Larache. **Asilah**, a growing tourist centre, is perhaps a little too exploited, though certainly worth time if you are travelling in August, when it is host to an **International Festival** – northern Morocco's major cultural event of the year. **Larache** is less well known, though a personal favourite, for its relaxed feel, fine beach and proximity to the ancient Carthaginian-Roman site of **Lixus**.

International zones

Northern Morocco has an especially quirky **colonial history**, having been divided into three separate zones. Tetouan was the administrative capital of the **Spanish zone**, which encompassed Chaouen (and the Rif) and spread south through Asilah and Larache – itself a provincial centre. The **French zone** began at Souk el Arba du Rharb, the edge of rich agricultural plains sprawling south toward the French Protectorate's capital, Rabat. **Tangier**, meanwhile, experienced **"International Rule"** under a group of European embassies.

One modern consequence of this past is that, although French is now the official second **language** (after Arabic) throughout Morocco, all but the younger generation in the northwest are more fluent in Spanish – a basic knowledge of which can prove extremely useful.

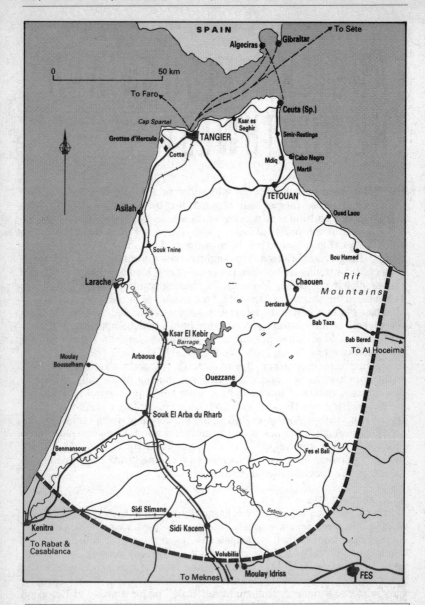

Train network note

ONCF, the Moroccan rail company, operates connecting buses twice daily between **Tetouan** and the station at **Sidi Tnine Lyamani**, just south of Asilah.

TANGIER AND THE COAST

Tangier – in addition to its international airport – has ferry connections with Algeciras, Faro and Sète, and (by catamaran) with Gibraltar. Unless you are bringing a car over from Spain (in which case Ceuta is more economic), it's the preferable crossing – both for the town, in its own right, and for the convenience in moving straight on into Morocco. Asilah is a mere forty minutes' ride on the train; Meknes, Fes, Rabat and Casablanca are all comfortably reached within the day, while if you are in a hurry to get south, there is a night express train for Marrakesh.

The **coast** detailed in this section is the **Atlantic** stretch south towards Rabat. Asilah, on the train line, is the easiest destination; Larache can be reached by bus or *grand taxi* only, either from Tangier or (simpler) from Asilah. A more distinctively Moroccan resort is **Moulay Bousselham**, south of Larache and accessible by bus or *grand taxi* via Souk el Arba du Rharb.

Tangier (Tanger, Tangiers)

For the first five decades of this century **TANGIER** was one of the stylish resorts of the Mediterranean – an "International City" with its own laws and administration, plus an eclectic community of exiles, expatriates and refugees. It was home, at various times, to Spanish and central European refugees; to Moroccan nationalists; and – drawn by loose tax laws and free-port status – to over seventy banks and 4000 companies, most of them dealing in currency transactions forbidden in their own countries. Writers also were attracted to the city: the American novelist Paul Bowles has lived in Tangier since the war, William Burroughs spent most of the 1950s here, and most of the Beats – Jack Kerouac, Allen Ginsberg, Brion Gysin and the rest – all passed through. Tangier was also the world's first and most famous gay resort, a role it maintains to a smaller degree.

When Moroccan independence was gained in 1956, however, Tangier's special status was removed. Almost overnight, the finance and banking businesses shifted their operations to Spain and Switzerland. The expatriate colony dwindled, too, as the new national government imposed bureaucratic controls and instituted a "clean-up" of the city. Brothels – previously numbering almost a hundred – were banned, and in the early 1960s "The Great Scandal" erupted, sparked by a handful of paedophilia convictions and escalating into a wholesale closure of the once outrageous gay bars.

These days there's a slight air of decay about the city, most tangible in the older hotels and bars, and a somewhat uncertain overall identity: a city that seems halfway to becoming a mainstream tourist resort – increasingly popular with holidaying Moroccans – but still retains hints of its dubious past amid the shambling 1930s architecture and style. It is, as already noted, a tricky place for first-time arrivals – hustling and mugging stories here should not be underestimated – but once you get the hang of it, Tangier is lively and very likeable, highly individual and with an enduring eccentricity.

POINTS OF ARRIVAL

By ferry

Disembarking at Tangier can be a slow process, with long queues for passport control and customs: be prepared. Most importantly, make sure that you have your **passport stamped** (and departure card collected) while *on board the ferry*; announcements to this effect are not always made in English, so make your way to the purser's office during the journey. If you miss out on this, you'll be left until last by the officials in Tangier.

Once ashore, and through customs, you pass into the **ferry terminal building**. There's a **bureau de change** here which sells dirhams at standard rates for most currencies and travellers' cheques (for credit card exchange you need a bank in the city, see "Directory", p.65). Also within the building is an **ONCF** office for **train tickets**, worth queuing for immediately if you're going straight on to Asilah, Rabat, Meknes or Fes; the afternoon train (for all destinations) currently leaves the **port station** (Gare du Port) at 4.10pm.

The Gare du Port is sited almost directly below the ferry terminal; you can't miss it as you come out. Nearby – and still inside the port enclosure – there are ranks for **grand and petit taxis** (see below for practicalities); they are best engaged here, before you get outside the enclosure to the hustling of the port gates.

By hydrofoil/catamaran

Hydrofoils (from Algeciras) and **catamarans** (from Gibraltar) dock close to the ferry terminal; passport control and customs clearance is usually fairly swift. If you want to change money and have ready cash, there's no special need to go and queue at the ferry terminal *bureau* – travel agents along the seafront will take pounds, pesetas and dollars, and so will most hotels.

By air

Tangier's **airport** is about 15km outside the city. There is a very sporadic bus (allegedly every 2hr), though if you arrive on a package tour you'll be met by a hotel shuttle. If you're on your own, either bargain with the **taxi** drivers, who *should* charge around 50dh (though tourists are often charged 70–80dh) for up to six passengers, or walk the two kilometres to the main road, where you can pick up the #17 or #70 **buses** to the Grand Socco (see "Orientation", opposite). The **bank** at the airport exchanges cash only.

A note on city taxis and buses

Grands taxis (large cream/beige Mercedes) are permitted to carry up to six passengers. The price for a ride should be fixed in advance – 7dh per person is standard for any trip within the city, including tip. Small blue/green **petits taxis** (which carry just three passengers) can be flagged down around the town. Most of these are metered – standard rate for a city trip is 5dh per person. On the streets you can **hail a taxi**, whether it has passengers or not; if it is going in your direction it will generally take you. If you join a taxi with passengers, you pay the full fare, as if it were empty. Both *grand* and *petit taxi* rates increase by fifty percent **after 9pm**.

A new privately operated **city bus service** has begun, operated by *Boughaz*. These "minibuses" run to a number of useful destinations – including the bus station and Cap Spartel; there is a stop just outside the port gate. Regular city bus services are less useful.

For details on the bus and taxi terminals for journeys out of Tangier, see "Leaving Tangier", on p.66–67.

Orientation

After the initial confusion of an unfamiliar Arab city, Tangier is surprisingly easy to find your way around. As with all the larger Moroccan towns, it's made up of two parts: the **Medina**, the original Moroccan town, and the **Ville Nouvelle**, built by its European colonisers. Inside the Medina, a classic web of alleyways and stepped passages, is the old fortified quarter of the **Kasbah**, with the former Sultanate's palace at its centre.

Together with the **beach** and the seafront **Avenue d'Espagne**, the easiest reference points are the city's three main squares – the Grand Socco, Petit Socco and Place de France. **Place de France** is a conventional, French-looking square at the heart of the Ville Nouvelle, flanked by elegant cafés and a terrace-belvedere looking out over the ocean. From here, **Boulevard Pasteur** (the main city street) leads off toward the post office and the ONMT tourist office a couple of blocks further up. In the other direction, **Rue de la Liberté** runs down to the **Grand Socco**, a fairly amorphous open space in front of the Medina. The north side of the square opens onto the Medina's principal street, **Rue es Siaghin**, which culminates in the **Petit Socco** – a tiny square of old cafés and cheap hotels.

Arriving

Arriving at the port or train station, it's easy enough to walk to a hotel on the seafront or in the Medina; places in the central Ville Nouvelle are a little further afield and you may want to take a taxi.

For the **seafront** places, simply follow the Avenue d'Espagne/Avenue des Forces Armées Royales (FAR). If you want to **stay in the Medina**, there's a choice of routes: either up Rue du Portugal to the Grand Socco, or up the steps behind the port entrance, round to the Grand Mosque and the junction of Rue des Postes/Rue Dar el Baroud. If you're unsure of yourself (and the walk to the Medina can be intimidating if this is your first visit to Morocco), it's best to take a taxi from the port.

STREET NAMES

Tangier **street-name signs** are the most confusing in the country, with the old French and Spanish colonial names still in use alongside their Arabicised successors. In addition *Rue* and *Calle* are both gradually being replaced by *Zankat; Avenue* and *Boulevard* by *Charih*.

Maps tend to use the new Arabic versions, though not all of the street signs have been changed. In the text and maps of this guide, we have used new names only when firmly established. Among the main street-name changes, note:

> **Rue de la Plage** – **Zankat Salah Eddine el Ayoubi**
> **Rue Rembrandt** – **Zankat el Jaba el Quatania**
> **Rue Goya** – **Zankat Moulay al Abdallah**
> **Rue de la Liberté** – **Zankat el Houria**
> **Rue Sanlucar** – **Zankat el Moutanabi**
> **Place de France** – **Place de Faro**
> **Grand Socco** – **Place de 19 Avril 1947**

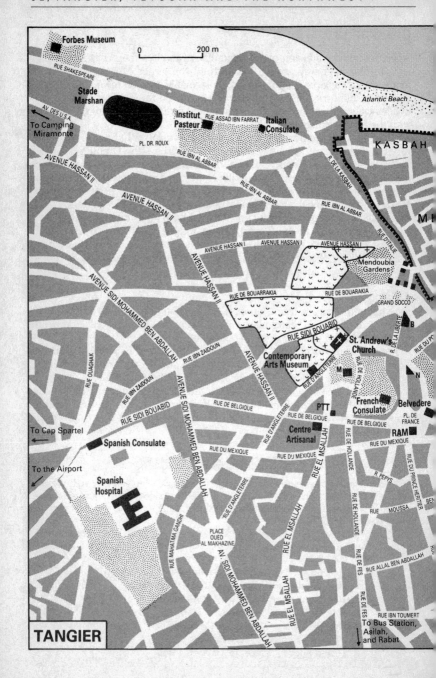

Forbes Museum

RUE SHAKESPEARE

0   200 m

Stade
Marshan

AV. DES U.S.A.

To Camping
Miramonte

PL. DR. ROUX

Institut
Pasteur

RUE ASSAD IBN FARRAT

Italian
Consulate

Atlantic Beach

KASBAH

RUE IBN AL ABBAR

AVENUE HASSAN II

AVENUE HASSAN II

RUE IBN AL ABBAR

RUE IBN AL ABBAR

R. DE LA KASBAH

RUE D'ITALIE

M...

AVENUE HASSAN I

AVENUE HASSAN I

AVENUE HASSAN I

Mendoubia
Gardens

AVENUE SIDI MOHAMMED BEN ABDALLAH

AVENUE HASSAN II

RUE DE BOUARRAKIA

RUE DE BOUARAKIA

GRAND SOCCO

B

RUE OUAGHAK

RUE IBN ZAIDOUN

RUE SIDI BOUABID

R. DE LA LIBERTÉ

RUE DU P...

Contemporary
Arts Museum

St. Andrew's
Church

RUE IBN ZAIDOUN

AVENUE SIDI MOHAMMED BEN ABDALLAH

AVENUE HASSAN II

RUE D'ANGLETERRE

RUE DE HOLLANDE

M

N

RUE SIDI BOUABID

RUE DE BELGIQUE

PTT

RUE DE BELGIQUE

French
Consulate

Belvedere

To Cap Spartel

RUE D'ANGLETERRE

RUE DE BELGIQUE

PL. DE
FRANCE

Centre
Artisanal

RUE EL MSALLAH

RUE DE HOLLANDE

RAM

To the Airport

RUE DU MEXIQUE

RUE D'ANGLETERRE

RUE DU MEXIQUE

RUE DU MEXIQUE

Spanish Consulate

R. PEPYS

Spanish
Hospital

RUE DU PRINCE HERITIER

BEN...

RUE
MOUSSA

RUE MAHATMA GANDHI

AV. SIDI MOHAMMED BEN ABDALLAH

PLACE
OUED
AL MAKHAZINE

RUE EL MSALLAH

RUE DE HOLLANDE

RUE DE FES

RUE ALLAL BEN ABDALLAH

RUE DE FES

RUE DE FES

RUE IBN TOUMERT

To Bus Station,
Asilah,
and Rabat

TANGIER

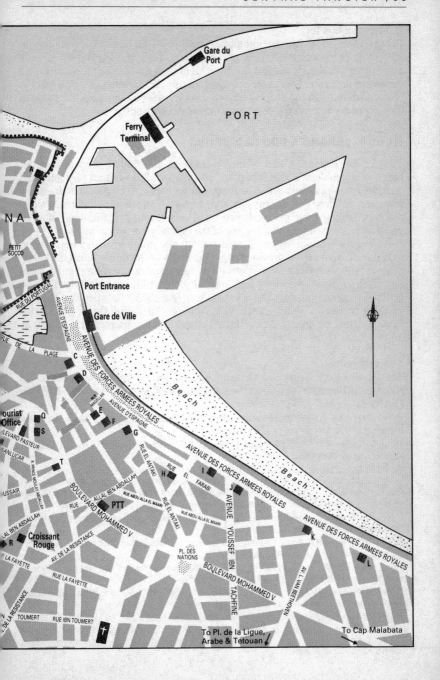

Guides and hustlers

Be prepared on arrival for unofficial **"guides"** – or hustlers – who can be incredibly persistent around the port entrance. They will tell you some fairly amazing tales: the hotels are full, the Medina is dangerous, the trains and buses are on strike. Don't take too much of this at face value, and don't feel in any way duty bound to employ anyone's services – you don't need a guide in Tangier and you certainly don't want one of the port hustlers.

Hotels, pensions and campsites

Tangier has dozens of **hotels and pensions**, and finding a room is never much of a problem: if the first place you try is full, ask them to phone and reserve you a place elsewhere – most will be happy to do so. The city does, however, get crowded during July and August, with some of the unclassified places doubling their prices. If you want a cheap bed at this time of year, you'll often do best by going for one of the officially classified hotels.

All **hotels** listed below are **keyed** by letter or number; letters correspond to the main map on the previous page, numbers to the more detailed Medina plan on p.59. A few places are detailed simply because they are regular package choices (which you may find yourself booked into); most, however, are positive recommendations. As always, there is a choice between the **Medina** or **Ville Nouvelle**. Hotels in the Ville Nouvelle, including the seafront area, have a virtual monopoly on comfort (and regular running water), as well as an easier, more familiar feel.

Seafront hotels

Almost all places below are along or just off the seafront, which begins as **Avenue d'Espagne** then becomes **Avenue des Forces Armées Royales (FAR)**.

Hôtel Bretagne (D), 92 Av. d'Espagne (☎323.39). Once grand, now a bit decayed, but friendly, clean and inexpensive. *1*B*.

Hôtel Valencia (C), 72 Av. d'Espagne (☎217.14). Recently renovated and very well situated; almost opposite the city train station. *2*A*.

Hôtel El Muniria (E), Rue Magellan. Friendly, excellent value and with a late-night bar that comes highly recommended. Burroughs, Kerouac and Ginsberg all stayed here when they first came to Tangier, Burroughs writing *The Naked Lunch* in room 9. (Rue Magellan zigzags up from the seafront behind the crumbling *Hôtel Biarritz*.) *Unclassified – 1*A prices*.

Hôtel Ibn Batouta (F), 8 Rue Magellan (☎371.70). Another good-value choice, just across the street from the *El Muniria*. *1*B*.

Hôtel El Djenina (G), 8 Rue Grotius. Dull, though well maintained (hot baths in all rooms, etc); a block up from Avenue d'Espagne. *2*A*.

Hôtel Miramar (J), Av. des FAR (☎389.48). By far the best budget hotel on the seafront – very 1930s and with big rooms with hot showers. *2*B*.

Hôtel El Farabi (H), 8 Rue Saidia/corner Rue El Farabi (☎345.66). Excellent, nearby alternative to the *Miramar*, if that's full. Clean, well run and friendly. *1*A*.

Hôtel Rif (I), Av. d'Espagne (☎359.08), *5**; **Hôtel Almohades** (K), Av. des FAR (☎403.30,) *5**; **Hôtel Solazur** (L), Av. des FAR (☎401.64), *4*A*. Three of the main package hotels on the seafront; official rates are high if you book independently, though they sometimes have special offers out of season.

Central Ville Nouvelle hotels

Most of these recommendations are within a few blocks of Place de France and the central Boulevard Pasteur. If you've got much luggage, a taxi could be a useful investment.

Hôtel Lutetia (Q), 3 Rue Moulay Abdallah (Goya) (☎318.66). Good for its category and well located – a block below Boulevard Pasteur. *2*A.*

Hôtel Maroc (S), Rue Moulay Abdallah (Goya). A block from the *Lutetia* – literally falling apart, but a nice place in its own way. *Unclassified.*

Grand Hôtel Villa de France (M), 143 Rue de Hollande (☎314.75). This is one of the most elegant hotels in the country (Matisse stayed in, and painted the view from, room 35), with gardens, swimming pool and a lively bar. It isn't, however, crammed with lifts and luxury fittings, and so remains moderately priced – around 200dh for a double room. Bookings are essential in midsummer. *4*A.*

Hôtel El Minzah (N), 85 Rue de la Liberté (☎358.85), *5**; **Hôtel Africa (O)**, 17 Av. Moussa Ibn Noussair (☎355.11), *4*B*; **Hôtel Chellah (R)**, Rue Allal Ben Abdallah (☎383.88), *4*A*; **Hôtel Tanjah Flandria (T)**, 6 Bd. Mohammed V (☎330.00), 4*A. The main package hotels in the centre. If you have unlimited money, the *Minzah* is Tangier's finest, with a wonderful garden pool overlooking the sea and town.

Rue de la Plage. This street (aka Zankat Salah Eddine El Ayoubi) runs up from the town train station to the Grand Socco and is lined with small **pensions**. Many of them charge outrageous prices to new arrivals sent over by port hustlers. Pensions *Miami* and *Talavera* are probably the best bets if rooms seem a problem elsewhere.

Medina hotels

With the exception of the *Continental* and the *Mamora,* these listings are unclassified and fairly basic – safe enough, though, and with distinct character if you have the (initial) confidence. See the Medina map for a key to the smaller places.

Hôtel Grand Socco (B on main map), Grand Socco. Not very salubrious but very central and extremely easy to find, with some rooms looking out over the square. Good deals on big rooms for three to five people. *Unclassified.*

Hôtel Mauretania (1), **Pension Becerra (2)**, **Hôtel Fuentes (3)**, all in the Petit Socco, at the heart of the Medina. *Fuentes*, with a terrace café above the square, is the friendliest, and also the oldest; Camille Saint-Saens was one of its Victorian residents. *Unclassified.*

Pension Palace (4), **Pension Marhaba (6)**, Rue des Postes. Best of a fairly bad bunch in a street that is a hotbed of hustling; the *Palace* is quite attractive, though, and *Marhaba*, in an alley to the left (just before reaching the Grand Mosque), has good views of town and sea from some rooms. *Unclassified.*

Hôtel Mamora (5), 19 Rue des Postes. Overpriced for the facilities (water is as erratic here as in the Socco dives above) but offers considerably more security and a bit more comfort at the heart of the Medina. *2*B.*

Hôtel Continental (A on main map), Rue Dar el Baroud (☎310.24). Founded in 1888, this was once the most fashionable hotel in Tangier, and it still has style, with a grand piano and huge parrot cage in the hall and a beautiful terrace overlooking the port. Over the last few years the hotel has been renovated – and slightly enlarged – and prices have crept higher than they should. However, it remains a personal favourite and by far the best choice if you have the confidence to stay in the Medina. To get there, either take a taxi from by the port entrance, or walk up to the Petit Socco and take Rue de la Marine to the left of Rue des Postes. Follow this around past the Grand Mosque and a terrace, and you'll come to the imposing old hotel gates. Bookings are recommended; ask for rooms 108 or 208, which are a *fin-de-siècle* treat – or, if they're gone, for any first- or second-floor seafront room; "back" rooms are not really worth the money. *As yet unclassified – 3*B prices.*

Campsites

Tangier's campsites are sited well outside the city – worth considering mainly if you are travelling in a campervan or with a caravan. For those with a tent, security is not great, and costs (especially if you have no transport) the equal of a reasonable budget hotel. Choices are:

Camping Miramonte (☎371.38). The closest and most popular campsite, 3km from the centre, to the west of the Kasbah; to get there, take local buses #2, #21, or preferably #1. The site, just behind the "Atlantic Beach", is fairly pleasant and there's a reasonable restaurant.

Camping-Caravaning Tingis (☎401.91). Six km east of the city, over towards Cap Malabata with its *Club Méditerranée* complex. *Tingis* itself is quite a sizeable "holiday village", complete with tennis court, shops and swimming pool. But it's a 2km walk from the beach (which, with the nearby woods, is highly unsafe at night), overpriced, and has a lot of mosquitoes.

Robinson Plage Camping, Cap Spartel. A relaxed, beachside campsite, 8km east of Tangier by the Caves of Hercules (see p.68). Take the *Bourghaz* minibus from the port; a *grand taxi* is pricey, unless you have a group to share costs.

The beach and Ville Nouvelle

Tangier's interest and attraction lies in the city as a whole: its café life, beach, and the tumbling streets of the Medina. The few specific "monuments", with the exception of the Dar el Makhzen palace, are best viewed as adding direction to your wanderings, while the markets, though novel and bright enough, are not on the whole great sources of bargains.

The town beach

It was the beach and mild climate which drew in Tangier's first expatriates, the Victorian British, who used to amuse themselves with afternoon rides along the sands and weekends of "pig-sticking" in the wooded hills behind. Today's pleasures come a little more packaged on the **town beach**, with camel rides and a string of club-like beach bars. However, by day the sands are diverting and fun, with Moroccans entertaining themselves in acrobatics and football.

It is compulsory to change in a cabin, so when you arrive you may feel like attaching yourself to one of the **beach bars**, most of which offer showers and deck chairs, as well as food and drink. Some of these are institutions, like *Emma's BBC Bar* (still serving up bacon-and-egg breakfasts), *The Sun Beach*, where Tennessee Williams reputedly wrote a first draft of *Cat on a Hot Tin Roof* or *The Windmill*, where Joe Orton knocked about. Others, like *The Macumba*, retain a predominantly gay clientele. Perhaps the most lively and pleasant is *Miami Beach*, with its gardens to laze around in, but the scenes change with the season, so look around and take your pick.

By day, it more or less goes without saying, don't leave anything on the beach unattended. By night, limit your exploration to the beach bars (a few of which offer evening cabarets – if Arabic Country & Western appeals), as the beach itself becomes a dangerous venue for rough trade.

The Grand Socco and Place de France

The **Grand Socco** is the obvious place to start a ramble around the town. Its name, like so many in Tangier, is a French–Spanish hybrid, proclaiming its origins as the main market square. The markets have long gone, but the square remains a meeting place and its cafés are good points to sit around and absorb the city's life. Flanking the Grand Socco are the luxuriant **Mendoubia Gardens**, nowadays part of the grounds of the city's law courts. They are closed to the public, though the caretaker can sometimes be persuaded to give a brief tour; knock at the low green gate in the wall.

Over in the **Place de France** the cafés are at their best in the late afternoon and early evening, when their regulars – an interesting mix of locals and expatriates – turn out to watch and be watched. The one to choose is the *Café de Paris*, which was a legendary rendezvous throughout the years of the International Zone, above all during World War II, when it was the centre of deal making and intrigue between agents from Britain, America, Germany, Italy and Japan. Later the emphasis shifted to Morocco's own politics: the first nationalist paper, *La Voix du Maroc*, surfaced at the café, and the nationalist leader Allal el Fassi, exiled in Tangier from the French-occupied zone, set up his Istiqlal party headquarters nearby.

Nearby markets and St Andrew's church

The old **markets** of the Grand Socco were moved partly into Rue de Portugal (running down to the port), partly on to cramped terraces beside Rue d'Angleterre. Most interesting of the latter is a small terrace on the left-hand side of the road, near the walls of the *Villa de France* hotel, where Berber women from the villages sell their red-, black- and white-striped *foutahs* – rough-weave blankets worn sometimes four to the body as skirt, shawl and head covering. Quality and prices for these are usually better in Tetouan, but the designs are much the same.

On the opposite side of Rue d'Angleterre is the Anglican church of **St Andrew**, one of the city's odder sights in its fusion of Moorish decoration and English country churchyard. There is generally a caretaker around to show off the church, notable for its rendition of the Lord's Prayer in Arabic script above the altar. In the graveyard, among the laments of early deaths from malaria, you come upon the tomb of **Walter Harris** (see *Contexts*), the most brilliant of the chroniclers of "Old Morocco" in the closing decades of the nineteenth century and the beginning of the twentieth. Another eccentric Briton, **Emily Keane**, is also commemorated. A contemporary of Harris, she lived a very different life, marrying in 1873 the Shereef of Ouezzane – at the time one of the most holy towns of the country (see p.94). Other graves reveal epitaphs to **Caid Sir Harry MacClean**, the Scottish military adviser to Sultan Moulay Abd el Aziz at the turn of the century, and to **Dean** of *Dean's Bar* ("Missed by all and sundry"). If you're intrigued by contemporary expat life, attend the Sunday service – which is followed by drinks in the graveyard. Master of Ceremonies is the Hon. David Herbert, second son of the Earl of Pembroke and expat society leader since the last war.

Further **market areas** are to be found in the Ville Nouvelle, if you follow Rue de la Liberté toward Place de France, and then turn left down a series of steps, past the *El Minzah* hotel. The terraces that you come out upon comprise the so-called **Fondouk Market**, a sequence of tiny stalls ranging from pottery to spectacle repairs, from fruit and vegetables to junk.

The Medina

The Grand Socco offers the most straightforward **approach to the Medina**. The arch at the northwest corner of the square opens onto Rue d'Italie, which becomes Rue de la Kasbah, the northern entrance to the Kasbah quarter. To the right, there is an opening onto Rue es Siaghin, off which are most of the *souks* (markets) and at the end of which is the Petit Socco, the Medina's principal landmark and square.

An alternative approach to the Medina is from the seafront: follow the steps up, walk round by the Grand Mosque, and Rue de la Poste will lead you to the Petit Socco.

Rue es Siaghin

Rue es Siaghin – Silversmiths' Street – was Tangier's main thoroughfare into the 1930s, and remains an active one today, with a series of fruit, grain and cloth markets opening off to its sides.

Halfway up, locked and decaying, is the old **Spanish Cathedral** and **Mission**; to the right, just before it, was formerly the **Mellah**, or Jewish quarter, centred around Rue des Synagogues. Moroccan Jews traditionally controlled the silver and jewellery trade – the "Siaghin" of the street name – but few remain in Tangier, having left at independence for Gibraltar, France and Israel. The street itself, well before that, had been taken over by tourist stalls; needless to say, it's a bad place to buy anything.

The Petit Socco

The **Petit Socco** (Little Market) seems too small ever to have served such a purpose. Old photographs, in fact, show it almost twice its present size: it was only at the turn of the century that the hotels and cafés were built. These, however, give the place its atmosphere: seedy, slightly conspiratorial and the location for many of the Moroccan stories of Mohammed Mrabet (see *Contexts*). In the heyday of the "International City", with easily exploited Arab and Spanish sexuality a major attraction, it was in the alleys behind the Socco that the straight and boy brothels were concentrated. William Burroughs used to hang out around the square dressed in old suits bought from Moroccans, sent over to them by American charities. "I get averages of ten very attractive propositions a day," he wrote to Alan Ginsberg, ". . . no stasis horrors here."

The Socco cafés (the *Central* was the prime Beat location) lost much of their allure at independence, when the sale of alcohol was banned in the Medina, but they remain a good place to sit around, talk and get some measure of the town.

Towards the Kasbah

It is beyond the Petit Socco that the Medina proper seems to start, "its topography", to quote Paul Bowles, "rich in prototypal dream scenes: covered streets like corridors with doors opening into rooms on either side, hidden terraces high above the sea, streets consisting only of steps, dark impasses, small squares built on sloping terrain so that they looked like ballet sets designed in false perspective, with alleys leading off in several directions; as well as the classical dream equipment of tunnels, ramparts, ruins, dungeons and cliffs".

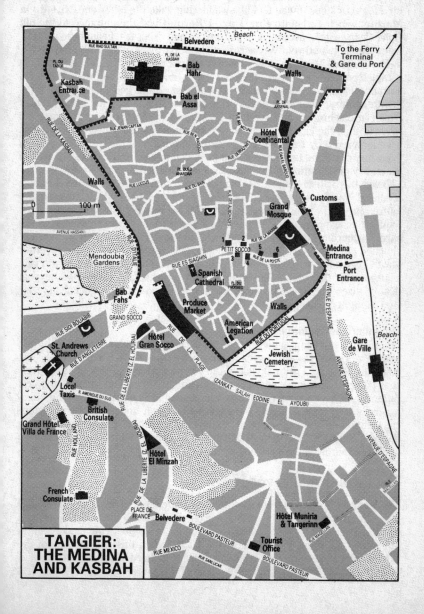

TANGIER:
THE MEDINA
AND KASBAH

Walking up from the Petit Socco, you can follow **Rue des Chrétiens** (aka Rue des Almohades) and its continuation **Rue Ben Raisouli** and emerge, with luck, around the lower gate to the Kasbah. Heading past the Socco toward the sea walls are two small streets straddled by the Grand Mosque. If you want to get out and down to the beach, follow **Rue des Postes** and you'll hit a flight of steps. If you feel like wandering, take the other one, **Rue de la Marine**, which curls into **Rue Dar el Baroud** and the entrance to the old *Hôtel Continental* – another fine place to sit and drink tea. From here it's relatively simple to find your way across to the square below the Kasbah Gate.

The **Grand Mosque** itself, though it spreads across a whole block, is completely screened from public view – and, as throughout Morocco, entrance is strictly forbidden to non-Muslims. Enlarged in the early nineteenth century, the mosque was originally constructed by the great Moulay Ismail in celebration of the return of Tangier to Moroccan control in 1685. Prior to this, the city had seen some two centuries of European rule: it was first conquered by the Portuguese in the aftermath of the Moors' expulsion from Andalusia and the Algarve, and in 1663 it passed to the British as part of the dowry of Catherine of Braganza, bride to Charles II.

It was the British – in just 22 years of occupation – who destroyed the city's medieval fortifications, including a great upper castle which covered the entire site of the present-day Kasbah. Under virtually constant siege, they found it an expensive and unrewarding possession: "an excrescence of the earth", according to Samuel Pepys, who oversaw the garrison's withdrawal, shocked at the women of the town ("generally whores") and at the governor ("with his whores at the little bathing house which he has furnished with jade a-purpose for that use"). Dining alone with the chaplain, Pepys had "a great deal of discourse upon the viciousness of this place and its being time for God Almighty to destroy it."

The American Legation

American history in Tangier is, by comparison, liberal, as evidenced by the **Old American Legation** (open daily 9am–1pm & 4–6.30pm; free), just inside the Rue du Portugal wall of the Medina. Morocco was the first overseas power to recognise an independent United States, and this was the first American ambassadorial residence, established in 1777. An interesting building in its own right, bridging the alleyway below, it houses excellent historical exhibits on the city's history, exhibits that include the correspondence between Sultan Moulay ben Abdallah and George Washington, and displays of Moroccan-resident American artists.

The Kasbah and beyond

The **Kasbah**, walled off from the Medina on the highest rise of the coast, has been the palace and administrative quarter since Roman times. It is a strange, somewhat sparse area of walled compounds, occasional colonnades, and a number of luxurious villas built in the 1920s, when this became one of the Mediterranean's most chic residential sites. Richard Hughes, author of *A High Wind in Jamaica* (and of a book of Moroccan tales), was the first

European to take a house here – his address fabulously titled "Numéro Zero, Le Kasbah, Tangier". Among those who followed was the eccentric Woolworth's heiress, Barbara Hutton, whose parties included a ball where thirty Reguibat camel drivers and racing camels were brought a thousand miles from the Sahara to form an honour guard.

Local guides point with some pride to these locations, but the main point of interest here is the former **Sultanate Palace**, or **Dar el Makhzen**, now converted to an excellent museum of crafts and antiquities (open, in theory at least, daily except Tuesdays, from around 9.30am to noon, and again from 3 to 6pm). It stands near the main gateway to the Medina, the **Bab el Assa**, to the rear of a formal court, or *mechouar*, where the town's pashas held public audience and gave judgement well into the present century. The entrance to the palace, a modest-looking porch, is in the left-hand corner of the court as you enter from the Medina – scores of children will probably direct you.

The Palace, gardens and *Café Detroit*

The Dar el Makhzen – built, like the Grand Mosque, by Moulay Ismail – last saw royal use as recently as 1912, with the residence of the Sultan Moulay Hafid, who was exiled to Tangier after his forced abdication by the French. The extraordinary negotiations which then took place are chronicled in Walter Harris' *Morocco That Was*. According to Harris, the ex-Sultan found it "an uncomfortable, out-of-date, and out-of-repair old castle, and it formed by no means a satisfactory place of residence, for it was not easy to install 168 people within its crumbling walls with any comfort or pleasure". Most of the 168 seem to have been members of the royal harem and well able to defend their limited privileges. Moulay Hafid himself ended up with "only a couple of very shabby rooms over the entrance", where he apologetically received visitors and played bridge with a small circle of Americans and Europeans.

However out of date and uncomfortable the palace may have been, it is by no means a poor example of Moroccan craftsmanship and architecture. The design is centred on two interior courtyards, each with rich arabesques, painted wooden ceilings and marble fountains. Some of the flanking columns are of Roman origin, particularly well suited to the small display of **mosaics and finds from Volubilis** (see Chapter Three). The main part of the museum, however, is devoted to **Moroccan arts**, laid out according to region and including an exceptional collection of ceramics from Meknes and Fes.

At the entrance to the main part of the palace is the **Bit el Mal**, the old treasury, and adjoining this is a small private **mosque**, near to which is the entrance to the herb- and shrub-lined palace **gardens**, shaded by jacaranda trees. If you leave this way, you will come out by the stairway to the **Café-Restaurant Detroit**, set up in the early 1960s by Beat writer Brion Gysin. Gysin created the place partly as a venue for the Trance Musicians of Jajouka, drummers and pipe-players from a village close to Tangier who achieved cult fame through an LP recorded by his friend, Rolling Stone Brian Jones, and who resurfaced on the Stones' recent *Steel Wheels* album. The café is now an overpriced tourist spot but worth the price of a mint tea for the views. Its main entrance is on Rue Riad Sultan, the street running alongside the outer walls of the Kasbah to the main gate and Rue de la Kasbah/Rue d'Italie.

The Forbes Museum and Jews' Beach

Leaving the Medina by the Kasbah gate, a ten- to fifteen-minute walk will bring you to the quarter known as the *marshan*, an exclusive residential quarter with a number of villas and consulates. The finest of the residences is the **Palais Mendoub** on Rue Shakespeare, former Tangerine home of the millionaire publisher Malcolm Forbes, who died in 1990, just months after his eightieth birthday party – the grandest in Tangier for decades, hosted with Elizabeth Taylor and featuring hundreds of musicians transported from the Anti-Atlas and Sahara.

Part of the palace houses (at least for the present) the **Forbes Museum of Military Miniatures** on Rue Shakespeare. This, the world's largest collection of toy soldiers, features a series of battle tableaux, many relating to Moroccan history. They include Hassan II's 1975 "Marche Verte," in which 350,000 unarmed Moroccans "reclaimed" the former Spanish Sahara (see *Contexts*). The museum (and part of the palace gardens) is open Monday to Saturday, 9am to 5pm; admission is free.

Rue Shakespeare runs on to the west of the museum, eventually giving out into a track that leads down to the **Jews' Beach** – so called from its role as the landing stage for Spanish Jews fleeing the Inquisition. There is a beach café here in summer.

Eating, drinking and nightlife

Tangier is not really a night-time city. If you're looking for international resort-style action, or the Tangier of sin-city legend, you'll be disappointed. There are nevertheless good and generally inexpensive **restaurants**, a fair scattering of **bars** and **discos**, and possibilities for films and the occasional concert.

Note that **alcoholic drinks** are not served in the Medina or Grand Socco restaurants.

Medina restaurants

As with most Moroccan cities, the cheapest places to eat are in the Medina. Make your way to the **Petit Socco**, head off left up Rue de la Marine and you've a choice of several hole-in-the-wall cafés on Rue de Commerce (the first alley to the left) or Rue des Chrétiens (aka Rue des Almohades). *Restaurant Andaluz* (7 Rue de Commerce) is about as simple as it's possible to be – and excellent, serving impeccably fried swordfish, grilled brochettes and salad. For a little more variety, the cafés around the Grand Socco are worth a look, too; most stay open all night.

Ville Nouvelle and seafront restaurants

There is a group of inexpensive Spanish seafood restaurants on Rue Sanlucar and its continuation, Rue Méxique, behind Place de France, and fair value set meals along the seafront. A handful of more upmarket places – some of them relics from the International days – add variety around the Ville Nouvelle.

Restaurant Africa, at the lower end of Rue de la Plage. A crowded, local place with no-nonsense Moroccan dishes. Inexpensive, and highly recommended.

Cleopatra's, Rue de la Plage. Good value alternative on the same street.

Restaurant Agadir, 21 Rue Prince Heritier (off Place de France); **Chellah Grill**, again on Rue Prince Heritier, next to the *Hôtel Chellah*. Two more good low-budget restaurants.

Hôtel-Restaurant L'Marsa, 92 Avenue d'Espagne (at the port end of the seafront). Excellent pizzas, cooked in a huge cone-shaped oven, and home-made ice cream to follow. Equally delicious croissants, *pains chocolats* and cakes for **breakfast** or tea.

Sol Beach Restaurant-Bar, 4km along the coast road towards Cap Spartel. If you have a car, this is worth a lunchtime or early evening trip – open year-round, 9am to 9pm, for grilled fish and beers.

Raihani's, Rue Ahmed Chaoki (opposite the terrace on Bd. Pasteur). A more upmarket choice for traditional Moroccan food – worth at least one meal for the superb *harira* (soup), *couscous* and *pastilla* (pigeon pie). Also a good French-based menu.

El Dorado, 21 Rue Allal ben Abdallah (by the *Hôtel Chellah*). Dependable Jewish-Moroccan/Spanish cooking. Mid-range.

San Remo, 15 Rue Ahmed Chaouki. The best Italian food in the city. Mid-range.

Hammadi's, Rue d'Italie (outside the west wall of the Medina). Traditional Moroccan dishes in a rather kitsch salon – and a worthwhile band of Andalusian musicians. Mid-range.

La Grenouille, Rue Rembrandt, just off Bd. Pasteur. Old-established French restaurant. Mid-range to expensive.

Romero's, Av. du Prince Moulay Abdallah (off Bd. Pasteur). Spanish seafood, served in vast portions. Mid-range to expensive.

Guitta's, 110 Sidi Bouabid. The restaurant most redolent of old International Zone Tangier. Mid-range to expensive.

Bars

Tangier **bars** have been much depleted over the last few years.*The Parade*, the most legendary, died with its owner in 1987, and *Dean's*, once the haunt of people like Tennessee Williams, Francis Bacon and Ian Fleming, has fallen into a not very interesting seediness. Possibilities remaining include:

Tangerinn, Rue Magellan, below the *Hôtel Muniria*. Deadpan imitation of a Brighton pub – quite an institution, run by an ex-Household Cavalry trooper and serving the expats for the last twenty years. Open 9pm–2am.

Club España, Rue Magellan. A new and younger innovation, adjoining the *Tangerinn*; beer, snacks and occasional Berber music. 5dh admission.

Carousel Bar, off Rue Prince Heritier. A recently-opened British-run wine bar.

Hôtel Miramar, Av. des FAR. The *Miramar's* seafront bar is a hard-drinking spot for Moroccans; occasionally interesting.

Caid's Bar in the *Hôtel Minzah*, 85 Rue de la Liberté. Long the chichi place to meet – ritzy decor and very expensive drinks.

Discos and clubs

The principal street for discos is Rue Sanlucar (aka Zankat Moutanabi), along with the neighbouring area around Rue Méxique; drinks at any of them are expensive – 50dh and up. For **late-night coffee** or **snacks**, *Café Atlas*, by the *Hôtel Rembrandt*, stays open till 4am, and the cafés in the Grand Socco more or less all night.

Scott's, Rue Sanlucar. Traditionally (though not exclusively) a gay disco, this is worth a look for its choice of paintings – Berber boys in Highland military uniform. Take care leaving late at night, as the street is none too safe; best idea is to tip the doorman 5dh to order you a taxi.

Regine's, Rue el Mansour Dahbi (opposite the Roxy Cinema); **Borsalino's**, Rue Prince Moulay Abdalah (off Bd. Pasteur). More mainstream discos.

Radio Club, Rue Prince Moulay Abdallah (off Bd. Pasteur). Attractively sleazy club with the chance of live Moroccan bands.

Morocco Palace, Rue Prince Moulay Abdallah. A clear winner if you want a folklore evening. This strange, sometimes slightly manic place puts on traditional Moroccan music for Westerners until around 1am, then a Western disco for the Moroccans.

Concerts and films

Music concerts – traditional and popular – are sporadic events in Tangier. The old Spanish bullring, out near the bus station in the Ville Nouvelle, has had a recent major refurbishment as an open-air concert hall, so it might be worth asking about events there at the tourist office. Events are also to be seen at the various consulates, including the Old American Legation (see p.60) and in the Mendoubia Gardens.

There are a dozen or so **cinemas** scattered about the Ville Nouvelle, in the grid around Boulevard Pasteur. Films are frequently shown in their original language, with Arabic subtitles, though some are dubbed into French. The cinema on the Grand Socco shows an exclusive and entertaining diet of Indian and Kung Fu films.

Shops and stalls

Many of the Tangier **market stalls and stores** are eminently avoidable, geared to selling tourist goods that wouldn't pass muster elsewhere. But a few are worthwhile, unique, or both.

Crafts and antiques

Ensemble Artisanal (Rue Belgique; left-hand side, going up from Place de France). Modern Moroccan crafts are displayed in this government-run store, as in other major cities. They are rarely the best or the cheapest available, but prices are (more or less) fixed, so this is a good first call if you feel you need to get an idea of quality and costs before bargaining elsewhere.

Bazaar Tindouf (64 Rue de la Liberté, opposite the *Hôtel Minzah*). One of the best quality junk-antique shops, with fine carpet-pillows and a tremendous selection of old postcards. Bargaining difficult but essential.

Unnamed junk-antique shop (24 Rue de Hollande). Another good second-hand shop for browsing. The **Fes Market**, adjoining, is a lively area for fruit and vegetables.

Bazaar Chaouen (116 Rue de la Plage). Good quality crafts and a very helpful owner, Abdeffamad.

Volubilis Boutique (in the Petit Socco, and another branch opposite *Romero's* restaurant in Rue Moulay Abdallah). Interesting mix of traditional Moroccan and western designer clothes and shoes.

Perfumerie Madini (14 Rue Sebou, in the Medina; from the Petit Socco take the alley between the *Tingis* and *Centrale* cafés, which leads into Rue Sebou, and look for the shop on your right). Madini makes inspired copies of brand-name perfumes from natural oils, which he sells at a fraction of the "real" price, as well as musk and traditional fragrances. Given a couple of days and a sample, he will reproduce any scent you like. Closed 1–4pm and Friday.

Rue Touahin (first right off Rue Saighin, entering the Medina from the Grand Socco). Line of jewellery stalls, which may turn up something appealing. Don't take silver, gold, or most stones at face value: judge on aesthetics.

See also the details on markets on p.57.

Listings

Airlines *Gib Air*, 83 Rue de la Liberté, operates a 16-seat Trislander to Gibraltar, twice daily for most of the year; their flights to London (direct, or via Gibraltar) are often good value. For domestic flights within Morocco (and some international destinations) contact *Royal Air Maroc* on Place de France. For flights to Spain (cheapest departures are from Melilla) try *Iberia* at 35 Bd. Pasteur. *Air France*, 20 Bd. Pasteur, may have good deals, too.

American Express Represented by *Voyages Schwartz*, 54 Bd. Pasteur (☎334.59). Open Mon–Fri 9am–noon and 3–7pm, Sat 9am–12.30pm only.

Banks Most are grouped along Bd. Pasteur/Bd. Mohammed V. The *BMCE bureau de change* on Bd. Pasteur is the most efficient, changing cash and travellers' cheques, and handling cash advances on *Visa* and *Access*; it's open 8am–2pm and 4–8pm every day of the week. The *SGMB* (opposite the post office on Mohammed V) takes some bank cheques backed by credit cards. *Crédit du Maroc,* Bd. Pasteur also handles *Visa* transactions.

Beer/wine Shop. The Spanish-run shop at 63 Rue Hollande has a good selection of bottles, wrapped discreetly for your travels.

Books *Librairie des Colonnes* , 54 Bd. Pasteur. Good range of English-language books, including some of Paul Bowles' Moroccan translations.

Car parking The *Hôtel Tanjah Flandria* (labelled T on the main plan) has an underground garage: 10dh for 24hr.

Car hire Most of the big companies have offices along Bd. Pasteur/Bd. Mohammed V – *Avis* at no. 54, *Hertz* at no. 36, *InterHire* at no. 87, among them. Cheaper and fairly reliable are *Leasing Cars* , 24 Rue Henri Regnault, and at the airport. Discounts are sometimes available if you arrange car hire through one of the package holiday representatives – contact them at any of the larger hotels (like the *Rif* on the seafront).

Car repairs and information Garages can be recommended by the *Royal Automobile Club de Maroc* at 8 Av. Prince Héritier. For Renaults, try *Tanjah-Auto* , 2 Av. de Rabat; Citroëns are at 33 Rue Victor Hugo (one block behind the post office).

Chemists There are several English-speaking chemists in the Place de France (try the Paris, opposite the *Café de Paris*) and along Bd. Pasteur.

Consulates *Great Britain,* 9 Rue Amérique du Sud (☎358.97 or 95; Mon–Fri 9am–12.30pm & 1–3.30pm). The *US* consulate has closed.

English-language newspapers are sold outside the post office, in various stores along Bd. Pasteur, and by news dealers around the *Café de France*.

Hospital Emergency number is ☎342.42; or for the Spanish Hospital (*Hôpital Español*), ☎310.18.

Post, Phones, Poste Restante All available at the main PTT, 33 Bd. Mohammed V; open Mon–Sat 8.30am–noon & 2.30–6.30pm; phone section is open 24hr. As Tangier has direct dialling you can phone (internationally) from any phone box or from one of the smaller PTTs; by day the PTT at the junction of Rue El Msala and Rue Belgique, opposite the Artisan Centre, is a quieter place to make phone calls – and, oddly, cheaper than at the main PTT.

Motorbike hire Bikes are available for short-term lease from the garage on Av. Youssef Ibn Tachfine.

Police Main station is on Rue Ibn Toumert. Emergency ☎19.

Tour companies *Nat Tours* (☎32068) is a reliable company which can arrange hotel bookings and most aspects of travel in Tangier and elsewhere in Morocco.

Tourist office There's an ONMT office at 29 Bd. Pasteur, just down from Place de France and open Mon–Sat 8am–2pm. English-speaking and helpful; ask for their free maps of Fes, Rabat-Salé and Marrakesh, all useful supplements to the ones we've printed.

LEAVING TANGIER

Travelling on **into Morocco** from Tangier is simplest either by **train** (the lines run to Meknes/Fes, or Rabat/Casablanca/Marrakesh; all trains stop at Asilah en route), or, if you are heading east to Tetouan, by shared **grand taxi**. Leaving the country, **ferries** run to Algeciras, Gibraltar, Faro (Portugal) and Sète (France).

Trains

There are two stations: the **Gare du Port** (by the port) and **Gare de Ville** (400 metres along the seafront from the port). At present the **4.10pm** (Rabat/Casablanca/Marrakesh; connection at Sidi Slimane for Meknes/Fes) and **11.15pm*** (Rabat/Casablanca/Marrakesh) trains leave from the Port station, calling at the Ville station ten minutes later. All other departures are from the Ville station only.

If you **arrive in Tangier by ferry and plan to travel straight on**, the 4.15pm train is likely to be the most convenient departure, though if you catch an early ferry you might just make the 2.15pm train to Meknes/Fes (change at Sidi Kacem). The 11.15pm* departure is essentially a night train to Marrakesh, and saves losing a couple of days' travel (and a night's hotel bill). If you take it, try to book a couchette, available as a supplement, which gives you a guaranteed booking and a separate carriage with an attendant – useful for baggage security. You're given a sheet, pillow and blanket; take your own toilet paper. There is a baggage *consigne* at the Ville train station, but it will accept locked luggage only; cafés across the road will oblige for a small fee.

*The 11.15pm night train leaves at 8.50pm during the winter months: check departure boards and don't rely on the timetable. For details of other departures, see the "Travel Details" at the end of this chapter.

Buses and *grands taxis*

Until recently, most of Tangier's **buses** left from down by the port entrance, but a recent shift has moved all departures to a new terminal by the Syrian Mosque at the end of Rue de Fes. This is some 2km from the centre of town, reached by following Rue de Fes to the Rue de Lisbonne roundabout where the road to the airport separates from that to Tetouan. It's a long walk, so either get a *petit taxi* (easily available if you arrive at the bus station) or one of the *Bourghaz* minibuses from the port entrance.

There are **grands taxis** leaving through the day to **Tetouan**, again from the bus station. To get a place in a taxi, just announce yourself to the driver at the head of the rank. You will then be crammed (with five other passengers) into the car. The cost is only slightly more than going by bus and journey time is considerably less.

Taxis can also be chartered here for expeditions further afield, direct to **Chaouen** or **Asilah** for example, and work out relatively economical shared between a group. On your own, heading for Chaouen, it's a lot cheaper to get a bus on from Tetouan. The cost of a place to Tetouan is a standard tariff (currently 20dh); all other destinations are negotiable.

For destinations in the immediate **vicinity of Tangier**, such as the Caves of Hercules or Cap Malabata, you need to negotiate a *grand taxi* at the rank by the *Grand Hôtel Villa de France* on Rue de Hollande.

Ferries

Tangier–Algeciras ferry: *Transmediterranea* (31 Rue Quevedo, off Bd. Pasteur) and *Limadet* (13 Rue du Prince Moulay Abdallah) operate three to four boats a day in spring and summer, down to two in the winter. You can buy **tickets** direct from the companies or (without commission) from any travel agent along Boulevard Pasteur or the seafront; there is also a ticket office at the entrance to the port (which accepts a mix of dirhams and pesetas, if you need to get rid of change). Cars and passengers carried.

Although boats invariably depart an hour or so late, you should **check in** at the port at least one hour before the official departure time to get through the chaos of official business. At the ferry terminal, you first have to get an embarkation card and departure card from the *depart* desk of the ferry companies. Take this, along with your passport, to the police *visa de passeport* desk on the same floor (opposite the bar), where you then need to have your passport stamped before going through customs to the boat. Arrive later than an hour before official departure time and you will probably find that the visa police have knocked off – which means you have to wait for the next ferry.

Tangier–Sète ferry: Similar procedures should be observed for the weekly ferry to Sète; times and tickets from *Voyages Comanav*, 43 Abou Alla El Maari (☎326.49 or 326.52).

Tangier–Algeciras hydrofoils: These cost about 30 percent more than the ordinary ferries, and don't run in bad weather, but are considerably quicker and more efficient. Spring and summer departures are at least daily to Algeciras (1hr); there are no services on Sundays. Again, you can buy tickets directly from the operator (*Transtour*, 54 Bd. Pasteur; ☎340.04) or from most travel agents. Passengers only.

Departures are from a separate dock, just in front of the ferry terminal building, where there's an individual *visa de passeport* office – normally open half an hour before the official (and, more often than not, actual) departure time.

Tangier–Gibraltar catamaran: Operated by *Gibline*, this has replaced the former ferry and hydrofoil services, taking an hour and an half for the crossing. Like the hydrofoils, it doesn't run in bad weather – but after initial teething problems it seems to run quite efficiently. Service is daily (except Thursday and Saturday) in season; three times a week at other times; no services during the boat's annual overhaul (normally for the month of February). Tickets from *Transtour* (see above) and most agents. Passengers only.

Tangier–Faro (Algarve, Portugal) ferry: Passengers and cars. Three departures weekly: Tues, Fri, Sun at 8am, arrives Faro 8pm. Reservations and tickets from *Voyages Comanav*, 43 Abou Alla El Maari (☎326.49 or 326.52).

For flights and car hire addresses see the "Listings", on the previous page.

Around Tangier: capes, caves and Ksar es Seghir

The Bay of Tangier curves around to a pair of capes – Malabata to the east, Spartel to the west. The best beaches are to be found at **Cap Malabata**, where much of the moneyed development of Tangier as a resort has been taking place; if you have transport, however, there is isolation to be found at **Ksar es Seghir**, beyond Malabata on the coast road to Ceuta.

The road west to **Cap Spartel** offers a longer, more exposed beach – **Robinson Plage** – and the picturesque **Caves of Hercules**; it's a pleasant route to fill a day waiting for a ferry or flight at Tangier.

West: the Caves of Hercules and "Atlantic Beach"

If the tourist board pushes one image of Tangier it must be the **Caves of Hercules**, whose strange sea window, shaped like a map of Africa, frames the cover of their official brochure. The name, like Hercules' legendary founding of Tangier, is purely fanciful, but the caves, 18km outside the city and above the "Atlantic Beach", make an attractive excursion. They're a good base, too, if you feel like camping for a few days by the sea; even in the middle of August, only stray groups of visitors share the long surf beaches. Take care with currents, which can be very dangerous even near the shore.

Getting there

The introduction of the local *Bourghaz* bus service has made Cap Spartel – and the caves – a lot more accessible. The bus (a 16-seater) runs regularly throughout the day from near the port gates. An alternative – if you get a group of people together – is to charter a *grand taxi* (from outside the *Grand Hôtel Villa de France*, or by the port gates). This should cost around 100dh for the 34-km return trip – for which price most drivers can be persuaded to drop you in the morning and pick you up in the late afternoon; pay at the end.

La Montagne, the Cape and Robinson Plage

The most interesting route to the caves and cape runs around and above the coast via the quarter known as La Montagne. From Place de France, take Rue Belgique to the beginning of Rue de la Montagne. **"The Mountain"**, less imposing than its name suggests, was a rebel base against the British and Portuguese occupations of Tangier, but is now thoroughly tamed; its cork and pine woods shield the city's most exclusive villas. Among them are two vast royal palaces, the first built by the Victorian British consul Sir John Hay and now one of King Hassan's roster, the other, heavily guarded, among the numerous retreats of the Saudi sheikhs.

After 11km, you reach a short turnoff to the lighthouse at **Cap Spartel** – a dramatic and fertile point, known to the Greeks and Romans as the "Cape of the Vines"; there is a café nearby. Beyond begins the vast and wild Atlantic Beach, or **Robinson Plage**, broken by a rocky spit and then rambling off for as far as you can see. There's a **campsite** on each side of the spit (both near reasonably priced **café-restaurants**) and two **hotels**: the expensive 3*A *Hôtel Grottes* and, beyond the caves, the cheaper *Hôtel Robinson* (2*A). The latter, also known as *Le Mirage*, has a **swimming pool**, open to anyone having a meal, and a bar; at its shop you can hire fishing tackle, or arrange for a horse (or, under supervision, camel) for a ride along the beach.

The Caves of Hercules
The **Caves of Hercules** are natural formations, occupied in prehistoric times, but most striking for a man-made addition – thousands of disc-shaped erosions created by centuries of quarrying for millstones. There were still Moors cutting stones here for a living until the 1920s, but by that time their place was beginning to be taken by professional guides and discreet sex hustlers; it must have made an exotic brothel. Today, there's a standard admission charge (9am–sunset), though you're unlikely to get away without a guide, too, whose descriptive abilities tend to be somewhat dwarfed by the utter obviousness of all there is to see ("wet cave", "dark cave", "sea", etc).

Ancient Cotta
Ten minutes' walk past the caves, the road turns inland from the beach and a rough farm track leads in 200m to the ruins of **Ancient Cotta**, a small, second- to third-century Roman town based around the production of *garum* (a kind of anchovy paste). Parts of the factory, and of a temple and baths complex, can be made out, but it's not a very inspiring or significant site.

East: Cap Malabata and Ksar es Seghir

There are few quicker contrasts than the bay east of Tangier. As you approach, **Cap Malabata** seems almost a different world to the city, dominated by a *Club Méditerranée* and a handful of huge modern hotel complexes. But once around the cape (and there is virtually no more development the whole way down the coast to Ceuta), there's a beautiful road winding above some tremendous stretches of beach, which if you're willing to camp for free – there are no organised sites – must be among the best in the north.

The only problem is a shortage of **buses**. Tangier and the Ceuta border crossing at Fnideq have no connecting service, and the only buses to Ksar es Seghir leave and return early in the morning.

Ksar es Seghir and Djebel Moussa
If you can overcome the transport problem, **KSAR ES SEGHIR** is as relaxed and picturesque a base as could be imagined, still largely enclosed by twenty-foot-high Portuguese walls. A small fishing port, it attracts a fair number of Moroccan summer campers, but few Europeans. There's a friendly café-restaurant on a terrace above the sea, occasional **rooms** to let (ask around), and, as long as you watch your possessions, infinite scope for camping.

South of Ksar es Seghir the road to Fnideq climbs around the **Djebel Moussa** – the mountain which, with Gibraltar, forms the so-called Pillars of Hercules, gateway to the classical world. Mythologies aside, the twin pillars effect remarkable thermal currents, speeding passage for **migratory birds** at this, the shortest crossing between Africa and Europe. A spring or autumn visit will almost guarantee sightings, as up to 200 species make their way across the Straits.

Asilah

The first town beyond Tangier – and the first stop on the railway – **ASILAH** is very much a resort: too much so in many ways, with local attitudes shaped by the possible rewards of package tourism. On the positive side, though, it is one of the most elegant of the old Portuguese Atlantic ports, with its square stone ramparts flanked by palms, and its beach is outstanding – an immense sweep of sand stretching halfway to Tangier. And the town itself is small and very easy to manage: hustlers limit themselves to souvenir selling and enthusiastic attendance at the tourist discos.

If you can visit in August (when the place is packed out) you'll coincide with the annual **International Festival**, a month-long event encompassing art exhibitions and a series of concerts – ranging from Lebanese singers to European jazz, Moroccan folk musicians to American university choirs. Programmes are available in the village, or ask for details at the tourist office in Tangier. The International Festival is followed by a three-day **horse fair**, with a traditional *fantasia* (horsemanship) display on each of the days.

Arriving and practicalities

The **train station** is 2km north of the town – an easy enough walk if you miss the connecting shuttle. Arriving by **grand taxi** (1hr from Tangier), you're dropped in a small square at the edge of the Medina, about 100m north of the ramparts; buses drop you in an adjacent street to this.

Hotels

Asilah can be packed full during the International Festival, but most of the year accommodation is easy enough to find and generally inexpensive. The following recommendations are in ascending order of price.

Hôtel Nasr, in the square facing the ramparts and the sea. A pretty basic place, but pleasantly run and with the cheapest accommodation around. *Unclassified*.

Pension Al-Karam (by the beach, behind the *Hôtel Oued el Makhasine* – see below). Straw-hut rooftop rooms. *Unclassified*.

Hôtel Marhaba, 9 Rue Zallakah (☎71.44). Down toward the ramparts from the bus station, this is slightly more expensive – and crazily decorated. *Unclassified*.

Hôtel Azilah, 79 Av. Hassan II (☎72.86). To the left of the *Marhaba*, opposite a small town gate. Rooms on a terrace above the walls make this the most attractive budget option. *1*B*.

Hôtel de l'Oasis, 8 Place des Nations Unies (☎70.69). A somewhat decaying old hotel in a square to the right (facing the sea) of the bus station; has a bar. *2*B*.

Hôtel Oued el Makhasine, Rue Melilla (☎70.90). Pleasant and comfortable hotel – probably the best choice if you can afford it. *2*A*.

Hotel Al Khaima, Route de Tanger (☎339.92). New and larger resort hotel out on the Tangier road. *3*A*.

Campsites

There are a string of campsites north of the train station. The closest, about 500 metres' walk, is *Camping Echrigui* (☎71.82), well maintained and as good a choice as any.

Restaurants, cafés, the market and *hammam*

The two most obvious **restaurants** – in the square outside the ramparts – are also generally the best. *El Espignon*, with outside tables, does good Spanish-style fried fish. *El Oceano*, opposite, is marginally cheaper.

Asilah's other diversions include a fine **music café**, *Café Haddou*, by the *Hôtel Azilah*, and a **disco**, *La Estrella*, on the beach. There's a Djebali villagers' **market**, at its liveliest on Thursday and Sunday, held on the far side of the Tangier–Rabat road. Ask directions to the town's small **hammam**, tucked down an alleyway in the north of the Medina. Unusually, the keeper charges westerners a group rate and gives you the place to yourselves.

The town

Before the tourists – and the International Festival – Asilah was just a small fishing port, quietly stagnating after the indifference of Spanish colonial administration. Whitewashed and cleaned up, it now has a prosperous feeling to it – the Grand Mosque, for example, is being rebuilt and doubled in size.

The circuit of **towers and ramparts** – built by the Portuguese military architect Botacca in the sixteenth century – are pleasant to wander around. The main keep, **El Hamra**, has been restored as a venue for the International Festival and has the occasional exhibition at other times of the year. It's an easily identifiable site as you walk into town through the ramparts. Continuing along the tiny network of streets, and down towards the platform overlooking the sea, you'll come upon at least a half-dozen **murals** painted and subsequently repainted) during the International Festivals; they form an intriguing mix of fantasy-representational art and geometric designs.

Palais de Raisuli

The town's focal sight – stretching over the sea at the heart of the Medina – is the **Palais de Raisuli**, built in 1909 with forced tribal labour by one Er Raisuli, a local bandit. Raisuli (or Raisuni) was one of the strangest figures to emerge from what was an almost routinely bizarre period of Moroccan government. He began his career as a cattle rustler, achieved notoriety with a series of kidnappings and ransoms (including the British writer Walter Harris and a Greek-American millionaire, Perdicaris, who was bailed out by Teddy Roosevelt), and was eventually appointed governor over practically all the tribes of northwest Morocco. Harris described his captivity in *Morocco That Was* as an "anxious time", made more so by being confined in a small room with a headless corpse. Despite this, captor and captive seem to have formed a real friendship, Harris finding Raisuli a "mysterious personage, half-saint, half-blackguard", and often entertaining him later in Tangier.

Another British travel writer, Rosita Forbes, visited Raisuli at his Asilah palace in 1924, later writing his biography. She described the rooms, today mostly bare, as hung with rugs "of violent colours, embroidered with tinsel", their walls lined with cushions stuffed with small potatoes. The decoration seems logical enough – the palace today still looks more like a glittering Hollywood set than anything real. The great reception room, a long glass terrace above the sea, even has dialogue to match: Raisuli told Forbes that he made murderers walk to their death from its windows – a ninety-foot drop to the rocks. One man, he said, had turned back to him, saying, "Thy justice is great, Sidi, but these stones are more merciful".

The palace overhangs the sea ramparts towards the far end of the Medina (away from the beach). It is used in August for the International Festival but is difficult to obtain entry to at other times. If you're interested, knock or ask around and you may strike lucky with the caretaker.

The beaches

As with Tangier, the **beach** is the main focus of life. The most popular stretches are to the north of the town, past the building works for a new marina and port complex and out towards the campsites. For more isolation, walk south, past the Medina ramparts, for about fifteen minutes.

Mzoura

If you have an interest in ancient sites, it's worth giving up a half-day to explore the prehistoric **stone circle of Mzoura**, south of Asilah. The site – its name in Arabic means "Holy Place" – comprises a central tumulus, assumed to be the tomb of some early Mauritanian king, and an elliptical circle of what were originally some 167 stones. The site bears strong resemblances to stone circles in Brittany and Britain, which would date it to around 1500–2000 BC. There are, however, no published reports.

To reach Mzoura, follow the P12 south of Asilah for 15km, turning east for 4km to the village of SOUK TNINE DE SIDI LYAMANI (also a station on the railway line). From here the site is 5km northeast, unsignposted and across a confusing network of tracks; it would be best to take on a guide in the village.

Larache

LARACHE is a relaxed, easy-going resort, its summer visitors primarily Moroccan tourists. In consequence it is one of the best towns of the north in which to spend a few days by the sea: the beach is superb and for once is very mixed, with as many women around as men – a reassuring feeling for women travellers looking for a low-key spot to bathe. Nearby, too, are the ruins of **ancient Lixus**, legendary site of the Gardens of the Hesperides.

Physically, the town looks like an amalgam of Tangier and Tetouan – an attractive place, if not spectacularly so. It was the main port of the northern Spanish zone and – though the central Plaza de España has become Place de la Libération – still bears much of its former stamp. There are faded old Spanish hotels, Spanish-run restaurants and Spanish bars, even an active Spanish cathedral for the small colony who still work at the docks. In its heyday it was quite a metropolis, publishing its own Spanish newspaper and journal, and drawing a cosmopolitan population that included the French writer Jean Genet, who spent the last decade or so of his life here.

Before the Spanish colonisation in 1911, Larache was a small trading port, its activities limited by dangerous offshore sand bars. Without these, it might have rivalled Tangier, for it is better positioned as a trade route to Fes. Instead, it eked out a living by building pirate ships made of wood from the nearby Forest of Mamora for the "Barbary Corsairs" of Salé and Rabat. There had been an earlier period of Spanish occupation in the seventeenth century, before it was reclaimed and repopulated by Moulay Ismail.

The town and beach

The **Château de la Cigogne** (Stork's Castle), a hulking, three-sided fortress compound, which you pass on the way into town, owes its origin to the first Spanish occupation. From the second, the most striking piece of colonial Spanish architecture is the town's main square, the circular **Place de la Libération** – set just back from the sea and a simple 200-metre walk from the (combined) bus station and *grand taxi* stand.

A high archway at the centre of the *place* leads into the **Medina**, a surprisingly compact wedge of alleys and stairways leading down towards the port. It is now the poorest area of Larache – better-off families have moved out to the new parts of town, leaving their houses here to the elderly – but it doesn't seem so bad a place to live, artfully shaded and airy in its design. The colonnaded market square, just inside the archway, was again built by the seventeenth-century Spanish.

The beach and coastline

The shore below Larache is wild and rocky, but cross its estuary and there are miles of fine sandy **beach** sheltered by trees and flanked by a handful of café-restaurants. You can go there by bus (#4 from the port, every 20min – some buses start from the *place*), a circuitous seven-kilometre route, or you can get straight over from the port in small fishing boats – one dirham per person. From the *place*, the quickest route down to the **port** is along a seafront path, past the crumbling **Fort Kebibat** (Little Domes), built by Portuguese merchants in the sixteenth century.

In summer, an oddity on the beach is the amount of foreign languages you hear – yet with so few foreigners around. The explanation is the number of migrant families, scattered about Europe, who return to the town for the holiday. As well as communities in Barcelona, Naples and Paris, Larache accounts for most of the Moroccan community in London, and on the beach you're likely to come upon kids with disarming English accents. Almost all of the London Moroccans come from the Westbourne Grove area.

For an alternative walk, head to the south of the town, **along the cliffs** to the **lighthouse** and past the jail, and you will eventually come to the Spanish cemetery, where **Jean Genet** is said to be buried. Another version has it that Genet made a deathbed conversion to Islam and is buried in the main Muslim cemetery.

Accommodation and practicalities

There are two **hotels** in the Place de la Libération: the once grand, still elegant *Hôtel España* (☎31.95; 1*A) and the rather grim *Cervantes* (unclassified). Cheaper and better than either of them is the *Pension Amal* (☎27.88; also unclassified); clean, quiet and friendly, it is signposted on the street from the bus station to the square, just off to the left along an alleyway. If you want to stay in the Medina, head for the *Pension Atlas*, just to the right of the square as you go in through the gate, though you probably won't pay much less than in the *Amal*.

The town's "smart" hotel, the 2*B *Hôtel Riad*, looks grand enough – it was the former mansion of the Duchesse de Guise, mother of the current pretender to the French throne – but it has fallen into decay and seems to be dropping stars by the year. It does, however, have quite a fine-looking bar.

Eating, except in the Medina cafés, or the sardine grills down by the port, remains resolutely Spanish. The cheapest cafés are in the Place de la Libération, around the entrance archway of the Medina. For seafood, try *Restaurant Larache* on Av. Moulay ben Abdallah, the street leading from the *place* to the bus station. The best value **bar** is on the same street as the *Hôtel Amal* (see above): it looks a dive but is friendly enough – and prices are half those in the *Riad*.

Ancient Lixus

Founded by Phoenician colonists around 1000 BC, **LIXUS** is thought to have been the first trading post of North Africa and was probably its earliest permanent settlement. It became an important Carthaginian and (later) Roman city, and was deserted only after the break-up of the empire in the fifth century AD. As an archaeological site it is significant, and the legendary associations are rich soil for the imagination, but it has to be said that the actual excavated ruins are not especially impressive. In fact, with the single exception of Volubilis (near Meknes), the best surviving monuments of Roman Africa are all to be found in Tunisia and Algeria.

Even so, if you're spending any amount of time in Larache, or passing through by car, the Lixus ruins are well worth an hour or two's exploration. They lie upon and below the summit of a low hill on the far side of the estuary leading south from the town, at the crossroads of the main Larache–Tangier road and the narrow lane to Larache beach. It's a four- to five-kilometre walk to the ruins from either the beach or town, or you can use the bus which runs between the two; alternatively, for about 75dh you could charter one of the boats to row you over from Larache, wait an hour or so, and then row you back to the town or beach. The site is not effectively enclosed, so there are no real opening hours.

Legendary associations

The **legendary associations** of Lixus – and the site's mystique – centre on the Labours of Hercules. For here, on an island in the estuary, Pliny and Strabo record reports of the palace of the "Libyan" (by which they meant

African) King Antaeus. Behind the palace stretched the **Garden of the Hesperides**, to which Hercules, as his penultimate labour, was dispatched. In the object of his quest – the Golden Apples – it is not difficult to imagine the tangerines of northern Morocco, raised to mythic status by travellers' tales. The site, too, seems to offer reinforcement to conjectures of a mythic pre-Phoenician past. Megalithic stones have been found on the Acropolis, and some early form of sun worship seems still to be echoed in the local name – *shamush*, "burned by the sun".

The site
The **Lower Town**, right beside the main road, consists largely of the ruins of factories for the production of salt – still being panned nearby – and, as at Cotta, anchovy-paste *garum*. The factories seem to have been developed in the early years of the first century AD by the Carthaginians, and they remained in operation until the Roman withdrawal.

A track, some 100m down the road to Tangier, leads up to the Acropolis (upper town), passing on its way eight rows of the Roman **theatre** and **amphitheatre**, unusually combined into a single structure. Its deep, circular arena was adapted for circus games and the gladiatorial slaughter of animals. Morocco, which Herodotus knew as "the wild-beast country", was the major source for these Roman *venationes*, and local colonists must have grown rich from the trade. Amid **baths** built into the side of the theatre, a mosaic remains in situ, depicting Neptune and the Oceans.

Climbing above the baths and theatre, you pass through ramparts to the main enceinte (fortifications) of the **Acropolis** – a somewhat confused network of walls and foundations – and **temple sanctuaries**, including an early **Christian basilica** and a number of **pre-Roman buildings**. The most considerable of the sanctuaries, with their underground cisterns and porticoed priests' quarters, were apparently rebuilt in the first century AD, but even then retained Phoenician elements in their design.

Heading south: Ksar el Kebir, Souk el Arba, Moulay Bousselham and some Roman sites

Heading south from Larache, the main road and most of the buses bypass **KSAR EL KEBIR** – and, unless it's a Sunday, when the town has one of the **region's largest markets**, it seems as well to accept the fact. However, as its name (the Great Enclosure) suggests, the town was once a place of some considerable importance. Founded in the eleventh century, it became an early Arab power base, enlarged and endowed by both Almohads and Merenids, and coveted by the Spanish and Portuguese of Asilah and Larache. It was here, in 1578, that the Portuguese fought the disastrous **Battle of the Three Kings**, the most dramatic in their nation's history – a crusading expedition which saw the death or capture of virtually the entire nobility; for the Moroccans it resulted in the fortuitous accession to power of Ahmed el Mansour, the greatest of all Merenid sultans.

Ksar el Kebir fell into decline in the seventeenth century, after a local chief incurred the wrath of Moulay Ismail, causing him to destroy the walls. Neglect followed, although its fortunes revived to some extent under the Spanish protectorate, when it served as a major barracks.

The **Sunday market** is held right by the bus and *grand taxi* terminals. On any morning of the week, however, there are lively **souks** around the main **kissaria** (covered market) of the old town – in the quarter known as *Bab el Oued* (the Gate of the River). There is also an active **tannery** on the south side of the Medina and a handful of minor Islamic monuments scattered about. With time to spare, there would probably be some reward in engaging a local to show you around.

If you want to stay, ask directions to the *Café-Hôtel Andaluz*, which has clean **rooms** and a fair bit of charm.

Arbaoua and Souk el Arba du Rharb

Beyond Ksar el Kebir, a decaying customs post at **ARBAOUA** marks the old colonial frontier between the Spanish and French zones. On the wooded hill nearby there is a group of French-built hunting lodges, a **hotel** (the *Hostellerie Route de France*; ☎18; 3* prices and excellent food) and a **campsite**. The land to the west is a hunting reserve – explore with care.

South again, **SOUK EL ARBA DU RHARB**, a sprawling roadside town where there are grill-cafés (and **hotels**, if you get stuck), is the first settlement of any size, though it is little more than its name suggests (Wednesday Market of the Plain). However, if you're making for either Ouezzane or Moulay Bousselham, this is the place to go for **transport**. To Ouezzane there are infrequent buses but pretty routine (and much quicker) *grands taxis*; Moulay Bousselham – an attractive resort (see below) – is well served by both.

Moulay Bousselham

Having pledged that buses to **MOULAY BOUSSELHAM** are numerous, it's perhaps worth adding that just because there's one around, this doesn't mean it's about to leave. The **Bousselham bus** – at least when I took it – was one of those classically timeless Moroccan exercises. It arrived out of nowhere, quarter-full and its engine revving up with urgency; after a flurry of action as everyone piled on, it slammed its doors shut and proceeded fifty metres down the road. There we all stopped, while the driver tried to persuade a handful of country women to get on; five eventually did; meanwhile, four other passengers had decided to stay in Souk el Arba. And so it continued, up and down the road to try and fill the bus before an eventual and furious altercation set everything smoothly in motion.

Even after this kind of a morning, though, Moulay Bousselham seems a worthwhile place to arrive in. A village-resort, it comprises little more than a single street, crowded with grill-cafés and sloping down to the sea at the side of a broad lagoon. The **beach** here is sheltered by cliffs – rare along the Atlantic – and there's an abrupt drop-off, which creates a continual thrash of breaking waves. While a lot of fun, the currents are also dangerous and the beach is strictly patrolled by lifeguards. For more practical swimming, you can wander over to the **lagoon**, full in summer with fishing boats and with **boat trips** offered to see the flamingoes from close range.

The village takes its name from the **Marabout Moulay Bousselham** – a tenth-century Egyptian saint, whose *koubba* is prominently positioned above the settlement. In July it sees one of the largest **moussems** – or religious festivals – in the region.

Accommodation

Most visitors to Moulay Bousselham are Moroccan – and you might find yourself the only Westerner here. Most people stay at the lagoon **campsite**, beautifully positioned and with a few facilities. If you don't want to camp, alternatives are distinctly limited: you might get a **room** above one of the cafés (or even a house if you stay a week or more: ask around), but otherwise there's just one small and expensive **hotel**, the 3*A *Le Lagon* (☎28). The hotel, incidentally, has the only **bar** in the place, along with a video room and a somewhat ritzy nightclub.

Banasa and Thamusida

Roman era enthusiasts might want to explore the minor sites of **Banasa**, south of Souk el Arba, and **Thamusida**, just west of the main P2 road, 13km before you arrive at Kenitra.

BANASA, reached along a vaguely signposted farm track off the S210, was a small settlement enlarged by Octavian (the future Emperor Augustus) into a colony for veterans. It retains traces of city walls, a forum, basilica and several baths. The custodian, who lives near the ruins, will probably notice your arrival and add a little life to the stones.

THAMUSIDA, again reached along a rough farm track (turn right by the petrol station in the hamlet of SOUK EL KHEMIS), was a fortified Roman camp. Again it preserves sections of wall, along with baths and a temple.

CEUTA, TETOUAN AND CHAOUEN

The Spanish enclave of **Ceuta** is a slightly frustrating port of entry. Although in Africa, you are not yet in Morocco, and you must make your way to the border at Fnideq, then on from there to **Tetouan**, the first Moroccan town. It can be a time-consuming business. However, if you are making for **Chaouen**, Tetouan has the advantage of regular bus connections.

An alternative, seasonal, port of entry is the village of **Mdiq**, north of Tetouan, which has a weekly (currently Thursday) catamaran connection with Gibraltar. This could be the gentlest of all introductions to Morocco. Mdiq apart, the **Mediterranean** here has few resorts of note, though **Martil** is pleasant enough, as (in its own, basic way) is the "travellers' resort" of **Oued Laou**, in the shadow of the Rif. All are easily reached from Tetouan.

Ceuta (Sebta)

A Spanish enclave since the sixteenth century, **CEUTA** (SEBTA in Arabic) is a curious political anomaly. Along with Melilla, east along the coast, it was retained by Spain after Moroccan independence in 1956 and today functions largely as a military base, its economy bolstered by a limited duty-free status. On a clear day you can almost see Gibraltar, which, in the absence of anything else of great interest, seems somehow symbolic.

Entering Morocco: the border at Fnideq

Since the Algeciras–Ceuta ferries and hydrofoils are quicker than those to Tangier (and the ferries significantly cheaper for cars), Ceuta is a popular **point of entry**. Coming over on a first visit to Morocco, however, try to arrive early in the day so that you have plenty of time to move on to Tetouan – and possibly beyond. There is no customs/passport check at the port. You don't officially enter Morocco until the border at **FNIDEQ**, 3km out of town, reached by local bus from the seafront.

Heading for the border, turn left as you come off the ferry or hydrofoil – the bus stop is about 200m down, in the second main square, Plaza de la Constitución. On the Moroccan side, formalities can be time-consuming, especially for car drivers, and there are sporadic searches of pedestrians, too. But stay patient: you should be clear (in either direction) within an hour. Once across, the easiest transport is a shared *grand taxi* to **Tetouan** (split six ways, that's currently 10dh each); buses are infrequent, though a couple of dirhams cheaper. There are **exchange facilities** (cash only) at the frontier. If you are driving, it is worth filling up with petrol – at lower prices – in Ceuta.

The town

In Ceuta itself there isn't a great deal to do. The local authorities are in the midst of creating a town beach, but at present there are no sands to speak of – locals go by bus to **Playa Benzou**, some way out of town. And, though the duty-free status draws many of the Tangier expatriates on day trips to buy cheap spirits, and Spanish day-trippers to buy radios and cameras, neither are very compelling pursuits for casual visitors. If you do want a cheap bottle for Moroccan travels, check the *Roma* supermarket on Paseo del Revellin.

Most of the town, which is surprisingly large, is modern, functional and provincial in the dullest Spanish manner. The **Cathedral** ("Our Lady of Africa") is in the main **Plaza de Africa** opposite the ferry dock, and an oldish quarter rambles up from the end of the long main street, **Paseo del Revellin**. Beyond this, you can walk out and around the peninsula in little over an hour. As the buildings, three to a dozen blocks in width, disappear from view, the land swells into a rounded, pine-covered slope, offering fine views out to the Rock of Gibraltar.

This part of Ceuta, **Monte Acho**, is occupied more or less exclusively by the military. Walking the circuit, signs direct you to the **Ermida de San Antonio**, an old convent completely rebuilt in the 1960s and dominated by a

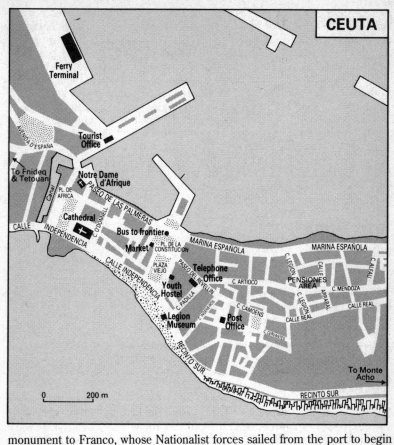

monument to Franco, whose Nationalist forces sailed from the port to begin the Spanish Civil War. Spanish–African military history is continued in the **Museu de la Legión** (Sat & Sun only 11am–2pm & 4–6pm), back in town on the Paseo de Colón; crammed with uniforms, weapons and paraphernalia of the Spanish Foreign Legion, it is quite intriguing.

Accommodation and ferries

If you plan to stay overnight in Ceuta, be warned that it isn't easy to find a room – and not cheap when you do. With its large garrison and its consumer goods, the town has a constant flow of Spanish families. Problems are compounded at **festival** times, the main event being the *Fiesta de Nuestra Señora* on August 5.

Most of the town's dozen or so **hotels**, **hostales** and **pensiones** are to be found along the main thoroughfare, Paseo del Revellin, or its extensions, Calle Camoens and Calle Real. A complete list (and a map of the town) is available at the **Oficina de Turismo** by the ferry dock; if it is closed you can consult the list displayed in its window. Two mid-range *pensiones* to try are the *Revellin* (2 Paseo del Revellin; ☎51.32.06) and the slightly more pricey *Atlante* (1 Paseo de las Palmeras, on the waterfront; ☎51.35.48). Other cheap *pensiones* and *Casas de Huespedes* (boarding houses – indicated by a blue *CH* sign), along with some good **tapas bars**, are tucked away in the streets just to the north of Calle Real. The **youth hostel** (*Pousada de Juventud*), at 27 Plaza Viejo, is at present open in July and August only. It has dormitory beds and low-priced rooms for two to six people; IYHA cards are required.

The only **campsite**, following the closure of the (still signposted) *Camping Municipal*, is *Camping Marguerita*, 3km west of the town. By car, follow the signs along the road to the west until you see a sign, "Camping: 300m". Don't follow this road: instead, look for the next turning, concealed between buildings opposite a point where you can see the sea, and follow this uphill, keeping right, until you come to the site.

Leaving Ceuta: the ferries

Leaving Ceuta **by ferry** for Algeciras, you can normally turn up at the port, buy tickets, and board a ferry within a couple of hours. The one time to avoid, as at Tangier, is the **last week of August**, when the ferries can be full for days on end with Moroccan workers returning to northern Europe.

If you plan to use the quicker **hydrofoil service** to Algeciras, it's best to book the previous day – though you should be okay outside the high season; details and tickets are available from 6 Muelle Caōnero Dato (☎51.60.41).

Be aware that all arrivals from Ceuta need to go through **customs at Algeciras** – and drug suspects are very thoroughly searched.

Tetouan

If you're a first-time Moroccan visitor coming from Ceuta, **TETOUAN** will be your introductory experience to a Moroccan city: a disadvantage that you'll quickly be made aware of. The Medina here seems – initially – overwhelming and totally unfamiliar, and the hustlers, often dealing large quantities of *kif* from the nearby Rif Mountains, have the worst reputation in Morocco. On the positive side, the city is home to a large university, so people you meet are just as likely to be genuine students – but you do need to keep your wits about you for the first few hours.

Physically, Tetouan is strikingly beautiful, poised atop the slope of an enormous valley against a dark mass of rock. Its name (pronounced *Tet-tá-wan*) means "open your eyes" in Berber, an apparent reference to the town's hasty construction by Andalusian refugees in the fifteenth century. The refugees, both Muslims and Jews, brought with them the most refined sophistication of Moorish Andalusia – an aristocratic tradition that is still reflected in the architecture of the Medina. Their houses, full of extravagant detail, are quite unlike those of other Moroccan towns; indeed, with their tiled lintels and wrought-iron balconies, they seem much more akin to the old Arab quarters of Córdoba and Seville.

Orientation and transport

Despite first impressions (particularly if you arrive at the chaotic bus station), and the "guides" and "students" who lay claim to new arrivals, Tetouan is not too hard a city in which to get your bearings – or to find your own way around.

The **Ville Nouvelle**, built by the Spanish as the capital of their colonial zone, follows a fairly straightforward grid. At its centre is **Place Moulay el Mehdi**, with the PTT (post/telephone office) and main banks. From here the grid stretches east toward the Medina, still partially walled and entered from a gateway on **Place Hassan II**. This square, sprawling with café tables, is the real heart of Tetouan – a gathering place during the evening, when half the town seems to be strolling through.

By day, at least, the Medina is good for just wandering around. It's not as large as it appears and you won't get lost for long without coming to an outer wall or gate, beyond which you can loop back to the Ville Nouvelle. Specific points of interest are detailed in the section following and are not too hard to find on your own. If this is your first day in Morocco, however, you might want to consider an easier introduction, arranging an **official guide** at the **tourist office**, a few metres down Bd. Mohammed V from Place el Mehdi. The office (Mon–Fri 8am–2pm and 3–6pm, Sat and sometimes Sun 8am–2pm) will also **change money** when the banks are closed.

If you run into trouble, the main **police station** is on Bd. Général Franco, opposite the *Hôtel Dersa*.

Points of arrival/departure

Arriving by **bus** or **grand taxi**, you'll find yourself on the edge of the Ville Nouvelle – slightly left of centre near the bottom of our town map. If you're moving on right away, there are regular **buses** from the station here to Chaouen, Meknes, Fes and Tangier; ask around at the various windows before buying a ticket because both *CTM* and private companies operate on each of these routes.

If you want to join the **train network**, make your way to the **ONCF office** near Place El Adala, three blocks northwest of Place El Mehdia in the Ville Nouvelle. This sells through tickets, including connecting buses (at 6.50am and 3.55pm) to the station of Tnine Sidi Lyamani, just south of Asilah. If tickets on the bus are sold out, as happens occasionally, you'll have to take a *grand taxi* to Tangier.

Heading for **Tangier** or **Ceuta** it's easiest to travel by **grand taxi**; these are routine runs – just go along to the ranks (see map) and get a place (currently 20dh and 12dh, respectively). Ceuta taxis (or buses) will drop you at the border; once there, you can just walk across and pick up a local Spanish bus for the 3km into town.

For the **beaches** at Martil, Cabo Negro and Mdiq – each easy day trips – buses leave frequently through the day in summer from behind the old train station on the road to Ceuta, or from the bus station in winter. For **Oued Laou**, there are two buses daily from the main station (8am and 5pm), or – considerably easier – you can share a *grand taxi* (from the Oued Laou road junction).

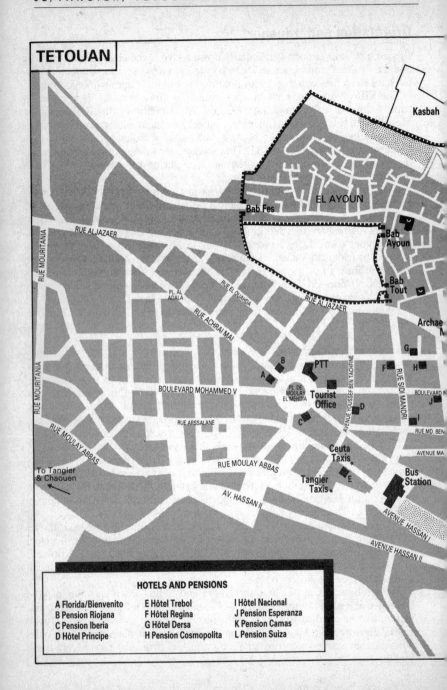

TETOUAN

Kasbah

Bab Fes

EL AYOUN

Bab Ayoun

Bab Tout

RUE MOURITANIA

RUE ALJAZAER

PL. AL ADALA

RUE EL OUAHDA

RUE ACHRAI MAI

RUE ALJAZAER

Archae

G

B

PTT

F

H

RUE SIDI MANDRI

RUE MOURITANIA

A

BOULEVARD MOHAMMED V

PL. DE MOULAY EL MEHDIA

Tourist Office

AVENUE YOUSSEF BEN TACHFINE

D

BOULEVARD

RUE ARSSALANE

C

J

I

RUE MD. BEN

RUE MOULAY ABBAS

Ceuta Taxis

AVENUE MA

To Tangier & Chaouen

RUE MOULAY ABBAS

Bus Station

Tangier Taxis

E

AV. HASSAN II

AVENUE HASSAN I

AVENUE HASSAN II

HOTELS AND PENSIONS

A Florida/Bienvenito   E Hôtel Trebol   I Hôtel Nacional
B Pension Riojana   F Hôtel Regina   J Pension Esperanza
C Pension Iberia   G Hôtel Dersa   K Pension Camas
D Hôtel Principe   H Pension Cosmopolita L Pension Suiza

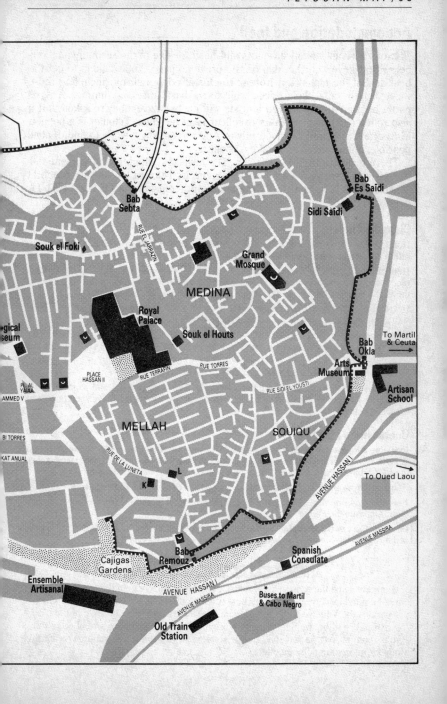

Bab Es Saïdi

Sidi Saïdi

Bab Sebta

RUE EL JARRAZIN

Souk el Foki

Grand Mosque

MEDINA

gical seum

Royal Palace

Souk el Houts

To Martil & Ceuta

Bab Okla

PLACE HASSAN II

RUE TERRAFIN

RUE TORRES

Arts Museum

Artisan School

EL AL YAIAA

AMMED V

RUE SIDI EL YOUSTI

BI TORRES

MELLAH

SOUIQU

KAT ANUAL

RUE DE LA LUNETA

L

K

AVENUE HASSAN I

To Oued Laou

AVENUE MASSIRA

Babg Remouz

Cajigas Gardens

Spanish Consulate

AVENUE MASSIRA

Ensemble Artisanal

AVENUE HASSAN I

Buses to Martil & Cabo Negro

AVENUE MASSIRA

Old Train Station

Accommodation and food

Try to ignore all offers from touts and head for one of the recommendations below and keyed on the map on the previous page. You're likely to get the best deal at the **classified hotels; unclassified pensions** (including those we've listed) raise their prices well above basic rates in summer. This is partly because newly arrived tourists will pay whatever they're asked, but it also reflects demand. With its excellent local beaches, Tetouan is a popular Moroccan resort and rooms in July or August can take a while to find. If at all possible, phone ahead and make a booking.

There is no **campsite** in the city. The nearest – which can be a useful fall-back if you have problems finding a room in Tetouan – is on the beach at **Martil**, 11km out. See the "Orientation and transport" section on p.81 for details on buses.

Classified hotels

Hôtel Trebol (E on the map), 3 Yacoub el Mansour (☎20.93). Right behind the bus station; safe, a little damp, but more or less adequate. *1*A*.

Hôtel Principe (D), 20 Youssef Tachfine (☎27.95). Much better in all respects: comfortable rooms and showers that function. Sited midway up from the bus station to the main *place* of the Ville Nouvelle. Has a ground-floor café for breakfast and snacks.*1*A*.

Hôtel Nacional (I), 8 Rue Mohammed Torres (☎32.90). Reasonable, old-fashioned hotel with a courtyard café; sometimes insists on full board in midsummer. *1*A*.

Hôtel Regina (F), 8 Rue Sidi Mandri (☎21.13). Used to be a good choice but standards have slipped (dirty rooms) and prices are now high for its category. Three blocks up from the bus station. *1*A*.

Hôtel Paris, 11 Rue Chkil Arsalane (☎67.50). *2*A*.

Hôtel Dersa (G), 8 Bd. General Franco (☎42.15). The city's oldest – and most elegant – hotel, with large rooms, a good (if pricey) restaurant and a rather distinguished basement bar. Sited opposite the *Regina*. *3*B*.

Unclassified pensions

Pension Riojana (B), **Pension Florida** (A), **Pension Bienvenito** (A), **Pension Iberia** (C; ☎36.79). All of these are in – or just off – the central Place Moulay el Mehdi. *Iberia*, above the *BMCE* bank, is the one to go for, if you can get one of its half- dozen rooms.

Pension Esperanza (J). Best of many overpriced places along Bd. Mohammed V.

Pension Cosmopolita (H), 5 Bd. General Franco. Slightly more expensive but spotlessly clean. Opposite the *Regina*.

Pension Camas (K), **Pension Suiza** (L), Rue Luneta. Both very basic – on a narrow street at the edge of the Medina, reached from the corner of Place Hassan II.

PENSIONS TO AVOID

There are some thirty or so other pensions, a few of them within the Medina itself – most around its periphery. The highest concentration is in **Place Hassan II**, which separates the Ville Nouvelle and Medina. These, the favourite choice of bus station hustlers, are to be avoided; if a guide brings you here, he'll have virtual access to your room as long as you stay, and he's *not* going to believe that you don't want to buy *kif*, or anything else on offer.

Restaurants

As ever, the cheapest food is to be found in the **Medina**, particularly the stalls inside Bab el Rouah and along Rue Luneta in the Mellah. For variety, try one of the many places on or around **Bd. Mohammed V/Bd. Mohammed Torres** in the Ville Nouvelle. Good choices here include:

Restaurant Moderne, Pasaje Acharc. One of the best budget restaurants in town. To find it, go through the arcades opposite Cinema Español on Place Hassan II. Open 9am–9pm.

Restaurant Zerhoun, 7 Bd. Mohammed Torres. A little pricier, though with a pleasant "traditional salon" and Spanish tapas in the bar. Open noon to midnight.

The Medina

Tetouan has been occupied twice by the Spanish. It was seized, briefly, as a supposed threat to Ceuta, from 1859 to 1862, a period which saw the Medina converted to a town of almost European appearance, complete with street lighting. Then in 1913 a more serious, colonial occupation began. Tetouan served first as a military garrison for the subjugation of the Rif, later as the capital of the **Spanish Protectorate Zone**, and as such almost doubled in size to handle the region's trade and administration.

"Native tradition" was respected to the extent of leaving the Medina intact, and even restoring its finer mansions, but in social terms there was very little progress. Spanish administration retained a purely military character, and only a handful of schools were opened throughout the entire zone. This legacy had effects well beyond independence in 1956, and the town, alongside its Rif hinterland, adapted with difficulty to the new nation, dominated by the old French zone. Its relationship with the central government continues to be uneasy, and it was at the centre of the 1984 riots.

Place Hassan II and the Mellah

Looking around Tetouan, the place to orientate yourself is **Place Hassan II**, the old meeting place and market square. This used to have a very Spanish character, formal gardens at its heart and a Mauresque Spanish Consulate taking up the east side, but in 1988 it was completely remodelled, with a pavement of Islamic motifs replacing the gardens, minaret-like floodlights at each corner and a brand new Royal Palace – replacing the Spanish Consulate and incorporating parts of an old nineteenth-century Caliphal Palace that stood beside it. It's all quite a shock if you've visited in the past.

The usual approach to the Medina is through **Bab el Rouah** (Gate of the Winds), the archway just south of the Royal Palace. The next lane south of this opens on to the main street of the **Mellah**, which was built as late as 1807, when the Jews were moved from an area around the Grand Mosque. Very few of the population remain today, although if you ask around someone will probably point out the old synagogues.

Into the Medina: the *souks*

Entering the Medina proper, at Bab el Rouah, you find yourself on **Rue Terrafin**, a relatively wide lane which (with its continuations) cuts straight across to the east gate, Bab el Oqla. To the left of Rue Terrafin, a series of alleys give access to most of the town's food and craft *souks*. The **Souk el Houts**, a small shaded square directly behind the grounds of the Royal Palace, is one of the most active: devoted to fish in the mornings, meat in the afternoons, and with an all-day smattering of local pottery stalls.

From the north side of the square, two lanes wind up through a mass of alleys, *souks* and passageways toward Bab Sebta. Following the one on the left for about twenty metres you'll see an opening (on the right) to another small square. This is the **Guersa el Kebira**, essentially a cloth and textile *souk*, where a number of stalls sell the town's exceptional *foutahs* – strong and brilliantly striped lengths of rug-like cotton, worn as a cloak and skirt by the Djebali and Riffian women.

Leaving the Guersa at its top right-hand corner, you should emerge more or less on **Place de l'Oussa**, another beautiful little square, easily recognised by an ornate, tiled fountain and trellis of vines. Along one of its sides is an imposing nineteenth-century **Xharia**, or almshouse; on another is an *artesania* shop, elegantly tiled and with good views over the quarter from its roof.

Beyond the square, still heading up toward Bab Sebta, are most of the specific **craft souks** – among them copper and brass workers, renowned makers of *babouches* (thick leather slippers), and carpenters specialising in elaborately carved and painted wood. Most of the shops along the central lane here – **Rue el Jarrazin** – focus on the tourist trade, but this goes much less for the *souks* themselves.

So, too, with the nearby *souks* around **Rue de Fes**, which is reached most easily by following the lane beside the Royal Palace from Place Hassan II. This is the main thoroughfare of a much more mundane area selling ordinary everyday goods, with the occasional villagers' **Joutia**, or flea market. At its main intersection – just to the right as you come out on to the lane up from Place Hassan II – is **Souk el Foki**, once the town's main business sector, though it's little more than a wide alleyway. Following this past a small perfume *souk* and two sizeable mosques, you meet up with Rue el Jarrazin just below **Bab Sebta**.

Walk out this way, passing (on your left) the superb portal of the **Derkaoua Zaouia** (no admission to non-Muslims), and you enter a huge **cemetery**, in use since at least the fifteenth century and containing unusually elaborate Andalusian tombs. Fridays excluded, non-Muslims are tolerated in most Moroccan cemeteries, and walking here you get illuminating views over the Medina and across the valley to the beginning of the Rif.

Had you proceeded along the main drag of Rue Terrafin/Rue Ahmed Torres/Rue Sidi el Yousti, you would have reached the eastern edge of the Medina at **Bab Okla**. The quarter to the north of here, below the Grand Mosque, was the Medina's most exclusive residential area and contains some of its finest mansions. Walking towards the gate you see signs for a *Palais*, one of the best of the buildings, but converted into a carpet and crafts warehouse aimed at tourists.

The Museum of Moroccan Arts and Crafts School

Considerably more authentic, and an interesting comparison for quality, is the **Museum of Moroccan Arts** (*Musée d'Art Marocain*), whose entrance is just outside Bab Okla. A former arms bastion, the museum has one of the more impressive collections around of traditional crafts and ethnographic objects. Take a look particularly at the *zellij* – enamelled tile mosaics – and then cross the road to the **Crafts School** (*Ecole de Métiers*), where you can see craftsmen working at new designs in the old ways, essentially unmodified since the fourteenth century. Perhaps owing to its Andalusian heritage, Tetouan actually has a slightly different *zellij* technique to other Moroccan cities – the tiles are cut before rather than after being fired. A slightly easier process, this is frowned upon by the craftsmen of Fes, whose own pieces are more brittle but brighter in colour and closer fitting.

Both school and museum are open 9am–noon and 2.30–5.30pm on Monday, Wednesday, Thursday and Friday; 9am–noon only on Saturday; closed Tuesday and Sunday; the school closes down for most of August.

Centre Artisanal and Archaeological Museum

Outside the Medina the most interesting sight is the **Centre Artisanal** on the main road below the town. The regular exhibits on the ground floor are well worth a check if you're planning to make purchases in the *souks* and want to assess prices and quality first. But where it scores most highly is in the displays of craftworking. Go up the stairs, either at the front or back of the main building, and you come to a fascinating array of carpet and embroidery workshops, while outside the building there are metalwork, basketry and musical instrument artisans at work.

If time needs filling, there is also a pleasant, if rather unmemorable, **Archaeological Museum** (same hours as Museum of Moroccan Arts, above). This was assembled during the Spanish protectorate, so it features exhibits from throughout their zone: prehistoric stones from the Western Sahara among them. Highlights, as so often in North Africa, are the Roman mosaics, mostly gathered from Lixus and the oft-plundered Volubilis.

The Tetouan beaches: Mdiq to Oued Laou

Despite the numbers of tourists passing through, Tetouan is above all a resort for Moroccans – a character very much in evidence at most of the beaches around. Throughout the summer, and particularly after Ramadan, whole villages of family tents appear at **Martil**, **Mdiq** and, further down the coast, around **Restinga-Smir**. At **Oued Laou**, 40km east of the town, there's a younger and slightly alternative atmosphere – something which is attracting small but growing groups of German, French and, to a lesser extent, British and American travellers.

See p.81 for details on transport to the resorts.

West: Martil, Cabo Negro and Mdiq

MARTIL, essentially Tetouan's city beach, was its port as well until the river between the two silted up. Throughout the Middle Ages it maintained an active corsair fleet, twice prompting Spanish raids to block the harbour.

Today it is a small but very active fishing village with a slightly ramshackle appearance, owing to the rows of tourist huts along the seafront. The beach, stretching all the way around to the fashionable villas of Cabo Negro, is superb – a stretch of fine, yellow sand that is long enough to remain uncrowded despite its summer popularity.

Martil's official **campsite**, *Camping Martil*, is set just back from the beach, by the river on the east side of town; it is friendly and cheap, though not a place to leave bags unattended. For a cheap **room**, try the *Hôtel Nuzha*, almost opposite the campsite on Rue Miramar; unclassified, it charges roughly 1*A prices for standard pension rooms. If it is full, they will probably find you a room nearby, or there are two cheapish places by the bus station: *Hôtel Rabat* and, preferable and cleaner, *Pension Rif*. North along the beach is a more upmarket **hotel**, the *Etoile de la Mer* (3* prices) and a good **fish restaurant**, the *Rio Martil*.

Cabo Negro

Most of the Martil buses go on to **CABO NEGRO**, an attractive alternative for lying around on the sands, but without casual places to **stay** other than the 3*A *Hôtel Petit Merou* (☎81.10). **Horses** can be hired at the *Horse Club* for rides along the beach.

Mdiq

MDIQ is a lovely coastal village and active fishing port. Though it is getting a little overdeveloped, with the encroaching hotel complexes, it remains a nice enough place to relax on the beach. If you want a **room**, the one cheap option is *Hôtel Playa* (☎85.10; 1*B); other than this, there are just package tourism enclaves and a large **campsite**. Every Thursday in season there are **catamarans** to and from **Gibraltar**.

Restinga-Smir

RESTINGA-SMIR is more a collective name for a length of beach than for an actual place or village: an attractive strip of the Mediterranean, but a little too dominated by package hotels and "holiday villages". Nevertheless, the *Al Fraia* **campsite**, set close by the *Club Mediterrané*, makes a good first or last stop in the country; it is inexpensive, well-equipped and secure.

East: in the shadow of the Rif

East of Tetouan the coastline is almost immediately distinct. For a few kilometres, the road follows the sea and the still more or less continuous beach, dotted with communities of tents. But very soon it begins to climb into the foothills of the Rif, a first taste of the crazily zigzagging Moroccan mountain roads. When you finally emerge at **OUED LAOU** (44km from Tetouan), you're unlikely to want to return too immediately.

A stay, anyway, is a positive option. Oued Laou is not an especially pretty place – Riffian villages tend to look spread out and lacking any core – but it has a terrific, near-deserted beach extending for miles on each side. There is a **campsite**, *Camping Laou*, just inland of the road, and a couple of small and very relaxed **hotels** by the sea, the *Hôtel-Café Oued Laou* and *Hôtel-Restaurant Laayoune*. If they're full, or if you want to pay less than their one-star equivalent prices, they'll find you **rooms** elsewhere – Oued Laou is a very easy-going sort of place. It is also one of the most accessible parts of the Rif and a good place to meet people and talk: hustlers have nothing to hustle except *kif* and rooms, and aren't too bothered about either; having come out here, off the tourist track, it is assumed that you're not completely innocent.

Oued Laou has a Saturday **souk**, held 3km inland of the beachside settlement, which draws villagers from all over the valley – and produces **bus connections with Chaouen**.

Towards El Jebha

It's possible to continue **along the coast to El Jebha** (see Chapter Two, *The Rif*); the road is now paved the whole way and there's a daily bus (which leaves Tetouan, currently, at 7am). En route, **KÂASERAS**, twenty minutes away from Oued.Laou, is a relaxed place, geared toward Moroccans camping on the beach, but with a few rooms available.

Chaouen (Chefchaouen, Xaouen)

Shut in by a fold of mountains, **CHAOUEN** becomes visible only once you have arrived – a dramatic approach to a town which, until the arrival of Spanish troops in 1920, had been visited by just three Europeans. Two of these were missionary explorers: Charles de Foucauld, who spent just an hour in the town, disguised as a rabbi, in 1883, and William Summers, an American who was poisoned by the townsfolk here in 1892. The third, in 1889, was the British journalist Walter Harris, whose main impulse, as described in his book, *Land of an African Sultan*, was "the very fact that there existed within thirty hours' ride of Tangier a city in which it was considered an utter impossibility for a Christian to enter".

This impossibility – and Harris very nearly lost his life when the town was alerted to the presence of "a Christian dog" – went right back to Chaouen's founding in 1471. The whole region hereabouts is sacred to Muslims due to the presence of the tomb of Moulay Abdessalam Ben Mchich – patron saint of the Djebali tribesmen and one of the "four poles of Islam" – and Chaouen was itself established by one of his Shereefian followers, Moulay Rachid, as a secret base from which to attack the Portuguese in Ceuta and Ksar es Seghir. Over the following century, the town's population grew increasingly anti-European with the arrival of refugees from Moorish Spain, and it became an important centre of pilgrimage and marabouts ("saints", believed to hold supernatural powers). It also became quite prosperous, and for a time was the centre of a semi-independent Emirate, exerting control over much of the northwest, in alliance with the Wattasid sultans of Fes.

The most startling fact about the town, however, was the extent of its recent isolation. When the Spanish began their occupation, they were astonished to find the Jews here speaking, and in some cases writing, medieval Castilian – a language extinct in Spain for nearly four hundred years.

These days, Chaouen is well established on the excursion routes and indeed becoming a little over-concerned with tourism. There are the inevitable _souks_ and stalls for the tour groups, a monstrous hotel that has been allowed to disfigure the twin peaks (_ech-Chaoua_: the horns) from which the town takes its name, and hustlers, sadly, have made an appearance. But local attitudes toward tourists, and to the predominantly backpacking travellers who stop over, are distinctly relaxed; pensions are among the friendliest and cheapest around, and to stay here a few days and walk in the hills remains one of the best possible introductions to Morocco.

Orientation and rooms

With a population of around 20,000 – a tenth of Tetouan's – Chaouen is more like a large village in size and feel, confusing only on arrival. **Buses** and **grands taxis** drop you at the marketplace, outside the walls of the town in a vague straggle of new buildings grouped about the Mosque of Moulay Rachid. There are a couple of **banks** here for money exchange: the _Banque Marocaine_ and _Banque Populaire_.

To reach the Medina, walk up across the marketplace to the tiny arched entrance, **Bab el Ain**, just beyond the prominent _Hôtel Magou_. Through the gate a clearly dominant lane winds up through the town to the main square, **Place Outa el Hammam** (flanked by the gardens and ruined towers of the **Kasbah**) and, beyond, to a second smaller square, **Place el Makhzen**.

Both along and just off this main route are a series of small, **unclassified pensions**, converted from private houses. These are the places to stay for anyone wanting to meet and mix with fellow travellers – rooms can be a bit cell-like, but most are exceptionally clean and remarkably inexpensive. For more comfort (and less "community life"), several of the **classified hotels** are good value, too.

Unclassified pensions

Hôtel Rachidia (B). The first pension you encounter, just inside the Medina walls to the right of Bab el Ain.

Pension Ibn Batouta (C). Possibly the quietest of the pensions – and with less feel of a "travellers' hang-out"; located in an alley to the left, about 30m along from Bab el Ain.

Hôtel Mauretania (D) (☎61.84). For the participatory – very relaxed place with a communal courtyard and rock music most hours. Down a network of alleys to the right of the street.

Hôtel Andaluz (E) (☎60.34). An excellent, comfortable pension, signposted to the left at the near end of Place Outa el Hammam.

Hôtel Kaskades (F). Just off Place Outa el Hammam – but not so clean as the rest and not highly recommended.

Pension Castellana (G) (☎62.95). Many travellers return loyally to the _Castellana_ each year, creating a distinctly laid-back and youthful atmosphere; others take one look and leave!

Classified hotels

Hôtel Rif (H), on the lower road (☎62.07). More modern and more comfortable, though still a mainly youthful clientele, attracted by a well-stocked sound system. Low rates for long stays, a bar, restaurant, and an exceptionally hospitable manager. _1*B_.

Hôtel Salam (I), again on the lower road (☎62.39). More mainstream hotel. _1*B_.

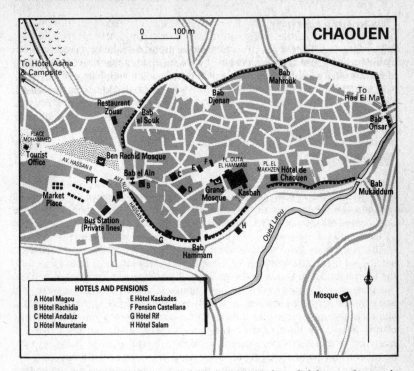

HOTELS AND PENSIONS

A Hôtel Magou
B Hôtel Rachidia
C Hôtel Andaluz
D Hôtel Mauretanie
E Hôtel Kaskades
F Pension Castellana
G Hôtel Rif
H Hôtel Salam

Hôtel Magou (A), just outside the Bab el Ain (☎62.39). Modern, slightly upmarket – and a little bit dull. *2*A*.

Hôtel de Chaouen, Place el Makhzen (☎61.36). The former Spanish "grand hotel", recently reconstructed for the package trade. Bar and swimming pool help justify the expense. *4*B*.

Campsite and Youth Hostel

Chaouen's **campsite** is on the hill above the town, by the big modern 4* *Hôtel Asma*; follow the signs to the *Asma* by the road, or cut through the cemetery on foot. It is inexpensive but can be crowded in midsummer. The **youth hostel** (*auberge de jeunesse*), adjoining, has dormitory beds for 6dh – only really worth considering if all the pensions are full.

Hammams

The uncertain showers in some of the pensions are mitigated by the ease of visiting the local **hammams**. The town, unusually, has separate *hammams* for men and women. The male one is next door to the *Pension Castellana,* off Place Outa el Hammam; the one for women, which is older and much more elaborate, is in the quarter of the *souks* – ask someone to show you the way because it totally defies written directions. Over the last couple of years, entrance to the *hammams* for non-Muslims has been limited, and sometimes refused unless you have a group and book the *hammam* together. Ask your pension/hotel for advice, or for someone to accompany you.

The town and river

Like Tetouan, Chaouen's architecture has a strong Andalusian character: less elaborate (and less grand), perhaps, but often equally inventive. It is a town of extraordinary light and colour, its whitewash tinted with blue and edged by soft, golden, stone walls – and it is a place which, for all its present popularity, still seems redolent of the years of isolation. The roofs of its houses, tiled and with eaves, are an obvious physical assertion, in contrast to the flat ones found everywhere else in Morocco. But it is something you can sense about life in general here, even about the people themselves – inbred over many generations.

The *souks* and Mellah

Since the Medina is so small, it is more than ever a place to explore at random: the things which draw your attention are not so much "sights" as unexpected strands of detail. At some point, though, head for the two main squares, and for the **souks** – just below Place Outa el Hammam.

There are basic town *souks* held on Mondays and Thursdays in the market square, so these, to some degree, have been set up for, or at least geared to, the tourist industry. But both the quality and variety are surprising. When the Spanish arrived – just seven decades ago – Chaouen craftsmen were still working leather in the manner of twelfth-century Córdoba, tanning with bark, and hammering silver to old Andalusian designs. Although you won't see any of this today, the town's carpet and weaving workshops remain active and many of their designs unchanged. Vendors are well used to haggling with travellers, and if you're staying for a few days, prices can fall dramatically.

It's interesting, too, to observe the contrasts in feel between the main, Arab part of Chaouen and the still modestly populated Jewish quarter of the **Mellah**. This is to be found behind the jewellers' *souk*, between the Bab el Ain and the Kasbah.

Place Outa el Hammam and the Kasbah

Place Outa el Hammam, the elongated main square, is where most of the town's evening life takes place, with its cafés overhung by upper rooms – some the preserve of *kif* smokers.

By day, the town's focus is the **Kasbah**, which occupies one side of the square. A quiet ruin with shady gardens, it was built, like so many others in northern Morocco, by Moulay Ismail. Off to the right, in the first of its compounds, are the old town prison cells, where Abd el Krim (see Chapter Two, *The Rif*) was imprisoned after his surrender in 1926. Five years earlier, he had himself driven the Spanish from the town, a retreat which saw the loss of nearly 20,000 of their troops.

The *place* was once the main market square, and off to its sides are a number of small **fondouks**; one of the more visible is at the beginning of the lane opposite the Kasbah (no. 34). The local Djebala tribesmen, who form most of the town's population, have a particular tradition of homosexuality, and there were boy markets held here until as recently as 1937, when they were officially banned by the Spanish administration.

Place El Makhzen and Ras el Ma

Place El Makhzen – the old "government square" – is in some ways a continuation of the marketplace, an elegant clearing with an old fountain, and pottery stalls set up for the package tourists.

If you leave the Medina at this point, it's possible to follow **the river** around the outside of the walls and up above Bab Onsar. Here, you reach **Ras el Ma** (the water-head), a small cascade in the mountainside with water so clear and cold that, in the local phrase, "it knocks your teeth out to drink it". Long a favourite spot – and, to an extent, a holy one due to the nearby marabout's tomb of Sidi Abdallah Habti – there are a couple of **cafés** close by to while away the midday hours.

Over to the south of the town, an enjoyable walk is to the ruined "**Spanish Mosque**". Set on a hilltop, its interior is covered in graffiti, but nevertheless it gives a good sense of the layout of a mosque – normally off-limits in Morocco. Nobody seems to mind you looking around.

Up into the hills

Further afield, a good **day's hike** is to head east, up over the mountains behind Chaouen. As you look at the "two horns" from town, there is a path winding along the side of the mountain on your left. A four-hour (or more) hike will take you up to the other side, where a vast valley opens up, and if you walk further, you'll see the sea. The valley, as even casual exploration will show, is full of small farms cultivating *kif* – as they have done for years. Walking in the area, you may occasionally be stopped by the military, who are cracking down on foreign involvement in the crop.

For more ambitious hikes – and there are some wonderful paths in the area – ask at the pensions about hiring a **guide**. Someone knowledgeable can usually be found to accompany you, for around 50–100dh a day. (The harder the climb, the more it costs!)

Food, transport and other practicalities

Compared to the hotels, Chaouen restaurants offer surprisingly little choice. In the Place Outa el Hammam a few of the cafés serve up regular Moroccan meals – *Restaurant Kasbah* is probably the best of these; some of the small pensions will arrange communal meals for guests; and the *Hôtel Rif* has a regular restaurant, too.

The indisputable best choice though – so long as you like its taste in music – is *Restaurant Zouar*, which is just outside the Medina, about 50m uphill, following the walls from the bus station square. If you want alcohol served with a meal, there's *Restaurant-Bar Omo Rabi* (again outside the Medina, on Rue Tarik Ibn Zaid) or the significantly more upmarket *Hôtel de Chaouen*.

Swimming

For **swimming**, the *Hôtel de Chaouen* has a pool, open (sometimes) to non-residents for 15dh a day. Locals share a taxi to a **pool in the river**, a few kilo-metres downstream – an excellent alternative for which any of the pension managers will give full instructions.

Festivals

As the centre of so much *maraboutism*, Chaouen and its neighbouring villages have a particularly large number of **moussems**. The big events are those in Moulay Abdessalam Ben Mchich (40km away: usually in May) and Sidi Allal El Hadj (August 9). There are dozens of others, however – ask around and you should come upon something.

Buses and grands taxis

Leaving Chaouen by **bus** can be difficult. Departures to Fes, and to a lesser degree, Meknes, are often full: try to get tickets the day before. Current departure times to Fes are around 6.30am and 10am; to Meknes at noon. If you can't get on any of these direct buses, an alternative is to take a *grand taxi* or local bus to Ouezzane and another from there, or to return to Tetouan (where most of the buses originate). For Tetouan, buses leave at least four times a day – much less of a problem – or you can share a *grand taxi*.

Daily buses also run to the Ceuta border at Fnideq (11am; 2hr) and to Oued Laou (5pm; 1hr 30min). If you like the idea of a dizzying ride through the Rif, and coming to a very small fishing village/beach at the end of it, you might also consider going on to El Djebha (see Chapter Two, *The Rif*), served by two buses a week, leaving around dawn.

For the more affluent, or anyone who can get a group of people together, *grands taxis* can be chartered – a stylish way to travel to Tangier or to Fes.

Ouezzane (Wazzan)

OUEZZANE, like Chaouen, has a fine, mountainous site, looping around an outreach of the Djebala mountains. It stands virtually at the edge of the Rif and formed the old traditional border between the *Bled es-Makhzen* (the governed territories) and the *Bled es-Siba* (those of the lawless tribes). As such, the town was an important power base, and particularly so under the last nineteenth-century sultans, when its local sheikhs became among the most powerful in Morocco.

The Ouezzani

The sheikhs – the *Ouezzani* – were the spiritual leaders of the influential **Tabiya brotherhood**. They were *shereefs* (descendants of the Prophet) and came in a direct line from the Idrissids, the first and founding dynasty of Morocco. This, however, seems to have given them little significance until the eighteenth century, when Moulay Abdallah es-Shereef established a *zaouia* (religious cult centre) at Ouezzane. It acquired a huge following, becoming one of the great places of pilgrimage and an inviolable sanctuary.

Unlike Chaouen, the town that grew up around this centre was not itself sacred, but until the turn of this century Jews and Christians were allowed to take only temporary residence in one of the *fondouks* set aside for this purpose. Walter Harris, who became a close friend of the Ouezzani *shereefs* in the late nineteenth century, found the town "the most fanatical that Europeans may visit" and the *zaouia* a virtually autonomous religious court.

Strange to relate, however, an Englishwoman, Emily Keane, married in 1877 the principal *shereef*, Si Abdesslem, whom she had met while out riding. For several decades she lived in the town, openly as a Christian, dispensing medical care to the locals. Her *Life Story*, written after her husband's death, ends with the balanced summing up: "I do not advise anyone to follow in my footsteps, at the same time I have not a single regret." She is buried in the Anglican church in Tangier.

The Zaouia, town and *souks*

The **Zaouia**, distinguished by an unusual octagonal minaret, is the most striking building in the town, and though the Tabiya brotherhood now maintain their main base elsewhere, it continues to function and is the site of a lively spring **moussem**, or pilgrimage festival. (As in the rest of Morocco, however, entrance to the *zaouia* area is forbidden to non-Muslims.)

The older quarters of Ouezzane – many of their buildings tiled, gabled and sporting elaborate doors – enclose and rise above the Zaouia, newer suburbs sprawling into the hills on each side. It's an attractive enough place, and if of little specific interest, has a definite grandeur in its site.

The *souks*

The main **souks** climb up from an archway on the main square, Place de l'Indépendance, behind the *Grand Hôtel*. Ouezzane has a local reputation for its woollen rugs – most evident in the weavers' *souk*, around Place Rouida near the top end of the town. Also rewarding is the metalworkers' *souk*, a covered lane under the Mosque of Moulay Abdallah Shereef; to find it, ask directions for the pleasant (and adjacent) *Café Bellevue*. The town also has a couple of Centres Artesanal – one facing Place de l'Indépendance, the other on Av. Hassan II.

There is a large **Thursday souk** on the Place de l'Indépendance.

Rooms and transport

Few tourists stay in Ouezzane, as it is only a couple of hours out of Chaouen, but there are worse places to be stranded. The bus and *grand taxi* terminal is about 50m below the **Place de l'Indépendance**, where you'll also find three reasonable, basic **hotels**, the *Marhaba*, *Horloge* and *El Elam*. There is little to choose between these, though all are preferable to the *Grand Hôtel* or *Hôtel de la Poste*, just off the square on Av. Mohammed V. There is a **hammam** opposite the *Hôtel de la Poste*, and numerous grill-cafés on the square.

Buses

Ouezzane provides a useful link if you're travelling by public **transport** (bus or *grand taxi*) between **Chaouen and the Atlantic coast**, or vice versa. There are a fair number of **buses** also to Meknes and Fes, but if you're stopping or staying, buy onward tickets well in advance; as with Chaouen it's not unusual for them to arrive and leave full.

travel details

Trains

Seven trains a day leave Tangier, all running through either SIDI KACEM or SIDI SLIMANE, where you may need to get a connection to the Fes/Meknes or Rabat/Casablanca/Marrakesh lines. The following timetable is current as of publication, and, though there may be small changes, its pattern should remain very similar

Tangier (12.10am), Asilah (12.57am), Meknes (5.07am), Fes (6.18am). Continues to Taza/Oujda (8.47am/12.39pm).

Tangier (7.22am), Asilah (8.01am), Sidi Slimane (10.26am: change for Meknes/Fes, arriving 11.55am/12.48pm), Rabat (11.49am), Casablanca Port (12.51pm).

Tangier (8.12am), Asilah (9.01am), Sidi Kacem (11.38am: change for Rabat/Casablanca Voyageurs/Marrakesh, arriving 2.29pm/3.51pm/ 9.09pm), Meknes (1.06pm), Fes (1.58pm). Continues to Taza/Oujda (4.47pm/8.12pm).

Tangier (2.15pm), Asilah (3.04pm), Sidi Kacem (5.42pm: change for Meknes/Fes, arriving 7.22pm/8.19pm).

Tangier (Port: 4.10pm; Ville: 4.22pm), Asilah (5.08pm), Sidi Slimane (7.41pm: change for Meknes/Fes, arriving 7.22pm/8.19pm), Rabat (9.09pm), Casablanca Port (10.12pm: change for Marrakesh, arriving 5.16am).

Tangier (8.50pm), arriving Asilah (9.39pm), Sidi Kacem (12.12am: change for Meknes/Fes, arriving 2.30am/3.34am). Continues to Taza/Oujda (6.07am/9.38am).

Tangier (Port: 11.15pm; Ville: 11.30pm), Asilah (12.14am), Rabat (4.18am), Casablanca Voyageurs (5.25am), Marrakesh (8.54am). *NB: This train leaves at 9.20pm in winter.*

Note: ONCF run connecting bus services to **Tetouan** from Tnine Sidi Lyamani, near Asilah.

Buses

From Tangier Asilah (7 daily; 1hr); Larache (6; 1hr 40min); Tetouan (12; 1hr 30min); Rabat (2; 5hr); Meknes (2; 7hr); Fes (2; 8hr).

From Asilah Larache (5 daily; 1hr).

From Larache Ksar el Kebir (3 daily; 40min); Souk el Arba (5; 1hr); Rabat (4; 3hr 30min); Meknes (2; 5hr 30min).

From Souk el Arba Moulay Bousselham (5 daily; 35min); Ouezzane (3; 1hr 30min).

From Ouezzane Meknes (2 daily; 4hr); Fes (2; 5hr 30min); Chaouen (4; 1hr 20min).

From Tetouan Tangier (12; 1hr 30min); Chaouen (10; 3hr); Fnideq (24; 25min); Oued Laou (2; 2hr).

From Chaouen Tetouan (10 daily; 3hr); Ketama/ Al Hoceima (2 ; 5hr/8hr); Meknes (1; 5hr 30min); Fes (2; 7hr); El Jebha (2 a week; 7hr).

Grands Taxis

From Tangier Regularly to Tetouan (1hr); less frequently to Larache, Rabat, and occasionally Fes.

From Ouezzane Regularly to Souk el Arba (1hr) and Chaouen (1hr 15min).

From Tetouan Regularly to Tangier (1hr), Oued Laou (1hr 20min) and Fnideq (Ceuta border) (20min).

From Souk el Arba Regularly to Moulay Bousselham (30min) and Larache (50min).

Ferries and Hydrofoils

From Tangier: FERRIES to Algeciras (4 daily; 2hr 30min); Gibraltar (3 per week; 2hr); Sète, France (weekly; 18hr). HYDROFOILS (in season) to Tarifa (3 daily; 30min); Algeciras (1 daily; 1hr); Gibraltar (1 daily; 1hr). See p.62 for details.

From Ceuta: FERRY to Algeciras (12 daily; 1hr 30min). HYDROFOILS (March–September) to Algeciras (30min).

From Mdiq HYDROFOILS daily in season to Algeciras (30min).

Flights

From Tangier Daily flights to Casablanca (and. from there on to Marrakesh, etc). International flights most days to London, Madrid, etc, and to Gibraltar (and on to London – fairly cheap on *Gib Air*).

TELEPHONE CODES	
ASILAH ☎091	SMIR-RESTINGA ☎096
CHAOUEN ☎098	SOUK EL ARBA ☎090
LARACHE ☎091	TANGIER ☎09
MDIQ ☎096	TETOUAN ☎096

CHAPTER TWO

THE RIF AND THE MEDITERRANEAN COAST

Goldshot green of the Rif's slant fields here, vapor-blossoms resinous and summery . . . "We've had a windfall of kif. Allah has smiled upon us".
Thomas Pynchon: *Gravity's Rainbow*

Anyone who has heard of the **Rif mountains** at all has usually done so in connection with Ketama, and the sale of **kif**, or hashish. There are towns enough in Morocco where you'll be offered *kif* for sale, but at Ketama it is simply assumed that this is why you are here. "How many kilos?" they ask. *Kif* and Ketama are big business.

Talking about the Rif you have to state this first, since it dominates much of the region's character. Even where uncultivated, *kif* plants grow wild around the stoney slopes – and there they seem to stretch forever. The cultivation itself is legal, but Moroccan laws forbid its sale, purchase and even possession outside of the region. Don't be blinded by the local ways: police roadblocks are frequent, informers almost as thick as the smoke.

An additional hazard are the drug industry's local mafiosos, cruising around the hills in their black Mercedes and not above a bit of traditional banditry. All through the year you hear stories of tourists driving along the road to Ketama and being stopped by a parked car or fallen tree. For them, "How many kilos?" ceases to be a joke. If you're driving and are reasonably cautious, it's wise to avoid the whole area around **Ketama** – bounded to the south by Had-Ikauen, to the east and west by Targuist and Bab Berred. If you're cautious and not driving, stay on the bus – it's a tremendous trip.

The **mountain range** itself is a vast, limestone mass, over 300km long, up to 2500m in height, and covered for the most part in dense upland forests. The whole impression is one of enormity, a grandiose place full of faintly outrageous views. You keep feeling it's far too hot for Alpine scenery and there are no horned, grazing cattle, just groups of workmen lying back on the pine needles, smoking *kif*. Travelling around, it's impossible to resist the feeling of nervous excitement – not just that the roads seem designed to terrify, but in a very real sense of isolation, unlike the mere remoteness of the Atlas.

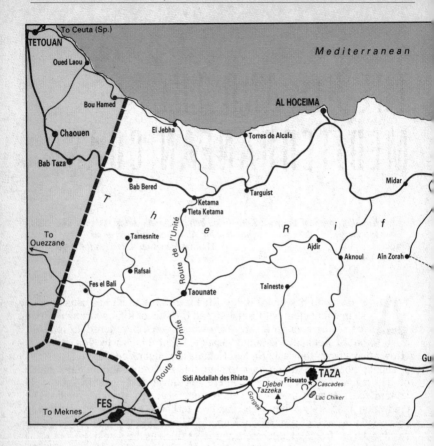

The Rif is, in fact, the natural boundary between Europe and Africa, and with the Sahara it cuts off central Morocco from Algeria and the rest of the Maghreb. In the past this was a powerful barrier – it took the first recorded European traveller three months to travel from Al Hoceima to Melilla – and it is sustained today by the extraordinary sense of independence and traditional xenophobia among the tribes. There is no other part of Morocco where you feel so completely incidental to ordinary local life, nor so on guard to offers. Do not, at any cost, accept the offers to visit a local farm.

Things are rather different with the **towns** to the east of the range. **Taza** and **Oujda**, important and historic posts on the "corridor" into Algeria, are among the most easy-going in the country – Oujda, in particular, with its large university population and proximity to Algeria's most liberal city, Oran. And there are relaxed times to be had, too, on those few points where the Rif gives way to the **Mediterranean coast**. Contrary to its daunting appearance from the great "backbone" roads, the Rif does have **beaches** – though they're few and far between, and virtually undeveloped east of Tetouan.

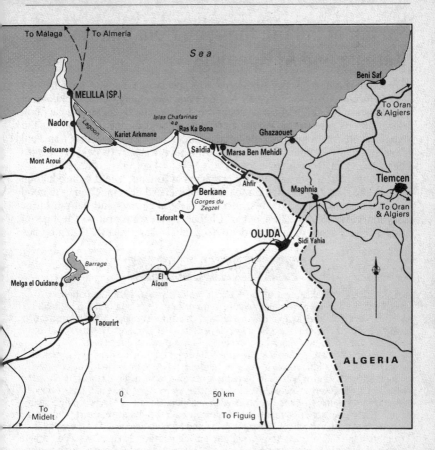

In this section of the guide, the only real beach resort is **Al Hoceima**, and even here the hotels spread for less than half a kilometre; elsewhere it's a question of a few sporadic campsites, the liveliest being at **Saïdia**, on the border with Algeria. These attract quite a number of Moroccan families during July and August and, if the season is right, at the end of Ramadan. Few tourists join them, though there's nothing to prevent you; unlike some of the Riffian mountain villages they are easy-going and friendly places – good points for meeting people, without any tourist hustling.

Lastly, the region has useful **ferry connections** with Spain at **Melilla** – which, like Ceuta, is Spanish territory. If you are bringing a car across from Spain, these are well worth considering. Fes is easily reached, either through the Rif, or by cutting down to the Taza road, and from Oujda there is a grand desert route **south to Figuig** and beyond to the oases of the Tafilalt (see Chapter Seven, *The Great Southern Routes*). In past years, car-less travellers wanting to go **on into Algeria** had to enter at Figuig, but with improved Moroccan–Algerian relations, the border at Oujda is now open to all.

On top of the Rif: the road from Chaouen to Ketama and Al Hoceima

There are very few journeys in Morocco as spectacular as that from Chaouen to Al Hoceima. The road literally – and perversely – follows the backbone of the Western Rif, the highest peaks in the north of the country. You can look down on one side to the Mediterranean coast, and on the other across the whole southern range; "big mountains and more big mountains", as Paul Bowles put it – "mountains covered with olive trees, with oak trees, with bushes, and finally with giant cedars".

Even without the drug industry problems of Ketama (see the introduction to this chapter), this is not a route for inexperienced drivers. Though in good condition, it seems to be constructed entirely of zigzags and hairpin turns. Beyond **BAB TAZA**, 23km out of Chaouen, you wind around the tops of ridges, sheer drops on either side to deep and isolated valleys. Going by bus

ABD EL KRIM AND THE REPUBLIC OF THE RIF

Up until the establishment of the Spanish protectorate in 1912, the **tribes of the Rif** existed outside government control – a northern heartland of the *Bled es-Siba*. They were subdued temporarily by *harkas*, the burning-raids with which sultans asserted their authority, and for a longer period under Emperor Moulay Ismail; but for the most part, bore out their own name of *Imazighen*, or "Free Ones".

Closed to outside influence, the tribes developed an isolated and self-contained way of life. The Riffian soil, stony and infertile, produced constant problems with food supplies, and it was only through a complex system of alliances (*liffs*) that outright wars were avoided. Blood feuds, however, were endemic, and a major contributor to maintaining a viably small population. Unique in Morocco, the Riffian villages are scattered communities, their houses hedged and set apart, and each family maintained a pillbox tower to spy on and fight off enemies. They were different, too, in their religion: the *Ulema*, the prayer said five times daily – one of the central tenets of Islam – was not observed. *Djinns*, supernatural spirits from pagan nature cults, were widely accredited, and great reliance was placed on the intercession of local marabouts.

It was an unlikely ground for significant and organised rebellion; yet, for over five years (between 1921 and 1927), the tribes forced the Spanish to withdraw from the mountains. Twice they defeated whole armies – bringing down the Madrid monarchy in the process – and it was only through the added intervention of France, and nearly half a million troops, that the Europeans won eventual victory. In the intervening years, the leaders of the revolt, the brothers **Mohammed and M'hamid Abd El Krim**, were able to declare a Republic of the Rif and to establish much of the apparatus of a modern state.

Well educated, and confident of the Rif's mineral reserves, they manipulated the *liff* system to forge an extraordinary unity among the tribes, negotiated mining rights in return for arms with Germany and South America, and even set up a Riffian State Bank. Still more impressive, they managed to impose a series of social reforms – including the destruction of family pillboxes and the banning of *kif* – which allowed the operation of a fairly broad administrative system. In their success, however, was the inevitability of defeat. It was the first nationalist move-the Riffians sleep or talk through it – a fact that seems almost as remarkable as the surrounding scenery.

Bab Berred and Ketama: the *kif* heartland

BAB BERRED, a smallish market village and former Spanish administrative centre, signals the real beginning of *kif* country – it is surrounded, in fact, by the plants – and at **KETAMA** you are at the epicentre. Arriving here, even in transit, is an initiation because absolutely everybody (passengers *and* staff) is involved in "Business". If you get off the bus, you will immediately be offered *kif* – immense, unbelievable quantities of it – and there is nobody who will believe that you are here for any other purpose.

This, really, is fair enough. Nobody does stay in Ketama unless they are doing business, and anywhere in Morocco, if people introduce themselves as being "from Ketama", there is no ambiguity about what they are offering. Dealers here are likely to try and get you to **stay at their farms** – something not be recommended, even if you've got an insatiable appetite and curiosity

---

ment in colonial North Africa, and although the Spanish were ready to quit the zone in 1925, it was politically impossible that the French would allow them to do so.

Defeat for the Riffians – and the exile of Mohammed Abd El Krim – brought a virtual halt to social progress and reform. **The Spanish** took over the administration en bloc, governing through local *caids* (district administrators), and although they exploited some mineral deposits there was no road-building programme or any of the other "civilising benefits" introduced in the French zone. There were, however, two important changes: migration of labour (particularly to French Algeria) replaced the blood feud as a form of population control, and the Riffian warriors were recruited into Spain's own armies. The latter had immense consequences, allowing General Franco to build up a power base in Morocco. It was with **Riffian troops** that he invaded Andalusia in 1936, and it was probably their contribution which ensured the fascist victory in the Spanish Civil War.

Abd El Krim was a powerful inspiration to later nationalists, and the Riffians themselves played an important guerrilla role in the 1955–56 **struggle for independence**. When, in April 1957, the Spanish finally surrendered their protectorate, however, the Berber/Spanish-speaking tribes found themselves largely excluded from government. Administrators were imposed on them from Fes and Casablanca, and in October 1958, the Rif's most important tribe, the Beni Urriaguel, rose in open **rebellion**. The mutiny was soon put down, but necessitated the landing at Al Hoceima of then-Crown-Prince Hassan and some two-thirds of the Moroccan army.

A quarter of a century later, the Rif is still perhaps the most unstable part of Morocco, remaining conscious of its under-representation in government and its underdevelopment, despite substantial school-building programmes, improved road communications, and a large, new, agricultural project in the plains south of Nador and Al Hoceima. Labour **emigration**, too, remains high – with Western Europe replacing Algeria as the main market – and (as in the rest of Morocco) there is widespread resentment at the difficulty of obtaining a passport for this outlet. With the growth of more sophisticated government systems, and a sizeable hierarchy of local administration, further tribal dissidence now seems unlikely. It is interesting to note, though, that it was in the Rif – above all in the towns of Nador, Al Hoceima and Tetouan – that the 1984 riots began, and it was here that the most serious disturbances were reported.

for *kif* production. Tales abound of travellers who have lost everything, often at knife-point, after taking up one of these offers.

The only **hotel** actually in Ketama is the old Spanish *parador*, the somewhat implausible four-star *Hôtel Tidighine* (☎10), complete with tennis court and swimming pool. Before *kif* took such a hold, it was popular with French tourists intent on the nearby skiing and boar hunting on **Djebel Tidirhine**; nowadays its rooms are rarely used. The Chaouen–Al Hoceima buses drop you right outside the hotel, a confusing stop since there's virtually nothing else in sight. The main village, with a scattering of cafés (and possible rooms), is, in fact, at **TLETA KETAMA**, 8km down the road to Fes.

KIF INDUSTRY DEVELOPMENTS

Some of the tribes in the mountains have always smoked hashish, though it was the Spanish who really encouraged its cultivation – probably to keep them placid. This situation was apparently accepted when Mohammed V came to power, though the reasons for his doing so are obscure. There is a story, probably apocryphal, that when he visited Ketama in 1957, he accepted a bouquet of *kif* as a symbolic gift; the Riffis add that this was because he feared their power, though this seems to have been swiftly forgotten amid the following year's rebellion.

Whatever, Ketama continued to supply the bulk of the country's *kif*, and in the early 1970s it became the centre of a significant drug industry, exporting to Europe and America. This sudden growth was accounted for by a single factor: the introduction, supposedly by an American dealer, of techniques for producing hash resin. Overnight, the Riffians had a compact and easily exportable product and, inevitably, big business was quick to follow. Large amounts of money are said to change hands between a whole network of officials, and there is a brisk trade among informants denouncing people. In fact, many of the large growers simply tell the police who they're selling to.

Targuist

Continuing east, with the cedar forests giving way to barren, stony slopes, you reach **TARGUIST**, Abd El Krim's last stronghold and the site of his surrender to the French. This is outside the dope triangle, and a much more relaxed base if you want to stay up in the mountains, without the all-pervasive "business". It is one of the larger villages of the Rif, with a couple of cafés, some **rooms** to rent, and the very basic *Hôtel Chaab*. There is a **hammam**, too.

Targuist also hosts one of the Western Rif's principal markets – a **Saturday souk** which draws villagers from the dozens of tiny communities in the neighbouring hills. If you've got transport, time, and the urge to see **more remote Riffian markets**, there are also smaller gatherings nearby: on Thursdays in ISAGEN, on Sundays in BENI BAR NSAR.

The beaches: Torres de Alcala and El Jebha

Scarcely less remote are the **beaches** reachable from the Ketama–Al Hoceima road. **El Jebha** can be reached by a turning 12km east of Ketama, or along the coast road from Tetouan and Oued Laou. **Torres de Alcala** and **Kalah Iris** are connected by a road just west of Targuist.

Torres de Alcala and Kalah Iris

TORRES DE ALCALA is the most enticing of these beaches – and easy enough to get to, with daily buses from Targuist, and soon, it is rumoured, from Al Hoceima as well. At present, however, it remains a quiet and very simple fishing village, with just a seasonal **campsite**, a small unclassified **hotel** and a few further rooms to rent at the cafés. Back in the sixteenth century, Torres was the main port for Fes, but it went into decline after the Turks established themselves on the offshore **Ile de la Gomera**, which they used into the nineteenth century as a base for piracy. The island – like those of Chafarinas and Al Hoceima nearby – remains Spanish territory.

At **KALAH IRIS**, an equally fine beach, 4km east on a paved road, there's another seasonal **campsite**, a restaurant and grocer's shop.

El Jebha

EL JEBHA is accessible by a more or less daily bus from Tetouan (and a twice-weekly service from Chaouen). It is a shabby sort of place – little more than a hamlet, with a group of fishermen's cottages – and one that very few outsiders visit. To be honest, there seems little to attract, with the beach sporadically polluted; however, the place has its devotees, who can reflect on the contrasts with Marbella and Torremolinos across the straits.

The Route de L'Unité: Ketama to Fes

At the end of the Spanish Protectorate in 1957, there was no north–south route across the Rif, a marked symbol both of its isolation and of the separateness of the old French and Spanish zones. It was in order to counteract these aspects – and to provide working contact between the Riffian tribes and the French-colonised Moroccans – that the great **Route de l'Unité** was planned, cutting right across the range from Ketama south to Fes.

The *route*, completed in 1963, was built with volunteer labour from all over the country – Hassan II himself worked on it at the outset. It was the brainchild of Mehdi Ben Barka, first President of the National Assembly and the most outstanding figure of the nationalist Left before his exile and subsequent "disappearance" in Paris in 1965. Ben Barka's volunteers, 15,000-strong for much of the project, formed a kind of labour university, working through the mornings and attending lectures in the afternoons.

Today the Route de l'Unité sees little traffic – travelling from Fes to Al Hoceima, it's quicker to go via Taza; from Fes to Tetouan, via Ouezzane. Nevertheless, it's an impressive and very beautiful road, certainly as dramatic an approach to Fes as you could hope for.

Taounate

Going by bus, the one village which might tempt a stop is **TAOUNATE**. The largest community along the way, it stands on a dark plateau above the valley of the Oued Sra (soon to be dammed up to form a vast, 35-kilometre-long lake). If you can make it for the huge **Friday market** here, you should be able to get a lift out to any number of villages in the region.

West: Rafsaï and Fes el Bali

A daily bus runs west from Taounate to Fes el Bali, making a detour to call in at **RAFSAÏ**, the last village of the Rif to be overrun by the Spanish and the site of a December **Olive Festival**. If you're into scenic roads and have the transport, a forty-kilometre dirt road extends out from here to the **Djebel Lalla Outka**, the peak reputed to offer the best view of the whole Rif range. The road is reasonable as far as the village of TAMESNITE but thereafter is very rough *piste* – accessible only in summer.

FES EL BALI is a useful connecting point with buses to the city of Fes and to Ouezzane. The village takes its name, *El Bali* (The Old), from an eleventh-century Almoravid fort, little of which remains. If you're stuck here, there's a cheap and basic **hotel**.

South of the town rises the **Djebel Amergou** (681m), which is capped by the ruins of another, more substantial **Almoravid fort**. It can be reached in a couple of hours' hiking from the roadside village of ET TNINE, about 15km south on the P26 to Fes.

East: Aknoul

Going **east from Taounate**, an attractive though less spectacular route heads through cork and holm oak forests toward the scattered and rather grim village of **AKNOUL**. From here you can pick up a bus or *grand taxi* down to Taza, or sporadic buses over to Nador or Al Hoceima.

Taza and the Djebel Tazzeka

TAZA was once a place of great importance: the capital of Morocco during parts of the Almohad, Merenid and Alaouite dynasties, and controlling the only practicable pass to the east. This, the Taza Gap, forms a wide passage between the Rif and Middle Atlas. It was the route into the country taken by Moulay Idriss and the first Moroccan Arabs, and the Almohads and Merenids both successfully invaded Fes from here. Each of these dynasties fortified and endowed Taza, but as a defensive position it was never very effective: the local Zenatta tribe were always willing to join an attack and, in the nineteenth century, they managed to overrun it completely, with centralised control returning only with the French occupation of 1914.

Modern Taza seems little haunted by this past, its monuments sparse and mostly inaccessible to non-Muslims. It is, however, a pleasant market town – an easy place to get acclimatised if you have arrived in Morocco at Oujda or Melilla – and its *medina* is saved from anonymity by a magnificent hilltop terrace site, flanked by crumbling Almohad walls. In addition, there is a considerable attraction in the surrounding countryside – the national park of **Djebel Tazzeka**, with its circuit of waterfalls, caves and schist gorges.

Orientation and practicalities

Taza splits into two parts, the **Medina** and the French-built **Ville Nouvelle**; the quarters are separated by nearly 3km of road and, to all intents, completely distinct. A shuttle bus runs between them, and another connects

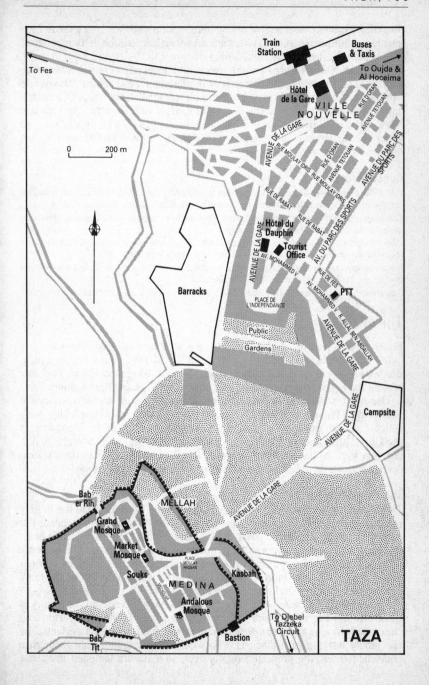

To Fes

Train Station

Buses & Taxis

To Oujda & Al Hoceima

Hôtel de la Gare

VILLE NOUVELLE

RUE D'ORAN

AVENUE TETOUAN

0   200 m

AVENUE DE LA GARE

RUE MOULAY IDRIS

RUE D'ORAN

RUE MOULAY IDRIS

AVENUE TETOUAN

AVENUE DU PARC DES SPORTS

RUE DE RABAT

RUE DE RABAT

Barracks

Hôtel du Dauphin

Tourist Office

AVENUE DE LA GARE

AV. MOHAMMED V

AV. DU PARC DES SPORTS

RUE DE FES

PLACE DE L'INDEPENDANCE

AV. MOHAMMED V

PTT

R. ALLAL BEN ABDALLAH

Public Gardens

AVENUE DE LA GARE

Campsite

AVENUE DE LA GARE

Bab er Rih

MELLAH

Grand Mosque

Market Mosque

Souks

PLACE MOULAY HASSAN

Kasbah

MEDINA

Andalous Mosque

Bab Tit

Bastion

To Djebel Tazzeka Circuit

TAZA

the Ville Nouvelle with the adjacent train station and bus and *grands taxis* terminal, 3km further away. *Petits taxis* are available, too, for getting between the stations, Ville Nouvelle and Medina.

The **Ville Nouvelle** was an important military garrison in the Riffian war and retains much of the barrack-grid character. Its centre, **Place de l'Indépendance**, actually serves a population of 40,000, but it's so quiet you'd hardly know it. There is a small, helpful **tourist office** on Av. de Tetouan. Most of the **restaurants** are grouped around the Place de l'Indépendance, or along Av. de Tetouan. The *Restaurant Majestic*, 26 Av. Mohammed V, has reasonable-value set meals.

Accommodation

Hôtel du Dauphine, Place de l'Indépendance (☎35.67). The definite first choice: a stylish, Art Deco building, with decent-sized rooms and an excellent café-bar downstairs. *2*A*.

Guillaume Tell, Place de l'Indépéndance. More or less opposite the *Dauphine*, this is an adequate (and cheaper) fallback. *Unclassified*.

Hôtel Friouato-Salam, Av. de la Gare (☎25.93). A concrete outpost in scrubland, between the campsite and Medina. Only the presence of a pool is a temptation. *3*A*.

Hôtel de la Gare, opposite the train station. Cheap, basic and pretty drab, but useful if you have to get the 4.30/5am bus to Nador. *Unclassified*.

Campsite, Av. de la Gare. Hardly more than scrub land – semi-fenced and not very inspiring.

The Medina

Buses from Place de l'Indépendance stop at **Place Moulay Hassan**, just below the **Mechouar** – the main street of the Medina. A modernised area, the Medina is compact and easy enough, though to locate and find your way around the few scattered sights it might be worthwhile to enlist a guide.

The most prominent building in the south section of the Medina is the **Andalous Mosque**, though its courtyards are characteristically well-concealed from public view. Close by, just off to the west of the Mechouar, is the **Bou Abul Hassan Medersa**. A somewhat inconspicuous Merenid building, it is hard to find and usually kept closed. If you can locate the *gardien*, there are rewards to be had in a classic court and beautiful *mihrab*.

The Palais Bou Hamra

To the rear of the Andalous Mosque is the **Palais Bou Hamra**, the largely ruined residence of the *Rogui* Bou Hamra, pretender to the throne in the early years of this century. There is little to see today, but for a decade or so this was a power base controlling much of eastern Morocco. Like most protagonists of the immediate pre-colonial period, Bou Hamra was an extraordinary figure: a former forger, conjurer and saint, who claimed to be the legitimate Shereefian heir and had himself proclaimed Sultan at Taza in 1902.

The name *Bou Hamra* – "man on the she-donkey" – recalled his means of travel around the countryside, where he won his followers by performing "miracles". One of these involved talking to the dead, which he perfected by the timely burying of a disciple, who would then communicate through a concealed straw; the pronouncements over, Bou Hamra flattened the straw with his foot (presumably not part of the original deal) and allowed the amazed villagers to dig up the by-then-dead witness.

Bou Hamra's own death – after his capture by Sultan Moulay Hafid – was no less melodramatic. He was brought to Fes in a small cage on the back of a camel, fed to the court lions (who refused to eat him), and was eventually shot and burned. Both Gavin Maxwell and Walter Harris give graphic accounts (see "Books" in *Contexts*).

Souks and the Grand Mosque

Taza's **souks** branch off to either side of the Mechouar, midway between the Andalous and Grand Mosques. Since there are few and sporadic tourists, these are very much working markets, free of the artificial "craft" goods so often found. In fact, one of the most memorable is a *souk* for used European clothing – a frequent feature of country and provincial markets, the more fortunate dealers having gained access to the supplies of international charities. The **granary** and the covered stalls of the **kissaria** are also worth a look, in the shadow of the Djemaa es Souk or Market Mosque.

The **Grand Mosque**, at the end of the Mechouar, is historically one of the most interesting buildings in the country – but, like that of the Andalous, so discreetly screened that it's difficult to gain any glimpse of the interior. Even the outside is elusive: shielded by a net of buildings, you have to walk up towards Bab er Rih for a reasonable impression of its ground plan. Founded by the Almohad sultan Abd el Moumen, it is probably the oldest Almohad structure in existence, predating even the partially ruined mosque at Tin Mal (see Chapter Five), with which it shares most stylistic features.

Bab er Rih and the bastions

Above the Medina, at **Bab er Rih** (Gate of the Winds), it is possible to get some feeling for Taza's historic and strategic significance. You can see up the valley towards the Taza Gap, Djebel Tazzeka and the Middle Atlas on one side, the reddish earth of the Rif behind, on the other.

The actual gate now leads nowhere and looks somewhat lost below the road, but it is Almohad in origin and design. So, too, is most of the circuit of walls, which you can follow around by way of a **bastion** (added by Moulay Ismail, in Spanish style) back to Place Moulay Hassan.

The Djebel Tazzeka . . . and beyond

A loop of some 123km around Taza, the **Cirque du Djebel Tazzeka** is really a car-driver's route, with its succession of mountain views, marking a transition between the Rif and Middle Atlas. However, it has a specific "sight" in the immense **Friouato Cave** (*Gouffre du Friouato*), 22km from Taza. This is a feasible hitch (stand at the turnoff just below the Medina) or a reasonable shared *grand taxi* ride (negotiate at the rank by the train station).

The cirque: cascades, a lake and Friouato

The **Tazzeka road** curls around below the Medina before climbing to a narrow valley of almond and cherry orchards. About 10km out of Taza you reach the **Cascades de Ras El Oued**, a series of small waterfalls reduced to a trickle in the dry summer months. Beyond this point, you loop up toward the first pass (at 1198m) and emerge beside the **Chiker Lake**, again pretty dry in midsummer.

The **Gouffre du Friouato** lies near the far end of this depression, along a short, signposted track to the right. Explored down to 180m, the cave complex is said to be the deepest in North Africa, and its entrance – over 30m wide – must certainly be the most impressive. The complex has not been developed as an attraction, but there is a guard around for most of the year who will steer you to some of the more spectacular caverns. You'll need a torch – if you don't have one, wait to see if some other tourists turn up.

Beyond Friouato, the cirque route runs through the dark schist **gorges of the Oued Zireg**. But the most dramatic and scenic stretch is undoubtedly the **ascent of the Djebel** itself. This is passable by car in dry weather but very dangerous at other times: a very rough, seven-kilometre road cuts its way up some 15km beyond Friouato, leading to a TV broadcasting tower near the summit. The view from the top, encased in forests of cedars, stretches to the Rif, to the mountains around Fes and to much of the eastern Middle Atlas.

Completing the cirque, you can rejoin the Fes–Taza road at SIDI ABDALLAH DES RHIATA.

A route to Midelt

For anyone with a car, there is an adventurous route from near the Chiker lake, leading off **through the Middle Atlas to Midelt**. This begins as a fairly reasonable paved road to MEGHRAOUA, where a dirt road (very rough) takes over to TALZEMT, eventually joining the P20 to Midelt at ENJIL DES IKHATARN.

Leaving Taza: transport and the route to Oujda

Taza is quite a transport junction, with good connections west to Fes, east to Oujda and north to Nador and Al Hoceima.

For **Fes** there's a wide choice of options. *Grands taxis* run throughout the day (just ask and wait for a place) from by the train station, arriving in Fes at Bab Ftouh (where you'll need to pick up a city taxi or bus to get to the hotels at Bab Boujeloud or the Ville Nouvelle). Fes is also served by four daily trains, plus a number of buses. **Oujda** is easiest reached by train – a quick route across the eastern steppes, through Guercif and Taourirt (see section following).

For the **Rif**, most buses leave very early in the morning. There are currently two to **Nador** (at 4.30 and 5am): one going via **Aknoul**, the other over a new and more direct road to the east of Taourirt (on the P1). There are also one or two buses each morning to **Al Hoceima**, via Aknoul. **From Aknoul** you can catch sporadic, local buses across the southern slopes of the Rif to Taounate on the Route de l'Unité.

All the **buses** leave from by the train station – whatever anyone may tell you about stops in the Ville Nouvelle!

Taza to Oujda

The route from **Taza to Oujda** is as bare as it looks on the map: a semi-desert plain, broken by little more than the odd roadside town.

MSOUN, just north of the main road, 29km east of Taza, is a rare point of interest. The village, inhabited by the semi-nomadic Haoura, is enclosed within a kasbah, built in the eighteenth century by Moulay Ismail. Further along the route, past the agricultural centre of **GUERCIF**, another brief detour from the road will bring you to the hamlet of **GOUTTITIR**, built around a **hot spring**, which serves as a *hammam* (for men during the day; women after dusk). There are **rooms** and **meals** to be had nearby at the *Café Sidi Chaffi*.

TAOURIRT, the largest town along the route, is a useful train and road junction, with buses running north to Nador connecting reasonably well with train arrivals from Oujda or Fes. The town itself is of little interest, with its kasbah still in use by the Moroccan military, though it does have a large **Sunday souk**. There are two **hotels** – the best of which is the *Gaada*, on the road leading south out of the town towards Debdou. If you have transport, however, a more tempting overnight stay would be to camp out beside the **Cascades** – and natural swimming pool – northwest of Taourirt. To reach them, drive west along the P1 back towards Taza, then turn north along the road to the MELGA EL OUIDANE barrage; they are 9km up this road.

Al Hoceima

After the somewhat epic existence of the Rif, **AL HOCEIMA** can be a bit of a shock. It is not quite, as the tourist board claim, "an exclusive international resort", but it is Mediterranean and developed enough to have little in common with the farming villages and tribal markets of the mountains.

If you're travelling through the Rif, you will probably want to stop here and rest a couple of days – maybe for longer. In late spring, or September, when the beaches are quiet, it's near idyllic. In midsummer, though, be warned that the town can feel cramped, its beaches are crowded with French package tourists and rooms are difficult to find. Nevertheless, even then, it does have a certain charm, and if you're deliberating on staying the night either here or in Nador, Al Hoceima is certainly the preferable choice.

Orientation

The town divides fairly naturally into two parts. Around the **bay** – which saw the Spanish invasion of the Rif in 1926, and Hassan's forces to quell the Riffians' revolt in 1958 – is a *Maroc-Tourist* complex with three luxury hotels (block-booked in season by package tours). Everything and everyone else is packed into the old Spanish fishing village of **Villa Sanjurjo** at the top of the hill. In midsummer this is a lively if slightly characterless place, full of young Moroccans; the rest of the year, it is almost empty, except for a handful of old, misplaced *Spaniolines* who, for one reason or another, wouldn't or couldn't leave with the rest in 1957. The town centre is up here – the **Place du Rif**, enclosed by cafés, grill-restaurants and hotels.

Accommodation

Hôtel Afrique, Place du Rif; **Hôtel Bilbao**, 28 Av. Mohammed V. Best of the cheap, unclassified hotels around the main square. Other cheap hotels are to be found up behind the square, along avenues Hassan II and Abd el Krim, and Rue de Rif.

Hôtel Karim, 27 Av. Hassan II (☎21.84). More comfort – and a bar. *2*B*.

Hôtel National, 23 Rue du Tetouan (☎24.31). Similar to the *Karim*. *2*A*.

Camping Plage El Jamil, 2km east of town along the main road. Set beside the Jamil beach – the best place for swimming. Unfortunately, the site is geared heavily toward caravans and overpriced for campers with tents. Summer only.

Camping Plage Cala Iris, a little way down the road, past the *Jamil*. The main, and much more popular, campsite is set beside another good beach; be very wary of leaving any possessions around. Again, summer only.

The beaches

Swimming – and walking in the olive-groved hills if you want a change – is the town's main attraction. If you wake early enough it is worth going down to the **bay** to watch the *lamparo* fishermen coming in; they work at night using acetylene lamps to attract and dazzle the fish. The other curiosity is the Spanish-owned islet of **Peñon de Alhucemas**, a perennial subject of dispute between the Spanish and Moroccans since the seventeenth century.

The best of the **beaches**, as mentioned above, is **Plage El Jamil**, east of the town by the campsite. There are others, though, within walking distance to the west, and another, a short ride by *petit taxi*, is just on the Al Hoceima side of the *Club Méditerranée*. All have **teahouses** where you can sip mint tea and gaze at the rocks and watch the waves hitting the coast of Africa.

Nightlife

For **nightlife**, you have a choice of the *Jupiter Disco* (at the main beach), discreet bars on the top floors of the smarter hotels (the *Mohammed V*, *Quemado* and *El Maghreb el Jàdid*), or sitting outside the *Café Florido* (which is decorated with Abd El Krim's truncated Star of David emblem), watching the somewhat illicit parade past the notorious *Hôtel Parador*.

Transport

As in the rest of the Rif, most **buses** leave Al Hoceima early – to Taza at 4am; to Fes (via the Route de l'Unité), Chaouen and Tetouan slightly later. If you're going to Chaouen, take one of the private buses rather than the *CTM*, which runs only to the Chaouen turnoff (a 9km walk). Al Hoceima's **tourist office**, by the prominent *Hôtel Quemado*, can give information and times.

If you need to get anywhere in a hurry, there are plenty of **grands taxis**, negotiable – even for Rabat and Casablanca. Al Hoceima also has an **airport**, out on the Nador side, with domestic flights as well as charters from France.

East to Nador and Melilla

There is little of apparent interest to slow your progress over the 164km stretch of the P39 from **Al Hoceima to Nador**. For anyone who has read about the events of the Rif War, however, the names of the villages will be familiar. This was the territory of Abd el Krim's first, dramatic rising – the so-called **Route of Annoual** – of July–August 1921. In those two months, the Spanish were forced back to Melilla, losing over 18,000 of their troops along the way. The occasional lookout post and barrack remain to be seen, if you follow the tracks inland.

Mont Araoui
MONT ARAOUI, where the road crosses the Oued Moulouya, marked the border of the old Spanish and French zones, a position still guarded by Moroccan sentries. A large and wonderful **Sunday souk** takes place here, with storytellers, dentists and a sort of roulette wheel ("spin the live rat in the pail"). There are also numerous café-restaurants.

Selouane
SELOUANE, 9km further east, at the junction of the roads to Al Hoceima and Oujda, has a Saturday *souk*, but is worth a couple of hours' visit on any day of the week. It boasts an interesting Kasbah, built by Moulay Ismail, used as a base by the bizarre pretender to the throne, Bou Hamra (see "Historical Framework" in *Contexts*), and now adapted as a storehouse. But perhaps the main reason for a visit is the very good, Belgian-run *Restaurant Brabo*.

South to Guercif
The road **south to Guercif**, heading off between Mont Araoui and Tiztoutine, is narrow and paved. It makes an interesting alternative to Taza or Oujda, with its vistas of palms and scrub, and the occasional wandering camel.

Nador

Entering or leaving Morocco at the Spanish enclave of Melilla you will have to pass through **NADOR**. If you're a birdwatcher, the marshes and dunes of Kariet Arkmane and Ras El Ma, east of the town, may well entice a stay of several days (see "Wildlife" in *Contexts*). If not, you will probably want to move straight out and on. Nador itself, landlocked by the shallow inland sea of Mar Chica, and rashly earmarked as a centre for economic development, is characterised by little more than the annoying, gritty wind floating down from the cement factory. It seems a depressed as well as a depressing place, and was the site of the first and main troubles in the 1984 riots.

When the Spanish left in 1957, Nador was just an ordinary Riffian village, given work and some impetus by the port of Melilla. Its choice as a provincial capital was unfortunate. There is little to do for the university students, while the iron foundry proposed to fuel the Rif's mining industry has yet to materialise. Add to this the creation of a population of over 100,000, drawn from the mountain villages, and you begin to see some of the problems.

Orientation, hotels and food
The bus station provides a focal point to Nador's uniform grid. Moving off from here toward the "sea", you reach the main boulevard with its banks and post office, and, at the end, the grandiose 4* *Hôtel Rif*. In the other direction,

along Av. Ibn Tachfine, are most of the cheaper **hotels**; the better unclassified ones, past a string of real dives, are about 100m down.

Among the **classified hotels** are:

Hôtel Khalid, 129 Ave. des FAR (☎67.26). One of the few non-luxury hotels in Morocco that
accepts credit card payment. *2*A*.

Hôtel Mediterranée, Rue Youssef Ibn Tachfine (☎64.95). Almost opposite the *Hôtel Rif.*
*2*A*.

Hôtel Mansour Ed Dahab, 101 Rue de Marrakech (☎24.09). *2*A*.

Hôtel Rif, Rue Youssef Ibn Tachfine (☎37.27). Extravagant and invariably empty. *4*A*.

The nearest **campsite** is at **Kariet-Arkmane**, 20km south (reached by *grand taxi*; see
below); if you have a car you can also camp at the **Cap des Trois Forches** on the Melilla
road – this has no campsite but Moroccan families descend on it with their tents in the
summer.

For **food**, try the seafood menus at *El Mahatta*, opposite the bus station, or
at *Romero's*, opposite the *souk*. There are restaurants and **bars**, too, at the *Ed
Dahab* and *Rif* hotels.

The only **bank** in town that will change money or travellers' cheques (no
plastic transactions) is the *Banque Populaire* on Rue de la Ligue Arabe.

Transport

All transport leaves Nador from the **bus station**, including local buses and
grands taxis to the Melilla border.

If you're heading for **Fes**, **Taza** or **Oujda**, the best course is to take the
buses run by *ONCF*, the rail company, to **Taourirt**, on the Fes–Oujda train
line. For **Tetouan** or **Chaouen**, it's best to break the trip in Al Hoceima (3hr
30min): both towns are still eight hours plus from there.

For details on the **Nador–Melilla border**, see "Melilla", following. In the
summer months, from June to mid-September, there are once- or twice-
weekly **ferries** from **Nador to Sète** in France (37hr).

Around Nador: Kariet Arkmane and Ras El Ma

The region around Nador is a lot more interesting than the town. **KARIET
ARKMANE**, to the east (past the airport), gives access to a sand/shell-packed
road along the spit of the lagoon. This is a desolate area but picturesque in its
own way, and with tangible attractions for birdwatchers, as flamingoes and
black-winged stilts are to be seen among the salt marshes. The road follows
the edge of the lagoon from Kariet, passing an old Spanish lookout post and –
just before it halts at a tiny fishing village, past a shell beach – it goes by a
popular spot with the Spanish from Melilla, who bring their tents and barbe-
cues at weekends. *Camping Karia Plage* is right on the beach.

The road east of Kariet is a pleasant drive, too, twisting into the hills, never
far from the sea, and eventually bringing you to **RAS EL MA** (or RAZ-KA-
BONA, as it is also known), another small fishing village with a good **beach**,
a smattering of cafés and street vendors, and a makeshift summer campsite.
You can complete a **loop back toward Nador** from here, following the
Oued Moulouya – or take the road across the river to the beaches around
Saïdia (see p.117).

Melilla: a Spanish possession

There ought to be an eccentric appeal to Spanish-occupied **MELILLA**, but even after Nador it's difficult to muster great enthusiasm. Together with Ceuta, it is the last of Spain's Moroccan enclaves, a former penal colony which saw prosperous days under the protectorate as a port for the Riffian mining industry. Since independence – and its retention as "sovereign Spanish territory" – Melilla's decline has been pretty wholesale. Resented by Morocco, whose claims are a fairly direct parallel to Spain's own on Gibraltar, it survives today on little more than the army, the duty-free tourist trade, and, of course, what's left of the Spanish colonial instinct. The current population of 70,000 is around half what it was in 1956.

Orientation

Melilla centres on the **Plaza de España**, overlooking the port, and **Avenida del Juan Carlos I**, leading inland off it. This is the most animated part of town, especially during the evening *paseo*, when everyone promenades up and down or strolls through the neighbouring **Hernandez Park**.

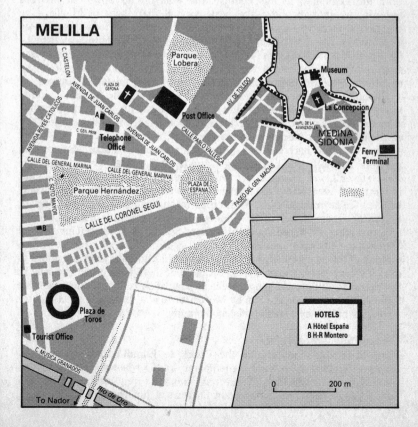

Accommodation

Rooms are generally hard to come by – and pricey by Moroccan standards. Most of the budget *hostales* and *pensiones* are down towards the port, in the side streets off the Paseo del Generál Macias. Others are scattered about the grid of streets radiating from the Plaza de España.

Among those worth trying are:

Hostal Montero, Av. del Generál Aizpuru. Cheap and good value.

Hostal España, corner of Av. Juan Carlos and c/del General Pareja (☎68.46.45). Similar – and with a bit more character.

Hôtel Miramar, Av. Generál Macias – facing the port. Slightly more upmarket.

Hôtel Parque, 15 Generál Marina (☎68.21.43). Similar.

Hôtel Nacional, 10 Av. Primo de Rivera (☎68.45.40). A further shift in price.

For a full list, call in at the **turismo** (Mon–Fri 9am–2pm, Sat 10am–noon) at c/del Generál Aizpura 20.

Medina Sidonia and the new town

Until the beginning of this century, the walled "Old Town" of **Medina Sidonia**, wedged in above the port, was all there was of Melilla. The enclave's security was always vulnerable, and at various periods of expansionist Moroccan rule – it was blockaded throughout the reign of Moulay Ismail – the Spanish population was limited to their fortress promontory and its sea approaches. The settlement was founded in 1497, a kind of epilogue to the expulsion of the Moors from Spain in the year that saw the fall of Granada.

The quarter's cramped, whitewashed streets suggest the Andalusian *medinas* of Tetouan or Chaouen, though inside, the design is much more formal; it was in fact laid out along the lines of a Castilian fort, following a major earthquake in the sixteenth century.

Steps near the harbour lead up to its main square, **Plaza Maestranza**, which is flanked by the tiny, Gothic **Capella de Santiago** (Saint James "the Moor-Slayer"), and beyond that, to an old barracks and armoury. If you follow the fortifications around, you'll come to another small fort, housing a somewhat miscellaneous **Museo Municipal** (Mon–Fri 9am–1pm and 3–6pm). Below this is the church of **La Concepçión**, crowded with baroque decoration, including a revered statue of *Nuestra Señora de Victoria* (Our Lady of Victory), the city's patroness.

None of this is especially striking – and there's nothing you can't afford to miss if you've just come over from Spain – but there is a certain curiosity in the **markets** up here. Although Melilla's population is almost ninety percent Spanish, most markets are run by Moroccans and – in the Mantelat quarter across the moat – by a small Indian community.

The new town: *Modernista*

Many of the buildings around the **Plaza de España** were designed by **Enrique Nieto**, a *modernista* contemporary of the renowned Catalan architect, Gaudí. His 1930s tile and stucco facades are a quiet delight of the New Town, though, sadly, often masked by the rows of duty-free shops.

Practicalities – food, ferries and flights

Melilla's **restaurants** are a little sparse, at least in the town centre, with most of the favoured local places a fair walk away, down at the beach. More **central options** include the always busy *Metropol* on Plaza de España and a clutch of no-nonsense bar-restaurants, including the highly recommended *Bodegas Madrid* on c/de Castelon, the street at the top left-hand corner of our map. Inside the fortress quarter of **Medina Sidonia**, there are a few bars; a good – though pricey – restaurant, the *Barbacoa de Muralla* (south corner of the ramparts); and a **folk music club**, the *Peña Francisco* (by the "A" of "SIDONIA" on our map).

Ferries and flights

In the summer, **ferries** leave Melilla daily for **Almería** (8hr; currently at 11.30am) and daily except Sundays for **Málaga** (10hr; currently at 8.30pm); in winter, ferries go on alternate nights to the two ports. Making advance bookings is critical in August (with possible three-day waits for a boat, if you just turn up), and at any time of year it is important to **check departure times** – which are highly variable.

Alternatively, for about the same cost, there are **flights to Málaga**; up to five a day in season, two or three daily out of season. Again, reserve ahead of time if possible, and be warned that flights don't leave in bad weather.

The Nador–Melilla border

The **Nador–Melilla border crossing** can take time and patience. During the summer it's always crowded, with Moroccans returning from (or going to) jobs in Europe, as well as travellers.

Formalities

Entering Melilla, allow for the possibility of a two-hour delay on the Moroccan side, while passports are collected, passed around and eventually stamped. Leave more time if you have a ferry connection to make. If you are just planning on a day trip to Melilla, on no account admit to it.

Entering Morocco, try to avoid the border in the hours immediately after the ferries arrive, and be prepared to show evidence of 3500dh in foreign currency or cheques (about £260); this seems to be the one frontier where such evidence is (sometimes) requested. If you have any problems, don't get involved in an argument but instead return later in the day for the next shift.

Getting to the border

To **get to the border** from Nador, there's a bus and numerous *grands taxis*; on the Spanish side there are buses to and from the Plaza de España. The frontier **currency exchange**, on both sides, is for cash only.

If you are **driving**, be aware that smuggling goes on at the border, with periodic police crackdowns. Driving at night, keep an eye out for road checks – not always well lit but usually accompanied by tyre-puncturing blockades. **Hire cars**, incidentally, are not allowed across the border.

The Zegzel Gorge, Berkane and Saïdia

The **route east from Nador to Oujda** is fast, efficient and well served by both buses and *grands taxis*. It holds little of interest along the way, but if you've got the time (or ideally a car), there's an attractive detour around Berkane into the **Zegzel gorge**, a dark limestone fault in the Beni Snassen mountains – the last outcrops of the Rif. And on the coast there is the considerable attraction of **Saïdia**, one of the country's most pleasant and relaxed seaside resorts.

The Gorge Route

The **Oued Zegzel** is a tributary of the Moulouya, which as it runs south of Berkane has carved out a fertile shaft of mountain valleys. These for centuries marked the limits of the Shereefian empire.

The route through these valleys is easily accessible today, though still forbiddingly steep: all traffic goes *down* (south from Berkane), climbing up again from the main road to Taforalt and winding from there to Berkane. If you've got a car, this is the route to follow. If not, stay on the bus to Berkane, where you can get a seat in a *grand taxi* to Taforalt and there negotiate another one back, via the gorge road. Neither is an expensive operation because the routes are used locally (and are popular with tourists).

Taforalt, the Grotte du Chameau and the gorge
TAFORALT is a quiet mountain village, active (or as active as it ever gets) only for the **Wednesday souk**. It does, though, have a reliable supply of *grands taxis*, and you should be able to move on rapidly towards the Zegzel.

Before setting on a price, get the driver to agree to stop off for a while at the **Grotte du Chameau** (15km), a cavern of vast stalactites – one of them remarkably camel-like in shape. The cave, with various tunnels leading off, is completely uncommercialised, so bring a torch if possible. Near the entrance is a hot stream, which locals use for bathing.

The gorge, or rather **gorges**, begin about a kilometre beyond the cave, scrupulously terraced and cultivated with all kinds of citrus and fruit trees. As the road crisscrosses the riverbed, they progressively narrow, drawing your eye to the cedars and dwarf oaks at the summit, until you eventually emerge (28km from Taforalt) on to the plain of Berkane.

Berkane
BERKANE is a strategic little market town, French-built and prosperous, set amid an extensive region of orchards and vineyards. If you stay, you're likely to be the only European in the town – in consequence there are no hustlers and people may even buy *you* a coffee. Good eating places are to be found in the long, unpaved street running uphill from Av. Hassan II, along with lots of very dark, tented *souks*. The best **place to stay** is the *Hôtel Najah* – very inexpensive. **Moving on** is similarly painless: there are frequent buses and *grands taxis* both to Oujda and Saïdia.

Saïdia

Sited right on the Algerian border, **SAÏDIA** is a good choice for staying put for a few days. Plans are apparently afoot for a Portuguese company to develop it as an international resort, with a marina, 5000-bed holiday village and 18-hole golf course. At present, however, it couldn't be more different: a one-street sort of place, rambling back from the sea in the shadow of an old and still occupied nineteenth-century kasbah. Moroccans proclaim that at Saïdia "we swim together with Algerians", which isn't exactly true, but not totally false either – there's a very similar resort over on the Algerian side.

Saïdia's **beach** explains the international interest. Immense and sandy, it stretches west toward the tiny Chafarinas islands, and east, across the Oued Kiss, into Algeria. The resort makes a good base for **birdwatchers**, too, with the marshes and woodland stretching behind the beach, out towards the Oued Moulouya (see"Wildlife" in *Contexts*).

Practicalities

In the summer months, Saïdia is very lively and a lot of fun; from mid-September through to May, in contrast, it becomes virtually deserted, with variable, rather windy weather.

There are three smallish **hotels**, the *Al Kalaa* (☎51.23; 2*A), *Hannour* (☎51.15; 2*A) and *Select* (☎51.10; 1*A) – the latter two closed out of season – and an expensive bungalow holiday complex. In summer, if you don't book a room in advance, you'll probably need to camp. In classic, local-resort fashion, Saïdia has two **campsites**, one for families only (off the main street), another (toward the kasbah) for single people – pick your category.

Liveliest of the town's **café-restaurants** are a group by the market, past the kasbah and looking across into Algeria. At night, the *Hôtel Hannour* is the centre of life, with its **bar**, restaurant and occasional entertainment.

There are regular **buses** and **grands taxis** between Saïdia and Oujda.

Oujda

Open and easy-going, with a large and active university, **OUJDA** has that rare quality in Moroccan cities – nobody makes demands on your instinct for self-preservation. After the Rif, it is a surprise, too, to see women in public again, and to re-enter a Gallic atmosphere – as you move out of what used to be Spanish Morocco into the old French zone. As Morocco's easternmost town, Oujda was the capital of French *Maroc Orient* and an important trading centre. Today it remains a lively and prosperous place, strikingly modern by Moroccan standards, and with a population approaching half a million.

With its strategic location at the crossroads of eastern and southern routes across Morocco-Algeria, Oujda, like Taza, was always vulnerable to invasion and has frequently been the focus of territorial claims. The Algerian Ziyanids of Tlemcen occupied the town in the thirteenth and fourteenth centuries, and Oujda was the first place to fall under French control when their forces moved into Morocco in 1907. In recent years, its proximity to the Algerian border and distance from the government in Rabat has led to its being a minor centre of dissidence and unrest. This was particularly evident during the Algerian border war in the early 1960s, and again, over recent years, in a series of student strikes. Much more striking, however, at least since the restoration of Moroccan–Algerian relations in 1988, is the upbeat and international tempo of the city, with Algerians coming in to shop, and Moroccans sharing in some of the cultural dynamism of neighbouring Oran, the home of Raï music.

Orientation and accommodation

Oujda consists of the usual **Medina** and **Ville Nouvelle**, the latter highly linear in its layout, having started out as a military camp.

The Medina, more or less walled, lies right in the heart of town, with the main square of the Ville Nouvelle, **Place du 16 Août 1953**, at its northwest corner. Around this square you'll find all the main facilities, including the **post office**, **banks** and **tourist office** (daily 8am–noon & 2.30–6.30pm).

Points of arrival

Arriving at the **train station** you are in easy walking distance of the centre. The new **bus station** (which now handles virtually all services) is more of a walk (or an inexpensive *petit taxi* ride), 500m southwest of the train station, across the Oued Nachef.

Oujda's **airport**, 15km north of the city off the P27, has flights to Casablanca most days – but, as yet, none direct to Algeria. The *RAM* office in town is inside the *Hôtel Oujda*.

Accommodation

The unclassified hotels in the Medina are poor value, but there are some good, inexpensive places just outside the walls, and, moving up the scale, a number of comfortable 4* hotels if you need some comfort after the Rif or a trip through Algeria. Booking ahead is a good idea for any class of hotel, as they're often full with Algerians on shopping sprees.

The following recommendations are in ascending order of price:

Hôtel du 16 Août; Hôtel Zegreg; Hôtel Marrakesh. Best of a strip of cheap hotels along Rue de Marrakech (between the main square and Place du Maroc); the *16 Août* is the one to go for as a first choice. *All unclassified.*

Hôtel Royal, 13 Bd. Zerktouni (☎22.84). Clean rooms with bathrooms, and an easy walk from the train station. *1*A.*

Hôtel Ziri, Av. Mohammed V (☎43.05). Close by the *Royal*, built into the town walls. *1*A.*

Hôtel Lutetia, 44 Bd. Hassan Loukili (☎33.65). Convenient position right by the train station. *2*B.*

Hôtel Al Massira-Salam, Bd. Maghreb Al Arabi (☎53.00). Modern hotel, with a pool and tennis court, run by a good chain. *4*A.*

Hôtel Oujda, Bd. Mohammed V (☎40.93). Similar to the above – again with a bar and pool. *4*B.*

Hôtel Terminus, Place de l'Unité Africaine (☎40.93). The best upmarket choice, opposite the train station, with a characterful bar and fine pool. *4*A.*

The closest **campsites** are in Saïdia (see previous page).

The town

Oujda's **Medina** is largely a French reconstruction – obvious by the ease with which you can find your way around. Unusually, though, it has retained much of the city's commercial functions and has an enjoyably active air. Entering from **Bab el Ouahab**, the principal gate, you'll be struck by the amazing variety of food – and it's well worth a look for this alone. Olives are Oujda specialities – wonderful if you're about after the September harvest. In the old days, more or less up until the French occupation, Bab El Ouahab was the gate where the heads of criminals were displayed. In the evenings it is still a square where storytellers and musicians come to entertain, an increasing rarity in post-independence Morocco.

Exploring the quarter, a good route to follow from the gate is straight down the main street toward **Place d'Attarine**, flanked by a *kissaria* and a grand *fondouk*. At the far end of the *souks* you come upon **Souk el Ma**, the

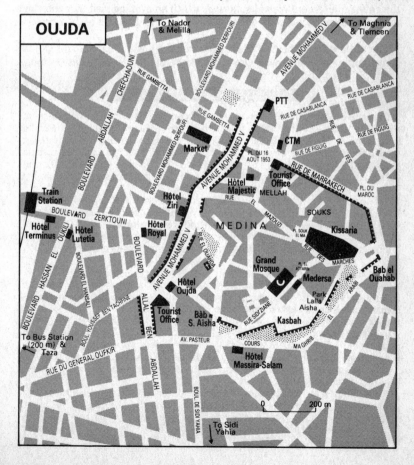

irrigation *souk,* where the supply of water used to be regulated and sold by the hour. Walking on from here, you'll arrive back at Place du 16 Août 1953.

Running along the outside of the Medina walls, the **Parc Lalla Aisha** is a pleasant area to seek midday shade. Following it around to the west, you reach the Bab Sidi Aicha, from which the Rue El Ouahda runs north to the old **French Cathedral**. This is an evocative place. Its present congregation numbers about ten, the fonts are dry, and the statue niches empty, but there is a beautiful chapel. It is kept locked; for admission, ring at the door of the presbytery at the back.

Food and entertainment

The focus of evening activity, as mentioned before, is the area around **Bab el Ouahab**. You can get all kinds of grilled food from stalls around the square and there are plenty of good eating places on, or just off, the Bd. Zerktouni; the coffee house *Les Pyramides,* here, is worth an evening visit. For entertainment with alcohol, ask someone to point you in the direction of the *Brasserie-Nightclub de France.*

Since the development of more open relations with Algeria, and Oujda's increasingly close links with Oran, across the border, the city has become a

---

CROSSING INTO ALGERIA

The state of Moroccan–Algerian relations has undergone a dramatic improvement over the last two to three years, making a border crossing at Oujda (or, 369km to the south, at Figuig) a relatively routine matter. There are still no **trains** running across the frontier, however. Instead, the line terminates at Oujda and restarts inside Algeria at Maghnia. For the missing 27km (15km in Morocco, 12km in Algeria), those without a car are dependent on hitching, taxis, or the somewhat sporadic local buses. It remains a time-consuming business.

The good news, though, is that **the Oujda–Maghnia border** is now routinely open. Until 1988, only car passengers could cross at this point, all "pedestrians" having to detour via Figuig. Hopefully, this will prove a permanent move, but before making hard and fast plans, it would be wise to ask fellow travellers and the tourist office in Oujda's main square (whose staff are usually well briefed and helpful).

Visas and currency exchange
Citizens of the UK, Ireland, USA, Canada, Australia, New Zealand and The Netherlands must obtain a **visa in advance** to enter Algeria; Scandinavian citizens can currently enter with a routine stamp at the border.

You can get a visa at any overseas Algerian consulate, including **Rabat** (where they are issued on the same day; see Chapter Four). The Algerian consulate in **Oujda** (11 Bd. de Taza; ☎37.40 or 37.41) can issue visas, too, but they take about a week to do so, as they have to send all the details to Rabat. If you are in Oujda without a visa, and in a hurry to cross into Algeria, it would be easier and quicker to get the night train up to Rabat and back.

Formalities at both borders are relatively quick and straightforward, at least for pedestrians, though there are random checks on the Algerian side for illegal importation of currency, etc. Car-drivers should allow three to four hours for registration. While in Algeria, you must **change** the equivalent of 1000 dinars (about promising place to catch performances of **Raï music** – a wild blend of traditional songs and rock, with a swirling funky beat, whose chief exponents include Oran-residents such as Cheb Khalaed (*the* superstar), Cheb Fadhela, Cheb Sahraoui and Chaba Fadhela. The music has taken recent hold in Morocco, and especially Oujda, where it is always worth asking about **concerts**. You may well catch a local Moroccan Raï group, or even one of the big Algerian stars, who occasionally give concerts at the Oujda football stadium.

Sidi Yahia: an oasis marabout

SIDI YAHIA, 6km outside Oujda, is an unexpected little oasis, with huge palms and ancient baobab trees breaking the wide empty plain. It's best visited in spring, when streams water the grass and flowers; in summer they can be down to a trickle.

The oasis has been a holy place since pre-Islamic times, the main object of veneration being the tomb of **Sidi Yahia** – a shadowy marabout, identified by local tradition with John the Baptist. Oujda's patron saint, he seems to have had a broad ecumenical appeal – Jews and Christians also made pilgrimage to the tomb over the centuries.

£80) at the official government rate (currently 12.5 dinar to £1 sterling). This can be at any time during your stay – you don't have to do it at the border, though this sum should last for a good week or so of travelling. Staying beyond that, many travellers pay for items in foreign currency or use the thriving black market (about three times the official exchange rate).

The Oujda-Maghnia border
Heading for the Oujda–Maghnia border, there are frequent *grands taxis*, leaving from the fountain at the end of Rue de Marrakech (5dh a place), and buses (no fixed timetable) from the main bus station. Better still, try and hitch a ride with other travellers – you can usually arrange this the night before by going around the better hotels (the *Terminus*, *Al Massira* and *Oujda*), and it should take you through to TLEMCEN, the first Algerian town of any size and a place well worth spending some time in (see "Onwards" in *Contexts*).

If you are driving, note that petrol is much cheaper in Algeria.

South to the Figuig border
Crossing over at FIGUIG (see Chapter Six) is by no means a bad option, though it's an unbelievably hot trip in the summer months. Despite its uncertain appearance on some maps, there is a fast new road down from Oujda – a 369km trek, but no more than seven hours by bus. Try and get the early-morning departure (currently at 6am); there are two later on, but by noon things can be pretty stifling. All of these buses leave from the *Gare Routière* in Place du Maroc.

En route, there are a few roadside settlements and mining towns – for coal and zinc. If you are driving, **AÏN BENIMATHAR**, 83km from Oujda, is a good point to break the journey: the village has a group of kasbahs, an important (and ancient) **Monday souk**, and, about 4km to the west, a small oasis, **Ras el Aïn**, with a highly seasonal waterfall. **TENDRARA**, 198km from Oujda, has a **Thursday souk** for the nomadic Beni M'Guil.

Nobody is quite sure where the saint is buried (several of the cafés stake an optimistic claim), but there is a profusion of reverence towards one of the great **wells**, said to be his water supply before the springs rose up after his death. On Fridays – and above all at the great **moussems** held here in August and September – this spot, together with almost every shrub and tree in the oasis, is festooned with little pieces of cloth, a ritual as lavish and extraordinary as anything in the Mediterranean church.

Scattered around the oasis are other lesser shrines – the tombs, *koubbas* (small domes) and hermitages of numerous saints who followed Sidi Yahia to live within the grove. Among them are a former hermitage of **Sidi Bel Abbes**, one of the patron saints of Marrakesh. There is also a cave known as the **Ghar el Houriyat**, identified with the *houris* – the obliquely sensual Handmaidens of Paradise promised to good Muslims in the Koran.

Regular **buses** run to Sidi Yahia from Oujda (from near the Bab el Ouahab), or, if you have the energy, it is only a little over an hour's walk down a broad (signposted) avenue.

travel details

Trains

From Taza Four trains daily to Oujda (3hr 30min), and in the other direction to Fes (2hr).
From Oujda Four trains daily to Taza (3hr 30min) and Fes (5hr 30min–6hr). Also a night train (mainly for freight) to Bouarfa (8hr).
Note: *ONCF* runs connecting bus services to Nador from Taourirt.

Buses

From Chaouen Ketama/Al Hoceima (2 daily; 5hr/8hr); El Jebha (2; 7hr).
From Ketama Fes (2 daily; 3hr 30min).
From Fes el Bali Daily to Taounate and Aknoul.
From Taza Fes (3 daily; 2hr 30min); Al Hoceima (2; 4hr 30min); Nador (2; 5–5hr 30min).
From Al Hoceima Nador (2 daily; 3hr 30min); Fes (1; 1hr 30min).
From Nador Berkane/Oujda (5 daily; 2hr/3hr); Melilla (local buses to the border); Fes (3; 8hr).
From Berkane Oujda (6 daily; 1hr); Saïdia (4; 1hr).
From Oujda Saïdia (6 daily, 1hr 20min); Figuig (3; 7hr); Midelt (1; 13hr).

Grands Taxis

From Taza Regularly to Fes (1hr 30min) and Oujda (2hr 30min). Occasionally to Al Hoceima.
From Al Hoceima Regularly to Nador (3hr). Infrequently to Fes and Taza.
From Nador Regularly to Oujda (2hr 30min) and Al Hoceima (3hr).
From Oujda Regularly to Saïdia (50min) and Taza (2hr 30min). Negotiable for the Algerian border.

Flights

From Oujda Casablanca (most days; **RAM** office at *Hôtel Oujda*).
From Melilla Málaga (4–6 daily; 35–40min); Almería (most days; 30min).

Ferries

From Melilla Daily except Sundays to Málaga (10hr) and Almería (6hr 30min). Drops to 3 times a week out of season.
From Nador Summer-only ferry to Sète (France). Sails once or twice weekly, from June to September.

TELEPHONE CODES

AL HOCEIMA ☎093	OUJDA ☎068
MELILLA ☎52	SAÏDIA ☎061
NADOR ☎060	TAZA ☎067

CHAPTER THREE

FES, MEKNES AND THE MIDDLE ATLAS

The imperial capital of the Merenid, Wattasid and Alouite dynasties, **Fes** has for ten centuries been at the heart of Moroccan history – and for five hundred years was one of the major intellectual and cultural centres of the West, rivalling the university cities of Europe. It is today unique in the Arab world, preserving the appearance and much of the life of a medieval Islamic city. In terms of monuments, above all the intricate university *medersas*, or colleges, Fes has as much as the other Moroccan imperial capitals together, while the city's *souks*, extending for over a mile, maintain the whole tradition of urban crafts.

In all of this – and equally in the everyday aspects of the city's life – there is enormous fascination, and, for the outsider, a real feeling of privilege. But inevitably, it is at a cost. Declared a historical monument by the French, and subsequently deprived of its political and cultural significance, Fes retains its beauty but is now in drastic and evident decline. Its university faculties have been dispersed around the country, with the most important departments in Rabat; the Fassi business elite have mostly left for Casablanca; and, for survival, the city depends increasingly on the tourist trade.

Fes's claims are well known, and, after Tangier, it is by far the most touristed city of the north. **Meknes**, in contrast, sees comparatively few visitors, despite being an easy and convenient stopover en route by train from Tangier or Rabat, or by bus from Chaouen. The megalomaniac creation of Moulay Ismail, most tyrannical of all Moroccan sultans, it is once again a city of lost ages, its enduring impression being that of an endless series of walls. But Meknes is also an important modern market centre and its *souks*, though smaller and less secretive than those of Fes, are almost as varied and generally more authentic. There are, too, the local attractions of **Volubilis**, the best preserved of the country's Roman sites, and the hilltop town of **Moulay Idriss**, the most important Moroccan shrine, forbidden to non-Muslims and hidden from Europeans until 1916.

South of the two imperial cities stretch the cedar-covered slopes of the **Middle Atlas**, which in turn gradually give way to the High Atlas. Across and around this region, often beautiful and for the most part remote, there are three main routes. The most popular, a day's journey by bus, skirts the range beyond the market town of **Azrou** to emerge via **Beni Mellal** at Marrakesh. A second one climbs southeastward from Azrou towards **Midelt**, an excellent carpet centre, before passing through great gorges to Er Rachidia and the

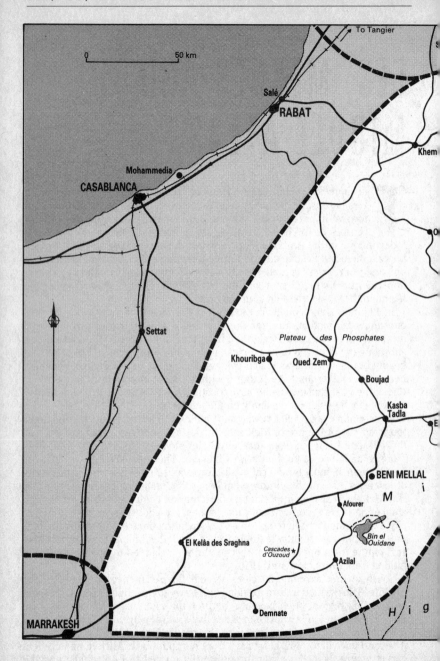

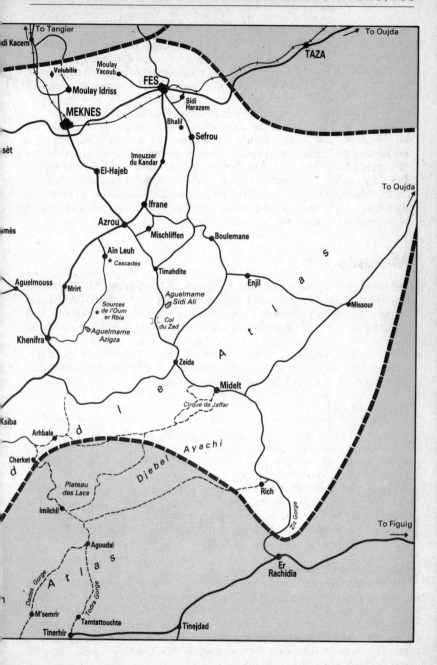

vast date palm oasis of Tafilalt – the beginning of a tremendous southern circuit (see Chapter Six). The third route, running between these two, is much more adventurous and is described (in reverse order) in the High Atlas section (see Chapter Five). Leaving the main Azrou–Marrakesh highway at **El Ksiba**, it follows a series of *pistes* (dirt roads) directly **across the Atlas** to Tinerhir. It is possible to cover this route – one of the great Moroccan journeys – by getting lifts over the various stages in local Berber lorries,

If you're travelling one of the main highways, and you've got the time, the Middle Atlas has other, definite attractions of its own. Close to Fes, **Immouzer** and **Ifrane** are popular summer resorts, their air and waters a cool escape from the city. The Berber market town of **Azrou** is host to a great **Tuesday souk** and surrounded by pine forests and mountain lakes. And just off the Marrakesh road, near Beni Mellal, are the **Cascades d'Ouzoud** – waterfalls which crash down from the mountains, even in midsummer, and beside which you can swim, camp and hike.

Meknes

Cut in two by the wide river valley of the Oued Boufekrane, **MEKNES** is a sprawling, prosperous provincial city. Monuments from its past – dominated by the extraordinary creations of Moulay Ismail (of whom more below) – well reward a day's rambling exploration, as do the varied and busy *souks* of its Medina. To get the most out of it all, though, it's best to visit before heading to Fes. Getting a grasp for Meknes prepares you a little for the drama of Fes, and certainly helps give an idea of quality (and prices) for crafts shopping; visited second, it is inevitably a little disappointing.

Orientation

Meknes is considerably simpler than it looks on the map. Its **Ville Nouvelle** stretches along a slope above the east bank of the river. The **Medina** flanked by its former Mellah occupies the west bank, with the walls of Moulay Ismail's **Ville Imperial** edging away, seemingly forever, to its south.

Focal point of the Medina is **Place el Hedim**, recently remodelled into a vast pedestrian plaza with fountains, decorated arcades and shops. The square is the best place to fix your bearings: downhill, *petits taxis*, *grands taxis* and buses operate to city and country destinations, including Volubilis; buses #5, #7 and #9 head up toward the main Ville Nouvelle avenues.

Points of arrival: transport
Arriving by **bus** you will be dropped at the terminal by **Place el Hedim** (actually just outside of the Bab Zein el Abidin), which seems to have taken over from the *CTM* station on Av. des Forces Armées Royales in the Ville Nouvelle (another possible setting-down point – if requested). **Grands taxis** (regular connections with Fes and Moulay Idriss) run from Place el Hedim, too. **Buses from Chaouen** (and some other private line services) may drop you on the Medina side of the bridge.

There are two **train stations**, both in the Ville Nouvelle on the east bank. The **main station** is a kilometre away from the central area; a smaller, more convenient one, the **Gare El Amir**, is a couple of blocks from the centre (behind the *Hôtel Majestic*); all trains stop at both.

Leaving Meknes for **Fes**, you have the choice of either taking a bus (8 *CTM* departures per day), train, or, quickest of all, *grand taxi*; the latter leave Meknes at Place el Hedim and arrive in Fes el Djedid at Place des Alaouites. *CTM* have at least daily departures, too, for **Azrou**, **Midelt**, **Rabat** and **Marrakesh**. Heading for **Chaouen**, check the timetable with the tourist office, and try to buy a ticket ahead of time – preferably the night before.

There is a **Syndicat d'Initiative** (☎201.91) inside the gates at the intersection of Av. Hassan II and Av. Moulay Ismail, and an **ONMT** tourist office on the Place d'Adminstrative.

Accommodation

Hotels are concentrated in the **Ville Nouvelle**, and if you want comfort and proximity to bars and restaurants this is the place to stay. However, it's a fair walk from here to the **Medina** and, for a short stay, there are more advantages in being close to the monuments and *souks*.

Medina hotels
See the Medina map on p.135 for locations.

Maroc Hôtel, 103 Av. Benbrahim – opposite the *Cinema Apollo* on Rue Rouamazin (☎307.05; keyed **H** on the main map). This is by far the cleanest and quietest of the Medina hotels. *Unclassified.*

Hôtel de Paris, Rue Rouamazin. Just up the street from the *Maroc* – and the best fallback if that's full. *Unclassified.*

Hôtel Agadir, Rue Dar Semen. The best of a bunch of three very basic hotels grouped at the corner of Rue Rouamazin/Rue Dar Semen. The other two are drab, showerless and stifling; the *Agadir* is, at least, friendly and has a bit of character. *Unclassified.*

Ville Nouvelle hotels
Most of the cheaper hotels are grouped in an area around the bus station and main avenues. Recommendations below, all keyed on the main map overpage, are in ascending order of price.

Youth Hostel (*Auberge des Jeunesses*), Av. Okba Ibn Nafi (☎217.43). A bit out of the way, but well maintained, with rooms around a courtyard. No curfew; reception closed 10am–noon & 4–7pm. YHA card necessary. Getting there, follow signs to the luxury *Hôtel Transatlantique*.

Hôtel Moderne (C), 54 Bd. Allal Ben Abdallah (☎217.43). Clean, balconied rooms – and the best cheap Ville Nouvelle choice. *Unclassified.*

Hôtel Excelsior (G), 57 Av. des Forces Armées Royales (☎219.00). Recently renovated – but retaining lowish prices. *1*A.*

Hôtel Continental (E), 92 Av. des Forces Armées Royales (☎202.00). Tucked behind the restaurant of the same name; large, clean rooms and reliable showers. *2*B.*

Hôtel Majestic (B), 19 Av. Mohammed V (☎220.35). Friendly, old-fashioned hotel, handy for the El Amir train station. *2*A.*

Hôtel Palace (A), 11 Rue du Ghana (☎223.88). Respectable enough, if a bit overpriced, but with a comfortable bar. *2*A.*

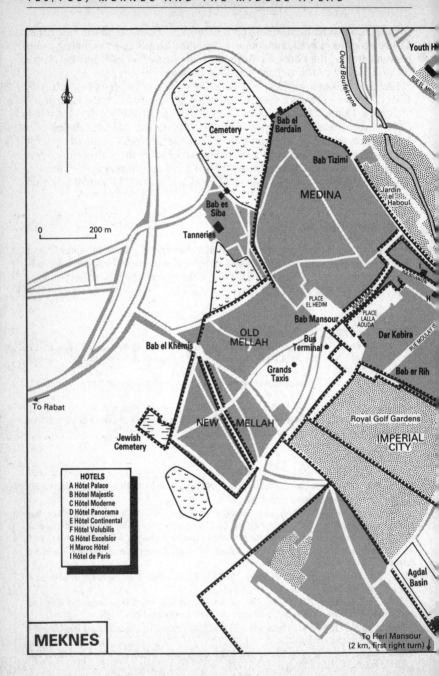

Oued Boufekrane

Youth H

RUE EL MRIN

Cemetery

Bab el Berdain

Bab Tizimi

MEDINA

Jardin el Haboul

Bab es Siba

Tanneries

RUE RAMMDO

PLACE EL HEDIM

PLACE LALLA AOUDA

Bab Mansour

Dar Kebira

H

OLD MELLAH

Bus Terminal

RUE MOULAY S

Bab el Khémis

Grands Taxis

Bab er Rih

To Rabat

NEW MELLAH

Royal Golf Gardens

IMPERIAL CITY

Jewish Cemetery

0   200 m

HOTELS
A Hôtel Palace
B Hôtel Majestic
C Hôtel Moderne
D Hôtel Panorama
E Hôtel Continental
F Hôtel Volubilis
G Hôtel Excelsior
H Maroc Hôtel
I Hôtel de Paris

Agdal Basin

To Heri Mansour
(2 km, first right turn)

MEKNES

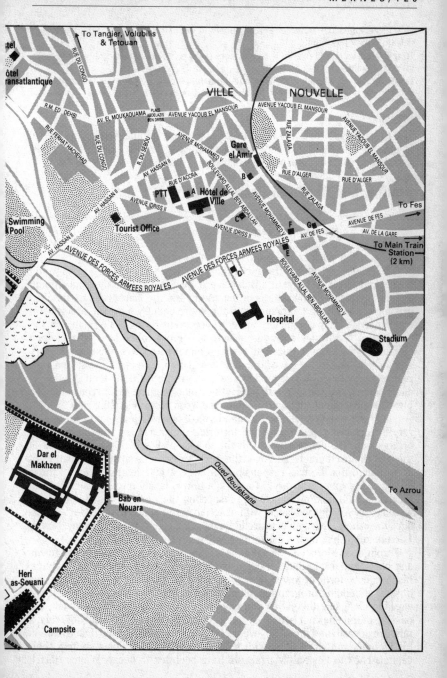

Hôtel Panorama (D), 9 Av. des Forces Armées Royales (☎227.37). Best of the 2* places, if you are looking for comfort. *2*A.*

Hôtel Volubilis (F), 45 Av. des Forces Armées Royales (☎201.02). Reasonably priced for its class, and again with a bar. *3*B.*

Hôtel Rif, Zankat Accra (☎225.91); **Hôtel Transatlantique**, Rue el Meriniyine (☎200.02/200.03). The two luxury options, both with pools, and, respectively 4 and 5 stars.

Camping

The town **campsite**, *Camping Aguedal*, is a twenty-minute walk from Place el Hedim (or an 8–10dh taxi ride), sited opposite the Heri as-Souani. It is a pleasant, shaded site, with reasonable facilities.

Moulay Ismail and the Imperial City

More than any other Moroccan town, Meknes is associated with a single figure, the **Sultan Moulay Ismail**, in whose 55-year reign (1672–1727) the city was built up from a provincial centre to a spectacular capital with twenty gates, over fifty palaces and some fifteen miles of exterior walls.

"The Sultan", wrote his chronicler, Ezziani, "loved Mequinez, and he would have liked never to leave it." But leave it he did, ceaselessly campaigning against the rebel Berber chiefs of the south, and the Europeans entrenched in Tangier, Asilah and Larache, until the entire country – for the first time in five centuries – lay completely under government control. His reign saw the creation of Morocco's strongest ever – and most coherent – army, which included a crack negro guard, the Abid regiment, and, it is reckoned, a garrison force of one in twenty of the male population. The period was, in a very real sense, Morocco's last golden age, though the ruthless centralisation of all decisions, and the fear with which the sultan reigned, led, perhaps inevitably, to a subsequent slide into anarchy and weak, inward-looking rule.

Ismail was a tyrant even by the standards of his own times – and contemporary Europeans were burning and torturing their enemies and putting them on the rack. His reign began with the display at Fes of 700 heads, most of them of captured chiefs, and over the next five decades, apart from battles, it is estimated that he was responsible for over 30,000 deaths. Many of these killings were quite arbitrary. Mounting a horse, Ismail might slash the head off the eunuch holding his stirrup; inspecting the work on his buildings, he would carry a weighted lance, with which to batter skulls in order to "encourage" the others. "My subjects are like rats in a basket", he used to say, "and if I do not keep shaking the basket they will gnaw their way through."

Throughout Morocco, the sultan was a tireless builder, constructing towns and ports, and a multitude of defensive kasbahs, palaces and bridges. By far his greatest efforts, however, were directed at Meknes, where he sustained an obsessive building programme, often acting as architect and sometimes even working alongside the slaves and labourers. Ironically, in Meknes itself, the passing of time has not been easy on his constructions. Built mainly of *tabia*, a mixture of earth and lime, they were severely damaged by a hurricane even in his lifetime, and since then, with subsequent Alaouite sultans shifting their capitals back to Fes and Marrakesh, have been left to decay. Walter Harris, writing only 150 years after Ismail's death, found Meknes "a city of the dead . . . strewn with marble columns, and surrounded by great masses of ruin". Even with its Ville Nouvelle across the river, built by the French as their chief military garrison, the city still has a feeling of emptiness.

The principal remains of Ismail's creation – the **imperial city** of palaces and gardens, barracks, granaries and stables – sprawl below the Medina amid a confusingly manic array of walled enclosures. It's a long morning's walk if you intend to take in everything, but a fairly straightforward one. Starting out from the Ville Nouvelle, make your way down to the main street at the edge of the Medina (**Rue Rouamazin/Rue Dar Semen**), and along to **Place el Hedim** and its immense gateway, **Bab Mansour**. There are usually **guides** hanging around here if you want to use one; you don't need to, but if you can find someone entertaining, he'll probably elaborate on the story of the walls with some superbly convoluted local legend.

Bab Mansour and around

Place el Hedim – the Square of Destruction – immediately recalls Moulay Ismail. Originally, it formed the western corner of the Medina, but the sultan demolished the houses here in order to form a grand approach to his palace quarter, the *Dar Kebira*. The square today, having been remodelled at the end of the 1980s, is rather less austere.

The centrepiece of the city's whole ensemble of walls and gateways is the great **Bab Mansour**, startlingly rich in its ceremonial intent, and almost perfectly preserved. Its name comes from its architect – one of a number of Christian renegades who converted to Islam and rose to high position at Ismail's court; there is a tale that when the sultan inspected the gate, he asked El Mansour whether he could do better – a classic catch-22, whose response ("yes") led to immediate and enraged execution. The story may be apocryphal, however, for the gate was actually completed under Ismail's son, Moulay Abdallah, a sultan who inherited some of his father's nastier habits. It was said that he had "a predilection for standing slaves in a row beside a wall he was about to demolish, and letting it fall about them."

Nevertheless, the gate is the finest in Meknes and an interesting adaptation of the classic Almohad design, flanked by unusually inset and fairly squat bastions, which are purely decorative, their marble columns having been brought here from Volubilis. The decorative patterns on both gate and bastions are basically elaborations of the *darj w ktarf* (a cheek-and-shoulder pattern, begun by the Almohads), the space between each motif filled out with a brilliant array of *zellij* created by a layer of cut-away black tiles, just like the ornamental inscription above, which extols the triumph of Ismail and, even more, that of Abdallah, adding that there is no gate in Damascus or Alexandria its equal. To the left of Bab Mansour is a smaller gateway in the same style, **Bab Djemaa en Nouar**.

Through Bab Mansour, and straight ahead through a second gate, you will find yourself in a large open square, on the right of which is a domed **Koubba** – once a reception hall for ambassadors to the imperial court. Below it, a stairway (small tip to the guide) descends into a vast series of subterranean vaults, known in popular tradition as the **Prison of Christian Slaves**.

This was probably, in fact, a storehouse or granary, although there were certainly several thousand Christian captives at Ismail's court. Most were captured by the Sallee Rovers (see "Rabat") and brought here as slave labour for the interminable construction projects; reputedly any of them who died while at work were simply buried in the walls they were building.

Ahead of the *koubba*, set within the long wall and at right angles to it, are two very modest **gates**. The one on the right is generally closed and is at all times flanked by soldiers from the royal guard; within, landscaped across a lake and the sunken garden of Ismail's last and finest palace, are the **Royal Golf Gardens** – private and generally *interdit*. The gate on the left opens on to an apparently endless corridor of walls and, a few metres down, the entrance to the **Mausoleum of Moulay Ismail**.

The Mausoleum

Together with the tomb of Mohammed V in Rabat, **Moulay Ismail's Mausoleum** (9am–noon & 3–6pm) is the only active Moroccan shrine that non-Muslims may visit. Even so, admission is occasionally refused; women especially must dress with total modesty.

The fact that Ismail's mausoleum, completed within his lifetime, has remained a shrine is itself perhaps puzzling. Yet, as Walter Harris wrote a century ago, this "deceased Sultan who, having killed more men, Christians and Moors, than any of his predecessors, having wasted more money on impossible palaces and such-like than could ever be counted, and, when tiring of a wife, having her for amusement tortured and killed before his very eyes, is reverenced as one of the greatest saints of the Moorish religious calendar." So it was, too, in Ismail's lifetime. His absolute tyranny of control, his success in driving out the Spanish from Larache and the British from Tangier, and his extreme observance of orthodox Islamic form and ritual all conferred a kind of magic on him.

Entering the mausoleum, you are allowed to approach the **sanctuary** in which the sultan is buried – though you cannot go beyond the annexe. Decorated in bright *zellij* and spiralling stuccowork, it is a fine if unspectacular series of courts and chambers. But what is most interesting, perhaps, is that the shrine was thoroughly renovated in the 1950s at the expense of Mohammed V, and also that the sarcophagus is still the object of prayer. You will almost invariably see country people here, especially women, seeking *baraka* (charismatic blessing) and intercession.

The Dar el Kebira

Past the mausoleum, a gate to your left gives access to the dilapidated quarter of **Dar el Kebira**, Ismail's great palace complex. The imperial structures – the legendary fifty palaces – can still be made out between and above the houses here: ogre-like creations, whose scale is hard to believe. They were completed in 1677 and dedicated at an astonishing midnight celebration, when the sultan personally slaughtered a wolf so that its head might be displayed at the centre of the gateway.

In the grandeur of the plan there is sometimes claimed a conscious echo of Versailles – its contemporary rival – though, in fact, it was another decade until the first reports of the French building reached the imperial court. When they did, Ismail was certainly interested, and in 1699 he even sent an ambassador to Paris with the task of negotiating the addition of Louis XIV's daughter, Princess Conti, to his harem. He returned without success.

On the opposite side of the long-walled corridor, beyond the Royal Golf Gardens, more immense buildings are spread out, making up Ismail's last great palace, the **Dar el Makhzen**. Unlike the Kebira, which was broken up by Moulay Abdallah in 1733, this has remained a minor royal residence – though Hassan II rarely visits Meknes. The most you can get are a few brief glimpses over the heads of the bored guards posted by occasional gates in the crumbling, twenty-foot-high wall. The corridor itself, which eventually turns a corner to bring you out by the campsite and the Heri as-Souani, may perhaps be the **"strangee"** which eighteenth-century travellers recorded. A mile-long terrace wall, shaded with vines, it was a favourite drive of the sultan, who, according to several sources, was driven around in a bizarre chariot drawn by his women or eunuchs.

At its end, and the principal "sight" of the imperial city, is the **Heri as-Souani** – often introduced by local guides as "Ismail's stables". The stables, in fact, are further south (see below), and the startling series of high vaulted chambers to be seen here were again a series of storerooms and granaries, filled with abundant provisions for siege or drought. A twenty-minute walk from Bab Mansour, they give a powerful impression of the complexity of seventeenth-century Moroccan engineering. Ismail's palaces each had underground plumbing (well in advance of Europe), and here you find a remarkable system, with chain-bucket wells built between each of the storerooms. One on the left, near the back, has been restored; there are lights you can switch on for a closer look.

Equally worthwhile is the view from the **roof** of the as-Souani, approached through the second entrance on the right. From the roof garden, with its **café**, you can gaze out across much of the Dar el Makhzen and the wonderfully still **Agdal Basin** – built as an irrigation reservoir and pleasure lake. Over to the southwest, in the distance, you can make out another seventeenth-century royal palace, the **Dar al-Baida** (the "White House"), now a military academy, and beyond it (to the right), the **Rouah**, or stables.

The Rouah

Known locally as the **Heri Mansour** (Mansour's Granary), the **Rouah** are a further twenty- to thirty-minute walk from the as-Souani. They are officially closed to visitors, though hang around for a while and the local guide will probably turn up. To find the site, follow the road which runs diagonally behind the campsite and Heri as-Souani for half a kilometre; when you reach a junction, turn right and you come out at the **Djemaa Rouah** (Stable Mosque), a large, heavily restored building preceded by a well-kept gravel courtyard. Walk around behind the mosque and you will see the stables off to your right – a massive complex perhaps twice as large as the as-Souani.

In contemporary accounts the Rouah was often singled out as the greatest feature of all Ismail's building projects: some three miles in length, traversed by a long canal, with flooring built over vaults used for storing grain, and space for over twelve thousand horses. Today, the province of a few scrambling goats, it's a conclusive ruin – piles of rubble and *zellij* tiles lining the walls and high arched aisles of crumbling *pisé* extending out in each direction. As such, it perhaps recalls more than anything else in Meknes the scale and madness of Moulay Ismail's vision. The sultan once decreed that a wall should be built from here all the way to Marrakesh – a convenient access for his carriage and a useful guide for the blind beggars to find their way.

The Medina

The Medina, although taking much of its present form and size under Moulay Ismail, bears less of his stamp. Its main sights – in addition to the **souks** – are a Merenid *medersa,* the **Bou Inania** and a nineteenth-century palace museum, the **Dar Jamai**.

The Dar Jamai

The **Dar Jamai** (9am–noon & 3–6pm; 10dh) stands at the back of Place el Hedim, from which it is reached down a stairway. One of the best examples of a nineteenth-century Moroccan palace, it was built by the same family of viziers (high government officials) who put up the Palais Jamai in Fes.

Its exhibits, some of which have been incorporated to recreate reception rooms, are predominantly of the same age, though some of the pieces of **Fes** and **Meknes pottery** date back more or less to Ismail's reign. These ceramics, elaborate polychrome designs from Meknes and strong blue and white patterns from Fes, make for an interesting comparison, and the superiority of Fes's handicrafts tradition during the last two centuries is clearly apparent. The best display here, however, is of **Middle Atlas carpets,** particularly from the Beni Mguild tribe. If at any time you're planning to buy a rug – and Meknes itself can be good place – take a long hard look at each of these; though you won't find anything to approach them, you'll get a good idea of what is really worth coveting.

The *souks*

To reach the *souks* from Place el Hedim, follow the lane immediately behind the Dar Jamai. You will come out in the middle of the Medina's major market street; on your right, leading to the Grand Mosque and Bou Inania Medersa, is **Souk es Sebbat**; on your left is **Souk en Nejjarin**.

Turning first to the left, you enter an area of textile stalls, which later give way to the carpenters' (*nejjarin*) workshops from which the *souk* takes its name. Shortly after this, you pass a mosque on your left, beyond which is an entrance to a parallel arcade. The **carpet market**, or **Souk Joutiya as-Zerabi**, is just off here to the left. Quality can be very high (and prices, too), though without the constant stream of tourists of Fes or Marrakesh, dealers are much more willing to bargain. Don't be afraid to start too low.

Out at the end of Souk en Nejjarin you come to another *souk*, the **Bezzarin**, which runs up at right angles to the Nejjarin, on either side of the city wall. This looks like a ramshackle, run-down neighbourhood, but if you follow the outer side of the wall, you'll come across an interesting assortment of crafts-

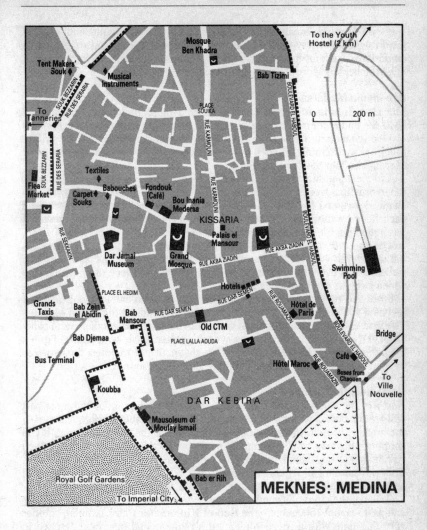

MEKNES: MEDINA

workers, grouped together in their own trading guilds and often with an old *fondouk* or warehouse to the front of them. As you proceed, there are **basket-makers**, **ironsmiths** and **saddlers**, while near **Bab el Djedid**, at the top, you'll find **tent makers** and a couple of **musical instrument workshops**.

Had you turned right beyond the Dar Jamai, onto **Souk es Sebbat**, you would have entered a classier section of the market – starting off with the *babouche* vendors, and then moving on to the fancier goods aimed at tourists near the *medersa*, finally exiting into the covered **kissaria**, dominated by caftan sellers. From here it is easy enough to find your way to the Bou Inania Medersa, whose imposing portal is visible on the left-hand side of the street.

If you want a break before doing that, there's a nineteenth-century **fondouk** a short way back which now doubles as a café and carpet/crafts emporium – look for its open courtyard. Meknes mint, incidentally, is reputed to be the best in Morocco and exported all around the north.

Bou Inania Medersa

The **Bou Inania Medersa** (9am–noon & 3–6pm; 10dh) was built around 1340–50, and is therefore more or less contemporary with the great *medersas* of Fes. It takes its name from the notorious Sultan Abou Inan (see p.159), though it was actually founded by his predecessor, Abou el Hassan, the great Merenid builder of Chellah in Rabat.

A modest and functional building, the *medersa* follows the plan of Hassan's other principal works, the Chellah *zaouia* and Salé *medersa*, in that it has a single **courtyard** opening on to a narrow **prayer hall**, and is encircled on each floor by the students' **cells**, with exquisite screens in carved cedar. It has a much lighter feel to it than the Salé *medersa*, and in its balance of wood, stucco and *zellij* achieves a remarkable combination of intricacy – no area is left uncovered – and restraint. Architecturally, the most unusual feature is a ribbed dome over the **entrance hall**, an impressive piece of craftsmanship which extends right out into the *souk*.

From **the roof**, to which there's usually access, you can look out (and you feel as if you could climb across) to the tiled pyramids of the Grand Mosque. The *souk* is mainly obscured from view, but you can get a good, general panorama of the town and the mosques of each quarter. Inlaid with bands of green tiles, the minarets of these mosques are distinctive of Meknes; those of Fes or Marrakesh tend to be more elaborate and multicoloured.

North from Bou Inania

North of the Medersa and Grand Mosque, the Medina is for the most part residential, dotted with the occasional fruit and vegetable market, or (up past the mosque of Ben Khadra) a carpenters' *souk*, for the supply of wood. If you continue this way, you'll eventually come out in a long, open square which culminates in the monumental **Bab el Berdain** (The Gate of the Saddlers). This was another of Ismail's creations, and echoes, in a much more rugged and genuinely defensive structure, the central section of Bab Mansour.

Outside, the city walls continue to extend up along the main road to Rabat, and past – about 1500m out – the **Bab el Khemis** (or Bab Lakhmis), another very fine gate with a frieze containing a monumental inscription etched in black tiles on the brickwork. Between the two gates, inside the wall on your left, you will catch occasional glimpses of an enormous **cemetery** – almost half the size of the Medina in extent. Non-Muslims are not permitted to enter this enclosure, near the centre of which lies the *zaouia* and shrine of one of the country's most famous and curious saints, **Sidi Ben Aissa**.

Reputedly a contemporary of Moulay Ismail, Ben Aissa conferred on his followers the power to eat anything, even poison or broken glass, without suffering any ill effects. His cult, the *Aissaoua*, became one of the most important in Morocco, and certainly the most violent and fanatical. Until prohibited by the French, some 50,000 devotees regularly attended the saint's annual *moussem* on the eve of Mouloud. Entering into a trance, they were known to pierce their tongues and cheeks with daggers, eat serpents and scorpions, or devour live sheep and goats. The only other confraternity to approach such frenzy was the *Hamacha* of Moulay Idriss, whose favourite rites included cutting off each other's heads with hatchets and tossing heavy stones or cannonballs into the air, allowing them to fall down on their skulls. Both cults continue to hold *moussems*, though successive Moroccan governments have effectively outlawed their more extreme activities.

Food and practicalities

For most practical needs, beyond a basic bed and meal, you'll need to cross the river to the Ville Nouvelle.

Medina café-restaurants

For straight Moroccan food pick from any of the café-grills along Rue Dar Semen, toward Place el Hedim, **in the Medina**. One place to avoid, despite the enthusiastic handbills given out at the *Maroc Hôtel*, is the *Rôtisserie Oumnia*. The *Café Bab Mansour*, near the gate of the same name, is among the best of the basic choices – and stays open late. *Restaurant Economique*, 123 Rue Dar Semen, is another reasonable cheapie.

Ville Nouvelle restaurants and bars

In the Ville Nouvelle, there are a handful of predominantly **French-menu restaurants** in and around Place de France. Rue du Ghana, which leads off from here past the PTT, has a couple of cheap places – *La Coupole*, towards the intersection with Av. Hassan II, is a good bet.

Others are to be found on Av. Hassan II itself – the unnamed restaurant at no. 12 is recommended. *Restaurant Marhaba* – on Av. Mohammed V, past the cinema, coming from the *CTM* station – is perhaps the best of the lot. For more **upmarket fare**, the Moroccan restaurant at the *Hôtel Transatlantique* is pretty reasonable, given the hotel's five-star status.

There are a surprising number of **bars**. Pick from the *Roi de la Bière*, Av. Mohammed V (but often closed in summer); the *Bar Continental* (corner of Av. des FAR/Av. Hassan II); the *Club de Nuit* (more or less opposite, on Av. Hassan II); the *Cabaret Oriental* (again Av. Hassan II), with bands sometimes playing till the early hours; or the *Novelty Bar-Restaurant* at 12 Rue de Marseille. There are also bars in the *Volubilis*, *Rif*, *Palace* and *Nice* hotels.

Listings

Banks are concentrated on Av. Mohammed V (the *Crédit du Maroc* is at no. 33) and Av. des Forces Armées Royales (*BMCE* at no. 98). Another *BMCE* branch is in the Medina, near the *Maroc Hôtel* at 66 Rue Rouamazin. The *Hôtel Rif* will exchange cash out of banking hours.

Festivals The city's **Ben Aïssa Moussem** (held over the Mouloud, see p.34) is one of the country's most impressive. Also worth planning for are the **Beni Rached Moussem** (seven days after Mouloud; at the village of Beni Rached, out of town on the Moulay Idriss road) and the **Moulay Idriss Moussem** (September).

Garages For Renault repairs try the garage on the Fes road; for VWs, *Maroc-France* on Av. Hassan II.

Hammam If you're staying in the Medina, the *Maroc Hôtel* should be able to steer you toward a *hammam*; in the Ville Nouvelle, you'll find a good one off Av. Hassan II, at 4 Rue Patrice Lumumba, with separate sections for women and men (both 7am–9pm).

Post Office The PTT, just off Place de France, is open Monday–Saturday 8am–2pm; its **phone** section stays open until 9pm.

Royal Air Maroc is at Av. Mohammed V (☎209.63).

Swimming Pools There are two public pools down by the river, reached along a lane from Bd. El Haboul or from the intersection of Av. Hassan II and Av. Moulay Ismail. The first you encounter is very cheap; a little further down there's another – classier, less crowded, and three or four times the price.

Volubilis and Moulay Idriss

The classic excursion from Meknes, **Volubilis** and **Moulay Idriss** embody much of Morocco's early history – Volubilis as its Roman provincial capital, Moulay Idriss in the creation of the country's first Arab dynasty. Their sites stand 4km apart, at either side of a deep and very fertile valley, about 30km north of Meknes.

Transport

You can take in both sites on a leisurely day trip from Meknes. **Grands taxis** (6dh a place to Moulay Idriss; frequent departures) and **buses** (4dh to Moulay Idriss; on the hour, last returning at 5pm) leave from the terminal area south of Place el Hedim.

It is simplest to visit Volubilis first, then to go on to Moulay Idriss, where you can pick up a bus or *grand taxi* returning to Meknes. Ask your bus or taxi driver to let you off at the turnoff for Volubilis, which is a couple of kilometres south of Moulay Idriss, on the left-hand (west) side of the road. One and a half kilometres from this main road turnoff, you'll come to a fork signposted "Aïn el Jamaa/Col du Zegotta": either road will bring you to Volubilis in about 2km. Taxi drivers might be persuaded to go this way to Moulay Idriss, though if you want to guarantee a ride the whole way the only sure answer is to get a group together and pay for the whole taxi.

Taxis from Moulay Idriss will not as a rule run to Fes, unless you're willing to pay for a *course* (the whole taxi). From Volubilis, however, Fes-bound hitchers may well strike lucky with a lift.

Accommodation

Non-Muslims are not officially permitted to stay overnight in the town of Moulay Idriss – the only place in Morocco to keep this status.

However, there is a pleasant, shaded **campsite**, *Camping Zerhoun* (no facilities, the bar has closed down), midway along the "outer road" between Moulay Idriss (11km) and Meknes. Roads here are slightly confusing, and it's a good idea to ask directions to the nearby *refuge Zerhoun*.

Volubilis

A striking site, visible for miles from the various bends in the approach road, **VOLUBILIS** occupies the ledge of a long, high plateau. Below its walls, towards Moulay Idriss, stretches a rich river valley; beyond lie dark, outlying ridges of the Zerhoun mountains. The drama of this scene – and the scope of the ruins – may well seem familiar. It was the key location for Martin Scorsese's film, *The Last Temptation of Christ*.

Some history

Except for a small trading post on the island off Essaouira, Volubilis was the Roman Empire's most remote and far-flung base. The imperial roads stopped here, having reached across France and Spain and then down from Tangier, and despite successive emperors' dreams of "penetrating the Atlas", the southern Berber tribes were never effectively subdued.

Direct Roman rule here, in fact, lasted little over two centuries – the garrison withdrew early, in 285 AD, to ease pressure elsewhere. But the town must have taken much of its present form well before the official annexation of North African Mauretania by Emperor Claudius in 45 AD. Tablets found on the site, inscribed in Punic, show a significant Carthaginian trading presence in the third century BC, and prior to colonisation it was the western capital of a heavily Romanised but semi-autonomous Berber kingdom, which reached into northern Algeria and Tunisia. After the Romans left, Volubilis saw very gradual change. Latin was still spoken in the seventh century by the local population of Berbers, Greeks, Syrians and Jews; Christian churches survived until the coming of Islam; and the city itself remained alive and active well into the eighteenth century, when its marble was carried away by slaves for the building of Moulay Ismail's Meknes.

What you see today, well excavated and maintained, are largely the ruins of second- and third-century AD buildings – impressive and affluent creations from its period as a colonial provincial capital. The land around here is some of the most fertile in North Africa, and the city exported wheat and olives in considerable quantities to Rome, as it did wild animals from the surrounding hills. Roman games, memorable for the sheer scale of their slaughter (9000 beasts were killed for the dedication of Rome's Colosseum alone), could not have happened without the African provinces, and Volubilis was a chief source of their lions. Within just two hundred years, along with Barbary bears and elephants, they became virtually extinct.

The Site

Open daily, sunrise–sunset; 20dh admission.

The entrance to the site is through a minor gate in the city wall, built along with a number of outer camps in 168 AD, following a prolonged series of Berber insurrections. Just inside are the **ticket office**, a shaded **café-bar** and a small, open-air **museum** of sculpture and other fragments.

The best of the finds made here – which include a superb collection of bronzes – have all been taken to the Rabat museum. Volubilis, however, has retained in situ the great majority of its **mosaics**, some thirty or so in a good state of preservation. You leave with a real sense of Roman city life and its provincial prosperity, while in the layout of the site it is not hard to recognise the essentials of a medieval Arab town.

Following the path up from the museum and across a bridge over the Fertassa stream, you come out on a mixed area of housing and industry, each

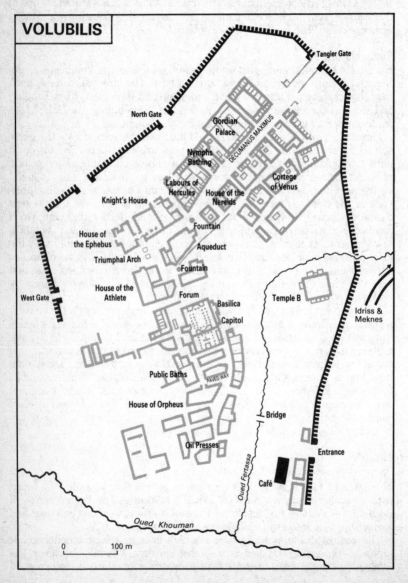

VOLUBILIS

Tangier Gate

North Gate

Gordian Palace

DECUMANUS MAXIMUS

Nymphs Bathing

Labours of Hercules

Cortege of Venus

Knight's House

House of the Nereids

House of the Ephebus

Fountain

Aqueduct

Triumphal Arch

Fountain

House of the Athlete

Forum

Temple B

West Gate

Basilica

Capitol

Idriss & Meknes

Public Baths

PAVED WAY

House of Orpheus

Bridge

Oil Presses

Entrance

Oued Fertassa

Café

Oued Khouman

0   100 m

of its buildings containing the clear remains of at least one **olive press**. The extent and number of these presses, built into even the grandest mansions, reflect the olive's absolute importance to the city and indicate perhaps why Volubilis remained unchanged for so long after the Romans' departure. A significant proportion of its 20,000 population must have been involved in some capacity in the oil's production and export.

Somewhat isolated in this suburban quarter is the **House of Orpheus**, an enormous complex of rooms just beside the start of a paved way. Although substantially in ruins, it offers a strong impression of its former luxury – an opulent mansion for perhaps one of the town's richest merchants. It is divided into two main sections – public and private – each with its separate entrance and interior court. The private rooms, which you come to first, are grouped around a small patio containing a more or less intact **dolphin mosaic**. You can also make out the furnace and heating system (just by the entrance), the kitchen with its niche for the household gods, and the **baths** – an extensive system of hot, cold and steam rooms. The public apartments, a bit further inside, are dominated by a large **atrium**, half reception hall, half central court, and again preserving a very fine mosaic, **The Chariot of Amphitrite drawn by a Seahorse**. The best example here, however, and the mosaic from which the house takes its name, is that of the **Orpheus Myth**, located to the south in a room which was probably the *tablinium*, or archives.

Above the Orpheus House, a broad, paved street leads up towards the main group of public buildings – the Capitol and Basilica, whose sand-coloured ruins dominate the site. Taking the approach on the left, you pass first through the remains of the city's main **Public Baths**. Restored by the Emperor Gallienus in the second century AD, these are clearly monumental in their intent, though sadly the mosaics are only fragmentary. The arrangement of the **Forum** is typical of a major Roman town: built on the highest rise of the city and flanked by a triumphal arch, market, capitol and basilica.

The **Capitol**, the smaller and lower of the two main buildings, is dated from inscriptions to 217 AD – a time at which this whole public nucleus seems to have been rebuilt by the African-born Severian emperors. Adjoined by small forum **baths**, it is an essentially simple building, a porticoed court giving access to a small temple and altar. Its dedication – standard throughout the Roman world – was to the official state cult of Capitoline Jove, Juno and Minerva. The large five-aisled **Basilica** to its side served as the courthouse, while immediately across the forum were the small court and stalls of the central **market**.

The **Triumphal Arch**, right in the middle of the town, had no particular purpose other than creating a ceremonial function for the principal street, the Decumanus Maximus – on whose side it is more substantially ornamented. Erected in honour of the Severian emperor, Caracalla, its inscription records that it was originally surmounted by a great bronze chariot. This, and the nymphs which once shot water into its basins below, are now gone, though with its tall Corinthian columns (of imported marble) and unashamed pointlessness, it is still an impressive monument. The medallions on either side, heavily eroded, presumably depict Caracalla and his mother, Julia Donna, who is also named in the inscription.

The finest of Volubilis's mansions – and its mosaics – line the **Decumanus Maximus**, fronted in traditional Roman and Italian fashion by the shops built in tiny cubicles. Before you reach this point, however; take a look at the remains of an **aqueduct** and **fountains** across from the triumphal arch; these once supplied yet another complex of public baths. Opposite them are a small group of **houses**, mostly ruined but retaining an impressive **Mosaic of an Athlete** or "chariot jumper" – depicted receiving the winner's cup for a *desultor* race, a display of great skill which entailed leaping on and off a horse in full gallop.

First of the Decumanus Maximus mansions, the **House of the Ephebus** takes its name from the bronze of a youth found in its ruins (and today displayed in Rabat). In general plan it is very similar to the House of Orpheus, once again containing an olive press in its rear section, though this building is on a far grander scale – almost twice the size of the other – with pictorial mosaics in most of its public rooms and an ornamental pool in its central court. Finest of the mosaics is a representation of **Bacchus Being Drawn in a Chariot by Panthers** – a suitable scene for the *cenacula*, or banquet hall, in which it is placed.

Separated from the Ephebus House by a narrow lane is a mosaic-less mansion, known after its facade as the **House of Columns**, and adjoining this, the **Knight's House** with an incomplete mosaic of **Dionysos Discovering Ariadne** asleep on the beach at Naxos; both houses are themselves largely ruined. More illuminating is the large mansion which begins the next block, similar again in its plan, but featuring a very complete mosaic of the **Labours of Hercules**. Almost comic caricatures, these give a good idea of typical provincial Roman mosaics – immediate contrasts to the stylish **Orpheus and Bacchus** and **Nymphs Bathing** of the second house down.

Beyond this area, approaching the partially reconstructed **Tangier Gate**, stands the **Palace of the Gordians**, former residence of the procurators who administered the city and the province. Despite its size, however, even with a huge **bath house** and pooled courtyards, it is an unmemorable ruin. Stripped of most of its columns, and lacking any mosaics, its grandeur and scale may have made it an all too obvious target for Ismail's building mania. Indeed, how much of Volubilis remained standing before his reign began is an open question; Walter Harris, writing at the turn of the twentieth century, found the road between here and Meknes littered with ancient marbles, left as they fell following the announcement of the sultan's death.

Back on the Decumanus, cross to the other side of the road and walk down a block to a smaller lane below the street. Here, in the third house you come to, is the most exceptional ensemble of mosaics of the entire site – the **Cortege of Venus**. You cannot enter the house but most of the fine mosaics can be seen by walking around the outside of the ruins. If you imagine walking into the main section of the house, a central court is preceded by a paved vestibule and opens on to another, smaller patio, around which are grouped the main reception halls (and mosaics). From the entrance, the **baths** are off to the left, flanked by the private quarters, while immediately around the central court is a small group of mosaics, including an odd, very worn representation of a **Chariot Race** – with birds instead of horses.

The villa's most outstanding mosaics lie beyond, in the "public" sections. On the left, in the corner, is a geometrical design, with medallions of **Bacchus Surrounded by the Four Seasons**; off to the right are **Diana Bathing** (and surprised by the huntsman Actaeon) and the **Abduction of Hylas by Nymphs**. Each of these scenes – especially the last two – is superbly handled in stylised but very fluid animation. They date, like that of the **Nereids** (two houses further down), from either the late second or early third century AD, and were obviously a very serious commission. It is not known for whom this house was built, but its owner must have been among the city's most successful patrons; here were found the bronze busts of Cato and Juba II which are now the centrepiece of Rabat's museum.

Leaving the site by a path below the forum, you pass close by the ruins of a **temple** on the opposite side of the stream. This was dedicated by the Romans to Saturn, but had probably previously been involved with the worship of a Carthaginian god; in its excavation several hundred votive offerings were discovered.

Moulay Idriss

MOULAY IDRISS takes its name from its founder, Morocco's most venerated saint and the creator of its first Arab dynasty. His tomb and *zaouia* lie right at the heart of the town, the reason for its sacred status and the object of constant pilgrimage – and an important September **moussem**. Even today, while open to non-Muslims for almost seventy years, it is still a place which feels closed and introspective, continuing with some dignity the business of religion. For the infidel, barred from the shrines, there is little specific that can be seen, and nothing that may be visited. But coming here from Volubilis, the site in itself is enough – a girdle of hills with no European building of any kind.

Moulay Idriss and the foundation of Morocco

Moulay Idriss el Akhbar (The Elder) was a great-grandson of the Prophet Muhammad; his grandparents were Muhammad's daughter Fatima, and cousin and first follower, Ali. Heir to the Caliphate in Damascus, he fled to Morocco around 787, following the Ommayad victory in the great civil war which split the Muslim world into Shia and Sunni sects*.

In Volubilis, then still the main centre of the north, Idriss seems to have been welcomed as an *imam* (a spiritual and political leader), and within five years had succeeded in carving out a considerable kingdom. At this new town site, more easily defended than Volubilis, he built his capital, and he also began the construction of Fes, later continued and considerably extended by his son Idriss II, that city's patron saint. News of his growing power, however, filtered back to the East, and in 792, the Ommayads had Idriss poisoned, doubtless assuming that his kingdom would likewise disap-

---

* Although of Shiite origin, the Moroccan tribes soon adopted the Sunni (or Malekite) system, in line with the powerful Andalusian Caliphate of Córdoba. Present-day Morocco remains orthodox Sunni.

pear. In this they were mistaken. Idriss had instilled with the faith of Islam the region's previously pagan (and sometimes Christian or Jewish) Berber tribes and had been joined in this prototypical Moroccan state by increasing numbers of Arab Shiites loyal to the succession of his *Alid* line. After his assassination, Rashid, the servant who had travelled with Idriss to Morocco, took over as regent until 807, when the founder's son, Idriss II, was old enough to assume the throne.

The town

Arriving in Moulay Idriss, you find yourself below an elongated *place* near the base of the town; above you, almost directly ahead, stand the green-tiled pyramids of the shrine and *zaouia*, on either side of which rise the two conical quarters of Khiber and Tasga.

The **souks**, such as they are, line the streets of the Khiber (the taller hill) above the *zaouia*, but apart from the excellent local nougat, made and sold here in great quantities, they're not of great interest.

Moulay Idriss' shrine and zaouia, rebuilt by Moulay Ismail, stands cordoned off from the street by a low, wooden bar placed to keep out Christians and beasts of burden. To get a true sense of it, you have to climb up toward one of the vantage points near the pinnacle of each quarter – ideally, the **Terrasse Sidi Abdallah el Hajjam** right above the Khiber. It's not easy to find your way up through the winding streets (most end in abrupt blind alleys), and, unless you're into the challenge of it all, you'd do better to enlist the help of a young guide down in the *place*.

Fes

> *The history of Fes is composed of wars and murders, triumphs of arts and sciences, and a good deal of imagination.*
>
> Walter Harris: *Land of an African Sultan*

The most ancient of the imperial capitals, and the most complete medieval city of the Arab world, **FES** is, for the moment at least, unique. It is a place that stimulates your senses – with haunting and beautiful sounds, infinite visual details and unfiltered odours – and it seems to exist suspended in time somewhere between the Middle Ages and the modern world. As is usually the case, there is a French-built Ville Nouvelle, but some 200,000 of the city's approximately half-million inhabitants continue to live in an extraordinary Medina-city – **Fes el Bali** – which owes absolutely nothing to the West besides its electricity and its tourists.

As a spectacle, this is an entirely satisfying experience, and it's difficult to imagine a city whose external forms (all you can really hope to penetrate) could be so constant and enduring a source of interest. But stay in Fes a few days and it's equally hard to avoid the paradox of the place. Like much of "traditional" Morocco, the city was "saved" and then re-created by the French – under the auspices of General Lyautey, the Protectorate's first Resident-General. Lyautey took the philanthropic and startling move of declaring the city a historical monument; philanthropic because he was certainly saving Fes el Bali from destruction (albeit from less benevolent Frenchmen), and startling because until then many Moroccans were under the impression that Fes was still a living city – the imperial capital of the Moroccan empire rather than a preservable part of the nation's heritage. In fact, this paternalistic protection conveniently helped to disguise the dismantlement of the old culture. By building a new European city nearby – the Ville Nouvelle – and then transferring Fes's economic and political functions to Rabat and the west coast, Lyautey successfully ensured the city's eclipse along with its preservation.

To appreciate the significance of this demise, you only have to look at the Arab chronicles or old histories of Morocco, every one of which takes Fes as its central focus. The city had dominated Moroccan trade, culture and religious life – and usually its politics, too – since the end of the tenth century. It was closely and symbolically linked with the birth of an "Arabic" Moroccan state due to their mutual foundation by Moulay Idriss I, and was regarded, after Mecca and Medina, as one of the holiest cities of the Islamic world. Medieval European travellers wrote of it with a mixture of awe and respect – as a "citadel of fanaticism" and yet the most advanced seat of learning in mathematics, philosophy and medicine.

The decline of the city notwithstanding, **Fassis** – the people of Fes – have a reputation throughout Morocco as being successful and sophisticated. Just as the city is situated at the centre of the country, so are its inhabitants placed at the heart of government, and most government ministries are headed by Fassis. What is undeniable is that they have the most developed Moroccan city culture, with an intellectual tradition, and their own cuisine (sadly not at its best in the modern city restaurants), dress and way of life.

The development of Fes

When the city's founder, Moulay Idriss I, died in 792, Fes was little more than a village on the east bank of the river. It was his son, **Idriss II**, who really began the city's development, at the beginning of the ninth century, by making it his capital and allowing in refugees from Andalusian Córdoba and from Kairouan in Tunisia – at the time, the two most important cities of western Islam. The impact on Fes of these refugees was immediate and lasting: they established separate, walled towns (still distinct quarters today) on either riverbank, and provided the superior craftsmanship and mercantile experience for Fes's industrial and commercial growth. It was at this time, too, that the city gained its intellectual reputation. The tenth-century Pope Silvester II studied here at the Kairouine University, and from this source he is said to have introduced Arabic mathematics to Europe.

The seat of government – and impetus of patronage – shifted south to Marrakesh under the Berber dynasties of the **Almoravides** (1068–1145) and **Almohads** (1145–1250). But with the conquest of Fes by the **Merenids** in 1248, and their subsequent consolidation of power across Morocco, the city regained its preeminence and moved into something of a "golden age". Alongside the old Medina, the Merenids began the construction of a massive royal city – **Fes el Djedid**, literally "Fes the New" – which reflected both the wealth and confidence of their rule. They enlarged and decorated the great Kairaouine Mosque, added a network of *fondouks* for the burgeoning commercial activity, and, above all, were responsible for the meteoric rise of the university – building the series of magnificent **medersas**, or colleges, to accommodate its students. Once again this was an expansion based on an influx of refugees, this time from the Spanish reconquest of Andalusia, and it helped to establish the city's reputation as "the Baghdad of the West".

It is essentially Merenid Fes which you witness today in the form of the city and its monuments. From the fall of the dynasty in the mid-sixteenth century, there was decline as both Fes and Morocco itself became isolated from the main currents of Western culture. The new rulers – the **Saadians** – in any case preferred Marrakesh, and although Fes re-emerged as the capital under the **Alaouites,** it had begun to lose its international stature. Moulay Ismail, whose hatred of the Fassis was legendary, almost managed to tax the city out of existence, and the principal building concerns of his successors lay in restoring and enlarging the vast domains of the royal palace.

Under **French colonial rule,** there were positive achievements in the preservation of the old city and relative prosperity of the Ville Nouvelle, but little actual progress. As a thoroughly conservative and bourgeois city, Fes became merely provincial. Even so, it remained a symbol of Moroccan pride and aspirations, playing a crucial role in the **struggle for independence** – events marvellously brought to life in Paul Bowles' novel *The Spider's House*.

Since **independence**, the city's position has been less than happy. The first sultan, Mohammed V, retained the French capital of Rabat, and with this signalled the final decline of the Fassi political and financial elites. In 1956, too, the city lost most of its Jewish community to France and Israel. In their place, the Medina population now has a predominance of first-generation, rural migrants, often poorly housed in mansions designed for single families but now accommodating four or five, while the city as a whole is increasingly dependent on handicrafts and the tourist trade. If UNESCO had not moved in over the last decades with its Cultural Heritage plan for the city's preserva-tion, it seems likely that its physical collapse would have become endemic and much more obvious than it appears today.

Orientation, arrival and guides

Even if you'd felt you were getting used to Moroccan cities, Fes is likely to prove bewildering. The basic layout is simple enough, with a Moroccan **Medina** and French-built **Ville Nouvelle**, but here the Medina is actually two separate cities: **Fes el Bali**, the oldest part, in the main stretch of the Sebou valley, and **Fes el Djedid**, the "New Fes" established on the edge of the valley in the thirteenth century.

Fes el Djedid, dominated by a vast enclosure of royal palaces and gardens, is relatively straightforward. **Fes el Bali**, however, where you'll want to spend most of your time, is an incredibly intricate web of lanes, blind alleys and *souks*. It takes two or three days before you even start to feel confi-dent in where you're going, and on an initial visit you may well want to pay for a guide (see section following) to show you the main sights and layout.

Maps

The **maps** we've printed are as functional as any available, though (like all maps of Fes) their network of lanes in the Medina areas is, by necessity, simplified. The free **ONMT map** (on the back of their Fes pamphlet) is a useful complement, folding out to show how each of the three cities (el Bali, Djedid and Ville Nouvelle) relate. It is available from the **ONMT office** on Place de la Résistance, in the Ville Nouvelle (open Mon–Fri 8am–noon & 2–6pm, Sat 8am–noon only).

Points of arrival

● **By train**. The train station is situated in the Ville Nouvelle, ten minutes' walk from the concentration of hotels around Place Mohammed V. If you prefer to stay in the Medina (see the following section), either take a *petit taxi* or walk down to Av. Hassan II, where you can pick up the #9 bus to Dar Batha/Place de l'Istiqlal, near Bab Boujeloud. Beware of unofficial taxi drivers who wait at the station and charge very unofficial rates for the trip into town; the standard fare for Boujeloud should be no more than 5dh. Be prepared, too, for hustlers: Fes is possibly the worst city in Morocco in this respect, and the station is a key locale.

    Leaving Fes, heading for **Nador/Melilla**, note that *ONCF* run connecting buses from Taorirt on the Oujda line; you can buy tickets straight through.

● **By bus**. Coming in by bus can be confusing, since there are terminals dotted all over the city – in the Ville Nouvelle and by the gates to the Medina. However, they have recently been reorganised, and you will more than likely arrive at the main **bus station** (or more accurately, "bus yard") in **Place Baghdadi**, by **Bab Boujeloud**, the western gate to Fes el Bali.

    The main exception is if you're coming from, or departing for, **Taza and the east**, for which buses use a terminal by the Medina's southeast gate, **Bab Ftouh**. Note also that convenient **night buses** cover routes to the south – to Marrakesh and Rissani, for example.

● **Grands taxis**, like buses, tend to operate in and out of **Place Baghdadi**, though they're tucked around the corner, downhill from Bab Boujeloud. Exceptions are those from/for **Azrou/Sefrou**, which use ranks on Rue de Normandes (between Place de l'Atlas and Bd. Mohammed V in the Ville Nouvelle) and at Bab Ftouh.

● **By air**. Fes's tiny **airport** is 11km south, off the P24 to Immouzer (☎247.12 or 247.99); it is easiest reached by *grand taxi* (30dh for the taxi; 5dh a place). There are various internal flight services – including Marrakesh and Er Rachidia – and a useful, weekly flight to Oran in Algeria. Details from the *RAM/Air France* office at 54 Av. Hassan II (☎255.16).

● **Driving**. Be prepared for "motorbike guides" – Morocco's most annoying hustlers – who haunt the approach roads to Fes, attach themselves to tourist cars and insist on escorting you to a hotel. They can be deeply unpleasant and are not best countered by aggression; on the whole, it's easier just to tell them where you're going (book your hotel in advance) and give them a small tip on arrival. Make it clear you do not want a subsequent tour of the city.

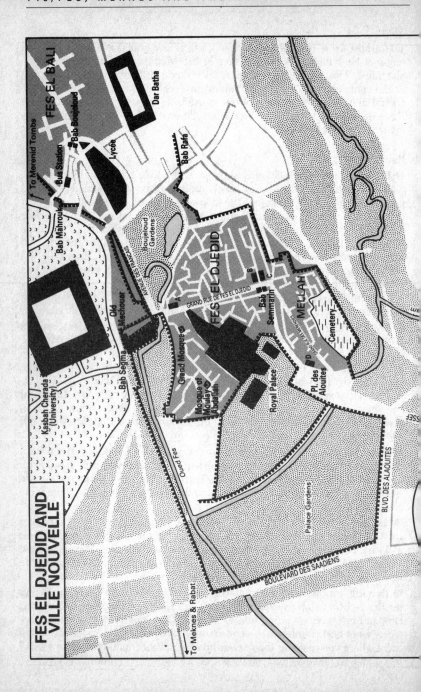

FES EL DJEDID AND VILLE NOUVELLE

FES EL BALI

FES EL BALI

Dar Batha

To Meranid Tombs

Bab Boujeloud

Bus Station

Lycée

Bab Mahrouk

Bab Rafa

Boujeloud Gardens

AVENUE DES FRANÇAIS

Old Mechouar

FES EL DJEDID

Kasbah Cherada (University)

Bab Segma

Grand Mosque

GRAND RUE DE FES EL DJEDID

Bab Semmarin

MELLAH

Cemetery

Mosque of Moulay Abdallah

Royal Palace

Pl. des Alaouites

Oued Fes

Palace Gardens

BLVD. DES ALAOUITES

BOULEVARD DES SAADIENS

To Meknes & Rabat

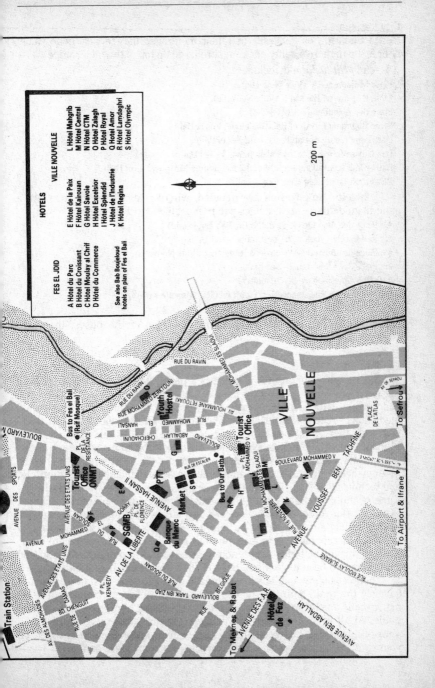

HOTELS

FES EL JDID

A Hôtel du Parc
B Hôtel du Croissant
C Hôtel Moulay al Chrif
D Hôtel du Commerce

See also Bab Boujeloud
hotels on plan of Fes el Bali

E Hôtel de la Paix
F Hôtel Kairouan
G Hôtel Savoie
H Hôtel Excelsior
I Hôtel Splendid
J Hôtel de l'Industrie
K Hôtel Regina

VILLE NOUVELLE

L Hôtel Mahgrib
M Hôtel Central
N Hôtel CTM
O Hôtel Zalagh
P Hôtel Royal
Q Hôtel Amor
R Hôtel Lamdaghri
S Hôtel Olympic

0   200 m

City transport

Petits taxis in Fes generally use their meters, so they're very good value; after 9.30pm, there's a fifty per cent surcharge on top of the meter price.

Useful *petit taxi* ranks include:

Place Mohammed V (Ville Nouvelle).

Main PTT on Av. Hassan II (Ville Nouvelle).

Place des Alaouites (Fes el Djedid).

Place Baghdadi (north of Bab Boujeloud, Fes el Bali)

Dar Batha (south of Bab Boujeloud, Fes el Bali).

Bab Guissa (north gate, by Palais Jamai, Fes el Bali).

Bab er Rsif (central gate, south of the Kairaouine Mosque, Fes el Bali)

Bab Ftouh (southeast gate, Fes el Bali).

Useful **city bus routes** are detailed, where relevant, in the text. As a general guide these are the ones you're most likely to want to use:

#1: Place des Alaouites–Dar Batha (by Bab Boujeloud).

#2: Rue Escalier (below the post office)–Dar Batha.

#3: Place des Alaouites–Place de la Résistance (Ville Nouvelle).

#9: Place de la Résistance–Dar Batha.

#10: Bab Guissa–Place des Alaouites.

#18: Place de la Résistance–Bab Ftouh (via Rsif Mosque square).

#19: Train station–Place des Alaouites.

Note: These numbers are marked on the sides of the buses; there are completely different numbers on the backs.

Guides

A half-day tour from an official guide is a useful introduction to Fes el Bali; the fee is just 50dh (90dh for a full day), no matter how many people are in your group. Official guides – who can identify themselves by round gold medallions – can be hired at the **Syndicats d'Initiatives** (Mon–Sat 8am–7pm) at Bab Boujeloud, the main entrance to Fes el Bali, or Place Mohammed V in the Ville Nouvelle, or outside the more upmarket hotels (such as the *Palais Jamai* or the *Merenides* above the Medina).

Anywhere else, guides who tout their services are likely to be **unofficial** and technically illegal. This doesn't necessarily mean they're to be avoided – some of those who are genuine students (as all guides claim to be) can be excellent. But you have to choose carefully, ideally by drinking a tea together, before settling a rate or declaring interest. An unpleasant trick, employed by the more disreputable, is to take you into Fes el Bali and, once you're disorientated, maybe with dusk descending, demand rather more than the agreed fee to take you back to your hotel. Don't allow yourself to be intimidated.

Whether you get an official or unofficial guide, it's essential to work out in advance the **main points you want to see**: a useful exercise would be to mark them on the map of Fes el Bali in this book and show this to your guide. At all events, make it absolutely clear that you're not interested in **shopping**; you can buy goods much more effectively, and much cheaper, on your own; see "Shopping for Crafts" on p.177 for some ideas on this.

Finding a place to stay

Staying in Fes, you have the usual choice between comfort (and reliable water supply) in the modern **Ville Nouvelle** hotels or lack of facilities in the basic, unclassified hotels in the **Medina**, ie **Fes el Bali** and **Fes el Djedid**. There is a shortage of hotel space in all categories, so be prepared for higher than usual prices and – if at all possible – phone ahead for a room.

If you are not overly concerned about the size and cleanliness of your room, then the **Medina** is definitely the place to be. You will be at the heart of the city's *souks* and traditional life, well placed to explore the monuments, and witness to the amazing sounds of the early morning calls of muezzins from the hundreds of mosques. On the negative side, you will be paying well over the odds – often 2* prices – for a distinctly flea-pit environment.

In the **Ville Nouvelle**, there is a much wider choice of hotels – most of them adequate but unexciting. A few of the better ones have swimming pools, which can be worth a bit of a splurge in midsummer, when the heat of this flat site can be overwhelming. There are also the advantages in proximity to restaurants and bars, and the train station.

The Ville Nouvelle

Recommendations below are in ascending order of price; letters in brackets refer to the main Ville Nouvelle/Fes el Djedid map on the previous page.

Youth Hostel (*Auberge de Jeunesse*), 18 Bd. Mohammed el Hansali (☎240.85). An easygoing, friendly hostel, which rents out space on the roof if the dormitories are full. If travelling on your own, you won't get a cheaper bed. Closes 10pm.

Hôtel Rex, Place de l'Atlas. A very basic, but very cheap, hotel. Cold showers only but very clean rooms. *Unclassified*.

Hôtel Savoie (G), just off Bd. Chefchaouni. After the Rex, this is the cheapest of the Ville Noubvelle hotels, though not exatly a bargain. Avoid the *Volubilis* next door like the plague. *Unclassified*.

Hôtel Regina (K), **Hôtel Maghrib (L)**, both on Av. Mohammed es Slaoui. Still unstarred but considerably better than the *Savoie*, with cool, spacious rooms. Both raise their prices a lot in the summer. *Unclassified*.

Hôtel de l'Industrie (J), Bd. Mohammed V. Similar to the above. *Unclassified*.

Hôtel Central (M), Rue Nador, off Bd. Mohammed V (☎223.3). The cheapest classified hotel – and for that reason very popular and often full. A good choice, nonetheless. *1*B*.

Hôtel Excelsior (H), Bd. Mohammed V (☎256.02). Standard for its class – fairly clean and with functional showers. *1*B*.

Hôtel CTM (N), Rue Ksar el Kbir/Av. Mohammed V (☎228.11). A little pricier than those above and very noisy, with a local bus depot below. *1*B*.

Hôtel Kairouan (F), 84 Rue du Soudan (☎235.90). Respectable if undistinguished. *1*A*.

Hôtel Amor (Q), 31 Rue du Pakistan (☎233.04/227.24). A bit of a jump in quality (as befits the rating); also has a small bar. *2*B*.

Hôtel Lamdaghri (R), 10 Kabbour El Mangad (☎203.10). Bigger rooms and better service than the *Amor* – perhaps the best of the two-star hotels. *2*B*.

Hôtel Royal (P), 36 Rue d'Espagne (☎246.56). Usefully situated for the train station – just off Av. de France – and tends to have space. Adequate but dull. *2*B*.

Hôtel Olympic (S), Bd. Mohammed V (☎245.29). A clean, reliable and functional hotel, with reasonable prices for its class. *2*A*.

Hôtel de la Paix (E), 44 Av. Hassan II (☎250.72). Straightforward tourist hotel, often full with groups, but considerably more comfortable than any of the above. *3*A*.

Hôtel Splendid (I), 9 Rue Abdelkrim (☎221.48). Excellent and friendly new hotel – with a garden, bar and swimming pool. *3*A*.

Hôtel Mounia, 60 Av. Asilah (☎248.38). New hotel with very helpful management. *3*A*.

Grand Hôtel, Bd. Chefchaouni (☎255.11). Old colonial hotel with good rooms and a bar.

Hôtel Zalagh (O), Rue Mohammed Diouri (☎228.10). With fine views across the valley to Fes el Djedid, this rather stylish 1930s hotel is the place to head for if you've got the money (but not enough for the *Palais Jamai*, see box on facing page). Its pool and bar are a favourite hangout for successful young Moroccans. *4*B*.

Medina hotels: around Bab Boujeloud

Bab Boujeloud is the western gateway to Fes el Bali, offering pedestrian access from Fes el Djedid, and the nearby **Place de l'Istiqlal** has bus and petit taxi ranks to the Ville Nouvelle. The half dozen **unclassified hotels** around the gate could all do with more regular cleaning and plumbing, and in summer their prices are ridiculous (groups of four taking a room do better). But, so long as your expectations are low, they're adequate enough – and in a great position. All are keyed on the map below.

Hôtel Jardin Publique (☎330.86). This is slightly tricky to find – signposted down a short lane by the Boujeloud Mosque – but it is a friendly place and is on the whole noticeably cleaner than the other Boujeloud hotels.

Hôtel National, Hôtel Erraha, Place Boujeloud. Probably the second choices – noisy but clean enough and the staff keep out hustlers.

Hôtel Kaskades, on the square inside the gate. Poor rooms but has a roof terrace and an old *hammam* on the second floor.

Hôtel Mauretania, on the square inside the gate. Very basic and tiny rooms.

Hôtel Marani, Talâa Seghira (the lower lane just within the Medina). Very basic and not for the claustrophobic. Usually has more Moroccan than Western guests.

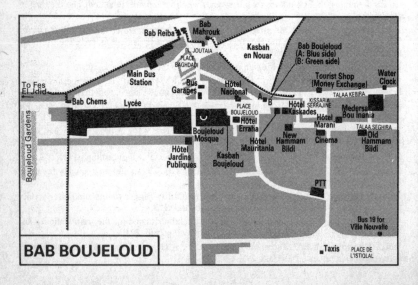

BAB BOUJELOUD

The problem of water (or lack of it) in many of these hotels is easiest over-come by taking a **hammam** (steam bath). Just through Bab Boujeloud, following the Talâa Seghira around to the left, you come to *Hammam Bildi*. This is open to foreigners, though it is best (especially for women) to ask someone at your hotel to escort you. Hours are 1pm to midnight for women, midnight to 1pm for men; bring a towel and a swimsuit.

The **Boujeloud cinema**, incidentally, if you need more entertainment than the city itself, shows an Indian and a Kung Fu film each day.

Fes el Djedid

As an alternative to the Boujeloud hotels – but still within a ten- to fifteen-minute walk of Fes el Bali – you might want to try one of the places in **Fes el Djedid**. Less well-known, these are generally cheaper, and even in midsea-son you've got a fair chance of finding an ordinarily priced single. Keyed letters refer to the Fes el Djedid/Ville Nouvelle map on the previous page.

Hôtel du Commerce (D), Place des Alaouites (☎222.31). The best of all the Fes Medina hotels, run by the same family for the last thirty years and, though summer puts a strain on the plumbing, usually functioning reasonably well. It is located opposite the royal palace.

Hôtel du Parc (A), Grand Rue des Merenides (Fes el Djedid's main street). The closest and best value alternative, though it gets very mixed reports on cleanliness.

Hôtel du Croissant (B), **Hôtel Moulay al Chrif (C)**, both on Grand Rue des Merenides. These two wouldn't win any health or safety awards either, but they've (just) enough charac-ter to save them from the squalor category. They are easy enough to find, on either side of Bab Semmarin at the south end of Grand Rue des Merenides.

The campsite

The Fes campsite, still noted on most maps in the Ville Nouvelle, is now 5km west of the city at **Aïn Chkeff**; it is pleasantly situated, in a forest, and there is plenty of space. Frequent buses run from opposite the new mosque on the Ifrane road in the Ville Nouvelle.

A DIFFERENT WORLD: THE HÔTEL PALAIS JAMAI

The **Hôtel Palais Jamai** (Bab Guissa; ☎343.31) is one of the three most luxurious hotels in Morocco (the others are the *Mamounia* in Marrakesh and the *Gazelle d'Or* in Taroudannt) and, uniquely, it more than justifies its reputation – and prices. If you were planning to spend one night in Morocco in pure and unalloyed splen-dour, this would be the place to do it. The beauty of the hotel lies partly in the build-ing and gardens – the basis of which is a nineteenth-century vizier's palace – and partly in the position, poised just above Fes el Bali, with panoramic views (and sounds) of the city below. The hotel, in addition, has a rare literary fame, having served as one of the principal settings for Paul Bowles' novel, *The Spider's House*.

Sadly, you do have to pay for the experience of a stay. Rooms on a weekly rate are offered for around £200–250 per person if booked through one of the specialist Morocco travel agents. However, if you book independently you should expect to pay upwards of £70 for a double per night – more if you want views directly over the Medina, and considerably more for one of the spectacular palace rooms or suites in the old part of the hotel.

The hotel is set just within the walls of Fes el Bali, by the north gate of Bab Guissa; see the Fes el Bali map on p.157.

Fes el Bali

With its mosques, *medersas* and *fondouks*, combined with a mile-long network of *souks*, there are enough "sights" in **Fes El Bali** to fill three or four days just trying to locate them. And even then, you'd still be unlikely to stumble across some of them by chance or through the whim of a guide. In this – the apparently wilful secretiveness – lies part of the fascination, and there is much to be said for Paul Bowles's somewhat lofty advice to "lose oneself in the crowd – to be pulled along by it – not knowing where to and for how long . . . to see beauty where it is least likely to appear." If you do the same, be prepared to really get lost. However, despite what hustlers may tell you, the Medina is not a dangerous place, and you can always ask a boy to lead you out toward one of its landmarks: **Bab Boujeloud**, **Talâa Kebira**, the **Kairaouine Mosque**, **Bab er Rsif** or **Bab Ftouh**.

Making your own way in purposeful quest for the *souks* and monuments, you should be able to find everything detailed in the following pages – with a little patience. As a prelude it's not a bad idea to head up to the **Merenid tombs** on the rim of the valley (see box below), where you can get a spectacular overview of the city and try to make out its shape. For a break or escape from the intensity of the Medina, head to the **Boujeloud Gardens** (officially retitled "Jardins de la Marche Verte"; open 9am–6pm), a real haven and with a pleasant open-air café, just to the east of the Bab Boujeoud.

THE MERENID TOMBS AND A VIEW OF FES

A crumbling and fairly obscure group of ruins, the **Merenid tombs** are not of great interest in themselves. People no longer know which of the dynasty's sultans had them erected and there is not a trace remaining of the "beautiful white marbles' vividly coloured epitaphs" which so struck Leo Africanus in his sixteenth-century description of Fes. Poised at the city's skyline, however, they are a picturesque focus and a superb vantage point. All around you are spread the Muslim cemeteries which ring the hills on each side of the city, while looking down you can delineate the more prominent among Fes's reputed 365 mosque minarets.

Getting up to the tombs is no problem. You can walk it in about twenty minutes from Bab Boujeloud, or take a taxi (around 10dh from the Ville Nouvelle). From the Boujeloud area, leave by **Bab el Mahrouk**, above the bus terminus, and once outside the walls, turn immediately to the right. After a while you come to a network of paths, climbing up toward the stolid fortress of **Borj Nord**. Despite its French garrison-like appearance, this and its southern counterpart across the valley were actually built in the seventeenth century by the Saadians. The dynasty's only endowment to the city, they were used to *control* the Fassis rather than to *defend* them. Carefully maintained, the Borj now houses the country's **arms museum** – an interminable display of row upon row of muskets, most of them confiscated from the Riffians in the 1958 rebellion.

Clambering across the hillside from Borj Nord – or following (by road) Route du Tour du Fes past the imposing and controversially located *Hôtel des Merenides* – you soon emerge at **the tombs** and an expectant cluster of guides. Wandering around here, you will probably be standing on the city's original foundations, before its rapid expansion under Moulay Idriss II. But it is **the view** across the deep bowl

There are four principal entrances and exits to Fes el Bali:

● **Bab Boujeloud**. The western gate, easily identified by its bright polychrome decoration and the hotels and cafés grouped on either side.

● **Bab er Rsif**. A central gate, by the square (and car park) beside the Mosque er Rsif, this is a convenient entrance, just a few blocks below the Kairaouine Mosque. Bus #19 runs between the square and Av. Mohammed V in the Ville Nouvelle.

● **Bab Ftouh**. The southeast gate at the bottom of the Andalous quarter, with potteries and cemetries extending to the south. Bus #18 runs between here and Dar Batha, near Bab Boujeloud, and there is also a *petit taxi* rank.

● **Bab Guissa**. The north gate, up at the top of the city by the *Hôtel Palais Jamai*: a convenient point to enter (or leave) the city from (or heading to) the Merenid tombs. *Petit taxis* are available by the gate.

Into the Medina: Bab Boujeloud and Dar Batha

The area around **Bab Boujeloud** is today the principal entrance to Fes el Bali: a place with a great concentration of cafés, stalls and activity where people come to talk and stare. Provincial buses leave throughout the day from**Place Baghdadi** (just west of the gate), while in the early evening there are occasional entertainers and a flea market spreading out toward the old Mechouar (the former assembly point and government square) and to **Bab el Mahrouk**, an exit onto the road to the Merenid tombs.

This focus and importance is all comparatively recent, since it was only at the end of the last century that the walls were joined up between Fes el Bali

of the valley below which holds everyone's attention – Fes el Bali neatly wedged within it, white and diamond shaped, and buzzing with activity.

Immediately below is Adourat el-Kairaouine, or the Kairaouine quarter: the main stretch of the Medina, where Idriss settled the first Tunisian refugees. At its heart, toward the river, stands the green-tiled courtyard of the **Kairaouine Mosque**, the country's most important religious building, preceded and partially screened by its two minarets. The main one has a dome on top and is whitewashed, which is an unusual Moroccan (though characteristically Tunisian) design; the slightly lower one to its right (square, with a narrower upper floor) is *Borj en Naffara* (The Trumpeter's Tower), from which the beginning and end of Ramadan are proclaimed. Over to the right of this, and very easily recognised, are the tall pyramid-shaped roof and slender, decoratively faced minaret of the city's second great religious building, the **Zaouia of Moulay Idriss II**.

The **Andalous quarter**, the other area settled by ninth-century refugees, lies some way over to the left of this trio of minarets – divided from the Kairaouine by the appropriately named **Bou Khareb** (The River Carrying Garbage), whose path is marked out by a series of minarets. **Djemaa el-Andalous**, the principal mosque of this quarter, is distinguished by a massive, tile-porched, monumental gateway, behind which you can make out the roofs enclosing its great courtyard.

Orientation aside, there is a definite magic if you're up here in the early evening or, best of all, at dawn. The sounds of the city, the stillness and the contained disorder below all seem to make manifest the mystical significance which Islam places on urban life as the most perfect expression of culture and society.

From the tombs you can enter Fes el Bali either through **Bab Guissa** (which brings you out at the Souk el Attarin), or by returning to **Bab Boujeloud.** There is a *petit taxi* stand by Bab Guissa.

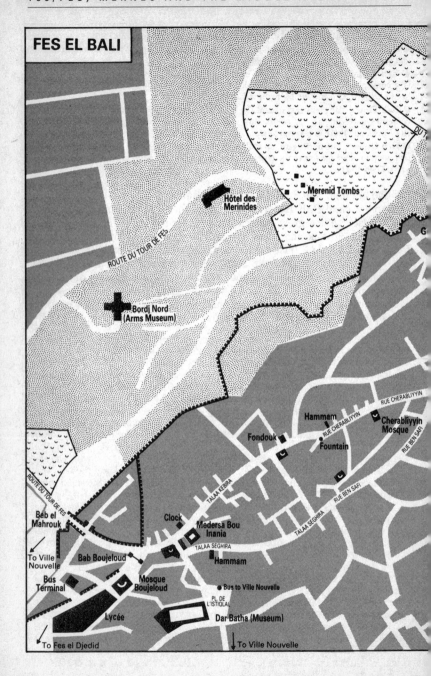

FES EL BALI

Merenid Tombs

Hôtel des
Merinides

ROUTE DU TOUR DE FES

Bordj Nord
(Arms Museum)

RUE CHERABLIYYIN

Hammam

RUE CHERABLIYYIN

Cherabliyyin
Mosque

Fondouk

RUE BEN SAFI

Fountain

ROUTE DU TOUR DE FES

TALAA KEBIRA

Bab el
Mahrouk

RUE BEN SAFI

Clock

TALAA SEGHIRA

Medersa Bou
Inania

To Ville
Nouvelle

TALAA SEGHIRA

Bab Boujeloud

Hammam

Bus
Terminal

Mosque
Boujeloud

Bus to Ville Nouvelle

PL. DE
L'ISTIQLAL

Lycée

Dar Batha (Museum)

To Fes el Djedid

To Ville Nouvelle

Dar Saada

Attarin Medersa

SOUK EL ATTARIN

SOUK EL ATTARIN

Souk el Henna

Misbahiya Medersa

KISSARIA

Zaouia Moulay Idriss

PL. EN NEJJARIN

Kairaouine Mosque

Titouani Fondouk

Fondouk

Palais de Fes

Cherratin Medersa

To the Tanneries

Oued Fes

Seffarine Medersa

PLACE SEFFARINE

Dyers' Souk

El Aouad Bridge

Palais Jamai

Walls

Fondouk Sagha

Oued Fes

Tanneries

ATTARIN

SOUK EL ATTARIN

Zaoula Moulay Idriss

Bein el Moudoun Bridge

Kairaouine Mosque

RUE SEFTAH

RUE SIDI YOUSSEF

RUE SEFTAH

0   200 m

Andalous Mosque

Sahrija Medersa

Bab er Rsif

Mosque er Rsif

Bus No. 19 to Ville Nouvelle

Non CTM buses to:
Taza, Oujda, Chaouen,
& Al Hoceima

To Ketama & Taza

BOULEVARD MOHAMMED EL ALOUI

PL. TAMDERT

Bab Ftouh

POTTERS' QUARTER

To Fes el Djedid & Route du Tour de Fes

To Ville Nouvelle

and Fes el Djedid and the subsequently enclosed area was developed. Nearly all the buildings here date from this period, including those of the elegant **Dar Batha** palace, designed for the reception of foreign ambassadors and now a very fine **Museum of Moroccan Arts and Crafts**.

DAR BATHA

The Dar Batha (open daily except Tues, 9–11.30am & 3–6pm; 10dh) is worth a visit both for its collections and for its courtyards and gardens, which offer useful respite from the general exhaustion of the Medina. The museum entrance is 30m up the narrow lane separating it from the Hôtel Batha.

The art and crafts collections are probably the finest anywhere in Morocco, concentrating on local artesan traditions. There are stunning collections of **carved wood,** much of it rescued from the Misbahiya and other *medersas;* another magnificent room of **Middle Atlas carpets**; and excellent examples of **zellij-work**, **calligraphy** and **embroidery**.

Above all, though, it is the **pottery** rooms which stand out. The pieces, dating from the sixteenth century to the 1930s, are beautiful and show the preservation of technique long after the end of any form of innovation. This timeless quality is constantly asserted as you wander around Fes. There is no concept here of the "antique" – something is either new or it is old, and if the latter, its age could be anything from thirty years to three centuries.

INTO THE MEDINA: TALÂA SEGHIRA AND TALÂA KEBIRA

Until you get a grasp of Fes el Bali, it's useful to stick with **Bab Boujeloud** as a point of entry and reference. Decorated with blue and gold tiles (green and gold on the inside face); it is a pretty unmistakable landmark, and once inside, things are initially straightforward. You will find yourself in a small square, flanked by the *Hôtel Kaskades* (on your right) and with a couple of minarets almost directly ahead. Just beyond the *Kaskades,* the square splits into two main lanes, traversed by dozens of alleys but running parallel for much of the Medina's length.

The lower (righthand) fork is **Talâa Seghira**, also known as the **Rue du Petit Talâa,** a street which begins with a handful of small foodstalls, where you can buy chunks of *pastilla,* the great Fassi delicacy of pigeon-pie; further down, the lane has little of specific interest until it rejoins the upper lane, Talâa Debira, just before Place Nejjarin.

Talâa Kebira, or **Rue du Grand Talâa**, is the major artery of the Medina, and with its continuations runs right through to the Kairaouine Mosque; for virtually its whole length it is lined with shops and stalls. About 100m down, too, it is host to the most brilliant of all the city's monuments, the **Medersa Bou Inania**. You can see the entrance to the *medersa,* down a step on your right, just before you come to a whitewashed arch-bridge over the road.

● **Access** Bus #18 from the Ville Nouvelle has a stop more or less outside Dar Batha in Place de l'Istiqlal, two minutes' walk below Bab Boujeloud. Here, and around the gate, you'll be pestered with offers of a **guide**. If you don't want one, be firm and explain that you're only going down to Bou Inania – which will probably be your first move anyway. Most hustlers give up after about 50m or so. If you do want a guide, arrange an official one at the tourist post by Bab Boujeloud. To get a **petit taxi** around Boujeloud, walk up to Place Baghdad by the Boujeloud bus terminal.

The Bou Inania Medersa and Clock

If there is just one building you actively seek out in Fes – or, not to put too fine a point on it, in Morocco – it is the **Bou Inania Medersa**. The most elaborate, extravagant and beautiful of all Merenid monuments, it comes close to perfection in every aspect of its construction – its dark cedar is fabulously carved, the *zellij* tilework classic, and the stucco a revelation. In addition, it is the city's only building still in religious use that you are allowed to enter, and so the nearest you'll come to sharing a mosque with Moroccans. You cannot, of course, enter the prayer hall – which is divided from the main body of the *medersa* by a small canal – but you can sit in a corner of the marble courtyard and gaze across to it. The **admission hours** are daily from around 8am until 5pm, with the exception of Friday mornings (closed) and times of prayer (when you might be asked to leave); as with all the *medersas* in Fes, there is now a standard 10dh admission fee.

The **medersas** – student colleges and residence halls – were by no means unique to Fes and, in fact, originated in Khorassan in Iran, gradually spreading west through Baghdad and Cairo. They seem to have reached Morocco under the Almohads, though the earliest ones still surviving in Fes are Merenid, dating from the fourteenth century. The word *medersa* means "place of study", and there may have been lectures delivered in some of the prayer halls. In general, however, the *medersas* acted as little more than dormitories, providing room and board to poor (male) students from the countryside and hence allowing them to attend lessons at the mosques. In Fes, where students might attend the Kairaouine university for ten years or more, rooms were always in great demand and "key money" was often paid by the new occupant. Although *medersas* had largely disappeared from the Islamic world by the late Middle Ages, most of those in Fes remained in use right up to the 1950s, and a few are still occupied by students today.

Set somewhat apart from the other *medersas* of Fes, the Bou Inania was the last and grandest built by a Merenid sultan. It shares its name with the one in Meknes, which was completed (though not initated) by the same patron, **Sultan Abou Inan** (1351–58). But the Fes version is infinitely more splendid. Its cost alone was legendary, and Abou Inan is said to have thrown the accounts into the river on its completion, claiming that "a thing of beauty is beyond reckoning".

At first glance, Abou Inan doesn't seem the kind of sultan to have wanted a *medersa* – his mania for building aside, he was most noted for having 325 sons in ten years, deposing his father, and committing unusually atrocious murders. The *Ulema*, the religious leaders of the Kairaouine Mosque, certainly thought him an unlikely candidate and advised him to build his *medersa* on the city's garbage dump, on the basis that piety and good works can cure anything. Whether it was this, or merely the desire for a lasting monument, which inspired him, he set up the *medersa* as a rival to the Kairaouine itself, and for a while it became the most important religious building in the city. A long campaign to have the announcement of the time of prayer transferred here failed in the face of the Kairaouine's powerful opposition; but the *medersa* was granted the status of a Grand Mosque – unique in Morocco – and retains the right to say the Friday *khotbeh* prayer.

The basic **layout** of the *medersa* is quite simple – a single large courtyard flanked by two sizeable halls and opening on to an oratory – and is essentially the same design as that of the wealthier Fassi mansions. For its effect it relies on the mass of decoration and the light and space held within. You enter the **courtyard** – the *medersa's* outstanding feature – through a stalactite-domed entrance chamber, a feature adapted from Andalusian architecture.

Off to each side of the courtyard are stairs to the upper floor, lined with student cells, and to the roof. Depending on the progress of restoration work, you may or may not be able to go up; if you can, head straight for the roof to get an excellent (and very useful) overview of this part of the city. The cells, as usual in *medersas*, are bare and monkish except for their windows and decorated ceilings.

In the courtyard, the **decoration**, startlingly well-preserved, covers every possible surface. Perhaps most striking in terms of craftsmanship is the wood carving and joinery, an unrivalled example of the Moorish art of *laceria*, "the carpentry of knots". The elegant, black Kufic script that rings three sides of the courtyard and divides the *zellij* (ceramic tilework) from the stucco adds a further dimension; unusually, it is largely a list of the properties whose incomes were given as an endowment, rather than the standard Koranic inscriptions. Abou Inan, too, is bountifully praised amid the inscriptions, and on the foundation stone he is credited with the title *caliph*, an emotive claim to leadership of the Islamic world followed by none of his successors.

THE WATER CLOCK AND LATRINES

More or less opposite the *medersa,* just across Talâa Kebira, Bou Inania's property continues with an extraordinary **water clock**, built above the stalls in the road. An enduring curiosity, this consists of a row of thirteen windows and platforms, seven of which retain their original brass bowls. Nobody has been able to discover exactly how it functioned, though a contemporary account detailed how at every hour one of its windows would open, dropping a weight down into the respective bowl.

Clocks had great religious significance during the Middle Ages in establishing the time of prayer, and it seems probable that this one was bought by Abou Inan as part of his campaign to assert the *medersa's* preeminence; there are accounts of similar constructions in Tlemcen, just across the border in Algeria. As to its destruction, Fassi conspiracy tales are classically involved – most of them revolve around the miscarriage of a Jewess passing below at the time of its striking and a Jewish sorcerer casting the evil eye on the whole device. The building to which the clock is fixed, which was, in fact, once owned by a rabbi, is popularly known as "The House of the Magician". (Note: at the time of writing, the clock has been removed for restoration.)

Completing the *medersa* complex, and immediately adjacent to the clock, are the original **public latrines** built for Friday worshippers. These have recently been closed, though it is possible that this will be temporary. Predating their use in the West by some four centuries, the "Turkish-style" toilets here were at last look very functional, flushed by quantities of running water. If they have reopened – and you're male – take a look inside at the large central patio with its ablutions pool and unexpectedly rich stucco ceiling.

Further Down Talâa Kebira

Making your way down **Talâa Kebira** – a straightforward route to follow – you will eventually emerge at the labyrinth of lanes around the Kairaouine Mosque and Zaouia Moulay Idriss II. It's interesting less for any specific "sights" than for the general accumulated stimuli for your senses. The diarist Anaïs Nin expressed her reaction in terms of odours: ". . . of excrement, saffron, leather being cured, sandalwood, olive oil being fried, nut oil so strong at first that you cannot swallow". To which might be added sound – the shouts of muleteers (*balak!* means "look out!"), mantric cries from the beggars, the bells of water vendors – and, above all, the sight of the people, seen in shafts of light filtered through the rush roofings which cover much of the Talâa's length.

Along the first (upward) stretch watch out for a very large **fondouk** on your left, just after a row of blacksmiths' shops, about 300m beyond Bou Inania. This was originally a **Merenid prison**, fitted out with suitably solid colonnades and arches; it is now home to people selling butter and honey out of large vats. Before the advent in Morocco of French-style cafés, at the beginning of this century, the *fondouks* (or *caravanserais* as they're called in the East) formed the heart of social life outside the home. They provided rooms for traders and richer students, and frequently became centres of vice, intrigue and entertainment. There were once some two hundred in Fes el Bali, but although many still survive, often with beautiful fourteenth- and fifteenth-century decorations, they tend now to serve as small factories or warehouses. Another **fondouk**, about 100m further down, is today used for curing animal skins (and smells awful).

RUE ECH CHERABLIYIN

A little way down, the street changes name – to **Rue ech Cherabliyin** – and, passing the oldest **hammam** still in use in Fes, you find yourself in a district of **leather stalls and shoemakers**. The Fassi *babouches*, leather slippers, are reputed to be the best in the country, and here, unusually, you'll find sophisticated-looking grey and black pairs in addition to the classic yellow and white. If you want to buy a good pair, you'll have to spend some time examining the different qualities; for the best, be prepared to bargain hard until you're down to around 150dh.

The **Cherabliyin** (Slippermakers') **mosque**, in the midst of the quarter, was endowed by the Merenid sultan, Abou el Hassan, builder of Rabat's Chellah. It has been substantially restored, though the minaret, its decoration inspired by the Koutoubia in Marrakesh, is original. If you've gazed at the Koutoubia, or the great Almohad monuments of Rabat, you'll recognise the familiar *darj w ktarf* motifs.

SOUK EL ATTARIN

Continuing, the lane is flanked by a drab series of "typical" handicraft shops before reaching, at the bottom of the hill, an arched gateway marked **Souk el Attarin**. The "Souk of the Spice Vendors", this is the formal heart of the city, and its richest and most sophisticated shopping district. It is around the grand mosque of a city that the most expensive commodities are traditionally sold and kept, and, approaching the Kairaouine, this pattern is more or less maintained. Spices themselves are still sold here, as well as Egyptian and Japanese imports, while in the web of little squares off to the left, you'll find all kinds of manufactured goods.

There are a few small cafés inside the *souk*, while returning to the Attarin you'll find **Dar Saada**, a large, nineteenth-century mansion now housing an expensive carpet shop and restaurant – you can look in or drink a cup of tea feeling only moderate pressure to buy something. Just beyond, this time on the right of the street, is the principal **kissaria**, or covered market, again dominated by textiles and modern goods; totally rebuilt after a fire in the 1950s, it lacks any particular character.

● **Access.** Reaching the end of Souk el Attarin you come to a **crossroads of lanes** lying slightly askew from the direction of the street. On your right (and ahead of you) are the walls of the **Kairaouine Mosque;** to your left, and entered a few yards up the lane, is the magnificent **Attarin medersa** (see below). First, however, it seems logical to take a look at the area below the Souk el Attarin – dominated, as it has been for five centuries, by the **shrine and zaouia of Moulay Idriss II,** the city's patron saint.

The Zaouia of Moulay Idriss II and around

The principal landmark to the south of the Souk el Attarin is the **Zaouia Moulay Idriss II**, one of the holiest buildings in the city. Although enclosed by a highly confusing web of lanes, it is not difficult to find: take the first lane to the right – Rue Mjadliyin – as soon as you have passed through the arch into the Attarin and you will find yourself in front of a wooden bar which marks the beginning of its *horm*, or sanctuary precinct. Until the French occupation of the city in 1911, this was as far as Christians, Jews or mules, could go, and beyond it any Muslim had the right to claim asylum from prosecution or arrest. These days non-Muslims are allowed to walk around the outside of the *zaouia* and, although you are not permitted to enter, it is possible to get a glimpse inside the shrine and even see the saint's tomb.

Passing to the right of the bar, and making your way around a narrow alleyway, you emerge on the far side of the *zaouia* at the **women's entrance.** Looking in from the doorway, the **tomb** of Moulay Idriss II is over on the left, and a scene of intense and apparently high-baroque devotion is usually going on all around it. The women, who are Idriss's principal devotees, burn candles and incense here and then proceed around the corner of the precinct to touch, or make offerings at, a round brass grille which opens directly on to the tomb. A curious feature, common to many *zaouias* but rarely within view, are the numerous European clocks – prestigious gifts and very popular in the last century, when many Fassi merchant families had them shipped over from Manchester (their main export base for the cotton trade).

There is no particular evidence that Moulay Idriss II was a very saintly marabout, but as the effective founder of Fes and the son of the founder of the Moroccan state, he obviously has considerable *baraka*, the magical blessing which Moroccans invoke. Originally it was assumed that Idriss, like his father, had been buried near Volubilis, but in 1308 an incorrupted body was found on this spot and the cult was launched. Presumably, it was an immediate success, since in addition to his role as the city's patron saint, Idriss has an impressive roster of supplicants. This is the place to visit for poor strangers arriving in the city, for boys before being circumcised, and for women wanting to facilitate childbirth; also, for some unexplained reason, Idriss is a national protector of sweetmeat vendors. The shrine itself was rebuilt in the eighteenth century by Sultan Moulay Ismail – his only act of pious endowment in this city.

PLACE NEJJARIN

Standing at the women's entrance to the *zaouia,* you'll see a lane off to the left – **Rue du Bab Moulay Ismail** – full of stalls selling candles and silverware for devotional offerings. If you follow this lane around to the wooden bar, go under the bar (turning to the right), and then, keeping to your left, you should come out in the picturesque square of **Place Nejjarin** (Carpenters' Square).

Here is the very imposing **Nejjarin Fondouk**, built in the early eighteenth century along with a beautiful canopied fountain on one side of the square. The *fondouk,* crumbling all around its courtyard, is generally closed, though it was in use up until a few years ago as a hostel for Kairaouine students.

In the alleys off the square, you'll find the **Nejjarin souk**, easiest located by the sounds and smells of the carpenters chiselling away at sweet-smelling cedar wood. They produce mainly stools and tables – three-legged so they don't wobble on uneven ground – along with various implements for winding yarn, wooden boxes for storage and coffins. If there's a wedding coming up, you may see them making special ornamented tables, with edges, used for parading the bride and groom at shoulder level – a Fassi custom. Parallel to this lane is a **metalworkers' souk**, where the men hammer patterns on to large iron tubs and implements.

To return to the Souk el Attarin, turn left at the point where you entered the Place Nejjarin.

SOUK EL HENNA

A similar arrangement of buildings characterises the **Souk el Henna**, a quiet, tree-shaded square adjoining what was once the largest madhouse in the Merenid empire.

The madhouse – which is now in use as a storehouse – is a surprisingly inappropriate setting for this *souk.* In addition to the sale of henna and the usual cosmetics (kohl, antimony, etc.), the stalls sell all of the more esoteric ingredients required for aphrodisiacs and other magical spells. If you get talking to the stallkeepers, you'll be shown an amazing collection of plant and animal (often insect) derivatives. On one side of the square there is a huge pair of scales used for weighing the larger deliveries.

Pottery stalls are gradually encroaching on this traditional pharmaceutical business. Cheap but often striking in design, the pieces include Fassi pots, which are usually blue and white or very simple black on earthenware; and others from Safi, the pottery most commonly exported from Morocco, distinguished by heavy green or blue glazes; and Salé, often elaborate modern designs on a white glaze.

To get down to the square, take the lane to the right immediately in front of the entrance arch to Souk el Attarin.

The Kairaouine Mosque

The largest mosque in the country*, and one of the oldest universities anywhere in the world, **El Kairaouine** remains the fountainhead of Moroccan religious life, governing, for example, the timings of Ramadan and the other Islamic festivals. The mosque was founded in 857 by a Tunisian woman, a wealthy refugee from the city of Kairouan, but its present dimensions, with sixteen aisles and room for 20,000 worshippers, are essentially the product of tenth- and twelfth-century reconstructions: first by the great Caliph of Cordoba, Abd er Rahman III, and later under the Almoravids.

Even if all the roads in Fes el Bali do lead to the Kairaouine – an ancient claim which retains some truth – the mosque remains a thoroughly elusive place to non-Muslims. The building is so enmeshed in the surrounding houses and shops that it is impossible to get any clear sense of its shape, and at most you can get only partial views of it from the adjoining rooftops or through the four great entrances to its courtyard. Surprisingly for such an important religious building, nobody objects (publicly, at least) to tourists gaping through the gates to look inside; inevitably, however, the centrepieces that would give order to all the separate parts – the main aisle and the *mihrab* – remain hidden from view.

The overall effect of this obscurity is compounded by the considerable amount of time you'll probably spend getting lost around this area. The best **point of reference** around the Kairaouine – and the building most worth visiting in its own right – is the Attarin Medersa, whose entrance (a fairly prominent bronze door) is just to the left (north) at the far (eastern) end of Souk el Attarin. From here you can make your way around the mosque to a succession of other *medersas* and *fondouks*, picking up glimpses of the Kairaouine's interior as you go.

The Attarin Medersa

The **Attarin Medersa** (daily, except Fri mornings, 9am–noon & 2–6pm; 10dh admission) is, after the Bou Inania, the finest of the city's medieval colleges. It has an incredible profusion and variety of patterning – equally startling in the *zellij,* wood and stucco. Remarkably, each aspect of the decoration seems accomplished with an apparent ease and the building's elegant proportions are never under threat of being overwhelmed.

The *medersa* was completed in 1325 by the Merenid sultan, Abou Said, and is thus one of the earliest in Fes. Interestingly, its general lightness of feel is achieved by the relatively simple device of using pairs of symmetrical arches to join the pillars to a single weight-bearing lintel – a design repeated in the upper floors and mirrored in the courtyard basin. The later Merenid design, as employed in the Bou Inania, was to have much heavier lintels (the timbers above the doors and windows) supported by shorter projecting beams; this produces a more solid, step-like effect, losing the Attarin's fluid movement.

The basic ground plan, however, is more or less standard: an entrance hall opening on to a courtyard with a fountain, off which to the left are the

---

*The new **Hassan II Mosque** in **Casablanca** will, when completed, remove this distinction from Fes.

latrines, and directly ahead the prayer hall. On your way in, stop a while in the **entrance hall,** whose *zellij* decoration is perhaps the most complex in Fes. A circular pattern, based on an interlace of pentagons and five-pointed stars, this perfectly demonstrates the intricate science – and the philosophy – employed by the craftsmen. As Titus Burckhardt explains (in his *Moorish Art in Spain*), this lies in direct opposition to the Western arts of pictorial representation:

> . . . with its rhythmic repetitions, [it] does not seek to capture the eye to lead it into an imagined world, but, on the contrary, liberates it from all the pre-occupations of the mind. It does not transmit specific ideas, but a state of being, which is at once repose and inner rhythm.

Burckhardt adds that the way the patterns radiate from a single point serves as a pure simile for the belief in the oneness of God, manifested as the centre of every form or being.

In the **courtyard** you'll notice a change in the *zellij* base to a combination of eight- and ten-pointed stars. This probably signifies the hand of a different *maallem* (master craftsman), most of whom had a single mathematical base which they worked and reworked with infinite variation on all commissions. In comparison with these outer rooms, the actual **prayer hall** is very bare and meditative, focusing on its *mihrab* (or prayer niche) flanked by marble pillars and lit by a series of small *zellij*-glass windows.

If you are allowed to go up the stairs in the entrance hall, do so. Around the second floor are **cells** for over sixty students, and these operated as an annexe to the Kairaouine University until the 1950s. Budgett Meakin (in 1899) estimated that there were some 1500 students in the city's various *medersas* – a figure which may have been overestimated since it was based not on an actual count of the students themselves but on how many loaves of bread were prepared for them each day. Non-Muslims were not allowed into the *medersas* until the French undertook their repair at the beginning of the protectorate, and were banned again (this time by the colonial authorities) when the Kairaouine · students became active in the struggle for independence.

VIEWS OF THE KAIRAOUINE
From the roof of the Attarin Medersa (not always open to visitors) you can get one of the most complete views possible of the **Kairaouine Mosque**.

Looking out across the mosque's green roof tiles there are three visible **minarets**. The square one on the left belongs to the Zaouia Moulay Idriss. To its right are the Kairaouine's Burj an-Naffara (Trumpeter's Tower) and original minaret. The latter, slightly thinner in its silhouette than usual – most minarets are built to an exact 5:1 (width:height) ratio – is the oldest Islamic monument in the city, built in 956. Below it, you can also make out a considerable section of the central courtyard of the mosque – the **sahn**.

For a closer glimpse of the *sahn* at ground level, the best vantage point is the Bab el Wad gate: 20m down from the Attarin entrance (turn left as you step out, then immediately left again). At the end of the courtyard, a pair of magnificent pavilions are visible – the last additions to the structure of the mosque, added by the Saadians in the sixteenth century. They are modelled on the Court of the Lions in Granada's Alhambra palace, and were perhaps constructed by Spanish Muslim craftsmen.

Around the Kairaouine and Place Seffarine

There is a further new angle on to the *sahn* of the Kairaouine from the **Bab Medersa**, near the end of this first stretch of the mosque wall. Opposite, as you'd expect, is another college – the semiderelict (but occasionally open) **Misbahiya Medersa**. It has some fine details, though much of its best wood carving is now displayed at the Dar Batha museum. The elegant central basin was brought over by the Saadians from Almeria in Spain; the marble floor in which it is set level came from Italy. Surprisingly large, with courtyards (and two latrines) at each corner, it was built a couple of years before Bou Inania, again by the Merenid sultan, Abou el Hassan.

TETOUANI FONDOUK AND PALAIS DE FES

Moving on around the corner of the Kairaouine, you pass the **Tetouani** (or *Istroihani*) **fondouk**, a well-preserved Merenid building where the traders from Tetouan used to stay. Now partially occupied by a carpet store, you can look inside without any obligation and you'll probably be shown the huge, ancient door lock which draws across its gateway.

A few doors down, past another, much smaller *fondouk,* is the so-called **Palais de Fes**, a grand nineteenth-century mansion now converted to a restaurant and rug shop. Again you can walk in, and if you ask you'll be allowed up to the **roof** to get a different view of the Kairaouine and an interesting exercise in orientation concerning the immediate area. There is a café-restaurant on the roof, which will serve tea and pastries outside meal times – highly recommended.

PLACE SEFFARINE AND THE KAIRAOUINE LIBRARY

Another gate to the Kairaouine, essentially of Almoravid construction, stands right opposite the Palais de Fes; it is one of the ten which are opened only for Friday prayers. Alongside, notice the cedar panelling, placed to guide the blind toward the mosque.

If you follow this around, through a tight-wedged alley, you soon emerge into a very distinctive open square, metalworkers hammering away on each of its sides, surrounded by immense iron and copper cauldrons and pans for weddings and festivals. This is **Place Seffarine** – almost wilfully picturesque, with its faience fountain and gnarled, old fig trees.

On the near side of the square a tall and very simple entrance in the white-washed walls leads into the **Kairaouine Library**, again a building frustratingly denied to non-Muslims. Established by the Kairouan refugees in the ninth century, and bolstered by virtually the entire contents of Córdoba's medieval library, it once held the greatest collection of Islamic, mathematical and scholarly books outside Baghdad. Amazingly, and somewhat pointedly marking Fes's decline, much of the library was lost or dissipated in the seventeenth century. Now restored and in use, it is one of the most important in the Arab world.

The **university** here has had its function largely usurped by the modern departments established around Fes el Djedid and the Ville Nouvelle, and dispersed throughout Morocco. However, until recent decades it was the only source of Moroccan higher education. Entirely traditional in character, studies comprised courses on Koranic law, astrology, mathematics, logic, rhetoric and poetry – very much as the medieval universities of Europe. Teaching was informal, with professors gathering a group of students around them in a corner of the mosque, the students contriving to absorb and memorise the body of the professors' knowledge. It was, of course, an entirely male preserve.

A good spot to get your bearings, Place Seffarine offers a number of possible routes. You can continue around the mosque by taking the first lane to the right as you enter the square – **Sma't el Adoul** (The Street of the Notaries). The notaries, professional scribes, are sadly out of business, but before looping back to reach the Attarin *medersa*, you will be able to peek through a number of gates revealing the Kairaouine's rush-matted and round-arched interior. If you don't take this turning but continue straight ahead, you enter an area of *souks* specialising in **gold and silver jewellery** and used metal goods – a magnificent range of **pewter teapots** among them. As this road begins to veer left down the hill, a right turn will lead you up to the **Cherratin Medersa** (and eventually to Zaouia Moulay Idriss).

First, though, it is worth taking a look at the **Seffarine Medersa**, right on Place Seffarine.

THE SEFFARINE MEDERSA

The **Seffarine Medersa** (same hours as Attarin; 10dh) is the earliest of these Fes colleges. Its entrance is fairly inconspicuous, and you might need it pointed out to you: leaving the Seffarine square at the bottom lefthand corner you follow a short lane down to the left and then briefly to the right – the door (studded and with an overhanging portico) is on your left.

Built around 1285 – twenty years before the Attarin, 42 before the Bou Inania – the Seffarine is unlike all the other *medersas* in that it takes the exact form of a traditional Fassi house, with an arched balcony above its courtyard. It is heavily decayed, though still with suggestions of former grandeur in the lofty prayer hall. Elsewhere, the wandering vine and delicate ablutions pool give it a domestic air; in the far left-hand corner are wash basins and latrines.

For a small tip, the custodian will unlock the door to the **roof**, an atmospheric place where you can look down on the Seffarine square and listen to the individual rhythms of the metalworkers. Next door to the building are two newer *medersas*, still used for housing groups of students from the Lycée.

THE CHERRATIN MEDERSA

Very different from the Seffarin, and indeed all the previous *medersas*, the **Cherratin** (see directions from Place Seffarine, above) dates from 1670 and the reign of Moulay er Rachid, founder of the Alaouite dynasty.

The whole design represents a shift in scope and wealth – to an essentially functional style, with student cells grouped around three corner courtyards and a latrine around the fourth. Comprising some 120 rooms (each with space for two students), the *medersa* was in use until very recently and the cells are still partitioned and occasionally provided with electric light. The craftsmanship here represents a significant decline, though there is some impressive woodwork around the individual courtyards. It is interesting, too, in a general way as a rare surviving building from this period.

This *medersa* has recently been closed for restoration: knock for admission and you might be able to tip a workman to let you look around.

● **Access.** Continuing down the lane **beyond the entrance to the Seffarine Medersa**, swinging down the hill to the right, you reach **Rue des Teinturiers** (The Dyers' Souk: see the following section) and a **bridge** over the Oued Fes, below which you can leave the Medina by the *place* beside the **Mosque er Rsif.**

South of the Kairaouine: The Dyers' Souk and tanneries

If you're beginning to find the medieval prettiness of the central *souks* and *medersas* slightly unreal, then this region, just below the Kairaouine, should provide the antidote. That's because the dyers' and tanners' *souks* – basis of the city's commercial wealth from the tenth to the nineteenth century – represent the nauseating underside of everything you've seen until now.

THE DYERS' SOUK

The **dyers' street** – **Souk Sabbighin** – is directly below the Seffarine Medersa. Continue down past the *medersa* to your left, and then turn right immediately before the bridge ahead.

The *souk* is short and very weird, draped with fantastically coloured yarn and cloth drying in the heat. Below, workers in grey, chimney-sweep-looking clothes toil over ancient cauldrons of multicoloured dyes. The atmosphere is thick and mysterious, and not a little disconcerting so close to one of the city's main entrances.

● **Access.** At the end of the Souk Sabbighin you come to a second bridge, the humpbacked **Qantrat Sidi el Aouad** – almost disguised by the shops built on and around it. Walking across, you'll find yourself in the **Andalous quarter** (see overpage), and if you follow the main lane up to the left, Rue Sidi Youssef, you'll come out at the Andalous Mosque. Staying on the Kairaouine side of the river and taking the lane down to your right at the end of the *souk,* you should emerge at the open **square by the Rsif Mosque**; from here, if you want to return to the Ville Nouvelle, you can get a #19 bus, or a *petit taxi*.

THE TANNERIES

For the tanneries quarter – the **Souk Dabbaghin** – return to Place Seffarine and take the righthand lane at the top of the square (the second lane on your left if you're coming from the Palais de Fes). This lane is known as **Darb Mechattine** (Combmakers' Lane), and runs more or less parallel to the river for 150m or so, eventually reaching a fork. The righthand branch goes down to the river and **Bein el Moudoun Bridge** – another approach to the Andalous Mosque. The left branch winds up amid a maze of eighteenth-century streets for another 150 to 200m until you see the tanneries on your right; it sounds a convoluted route but is in fact a well-trodden one.

The most physically striking sight in Fes, the **tanneries** are constantly being visited by groups of tourists, with whom you could discreetly tag along for a while if you get lost. Otherwise, follow your nose or accept a guide up from the Seffarine. The best time to visit is in the morning, when there is most activity.

Inside the tanneries, there is a compulsive fascination about everything. Gigantic streams of water pour through holes that were once the windows of houses; hundreds of skins lie spread out to dry on the rooftops; while amid the vats of dye and pigeon dung (used to to treat the leather) an unbelievably gothic fantasy is enacted. The rotation of colours in the enormous honey-combed vats follows a traditional sequence – yellow (saffron), red (poppy), blue (indigo), green (mint) and black (antimony) – though vegetable dyes have mostly been replaced by chemicals. This innovation and the occasional rinsing machine aside, there can have been little change here since the sixteenth century, when Fes took over from Cordoba as the pre-eminent city of leather production. As befits such an ancient system, the ownership is also intricately feudal: the foremen run a hereditary guild and the workers pass down their specific jobs from generation to generation.

The processes can best be seen from surrounding terrace rooftops, where you'll be directed along with the other tourists. There is, oddly enough, a kind of sensuous beauty about it – for all the stench and voyeurism involved. Sniffing the mint that you are handed as you enter (to alleviate the nausea) and looking across at the others doing the same, however, there could hardly be a more pointed exercise in the nature of comparative wealth. Like it or not, this is tourism at its most extreme.

North to Bab Guissa and the Palais Jamai

This region – **north from Souk el Attarin** toward Bab Guissa and the Palais Jamai Hôtel – is something of a tailpiece to the Kairaouine quarter of Fes el Bali. It is not a route which many tourists take, scattered as it is with curiosities rather than monuments, but in this itself there's a distinct attraction. Additionally, leaving the city at Bab Guissa you can walk out and around to the **Merenid Tombs**, a beautiful walk as the sun is going down on the city.

A ROUTE TO BAB GUISSA – AND THE JEWELLERS' SOUK

From **Souk el Attarin,** there are dozens of lanes climbing up in the general direction of Bab Guissa, many of them blind alleys which send you scuttling back to retrace your steps. One of the more interesting and unproblematic approaches is to take the first lane to your left just inside the entrance arch to the *souk* (that is, about 15m before you come to the *Dar Saada* palace restaurant). Following this as directly as you can, you will soon emerge at the **Joutia**, the ancient fish and salt market.

Spreading out above here is the **Sagha** – the **jewellers' quarter** – which curves around to the right into a small square flanked by an eighteenth-century **fondouk** and fountain. The *fondouk* is now used as a wool store-house, though you can wander in to take a look at the elegant cedar wood-work and (heavily restored) stucco.

Back at the main lane – Place Sagha and its *fondouk* are about 20m off to the right – you pass a series of small café-restaurants and a cinema near **Place Achabin**, the herbalists' square, where remedies and charms are still sold.

The **café-restaurants** in this area are among the best value in Fes el Bali, serving good solid meals, and many double as *pâtisseries*, good for a mint tea or some fresh orange while rambling around the Attarin/Kairaouine area. Most of them are located in Rue Hormis.

Beyond Place Achabin, the road continues uphill, through an area filled with carpenters' workshops, toward Bab Guissa. On your way, look out for the **Fondouk Guissa** – or *Fondouk el Ihoudi* (The Jews' Fondouk) – on the lefthand side of the road. This dates back to the thirteenth century and was at the centre of the city's Jewish community until their removal to the Mellah in Fes el Djedid. It is used today for the sorting and storing of skins brought up from the tanneries: not a building for the queasy.

BAB GUISSA AND THE HÔTEL PALAIS JAMAI

The **Bab Guissa and Mosque**, at the top of the hill, are of little interest, rebuilt in the nineteenth century to replace a string of predecessors which have occupied this site for 800 years.

A quick right just before the gate, however, takes you up to the **Hôtel Palais Jamai** – a building whose luxury comes as quite a shock after a day's rambling through the Medina below. It was built toward the end of the last century by the Jamai brothers, viziers to Sultan Moulay Hassan and, in effect, the most powerful men in the country. Fabulously rapacious, the brothers eventually fell from power amid spectacular intrigues at the accession of Abdul Aziz in 1894. Walter Harris records the full story in *Morocco That Was*, dwelling in great detail on the brothers' ignominious fate – "perhaps the blackest page of Moulay Abdul Aziz's reign."

> *They were sent in fetters to Tetouan, and confined, chained and fettered, in a dungeon. In the course of time – and how long those ten years must have been – Hadj Amaati (The Elder) died. The governor of Tetouan was afraid to bury the body, lest he should be accused of having allowed his prisoner to escape. He wrote to the court for instructions. It was summer, and even the dungeon was hot. The answer did not come for eleven days, and all that time Si Mohammed remained chained to his brother's corpse! The brother survived. In 1908 he was released after fourteen years of incarceration, a hopeless, broken, ruined man. Everything he had possessed had been confiscated, his wives and children had died; the result of want and persecution. He emerged from his dark dungeon nearly blind, and lame from the cruel fetters he had worn. In his days of power he had been cruel, it is said – but what a price he paid!*

In overt and dramatic contrast to this tale, you can wander in to the hotel for a drink. Ask to do so on the terrace beside the old palace, now dwarfed by a huge modern extension. An hour in the gardens here, with their box-hedge courtyards and fountains, really does merit the bar prices. The palace quarters themselves are used as special suites and conference rooms, but if they're unoccupied you may be able to look around one or two – ask at reception if a porter can show you the "Royal Suites"; a tip will be expected.

● **Access.** From **Bab Guissa** you can take a shortcut across through the hill cemetery to the Merenid tombs, or you can follow the road up and around. At **Bab Ferdaous**, just outside the *Palais Jamai,* there's a *petit taxi* stand, and from here **bus #10** runs to Place des Alaouites in Fes el Djedid.

The Andalous Quarter

Coming across the **Bou Khareb** river from the Kairaouine to the **Andalous bank** is not quite the adventure it once was. For the first three centuries of their existence, the two quarters were entirely separate walled cities and the intense rivalry between them often resulted in factional strife. The rivalry still lingers enough to give each a distinct identity, though since the thirteenth century this has been a somewhat one-sided affair: as the Fassis tell it, the Andalusians are known for the beauty of their women and the bravery of their soldiers, while the Kairaouinis have always had the money.

Whatever the reasons, the most famous Andalusian scholars and craftsmen have nearly all lived and worked on the other side of the river and as a result the atmosphere has a somewhat provincial character. Monuments are few and comparatively modest, and the streets are quieter and predominantly residential. As such, it can be a pleasant quarter to spend the early evening – and to get caught up in the ordinary, daily life of Fes el Bali. Street trading here (and in the southern quarters of the Kairouine side, too) tends to revolve around daily necessities, providing a link between the "medieval" town and continuing urban life. And your relationship with the city changes alongside, as you cease for a while to be a consuming tourist – a factor reflected also in the near total absence of "guides" and hustlers.

There are four principal **approaches to the quarter**, all providing more or less direct access to the area around the Andalous Mosque.

• **Cross the river at the El Aouad Bridge**. From here, take **Rue Sidi Youssef** up the hill to the right, and keep going straight to the top, where you'll come into line with the minaret of the Andalous Mosque. At this point, veer left, and you will see (on your right) the elaborate facade of the **Sahrija Medersa.**

• **Cross the river to the north, near the tanneries, on the Bein el Moudoun Bridge** (The Bridge Between the Cities). Then follow the main street, **Rue Seftah,** all the way up the hill as it winds around to the Andalous Mosque.

• **Start at the square by Mosque er Rsif.** From here you can get to **Rue Sidi Youssef** by going through the gate opposite the mosque entrance, then taking a first left by the first mosque (Sidi Lemlili) you come to, followed by a right turn up the hill. The square can be reached (somewhat circuitously) from the area around the Kairaouine Mosque, or you can get a **bus** to it (#19) from the Ville Nouvelle.

• **Start at Bab Ftouh, at the bottom of the quarter, and head north to the Andalous Mosque.** Bab Ftouh is connected by **bus** #18 to the Place de l'Istiqlal, by the Dar Batha; a handy point from which to leave Fes el Bali.

THE SAHRIJA MEDERSA AND ANDALOUS MOSQUE

If you are seeking direction for your wanderings in the Andalous Quarter, the **Sahrija Medersa** (or *Medersa Es-Sihrij*) is the quarter's most interesting monument and is generally rated the third finest *medersa* in the city, after the Attarin and Bou Inania. Anywhere else but Fes it would be a major sight, though here, perhaps because of its state of dilapidation, it fails to stand out as much as it should.

Still, it is currently undergoing restoration, and there's a considerable range and variety of original decoration. The *zellij* is among the oldest in the country, while the wood carving harkens back to Almohad and Almoravid motifs with its palmettes and pine cones. Built around 1321 by Sultan Abou el

Hassan, it is slightly earlier than the Attarin and a more or less exact contemporary of the *medersa* in Meknes – which it in many ways resembles.

There is frustratingly little to be seen of the nearby **Andalous Mosque**, other than its monumental entrance gates, as it is built right at the highest point of the valley. Like the Kairaouine, it was founded in the late ninth century and saw considerable enlargements under the Almoravids and Merenids. The Sahrija and the adjoining Sebbayin Medersa (which is currently in use for Lycée students) both served as dormitory annexes for those studying at the mosque's library and under its individual professors.

TOWARDS BAB FTOUH AND THE POTTERS' QUARTER

South from the Andalous Mosque – out toward **Bab Ftouh** – you emerge in a kind of flea market: clothes sellers at first, then all variety of household and general goods and odds and ends. At the top of the hill, on the edge of a cemetery area, there are often entertainers – clowns, storytellers, the occasional musician, all performing to large audiences.

This region of the city, a strange no-man's land of **cemeteries** and run-down houses, was once a leper colony, and traditionally a quarter of necromancers, thieves, madmen and saints. At its heart, close by Bab Ftouh, is the whitewashed **koubba of Sidi Harazem**, a twelfth-century mystic who has been adopted as the patron saint of students and the mentally ill. The saint's *moussem*, held in the spring, is one of the city's most colourful and was in the past a frequent spark for rioting.

About 1500m out beyond Bab Ftouh, and easily distinguished by the smoke from its kilns, is the **Potters' quarter** (*quartier des potiers*). If you're interested in the techniques – the moulding, drying and decorating of the pots and tiles – follow the road and wander up to some of the workshops. The quarter itself is actually quite new, the potters having been moved out of an enclosure by Bab Ftouh only a few years ago, though the designs and workmanship remain traditional.

● **Access.** At **Bab Ftouh** you can pick up a *petit taxi* to any part of town (the route up to the Merenid tombs is good for its views), or you can catch bus #18 back to the Ville Nouvelle.

Fes el Djedid

Unlike Fes el Bali, whose development and growth seems to have been almost organic, **Fes el Djedid** – "Fes the New" – was an entirely planned city, built by the Merenids at the beginning of their rule, both as a practical and symbolic seat of government. The work was begun around 1273 by the dynasty's second ruling sultan, Abou Youssef, and in a manic feat of building was completed within three years. The capital for much of its construction came from taxes levied on the Meknes olive presses; the Jews were also taxed to build a new grand mosque; and the labour, at least in part, was supplied by Spanish Christian slaves.

The site which the Merenids chose for their city lies some distance from Fes el Bali. In the chronicles this is presented as a strategic move for the defence of the city, though it is hard to escape the conclusion that its main function was as a defence of the new dynasty against the Fassis themselves. It was not an extension for the people, in any real sense, being occupied largely by the **Dar el Makhzen,** a vast royal palace and by a series of army garrisons. With the addition of the **Mellah** – the Jewish ghetto – at the beginning of the fourteenth century, this process was continued. Forced out of Fes el Bali following one of the periodic pogroms, the Jews could provide an extra barrier (and scapegoat) between the sultan and his Muslim faithful, as well as a useful and close to hand source of income.

Over the centuries, Fes el Djedid's fortunes have generally followed those of the city as a whole. It was extremely prosperous under the Merenids and Wattasids, fell into decline under the Saadians, lapsed into virtual ruin during Moulay Ismail's long reign in Meknes, but revived with the commercial expansion of the nineteenth century – at which point the walls between the old and new cities were finally joined.

Events this century, largely generated by the French Protectorate, have left Fes el Djedid greatly changed and somewhat moribund. As a "government city", it had no obvious role after the transfer of power to Rabat – a vacuum which the French filled by establishing a huge *quartier reservé* (red-light district) in the area around the Grand Mosque. This can have done little for the city's identity, but it was not so radical or disastrous as the immediate aftermath of independence in 1956. Concerned about their future status, and with their position made untenable by the Arab-Israeli war, virtually all of the Mellah's 17,000 **Jewish population** emigrated for Israel, Paris, or Casablanca; today only a few Jewish families remain in the Mellah, though there is still a small community in the Ville Nouvelle.

● **Access.** You can reach Fes el Djedid in a ten-minute walk from **Bab Boujeloud** (the route outlined below), or from the Ville Nouvelle by walking up or taking a **bus** (#3 from Place de la Résistance) to **Place des Alaouites** beside the Mellah.

West from Boujeloud

Walking down to Fes el Djedid from **Bab Boujeloud** involves a shift in scale. Gone are the labyrinthine alleyways and *souks* of the Medina, to be replaced by a massive expanse of walls. Within them, to your left, are a series of gardens: the private **Jardins Beida**, behind the Lycée, and then the public **Jardins de Boujeloud** with their pools diverted from the Oued Fes. The latter have an entrance toward the end of the long Av. des Français, and are a vital lung for the old city. If everything gets too much, wander in, lounge about on the grass, and spend an hour or two at the tranquil **café**, by an old waterwheel, at their west corner.

THE PETIT MECHOUAR

Moving on, near the end of the gardens, you pass through twin arches to reach a kind of square, the **Petit Mechouar**, which was once the focus of city life and still sees the occcasional juggler or storyteller during Ramadan evenings. To its left, entered through another double archway, begins the main street of Fes el Djedid proper – the **Grande Rue.** To the right is the monumental **Bab Dekakine** (Gate of the Benches), a tremendous Merenid structure which was, until King Hassan realigned the site in 1967–71, the main approach to the Royal Palace and Fes el Bali. It was on this gate that the Infante Ferdinand of Portugal was hanged, head down, for four days in 1437. He had been captured in an unsuccessful raid on Tangier and his country had failed to raise the ransom required. As a further, salutary warning, when his corpse was taken down from the Bab, it was stuffed and displayed beside the gate for the next three decades.

THE VIEUX MECHOUAR

Through the three great arches you will find yourself in another, much larger **Mechouar** (the *Vieux Mechouar*). Laid out in the eighteenth century, this is flanked along the whole of one side by an old arms factory – the Italian-built *Makina* – which is today partially occupied by a rug factory and various local clubs. A smaller gate, the nineteenth-century **Bab as Smen**, stands at the far end of the court, forcing you into an immediate turn as you leave the city through the Merenid outer gateway of **Bab Segma** (whose twin octagonal towers slightly resemble the contemporary Chellah in Rabat).

If you are making your way up to the **Merenid tombs** from here, turn sharp right. Directly ahead, and closed to the public, is the huge **Kasbah Cherrada**, a fort built by Sultan Moulay Rashid in 1670 to house – and keep at a distance – the Berber tribes of his garrison. It is now the site of a hospital, school and annexe of Kairaouine University.

QUARTIER MOULAY ABDALLAH AND THE SOUKS

Back at the Petit Mechouar – and before turning through the double arch on to the Grande Rue of Fes Djedid – a smaller gateway leads off to the right at the bottom of the square. This gives entrance to the old *quartier reservé* of **Moulay Abdallah**, where the French built cafés, dance halls and brothels. The prostitutes were mostly young Berber girls, drawn by a rare chance of quick money, and usually returning to their villages when they had earned enough to marry or keep their families.

The quarter today has a slightly solemn, empty feel about it, with the main street twisting down to Fes el Djedid's **Great Mosque**.

Within the main gateway, the **Grand Rue** zigzags slightly before leading straight down to the Mellah. There are **souks**, mainly for textiles and produce, along the way but nothing very much to keep you. Just by the entrance, though, immediately to the left after you go through the arch, a narrow **lane** curves off into an attractive little area on the periphery of the Boujeloud gardens. There's an old **water wheel** here which used to supply the gardens, and the small café (mentioned above) in the gardens nearby. On the way down, you pass a handful of stalls; among them are, traditionally, the *kif* and *sebsi* (kif pipe) vendors.

The Mellah and Royal Palace

With fewer than a dozen Jewish families still remaining, the **Mellah** is a rather melancholic place – resettled by poor Muslim emigrants from the countryside.

The quarter's name – *mellah*, "salt" in Arabic – came to be used for Jewish ghettos throughout Morocco, though it was originally applied only to this one in Fes. In derivation it seems to be a reference to the job given to the Fassi Jews of salting the heads of criminals before they were hung on the gates.

The enclosed and partly protected position of the Mellah represents fairly accurately the Moroccan Jews' historically ambivalent position. Arriving for the most part together with compatriot Muslim refugees from Spain and Portugal, they were never fully accepted into the nation's life. Nor, however, were they quite the rejected people of other Arab countries. Inside the Mellah they were under the direct protection of the sultan (or the local *caid*) and maintained their own laws and governors.

Whether the creation of a ghetto ensured the actual need for one is, of course, debatable. Certainly, it was greatly to the benefit of the reigning sultan, who could both depend on Jewish loyalties and manipulate the international trade and finance which came increasingly to be dominated by them in the nineteenth century. For all this importance to the sultan, however, even the richest Jews had to lead extremely circumscribed lives. In Fes before the French Protectorate, no Jew was allowed to ride or even to wear shoes outside the Mellah, and they were severely restricted in their travels elsewhere.

HOUSES, SYNAGOGUES AND CEMETERIES

Since the end of the Protectorate, when many of the poorer Jews here left to take up an equally ambivalent place at the bottom of Israeli society (though this time above the Arabs), memories of their presence have faded rapidly. What still remain are their eighteenth- and nineteenth-century **houses** – immediately and conspicuously un-Arabic, with their tiny windows and elaborate ironwork. Cramped even closer together than the houses in Fes el Bali, they are interestingly designed if you are offered a look inside.

It is worth weaving your way down toward the **Hebrew cemetery**, too, with its neat, white, rounded gravestones restored to pristine condition as part of the UNESCO plan.

There are also two surviving **synagogues**: the *Fassiyin* (which is now a carpet workshop) and the *Serfati*, slightly grander but currently occupied by a Muslim family. If you hire a guide, offer him a few dirhams and you may be able to see them both.

THE ROYAL PALACE

At the far end of the Mellah's main street – Grand Rue des Merenides (or Grand Rue de Mellah) – you come into **Place des Alaouites**, fronted by the new ceremonial gateway to the **Royal Palace**. The palace is one of the most sumptuous complexes in Morocco, set amid vast gardens, with numerous pavilions and guest wings.

In the 1970s, it was sometimes possible to gain a permit to visit part of the palace grounds – described in Christopher Kininmonth's *Traveller's Guide* as "the finest single sight Morocco has to offer . . . , many acres in size and of a beauty to take the breath away." Today, the palace complex is strictly off limits to all except official guests, it is reputedly little used by Hassan II, the present king, who divides most of his time between his palaces in Ifrane, Rabat and Marrakesh.

The Ville Nouvelle

By day at least, there's little to keep you in the **Ville Nouvelle**, the new city established by Lyautey at the beginning of the protectorate. Unlike Casa or Rabat, where the French adapted Moroccan forms to create their own show-places, this is a straightforward and pretty dull European grid.

The Ville Nouvelle is, however, home to most of the faculties of the city's university, and is very much the city's business and commercial centre. If you want to talk with Fassis on a basis other than that of guide to tourist, you'll stand the most chance in the cafés here. It's more likely, too, that the students you meet are exactly that – rather than the "friends" who want to walk with you, fare-meters rolling, in the Medina.

Eating and drinking

The **Ville Nouvelle** is also the centre for most of the cities restaurants, cafés, bars and other facilities. **Fes el Bali** and **Fes el Djedid** are quieter at night, except during Ramadan (when shops and stalls stay open till 2 or 3am). They have, of course, no bars, and with the exception of a scattering of touristic "Palace-Restaurants", fairly basic eating places.

Ville Nouvelle restaurants

The Ville Nouvelle has quite a selection of restaurants – though few go any way toward justifying the city's reputation as the home of the country's most exotic cooking.

For a **cheap, solid option**, try one of the handful of café-restaurants near the municipal market – on the lefthand side of Bd. Mohammed V as you walk down from the post office. Good possibilities include:

Restaurant Chamonix, 5 Rue Kaid Ahmed; **Casse-Croute Balkhaiat**, 41 Rue Kaid Ahmed. Reliable Moroccan dishes. The *Chamonix* stays open to midnight.

Restaurant du Centre, 105 Bd. Mohammed V. Copious portions.

Chawarma Sandwich, 42 Rue Normandie (off Place de l'Atlas). Modern and unatmospheric, but very friendly; serves good fish and Moroccan dishes at low prices.

Restaurant Mounia, 11 Bd. Mohammed Zerktouni (near the *Hôtel Zalagh*).

Restaurant Marrakech, Rue Ksar El Kbir (opposite the *Hôtel CTM*).

Moving a little upmarket, you might take a look at:

Le Tour d'Argent, 40 Av. Slaoui. Once-famous but now unlicensed restaurant, which retains a fair bit of style and serves massive portions of food.

Café-Restaurant Mounia, 11 Bd. Zerktouni. Reliable and licensed.

Roie de la Bière, 59 Bd. Mohammed V. Another old-style place and again licensed.

Chez Vittorio, Rue Nador (opposite the Hôtel Central). Respectable-looking pizzas.

Ville Nouvelle cafés and bars

Cafés are plentiful in the Ville Nouvelle, with some of the most popular around Place Mohammed V (the *Café de la Renaissance* here was an old Foreign Legion hangout), along Av. Mohammed es Slaoui and Bd. Mohammed V (both of which run between the *place* and Av. Hassan II).

For **bars**, you have to look a little harder. There are a couple along the Av. Slaoui (the *Es Saada* here is usually lively) and the pretty seedy, but cheap, *Dalilla* at 17 Bd. Mohammed V, its upstairs bar a place for serious Moroccan drinking. Beyond these, you're down to the handful of hotel bars – among them the *Hôtel Zalagh* (outdoors, by the swimming pool), *Hôtel Amor*, *Hôtel Splendid*, *Grand Hôtel* and the upmarket and rather dull *Hôtel de Fes*.

Fes el Bali and Fes el Djedid cafés and restaurants

Fes el Bali has two main areas for **budget eating**: around Bab Boujeloud, and along Rue Hormis (which runs up from Souk el Attarin toward Bab Guissa: see "North from the Attarin"). The places around Boujeloud have seen too many tourists to remain particularly good or cheap, though there is always plenty going on. *Restaurant Bouayad*, next to the *Hôtel Kaskades,* is about the best one there, with a decent *tajine;* it's also open pretty much through the night. If your money doesn't allow a full meal, you can get a range of **snacks** around Boujeloud, including chunks of *pastilla* from the stalls near the beginning of Talâa Seghira; ask prices before you're served and they'll probably work out lower.

In **Fes el Djedid** there are fewer – but much less touristy – places, most of them concentrated around Bab Semmarine. The unnamed restaurant opposite the *Hôtel Moulay al Chrif* is basic but wholesome.

For a real **Fassi banquet**, in an appropriate palace setting, reckon on spending 100–150dh a head. If you're interested, phone ahead for a table and try one or other of the following:

Palais de Fes, 16 Rue Boutouil-Kairaouine (☎347.07). Caters largely for tour groups, but the rooftop setting is as good as any in the city. Located by the Kairaouine Mosque and labelled on the Fes el Bali map.

Dar Saada, 21 Souk el Attarin (☎333.43). Wonderful *pastilla* or (ordered a day in advance) *mechoui*. All their portions are vast, and two people can do well by ordering one main dish and a plate of vegetables. Located in the Souk el Attarin and labelled on the Fes el Bali map.

Restaurant Al Fassia, in the Hôtel Palais Jamai (☎343.31). A distinguished Moroccan cuisine restaurant, with a terrace overlooking the Medina. There are few more stylish ways to spend an evening, but count on at least 120dh each, and considerably more if you get the full courses.

Restaurant Firdaous, Bab Guissa (☎343.43). Less ethereal, but with music and belly dancing. 55dh buys admission and a drink, 110dh a full meal. Located just below the Bab Guissa, near the *Hôtel Palais Jamai.*

Shopping for crafts

Fes has a rightful reputation as the centre of Moroccan traditional crafts but if you're buying rather than looking, bear in mind that it also sees more tourists than any of its rivals. Rugs and carpets, however much you bargain, will probably be cheaper in Meknes, Midelt, or Azrou; and although the brass, leather and cloth here are the best you'll find, you will need plenty of energy, a good sense of humour and a lot of patience to get them at a reasonable price.

Fassi dealers are expert hagglers – making you feel like an idiot for suggesting such a low price, jumping up out of their seats and pushing you out of the shop, or lulling you with mint tea and elaborate displays. All of this can be fun but you do need to develop a certain confidence and have some idea of what you're buying and how much to pay for it. As a preliminary check on quality (which may put you off buying anything new at all), take a look around the **Dar Batha** museum.

It can also be worth taking a careful look at the various shops along Av. Mohammed V in the **Ville Nouvelle**, before setting out to haggle in Fes el Bali. Shops here tend to have more fixed prices and are a lot easier to leave.

Listings

Banks Most of the banks are grouped along Bd. Mohammed V. As always, the *BMCE* (on Place Mohammed V) is best for exchange and handles *VISA/Access* transactions, as well as travellers' cheques. Others include: *Banque Populaire* (Av. Mohammed V; quick service for currency and travellers' cheques), *Crédit du Maroc* (Av. Mohammed V; also handles *VISA*) *SGMB* (at the intersection of Av. de France and Rue d'Espagne; again, handles VISA). *Crédit du Maroc* also has a branch in Fes el Bali (currency exchange only), in the street above the Cherratin Medersa.

Books The *English Bookshop* (68 Av. Hassan II; by Place de la Résistance) has a great selection of English novels, stocked for the city's students, and carries a fair number of North African writers. *Librairie du Centre* (60 Bd. Mohammed V; near the post office) and the boutique inside the *Hôtel de Fes* (Av. des FAR) can also be worth trying.

Car Hire Fes has quite a number of hire companies, though none are as cheap as the best deals in Casa. Call the following, which all allow return delivery to a different centre: *Tourvilles* (15 Rue Houmam Fetouaki, off Bd. Mohammed V; ☎266.35); *Zeit* (35 Av. Slaoui; ☎236.81/☎255.10); *Transcar* (21 Rue Edouard Escalier; ☎217.76); *Avis* (23 Rue de la Liberté; ☎227.90); *Tourist Cars* (Grand Hôtel, Bd. Mohammed V; ☎229.58); *Hertz* (Hôtel de Fes, Av. des FAR; ☎228.12); or *Caravan Maroc* (21 Rue de la Liberté).

Car Repairs *Mécanique Générale* (22 Av. Cameroun, Ville Nouvelle) is highly recommended: excellent mechanics and fair prices. Try also *Source Pièce Auto* (50 Rue Zambia, Labeta, Ville Nouvelle) for car parts and advice.

Chemist Among numerous ones throughout the Ville Nouvelle, there's the all-night *Pharmacie du Municipalité* just up from Place de la Résistance, on Bd. Moulay Youssef.

Cultural Events are relatively frequent, both Moroccan- and French-sponsored. Ask for details at one of the tourist offices.

Festivals The big events are the **Students' Moussem of Sidi Harazem** (held outside the city at Sidi Harazem – see following section – at the end of April) and the **Moulay Idriss II Moussem** and **Sidi Ahmed el Bernoussi Mousseum** (both held in the city, in September). There are others locally – ask at the tourist office for details.

Newspapers British papers and the *International Herald Tribune* are sold at the *Hôtel de Fes* boutique (in the Ville Nouvelle) and at some of the newsstands along Bd. Mohammed V.

Police *Commissariat Central* is on Av. Mohammed V; ☎19.

Post Office The main **PTT** is on the corner of Bd. Mohammed V/Av. Hassan II in the Ville Nouvelle (open summers 8am–2pm; winters 8.30am–noon and 2.30–6pm). Poste Restante is next door to the main building; the **phones section** (open until 9pm) has a separate side entrance when the rest is closed.

Swimming Pools Cheapest is the **Municipal Pool** (on Av. des Sports, just west of the train station; open mid-June to mid-Sept). For more space you can pay a bit extra to use the pool at the *Hôtel Zalagh* (close to the Youth Hostel).

THE MIDDLE ATLAS

Heading south from Fes, most people take a bus straight to **Marrakesh** or to **Er Rachidia**, the start of the great desert and *ksour* routes. Both journeys, however, involve at least ten to twelve hours of continuous travel, which, in the summer at least, is reason enough to stop off along the way.

The second, stronger reason, if you have the time (or, ideally, a car), is to get off the main routes and up into the mountains. Covered in forests of oak, cork and giant cedar, the **Middle Atlas** is beautiful and relatively little-visited. The brown-black tents of nomadic Berber encampments immediately establish a shift from the European north, the plateaux are pockmarked by dark volcanic lakes, and, at **Ouzoud** and **Oum er Rbia,** there are some magnificent waterfalls. If you just want a day trip from Fes, the Middle Atlas is most easily accessible at **Sefrou**, a relaxed market town, 28km southeast.

On the practical front, you'll probably hear that it's difficult to stop en route to Marrakesh, since many of the **buses** arrive and depart full. This is true to an extent, but by taking the occasional *grand taxi* or stopping for a night to catch a dawn bus, you shouldn't find yourself stuck for long. Along the Fes–Azrou–Midelt–Er Rachidia route, buses are no problem.

Around Fes: two spa centres

You need a sense of purpose to break out from the all-enveloping atmosphere of Fes's Medina. The surrounding countryside – the foothills of the Middle Atlas – is pleasant but is explored most easily by car; local buses can be tiresome and day trips something of an effort. The spa villages of **Sidi Harazem** and **Moulay Yacoub**, however, are easy escapes from the summer heat.

Sidi Harazem

The eucalyptus-covered shrine of **SIDI HARAZEM** was established by Sultan Moulay er-Rachid in the seventeenth century, though the centre owes its current fame to being the home of Morocco's best-selling mineral water. Fifteen kilometres from Fes, it is served by frequent **buses** from the CTM station in the Ville Nouvelle and from Bab Boujeloud, and by private ones (and *grands taxis*) from Bab Ftouh.

The oasis is today rather heavily orientated towards its health industry. The old **thermal baths** have an appeal, still, but in summer they are crowded and not very health-inspiring. Hotels are modern and functional affairs, too. If you visit from Fes, it's best to plan to return the same day.

Moulay Yacoub

MOULAY YACOUB, 20km to the northwest of Fes, revolves around its sulphurous springs. These have been channeled into a swimming pool (2dh admission) and alongside is a large hammam, with separate sections for women and men (7dh admission). Even if you don't want to make use of these facilities, the village is an enjoyable and colourful place for a daytrip.

The easiest **access** is by *grand taxi* – negotiable in Fes at the stands by Boujeloud or in the Ville Nouvelle. There are four small, unclassified **hotels**, best of which is *Hôtel Lamrhani* (☎06/122), and numerous café-restaurants.

Sefrou

SEFROU, an hour by bus to the south of Fes, is a very ancient walled town, the first stop on the caravan routes to the Tafilalt, and, until the Protectorate, marking the mountain limits of the **Bled el Makhzen** – the governed lands. Into the 1950s, it was also a predominantly Jewish town; there was an indigenous Jewish-Berber population here long before the coming of Islam and, although subsequently converted, a large number of Jews from the south again settled in the town under the Merenids.

Orientation and practicalities

Although Sefrou is not a large place – the population is only 40,000 – its general layout is confusing. If you are coming in by bus the first stop is usually in **Place Moulay Hassan** – the main entrance to the Medina, whose walls (and two gates) you see below. Beyond, the road and most of the buses continue around a loop above the town and valley, crossing the river and straightening out on to **Bd. Mohammed V**. This, as you'd expect, is the principal street of the Ville Nouvelle and contains all the usual facilities.

On the right, about 300m along, is the **post office**, next door to which is the *Hôtel des Cerises*, the only cheap and central **place to stay**. Ask to be let off here, if possible – it'll save the kilometre's walk from the *place*. If you can afford it, there's an alternative choice, halfway between the two, in the 3* *Hôtel Sidi Lahcen Lyoussi* (☎604.97); this has an alpine chalet feel, with its wooden 1950s' fixtures, and a good restaurant, though don't count on its swimming pool being filled. Back by the bridge, you'll find a sporadically open **Syndicat d'Initiative** in the isolated, white building.

Out from the centre, on the hill to the west of the town, there is also a semi-maintained **campsite**, and, close by the koubba detailed on the facing page, the *Hôtel-Café Boualserhin* – a cheap, attractive spot, with a tremendous view of the valley. Both campsite and hotel are about 2km from the centre on the hill west of town; the campsite is signposted on the road leading up behind the PTT.

The Medina and Mellah

In many ways it's a pity that Sefrou's **Medina** is so close to Fes el Bali – in comparison with which it inevitably suffers. It is, though, on its own modest scale, equally well-preserved, and the untouristy atmosphere – despite a straggle of hustlers – makes it a very pleasant place to explore. The **Thursday souk**, for example, remains very much a local affair, drawing Berbers from the neighbouring villages to sell their garden produce and buy

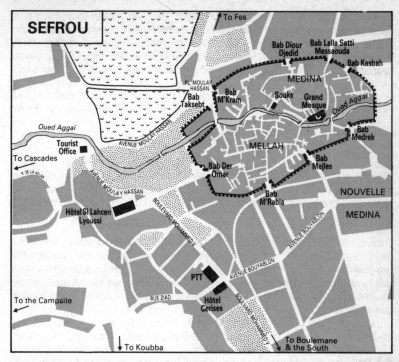

basic goods. The one time the town draws crowds is for the annual **Fête des Cerises** – the cherry festival, usually held in June and accompanied by various music and folklore events.

Enclosed by its nineteenth-century ramparts and split in two by the river, the Medina isn't difficult to find your way around. Coming from the post office on Bd. Mohammed V, you can take a shortcut down on the right of the road straight into the Mellah; if you were to turn up to the left, this would eventually lead you to Place Moulay Hassan. The most straightforward approach, though, is through **Bab M'Kram** in Place Moulay Hassan – on your left as you face the walls.

Entering at Bab M'Kram, you find yourself on the main street of the old Arab city, which winds down to the river, passing through a region of **souks**, to emerge at the **Grand Mosque**. The *souks* include some impressive ironwork stalls and, reflecting the traditional Jewish heritage, a number of silversmiths.

The Mellah

The **Mellah**, a dark, cramped conglomeration of tall, shuttered houses and tunnel-like streets, lies across the river from the Grand Mosque. It is today largely occupied by Muslims, though many of Sefrou's Jews only left for Israel after the June 1967 Six-Day War, and the quarter still seems distinct.

Over the years of the French Protectorate, the Jews had become quite well off, owning good agricultural land in the environs. But when most of the houses were built, in the mid-nineteenth century, the people's living conditions must have been pretty miserable. Edith Wharton, visiting in 1917, found "ragged figures . . . in black gabardines and skull-caps" living one family to a room in most of the mansions, and the alleys were lit even at midday by oil lamps. "No wonder", she concluded, "[that] the babies of the Moroccan ghettoes are nursed on date-brandy, and their elders doze away to death under its consoling spell."

Into the hills – and Bhalil

High enough into the Middle Atlas to avoid the dry summer heat, Sefrou is a place where you might actually want to do some walking. There are dozens of **springs** in the hills above the town and, for part of the year, active waterfalls.

Walks

For a relatively easy target, take the road up behind the post office, which will divide into a fork after about a kilometre. The right branch goes up past the campsite; the left leads to a small, French-built fort, known as the *Prioux* and still in military use, and to the **Koubba of Sidi Boualserhin**. A strange and ancient *moussem* takes place here, involving the ritual sacrifice of a black hen and white cock.

Another good walk is to go up in the hills above the river, a path followed by **Rue de la Kelaa** (just before the bridge, coming from the post office). There are gorges, coves and waterfalls in this direction (for which the *Syndicat* may be able to give more detailed directions or suggest a guide).

Bhalil

BHALIL, 8km to the north of Sefrou, claims pre-Islamic Christian origins and, more visibly, retains a number of troglodyte (cave) dwellings. If you have a car, this is worth a brief detour on your way from Fes; it is signposted to the right 5km before Sefrou. The **cave houses** are to the rear of the town, reached by a dirt road; ask directions to Mohammed Chraibi (B.P.42), the town's official guide, who will show you his own cave home.

South from Sefrou: Boulemane and the Massif du Kandar

Going **south from Sefrou** can be frustrating. There is a daily bus to Midelt, but no regular connection onto the Fes–Marrakesh road. If you want to cross over to the Marrakesh route, either take the Midelt bus, or a *grand taxi* to the garrison town of **BOULEMANE**, set at the foot of the Djebel Tichoukt in the Recifa gorge. This has a couple of garages and café-restaurants. Connections by *grand taxi* and bus are possible from there.

The Massif du Kandar road

Alternatively, if you have transport, or can afford to charter a *grand taxi*, you can travel south over to Immouzer du Kandar (see below) across the 34km of *piste* road (the P4620) over the mountainous **Massif du Kandar**. If you're driving, check out the state of the road before setting out – in winter it can be impassable.

The P4620 turns off from the Midelt road 12km after Sefrou, climbing up into the hills around the **Djebel Abad** (1768m) before descending to Immouzer. If you reckon your car can make it – or you feel like walking – there's a rocky road almost to the summit of the mountain (4km each way), on the right of the road, 10km down the P4620.

Immouzer du Kandar, Ifrane and the Mischliffen

The first hills you see of the Middle Atlas, heading directly south from the plains around Fes, seem perversely un-Moroccan. In **Ifrane** the king has a summer palace; in **Mischliffen** there's a ski centre; and the road up to both of them is almost ceremonial. **Immouzer du Kandar**, en route, is a little more approachable and mundane.

Immouzer du Kandar

Just under an hour by bus from Fes, **IMMOUZER DU KANDAR** is a one-road, one-square kind of place, where Fassis come up to swim, picnic and spend a few days.

There are a handful of **hotels** if you feel like doing the same. The 2*A *Hôtel des Truites* (☎630.02), near the beginning of town, is the best choice, with a bar and well reputed restaurant; a pricier alternative (with few advantages) is the 3*B *Hôtel Royal* on Av. Mohammed V. Cheaper rooms are to be had at the unclassified *Hôtel du Centre*, right beside the bus stop.

Other descriptions of Immouzer come down to facilities, too. The municipal **swimming pool**, near the centre, is open from mid-June to mid-September and filled, like everything here, with natural spa water. There's a famous **restaurant**, the *Auberge de Chambotte*; a small Monday **souk**, held within the ruined kasbah; and a July **festival**, the *Fête des Pommes*, which takes in a number of music and dance events.

Dayet Aouwa

A good excursion from Immouzer, or an alternative place to break your journey, is the **Dayet Aouwa**, a beautiful freshwater lake just to the left of the Ifrane road, 9km south of Immouzer. You can camp around the lakeside or stay at the 2*A *Chalet du Lac* (☎056/0 for the Ifrane post office, who will connect you), an old-style French-run hunting lodge with a bar whose walls are covered in stuffed animals, and a restaurant.

Like other lakes in the Ifrane area, Aouwa is a rewarding **birdlife habitat**, attracting breeding birds, ducks in passage, waders and terns. Particular species to sight include crested coot and grebes, ruddy shelduck and marbled teal. The chalet rents out **boats** for trips on the lake.

On to Ifrane

With a car it's possible to reach Ifrane by following the *piste* (P4628) up behind the **Dayet Aouwa**, then looping to the right, past another lake, **Dayet Ifrah**, before joining the last section of the road in from Boulemane. By bus the approach is simpler, the main road climbing through more and more dense shafts of forest before emerging in a bizarre clearing of pseudo-Alpine chalets and broad, suburban streets.

Created in 1929, this is **IFRANE**, a self-conscious *"poche de France"*, whose affluent villas were taken over after independence by Moroccan government ministries and the wealthier bourgeoisie. If you are into **skiing**, the town is the main base for the Mischliffen – Morocco's best slopes after Oukaïmeden in the High Atlas. For the average traveller, though, there's not a lot of interest here, beyond glimpses of the royal hunting lodge across the valley, the cool air and an excellent municipal **swimming pool**.

Practicalities

If you find yourself stranded at Ifrane – which, with four buses daily to Azrou and Fes, is unlikely – finding a room can be a problem. Besides the **youth hostel** (sporadically open: ask at the *Syndicat* in the centre of town), the only cheap **accommodation** is at the unclassified *Hôtel Tilleuls*, which in midsummer (and in the ski season) is frequently full. Other than this there are just three resort **hotels**, all generally full in the skiing season, the June to September summer season and at any time when the king is in town. These are the 2*A *Hôtel Perce Neige*, Rue des Asphodelles (☎64.04 or 62.10), and *Grand Hôtel*, Av. de la Marche Verte (☎64.07 or 62.03), and the 5* luxury *Hôtel Mischliffen* (☎64.16 or 64.18).

A useful summer alternative is the **campsite**, signposted just off the principal street through the town.

Skiing at Mischlifen

During the skiing season (Jan–March) there are taxis up to Mischliffen's **refuge/club** (food and drink; no accommodation) and **ski lifts**. You can **hire equipment** in town from the *Café-Restaurant Chamonix*. Snow cover on the slopes is unpredictable.

Skiing aside, Mischliffen has little of interest – it is merely a shallow bowl in the mountains, the crater of an extinct volcano, enclosed on all sides by cedar forests: there's no village and few buildings.

Azrou

AZROU, the first real town of the Middle Atlas, stands at a major junction of routes – north to Meknes and Fes, south to Khenifra and Midelt. As might be expected, it's an important market centre (the main *souk* is held on Tues), and it has long held a strategic role in controlling the mountain Berbers. Moulay Ismail built a Kasbah here, the remains of which still survive, while more recently the French established the prestigious **Collège Berbère** –

part of their attempt to split the country's Berbers from the urban Arabs. The *collège*, still a dominant building in the town, provided many of the Protectorate's interpreters, local administrators and military officers, but in spite of its ban on using Arabic and any manifestation of Islam, the policy proved to be a failure. Azrou graduates played a significant role in the nationalist movement – and were uniquely placed to do so, as a new French-created elite. Since independence, however, their influence has been slight outside of the army; many of the Berber student activists followed Mehdi Ben Barka's ill-fated, socialist UNEP party (see *Contexts*).

Practicalities

Arriving in the town, the feature you immediately notice is a massive outcrop of rock – the *azrou* ("rock" in Berber) from which the town takes its name. The bus drops you off just in front of it, at the end of the main square, **Place Mohammed V**.

The best cheap **hotel**, the 1*A *Hôtel des Cèdres* (☎23.26) is on Place Mohammed V. Around the corner on a smaller, adjacent square are the more basic and unclassified *Hôtel Ziz* , *Hôtel Beausejour*, *Hôtel Atlas* and (marginally preferable of these four) *Hôtel Salam*. There is also a **youth hostel** (*Auberge de Jeunesse*; ☎83.82), on the outskirts of town; to get there, walk out from the centre towards the roads to Fes and Midelt – it's about 1km uphill on the left. The only other hotels in town, the 1*A *Hôtel Azrou* (☎21.16) and 3*B *Hôtel Panorama* (☎20.10), are both well out from the centre, too.

Inexpensive **food stalls** are clustered around the bus station and there's a **restaurant** (keeping erratic hours) in the *Cèdres* with the sometimes expensive *Relais Forestier* bar/restaurant next door. The unnamed *café-patisserie* on the corner of the main square, near the *CTM* office, is plush by Moroccan standards, but prices are normal and the coffee and croissants superb.

Azrou has two **bus stations**, both of them in Place Mohammed V. Between them, you can choose from five buses per day to Midelt, Er Rachidia and Rissani, and it's not usually a problem to get a bus to Fes (or, less frequently, to Meknes). For Marrakesh, you should ask around and try to buy tickets the night before you plan to leave; several of the buses tend to arrive full, though there is one (currently departing at 4am, arriving in Marrakesh at 10.30–11am) which starts at Azrou. Around the other side of the rock, there is a **grand taxi** stand, with regular departures for Ifrane and Fes; sporadic (but possible) ones for Khenifra.

The *Souk* and the Town

If you can manage it, by far the best time to be in Azrou is for the **Tuesday souk**, which draws Berbers from all the surrounding mountain villages. It's held a little above the main part of town – just follow the crowds up to the quarter across the valley. The fruit and vegetable stalls sprinkled all over the main area seem at first to be all there is; look further, though, and you'll see a stretch of wasteland (usually filled with musicians and storytellers), beyond which is a smaller section for carpets, textiles and general goods. The **carpet stalls**, not particularly geared towards tourists, can turn up some beautiful items; reasonably priced if not exactly bargains.

For a more modern selection of rugs and carpets – including high-quality, heavy woollen local rugs – take a look, too, at the **Cooperative artesanale** (open daily 8.30am–noon and 2.30–6pm) back in Place Mohammed V, to the left of the rock. This is one of the best crafts cooperatives in the country, and quite a contrast to the usual junk in the tourist shops. In addition to the rugs, containing bright, geometric designs based on the traditional patterns of the Beni M'Guild tribe, there are impressive cedar and stone carvings.

There is little else to do in the town, though you can spend most of the day climbing around the hills (which again have seasonal springs) or wandering down to the river, reputedly well stocked with trout. Local guides tout the cedar forest and, above all, a very ancient and massive tree known as the **Cèdre Gouraud**, after one of Lyautey's generals; it's a 14km–hike or taxi ride (8km up the Midelt road and then down a signposted track to the left).

Stopping off for a rest from the Fes–Marrakesh/Midelt journey, you might find the **swimming pool** (behind the rock) equally tempting.

Aïn Leuh and the waterfalls of Oum er Rbia

South of Azrou lies some of the most remote and beautiful country of the Middle Atlas – dotted with cedar forests and home to numerous groups of monkeys (often to be seen even on the outskirts of Azrou). At the heart of the region are the magnificent waterfalls of **Oum er Rbia**, the source of Morocco's largest river.

There's a daily **bus** from Azrou to Aïn Leuh, 30km along the route to the Oum er Rbia and with some minor falls of its own, or you can charter a **grand taxi** straight through. The road has recently been paved along its whole course but it can still become waterlogged and impassable in winter.

Aïn Leuh
AÏN LEUH (17km down the main Khenifra road, then left along the S303) is a large Berber village, typical of the Middle Atlas, with its flat-roofed houses tiered above the valley. As at Azrou, there are ruins of a Kasbah built by Moulay Ismail; and in the hills behind the town there are **springs** and a more or less year-round waterfall.

Aïn Leuh's **souk** is held on Wednesday (a good day to hitch), though it can extend a day in either direction. It is the weekly gathering point of the **Beni M'Guild** tribe – still semi-nomadic in this region, and to be seen camping out beside their flocks in heavy, dark tents. As a colonial *zone d'insécurité*, this part of the Atlas was relatively undisturbed by French settlers and the traditional balance between pasture and forest has remained largely intact.

To the Oum er Rbia
The road to the **Sources de l'Oum er Rbia** begins just before you reach Aïn Leuh and is signposted "Aguelmane Azigza/Khenifra". It runs mostly through mountain forest, where you're almost certain to come across Middle Atlas monkeys. About 20km from Aïn Leuh, to the left of the road, there's a small lake – **Lac Ouiouane** – with scope for camping in perfect isolation.

Thirteen kilometres from here, you come to a sizeable **bridge** over the Oum er Rbia; stay on the road until you reach a second, concrete bridge, with a small parking area by the river; the footpath on the far side of the bridge leads after a fifteen-minute walk to the **waterfalls**. These are truly spectacular – forty or more cascades, shooting out from an enormous limestone cliff. The basin below, sculpted by the adjacent rocks, seems like a tempting place to have a swim, though be warned that the currents here are extremely strong; there are smaller, natural pools nearby. The water, full of salt sediments, is not drinkable.

Aguelmane Azigza and beyond

On past the bridges, the main road heads off to the west, crossed by a confusing array of *pistes*. After 18km, a turnoff on the left leads to the **Aguelmane Azigza**, a dark and very deep lake, where again you can camp – and swim, as many Moroccans do, or stay at the brand new **lodge–café**.

From the Azigza turnoff, it's a further 24km to Khenifra. Alternatively, for the exploring minded, there's a *piste* (3km past the Azigza turnoff) which leads into the mountains to emerge eventually near the junction of the Azrou and Khenifra roads to Midelt; this, however, is a very rough road and suitable only for vehicles with four-wheel drive.

Midelt and the route to Er Rachidia

If you're travelling the southern circuits of the *ksour* and *kasbahs* of the sub-Sahara, you're almost certain to take this route in one direction or the other. It's 125km from **Azrou to Midelt** and a further 154km to **Er Rachidia** – quite feasible distances for a single bus trip or a day's driving, but much more satisfying when taken in a couple of stages. You cross passes over both the Middle and High Atlas ranges, catch a first glimpse of the south's extraordinary *pisé* architecture and end up in the desert.

Azrou to Midelt

Climbing up from Azrou, the Midelt road follows a magnificent stretch of the Middle Atlas, winding through the pine and cedar forests around the town to emerge at the river **valley of the Oued Gigou**, the view ahead taking in some of the range's highest peaks.

By bus you have little alternative but to head straight to Midelt, reached in around two hours, via the market village of **TIMADHITE** (with a large **Thursday souk**). With a car, there are two very brief and worthwhile detours. Fifty-two kilometres from Azrou, as the road levels out on a strange volcanic plateau littered with dark pumice rock, there's a turnoff on the left marked **Aguelmane Sidi Ali.** This is a mountain lake, the largest of many formed in the extinct craters of this region. It's only a kilometre from the road – long, still and eerily beautiful. Besides an occasional shepherd's tent and flock, there is unlikely to be anything or anyone in sight; if you can improvise a fishing rod, there are reputed to be plenty of trout, pike and perch.

The other point where you might want to leave the road is 24km further down, just before the junction with the old road (and caravan route) from Sefrou and Boulemane. Six kilometres off to the right here is the small village of **ITZER**, whose **market** is one of the most important in the region. Held on Mondays and Thursdays, it can be a good source of Berber rugs and carpets.

Midelt

At **MIDELT**, approached through a bleak plain of scrub and desert, you have left the Middle Atlas behind. Suddenly, through the haze, appear the much greater peaks of the High Atlas rising sheer behind the town to a massive range, the **Djebel Ayachi**, at over 3700m.

The drama of this site, tremendous in the clear, cool evenings, is the most compelling reason to stop over, for the town itself initially looks very drab – one street with a couple of cafés and hotels and a small *souk*. In fact, it's a very pleasant place to stay – partly because so few people do, partly because it's the first place where you become aware of the much more relaxed (and largely Berber) atmosphere of the south. The best time to be here is for the huge **Sunday souk**, which spreads back along the road towards Fes.

The town: carpet shopping

The most interesting section of town, meriting at least a stop between buses, is the old *souk* – **Souk Djedid** – behind the stalls opposite the bus station. This is exclusively a **carpet market**, the wares slung out in rotation in the sunlight (for natural bleaching) and piled up in bewildering layers of pattern and colour in the various shops to the rear. It's a relaxed place for shopping and the rugs are superb – mostly local, geometric designs from tribes of the Middle Atlas. Ask to see the "antique" ones – few will be more than ten or twenty years old, but they are usually the most idiosyncratic and inventive.

More carpets – and traditional-styled blankets and textiles – can be seen or bought at the **Atelier de Tissage** run by a group of French Franciscan nuns in a convent just off to the left on the road to **Tattiouine** (signposted "Cirque Jaffar;" first right after the bus station). Many of the nuns have been living here for years, and will happily talk about Morocco for hours.

If you follow the Tattiouine road a couple of kilometres further, you find yourself in countryside very different from that around Midelt, with eagles soaring above the hills and mule tracks leading down to the valleys, and an occasional *kasbah*. There are more ambitious hikes up into the **Djebel Ayachi**, best approached by getting a taxi up to the village of Tattiouine.

Practicalities

There are food stalls and a cheap, unnamed **hotel** by the bus station (midway through the town); another hotel, *El Aghouar*, is a little further into town. The preferable options, though, are the *Roi de la Bière* and *Occidentale* (clean and with a café – highly recommended), both near the **campsite** (cheap but lacking facilities), 2km out on the road to Er Rachidia. The only classified hotel is the 3*A *Hôtel Ayachi* (☎21.61), on the southern edge of town. The town has separate **hammams** for women and men – ask directions at your hotel.

For **food**, choose between *Restaurant Fes* (with a massive *menu du jour*), on Rue des Essayaghane and *Brasserie Chez Aziz*, on the Er Rachidia road.

The Cirque Jaffar

The most adventurous route from Midelt is the **Cirque Jaffar** road – a very poor *piste*, practicable only in dry weather, which leaves the Tattiouine road to edge its way through a kind of hollow in the foothills of the Djebel Ayachi. If you have a car, there's a classic route around the *cirque*, which loops back to the Midelt–Azrou road after 34km (turn right, on to the 3426, near the *Maison Forestière de Mitkane*); it is only 79km in all back to Midelt, though it'll take you at least half a day to get around it.

Alternatively – and highly recommended for the more intrepid – you can continue along the *Cirque* road right **over the backbone of the Atlas**, eventually reaching Arhbala and El Ksiba, or Imilchil up in the High Atlas (see Chapter Six). To take this route, you don't need a car; as long as you have the time, it's possible to ride in Berber lorries (for which you pay as if they were buses) over the various stages. Bear in mind, however, that you'll be largely dependent on the patterns of local markets, and reckon on three, perhaps four days up to Imilchil, and a similar number from there down to the fabulous Todrha Gorge and Tinerhir (again, see Chapter Six). It will help, too, if you decide that, for at least part of the way, you'll walk.

If, incidentally, you set out to **hike** the whole way, you might want to acquire Michael Peyron's *Grand Atlas Traverse* guides (see p.15), which detail the whole zone between Midelt and the Toukbal massif.

South towards Er Rachidia

There's rather less adventure in continuing the trip **south from Midelt to Er Rachidia,** though it is still a memorable route, marking a transition to the south and the sub-Sahara. It was the traditional territory of the Aït Haddidou tribes, notorious raiders, who were only really "pacified" in the 1930s. The area, in conseqence, is dotted with old French Foreign Legion posts.

Tizi n'Talrhmeht

You cross one of the lower passes of the High Atlas, **Tizi n'Talrhmeht** (Pass of the She-Camel) some 30km south of Midelt, descending to what is essentially a desert plain. At **AÏT MESSAOUD**, just beyond the pass, there's a Beau Geste-like military fort, and a few kilometres further down, you come across the first southern *ksar*, **AÏT KHERROU**, a river oasis at the entrance to a small gorge. After this, the *ksour* (plural form for these fortified villages) begin to dot the landscape as the road follows the path of the great Ziz River.

Rich

Before arriving at Er Rachidia, there is the possible, if distinctly quixotic, prospect of a stopover in **RICH**: a small (and inappropriately named) market town, which is approached from the main road by a vast and bizarre red-washed esplanade. Utterly desolate, with mountains stretching off into the distance, this seems a perfect stage for some fatalistic gesture; staying here – there are two basic **hotels** – would probably be enough.

On a more prosaic level, the *piste* behind the town, trailing the last section of the Oued Ziz, offers an alternative approach to Imilchil – less dramatic than that from Midelt but said to be passable for most of the year.

The Ziz Gorge

One last highlight of this route is the **Ziz Gorge**, which begins 25km from the Rich turnoff, and 54km before Er Rachidia: a tremendous erosion of rocks cutting its way through the final stretch of the Atlas. Impressive at any time of day, it's unbelievably majestic in the late afternoon, with great shafts of sunlight shining through the valleys.

ER RACHIDIA (see Chapter Six) sprawls out ahead of you as you emerge, past a huge dammed reservoir. Unless you arrive late in the day, you'll probably want to press straight on to MESKI or ERFOUD (again, see Chapter Six).

Towards Marrakesh: the Routes from Azrou and the Cascades d'Ouzoud

The **main route from Azrou to Marrakesh** – the **P24** – skirts well clear of the Atlas ranges, its interest lying in the subtle changes of land, cultivation and architecture on the plains as you move into the south. The towns along the way are hot, dusty, functional market centres, unlikely to tempt you to linger. However, once again, contact with the Middle Atlas is close at hand, if you leave the main road and take to the *pistes*. A great network of them spreads out behind the small town of **El Ksiba**, itself 8km off the P24 but easily hitched to from the turnoff or reached by bus from Kasba Tadla.

Khenifra – and a side trip to Oulmes

It's unlikely that you'll get stranded in **KHENIFRA** and it's equally difficult to imagine any other reason to stay there. It is a dull-looking market town, whose reputation for providing some of the best Moroccan musicians (including the star, Rouisha), seems hard to credit. From an outsider's perspective, the only bit of life to be seen is at the twice weekly **souks** (Wed and Sun) or the Saturday afternoon rug auction, put on by Berber women just across the bridge from the highway which bypasses the town. Historically, the town's chief claim to fame is as a focus of resistance, as the fiefdom of one Moha ou Hammou, in the early years of the Protectorate. The French suffered one of their worst military defeats here, losing 600 men when they took the town in 1914.

If you're following this chapter in reverse (from Marrakesh) note that you can approach the Cascades of Oum er Rbia (see p.167) from Khenifra. If you've just done this, or plan to do so, you might just want to use the local accommodation: a particularly gloomy **hotel** by the *CTM* station at the end of town, or a couple of somewhat more enticing ones (each with a restaurant) down by the river – the *Voyageurs* and the *France* – all unclassified. The only starred hotel is the 4*B *Hôtel Hamou* (☎60.20) in the hilllside new town.

Northwest to Oulmes

Northwest of Khenifra, a road leads through forested outcrops of the Middle Atlas, the Djebel Mouchchene, towards Rabat. This is an attractive route through countryside cut by mountain rivers and ravines, and with wild boar in the hills. There is a major **souk** at the crossroads settlement of **AGUELMOUSS** each Saturday.

Midway along the route is the small town of **OULMES** and – 4km distant – the spa-hamlet of **OULMES-TARMILATE**, home of Morocco's most popular sparkling water. The spa makes a good stop, if you can afford 3*A **hotel** prices at the *Hôtel les Thermes* (☎901; closed July–Aug). Below the hotel you can walk down to a spot known as **Lalla Haya**, where Oulmes water cascades out from the rocks.

El Ksiba, Arhbala and across the Atlas

EL KSIBA, a sizeable and busy Berber village with a **Sunday souk**, has no great lure of its own, though the approach up here, hemmed in by dense woods, gives a hint of the dramatic Atlas countryside beyond. There is a pleasant, small **hotel**, the 2*B *Hostelerie Henri* IV (☎2), on a loop road which bypasses the main part of the village, but if you arrive here early enough in the day, you should be able to get a bus or lift straight to the market village of Arhbala, in the Atlas proper. En route to Arhbala, the road passes a series of **campsites** hidden in the wooded Atlas slopes.

ARHBALA itself lies at the beginning of the **piste to Midelt**, and if you are heading for Imilchil and the Plateau des Lacs (see Chapter Six), you can either try and get a lift from a lorry here (most likely on Wed, when Arhbala has its *souk,* or Fri when there's a *souk* at Imilchil), or take a chance by getting out at the Imilchil turnoff – 50km from El Ksiba and 13km before Arhbala. The usual route from the turnoff to Imilchil – see the map in Chapter Six – goes via the villages of CHERKET and TASSENT; there's a Berber lorry/bus along each stage at least every other day.

Kasba Tadla

KASBA TADLA was created by Moulay Ismail, and takes its name from a fortress he built here, strategically positioned beside the Oum er Rbia river. It remains a military town, with all the life that entails, and is scarcely a place to linger. However, if you have a car or are between buses, you might as well take the odd hour to look around. The **Kasbah** is only a few blocks from the bus station – a massive, crumbling quarter, whose palace and even mosque have lapsed into dereliction, their shells now occupied by small farmholdings and cottages.

For anyone stranded, there are two cheap and very basic **hotels** right by the bus station, and another, the *Hôtel des Alliés*, just around the corner. There is a pleasant **Monday souk**.

Beni Mellal

BENI MELLAL is one of Morocco's fastest-growing towns, with a population of some 250,000. It has few specific sights – and few tourists – and makes an easy, restful stop en route to Marrakesh. As a centre for the broad, prosperous flatlands to the south, it hosts a sizeable **Tuesday souk** – particularly good for blankets, which feature some unusual Berber designs. It is also useful for its transport links, with a regular bus towards the wonderful Cacades d'Ouzoud (see overpage).

As far as sights go, the town's **Kasbah**, again built by Moulay Ismail, has been often restored and is of no great interest. Time would be better spent by walking up to the smaller, ruined **Kasbah de Ras el Aïn**, set above gardens, and to the spring of **Aïn Asserdoun**, to the south of town.

Practicalities

The **bus station**, as so often, has been recently implanted to the edge of town, on the P24 bypass road; to get into the centre, best take a *petit taxi*.

Half a dozen reasonable and inexpensive **hotels** are scattered around the town. In the centre, the unclassified *Hôtel El Amria* (☎35.51), on Av. des Far, is clean, simple and very sympathetically run, while along the main thoroughfare of Av. Mohammed V are the 1*A *Auberge du Vieux Moulin* (☎27.88), at the Kasba Tadla end of the street, and the more central, 2*B *Hôtel Gharnata* (☎34.82). In the "new medina" you'll find the unrated *Hôtel Afrique* and 1*A *Hôtel de Paris* (☎22.45). For food, you're best off at the *Auberge du Vieux Moulin*, which also has an unintimidating **bar**.

Oulad Nemâa: a Saturday *souk*

If you're in Beni Mellal on a Saturday, it's worth a trip to what is traditionally the Middle Atlas's largest weekly **market**, held 35km southwest of the town at **SOUK SEBT DES OULAD NEMÂA**. There are regular buses.

The Cascades d'Ouzoud

The **Cascades d'Ouzoud** are a fairly long detour from the Beni Mellal–Marrakesh road – at least half a day's journey if you're going by local bus and taxi. But there are few places in Morocco so enjoyable and easy-going as these fallls, with their seasonal campsites, and in midsummer it's incredible to encounter the cool air here, with the water crashing down on to a great drop of rocks amid thickets of lush green trees and vegetation.

Getting There

Getting to Ouzoud by bus is simplest from Beni Mellal. There's a regular service to AZILAL (a winding 63km), where you can generally get a place in a *grand taxi* to the springs (5dh a place or 30dh for the taxi). There is also a bus twice a day from Marrakesh along the old S508 road, which passes by Azilal. Getting back to Azilal is generally no problem, with *grands taxis* regularly shuttling from the Cascades.

Bin el Ouidane

On the way from Beni Mellal to Azilal, the road climbs almost straight up from the plain, zigzagging through the hills and crossing an immense dammed lake at **BIN EL OUIDANE** (Aït Maazik in Berber), where there's a small **1*A hotel**, the *Auberge du Lac* (open year-round; no phone), with a bar, a good restaurant, river fishing/swimming and boats for hire; be warned that in winter it's cold, with hot water but no room heating. There's also a summer **campsite**. The barrage, one of the earliest (1948–55) and most ambitious of the country's irrigation schemes, has changed much of the land around Beni Mellal – formerly as dry and barren as the phosphate plains to the west – and provides much of central Morocco's electricity.

Azilal

AZILAL is just a small village, with a garrison, a Thursday *souk* and transport links. If you find yourself stranded, there's a single 2*A **hotel**, the *Tanout*, on the Beni Mellal road.

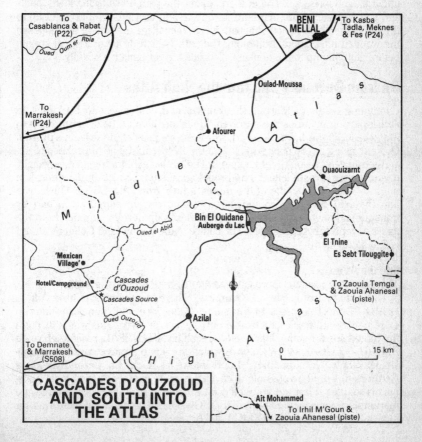

The Cascades

OUZOUD is a popular place to camp in the summer, as the air is cooled by the falls and altitude, and it is refreshingly uncommercialised. At the roadside, there is a small **café-hotel**, but to get the most from the location you really need to camp. Two or three seasonal and makeshift **campsites** (open March–Sept) are poised on trellis-covered terraces right above the springs. Both sell drinks and hot food, and, with a predominantly young Moroccan/European clientèle, are very relaxed.

From the campsites, a series of signposted paths wind down to the valley and the great basins below the **cascades**. You can swim in one of these – a fabulous natural pool, and if you don't mind the occasional monkey (still a fairly common sight in this stretch of hills), you could pitch a tent under the oak and pomegranate trees.

The most memorable hike, however, is to go beyond the lower pools to the so-called **"Mexican Village"** – a fascinating place connected by semi-underground passages. To get there, follow the path down to the lower pools and you will see a path climbing up on the left, past a farmhouse and up to the top of the plain. Follow this path west. The village is sited on the slopes of the wooded hills, about 1km along the path (which drops to a small stream before climbing up to the houses). Tourists are very much a novelty.

On from Ouzoud – and into the High Atlas

Continuing south to Marrakesh from Ouzoud, it's easiest to backtrack to Azilal, picking up a bus there to Beni Mellal or (if you time it right) direct to Marrakesh. If you have transport, however, it's possible to drive north from Ouzoud, along a very poor *piste*, to join the P24 Beni Mellal–Marrakesh road.

Alternatively, if you're into a spot of High Atlas exploration, and especially if you've read Ernst Gellner's anthropological study, *Saints of the Atlas*, you might be tempted by one of the **pistes south from the S508**. These lead into the **Irhil M'Goun** mountains, a remote region, populated in part by transhumant shepherds who bring their flocks up here in summer from the oases beyond the Atlas ranges. The centre of the region (and Gellner's study) is Zaouia Ahanesal.

Into the Atlas

There are two possible approaches to the High Atlas from the S508.

The first is **from Bin el Ouidane**, where a minor road turns off to OUAOUIZARNT, crosses to the south of the lake and then turns into an extremely rough track, practicable only by jeep or lorry. This winds through the mountains for some 70km before reaching AHANESAL, passing en route ZAOUIA TEMGAL (40km), above which are some strange rock formations shaped like a Gothic cathedral and known as such: **La Cathédrale Des Rochers**. It would be possible to cover this route in stages, using local transport resources. First get yourself a lift to Ouaouizarnt, then ask around the marketplace for a jeep going to TILOUGGITE, then ask around and wait for lorries (*camions*) going to TEMGA and beyond.

The second is to take a **dirt track southeast of Azilal**, which leads to the village of AÏT MEHAMMED and then on to TAMDA, before joining the *piste* running south from AHANESAL. Continuing up into the Central Atlas from Aït Mehammed, another difficult *piste* leads to the **Bou Goumez valley**, a possible hiking/climbing base for the 4000m peaks of the **Irhil M'Goun** – the highest in Morocco outside the Toubkal massif. If you're interested in exploring this range (Imelghas, Aït Bou Goumez, Azilal), Mohammed Achari is a **mountain guide** and has mules for hire.

Azilal to Marrakesh: Demnate

Having come as far as Azilal and the cascades, it is easier to continue along the S508 road to Marrakesh rather than try and cut back on to the main road from Beni Mellal. It is in any case the more interesting route.

Demnate

You'll probably have to change buses along the way at **DEMNATE**, a walled market town whose **Sunday souk** is by far the largest in the region and an interesting, unaffected event that is well worth trying to coincide with. It is held just outside the ramparts, the stalls spreading out into the town streets with their used clothes and other goods, together with enormous stacks of fresh produce.

Demnate has a small **hotel**, close by the bus station, and if you have the time and the transport, a road up above the town climbs after 6.5km to a curious-looking natural bridge – **Imi n'Ifri**. Close to a series of springs, which account for the Demnate Valley's prosperous and intense cultivation, this is the site of a large *moussem* held two weeks after the Aïd el Kebir.

Demnate to Marrakesh

The land between Demnate and Marrakesh is generally poor and rocky, distinguished only by sporadic clusters of farmhouses or shepherds' huts. If you take the bus, it might follow either of the routes to Marrakesh – via Tamelelt (where you rejoin the P24) or a perfectly well-paved road via Tazzerte and Sidi Rahhal.

Given the choice, go for the latter. An old Glaoui village, **TAZZERTE** is fronted by four crumbling Kasbahs, from which the clan (see "Telouet" for its history) used to control the region and the caravan routes to the north. There is a small Monday market held here, and a larger one on Fridays at Sidi Rahhal, 7km further down.

SIDI RAHHAL, named after a fifteenth-century marabout, is also a point of significant local pilgrimage and host to an important, week-long *moussem* (flexible date in the summer). The saint, in whose honour the festivities take place, has an unusual Judeo-Muslim tradition, and a multitude of stories told about him. All are timeless in their evocations of magic and legend. The most popular ones recount how he had the power to conduct himself and other creatures through the air – a "talent" which led to a minor incident involving the Koutoubia minaret in Marrakesh, whose upper floor one of his followers is supposed to have knocked down with his knee.

Coming into Marrakesh from either Demnate or Beni Mellal, you skirt part of the huge **palmery** which encloses the northern walls of the city. Arriving by bus, you will almost certainly find yourself at the main **bus station** by Bab Doukkala – a ten-minute walk from the centre of Gueliz (or the Ville Nouvelle), or twenty minutes (or an 8–10dh taxi ride) from Place Djemaa el Fna and the Medina.

travel details

Trains

Fes–Meknes Seven daily in each direction (around 45min).

Fes–Rabat/Casablanca Six daily (around 4hr 30min–5hr/6hr); all via Meknes, Sidi Kacem (2hr 30min), Kenitra (3hr 30min) and Salé (4hr).

Fes–Taza/Oujda Four daily (2–2hr 15min/5hr 45min–6hr).

Fes–Tangier Three daily (around 6hr); all via Meknes, Sidi Kacem (3hr 30min) and Asilah (5hr).

Fes/Marrakesh Three daily via Marrakesh (around 11hr 30min).

Meknes–Marrakesh No direct bus.

Buses

From Meknes Fes (hourly; 50min); Larache/Tangier (2 daily; 5hr 30min/7hr); Rabat (3; 4hr); Ouezzane (2; 4hr); Chaouen (1; 5hr 30min); Azrou (4; 3hr 30min); Midelt (1; 5hr 30min); Beni Mellal/Marrakesh (1; 6hr/9hr).

From Fes Chaouen (2; 5hr); Mdiq (1; 5hr); Larache/Tangier (2; 4hr 30min/6hr); Rabat (6; 5hr 30min); Casa (8; 7hr); Taza (3; 2hr 30min); Al Hoceima (1; 11hr 30min); Sefrou (3; 1hr 30min); Immouzer/Ifrane (5; 1hr/1hr 30min.); Azrou (5; 2hr 30min); Midelt/Er Rachidia (3; 5hr 30min/8hr 30min); Beni Mellal/Marrakesh (3; 8hr 30min/11hr).

From Sefrou Boulemane/Midelt (2hr/5hr).

From Azrou Ifrane/Immouzer (4 daily; 1hr/1hr 30min); Midelt/Er Rachidia (5; 2hr/5hr); Khenifra/Kasba Tadla/Beni Mellal/Marrakesh (3; 3hr/4hr/4hr 30min/7hr).

From Midelt Er Rachidia (2; 3hr), Oujda (1; 13hr.).

From Kasbah Tadla El Ksiba (3 daily; 20min); Beni Mellal (4; 1hr).

From Beni Mellal Demnate (4 daily; 3hr); Marrakesh (6; 6hr).

Grands Taxis

From Meknes Regularly to Fes (40min) and Volubilis/Moulay Idriss (35min).

From Fes Regularly to Meknes, Sefrou (1hr), Immouzer/Ifrane (1hr 20min/1hr 40min) and Taza (1hr 40min).

Other **local and Middle Atlas** routes are specified in the text.

Flights

From Fes Daily to Casablanca (and on from there to Marrakesh, etc.).

TELEPHONE CODES	
AZROU ☎056	KHENIFRA ☎058
BENI MELLAL ☎048	MEKNES ☎05
FES ☎06	MIDELT ☎058
IFRANE ☎056	SEFROU ☎06

CHAPTER FOUR

THE WEST COAST: FROM RABAT TO ESSAOUIRA

This chapter takes in almost five hundred kilometres of **Atlantic coastline** – from Kenitra in the north down to Essaouira in the south. It is, inevitably, a mix of influences, characters and landscapes, ranging through Morocco's urban heartland to long stretches of scarcely developed lagoons and sands.

Rabat and **Casablanca** form the power base of the nation – the respective seats of government and of industry and commerce. The two cities, together with the neighbouring towns of **Salé**, **Kenitra** and **Mohammedia**, have a combined population of over four million – a fifth of the country's total. They have acquired this preeminence almost entirely within the last fifty years. At the turn of the century, Rabat was a straggling port with a population of 30,000 (today it is 518,000); Casablanca, Morocco's largest city (2,140,000), was a minor harbour town of 20,000 inhabitants.

Inevitably, given this rapid and immense development, it is French and post-colonial influences which are dominant in this conurbation. Don't go to "Casa" (as it's popularly known) expecting it to "look Moroccan" – it doesn't; it looks very much like Marseille. Likewise Rabat, which the French developed as an administrative capital to replace the old imperial centres of Fes and Marrakesh, and whose cafés and avenues are recognisably European. All of which may suggest the briefest of stops. Yet, if you want to get a real idea of what Morocco is all about – and of how most Moroccans now live, these, at some stage, are places to spend time. **Casa** is perhaps best visited after spending some time in the country – when you'll find its beach clubs and bars a novelty, and appreciate both its differences and its fundamentally Moroccan character. **Rabat**, on the other hand, is one of the best places to make for as soon as you arrive in the country: well connected by train with Tangier, Fes and Marrakesh, it makes an easy cultural shift in which to gain some initial confidence. With the old port of **Salé**, facing Rabat across a river estuary, it also has some of Morocco's finest and oldest monuments, dating from the Almohad and Merenid dynasties.

As you move **south along the coast**, populations and towns thin out, as the road skirts a series of beaches and dunes, with the odd detour inland when cliffs take hold. **Essaouira**, easily accessible from Marrakesh, is a long-established backpackers' resort, and more recently a major centre for windsurfers. For most independent travellers, it is Morocco's coastal highlight,

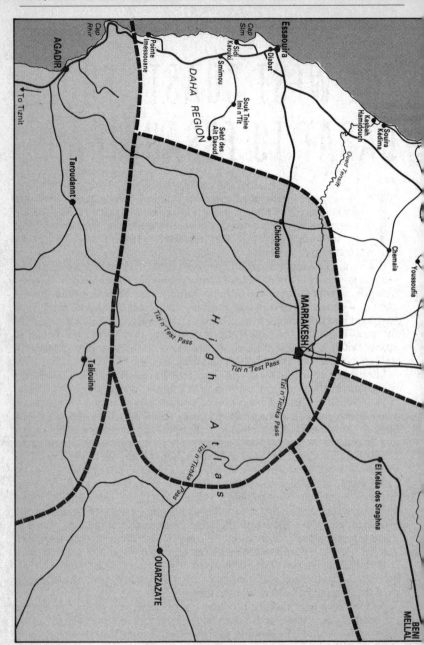

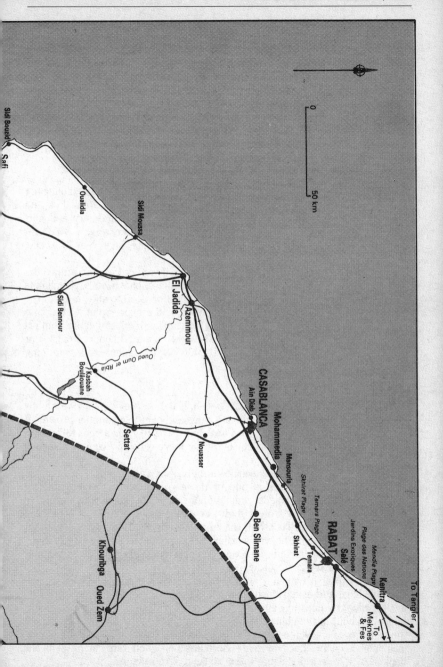

blending as it does a slightly alternative feel with the air of a traditional provincial town. **El Jadida**, established as a beach resort by the French, is more the preserve of people from Casablanca; it sees fewer foreign visitors and, oddly, is more expensive and exclusive. **Oualidia**, to its south, has a similar, though more relaxed and small-scale, style. **Safi**, between El Jadida and Essaouira, is a quirkier choice for a visit, with its predominantly industrial base, but a friendly place, and with excellent beaches nearby for those with the transport to reach them.

The road to Rabat: Kenitra and Mehdiya

KENITRA was established by the French as Port Lyautey – named after the resident general – with the intention of channelling trade from Fes and Meknes. It never quite took off, however, losing out in industry and port activities to Casablanca, and today maintains a population of around 300,000 – many of them dependent on the naval and military base, shared by Morocco, since the 1970s, with the US.

Most tourists pass straight through the town, by rail or bus, and indeed the garrison presence, reflected in an unusual number of bars, hotels, pizza joints and discos, has little to recommend. If you want or need to stay, most of the **hotels** are to be found along Av. Mohammed V, the main street leading into town from the bus station. The majority are unclassified. For more comfort head for the 2*B *Hôtel La Rotonde* at 60 Av. Mohammed Diouri (☎33.43) or the 3*B *Hôtel Mamora* on Av. Hassan II (☎30.70), the latter with a swimming pool and lively bar.

Mehdiya

MEHDIYA PLAGE, Kenitra's local beach, is a dull, greyish strip with a few houses and chalets, intermittent beach cafés and plenty of summer crowds. It is reached easily enough by *grand taxi*, but if you're after a spot to break a journey and swim, you'd be better off at the more relaxed Plage des Nations (towards Rabat, see p.221).

There is some appeal, however, to a night – or an evening – spent at the 2*B *Hôtel Atlantique*. This is one of those odd locations which has, for reasons unknown, developed a reputation for authentic **Moroccan music**. In summer there are bands most night, covering the spectrum of Moroccan trends – including, on occasion, the Algerian imported Rai style. The other **hotel** at the resort is the unclassified but dependable *Auberge de la Foret* (☎106); similar prices but more likelihood of a room. There is also a summer campsite on the outskirts of town.

As for sights, Mehdiya – which long predates Kenitra – has a ruined **Kasbah**, near the estuary, which was built by the Portuguese, extended by the Spanish, demolished and then restored by Moulay Ismail, and, finally, knocked about in the course of US troop landings in the last war; it shelters the remains of a seventeenth century governor's palace. A couple of kilometres inland is the **Lac de Sidi Bourhaba** – good birdwatching locale, flanked by a *koubba* that is the site of an August **moussem**.

Rabat

Capital of the nation since independence – and, before that, from 1912 to 1956, of the French Protectorate – **RABAT** is in many ways the city you'd expect: elegant in its spacious European grid, slightly self-conscious in its civilised modern ways, and, as an administrative centre, a little bit dull. If you arrive during Ramadan, you'll find the main boulevards an astonishing night-long promenade – at other times, it's hard to find a café open past ten at night. Rabat, as they tell you in Casa, is *provincial*.

None of this makes any difference to the city's considerable historic and architectural interest, though it does leave little choice but to act the tourist: unlike Fes or Marrakesh, there's no involved city life to drift along with. You can, however, get around the place quite happily without a guide; talk in cafés with people who do not depend on tourist money; and spend an easy few days seeing the monuments and lying on the excellent nearby beaches.

Some history

Rabat's **monuments** punctuate the span of Moroccan history. The plains inland of the city, designated *Maroc Utile* by the French, have been occupied and cultivated since Paleolithic times, and both Phoenicians and Carthaginians established trading posts on modern day Rabat's estuary site.

The earliest known settlement, *Sala*, occupied the citadel known today as **Chellah**. Here, after the demise of the Carthaginians, the **Romans** created their southernmost colony. It lasted well beyond the breakup of the empire in Africa and eventually formed the basis of an independent Berber state, which reached its peak of influence in the eighth century, developing a code of government inspired by the Koran but adapted to Berber customs and needs. It represented a challenge to the Islamic orthodoxy of the **Arab** rulers of the interior, however, and to stamp out the heresy, a *ribat* – the fortified monastery from which the city takes its name – was founded on the site of the present-day Kasbah.

The *ribat's* activities led to Chellah's decline – a process hastened in the eleventh century by the founding of a new town, **Salé**, across the estuary. But with the arrival of the **Almohads** in the twelfth century, the Rabat Kasbah was rebuilt and a city again took shape around it. The Almohad fort, renamed **Ribat el Fathi** (Stronghold of Victory), served as a launching point for the dynasty's Spanish campaigns, which by 1170 had brought virtually all of Andalusia back under Muslim rule.

Under the Almohad Caliph **Yacoub el Mansour,** a new imperial capital was created. Its legacy includes the superb **Oudaïa Gate** of the Kasbah, **Bab er Rouah** at the southwest edge of town, and the early stages of the **Hassan Mosque.** Until recent years, this was the largest ever undertaken in Morocco and its minaret, standing high above the river, is still the city's great landmark. Mansour also erected over five kilometres of fortifications – but neither his vision nor his success in maintaining a Spanish empire were to be lasting. He left the Hassan Mosque unfinished, and only in the last sixty years has the city expanded to fill his dark circuit of *pisé* walls.

After Mansour's death, Rabat's significance was dwarfed by the imperial cities of Fes, Meknes and Marrakesh, and the city fell into neglect. Sacked by the Portuguese, it was little more than a village when, as New Salé, it was resettled by seventeenth-century Andalusian refugees. In this revived form, however, it entered into an extraordinary period of international piracy and local autonomy. Its corsair fleets, the **"Sallee Rovers",** specialised in the plunder of merchant ships returning to Europe from West Africa and the Spanish Americas, but on occasion raided as far afield as Plymouth and the Irish coast – Defoe's Robinson Crusoe began his captivity "carry'd prisoner into Sallee, a Moorish port".

The Andalusians, owing no loyalty to the Moorish sultans and practically impregnable within their Kasbah perched high on a rocky bluff above the river, established their own pirate state, the **Republic of the Bou Regreg**. They rebuilt the Medina below the Kasbah in a style reminiscent of their homes in Spanish Badajoz, dealt in arms with the English and French, and even accepted European consuls, before, under Moulay Rashid, and his successor, Moulay Ismail, the town finallly reverted to government control.

Arriving, orientation and hotels

With its **Medina** and **Ville Nouvelle** bounded by the river and Almohad walls, central Rabat never feels like a big city, and indeed all the city's points of interest are withineasy walking distance.

Points of arrival

● **By train**. By far the easiest way to arrive. The Rabat Ville station (don't get off at Rabat-Salé) is at the heart of the Ville Nouvelle, with most hotels a few minutes' walk. Unusually, there are luggage lockers.

● **By bus**. The main bus terminal is located in Place Zerktouni – 3km out from the centre by the road junction for Casa and Beni Mellal. To get into town from here (or vice versa), you'll have to take a local bus (#30 and others stop along Bd. Hassan II by the *Hôtel Majestic*) or compete for a *petit taxi* (6dh or so – usually metered – for up to three people). Easier, if you are coming by bus from the north, is to get off in **Salé** (see p.218) and take a *petit taxi* from there into Rabat; the distance is no greater.

● **By grand taxi.** Taxis for non-local destinations operate from outside the main bus station (see above). Those from/to Casa cost only a couple of dirhams more than the bus and leave more or less continously through the day. *Grands taxis* to Skhirat, Bouknadel and other local destinations leave from the lengthy and chaotic stand on Bd. Hassan II.

● **By air.** From the **Mohammed V Airport** (out towards Casablanca), buses run to the square outside the *Hôtel Terminus* (by the train station); journey time is approximately 90 minutes. Departures **to the airport** from Rabat are (currently) at 5am, 6.30am, 8.30am, 10am, 12.30pm, 3.30pm, 6.30pm; tickets are sold at the kiosk by the departure point, immediately before the bus leaves. In both directions, specify *le prochain depart*. *Grands taxis* are an expensive alternative (400dh), unless you can split the fare.

Local bus services radiate out from Bd. Hassan II. Buses #1, #2 and #4 run from here (via Allal Ben Abdallah) to Bab Zaer, by way of Chellah; #6 and #12 cross the bridge to Salé; and #17 heads south to Temara Beach. *Petit taxis* can also be found on Bd. Hassan II; they are nearly always metered.

Finding a room

Accommodation can be tight in midsummer and especially in July, when rooms in the Ville Nouvelle budget hotels go early in the day and prices are hiked to absurd levels at the unclassified Medina places. It's perhaps best, at any time of year, to concentrate your search on the classified hotels and, if at all possible, to make an advance reservation by phone.

Recommendations below are in roughly ascending price order (the better ones are keyed on the map overpage). Anything upmarket of the *Hôtel Balima* is not especially worth your money – there are better cities to splurge.

MEDINA HOTELS

Hôtel France, Hôtel Algers, Hôtel du Marché. These three are all on the second turnoff to the left on Rue Mohammed V, the extension of Av. Mohammed V; continue on a bit and there are several more. None are especially inviting.

Hôtel el Alam (H), Hôtel Marrakech, Hôtel Regina. Another group, one street beyond those above, off to the right on Rue Gebbali. *El Alam*, outrageously decorated, is usually very cheap; *Marrakech* has better rooms but is overpriced for the (lack of) facilities.

Hôtel Darna (I), 24 Bd. el Alou (☎224.56). Just inside Bab el Alou at the far side of the Medina. By far the best of another small cluster of hotels. *2*A*.

Hôtel des Oudaïas (I), 132 Bd. El Alou (☎323.71). Conveniently sited, just across from the Kasbah area, and much more luxurious than other hotels in the Medina. *2*A*.

VILLE NOUVELLE HOTELS

Youth hostel (*Auberge de Jeunesse*), 34 Bd. Misr (☎257.69). Well-sited – just outside the Medina walls, a block to the north of Bd. Hassan II. However, standards of cleanliness leave a lot to be desired and the staff have a penchant for all night parties.

Hôtel Majestic (F), 121 Bd. Hassan II (☎229.97). Old hotel with a faded charm: the best budget choice – though you'd be lucky to find a room much after midday. *1*B*.

Hôtel Central (B), 2 Rue el Basra (☎221.31). Another useful budget choice – larger and so more likely to have space. Decent, clean rooms and nicely located by the *Hôtel Balima*. *1*A*.

Hôtel Gauloise (E), 1 Zankat Hims (☎230.22). Best value of a cluster of eight 1* and 2* hotels at the top of Av. Mohammed V. *1*A*.

Hôtel de la Paix (C), 2 Rue Ghazza (☎229.26). Adequate; useful for single rooms. *2*A*.

Hôtel Splendid (D), 24 Rue Ghazza (formerly Rue du 18 Juin) (☎232.83). Large rooms – ask for one overlooking the garden. *2*A*.

Hôtel Balima (A), Rue Jakarta, just behind Av. Mohammed V (☎216.71). This was Rabat's top hotel into the 1960s. Today, though faded and superseded, it retains a deco grandeur – as well as moderate-priced *suites*! Thami el Glaoui, Pasha of Marrakesh, stayed in one on his visits to the city in the 1950s. If you have the money, do the same. *3*B*.

Hôtel d'Orsay, 11 Av. Moulay Youssef/Place de la Gare (☎613.19). Conveniently located behind the station. A bit pricey but a good alternative if the *Balima* is full. *3*B*.

Camping

The nearest is a drab site across the river at **Salé** (see p.218). A better alternative, if you have transport, is at **Temara Plage**, 15km south (see p.222).

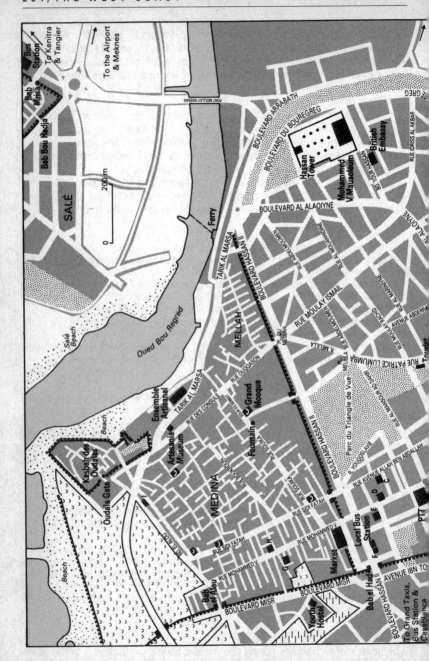

RABAT

Chellah

Bab Zaers

BOULEVARD MOUSSA IBN NOSSAIR

BOULEVARD TARIK IBN ZIAD

Algerian Embassy

Tourist Office

PLACE LINCOLN

RUE AL JAZAIR

AVENUE DE FES

AVENUE DE FES

AVENUE MARRAKECH

RUE PRES. ROOSEVELT

French Embassy

RUE D'OUARZAZATE

American Bookstore

RUE YOUSSEF BEN TACHFINE

RUE TANJA

AVENUE MOHAMMED V

AV. AS. SAOUIA

Archaeological Museum

R. MOULAY ABDELAZIZ

AVENUE MOHAMMED V

RUE TANJA

AVENUE YACOUB AL MANSOUR

AVENUE YACOUB AL MANSOUR

Grand Mosque

AVENUE MOULAY HASSAN

American Embassy

RUE ABOU INAN

RUE PATRICE LUMUMBA

AVENUE MOULAY HASSAN

AVENUE ALLAL BEN ABDALLAH

MECHOUAR

Royal Palace

AV. MY. ABDALLAH

AVENUE MOHAMMED V

Bab er Rouah

AVENUE MOULAY YOUSSEF

Train Station

English Bookshop

British Council

PLACE AN NASR

AVENUE IBN TOUMERT

AVENUE IBN TOUMERT

AV. JEAN JAURES

AV. AN NASR

To Casablanca

MOULAY ISMAIL

BOULEVARD

EGGAY

The Medina and Souks

Rabat's **Medina** – all that there was of the city until the French arrived in 1912 – is a compact quarter, wedged on two sides by the sea and the river, on the others by the Almohad and Andalusian walls. It is not the country's most interesting – open and orderly in comparison to those of Fes or Marrakesh – but coming here from the adjacent avenues of the modern capital is always a surprise. In appearance, it is still essentially the town created in the seventeenth century by Muslim refugees from Badajoz in Spanish Andalucia, and with these external features intact, its way of life seems remarkably at odds with the government business and cosmopolitanism of the Ville Nouvelle.

That this is possible – here and throughout the old cities of Morocco – is largely due to **Marshal Lyautey**, the first, and certainly the most sympathetic to the indigenous culture, of France's resident generals. Colonising Algeria over the previous century, the French had destroyed most of the Arab towns, replacing their traditional structures (evolved through the needs of Islamic customs) with completely European plans.

In Rabat, Lyautey found this system already in operation, the builders tearing down parts of the Medina for the construction of a new town and administrative quarters. Realising the aesthetic loss – and perhaps, too, the arrogance of "Europeanisation" – he ordered work to be halted and the Ville Nouvelle built outside the walls. It was a precedent accepted throughout the French and Spanish zones of the colony, a policy which inevitably created "native quarters", but one which also preserved continuity, maintained the nation's past and, at least so Lyautey believed, showed the special relationship of the Protectorate.

Into the Medina

The basic grid-like regularity of the Medina, cut by a number of long main streets, makes this a good place to get to grips with the feel of a Moroccan city. In plan it is typical, with a main market street – **Rue Souika** and its continuation **Souk es Sebbat** – running beside the Grand Mosque, and behind it a residential area scattered with smaller *souks* and "parish" mosques. The buildings, characteristically Andalusian, in the style of Tetouan or Chaouen, are part stone and part whitewash, with splashes of yellow and turquoise and great, dark-wood studded doors.

From **Bd. Hassan II**, a series of streets give access to the Medina, all of them leading more or less directly through the quarter, to emerge near the Kasbah and the old, hillside cemetery.

The two main streets on the west side – **Rue Mohammed V** and **Rue Sidi Fatah** – are really continuations of the main Ville Nouvelle avenues, though, flanked by working-class café-restaurants and cell-like hotels, their character is immediately different. Entering along either, past a modern food market and a handful of stalls selling fruit, orange juice and snacks, you can turn very shortly to the right and come out on the cubicle shops of **Rue Souika**. Dominated by textiles and silverware along the street's initial stretch, these give way to a concentration of *babouche* and other shoe stalls as you approach the Grand Mosque. They are all fairly everyday – though quite high quality –

shops, not for the most part geared to tourists. The cheaper goods and the *joutia* (flea market – see below) are off towards the river, around the old Jewish quarter of the Mellah. Along the way are few buildings of particular interest, most of the medieval city (which predated that of the Andalusians on this site) having been destroyed by Portuguese raids in the sixteenth century.

The **Grand Mosque**, founded by the Merenids in the fourteenth century, is a partial exception, though it has been considerably rebuilt – its minaret, for example, was only completed in 1939. Entry to the mosque is, as throughout Morocco, forbidden to non-Muslims. Opposite, there is a small example of Merenid decoration in the stone facade of a public **fountain**, now forming the front of an Arabic bookshop.

The Mellah and Joutia

The most direct approach from Bd. Hassan II to the Grand Mosque is a broad, tree-lined, pedestrian way, about halfway up the boulevard – facing the northeast corner of the Parc du Triangle de Vue. Alternatively, continuing a couple of blocks (past the *Hôtel Rex*), you can go in by the Mellah, alongside Rue Ouqqasa.

The poorest and most rundown area of the city, the **Mellah** no longer has a significant Jewish population, though some of its seventeen synagogues still survive in various forms. The only one active today is in a modern building, a block away in the Ville Nouvelle. The quarter itself, where all of the city's Jews were once required to live, was created only in 1808; Jews previously owned several of the mansions along Rue des Consuls, a bit further up. With its meat and produce markets, it looks a particularly impenetrable area, but it is worth walking through towards the river.

The **joutia**, or **flea market**, spreads out here along the streets below Souk es Sebbat, down to Bab el Bahr. There are clothes, pieces of machinery whose parts can no longer be replaced and (something you don't see too often) a number of vendors touting wonderful 1950s and 1960s movie posters, garishly illustrating titles like *Police Militaire* and *La Fille du Désert*.

Towards the Kasbah: Rue des Consuls

Beyond the Mellah, heading towards the Kasbah, you can walk out by **Bab el Bahr** and follow an avenue near the riverside up to the Oudaïa Gate; to the left of this road is a small **crafts museum** (officially 9am–noon & 3–6pm but often closed), to the right a run of the mill **Centre Artesanal.**

Rue des Consuls, a block inland, is a more interesting approach; like the Mellah, this, too, used to be a reserved quarter – the only street of the nineteenth-century city where European consuls were permitted to live. Many of the residency buildings survive, as do a number of impressive merchants' *fondouks* – most in the alleys off to the left. The main street, particularly at its upper end, is today largely a centre for **rug and carpet shops** and on Tuesday and Thursday mornings becomes a **souk,** with local people bringing carpets – new and old – to sell. Rabat carpets, woven with very bright dyes (which, if vegetable-based, will fade with time), are a traditional cottage industry in the Medina, though they're now often produced in factories, one of which you can take a look at on the Kasbah's *platforme* (see overpage).

The Kasbah des Oudaïas

The site of the original *ribat* and citadel of the Almohad, Merenid and Andalusian towns, the **Kasbah des Oudaïas** is a striking and evocative quarter. Its principal gateway, the Bab el Kasbah (or Oudaïa Gate), is perhaps the most beautiful in the Moorish world, and within the kasbah walls is one of the country's best craft museums and a perfect Andalusian garden.

The Oudaïa Gate

The **Oudaïa Gate**, like so many of the great external monuments of Morocco, is of Almohad foundation. Built around 1195, concurrently with the Hassan Tower, it was inserted by Yacoub el Mansour within a line of walls already built by his grandfather, Abd el Moumen. The walls in fact extended well to its west, leading down to the sea at the edge of the Medina, and the gate cannot have been designed for any real defensive purpose – its function and importance must have been purely ceremonial. It was to be the heart of the Kasbah, its chambers acting as a courthouse and staterooms, with everything of importance taking place within its immediate confines. The **Souk el Ghezel** – the main commercial centre of the medieval town with its wool and slave markets – was located just outside, while the original sultanate's palace stood immediately inside it.

The effect of the gate is startling. It doesn't impress so much by its size, which is not unusual for an Almohad structure, as by the visual strength and simplicity of its decoration. This is based on a typically Islamic rhythm, establishing a tension between the exuberant, outward expansion of the arches and the heavy, enclosing rectangle of the gate itself. Looking at the two for a few minutes, you begin to sense a kind of optical illusion – the shapes appear suspended by the great rush of movement from the centre of the arch. The basic feature is, of course, the arch, which here is a sequence of three, progressively more elaborate: first, the basic horseshoe; then, two "filled" or decorated ones, the latter with the distinctive Almohad *darj w ktarf* patterning, a cheek-and-shoulder design somewhat like a fleur-de-lis. At the top, framing the design, is a band of geometric ornamentation, cut off in what seems to be an arbitrary manner but which again creates the impression of movement and continuation outside the gate.

The dominant motifs – scallop-shell-looking palm fronds – are also characteristically Almohad, though without any symbolic importance; in fact, there's very little that's symbolic in the European sense in any Islamic decoration, the object being merely to distract the eye sufficiently to allow contemplation.

Around the Kasbah

You can enter the **Kasbah** proper through the Oudaïa Gate (or, if it's closed, through the small gateway on its right), or by a lower, horseshoe arch at the base of the ceremonial stairway. This latter approach leads directly to the **Andalusian gardens** and **palace museum**, which can also be reached fairly easily after a brief loop through the Kasbah.

An airy, village-like part of the city, the Kasbah is a pleasant quarter in which to wander – and not remotely dangerous or "closed to visitors", as the

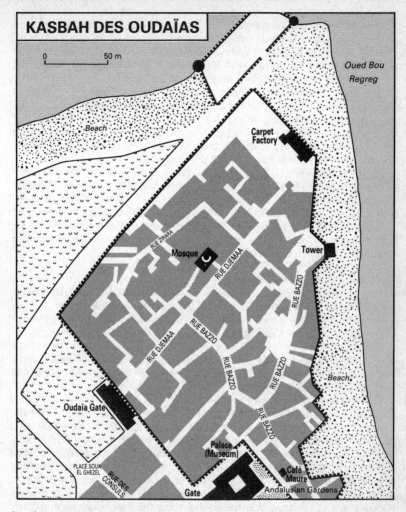

KASBAH DES OUDAÏAS

0   50 m

Oued Bou Regreg

Beach

Carpet Factory

RUE ZIRARA

Mosque

RUE DJEMAA

Tower

RUE BAZZO

RUE DJEMAA

RUE BAZZO

RUE BAZZO

RUE BAZZO

Beach

Oudaïa Gate

RUE BAZZO

PLACE SOUK EL GHEZEL

RUE DES CONSULS

Palace (Museum)

Café Maure

Gate

Andalusian Gardens

hustlers around the gate may try to suggest. Hardly more than 150m from one end to the other, it's not a place where you really need a guide; but if you're approached, talk to the hustlers, be easygoing and explain you're only wandering down to *le platforme*.

Once inside the Oudaïa Gate, it would actually be hard not to find the way down to the *platforme* since there's just one main street, **Rue Djemaa** (Street of the Mosque), which runs straight down to a broad belvedere/terrace commanding views of the river and sea. Along the way, you pass by the **Kasbah Mosque**, the city's oldest, founded in 1050, though rebuilt in the eighteenth century by an English renegade known as Ahmed el Inglise – one of a number of European pirates who joined up with the Sallee Rovers.

El Inglizi was also responsible for several of the forts built below and around the **Platforme**, their gun positions echoed across the estuary in Salé. The Bou Regreg (literally, Father of Reflection) river is quite open at this point and it would appear to have left the corsair fleets vulnerable, harboured a little downstream, where the fishing boats today ferry people across to Salé. In fact, a long sandbank lies submerged across the mouth of the estuary – a feature much exploited by the low-keeled pirate ships, which would draw the merchant ships in pursuit, only to leave them stranded within the sights of the city's cannon. This is action which you can still imagine, up here amid the low-lying alleys and the sea towers, though, as so often in Morocco, it is hard to come to terms with just how recent this past was.

From the *platforme*, it is possible to climb down towards the *Caravelle Restaurant* (a good lunch stop) and the **beach**, crowded with locals throughout the summer, as is the Salé strip across the water. Neither of these beaches, however, is particularly inviting, and if you're more interested in swimming than in keeping your head above the polluted water, you'd be better off at the more relaxed (and less exclusively male) sands at Bouknadel or Temara (see "Around Rabat", p.222).

The Palace Museum and Gardens

Getting down to the **Palace Museum** and gardens is fairly straightforward: from the main Kasbah street, Rue Gazzo zigzags down towards them.

Depending on which fork you take, you'll come out either by the entrance to the palace or at the **Café Mauré** – beside the gardens. Oddly enough, the café is not at all "Moorish", but it's a wonderful place in which to retreat: high on a terrace overlooking the river, serving excellent mint tea, Turkish coffee and great trays of traditional pastries. It is used as much by Moroccans as tourists, and is ordinarily priced.

The **Palace** itself is seventeenth-century, one of many built by Moulay Ismail, the first sultan since Almohad times to force a unified control over the country. Ismail, whose base was at Meknes, gave Rabat – or New Salé, as it was then known – a relatively high priority. Having subdued the pirates' republic, he took over the Kasbah as a garrison for the Oudaïas – Saharan tribesmen who accepted military service in return for tax exemption, and who formed an important part of his mercenary army. This move was in part because they proved uncontrollable in Fes or Meknes, but it was also an effective way of ensuring that the pirates using the port below kept up their tribute with a constant supply of slaves and booty.

Now housing a **Museum of Moroccan Arts** (8.30am–noon & 3–6pm; closed Tues; 10dh), the palace is an interesting building in its own right. Its design is classic: a series of reception rooms grouped around a central court, giving access to the private quarters where you can take a look at the small *hammam* – a feature of all noble mansions. The displays within the main building include collections of Berber and Arab jewellery from most of the regions of Morocco, while the main reception hall has been furnished in the styles of nineteenth-century Rabat and Fes. A room just off to the left as you're leaving is often kept shut, though opened on request; once the palace mosque, it houses a very fine display of local carpets.

The museum collections – including groups of traditional costumes, which again reveal the startling closeness of a medieval past – are continued in a series of rooms bordering on the beautiful "**Andalusian Garden**". Occupying the old palace grounds, this was actually constructed by the French in the present century – though true to Spanish-Andalusian tradition, with deep, sunken beds of shrubs and flowering annuals. If you've come here from Granada, it is illuminating to compare this (the authentic Moorish concept) with the neat box hedges with which the Alhambra has been restored. But historical authenticity aside, it is a really delightful place, full of the scent of datura, bougainvillea and a multitude of herbs and flowers. It has a definite role, too, in modern Rabat, as a meeting place for women, who gather here in dozens of small groups on a Friday or Sunday afternoon.

The Hassan Mosque and Mohammed V Mausoleum

The most ambitious of all Almohad buildings, the **Hassan Mosque** and its vast minaret dominates almost every view of the capital – a majestic sight from the Kasbah, from Salé, or glimpsed as you arrive across the river by train. If it had been completed, it would (in its time) have been the second largest mosque in the Islamic world, outflanked only by the one in Smarra, Iraq. Even today its size seems a novelty.

There is also the poignancy of its ruin. Designed by El Mansour as the centrepiece of the new capital and as a celebration of his great victory over the Spanish kings at Alarcos, the mosque's construction seems to have been more or less abandoned at his death in 1199. The tower was probably left much as it appears today; the mosque's hall, roofed in cedar, was used until the Great Earthquake of 1755 (which destroyed central Lisbon) brought down its central columns. Its extent, however, must always have seemed an elaborate folly. Morocco's most important mosque, the Kairaouine in Fes, is less than half the Hassan's size, but served a much greater population, with adequate space for 20,000 worshippers. Bearing in mind that it is only men who gather for the weekly Friday prayer – when a town traditionally comes together in its Grand Mosque – Rabat would have needed a population of well over 100,000 to make adequate use of the Hassan's capacity. As it was, the city never really took off under the later Almohads and Merenids, and when Leo Africanus came here in 1600, he found no more than a hundred households, gathered for security within the Kasbah.

The **tower**, or minaret, was begun by Yacoub el Mansour in 1195 – at the same time as the Koutoubia in Marrakesh and the Giralda in Seville – and it is one of the few Moroccan buildings which approach the European idea of monumentality. This is due in part to its site, on a level above the river and most of the city, but perhaps equally to its unfinished solidity. The other great Moroccan minarets, perfectly balanced by their platform decoration and lanterns, are left "hanging" as if with no particular weight or height. The Hassan Tower, with no such movement, stands firmly rooted in the ground.

The minaret is unusually positioned at the centre rather than the northern corner of the rear of the mosque. Some 50m tall in its present state, it would probably have been around 80m if finished to normal proportions – a third again the height of Marrakesh's Koutoubia. Despite its apparent simplicity, it is perhaps the most complex of all Almohad structures. Each facade is different, with a distinct combination of patterning, yet the whole intricacy of blind arcades and interlacing curves is based on just two formal designs. On the south and west faces these are the *darj w ktàrf* of the Oudaïa Gate; on the north and east are the *shabka* (net) motif, an extremely popular form adapted by the Almohads from the lobed arches of the Cordoba Grand Mosque – and still in modern use.

The Mohammed V Mausoleum

Facing the tower – in an assertion of Morocco's historical independence and continuity – are the **Mosque** and **Mausoleum of Mohammed V**, begun on the sultan's death in 1961 and dedicated six years later. The **mosque**, extending between a pair of stark white pavillions, gives a somewhat foreshortened idea of how the Hassan Mosque must once have appeared, roofed in its traditional green tiles.

The **Mausoleum**, designed, oddly, by a Korean architect, Vo Toan, was one of the great prestige projects of modern Morocco. Its brilliantly surfaced marbles and spiralling designs, however, seem to pay homage to traditional Moroccan techniques, while failing to capture their rhythms and unity. It is, nevertheless, an important shrine for Moroccans – and one which, unusually, non-Muslims are permitted to visit. You file past the fabulously costumed royal guards to an interior balcony. The tomb, carved from white onyx, lies below, groups of old men squatting beside it, reading from the Koran.

Around the Ville Nouvelle

French in construction, style and feel, the **Ville Nouvelle** provides the main focus of Rabat's life, above all in the cafés and promenades of the broad, tree-lined Avenue Mohammed V, and in the parks opposite the south wall of the Medina – popular afternoon meeting places (they close around 6pm). There's a certain grandeur in some of the old, *Mauresque* public buildings here, built with as much desire to impress as any earlier epoch, but it is the Almohad walls and gates, the citadel of Chellah (see the following section) and the excellent Archaeological Museum which hold the most interest.

The walls and gates

More-or-less complete sections of the **Almohad walls** run right down from the Kasbah to the Royal Palace and beyond – an extraordinary monument to Yacoub el Mansour's vision.

Along their course four of the original **gates** survive. Three – **Bab el Alou, Bab Zaer** and **Bab el Had** – are very modest. The fourth, **Bab er Rouah** (Gate of the Wind), is on an entirely different scale, recalling and in many ways rivalling the Oudaïa. Contained within a massive stone bastion, it again achieves the tension of movement – with its sunlike arches contained within a square of Koranic inscription – and a similar balance between simplicity and ornament. The east side, approached from outside the walls, is the main facade, and must have been designed as a monumental approach to the city;

the shallow-cut, floral relief between arch and square is arguably the finest anywhere in Morocco. Inside, you can appreciate the gate's archetypal defensive structure – the three domed chambers aligned to force a sharp double turn. They are used for art exhibitions and usually open.

From Bab er Rouah, it's a fifteen-minute walk down towards the last Almohad gate, the much-restored **Bab Zaer**, and the entrance to the **Necropolis of Chellah.** On the way, you pass a series of modern gates leading off to the vast enclosures of the **Royal Palace** – which is really more a collection of palaces, built mainly in the nineteenth century and decidedly off-limits to casual visitors – and, off to the left (opposite the *Hôtel Chellah*), the Archaeological Museum.

The Archaeological Museum

Rabat's Archaeological Museum (8.30am–noon & 2.30–6pm; closed Tues; 10dh) is by far the most important in Morocco. Although small – surprisingly so in a country which saw substantial Phoenician and Carthaginian settlement and three centuries of Roman rule – it houses a quite exceptional and beautiful collection of Roman era bronzes.

The bronzes – displayed in an annexe distinct from the main collections – date from the first and second centuries AD and were found mainly at the provincial capital of Volubilis (see p.139), though there are a few pieces from Chellah and the small coastal colonies of Banasa and Thamusidia. Highlights include superb figures of a guard dog and a rider, and two magnificent portrait heads, reputedly those of Cato the Younger (Caton d'Utique) and Juba II – the last significant ruler of the Romanised Berber kingdoms of Mauretania and Numidia before the assertion of direct imperial rule. Both of these busts were found in the House of Venus at Volubilis.

The Chellah Necropolis

The most beautiful of Moroccan ruins, **Chellah** (open sunrise to sunset; 10dh) is a startling sight as you emerge from the long avenues of the Ville Nouvelle. Walled and towered, it seems a much larger enclosure than the map suggests, and it feels for a moment as if you've come upon a second Medina. The site is, in fact, long uninhabited – since 1154, when it was abandoned in favour of Salé across the Bou Regreg. But for almost a thousand years prior to that, Chellah (or *Sala Colonia*, as it was known) had been a thriving city and port, one of the last to sever links with the Roman Empire and the first to proclaim Moulay Idriss founder of Morocco's original Arab dynasty. An apocryphal local tradition maintains that the Prophet himself also prayed at a shrine here.

Under the Almohads, the site was already a royal burial ground, but most of what you see today, including the gates and enclosing wall, is the legacy of the Merenid sultan, **Abou el Hassan** (1331–51). The greatest of Merenid rulers, conquering and controlling the Maghreb as far east as Tunis, Abou el Hassan, "The Black Sultan", was also their most prolific builder. In addition to Chellah, he was responsible for important mosques in Fes and Tlemcen, as well as the beautiful *medersas* of Salé and Meknes.

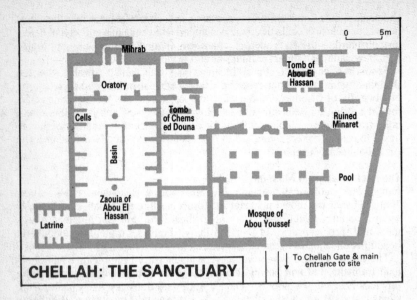

0   5m

Mihrab

Oratory

Tomb of
Abou El
Hassan

Cells

Tomb
of Chems
ed Douna

Ruined
Minaret

Basin

Pool

Zaouia of
Abou El
Hassan

Latrine

Mosque of
Abou Youssef

To Chellah Gate & main
entrance to site

CHELLAH: THE SANCTUARY

The **main gate** here is the most surprising of Merenid monuments, its turreted bastions creating an almost Gothic appearance. Its base is recognisably Almohad, but each element has become inflated, and the combination of simplicity and solidity has gone. In its original state, with bright-coloured marble and tile decoration, the effect must have been incredibly gaudy – a bit like the nineteenth-century palaces you see today in Fes and Marrakesh. An interesting technical innovation, however, are the stalactite (or "honeycomb") corbels which form the transition from the bastion's semioctagonal towers to their square platforms; these were to become a feature of Merenid building. The Kufic inscription above the gate is from the Koran and begins with the invocation: "I take refuge in Allah, against Satan, the stoned one . . . "

There are usually a number of guides hanging around the gate, but hiring them is not mandatory – once inside, things are clear enough. Off to your left, in a state of long-suspended excavation, are the main **Roman ruins** (currently closed for excavation), including the visible outlines of a forum, temple and craftsmen's quarter. The **Islamic ruins** are down to the right, within a second inner sanctuary approached along a broad path through half-wild gardens of banana, orange and ancient fig trees, sunflowers, dahlias and datura plants. Their most prominent and picturesque feature is a tall stone-and-tile minaret, a ludicrously oversized stork's nest perched invariably on its summit. Storks, along with swallows and crows, have a certain sanctity in Morocco, and their presence on minarets is a sign of good fortune.

The Sanctuary

The sanctuary itself appears a confusing cluster of tombs and ruins, but it is essentially just two buildings: a mosque, built by the second Merenid sultan,

Abou Youssef (1258–86), and a *zaouia*, or mosque-monastery, added along with the enclosure walls by Abou el Hassan. You enter directly into the *sahn*, or courtyard, of **Abou Youssef's Mosque**, a small and presumably private structure built as a funerary dedication. It is now very much in ruins, though you can make out the colonnades of the inner prayer hall with its *mihrab* to indicate the direction of prayer. Off to the right is its minaret, now reduced to the level of the mosque's roof.

Behind, both within and outside the sanctuary enclosure, are a series of scattered **royal tombs** – each aligned so that the dead, dressed in white and lying on their right hand sides, may face Mecca to await the Call of Judgment. Abou Youssef's tomb has not been identified, but you can find those of both **Abou el Hassan** and his wife **Shams ed Douna**. Hassan's is contained within a kind of pavilion whose external wall retains its decoration, the *darj w ktarf* motif set above three small arches in a design very similar to that of the Hassan Tower. Shams ed Douna, (Morning Sun) has only a tomb-stone – a long, pointed rectangle covered in a mass of verses from the Koran. A convert from Christianity, Shams was the mother of Abou el Hassan's rebel son, Abou Inan, whose uprising led to the sultan's death as a fugitive in the High Atlas during the winter of 1352.

The **Zaouia** is in a much better state of preservation, its structure, like Abou el Hassan's *medersas,* that of a long, central court enclosed by cells, with a smaller oratory or prayer hall at the end. Each of these features is quite recognisable, along with those of the latrine, preceding the main court, for the worshippers' purification. There are fragments of *zellij* (mosaic tile-work) on some of the colonnades and on the minaret, which again give an idea of its original brightness, and there are traces too of the *mihrab's* elaborate stucco decoration. Five-sided, the **mihrab** has a narrow passageway (now blocked with brambles) leading to the rear – built so that pilgrims might make seven circuits around it. This was once believed to give the equivalent merit of the *hadj*, the trip to Mecca: a tradition, with that of Muhammad's visit, probably invented and propagated by the *zaouia's* keepers to increase their revenue.

Off to the right and above the sanctuary enclosure are a group of **koubbas** – the domed tombs of local saints or *marabouts* – and beyond them a **spring pool**, enclosed by low, vaulted buildings. This is held sacred, along with the eels which swim in its waters, and women still bring hard-boiled eggs to invoke assistance in fertility and childbirth.

Eating and drinking

For a capital city, Rabat's potential for fun – and even for eating well – is not very impressive. The city's practical attractions rest mainly in its cafés and in its access to beaches (see the sections following).

Restaurants

As ever, the cheapest restaurants are to be found **in the Medina**. Just on the edge of the quarter, down Rue Mohammed V and along Rue Souika, there are a string of good everyday café-restaurants – clean enough and serving regular Moroccan fare. They are excellent value at lunchtime, when many have fixed-price meals for the office and shop workers. Alternatively, for only a few dirhams, you can pick up a range of snacks and juices just inside the Medina walls (by the market on our map).

In the **Ville Nouvelle** most of the restaurants are grouped around the train station and Avenue Moulay Youssef (the diagonal street behind it); except during Ramadan, most stop serving about 9.30–10pm. Worthwhile choices include:

Restaurant l'Oasis, 7 Rue Al Osquofiah (close to the train station). Well-prepared and inexpensive Moroccan food.

Restaurant El Bahia, Bd. Hassan II (built into the walls, with a courtyard, close by the junction with Av. Mohammed V). Reasonably priced *tajines*, kebabs and salads, of fluctuating quality. Popular with travellers.

Le Clef, just off Av. Moulay Youssef; **Restaurant Saadi**, 87 Av. Allal Ben Abdallah; **Les Fouquets**, 285 Av. Mohammed V. These are all slightly classier but still with good value set meals.

Hôtel Balima, Av. Mohammed V. Inexpensive dishes in the snackbar; pricier ones (and full service) in the main restaurant (open from 8.30pm).

Restaurant Saïdoune, set back in a mall off Av. Mohammed V, opposite the *Hôtel Terminus*. Excellent and not too expensive Lebanese restaurant.

Le Pagode, 5 Rue de Baghdad; **Le Mandarin**, 44 Av. Abdel Krim El Khattabi. Two Chinese restaurants for a change of cuisine.

Cafés, bars and nightlife

Avenues Mohammed V and Allal Ben Abdallah have some excellent **cafés**, though **bars** (outside the main hotels) are few and far between. The one at the *Hôtel Balima* is as good a place as any; it tends to stay open late, if there are customers, and it is popular with Moroccans – many of whom come to watch Sky Channel on its TV.

After the *Balima* has closed, about the only **late-night options** are a string of **disco-bars** around Place de Melilla (east of the Parc du Triangle de Vue) and on Rue Patrice Lumumba – where you'll find the *Biba* and *Jefferson* discos. The *Baghdad Bar* on Zankat Tanto might also fill the odd hour.

Listings

Airlines *Royal Air Maroc* is just down from the train station on Av. Mohammed V; *Air France* is on the same avenue at no. 281; *Iberia* at no. 104 (2nd floor).

American Express had an office in the *Rabat Hilton,* but the hotel is currently closed for refurbishment and *AmEx* temporarily unrepresented. Check with the tourist office (see below) for any change. Otherwise, Casablanca has the nearest office.

Banks Most are along Av. Allal Ben Abdallah and Av. Mohammed V. The *BMCE* (change facilities open daily 8.30am–2pm and 3–8pm) have offices at 241 Av. Mohammed V and at the port train station; they handle *VISA/Mastercard*, travellers' cheques and cash.

Beaches Nearest are the Kasbah and Salé beaches, with the latter best reached by the ferry leaving from below the Mellah. For clearer waters, head by bus to either Plage des Nations or Temara, detailed in the section following Salé.

NORTH AND WEST AFRICAN VISAS

The following North and West African nations have consulates, with visa issuing facilities, in Rabat:

Algeria, 46 Bd. Tariq Ibn Ziad (☎650.92).

Côte d'Ivoire, BP 192, 21 Zankat Tiddas (☎631.51).

Guinea, 2 Zankat Mokla, Orangers (☎327.05).

Mauritania, 6 Rue Thami Lamdouar, Souissi (☎568.17).

Nigeria, BP 347, 70 Av. Omar Ibn al-Khattab, Agdal (☎718.56).

Senegal, 17 Rue Cadi ben Hammadi Senhadji, Souissi (☎541.48).

Tunisia, 6 Av. de Fass (☎256.44).

The **French Consulate** at 3 Rue Sahnoun (☎778.22) issues visas for most of the other West African states, other than Sierra Leone, for which visas are issued by the **UK Consulate**, 17 Bd. Tour Hassan (☎209.05).

The **Algerian consulate** is open Mon–Fri 9.30am–2.30pm. Getting a visa is straightforward enough, and if you turn up at 8.30am, you should be able to collect it the same day: take along four passport photographs and the 60dh fee.

The **Tunisian consulate** issue visas on the spot (26dh for a week, 34dh a month).

Books The *American Bookstore* (Rue Tanja: see map) has a good selection of Penguin novels, etc., along with an enterprising shelf on Moroccan architecture, Islam and some of Paul Bowles's translations of Moroccan fiction. Another useful bookshop is to be found at 7 Zankat Alyamama, just behind the British Council (see below and map); this stocks and exchanges a wide selection of secondhand paperbacks.You can get Moroccan Arabic-French phrasebooks from several of the bookshops along Av. Mohammed V.

British Council, 3 Zankat Descartes, one block from the town train station (☎693.61). Operates a small library, with UK papers available for browsing, and puts on various films and events in English. Also a possible source of information if you want to stay on in Morocco and teach English. Open Mon–Fri 9.30am–noon and 2.30–5.45; closed Monday mornings. There are papers available, too, at the George Washington Library, 35 Av. de Fass.

Car hire *Leasing Cars,* usually the cheapest option, have an office in Casa (see that city's listings) but not in Rabat. Here, you're dependent on the usuals: *Hertz* (467 Av. Mohammed V; ☎344.75), *Avis* (7 Rue Abou Faris Al Mairini; ☎697.59) and *Marloc/InterHire* (inside the *Hôtel Tour Hassan*, Av. Annegai; ☎223.228). *Tourist Cars* (inside the *Hôtel Rex*, 1 Rue de Nador; ☎241.10) may be able to offer slightly better rates.

Car repairs Try *Concorde* (6 Av. Allal Ben Abdallah) or, particularly for Renaults, the garage at 14 Av. Misr.

Embassies and Consulates *Great Britain* (17 Bd. Tour Hassan; ☎209.05 or 314.03); *Ireland* (representation c/o Britain); *Australia* (representation c/o Canada). *U.S.* (2 Av. de Marrakesh – near the far end of Allal Ben Abdallah; ☎622.65); *Canada* (13 Zankat Joafar Essadik; ☎713.75); Most are open from around 8.30–11.30am, Mon–Fri, though you can phone at any time in an emergency. See box above for African consulates.

Galleries Unusual for Morocco, Rabat has a number of worthwhile art galleries, showing works by contemporary artists. *L'Atelier* (16 Rue Annaba) is the major dealer; try also *Galerie Marsam* (6 Rue Oskofiah) and *Galerie Le Mamoir* (7 Rue Baitlahm).

Golf The *Royal Dar es Salaam* golfcourse, on the outskirts of Rabat, is the country's finest – featuring two 18-hole and one 9-hole course designed by Robert Trent-Jones.

Libraries Both the *British Council* (6 Av. Moulay Youssef) and the *American Embassy* (Annex on Av. Allal Ben Abdallah) have library rooms where you can walk in and read newspapers and magazines. They can also put you in touch with people if you want to take **lessons in Moroccan Arabic**.

Hiking maps Topographic maps used to be sold, on production of a passport, at the *Division de la Cartographie*, Ministère de l'Agriculture et de la Réforme Agraire (MARA), 31 Av. Moulay Hassan. At present sales of survey maps are suspended – but if you are planning to hike in the Atlas, the office may still be worth a call.

Police Central office in Rue Soekarno, a couple of blocks from Av. Mohammed V. ☎19.

Post office The *PTT Centrale* – 24hr a day for phones – is halfway down Av. Mohammed V. The *poste restante* section is across the road from the main building. The PTT also maintains a small **philatelic museum**, with displays and sales of Moroccan stamps.

Public baths Beside the *Hôtel Rex,* just off Bd. Hassan II.

Tourist offices *ONMT* (22 Av. Al Jazair); *Syndicat d'Initiative* (Rue Patrice Lumumba); both are open Mon–Sat 8am–noon, with the *Syndicat* open on weekday afternoons as well. The *ONMT Dépot* in Av. Moulay Ismail (next to a branch of the Banque Populaire, a short walk from Place Melilla) has a "cave" full of the whole range of Moroccan tourist posters and will give you as many as you can carry away.

Salé

Although it is now essentially a suburb of Rabat, **SALÉ** was the pre-eminent of the two right through the Middle Ages, from the decline of the Almohads to the town's uneasy alliance in the pirate republic of Bou Regreg. Today, largely neglected since the French creation of a capital in Rabat, it looks and feels very distinct. The spread of a Ville Nouvelle outside its walls has been restricted to a small area around the bus station and the north gates, and the *souks* and life within its medieval limits remain surprisingly traditional.

Access and orientation

From Rabat you can cross the river to Salé by **boat** (see the map), or take a **bus** (#6 or #12) from Bd. Hassan II. The boats charge one dirham per person and drop you close to the Salé beach; from here it's a steep walk up to **Bab Bou Haja**, one of the main town gates. Both buses drop you at an open terminal just below the train station, opposite another major gate, **Bab Fes**, which leads straight towards the *souks*.

Salé has a basic and somewhat shadeless **campsite**, *Camping de Salé*, at its beach, and a small **hotel**, the *Saadiens*, by the bus station. But unless you want to use the campsite as a base for Rabat, there seems little reason to stay. It is an interesting town to wander through for an afternoon, and you can eat at one of the many workers' **cafés** along Rue Kechachin, but, if anything, its streets empty even earlier than Rabat's.

Into the Medina: the *Souks*

The most interesting point to enter Salé's Medina is through **Bab Mrisa**, just south of the bus terminal. The gate's name – "of the small harbour" – recalls the marine arsenal which used to be sited within the walls, and explains the

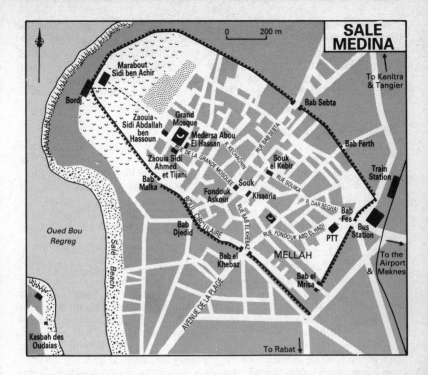

gate's unusual height. A channel running here from the Bou Regreg has long silted up, but in medieval times it allowed merchant ships to sail right into town, a device that must have been useful during the years of the pirate republic. The gate itself is a very early Merenid structure of the 1270s, its design and motifs (palmettes enclosed by floral decoration; bands of Kufic inscription and *darj w ktarf*, etc.) still inherently Almohad in tone.

Inside the gate you'll find yourself in a small square, at the bottom of the old Mellah quarter. Turning to the left and continuing close to the walls, you come out after around 350m at another gate, **Bab Bou Haja**, beside a small park. If you want to explore the *souks* – the route outlined below – take the road along the left hand side of the park. If not, continue on just inside the walls to a long open area; as this starts to narrow into a lane (about 40m further down) veer to your right into the town. This should bring you out more or less at the **Grand Mosque,** opposite which (see overpage) is the **Medersa of Abou el Hassan.**

The park-side street from Bab Bou Haja is **Rue Bab el Khabaz** (Street of the Bakers' Gate), a busy little lane which emerges at the heart of the **souks** by a small *kissaria* (covered market) devoted mainly to textiles. Most of the alleys here are grouped around specific crafts, a particular speciality here being the pattern-weave mats produced for the sides and floors of mosques.

From the *kissaria,* the Medina's main street, **Rue de la Grande Mosque** leads uphill through the middle of town to the Grand Mosque. This is the simplest approach, but you can take in more of the *souks* by following **Rue Kechachin,** parallel but slightly above it (away from the river walls). Along Kechachin are located the carpenters and stone-carvers, as well as other craftsmen. In **Rue Haddadin,** a fairly major intersection which leads off to its right up towards Bab Sebta, you'll come upon gold- and coppersmiths.

The Grand Mosque and Medersa

As far as buildings go, the **Grand Mosque** marks the most interesting part of town, its surrounding lanes fronting a concentration of aristocratic mansions and religious *zaouia* foundations. Almohad in origin, the mosque is one of the largest and earliest in Morocco, though what you can see as a non-Muslim (the gateway and minaret) are recent additions.

You can, however, visit its **Medersa** (10dh admission), opposite the mosque's monumental, stepped main entrance. Salé's main monument and recently restored, it was founded in 1341 by Sultan Abou el Hassan (see Chellah, in Rabat), and is thus more or less contemporary with the Bou Inania *medersas* in Meknes and Fes. Like them, it follows the basic Merenid plan of a central courtyard opening on to a prayer hall, with a series of cells for the students – for whom these "university halls" were endowed – around its upper floors. If this is the first example you've seen, it will come as a surprise after the sparse Almohad economy of the monuments in Rabat. The great Merenid *medersas* are all intensely decorated – in carved wood, stucco and *zellij* – and this is no exception. As you stand within the entrance gate, there is hardly an inch of space which doesn't draw the eye away into a web of intricacy.

What is remarkable, though, despite a certain heaviness which the great Merenid *medersas* manage to avoid, is the way in which each aspect of the workmanship succeeds in forging a unity with the others, echoing and repeating the standard patterns in endless variations. The patterns, for the most part, derive from Almohad models, with their stylised geometric and floral motifs, but in the latter there is a much more naturalistic, less abstracted approach. There is also a new stress on calligraphy, with monumental inscriptions carved in great bands on the dark cedarwood and incorporated within the stucco and *zellij.* Almost invariably these are in the elaborate cursive script, and they are generally passages from the Koran. There are occasional poems, however, such as the beautiful foundation inscription, set in marble against a green background, on the rear wall of the court, which begins:

> *Look at my admirable portal!*
> *Rejoice in my chosen company,*
> *In the remarkable style of my construction*
> *And my marvellous interior!*
> *The workers here have accomplished an artful*
> *Creation with the beauty of youth. . . .**

---

* Quoted in translation from a French book by Charles Terrasse in Richard B. Parker's *Islamic Monuments in Morocco* (Baraka Press, Virginia).

The *medersa* is only sporadically visited and you'll probably have it to yourself (except for the sparrows and the caretaker) – a quiet, meditative place. Close to its entrance there is a stairway up to the old, windowless cells of the students and to the **roof**, where, looking out across the river to Rabat, you sense the enormity of the Hassan Tower.

Marabouts and Moussems

Out beyond the *medersa,* a street runs down the near side of the Grand Mosque to emerge amid a vast and very ancient **cemetery**, at the far end of which you can see (though you should not approach) the white *koubba* and associated buildings of the **Marabout of Sidi ben Achir**. Sometimes known as "Al Tabib" (The Doctor), Ben Achir was a fourteenth-century ascetic from Andalusia. His shrine, said to have the ability to attract shipwrecks and quell storms – good pirate virtues – is a reputed cure for blindness, paralysis and madness. Enclosed by nineteenth-century pilgrim lodgings, it still has its devotees and a considerable annual *moussem*, or pilgrimage festival.

The most important of Salé's *moussems,* however, is that of its patron saint, **Sidi Abdallah ben Hassoun**, whose **zaouia** stands just to the right of the road, a few steps before you come out at the cemetery. The saint, who for Muslim travellers plays a role similar to St. Christopher, lived in Salé during the sixteenth century, though the origins and significance of his *moussem* are unclear. Taking place each year on the eve of *Mouloud* – the Prophet's birthday – it involves a spectacular procession through the streets of the town with local boatmen, dressed in corsair costumes, carrying huge and elaborate wax lanterns mounted on giant poles.

North of Rabat: the Jardins Exotiques and Plage des Nations

Respectively 12km and 18km from Rabat, the **Jardins Exotiques** and **Plage des Nations** provide the capital's most enjoyable excursions. The first, as its name suggests, is a French colonial creation of botanical extravagance; the second, an immense stretch of fine shore, which, together with Temara (see the next section), is *the* sophisticated local beach.

Both gardens and beach can be reached by bus #28 from the **Salé terminal** (every 20min). The bus stops and turns around a few kilometres before it reaches the turnoff for the **Plage** (which is where everyone will be heading). For the **Jardins** you'll have to ask the driver to let you off – the entrance is just to the left of the road and there's a bus stop 20m beyond the turning. Alternatively, there are regular *grands taxis* direct to the beach from Salé, or you could charter a taxi from Rabat.

The Jardins Exotiques

The **Jardins Exotiques**, laid out by one M. François in the early 1950s, in what the French guidebooks call *"une manière remarquable"*, have obviously seen better days – a fact which adds considerably to their charm.

They are crowded with precarious bamboo bridges and bizarre, dot-directed routes which direct you (in various time permutations) through a sequence of brilliant regional creations. There is a Brazilian rain forest, dense with water and orchids; a formal Japanese garden; and then suddenly a great shaft of French Polynesia, with rickety summerhouses set amid long pools, turtles paddling past you, palm trees all around and terrific flashes of bright-red flowers. And, finally, on a more local level, there is also a superbly maintained Andalusian garden and a fine collection of Moroccan plants.

The gardens are open daily from sunrise to sunset; 10dh admission.

On to Plage des Nations

There is a good modern road right down to the Plage des Nations, but the #28 bus (which you can hail from the stop outside the Jardins) turns round some way before this turnoff – just after the village of BOUKNADEL, by a café in what seems to be the middle of nowhere. Everybody gets out here and takes the diagonal path off towards the sea and a cape past a couple of farms, around some woods and then joining the tail end of the asphalt road down to the beach itself.

After this approach, you imagine a rather wild beach, with battered cliffs and a few picnic groups. **PLAGE DES NATIONS**, or SIDI BOUKNADEL as it's also known, is nothing of the kind. Flanked by a couple of beach cafés and the 4*A *Hôtel Firdaous* (☎451.86), a slick modern complex with a freshwater pool (open to all for a small charge), it seems more westernised than Rabat itself. Certainly, unlike the Kasbah or Salé beaches, it's a resort where young Rabat women feel able to come out for the day, rather than suffer the uncontestedly male domination of the city's beaches. And with everyone here to take a day's holiday, it's a very relaxed and friendly sort of place. The beach itself is excellent, with big, exciting waves – but dangerous currents, so it is patrolled by lifeguards along the central strip.

South towards Casablanca

It's a little over an hour by *grand taxi* from Rabat to Casa (under an hour by express train) and there's little en route to delay your progress. The landscape, wooded in parts, is a low, flat plain, punctuated only by the resort centre and industrial port of **Mohammedia**, and turnoffs for a few, local beach resorts, like **Temara** and **Skhirat**. These are popular weekend escapes from Rabat and Casablanca, and as such, have an attraction. In summer, especially, they can be lively – and remain so well into the night.

Rabat to Mohammedia

TEMARA PLAGE, 16km southwest of Rabat (just twenty minutes by *grand taxi* from the rank on Bd. Hassan II), is probably the best of the bunch. Flanked by a number of discos, it also provides a summer alternative to the lack of action in Rabat. Few people stay here overnight, other than the local rich at their summer villas, though if you want to, there's a **campsite** and two

hotels, the 3*A *La Felouque* and unrated *Hôtel Casino*. The *Felouque* has an excellent French-style restaurant.

Bus #17 leaves Rabat from Av. Hassan II, running past a turnoff to Temara Zoo (best avoided) before arriving at the small town of TEMARA VILLE, with its Kasbah ruins and a very swish French restaurant, *Le Provencal*. From the town, it's a four-kilometre walk to the beach.

Ech Chiana

ECH CHIANA, 9km south from Temara, is in a smaller but similar vein; again with a luxury **hotel** (the 4*B *Kasbah Club*, ☎416.33 – largely frequented by French package tourists), a cheap **auberge** (the unclassified *Gambusia*) and small, well maintained **campsite** (☎423.07).

Skhirat Plage

There is a distinctly classier shift as you approach **SKHIRAT PLAGE** and Hassan II's summer **Royal Palace**, the site of a notorious coup attempt by senior Moroccan generals during his birthday celebrations in July 1971. The coup was mounted using a force of Berber cadets, who took over the palace, imprisoned King Hassan and massacred a number of his guests. It came within hours of being successful, being thwarted, ironically, by the apparently accidental shooting of the cadets' leader, General Mohammed Medbuh.

The palace today still forms the centrepiece of a somewhat exclusive resort. However, there are two regular **hotels** – the unclassified *Auberge Potinière* and, south of the town, the 3*B *Amphitrite* (☎422.36).

The easiest access to Skhirat Plage is by train. All slow trains on the Rabat-Casa line run through the town of SKHIRAT, a couple of kilometres from the beach. If you are driving, there are a couple of further turn-offs to beaches at BOUZNIKA (*Camping Dahoney*) and ESSANOUBAR, before you reach Mohammedia.

Mohammedia

The port of **MOHAMMEDIA** has a somewhat split identity. Boosted by its proximity to Casablanca and the Plateau des Phosphates inland, it has developed a considerable industrial and commercial base, including major petrochemical refineries, and a population of some 70,000. Yet it also has one of the best beaches on the Atlantic and has long been a holiday pleasure ground for Casablanca. In addition to its excellent five-kilometre-long beach, the city boasts a racecourse, 18-hole golf course, casino and yacht marina.

For foreign visitors, there is no great attraction, and there are no monuments to speak of, save for a Portuguese-built Kasbah. If you do want to stay, check the ONMT hotel list for facilities at any number of big luxury hotels, which, together with dozens of restaurants and discos, line the beach. Cheaper **hotels** are scattered about the area inland from the Kasbah, close by the **train station**; try the *Hôtel Ennasr*, or, as fallback choices, the *Hôtel des Voyageurs* or *Hôtel Castel*.

The best **restaurant** in the town, if you are willing to pay high prices for well-prepared fish, is *Chez Irene*, by the port.

Casablanca (Casa, Dar El Baida)

The principal city of Morocco, and capital in all but administration, **CASABLANCA** (*Dar el Baida* in its literal Arabic form) is now the largest port of the Maghreb – busier even than Marseilles, the city on which it was modelled by the French. Its development, from a town of 20,000 in 1906, has been astonishingly rapid and quite ruthlessly deliberate. When the French landed their forces here in 1907 (and established their Protectorate five years later), it was Fes which was Morocco's commercial centre, and Tangier was its main port. Had Tangier not been in international hands, this probably would have remained the case. Instead, the demands of an independent colonial administration forced the French to seek an entirely new base. Casa, at the heart of *Maroc Utile*, the country's most fertile zone and centre of its mineral deposits, was a natural choice.

Superficially, Casa is today much like any other large Western city – a familiarity which makes it fairly easy to get your bearings and a revelation as you begin to understand something of its life. It is a genuinely dynamic city, still growing at a rate of 50,000 people a year. Arriving here from the south, or even from Fes or Tangier, most of the preconceptions you've been travelling around with will be happily shattered.

Casa's Westernised image – with the almost total absence of women wearing veils and its fancy beach clubs – shields, however, what is still substantially a "first-generation" city and one which inevitably has some of Morocco's most intense social problems. Alongside its wealth and a handful of showpiece developments – it recently hosted the Mediterranean Games – it has had since its formation a reputation for extreme poverty, prostitution, *bidonville* shantytowns and social unrest. The *bidonville* problem resulted partly from the sheer extent of population increases (over 1 million in the 1960s), partly because few of the earlier migrants intended to stay permanently – sending back most of their earnings to their families in the country*.

The pattern is now much more towards permanent settlement, and this, together with a strict control of migration and a limited number of self-help programmes, have eased and cleared many of the worst slums. The problem of a concentrated urban poor, however, is more enduring and represents, as it did for the French, an intermittent threat to government stability. Casa, through the 1940s and 1950s, was the main centre of anti-French rioting, and it was the city's working class, too, which formed the base of Ben Barka's Socialist Party. There have been strikes here sporadically since independence, and on several occasions, most violently in the food strikes of 1982, they have precipitated rioting. Whether Casa's development can be sustained, and the lot of its new migrants improved, must decide much of Morocco's future.

---

* **Bidonville dwellers** have been accorded increasing respect in recent years. They cannot be evicted if they have lived in a property over two years, and after ten years they acquire title to the land and building, which can be used as collateral at the bank for loans. The dread of every bidonville family is to be evicted and put in a high rise block, which are regarded as the lowest of the low on the housing ladder.

Arrival, orientation and hotels

A large city by any standards, Casa can be a confusing place in which to arrive – particularly if you're on one of the trains that stop at the main **Gare des Voyageurs** (2km from the centre) rather than continuing on to the better-situated **Gare du Port.**

Once you're in the city, though, things are pretty simple. There are two main squares – **Place Mohammed V** and **Place des Nations Unies** – and most of the places to stay, to eat, or (in a rather limited way) see, are located in and around the avenues off to their sides. The **Old Medina**, *the* town of Casablanca until around 1907, remains largely within its walls behind Place Mohammed V (which was formerly the site of its weekly *souk*). The **New Medina**, an entirely French creation, lies a couple of kilometres south. And beyond this, it is only the beach suburb of **Aïn Diab**, west of the port, which you're likely to want to explore.

The Casablanca tourist pamphlet has a fairly clear map of the city, covering a larger area than ours and detailing Aïn Diab, the Gare des Voyageurs and the New Medina (labelled *Habbous*, its local name). You can pick this up in advance from any Moroccan tourist office, or here from the **ONMT** (55 Rue Omar Slaoui) or **Syndicat d'Initiative** (98 Bd. Mohammed V).

Getting around within the city, **petits taxis** are easy to find along the main avenues and are invariably metered – as long as the meter is switched on you will rarely pay more than 6dh per taxi for a trip around town. For Aïn Diab the fare is currently 16dh (2–3dh extra if you get the driver to detour en route around the new Hassan II Mosque). There is a 20 percent surcharge at night.

Points of arrival

● **By train.** Most of the **trains** from Marrakesh run to both stations, allowing you to stay on until the **Gare du Port**, 150m from Place Mohammed V. From Rabat (and Fes/Tangier), however, trains sometimes terminate at the **Gare des Voyageurs**, at the far end of Bd. Mohammed V. From here, if you're quick and very determined, you might just get a place on bus #30, which runs into town from the square in front of the station; otherwise, reckon on a twenty-minute walk or a *petit taxi* ride. Bd. Mohammed V runs straight ahead from the square in front of the station, curving slightly to the left as you come to the next main square (Place Albert 1er).

● **By bus.** Bus stations are more central and straightforward. All the *CTM* buses arrive at the *CTM Gare Routière* on Rue Léon l'Africain (off Rue Colbert, centre-right on our map). Private line buses use a terminal below Place de la Victoire (in the Alsace-Lorraine quarter).

● **By grand taxi.** *Grands taxis* usually stop just behind the *CTM Gare Routière* (see buses, above), by the *Hôtel Safir*.

● **By air.** Coming from the **Aeroport Mohammed V**, used by all international and most domestic flights, there is a shuttle bus to/from the CTM Gare Routière. Specify you want *le prochain départ*. For flights at odd hours, or if you can share costs, a *grand taxi* (200dh for the whole taxi) can be a reassurance, especially if you are catching a flight out of the country.

CASABLANCA

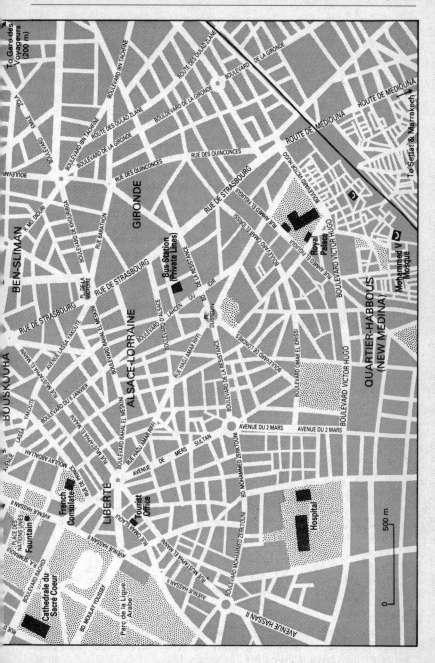

To Gare des
Voyageurs
(200 m)

BEN-SLIMAN

BOUSKOURA

BOULEVARD EMILE ZOLA

BOULEVARD IBN TACHFINE

BOULEVARD IBN TACHFINE

ROUTE DES OULAD ZIANE

BOULEVARD DE LA GIRONDE

BOULEVARD

R. MD DIOURI

BOULEVARD DE KHOURIBGA

RUE BARATHON

PL. DE LA
VICTOIRE

RUE DES QUINCONCES

RUE DES QUINCONCES

RUE DE STRASBOURG

GIRONDE

RUE DE STRASBOURG

Bus Station
(Private Lines)

RUE DE STRASBOURG

RUE DE STRASBOURG

BOULEVARD D'ALSACE

BOULEVARD RAHAL EL MESKINI

AVENUE LASSA YAQUTE

ALSACE-LORRAINE

BOULEVARD DU 11 JANVER

RUE MUSTAPHEL MANN

RUE MUSTAPHA EL MAANI

RUE HADJ AMAR RIFFI

RUE HADJ AMAR RIFFI

BOULEVARD RAHAL EL MESKINI

BOULEVARD D'ALSACE

BOULEVARD DE LAHCEN OU

BD DIR

DUBREUIL

DE LA RESISTANCE

BOULEVARD DE LA RESISTANCE

BOULEVARD DE LONDRES

RUE AHMED EL FIGUIGUI

BOULEVARD OMAR EL DRISSI

RUE AHMED EL DRISSI

BOULEVARD VICTOR HUGO

Royal
Palace

ROUTE DE MEDIOUNA

ROUTE DE MEDIOUNA

RUE DE STRASBOURG

BOULEVARD VICTOR HUGO

BOULEVARD OMAR EL DRISSI

Mohammed V
Mosque

QUARTIER-HABBOUS
(NEW MEDINA)

To Settat & Marrakech

AVENUE DU 2 MARS

AVENUE DU 2 MARS

AVENUE DE MERS SULTAN

BOULEVARD MOHAMMED ZERKTOUNI

BD. MOHAMMED ZERKTOUNI

Hospital

AVENUE HASSAN II

RUE MUSTAPHA EL MANN

BOULEVARD MOHAMMED ZERKTOUNI

AVENUE HASSAN II

500 m

0

French
Consulate

LIBERTÉ

Tourist
Office

RUE OMAR SLAOUI

AVENUE HASSAN II

RUE DE FRANCE

MOULAY ABDALLAH

AVENUE H LASSA YAQUTE

AVENUE HASSAN II

Fountain

PLACE DES
NATIONS UNIES

BD MOULAY YOUSSEF

Parc de la Ligue
Arabe

Cathédrale du
Sacré Coeur

BOULEVARD RACHDI

LA SEMBRAUK

BD. MOULAY YOUSSEF

RUE D

Hotels

Hotels are plentiful in Casa, though they operate at near capacity for much of the year. If at all possible, phone ahead for a room, or at least arrive fairly early in the day.

All of the recommendations below are for hotels in the main, **central area** of the city and are listed in ascending order of price. As in Rabat, the Medina hotels are overpriced, with most of them charging the equivalent of 2* prices for miserable rooms; many of the cheaper one- and two-star places, by contrast, are quite stylish art deco buildings.

Youth Hostel (*Auberge de Jeunesse*), 6 Place Admiral Philbert (☎22.05.51). A friendly, airy place, nicely sited just inside the Medina, and – after a very ropey period – currently well maintained. To reach it from Gare du Port, walk up Bd. Houphouet Boigny, then turn left along Bd. des Almohades and take the first opening on the Medina walls to your left. The hostel's on your right at the near side of a square.

Hôtel Les Negociants (E), Hôtel Bon Reve (F), Rue Allal Ben Abdallah. The two best options in a promising area for cheap, more or less reasonable, hotels. A third choice, the **Hôtel Kon Tiki**, is further down the same street at no. 89. *All unclassified.*

Hôtel du Périgord (B), 56 Rue de Foucauld. Arguably the best of the unstarred hotels. *Unclassified.*

Hôtel du Louvre (I), 36 Rue Nationale (☎27.37.47). Standard prices for its class, but not much to be said for the rooms. *1*B.*

Hôtel de Foucauld (C), 52 Rue de Foucauld (☎22.26.66). Next door to the *Périgord*. *1*A.*

Hôtel Touring (D), 87 Rue Allal Ben Abdallah (☎31.02.16). A popular choice, with Art Deco touches. Best try this before its unclassified neighbours – whose prices are similar. *1*A.*

Hôtel Colbert, 30 Rue Colbert (☎31.42.41). Useful location if you arrive by bus – it's just around the corner from the CTM. A bit gloomy but more or less clean rooms. *1*A.*

Hôtel Rialto (G), 9 Rue Claude (☎27.51.22). A good, safe bet, with a *hammam* next door. *1*A.* (The unclassified *Hôtel de France*, opposite, is tolerable).

Hôtel Guynemer, 2 Rue Pégoud (☎27.57.64). Pleasant, clean rooms in an attractive, "seen-better-days" hotel. *2*B.*

Grand Hôtel de Paris, 2 Rue Branly (☎27.38.71). Smaller rooms, otherwise pretty similar to the *Guynemer*. *2*B.*

Hôtel Excelsior (A), 2 Rue Nolly, on Place Mohammed V (☎27.65.43 or 27.18.54). Strongly recommended if you can afford it; this (like the *Balima* in Rabat) used to be the city's "Grand Hotel" until the big chains moved in. Pleasant café downstairs, too. *2*A.*

Hôtel Georges V, 1 Rue Sidi Belyout/corner Av. des FAR (☎31.24.48). Across the road from the *Excelsior*, if you strike unlucky there. Very reasonable. *2*A.*

Hôtel Windsor, 93 Place Oued El Makhazine (☎27.88.74). Large rooms with showers/bathrooms. A bit pricey, but good. *3*B.*

Hôtel Plàza (J), 18 Bd. Houphouet Boigny (☎22.02.26). Again, good rooms and facilities and fairly priced for its class. *3*A.*

Hôtel Transatlantique, 79 Rue Colbert (☎22.07.64). Another grand 1930s hotel, with a period bar and large, appallingly decorated rooms. *4*B.*

Camping

The nearest campsite – **Camping Oasis**, Av. Mermoz – is miles out on the road to El Jadida. If you're using it as a last resort and dependent on public transport, take bus #31 from the *CTM* terminal.

Around the city

It used to be said, with some amazement, that Casa had not a single "real" monument. Given the scale and success of the 1930s Art Deco landmarks of the city centre, designed by the French architect d'Henri Prost, this was never quite true. However, the city did undoubtedly lack any one single, great building: a position that, in part, may have prompted King Hassan II's decision to construct here the world's largest-ever mosque. Set beside the sea, out on the road to Aïn Diab, this building is nearing completion – and, if your architectural curiosity leads no further in this city, must be seen.

The Hassan II Mosque

The **Hassan II Mosque**, begun in 1980 and scheduled for completion some time in 1991, represents the present monarch's most ambitious building project and will surely be his legacy to Moroccan architecture. It is a startling endeavour, even in the bare facts of its construction. The minaret has a height of 172 metres – making it the tallest building in the country and the world record for any mosque – and at its summit, a laser projects its beams, visible for thirty miles out to sea, towards Mecca. The mosque itself has space for 80,000 worshippers and is to be the centre of a cultural complex that will eventually include a major library and museum, complete with sections of glass flooring revealing the ocean below. The design is by a French architect, Michel Pinseau, and the work has employed no less than 25,000 labourers, including 10,000 master craftsmen.

Equally extraordinary is its cost – an estimated £320m – and the fact that this was raised entirely by public subscription. Press reports outside Morocco have alleged resentment towards an over-enthusiastic sponsoring operation. This generated donations through non-voluntary deductions from wages, as well as door to door collections – including approaches to expatriate workers from Germany to Saudi Arabia; at one stage the level of donations was so high that it temporarily reduced Morocco's money supply and brought down inflation. However, in Morocco there is certainly a genuine pride in the project, and pictures of the mosque are displayed in homes and cafés throughout the nation.

That the mosque bears Hassan's name has inspired rumours that it is designed in part as his mausoleum, along the lines of that of his father, Mohammed V, in Rabat. But it is important to add that in addition to his secular positon, Hassan is also "Commander of the Faithful", the spiritual leader of Moroccan Muslims. And the building's site, in addition to reflecting Hassan's stated intent to "give the city a heart", is designed to illustrate the Koranic saying, "Allah has his throne on the water".

Mauresque: the central squares

The French city centre and its formal colonial buildings already seem to belong to a different and distant age. Grouped around **Place des Nations Unies**, they served as models for administrative architecture throughout Morocco, and to an extent still do. Their style, heavily influenced by Art Deco, is known as *Mauresque* – a French idealisation and "improvement" on

Moorish design. The effect of the central ensemble, orchestrated on a *son et lumière* fountain three nights a week, is actually very impressive, the only intrusively French feature being a clocktower in the *préfecture* – an irresistible colonial addition. Other impressive Mauresque buildings are to be seen along Boulevard Mohammed V, including a couple of the older hotels.

More European in style, though again adopting traditional Moroccan forms, is the old **Cathedral of Sacre Cœur** at the far end of the **Parc de la Ligue Arabe**. Now used as a school, it is a wonderfully balanced and airy design, paying homage to its Moroccan setting and very much out of character with the repressive colonialism of its age.

Habbous: the New Medina

If you have time to spare, visit the **New Medina** – or **Quartier Habbous** – which displays a somewhat bizarre extension of *Mauresque*. Built in the 1930s as a response to the first *bidonville* crisis, it is an odd recreation of what the French felt domestic Moroccan architecture should be like. The streets, laid out in neat little rows, now have a somewhat twee, shopping-centre feel to them – not at all Moroccan even with the years. What's actually unreal, however, is the neighbourhood mosque, flanked by a tidy stretch of green as though it were a provincial French church.

The Old Medina

The **Old Medina**, lapsing into dilapidation above the port – and apparently to be part demolished to form an approach to the Hassan II Mosque, is largely the product of the late nineteenth century, when Casa began its modest growth as a commercial centre. Before that, it was little more than a group of village huts, half-heartedly settled by local tribes after the site was abandoned by the Portuguese in 1755. *Casa Branca*, the town the Portuguese founded here in the fifteenth century, had been virtually levelled by the great earthquake of that year (which also destroyed Lisbon). Only its name ("The White House"; *Casablanca* in Spanish; *Dar el Baida* in Arabic) survives.

Now relatively underpopulated, the Medina has a slightly disreputable, if also fairly affluent, air. It is said to be the place to go to look for any stolen goods you might want to buy back – a character well in keeping with many of the stalls. There's nothing sinister though, and it can be a good source for cheap snacks and general goods. A single main street, **Rue Djemaa ech Chleuh**, edges its way right through the quarter, past most of the market stalls and the principal mosque from which it takes its name.

Whilst in the port area, incidentally, do not on any account miss the **Centre 2000** complex, by the Gare du Port. This late 1980s emporium, featuring dozens of expensive shops and three (quite reasonable) restaurants, is Moroccan taste at its tackiest and most extreme.

Aïn Diab: the beach

You can get out to the beach suburb of **Aïn Diab** by bus (#9 from Bd. de Paris; see our map), by *petit taxi* (wait around Place Mohammed V), or by foot. The beach starts around 3km out from the port and Old Medina, past the Hassan II Mosque, and continues for about the same distance.

A beach right within Casa may not sound alluring – and it's certainly not the cleanest and clearest stretch of the country's waters. But Aïn Diab's big attraction is not so much the sea (in whose shallow waters Moroccans gather in phalanx formations, wary of the currents), as the **beach clubs** along its front. Each of these has one or more pools, usually filled with filtered seawater, a restaurant and a couple of snack bars; in the fancier ones there'll also be additional sports facilities like tennis or volleyball and perhaps even a disco. The novelty of coming upon this in a Moroccan city is quite amazing and it's a strange sight to see women veiled from head to toe looking down on to the cosmopolitan intensity unfolding beneath them.

The prices and quality of the **beach clubs** vary enormously and it's worth wandering around a while to check out what's available. Most locals have annual membership and for outsiders a day or weekend ticket can work out surprisingly expensive (£5–10 a day). But there's quite often one place which has thrown its doors open for free in an attempt to boost its café business. *Piscine Eden Roc,* the first you encounter coming from the port, is often among the cheapest, though it's a little dull and away from the centre. If you're taking a *petit taxi,* ask to be let off a kilometre or so further down the corniche, at one of the group of clubs near *Le Lido* or *Kon Tiki.*

And finally, an oddity. If you feel like practising your English with Moroccans, in the premises of a British "club", call in at the **Churchill Club** on Rue Pessac, Aïn Diab. Established in 1922, this was formerly the "British Bank Club". Its one condition of membership is that "the English language only should be spoken on the premises".

Eating and nightlife

Casa has the reputation of being the best place to eat in Morocco, and if you can afford the fancier restaurant prices, this is certainly true. There are some excellent seafood restaurants along the *corniche* (coast) road at Aïn Diab and the bays beyond and some very stylish, old French colonial ones around the central boulevards.

Restaurants

For anyone keeping to a **budget**, some of the best restaurant possibilities lie in the smaller streets off Bd. Mohammed V. Promising streets include:

Rue Mohammed el Quori (by the Hôtel de France, keyed 9 on our map). Numerous caférestaurants, plus the reliable *Brasserie el Sphinx* and, signposted just off the street, the *Restaurant Ouarzazate.*

Rue Colbert (between Bd. Mohammed V and Rue Allal ben Abdallah). A good, safe and inexpensive locale. On one side of the street are *rotisseries* for chicken and olives and (at the junction of Mohammed V and Ben Abdallah) the *Café Intissar,* which offers delicious *harira* and a cheapish menu upstairs. On the other side of the street, more typically Moroccan hole-in-the-wall eateries are interspersed with some wonderful florist shops. There are further Moroccan eateries backing on to the **Marché Central,** which is worth a visit in itself, groaning under the weight of the freshest and best produce in Morocco. The market is open daily from the early hours until around 2pm.

Old Medina. For rock-bottom Moroccan standbys, there are cafés near the beginning of Rue Djemaa ech Chleuh and (further down) on Rue Centrale.

Pricier, regular **restaurants around the centre** include:

L'Etoile Marocaine, 107 Rue Allal Ben Abdallah. Good value for dishes like pastilla. Unlicensed.

Al Mounia, 95 Rue du Prince Moulay Abdallah. More upmarket Moroccan cuisine.

Las Delicias, 18 Bd. Mohammed V. An old established Spanish restaurant, serving vast salads and almost intimidating plates of fried fish.

Le Petit Poucet, 8 Bd. Mohammed V. A slice of old Casablanca style, this French restaurant is dressed up like a 1920s Parisian salon (which is really what it was). It offers plentiful portions and service and also has a (much cheaper) snack bar next door – one of the best places around for some serious drinking. It was in *Le Petit Poucet* that the French aviator and writer Sainte-Exupery used to recuperate between his flights south to the Sahara.

Le Marignan, 63 Rue Mohammed Smiha, corner of Bd. Mohammed V. Excellent and surprisingly reasonably priced Korean and Japanese food, cooked at the tables.

Centre 2000, alongside the Gare du Port. This shopping complex includes three restaurants – Moroccan (the good value *La Tajine*), French and Vietnamese (with plastic pagodas).

If you have serious money to spend, then **Aïn Diab**, and the bay beyond, known as Sidi Abderrahman or El Hank, is the place to go.

Ma Bretagne, Sidi Abderrahman (☎36.21.12). The only restaurant in Africa with a Michelin star.

Le Calbestan (☎36.32.65); **La Mer** (☎36.33.15); both at El Hank. These have also had good reports for their seafood.

Ice cream and patisseries

Casa has a reputation for its **ice cream parlours** and **pâtisseries**, too.

Oliver's, Av. Hassan II; **L'Igloo**, Bd. du Janvier (below the Place des Nations Unies). The two best ice cream parlours in the city.

Gâteaux Bennis, 2 Rue Fkih El Gabbas, in the Quartier Habbous.

Nightlife

For a city with such a glamourous film image, Casa has a surprisingly elusive **nightlife** – at least in the centre.

Bd. Mohammed V. Bars worth trying here include *Le Sphinx* and *Rich Bar*.

La Fontaine, Bd. Houphouet Boigny (off Place Mohammed V). One of the more conspicuous strip joints, if you're curious for Casa low life. Belly dancing, live music and obligatory drinks for the barwomen.

Don Quichote, 44 Place Mohammed V; **The Embassy**, 2 Bd. Mohammed V; **Le Negresco**, Rue Poincaré. In a similar mould to *La Fontaine*.

La Cage, in the *Centre 2000*, by the Gare du Port. A regular Moroccan disco; if you want to see what young Casa is wearing, this is the place to come.

Rick's Bar, in the Hôtel Hyatt Regency on Place Mohammed V. If you can't leave Casa without a visit to Rick's Bar, some salutary news. The bar never existed. For a session of postcard-writing, your only option is this very contrived bar, touting the legendary monicker and open from 10pm. It is a little staid and pricey, to say the least.

Hôtel Safir, Av. des F.A.R. Features another expensive, very swish (and also pretty tasteful) bar – as well as a disco.

In **Aïn Diab** there's usually more happening:

Le Balcon; Zoom Zoom. Two of the liveliest regular discos.

Palm Beach Beach Club. If you want to live a little more dangerously, try this beerhall of an evening, with its belly dancers, sleazy, heavy-drinking crowd and police on the door to prevent trouble.

And lastly, for a spot of culture, prestige **concerts** are performed at the **Théâtre Mohammed V** on the Av. des F.A.R.

Listings

Airlines *Royal Air Maroc*, 44 Av. des F.A.R.; *Air France*, Av. des F.A.R.; *British Airways,/GB Air*, 57 Place Zellaqa (in the *Tour Atlas* building, 6th floor), Air Afrique (Tour Atlas, Place Zellaka; ☎24.96.35). *Royal Air Maroc* fly to a range of destinations from Casa, including Oran and Algiers (Algeria) and Nouadhibou (Mauretania).

American Express *Voyages Schwarz*, 112 Av. Moulay Abdallah (☎743.33); open Mon–Sat 8.30am–noon and 2.30–6.30pm.

Banks *SGMB*, 84 Bd. Mohammed V; *Crédit du Maroc*, 48–58 Bd. Mohammed V; others along the same boulevard. The *Hôtel Safir* (160 Av. des F.A.R.) will often change money outside banking hours, if you are supplicative and look sufficiently well dressed.

Books and Newspapers For English-language **books** try *English Forum* (27 Rue Clémenceau) or the *American Language Centre Bookstore* (Bd. Moulay Youssef), both of which have a good range of paperbacks and fair sections on Morocco. *Librairie Farairie* (near Place Mohammed V, between Bd. Mohammed V and Av. des F.A.R.) and *Librairie Nationale* (Av. de Mers Sultan) are also good for a browse. Some British **newspapers** and the *International Herald Tribune* are available from stands around Place Mohammed V.

Car Hire Cheapest is *Leasing Cars*, 100 Bd. Zerktouni (☎265-331; go by *petit taxi* from the centre – it's a long way out). Others are mostly concentrated along Av. des F.A.R. They include *Atlas Cars* (no. 52; ☎757.98), *Europ-Cars* (no. 144; ☎36.79.73), *Intercars* (no. 61; ☎27.54.19), *Inter-Rent/Marloc* (no. 44; ☎31.37.37) and *Sahara Tours* (no. 227; ☎27.19.47). *Hertz/Starc* are at 25 Rue de Foucault (☎22.32.20); *Avis* at the airport.

Car Repairs Garages include *Renault-Maroc* on Place de Bandoeng (just off our map, below Place Paquet). For information and addresses, contact the *Touring Club du Maroc* (3 Av. des F.A.R.) or *R.A.C. du Maroc* (3 Rue Lemercier).

Consulates *Great Britain* (60 Bd. d'Anfa; ☎22.16.53 or 22.17.41); *U.S.* (8 Bd. Moulay Youssef; ☎22.41.49).

Department Stores *Alpha 55* (Av. de Mers Sultan; with a good, 7th-floor restaurant) and *Centre 2000* (near the Gare du Port) can be useful for stocking up on supplies before heading south.

Ferry agent *Comanav Voyages*, 43 Av. des F.A.R. (%31.20.50) will give details and sell tickets for most ferry departures from Morocco.

Hammams Every neighbourhood has several; the best is reputed to be *Hay Ali* in the Maarif area – ask a *petit taxi* to take you there.

Medical Aid Dial ☎15 for emergency services. Addresses of doctors from the larger hotels, or from the *Croissant Rouge* (Cité Djemaa, 44 Av. E.; ☎340.914). All-night *pharmacie* is open in Place des Nations Unies.

Police Phone ☎19. Main station is on Bd. Brahim Roudani.

Post Office The main *PTT* (for phones/*poste restante*) is in Place des Nations Unies. Open Mon–Thur 8.30am–12.15pm, Fri 8.30–11.30am.

Sports Casa is the best place in Morocco to see Moroccan football; matches are played at the Marcel Cédan stadium (check the local press for details). The city also boasts a racecourse, the Hippodrome, at Anfa (active some Sundays) and, beside it, an 18-hole golfcourse.

MOVING ON FROM CASA

Moving on from Casa, *CTM* run **buses** to just about everywhere, including El Jadida, Agadir, Tiznit and various European destinations; tickets and times from the terminal on Rue Léon l'Africain (see map). If you are heading south for Essaouira, the best service is the *CTM* "Mumtaz Express", which leaves at 4.30pm, arriving 10pm at Essaouira; most other services run via El Jadida. In Casa, negotiate at the main stand for Rabat taxis (see above).

For Rabat, Tangier, Meknes, Fes, or Marrakesh, you'll probably want to go **by train**. Check times in advance at the *Gare du Port*, above Place Mohammed V, and try to find one that's leaving from this station rather than from the *Voyageurs*.

Casablanca to Marrakesh: Boulaouane

The road and railway speed south across the plains from Casa to Marrakesh – and few people think of stopping along the way. To the east lies the phosphate mining region, the Plateau des Phosphates, whilst along the road you pass scarcely more than a handful of local, market centres for the (initially quite fertile) agricultural villages, watered by Morocco's greatest river, the Oum er Rbia.

If you are driving, the one detour to consider is to the **Kasbah de Boulaouane**, 50km west of the region's main town, Settat. The Kasbah was one of Moulay Ismail's grandest and most strategic, protected on three sides by a loop in the Oum er Rbia. It has a well preserved gateway and, within, remains of a palace, vaulted underground chambers and a hammam.

SETTAT itself is a sizeable town – with a population of 150,00 and a single classified **hotel**, the M'Zamza (1km out on the Casa road; ☎040/23.66).

On the **coast**, the one major point of interest is the town of **AZZEMOUR**, 83km south of Casa and 16km north of El Jadida. On local transport, it is easiest approached by bus from El Jadida.

El Jadida

The most popular and developed of the "central" Atlantic resorts, **EL JADIDA** is a stylish and beautiful town, retaining the lanes and ramparts of an old Portuguese Medina. Known as Mazagan under the Portuguese, it was renamed *El Jadida* – "The New" – after being resettled, partly with Jews from Azzemour, by the nineteenth century Sultan Abd er Rahman. Under the French, it grew into a quite sizeable adminsistrative centre and a popular beach resort.

Today it's the beach that is undeniably the focal point. Moroccans from Casablanca and Marrakesh, even Tangier or Fes, come here in droves, and, alongside this cosmopolitan mix, there's an unusual feeling of openness. The bars are crowded (an unusual feature in itself), there's an almost frenetic evening promenade and – as at Casa – Moroccan women are visible and active participants.

Orientation and accommodation

Orientation is straightforward, with the old **Portuguese Medina**, walled and looking out over the port, and the **Ville Nouvelle** spreading to its south along the seafront. By public transport, you will almost certainly arrive at the **main bus station** at the southern end of town (bottom-centre on our map overpage). From here it's a ten-minute walk to the Medina or to most hotels.

In summer, you'd be well advised to make a **hotel** booking – rooms can be very hard to find in July and August – and at all times you may prefer to make some phone calls before pacing the streets, as the town extends for some distance along the seafront.

Hotel options, in ascending order of price, are:

Hôtel d'El Jadida (A), Av. Zerktouni. **Hôtel du Maghreb (C)**, **Hôtel du Port (D)**, Bd. de Suez. Three unclassified hotels, which are often the last to fill. The *El Jadida* is basic but reasonable; the others are basic and a bit seedy – not recommended for women travellers.

Hôtel de la Plage (H), Av. Al Jamia al Arabi (☎26.48). Formerly a *1*B* hotel, this has just slipped to become unclassified. It's clean enough and again a good fallback.

Hôtel Provence (F), 42 Av. Fqih Mohammed Errafi (☎23.47). British-run hotel: clean and central, with a good restaurant and covered parking nearby (10dh for 24hr). The best budget choice – phone in advance. *1*B*.

Hôtel Bruxelles (E), 40 Rue Ibn Khaldoun (☎20.72). Pleasant, clean rooms – and balconied at the front. *1*B*.

Hôtel Royal (G), 108 Av. Mohammed V (☎28.39). A bit pricier but large rooms and generally functional showers. *1*A*.

Hôtel Suisse (B), 145 Bd. Zerktouni (☎28.16). Similar to the above, in a useful central location. *1*A*.

Hôtel Le Palais Andalous, Av. de la Nouie (☎39.06 or 37.45). Converted 1930s palace with a touch of fantasy and an excellent bar. Very good value out of season. *3*A*.

Hôtel-Club Doukkala Salam, Rue de la Ligue Arabe (☎37.37). Modern package hotel with tennis courts and swimming pool. Well maintained, as ever with the *Salam* group. *4*B*.

The town **campsite**, *Camping International* (Av. des Nations Unies; ☎25.47) is well-equipped, if a bit expensive, with a pool, bar and restaurant. It is signposted – a five-minute walk south from the bus station.

Food and other practicalites

For a largish resort, it's surprisingly hard to find anywhere good to eat. Possibilities include:

Restaurant Chahrazad, 38 Place el Hansali. Good basic meals in a central location; other café-restaurants are to be found nearby or by the souks, just off Av. Zerktouni.

Safari Pub, Av. Mohammed Er Riffi; **Restaurant du Port** (below the citadel). Reasonable prix fixe meal and full licences.

Hôtel du Provence (see above). Well prepared, French-inspired meals, open to non-residents. Again, licensed.

Bars are to be found mainly in the hotels – try the *Hôtel de la Plage* (lively) and *Palais Andalous* (refined). Since El Jadida is very much a resort, prices at most establishments tend to the high side, even for standard café drinks.

And lastly, a few other details. The **PTT** is in Place Mohammed V. **Bus tickets** for Casa or Marrakesh should be bought in advance (from the main station). There's a **Wednesday souk**, held out by the lighthouse southwest of town. And there's no tourist office.

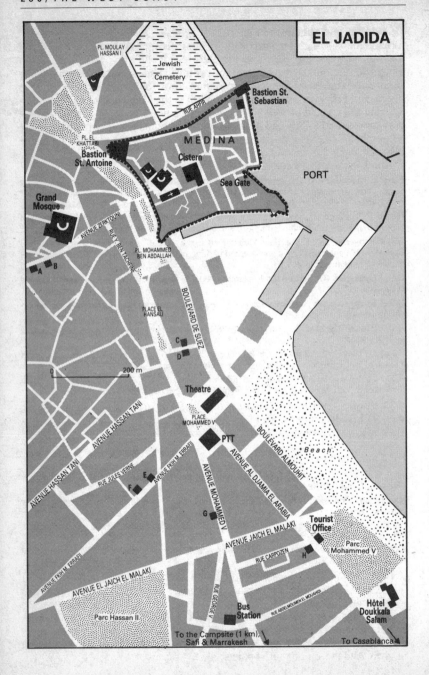

EL JADIDA

PL. MOULAY
HASSAN I

Jewish
Cemetery

RUE AFRIK

Bastion St.
Sebastian

PL. EL
KHATTABI

Bastion
St. Antoine

M E D I N A

Cistern

AVENUE ZERKTOUNI

Grand
Mosque

Sea Gate

PORT

RUE Y. BEN TACHFINE

PL. MOHAMMED
BEN ABDALLAH

A B

PLACE EL
HANSALI

BOULEVARD DE SUEZ

C

D

200 m

Theatre

AVENUE HASSAN TANI

PLACE
MOHAMMED V

AVENUE HASSAN TANI

AVENUE FKIH M. ERRAFSI

PTT

RUE JULES VERNE

E

Beach

F

AVENUE FKIH M. ERRAFSI

BOULEVARD ALMOUHIT

AVENUE AL DJAMIA EL ARABIA

AVENUE MOHAMMED V

G

Tourist
Office

AVENUE JAICH EL MALAKI

Parc
Mohammed V

RUE CARPOZEN

H

AVENUE FKIH M. ERRAFSI

AVENUE EL JAICH EL MALAKI

RUE GEORGE V

Bus
Station

RUE ABDELMOUMEN EL MOUAHID

Hôtel
Doukkala
Salam

Parc Hassan II

To the Campsite (1 km),
Safi & Marrakesh

To Casablanca

The Cité Portugaise

El Jadida's Medina is the most European-looking in Morocco: a quiet, walled and bastioned seaside village, with a handful of churches scattered on its lanes. It was founded by the Portuguese in 1513 – and retained by them until 1769 – and it is still popularly known as the **Cité Portugaise**. The Moors who settled here after the Portuguese withdrawal tended to live outside the walls. Budgett Meakin, writing in the 1890s, found an "extensive native settlement of beehive huts, or *nouallahs*" spreading back from the harbour, while European merchants had re-established themselves in the "clean, prosperous and well-lighted streets" of the Medina. As in all the "open ports" on this coast, there was also an important Jewish community handling the trade with Marrakesh; uniquely, Mazagan had no separate Jewish quarter, or *Mellah*.

The *cité* today – decaying and insignificant – is not of enormous interest, though it does have one distinct and very beautiful sight. This is the **Portuguese Cistern**, a dramatic subterranean vault that mirrors its roof and pillars in a shallow film of water covering the floor – a startling effect that Orson Welles used in his *Othello*, staging a riot here and filming it from above. Open on weekdays from 8am–noon and 2–6pm (4dh admission), the cistern is entered midway down the main street, on the left (going down), opposite a small souvenir shop.

If you walk further up this street, you'll come to the old **Porte de la Mer**, a sea gate opening on to the port. The churches and chapels, long converted to secular use, are generally closed; the **Grand Mosque** here was once a lighthouse – and looks like it.

The beaches – and south to Tit

El Jadida's **beach** spreads north from the *cité* and port, well beyond the length of the town. It's a popular strip, though from time to time polluted by the ships in port.

If it doesn't look too good, or you feel like a change, take a *petit taxi* 3km south along the coastal road to **PLAGE SIDI OUAFI**, a broader strip of sand where dozens of Moroccan families set up tents for the summer. There is good swimming to be had here and cheap food from makeshift beach cafés.

Sidi Bouzid, Moulay Abdallah and Tit

If you decide to head on from Sidi Ouafi, you can usually find *grands taxis* leaving for Sidi Bouzid and Moulay Abdallah (5km and 11km respectively from El Jadida). **SIDI BOUZID** is another beach, but much more developed than Sidi Ouafi, with fancy villa-bungalows, a chic bar and fish restaurant, *Le Requin Bleu*, and a summer campsite.

MOULAY ABDALLAH, in contrast, is a tiny fishing village – dominated, to its left, by a large *zaouia* complex and partially enclosed by a circuit of walls in ruins. These span the site of a twelfth-century *ribat,* or fortified monastery, known as **Tit** ("eyes" or "spring" in the local Berber dialect), and built, so it is thought, in preparation for a Norman invasion: a real threat at the time – the Normans had already launched attacks on Tunisia – but one which never materialised.

Today, there is little to see, though the minaret of the modern **zaouia** (prominent and whitewashed) is Almohad in origin; behind it, up through the graveyard, you can walk to a second, isolated minaret, which is thought to be even older. If it is, then it is perhaps the only one surviving from the Almoravid era – a claim considerably more impressive than its simple, block-like appearance might suggest. At the *zaouia* an important **moussem** is held towards the end of August.

To **reach Sidi Bouzid** direct from El Jadida, catch the local #2 bus from Place Mohammed Ben Abdullah.

Azzemour

AZZEMOUR, 16km north of El Jadida, has an oddly remote feel, considering its strategic site on the great Oum er Rbia river. It has long been outside the mainstream of events. When the Portuguese controlled El Jadida, Safi and Essaouira, they stayed in Azzemour for under thirty years; later, when the European traders moved in on this coast, the town remained a "closed" port. Today, it sees possibly fewer tourists than any other Moroccan coastal town.

Practicalities

The town is easily reached by **bus** from El Jadida, and, once there, getting your bearings is straightforward. You are dropped on Av. Mohammed V, the main thoroughfare of the new town. At its end, past a tiny **Syndicat d'Initiative** (at no 141), you emerge at a garden square, with the **Medina** straight ahead.

To stay in Azzemour, you'd probably be better off camping down at the beach (see below). There are, however, a couple of small, basic **hotels** – the best of which is the *Hôtel de la Victorie*, close by the bus station at 308 Av. Mohammed V.

The Medina

The Portuguese stayed long enough to build Azzemour's circuit of walls, which are stacked directly above the banks of the river and dramatically extended by the white, cubist line of the **Medina**. The best view of all this – and it is impressive – is from across the river, on the way out of town towards Casablanca. To look around the town, however, make your way down from the bus station to the main (landward) side of the ramparts.

At the far corner are the former **Kasbah** and **Mellah** quarters, now largely in ruins, but safe enough to visit. If you wait around, the local *gardien* will probably arrive, open things up and show you around; if he doesn't turn up, you can find him by asking at the syndicat. Once inside the ruins, you can follow the parapet wall around the ramparts, with views of the river and the gardens, including henna orchards, along its edge. You'll also be shown **Dar el Baroud** (The House of Powder), with its ruined Gothic window, and, nearby, the old town **synagogue**.

It might not sound like much, and you'll have to negotiate the final tip, but all in all it's an interesting and enjoyable break from El Jadida, and easily combined with a swim.

The beach

The river currents at Azzemour are notoriously dangerous, but there's a fabulous stretch of **beach** half an hour's walk through the eucalyptus trees above the town. If you go by road, it's signposted *"Balneaire du Haouzia"*, a small complex of cafés and cabins occupying part of the sands.

For **birdwatchers** (see also Oualidia, below), the scrub dunes around the mouth of the river are rewarding territory – with the possibility of sighting the rare slender-billed curlew in autumn or winter.

South to Oualidia and Safi

For one reason or another, few tourists take the road between El Jadida and Essaouira. Even though El Jadida is an attractive, lively resort, few people seem to want to spend time both there and in Essaouira.

Enthusiastic birdwatchers, however, may find the route itself an attraction. For the 70km of coast between SIDI MOUSSA (36km south of El Jadida) and CAP BEDDOUZA (34km south of Oualidia) are among the richest **birdlife habitats** in the country. The coast is backed almost continuously by huge dunes, which have cut off a long expanse of salt marshland north of Oualidia. These wetlands, and the lagoons at Sidi Moussa and Oualidia, shelter a huge range of species – storks, waders, terns, egrets, warblers – and there are sometimes flocks of shearwaters to be seen not far offshore. The best watching locations are the lagoons and the rocky headland at **Cap Beddouza**.

Along the route, there are a scattering of summer **campsites** and a rather wonderful old French **auberge**, *Le Relais* (26km south of El Jadida), offering superb seafood meals and a handful of rooms.

Oualidia

OUALIDIA, 78km from El Jadida (regular buses), is a picturesque little resort – a fishing port and lagoon beach, flanked by an old Kasbah and a (now unused) royal villa, built by Hassan II's father, Mohammed V. It deserves to be better known: the beach is excellent, the atmosphere relaxed, and swimming is safe and easy.

Most of the tourists who come here are Moroccan families and they settle into summer colonies in the two sizeable **campsites**: a standard *Camping Municipal* and, nearer the beach and a bit fancier, the *International Camping Chems*, with a few cabins. There are also three **hotels**, all of which have enticing seafood restaurants: the 1*A *Auberge de la Lagune* (☎105), 2*A *Hôtel Hippocampe* (☎111) and newer *Motel de l'Araigné Gourmande*. The *Hippocampe* is the most pleasant place to stay, good value for its class and with a terrace overlooking the lagoon; the *Lagune* has the better cooking – including local oysters in season.

Twelve kilometres further south, just before you reach Cap Beddouza, there's another **campsite** and an unclassified roadside **auberge**, by the little village of SIDI BOUCHTA. The beach here, however, is more exposed, with long stretches of weed-strewn sands, backed by parched wasteland.

Safi

Flanked by a long stretch of sulphur-spewing chimneys and vast sardine-canning factories, **SAFI** is not the prettiest of Moroccan towns. It does, however, provide a glimpse of an active, modern and working community and the old Medina in its centre, walled and turreted by the Portuguese, holds a certain interest.

In the Medina, too, there is an industrial tradition, with a whole neighbourhood above the walls still devoted to the town's **pottery workshops**. These have a virtual monopoly on the green, heavily-glazed roof tiles used on palaces and mosques, as well as providing Morocco's main pottery exports, in the form of bowls, plates and garden pots.

Practicalities

Arriving by **bus**, you'll find yourself at one of the terminals in Place Ibnou Sina, a busy roundabout about 1km south of the Medina, or on the nearby Av. du President Kennedy. The **train station** (connections to the Casa–Marrakesh line at Benguerir) is a similar distance. It's easiest to get on a local bus, or hire a *petit taxi*, to the central Place de l'Indépendance.

Most of the cheap **hotels** are grouped in the Medina, either around Rue du Socco or on the street to its east. All are fairly basic, though the *Hôtel de Paris* and the *Hôtel Majestic* (both unrated) are clean enough. The classified alternatives are upmarket: 3*B *Hôtel Les Mimosas* (☎32.08) on Rue Ibn Zaidoun, with a bar; 4*B *Hôtel Atlantide* (Rue Chaouki; ☎21.60); and the new 4*A *Hotel Safir* (☎42.99) on Av. Zerktounil, twenty minutes walk from the centre, with a bar, tennis courts and pool. If you want to **camp**, there's a year-round site near the beach of Sidi Bouzid (see below), 3km north of town.

For basic **meals**, try the cafés along Rue du Socco, in the Medina. For more formal restaurant fare, *Restaurant Calypso*, in a courtyard just off Place de l'Independance, and the restaurant in the *Hôtel Les Mimosas* are reasonable value. If you have transport, there's a fine seafood restaurant, *Le Refuge*, on the cliffs at Sidi Bouzid.

Banks, including a BMCE, are located on Place Ibnou Sina, and there are a couple of **car hire** companies here too: *Safi Voyages/Europcar* (☎29.35) and *Hertz* (14 Rue de l'Industrie; ☎38.25).

The Medina

The old port is dominated by the waterfront **Dar el Bahar** fortress (Mon–Fri 9am–noon & 2–4pm; 4dh), the main remnant of the town's brief Portuguese occupation (1508–41) and well maintained following long use as a fortress and prison. From here on back, the old walls continue up, enclosing the Medina, to another and larger fortress known as **Kechla** – again, Portuguese in origin, but this time housing the town's modern prison.

The **Quartier des Potiers** sprawls above the Medina and is impossible to miss, with its dozens of whitewashed kilns and chimneys. The processes here, certainly for tile production, remain traditional and are worth at least the time it takes to wander up. The colour dyes, however, and the actual

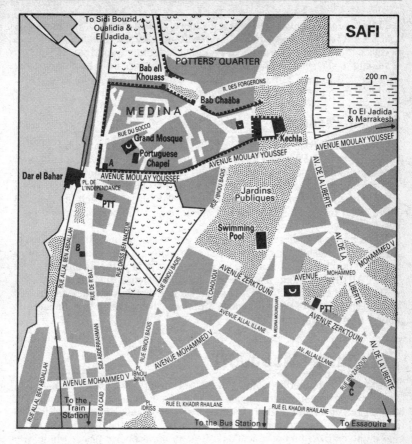

pottery designs are hardly comparable to the beautiful old pieces you see around the country's crafts museums.

Potteries apart, there's little particular to say about Safi's Medina – or about the extensive suburbs of the new city. The **souks**, ordinary food and domestic-goods markets, are grouped around the Medina's main street, Rue du Socco, which runs up from a small square by Dar el Bahar to the old city gate of Bab Chaaba and the potteries.

Beaches north of Safi

The coast immediately south of Safi is heavily polluted and industrialised, and for a beach escape you'll want to head north. Local buses #15 runs to Lalla Fatima and Cap Beddouza from the Place de l'Indépendance.

SIDI BOUZID, 4km north of town, is the main local beach, but, a couple of pleasant restaurants – notably *Le Refuge* – notwithstanding, there are better targets just around Cap Safi.

Fifteen kilometres north of Safi is a superb, cliff-sheltered beach known as **LALLA FATMA** – totally undeveloped, with nothing more than a *koubba*, an occasional summer café and a few Moroccan campers in sight. If you are intending to stay, you'll either need your own transport, or to take provisions. The beach is a steep 2km descent from the road; camping, make sure you've pitched your tent far enough back from the tides.

South to Essaouria

A minor coastal road runs for around 30km south of Safi, past a brief industrial strip, to **SOUIRA KEDIMA** (daily bus from Safi), a fine beach, backed by dunes, with a summer campsite and café-restaurant. Beyond here, the road's path is washed away most years by the Oued Tensift, which you'd have to ford in order to avoid backtracking 10km or so to reach the main P8 inland road to Essaouria. South of Souira Kedima the coast is mostly inaccessible cliffs.

If you have a car, there is a worthwhile excursion to **Kasbah Hamidouch**, a large and isolated fortress, built, like so many on this coast, by Moulay Ismail. It is situated just south of the Oued Tensift, near the fishing village of DAR CAID HADJI, 2km from the P8 and signposted to the left as you pass DAR TAHAR BEN ABBOU. The fort's main function was to guard the mouth of the Tensift, one of the most active Moroccan rivers, which here finishes its course from Marrakesh.

Essaouira (Mogador)

Apart from the immediate impact of the sea air and the friendly animation of the town, the predominant images of **ESSAOUIRA** are of the Atlantic – of the rugged coast and offshore islands, the vast expanse of empty sands trailing back along the promontory to the south and the almost Gothic scenery of the eighteenth-century fortifications. It is an atmospheric place, windblown and a little melancholic out of season but, with its whitewashed and blue-shuttered houses and lines of arcaded shops, thoroughly likeable. The mixture of Berber villagers, sardine fishermen and Marrakchi and European tourists – almost all independent rather than packaged – seems easy and uncomplicated, and the handful of local hustlers almost apologetic.

Over the last few years Essaouira has been discovered by **windsurfers**, for whom the wind – which frustrates beach lounging – is of course an asset. The town actively promotes itself as "Windy City, Afrika", the German spelling of the name being significant, as it is German windsurfers who come in the biggest numbers, followed by the French and an increasing number of British, Americans and Australians. The windsurfers are, inevitably, changing the town's character, as villas spring up along the corniche to cater for their needs, but they form a clientele which fits in easily enough with the established image. Depending on your attitude to a town dominated by travellers in their early 20s to late 30s, you'll either want to stay for a week or more or take the first bus out.

Orientation and transport

Still largely enclosed by its eighteenth century ramparts, Essaouira is a pretty simple place to get to grips with. At the north end of town is the **Bab Doukkala**, at the south, the main square, Place Moulay Hassan, and the harbour. Between the two run two main, parallel streets – **Rue Mohammed Zerktouni** and **Av. Mohammed Ben Abdallah**.

Buses (both *CTM* and the private companies) arrive at a new bus station, inconveniently sited on the outskirts of the town, about a mile north of the Bab Doukkala in the Quartier Industrielle. It is unsignposted and reached along a very ill-lit and in parts unmetalled road, past a shanty quarter. Especially at night, it's well worth taking a *petit taxi* into or out from town; the charge is only 5–6dh (8dh at night). **Grands taxis** also operate from the bus station, though they will normally drop arrivals in central Essaouira. If you're driving, there is a **car park**, manned around the clock, near Place Moulay Hassan (5dh for 24hr). There is a *petit taxi* rank by the clocktower.

Leaving Essaouira, there are only private bus company services to Marrakesh (no *CTM* departures). For Casablanca, the best services are the *CTM* "Mumtaz Express" (leaves daily at 11pm, arriving Casa at 5am) and the night *Pullman du Sud*; they cost around 10dh more than other departures – money that you will, in any case, save on baggage loading. The other *CTM* services to Casa are second class and considerably slower.

Accommodation

Accommodation can be difficult in midsummer, given the town's increasing popularity, but at the end of the day there usually seem to be rooms available. Many of the windsurfers arrive in campervans and others rent out villas and apartments through the local windsurfing organisation, housed in a white building about 100m south along the beach from the Café de la Plage.

The following is a selective list of hotels, as usual in roughly ascending order of price; see the map overpage for keyed letters. If all of them are full – which is unlikely – there are half a dozen other basic hotels in the alleyways between the two main Medina streets.

Hôtel Beau Rivage (C), Place Moulay Hassan. Inexpensive hotel, with rooms looking out onto the main square and its own café above; no hot water. *Unclassified*.

Hôtel des Remparts (A), 18 Rue Ibn Rochd (no phone). As the name suggests, the *Remparts* is built right into the walls overlooking the sea. It was once quite grand, but has decayed and is a bit seedy, with everything at times just a bit too damp. On the plus side, it has a rooftop terrace where you can sunbathe out of the wind. *1*B*.

Pension Smara (H). Next to the *Cinema Skala*, off Rue Laalouj. Similarly priced and again with some of its rooms overlooking the sea. Clean and good value. *Unclassified*.

Hôtel Majestic (B), on an alley south of Rue Laalouj. Hot showers, clean rooms and a central location mean that this fills up fast in summer. *Unclassified*.

Hôtel du Tourisme (D), Rue Mohammed Ben Messaoud (☎20.75). Clean and cheap, located within the southeast corner of the ramparts. *Unclassified*.

Hôtel Tafraout (G), 7 Rue Marrakech (☎21.20). In the heart of the Medina, with rather cell-like rooms. A women's *hammam* is right next door. *1*A*.

Hôtel Mechouar (F); ☎20.18. **Hôtel Sahara** (☎23.79). These are next door to each other on Rue Okba Ibn Nafia, just off Avenue de l'Istiqlal. They're a bit more upmarket with rather glitzy decor – but clean and pleasant enough. Respectively, *1*A, 2*B*.

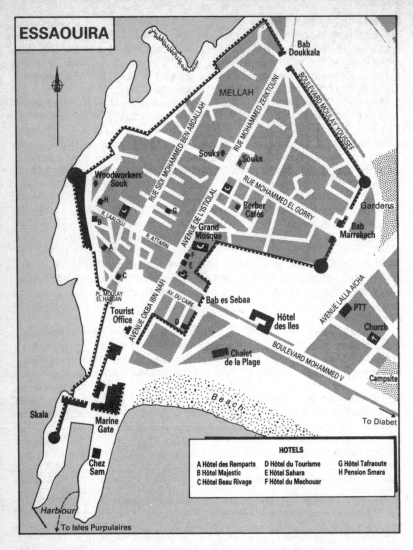

ESSAOUIRA

Bab Doukkala

MELLAH

BOULEVARD MOULAY YOUSSEF

Souks

Souks

RUE SIDI MOHAMMED BEN ABDALLAH

RUE MOHAMMED ZERKTOUNI

RUE MOHAMMED EL GORRY

Woodworkers' Souk

H

R. LAALOU

B

G

AVENUE DE L'ISTIQLAL

R. ATTARIN

Berber Cafés

Gardens

Bab Marrakech

A

Grand Mosque

F
E

C

AVENUE OKBA IBN NAFI

AV. DU CAIRE

PL. MOULAY EL HASSAN

Bab es Sebaa

Tourist Office

D

Hôtel des Iles

AVENUE LALLA AICHA

PTT

Church

BOULEVARD MOHAMMED V

Chalet de la Plage

Campsite

Skala

Beach

Marine Gate

To Diabet

Chez Sam

HOTELS

A Hôtel des Remparts	D Hôtel du Tourisme	G Hôtel Tafraoute
B Hôtel Majestic	E Hôtel Sahara	H Pension Smara
C Hôtel Beau Rivage	F Hôtel du Mechouar	

Harbour
↓ To Isles Purpulaires

Hôtel Villa Maroc (I), near the clocktower. New, English-owned hotel, decorated as a traditional Moroccan home, with comfortable rooms, heated in winter, grouped around a garden courtyard. The hotel has a terrace for sunbathing and its own *hammam*. Prices of 225dh per person (325dh per person in room with shower and toilet) include a five course meal (cooked by a fine Belgian chef) in the evening. In low season prices can be negotiated – you don't always have to take the meal. *As yet unclassified.*

Hôtel **Tafoukt** (☎25.04), **Hôtel des Iles** (☎23.29). The two more expensive hotels, both on Boulevard Mohammed V. The latter has a swimming pool; both have bars. Facing the beach, south of town. Respectively, *3*A, 4*A*.

The town **campsite is** 200m east along the seafront, pas the *Hôtel des Iles*. Cheap and reasonably secure. An alternative is to camp at the *Auberge Tangaro* in Diabat (see overpage).

The town

With its dramatic sea bastions and fortifications, Essaouira seems a lot older than it is. Although a series of forts had been built here from the fifteenth century on, it was only in the 1760s that the town, then known as Mogador, was established and the present circuit of walls constructed.

Mogador's original function was military – Agadir was in revolt at the time and Sultan Mohammed Ben Abdallah needed a local base – but this was soon preempted by commercial concerns. During the nineteenth century, it was the only southern port open to European trade: its harbour was free from customs duties, British merchants lived in the town and a large Jewish community settled. With the coming of the French Protectorate and the emergence of Casablanca, decline set in. After Independence, and the exodus of the Jewish community, it declined to a role as a fishing port and market town, growing again only with the recent impetus of tourism.

The Skala and Souks

There are few formal "sights" in the town – it's more a place just to walk around in, exploring the *souks* and ramparts or wandering along the immense beach. At some point, though, make your way down to the **harbour,** where fresh sardines (and all variety of other fish) are cooked on the quays, and climb up to the **Skala**, the great sea bastion which runs back from it along the northern cliffs. Orson Welles filmed much of his *Othello* here, staging a bizarre (but very Moroccan) "punishment" of Iago, suspended above the sea and rocks in a cramped metal cage. Along the top of the Skala are a collection of European cannon, most of them presented to Sultan Mohammed Ben Abdallah by ambitious nineteenth-century merchants.

Underneath the Skala, towards the "angle" of the ramparts, are a group of cedar and *thuya* **craftsmen**, long established in Essaouira, who produce some amazingly painstaking and beautiful marquetry work. Quite justifiably, they claim this is the best in the country, and if you see good examples elsewhere they've probably come from here. If you're thinking of buying – boxes and chess sets are for sale, as well as traditional furniture – this is the best place to do it, after checking out the *Ensemble Artisanal* (see below).

The town's **other souks** spread around two arcades, on either side of Rue Mohammed Zerktouni and up towards the old Mellah – an interesting area and a good place to start thinking about food (see below). Worth particular attention are the **Marché d'Épices** (spice market) and **Souk des Bijoutiers** (jewellers' market).

The Museum and Artisanal

Just recently opened, the **Musée Sidi Mohammed Ben Abdallah** (8.30am– noon & 2.30–6pm; closed Tues) is worth visiting. Featuring excellent displays of marquetry, as well as standard handicrafts collections, it is housed in a nineteenth-century mansion on the road running down from the ramparts to Av. de l'Istiqlal. Next door is the **Ensemble Artisanal**, exhibiting local crafts.

The Isles Purpuraires

Out across the bay lie the **Isles Purpuraires**: two rocky islets, the larger dominated by a fortress-like building which saw intermittent use as a state prison and a quarantine station for pilgrims returning from Mecca. The islands are semiprotected as a nature reserve, since they are the only non-Mediterranean breeding site of Eleonora's falcon – clearly visible, with binoculars, from the town.

If you want to visit the isles (and this is strongly discouraged, in summer), you'll have to get a *permet d'autorisation* from the tourist office (50dh) before beginning to negotiate for the boat ride. Don't pay for the ride until you're collected and returned to the town!

Food and other practicalities

With its fishing fleet and market, Essaouira offers a good range of food and restaurants. The grills down at the port have been mentioned already. Another pleasantly informal Essaouira institution are a series of **"Berber Cafés"**, off to the right (if you're walking up from the harbour) of the Rue Zerktouni *souks*. Amounting to little more than a street of tiny rooms covered with matting, these serve soup, tea and a variety of *tajines* – or anything you present to be cooked. Some of them are a bit of a tourist trap (and a few are haunted by hustlers peddling dope), but they are frequented also by local fishermen and workers.

Among the more mainstream **restaurants**, pick from:

Café-Restaurant Essalam, Place Moulay Hassan. The cheapest set meals in town, if not the most co-operative service.

Mustafa's, corner of Rue Sidi Mohammed Ben Abdallah and Rue Zayane. A good, cheap place where a lot of Moroccans eat. It looks like a typical hole-in-the-wall but a door by the counter leads to a masasive complex of rooms and alcoves. The *harira* is excellent and all the food is fresh daily, as Mustafa gives away anything unsold to the poor.

Restaurant Miami, 107 Rue du Mellah. New restaurant in the heart of Medina, with a good set menu. To find it, follow Rue Sidi Mohammed ben Abdallah to its (north) end, then carry on uphill and look for the signpost.

Café l'Horloge, just inside the clocktower gate. A former synagogue – and worth a look if only for the setting. It is unlicensed, though you can bring wine (or send out for it).

Restaurant Riad, 18 Rue Zayane, off Av. Allal Ben Abdallah. Imaginative French-Moroccan dishes in beautiful, traditionally decorated rooms, with rare antiques.

Restaurant El Khaima, Place Moulay Hassan. More upmarket but good cuisine, extravagant draperies and licensed to sell alcohol. The restaurant often stays open serving coffee after the other cafés have closed.

Chez Sam, at the end of the harbour. Seafood restaurant and bar, serving huge portions of fish and (at a price) lobster. A bit unpredictable – but good when it's good.

Beyond *Sam's* and the *Bar Lachouar*, places to have a **drink** are limited. There is a restaurant-bar, the *Chalet de la Plage*, just off the beach, opposite the *Hôtel des Iles*; another attached to the *Iles* itself, where Moroccans gather to drink beer and play chess and draughts; and a cheaper and extremely seedy one at the *Hôtel Sahara*.

If you want to buy your own beer or wine, at very much lower prices, head for the *épicerie*, 200m north of the Bab Doukkala. This supplies most of the town's restaurants.

Still on the practical front, **Jack's Kiosk** on Place Moulay Hassan operates as a small travel agency, giving out information on local trips, reconfirming flights, etc, as well as a bookshop and as an international phone centre. It charges ten percent more for calls than the PTT but rarely has any queues.

The **Club Equestre Sidi Mgdoul**, out of town on Marrakesh road, hires out horses for riders of all levels of experience. And lastly, a **hammam** (for men and women), offering robust massages, is to be found in the area just north of Bab Doukkala.

The beach, Diabat and Cap Sim

Essaouira's **beach** extends for miles south of the town, towards Cap Sim. The sands are fine and safe, though at times (especially in early summer) the wind can be pretty relentless – making sunbathing, at least, impossible. But windiness is a complaint that could be levelled generally against most of the Atlantic coast, and it does keep temperatures cool (70° F is about average).

The main activity, as ever in Morocco, is **football**. There's virtually always a game in progress and at weekends a full scale local league, with a dozen matches side by side and kick-offs timed by the tides. If you're a player, you'll be encouraged to join in, but the weekend games are fun just to watch, and on occasions seemingly half the town seems to turn out.

Walking further along the beach, past the pitches and the crowds, you pass the ruins of an old fort and royal summer pavilion half buried in the sand – the inspiration, apparently, for Jimi Hendrix's *Castles in the Sand*. Further still you reach the riverbed, just south of Diabat, which is well reputed for its **birdlife**, with a variety of waders and egrets, and numerous warblers in the scrub behind.

Diabat

In the direction of Cap Sim, an hour's walk along the beach and then a kilo-metre's climb, over a path through thorny scrub, is the village of **DIABAT**. This was once a legendary hippie hangout, popularised by Jimi Hendrix, who spent a while in the colony here. These days, it has reverted back to an ordi-nary Berber farming village, a ragged sort of place which (since a police crackdown in the early 1970s) is no longer permitted to rent rooms.

Three kilometres south of the village, however, is the French-owned and rather chic *Auberge Tangaro*, a tempting alternative to staying in Essaouira, especially if you have transport of your own. Little used except at weekends, when groups of French and German windsurfers come down from Casablanca and Marrakesh, the *auberge* has a number of chalet **rooms**, and it serves excellent meals throughout the day. Next door is a small, rather primitive **campsite**. Coming by car, take the Agadir road for about 6km out of Essaouira and then turn off to the right; the "direct" approach from Essaouira is no longer possible after the collapse of a bridge just below Diabat. There is a good **beach** a half-hour hike from the campsite and *auberge*.

Cap Sim

There is no road or track access to **Cap Sim** from Diabat. To get there, you need to drive, hitch or taxi south for 12km along the Agadir road and then take a right fork, signposted Sidi Kaouki – a *marabout* near the cape which has the reputation of curing sterility in women.

SIDI KAOUKI is reckoned the best spot on the Moroccan coast for **wind-surfing** and attracts most of the devotees of the sport from Essaouira. Camper vans are to be found here, virtually year round, parked a short way back from the beach.

At **CAP SIM** itself, there are usually just a couple of **camels** and their drivers, who hire out the beasts to tourists. The trip that's touted is actually quite fun – a four-hour return ride to (otherwise hard of access) **dunes**.

South to Agadir

The main road south from Essaouira to Agadir runs inland, with just the occasional *piste* leading down to fishing hamlets scattered along the rugged, cliff-lined coast. This region, known as the Haha, and populated by Tachelhaït-speaking Berbers, is actually the westernmost range of the High Atlas. Its slopes are covered in argan trees, which are often to be seen with a goat halfway up, nibbling away at the fruit.

Inland from the P8, very rough *pistes* lead off east into the hills, struggling over the mountains to meet the Tizi Machou road from Marrakesh to Agadir. On the P8 itself, there is little of interest. **SIMMOU** has a petrol station and roadside café-restaurants – and one of the better roads into the hills, leading to SOUK TNINE IMI N TLIT, where one of the largest souks take place on Mondays. **TAMANAR** (63km) has a petrol station and café-restaurants, too, as well as a very basic hotel, the *Etoile du Sud*.

Continuing south, 16km on from Tamanar, a road cuts down to the coast at **POINTE IMESSOUANE**, where there is a small fishing village and a very simple café-hotel, with meals and a few beds. Just east of the village is a bay known as **Imoucha**, which, like Sidi Kaouki, has become a centre of **wind-surfers** – and, to a lesser degree, surfers.

A few kilometres beyond the roadside settlment of **TAMRI** (117km), the road rejoins the coast, and widens, passing through the fishing village of TARHAZOUTE (see *Chapter Seven*) before the final run to Agadir.

travel details

Trains

Rabat–Casablanca More or less hourly departures (50min–1hr 30min). Most run to/from *Casa-Port*, though a few exclusively to/from *Voyageurs*.
Casablanca–Tangier Four daily, via Rabat, Mohammedia, Salé, Kenitra, Asilah and Tangier.
  7.15am Casa–Port, arrives Rabat (8.15am), Asilah (12.13pm) and Tangier (1.15pm).

12.45pm Casa-Voyageurs, arrives Rabat (2.03pm), Sidi Slimane (4.18pm: change for Asilah/Tangier, 6.59pm/7.55pm).
3.15pm Casa-Voyageurs, arrives Rabat (6.12pm: change for Asilah/Tangier, 10.42pm/11.26pm).
11.10pm Casa-Voyageurs, arrives Rabat (12.08am), Asilah (4.43am), Tangier (5.37am).

Casablanca–Fes/Meknes Five daily, via Rabat, Salé and Kenitra; all from **Casa-Voyageurs:**

6am, arrives Rabat (7.18am), Meknes (10.36am) and Fes (11.33am).

12.45pm, arrives Rabat (2.03pm), Meknes (5.38pm) and Fes (6.40pm).

5.15pm, arrives Rabat (6.12pm), Meknes (4.09pm) and Fes (5.16pm).

10.05pm, arrives Rabat (11.17pm), Meknes (2.30am), Fes (3.34am).

Rabat/Casablanca–Marrakesh Seven daily in 4–6hr (from Rabat), 5hr–7hr 30min (from Casablanca). Departures from Rabat/Casablanca-Voyageurs at: 4.18am/5.25am (arrives Marrakesh 8.54am), 5.18am/7:54am (11.31am), 8.45am/9.39am (12.43pm), 11.03am/12.08pm (3.13pm), 2.34pm/17.16pm (9.09pm), 6.19pm/7.13pm (10.17pm) and 10.52pm/1.23am (changing at Casa, 5.16am).

Casablanca–El Jadida Three daily (8.52am from Port, arrives Azzemour 10.13am, El Jadida 10.25am; 6.20pm from Port, arrives Azzemour 7.47pm, El Jadida 8pm; 8.05pm from Casa-Voyageurs, arrives Azzemour 9.02pm, El Jadida 9.12pm).

Buses

From Rabat Tangier (2 daily; 5hr); Larache (4: 3hr 30min); Salé (frequent; 15min); Casablanca (10; 1hr 40min); Meknes (3; 4hr); Fes (6; 5hr 30min).

From Casa Dozens of destinations, including Tangier (2 daily; 6hr 30min); Rabat (10; 1hr 40min); El Jadida (3; 2hr); Essaouira (3; 5–7hr; best is the *SATAS*); Agadir (1; 10hr); Marrakesh (3; 4hr).

From El Jadida Casablanca (3 daily; 2hr 30min); Rabat (2; 4hr); Oualidia (daily; 1hr 30min).

From Safi Oualidia/El Jadida (3 daily; 1hr 25min/ 2hr 30min).

From Essaouira Agadir (6 daily; 3hr 30min); Safi (2; 6hr); El Jadida (2; 8hr); Casablanca (4; 5–9hr); Tiznit (1; 7hr). **Note**: Most Essaouira–Marrakesh services (6 daily; 3hr) are non-*CTM* buses.

Grands Taxis

Rabat–Casablanca Regular route, 1hr 20min

From El Jadia Negotiable to Casablanca.

Flights

Rabat/Casa Mohammed V Airport: International flights to London, Paris and most major destinations. Domestic flights to all major cities in Morocco.

TELEPHONE CODES	
CASABLANCA ☎0	SAFI ☎046
ESSAOUIRA ☎047	SALÉ ☎07
KENITRA ☎016	SKHIRAT ☎07
MOHAMMEDIA ☎032	TÉMARA ☎07
RABAT ☎07	

CHAPTER FIVE

MARRAKESH AND THE HIGH ATLAS

Marrakesh – "Morocco City", as the early travellers called it – has always been something of a pleasure city, a marketplace where the southern tribesmen and Berber villagers bring in their goods, spend their money and find entertainment. For tourists it's an enduring fantasy – a city of immense beauty, low, pink and tentlike before a

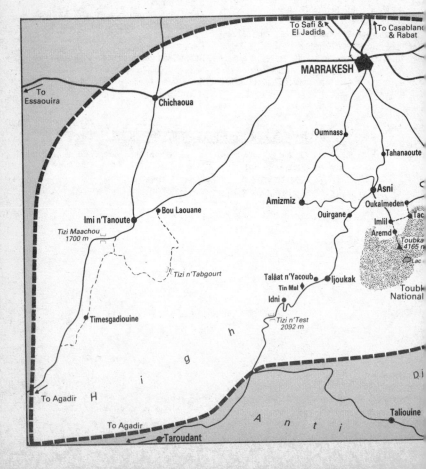

great shaft of mountains – and immediately exciting. At the heart of it all is a square, **Djemaa el Fna**, really no more than an open space in the centre of the city, but the stage for a long-established ritual in which shifting circles of onlookers gather around groups of acrobats, drummers, pipe musicians, dancers, storytellers and comedians. However many times you return there, it remains compelling. So, too, do the city's architectural attractions: the immense, still basins of the **Agdal** and **Menara** parks, the delicate Granadine carving of the **Saadian Tombs** and, above all, the **Koutoubia Minaret**, the most perfect Islamic monument in North Africa.

Some 50km south of Marrakesh rise the **High Atlas**, the grandest and most rewarding Moroccan mountain range. Its foothills and the lush summer pleasureground of **Ourika Valley** can be reached in just an hour by bus or *grand taxi*. Or, within the space of a morning, you can leave the city and get up to the **hiking trailheads** of **Asni**, **Imlil** or **Ijoukak**. From here, a network of trails – mulepaths, ridgewalks and climbing routes – radiate across the

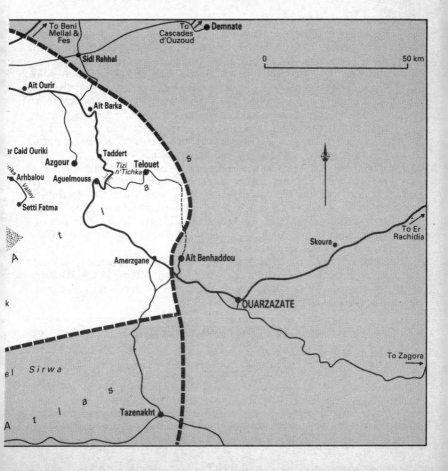

valleys and mountains. The most popular trek – which forms the basis of most walking holidays in the region – is from Imlil to **Djebel Toubkal**, at 4165m the tallest Atlas peak and one of the highest in Africa. This is a well-established route, snow-covered and limited to those with climbing experience in winter, but accessible to walkers from spring to autumn. Elsewhere, there is scope for any number of hikes, to match any level of expertise and' commitment, from casual daytrips to week-long expeditions.

The High Atlas as a whole, is a surprisingly populated region, its slopes dropping away to valleys and streams, with small **Berber villages** (where you can usually find basic accommodation) terraced into their sides. Increasingly, too, there is a local infrastructure of guides and mule hire, though, it must be stressed, part of the attraction of **Atlas hiking** is that it remains wonderfully undeveloped in comparison to, say, the Pyrenees or Alps. Moving a little away from the beaten track, you still get a real sense of exploration. For practicalities on hiking in the region, see p.292.

The passes

The remoteness of these mountain villages is reflected also in the great **High Atlas road passes** (*tizis* in Berber, *cols* in French) that cross the range to reach the desert and oasis routes detailed in chapters six and seven.

Tizi n'Test, the pass which runs beyond Asni and Toubkal over to Taroudannt, is the steepest – a spectacular, adrenalin-plugged switchback of almost continuous hairpin curves. If you drive along this road, be aware of what's in store; it's pretty alarming even on the bus. Hiking detours aside, the route has a major (and easily accessible) attraction in the ruins of the twelfth-century mosque of **Tin Mal**, the base from which the Almohads swept down to take Marrakesh and, ultimately, to reconquer Spain.

Tizi n'Tichka, which cuts across to the east to reach Ouarzazate and today bears most of the traffic, has a more recent but equally evocative history. It was built to replace the old caravan route to Tafilalt, which was controlled over the last century and for much of the present by the legendary Glaoui family, "the Lords of the Atlas". Their Kasbah, a bizarre cluster of crumbling towers and kitschy-looking 1930s reception halls, is still to be seen at **Telouet**, just an hour from the main road.

The third Atlas pass, the **Tizi Maachou**, has less drama, unless you leave the main road behind to get into the hills for some hiking in the Western Atlas, the least known part of the range. For most travellers it simply offers a fast and convenient approach to Agadir.

WINTER TRAVELLING

Note that the High Atlas is subject to snow from November to the end of February, and even the major Tizi n'Tichka pass can be closed for periods of a day or more. Flash floods, too, can present problems, when the snows melt in February–March. If you get caught by the snow, the easiest route from Marrakesh to the south is road 6543 to Agadir, then the P32 through Taroudannt and Taliouine.

For information on hiking seasons – and winter treks above the snow line are a serious endeavour here – see the "Hiking Practicalities" box, on p.292–93.

Marrakesh (Marrakech)

Unlike Fes, for so long its rival as the nation's capital, **MARRAKESH** exists very much in the present. Its population is rising, it has a thriving industrial area and it remains the most important market and administrative centre of southern Morocco. None of this is to suggest a bland prosperity – there is heavy unemployment here, as throughout the country, and intense poverty, too – but travelling through it leaves you with a vivid impression of life and activity. And for once this doesn't apply exclusively to the new city, **Gueliz**; the **Medina**, substantially in ruins at the beginning of this century, was rebuilt and expanded during the years of French rule and retains no less significant a role in the modern city.

The Koutoubia excepted, Marrakesh is not a place of great monuments. Its beauty and attraction lie in the general atmosphere and spectacular location – with the tallest, sheerest peaks of the Atlas rising right up behind the city, towering through the haze. The feel, as much as anything, is a product of this. Marrakesh is a **Berber** rather than an Arab city: long the metropolis of Atlas tribes, Mahgrebis from the plains, Saharan nomads and former slaves from Africa beyond the desert – Sudan, Senegal and the ancient kingdom of Timbuktu. All of these strands have shaped the city's *souks* and its way of life, and in the crowds and performers in Djemaa el Fna, they can still occasionally seem distinct.

For most travellers, Marrakesh is the first experience of the south and – despite the inevitable guides and hustlers – of its generally more relaxed atmosphere and attitudes. **Marrakchis** are renowned for their warmth and sociabililty, their humour and directness – all qualities that (superficially, at least) can seem absent among the Fassis. There is, at any rate, a conspicuously more laid-back feel than anywhere in the north, with women, for example, having a greater degree of freedom and public presence, often riding mopeds around on the streets. And compared to Fes, Marrakesh is much less homogenous and cohesive. The city is more a conglomeration of villages than an urban community, with quarters formed and maintained by successive generations of migrants from the countryside.

Some history

The original date of Marrakesh's **foundation** is disputed, though it was certainly close to the onset of **Almoravid** rule – around 1062–70 – and must have taken the initial form of a camp and market, a *ksour*, or fortified town gradually developing around it.

Its founder (as that of the Almoravid dynasty) was **Youssef bin Tachfine**, a restless military leader who conquered northern Morocco within two years and then, turning his attention towards Spain, defeated the Christian kings, to bring Andalusia under Moroccan rule. Tachfine maintained as bases for his empire both Fes and Marrakesh, but under his son, the pious **Ali ben Youssef**, Marrakesh became very much the dominant centre. Craftsmen and architects from Cordoba worked on the new city: palaces, baths and mosques were built; a subterranean system of channels was constructed to provide water for the growing palmery; and, in 1126–27, the first, seven-kilometre **circuit of walls** was raised, replacing an earlier stockade of thorn bushes. These, many times rebuilt, are essentially the city's present walls – made of *tabia*, the red mud of the plains, mixed and strengthened with lime.

Of the rest of the Almoravid's building works, there remains hardly a trace. The dynasty that replaced them – the orthodox and reforming **Almohads** – sacked the city for three days after taking possession of it in 1147. Once again, though, Marrakesh was adopted as the empire's preeminent capital, its domain stretching as far as Tripolitania (modern Libya) in the wake of phenomenal early conquests. With the accession to the throne in 1184 of **Yacoub el Mansour**, the third Almohad sultan, the city entered its greatest period. Under this prolific builder, *kissarias* were constructed for the sale and storage of Italian and oriental cloth, a new Kasbah was begun, and a succession of poets and scholars arrived at the court – among them Averroes, the most distinguished Arabic medieval philosopher. Mansour's reign also saw the construction of the **Koutoubia Mosque** and minaret.

It is astonishing, though, to think that this whole period of Almoravid and Almohad rule – so crucial to the rise of both the city and the nation – lasted barely two centuries. By the 1220s, the empire was beginning to fragment amid a series of factional civil wars, and Marrakesh fell into the familiar pattern of pillage, ruination and rebuilding. It revived for a time to form the basis of an independent **Merenid** kingdom (1374–86) but overall it gave way to Fes until the emergence of the Saadians in the early sixteenth century.

Taking Marrakesh, then devastated by famine, in 1521, and Fes in 1546, the **Saadians** provided a last burst of imperial splendour. Their first sultans regained the Atlantic coast, which had been extensively colonised by the Portuguese; **Ahmed el Mansour**, the great figure of the dynasty, led a conquest of Timbuktu, seizing control of the most lucrative caravan routes in Africa. The **El Badi Palace** – Marrakesh's largest and greatest building project – was constructed from the proceeds of this new wealth, though it again fell victim to dynastic rivalry and, apart from its mausoleum (the **Saadian Tombs**), was reduced to ruins by Moulay Ismail.

Subsequent history under the **Alaouites** – the dynasty perpetuated today by King Hassan – is for the most part less distinguished. Marrakesh remained an imperial capital, and the need to maintain a southern base against the tribes ensured the regular, alternating residence of its sultans. But from the seventeenth to the nineteenth century, it shrank back from its medieval walls and lost much of its former trade. A British traveller's description of the city at the turn of the century as "a squalid, straggling, mazy kind of open cesspool about the size of Paris" is probably not inaccurate, though for the last decades prior to the protectorate, it enjoyed a return to favour with the Shereefian court. **Moulay Hasan** (1873–1894) and **Moulay Abd el Aziz** (1894–1908) both ran their governments from here in a bizarre closing epoch of the old ways, accompanied by a final bout of frantic palace building.

On the arrival of **the French**, Marrakesh gave rise to a short-lived pretender, the religious leader El Hiba, but for most of the colonial period it was run as a virtual fiefdom of its pasha, **T'hami el Glaoui** – the most powerful, autocratic and extraordinary character of his age (see p.271 and p.311).

Since **Independence**, the city has undergone considerable change, with rural emigration from the Atlas and sub-Sahara, new methods of cultivation in the plains and the development of a sizeable tourist industry combining to give it today the country's largest modern trading base and population (1,425,000 at the last estimate) after Casablanca.

Orientation and transport

Despite its size – and the tortuous maze of its *souks* – Marrakesh is not too difficult to find your way around. The broad, open space of **Djemaa el Fna** lies right at the heart of the Medina, and almost everything of interest is concentrated in the web of alleyways above and below it. Only in the *souks* (see section following) might you want to consider taking a guide.

Just to the west of the Djemaa, an unmistakable landmark, is the minaret of the **Koutoubia** – in the shadow of which begins **Avenue Mohammed V**, leading out of the Medina and up the length of the new city, **Gueliz**.

Getting around

It is a fairly long walk between Gueliz and the Medina, but there are plenty of **petits** and **grands taxis** (ranks by the post office in Gueliz and at Djemaa el Fna; 6–8dh) and a regular **bus** (#1 runs between the Koutoubia/Place de Foucauld in the Medina and the main squares in Gueliz).

In addition, there are **calèches**, horse-drawn cabs which line up near the Koutoubia, the Badi Palace and some of the fancier hotels. These can take up to five people and are often no more expensive than *petits taxis* – though again bargain and fix the price before setting out, particularly if you want a tour of the town or a trip to one of the sights.

Note that very few of the *petits taxis* are metered (or admit to their meter working); you either have to fix a price in advance, haggle on arrival, or just decide on what you're paying and hand it over at the end of the trip. *Grands taxis* and *calèches* have, by law, to display standard prices for specified trips. All prices shown are per trip and not per person, as drivers often claim.

For exploring the more scattered city sights – the Agdal and Menara gardens, for example, or the palmery – the ideal transport is a **bike**. You can hire bikes by the day from the *Hôtel Foucauld* (in the Medina), from the hotels *Toubkal, Sigha,Andalous* and *Aghdal* in Gueliz, and from various stores along Av. Mohammed V (try *Peugeot* at no. 225). **Grands taxis** can also be chartered by the day for around 100–120dh

Points of arrival

● **By bus**. The bus terminal (for all long distance services) is located just outside the walls of the Medina by Bab Doukkala. You can walk into the centre of Gueliz from here in around ten minutes by following Av. des Nations Unies; to the Djemaa it's around twenty to twenty-five minutes, most easily accomplished by following the Medina walls down to Av. Mohammed V. Alternatively, catch the #3 or #8 bus, which run in one direction to the Koutoubia, in the other to Gueliz; or take a *petit taxi* (6–8dh).

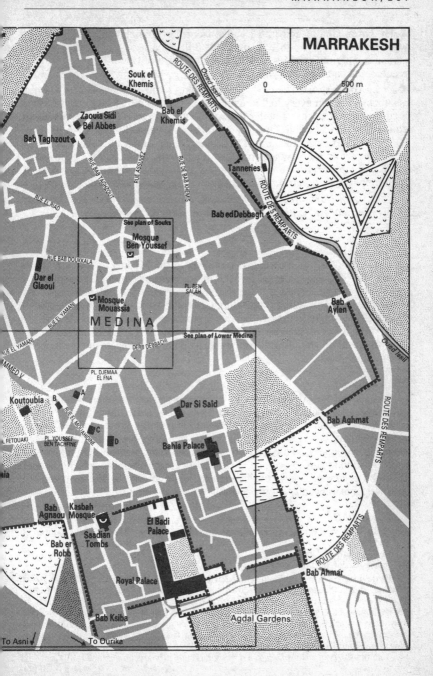

MARRAKESH

0   500 m

Souk el Khemis

ROUTE DES REMPARTS

Oued Issil

Zaouia Sidi Bel Abbes

Bab el Khemis

Bab Taghzout

RUE BAB TAGROUT

RUE ASSOUEL

RUE DE BAB KHEMIS

Tanneries

RUE EL RIAD

Bab ed Debbagh

ROUTE DES REMPARTS

See plan of Souks

Mosque Ben Youssef

RUE BAB DOUKKALA

Dar el Glaoui

PL. BEN SALAH

RUE EL YAMANI

Mosque Mouassia

MEDINA

Bab Aylen

See plan of Lower Medina

DERB DEBBACHI

RUE EL YAMAN

MMED V

PL. DJEMAA EL FNA

Oued Issil

Koutoubia   B

A

RUE EL MOUAHIDINE

Dar Si Saïd

Bab Aghmat

L FETOUAKI

C

PL. YOUSSEF BEN TACHFINE

D

Bahia Palace

ROUTE DES REMPARTS

Bab Agnaou

Kasbah Mosque

El Badi Palace

Bab er Robb

Saadian Tombs

Bab Ahmar

Royal Palace

Bab Ksiba

Agdal Gardens

To Asni   To Ourika

● **By train**. Getting into the Djemaa from the train station you'll certainly want transport (#3 or #8 bus, or about 8dh for a *petit taxi*). However, the station is only ten minutes' walk from the centre of Gueliz, and within easy reach of the campsite and youth hostel.

● **From the airport**. The city's airport is 5km to the southwest. The #11 bus is supposed to run every half hour to the Djemaa, but it is very erratic. *Petits taxis* or *grands taxis* are a better option, though you will need your wits about you to pay a reasonable fare. The *grands taxis* currently display a price of 20dh for the trip from the airport to Gueliz; try not to pay a lot more. Arriving at the airport on a Friday afternoon, or after about 6pm any day of the week, you'll find the **bureau de change** closed; taxis will accept pounds or dollars, though they will charge significantly more than the equivalent dirham rate.

For details on transport out of Marrakesh, and buses to local destinations like Asni or Ourika, see "Leaving Marrakesh", under "Practicalities".

Hotels

As usual, there is a choice between staying in the Medina or the new town, Gueliz. The Medina, as ever, has the main concentration of cheap places – most of them quite pleasant (though freezing in winter) – and, unusually, has a fair number of classified hotels, too. Given the attractions of the Djemaa el Fna and the souks, it has to be the first choice. The main advantages of Gueliz hotels are their convenience if you are arriving late at night, particularly at the train station, and, in the more upmarket choices, the presence of a swimming pool.

Medina hotels

Virtually all of the Medina area hotels are keyed on the map opposite – a compact, easily walkable area just south of the Djemaa el Fna. If you are after one of the **classified hotels**, try to phone ahead and book. For the **cheap hotels** – most of which are small, youth-oriented places, with eight or ten rooms grouped around a courtyard – it is a question of pacing the alleyways: if you're in company, leave one person at a café with your bags. The best of them are reviewed below; you may strike lucky at others, though some are distinctly miserable and overpriced.

UNCLASSIFIED

Hôtel du Café de France and **Hôtel Oukaïmeden**. These are actually in the Djemaa el Fna and have some rooms overlooking the square. The *Café de France* has poor rooms, with cockroaches and cold water showers. The *Oukaïmeden* is a bit better, over on the far side of the square, beside the huge, strictly guarded *Club Med* complex.

Hôtel de France, 197 Rue Zitoun el Kedim (☎430.67); **Hôtel Chellah** (☎419.77); **Hôtel Medina**. Facing the *Hôtel CTM*, turn down the arched lane to its left, Rue Zitoun el Kedim. The *Hôtel de France* (not to be confused with the *Hôtel Café de France* listed above) is near the beginning of this street: one of the best of the cheapies, recently modernized and secure. Fifty metres down, the *Chellah* is signposted on an alley to the left: it can be a bit hustley, but is again cheap, and a nice building. The *Hôtel Medina* , in the first alley to the right, heading down Rue Zitoun el Kedim, is a real gem – small, clean, family-run and friendly; good value, too, with hot showers included. *Hôtel des Amis*, en route, is not recommended.

> **Note**. At most times of year, the city has a shortage of space in the classified hotels (the Medina places are less of a problem), so **advance bookings** are a wise idea, especially if you want to stay in one of the classified Medina hotels. The worst times are around the **Christmas/New Year** and **Easter** holiday periods, when you may arrive and find virtually every hotel full to capacity. Prices at these times are inflated for just about everything – from orange juice in the Djemaa el Fna to car hire (which at peak times can be virtually impossible to arrange).

Hôtel de la Jeunesse (☎436.31); **Hôtel Afriquia**; **Hôtel Nouzah** and **Hôtel Eddakla**; all in Rue de la Recette. The best in a zigzagging lane of small, cheap hotels entered (coming from the Djemaa) through the first alley on your left off Rue Bab Agnaou. The hotels offer similar, clean but basic, facilities. The *Afriquia* has a pleasant courtyard, with orange trees; the *Nouzah* is youth-oriented, with a questionable taste for 1970s rock on its tape system.

Hôtel Souria; **Hôtel Hillal**; **Hôtel El Farah** and **Hôtel El Allal**; These are scattered along the next lane down off Rue Bab Agnaou – reached through a smaller, arched entrance opposite the *Hôtel du Tourisme* (and just before you come to the Banque Populaire). The *Souria* is by far the best, run by a grand old *patronnne* who is selective about her guests and imposes an 11pm curfew; the *Allal* is friendly and secure.

CLASSIFIED

Hôtel CTM, Place Djemaa el Fna (☎423.25). Located above the old bus station. Good-sized rooms, clean and as cheap as many unclassified places. *1*A*.

Hôtel Gallia, Rue de la Recette (☎459.13). Follow directions as for the *Souria*, etc, above; the *Gallia* is on the left at the end of the lane. Pleasant building and worth the extra money over its neighbours if you are offered one of the larger, better rooms. *2*B*.

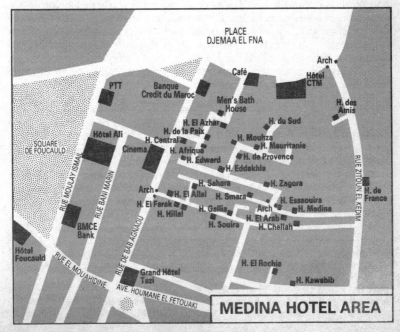

MEDINA HOTEL AREA

Hôtel de Foucauld (B, on main plan), Rue El Mouâhidine (☎454.99). Good location and a fine (if variable) restaurant attached. Rooms are on the small side and there are frequent problems with the water supply, but it's a reliable choice – and excellent value if you have a group of three or four to share one of the multi-bedded rooms. *2*B.*

Grand Hôtel Tazi (C, on main plan), Rue Bab Agnaou/corner of Av. Hoummam el Ftouaki (☎451.52/427.87). Same management as the *Foucauld* though rather more expensive – for larger rooms, with hot showers, heating in winter, a garage to the rear and a rooftop bar. When busy, they may insist on you taking half-board. *2*A.*

Hôtel Ali (A, on main plan), 10 Rue Dispensaire/Place de Foucauld (☎449.79). A fairly new and very popular small hotel; rooms with reliable en suite showers and heating in winter; rooftop sun terrace and excellent breakfasts. Good, inexpensive Moroccan meals in its restaurant, too. The hotel is used as a pick-up point for various hiking tours to the High Atlas, which could be useful for independent travellers heading that way. *2*A.*

Hôtel Minaret, 10 Rue du Dispensaire. Another new – and recommended – hotel, in the street behind the *Tazi*. *2*A.*

Hôtel Yasmine, 8 Bd. de la Madeleine, south of Place de la Liberté (☎461.42). A new and very attractive hotel, only 400m from the Djemaa and with a garden, bar, tennis court and swimming pool, plus parking space. *As yet unclassified: 3*A prices.*

Hôtel Mamounia, Av. Bab Jdid (☎489.81). Something of a legend, set within its own palace grounds, this is – alongside the *Palais Jamai* in Fes – the most beautiful hotel in Morocco. It is also the most expensive, with doubles from 2500dh if you book independently. Room prices drop a bit during the low season, or if you book as part of a holiday package – but they are still pretty astronomical. For the merely curious, tea in the gardens comes a lot cheaper, if the staff deign to let you in; no jeans, shorts, or trainers allowed.

Gueliz/Hivernage hotels

If you are thinking of splashing out on a few **luxury nights** in Morocco, Marrakesh is one of the best places to do so – particularly in summer, when temperatures hover around 100°F, with midday bursts of 120-130°F. Your main criterion will be a swimming pool, which means headintg for **Gueliz** or the upmarket "hotel quarter" of **Hivernage**, to its south, unless you can get a room at the *Yasmine* or afford the *Mamounia* (see above).

The following recommendations are in roughly ascending order of price; keyed letters refer to the main map on p.256–57.

Youth Hostel (K), Rue el Jahid (☎328.31). Quiet, clean and friendly, this is a useful first-night standby if you arrive late by train. Located five minutes' walk and three blocks from the train station: closes 10pm in the winter, around midnight in the summer. To get to the Djemaa from here, take the # 3 or #8 bus near the station. IYHF cards compulsory.

Hôtel du Haouz, 66 Av. Hassan II. Respectable, if dull; on the road leading into central Gueliz from the train station. *Unclassified.*

Hôtel Franco-Belge, 62 Bd. Zerktouni (☎484.72); **Hôtel des Voyageurs**, 40 Bd. Zerktouni (☎472.18). Unexciting but cheap; on a main thoroughfare. *Both 1*B.*

Hôtel Oasis (E), 50 Av. Mohammed V (☎471.79). Better rooms, clean and well run. Also has a bar and good value restaurant. *1*A.*

Hôtel la Palmeraie, 8 Rue Souraya, parallel to Bd. Zerktouni, two blocks south (☎310.07). Good-value basic rooms, and a few more expensive ones with showers. *1*A.*

Hôtel Excelsior, Tarik Ibn Zaid/Ibn Aicha, parallel to Av. Mohammed V, a block above; and a block above Bd. Zerktouni (☎317.33). Popular French-run hotel with slightly kitsch, Moorish decor. *2*A.*

Hôtel Koutoubia (J), 51 Av. El Mansour Eddahbi (☎309.21). Vaguely stylish and set amid gardens, though sadly, its pool always seems empty and prices therefore a little high. *2*A.*

Grand Hôtel Imilchil, Av. Echouhada (☎314.50 or 314.70). One of the least expensive hotels with a reliably full, if rather small, swimming pool. *3*A*.

Hôtel Oudaia, 147 Rue Mohammed el Beqal (☎487.51). New hotel with rooms overlooking a pleasant, courtyard pool. *3*A*.

Hôtel Siaha Safir, Av. Kennedy, Hivernage (☎489.52). A good hotel, with its own hammam, as well as a fine pool – and not that expensive for its classification. *4*A*.

Hôtel Semiramis Meridian, Route de Casablanca (☎313.77). Arguably the best swimming pool in the city – which might tempt a couple of nights' stay in summer. Summer prices can drop to £60–70 a night for doubles, which can be shared between three people.

Hôtel Es Saadi (M), Av. Qadissia, Hivernage (☎488.11). The most elegant hotel in Hivernage, with a beautiful garden and prices a fair bit below the *Mamounia*, despite luxury classification. *5**.

Campsite

The **Camping Municipal** is located on Av. de France, a couple of blocks south of Av. Hassan II, so just a five minute walk if you arrive at the train station. It's a reasonable site – good for meeting people for information and possible lifts – and has a café-restaurant and small pool (not always full). Bus #3 or #8 runs from the corner of Av. de France/Av. Hassan II to the Djemaa.

The Djemaa el Fna and Koutoubia

There's nowhere in North Africa like **Djemaa el Fna** – no place that so effortlessly involves you and keeps you coming back. By day it's basically a market, with a few snake charmers and an occasional troupe of acrobats. In the evening it becomes a whole carnival of musicians, clowns and street entertainers. When you arrive in Marrakesh, and after you've found a room, come out here and you'll get straight into the ritual: wandering around, squatting amid the circles of onlookers, giving a dirham or two as your contribution. If you get tired, or if things slow down, you can move over to the rooftop terraces of the *Café de France* or. the *Restaurant Argana* to gaze at it all and admire the frame of the Koutoubia Minaret.

What you are part of is a strange process. Tourism is probably now vital to the Djemaa's survival, yet apart from the snake charmers, water vendors (who live by posing for photographs) and the hustlers, there's little that has compromised itself for the West. In many ways it actually seems the opposite. Most of the people gathered into circles around the performers are Moroccans – Berbers from the villages and lots of kids. There is no way that any tourist is going to have a tooth pulled by one of the dentists here, no matter how neat the piles of molars displayed on their square of carpet. Nor are you likely to use the scribes or street barbers or understand the convoluted tales of the storytellers, around whom are gathered perhaps the most animated crowds in the square.

Nothing of this, though, matters very much. There is a fascination in the remedies of the herb doctors, with their bizarre concoctions spread out before them. There are **performers,** too, whose appeal is universal. The Djemaa acrobats, itinerants from the Tazeroualt, have for years supplied the European circuses – though they are probably never so spectacular as here, thrust forward into multiple somersaults and contortions in the late afternoon heat. There are child boxers and sad-looking trained monkeys, clowns and Chleuh boy dancers – their routines, to the climactic jarring of cymbals, totally sexual (and a traditional invitation to clients).

And finally, the Djemaa's enduring sound – the dozens of **musicians** playing all kinds of instruments. Late into the night, when only a few people are left in the coffee stands at the centre of the square, you can encounter individual players, plucking away at their *ginbris,* the skin-covered, two- or three-string guitars. Earlier in the evening, there are full groups: the *Aissaoua,* playing oboe-like *ghaitahs* next to the snake charmers; the Andalusian-influenced groups, with their *aouds* and crude violins; and the predominantly black *Gnaoua,* trance-healers who beat out hour-long hypnotic rhythms with iron clanging hammers and pound tall drums with long curved sticks.

If you get interested in the music there's a small section in the Djemaa, near the entrance to the *souks,* where stalls sell recorded **cassettes**. Most of these are by Egyptian or Algerian Raï bands, the pop music that dominates Moroccan radio, but if you ask they'll play you Berber music from the Atlas, classic Fassi pieces, or even Gnaoua music – which sounds even stranger on tape, cut off only by the end of the one side and starting off almost identically on the other. These stalls apart, and those of the nut roasters, whose massive braziers line the immediate entrance to the potters' *souk,* the **market** activities of the Djemaa are mostly pretty mundane.

Not to be missed, however, even if you lack the stomach to eat at any of them, are the rows of makeshift **restaurants** that come into their own towards early evening. Lit by enormous lanterns, their tables piled high with massive bowls of cooked food, each vendor extols his own range of specialities. If you're wary, head for the orange and lime juice vendors opposite the Café de France, or go for a handful of cactus fruit, peeled in a couple of seconds at the stalls nearby. For details on more substantial eating in the Djemaa and elsewhere, see p.282.

Nobody is entirely sure when or how Djemaa el Fna came into being – nor even what its name means. The usual translation is "assembly of the dead", a suitably epic title that seems to refer to the public display here of the heads of rebels and criminals. This is certainly possible, since the Djemaa was a place of execution well into the last century; the phrase, though, might only mean "the mosque of nothing" (*djemaa* means both "mosque" and "assembly" – interchangeable terms in Islamic society), recalling an abandoned Saadian plan to build a new grand mosque on this site. Whichever is the case, as an open area between the original Kasbah and the *souks,* the *place* has probably played its present role since the city's earliest days. It has often been the focal point for rioting – even within the last decade – and every few years there are plans to close it down and to move its activities outside the city walls. This, in fact, happened after Independence in 1956, when the new "modernist" government built a corn market (which still stands) on part of the square and tried to turn the rest into a car park. The plan, however, lasted for only a year. Tourism was falling off and it was clearly an unpopular move – it took away one of the people's basic psychological needs, as well as eliminating a perhaps necessary expression of the past.

The Koutoubia

The absence of any architectural feature in the Djemaa – which even today seems like a haphazard clearing – serves to emphasise the drama of the **Koutoubia Minaret**, the focus of any approach to the city. Nearly seventy metres high and visible for miles on a clear morning, this is the oldest of the three great Almohad towers (the others being in Rabat and Seville) and the most complete. Its proportions – a 1:5 ratio of width to height – established the classic Moroccan design. Its scale, rising from the low city buildings and the plains to the north, is extraordinary, and the more so the longer you stay and the more familiar its sight becomes.

Completed by Sultan Yacoub el Mansour (1184–99), work on the minaret probably began shortly after the Almohad conquest of the city, around 1150. It displays many of the features that were to become widespread in Moroccan architecture – the wide band of ceramic inlay near the top, the pyramid-shaped, castellated *merlons* rising above it, the use of *darj w ktarf* and other motifs – and it also established the alternation of patterning on different faces. Here, the top floor is similar on each of the sides but the lower two are almost eccentric in their variety; the most interesting is perhaps the middle niche on the southeast face, a semicircle of small lobed arches, which was to become the dominant decorative feature of Almohad gates.

If you look hard, you will notice that at around this point, the stones of the main body of the tower become slightly smaller. This seems odd today but originally the whole minaret would have been covered with plaster and its tiers of decoration painted. To see just how much this can change the whole effect – and, to most tastes, lessen much of its beauty – take a look at the Kasbah mosque (by the Saadian Tombs) which has been carefully but completely restored in this manner.

There have been plans over the years to do the same with the Koutoubia and the local press have recently been running a number of articles on various schemes, possibly involving a restoration of the whole mosque area. At present, however, the only parts of the structure that have been renovated are the three gilt balls made of copper at the summit. These are the subject of numerous legends, mostly of supernatural interventions to keep away the thieves. They are thought originally to have been made of gold and were possibly the gift of the wife of Yacoub el Mansour, presented as a penance for breaking her fast for three hours during Ramadan.

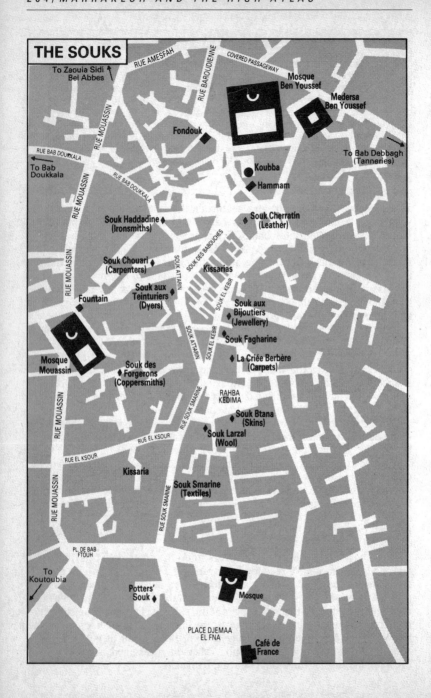

THE SOUKS

RUE AMESFAH

RUE BAROUDIENNE

COVERED PASSAGEWAY

To Zaouia Sidi
Bel Abbes

Mosque
Ben Youssef

Medersa
Ben Youssef

Fondouk

RUE BAB DOUKKALA

RUE MOUASSIN

To Bab
Doukkala

RUE BAB DOUKKALA

To Bab Debbagh
(Tanneries)

Koubba

Hammam

Souk Haddadine
(Ironsmiths)

Souk Cherratin
(Leather)

SOUK DES BABOUCHES

Souk Chouari
(Carpenters)

SOUK ATTARIN

Kissarias

RUE MOUASSIN

Souk aux
Teinturiers
(Dyers)

SOUK EL KEBIR

Souk aux
Bijoutiers
(Jewellery)

Fountain

Souk Fagharine

SOUK ATTARIN

SOUK EL KEBIR

La Criée Berbère
(Carpets)

Mosque
Mouassin

Souk des
Forgerons
(Coppersmiths)

RAHBA
KEDIMA

RUE MOUASSIN

Souk Btana
(Skins)

RUE SOUK SMARINE

Souk Larzal
(Wool)

RUE EL KSOUR

RUE EL KSOUR

Kissaria

RUE MOUASSIN

Souk Smarine
(Textiles)

RUE SOUK SMARINE

PL. DE BAB
FTOUH

To
Koutoubia

Potters'
Souk

Mosque

PLACE DJEMAA
EL FNA

Café de
France

The *souks* and northern medina

It is spicy in the souks, and cool and colourful. The smell, always pleasant, changes gradually with the nature of the merchandise. There are no names or signs; there is no glass . . . . You find everything – but you always find it many times over.

Elias Canetti: *The Voices of Marrakesh*

The **souks** of Marrakesh sprawl immediately north of Djemaa el Fna. They seem vast the first time you venture in, and almost impossible to navigate, though, in fact, the area that they cover is pretty compact. A long, covered street, **Rue Souk Smarine**, runs for half their length and then splits into two lanes – **Souk el Attarin** and **Souk el Kebir**. Off these are virtually all the individual *souks:* alleys and small squares devoted to specific crafts, where you can often watch part of the production process. At the top of the main area of *souks*, too, you can visit the Saadian **Ben Youssef Medersa** – the most important monument in the northern half of the Medina and arguably the finest building in the city after the Koutoubia Minaret.

If you are staying for some days, you'll probably return often to the *souks* – and this is a good way of taking them in, singling out a couple of specific crafts or products to see, rather than being swamped by the whole. To come to grips with the general layout, though, you might find it useful to walk around the whole area once with a **guide** (see below). Despite the pressure of offers in the Djemaa, don't feel that one is essential, but until the hustlers begin to recognise you (seeing that you've been in the *souks* before), they'll probably follow you in; if and when this happens, try to be easygoing, polite and confident – the qualities that force most hustlers to look elsewhere.

The most interesting **times** to visit are in early morning (between 5 and 8am if you can make it) and late afternoon, at around 4 to 5pm, when some of the *souks* auction off goods to local traders. Later in the evening, most of the stalls are closed, but you can wander unharassed to take a look at the elaborate decoration of their doorways and arches; those stalls that stay open, until 7 or 8pm, are often more amenable to bargaining at the end of the day.

CRAFTS, "GUIDES" AND THE SOUKS

Like Fes, Marrakesh can be an expensive place to **buy craft goods** – though if you have anything to barter (designer T-shirts, trainers, rock music cassettes, etc.), you'll find people eager enough to arrange an exchange. Before setting out into the souks in search of rugs, blankets, or whatever, check out the classic designs in the **Dar Si Said** museum (see p.279) and take a look at the (higher than reasonable) prices in the official state-run **Centre Artesenal** – just inside the ramparts beside Av. Mohammed V.

Official **guides** (10dh for 2 hours) can be arranged at the ONMT or S.I. tourist offices (see "Listings") or large hotels, unofficial ones in Djemaa el Fna and almost anywhere you're seen looking perplexed. Some of the latter can be fine, others a struggle, as you are escorted into shop after shop; fix a price in advance. A favourite recommendation of the hustlers is the so-called Berber market – "only today", they'll tell you, with great urgency. In fact, all the main **souks** are open every day, though they're quiet on Friday mornings. Even the big Souk el Khemis (the Thursday Market, held outside Bab Debbagh) now operates most days of the week.

Towards Ben Youssef: the main souks

On the corner of Djemaa el Fna itself there is a small potters' *souk,* but the main market area begins a little further beyond this. Its **entrance** is initially confusing. Standing at the *Café de France* (and facing the mosque opposite), look across the street and you'll see the *Café el Fath* and, beside it, a building with the sign "Tailleur de la Place" – the lane sandwiched in between them will bring you out at the beginning of Rue Souk Smarine.

SOUK SMARINE AND THE RAHBA KEDIMA

Busy and crowded, **Souk Smarine** is an important thoroughfare, traditionally dominated by the sale of textiles. Today, classier tourist "bazaars" are moving in, with *American Express* signs displayed in the windows for the guided hordes, but there are still dozens of shops in the arcades selling and tailoring shirts and caftans. Along its whole course, the street is covered by a broad, iron trellis that restricts the sun to shafts of light; it replaces the old rush (*smar*) roofing, which along with many of the *souks'* more beautiful features was destroyed by a fire in the 1960s.

Just before the fork at its end, Souk Smarine narrows and you can get a glimpse through the passageways to its right of the **Rahba Kedima**, a small and fairly ramshackle square with a few vegetable stalls set up in the middle of it. Immediately to the right, as you go in, is **Souk Larzal**, a wool market feverishly active in the dawn hours, but closed for most of the rest of the day. Alongside it, easily distinguished by smell alone, is **Souk Btana,** which deals with whole sheepskins – the pelts laid out to dry and be displayed on the roof. You can walk up here and take a look at how the skins are treated.

The most interesting aspect of Rahba Kedima, however, are the **apothecary stalls** grouped around the near corner of the square. These sell all the standard traditional cosmetics – earthenware saucers of cochineal (*kashiniah*) for rouge, powdered *kohl* or antimony for darkening the edges of the eyes, *henna* (the only cosmetic unmarried women are supposed to use) and the sticks of *suak* (walnut root or bark) with which you see Moroccans cleaning their teeth. But, in addition to such essentials, they also sell the herbal and animal ingredients that are still in widespread use for manipulation, or spellbinding. There are roots and tablets used as aphrodisiacs, and there are stranger and more specialised goods – dried pieces of lizard and stork, fragments of beaks, talons and gazelle horns. Magic, white and black, has always been very much a part of Moroccan life, and there are dozens of stories relating to its effects, nearly always carried out by a wife on her husband.

LA CRIÉE BERBÈRE

At the end of Rahba Kedima, a passageway to the left gives access to another, smaller square – a bustling, carpet-draped area known as **la Criée Berbère**.

It was here that the old **slave auctions** were held, just before sunset every Wednesday, Thursday and Friday, until the French occupied the city in 1912. They were conducted, according to Budgett Meakin's account in 1900, "precisely as those of cows and mules, often on the same spot by the same men . . . with the human chattels being personally examined in the most disgusting manner, and paraded in lots by the auctioneers, who shout their attractions and the bids". Most had been kidnapped and brought in by the caravans from Guinea and Sudan; Meakin saw two small boys sold for £5 apiece, an eight-year-old girl for £3 and 10 shillings and a "stalwart negro" went for £14; a beauty, he was told, might exceptionally fetch £130 to £150.

These days, **rugs and carpets** are about the only things sold in the square, and if you have a good deal of time and willpower you could spend a the best part of a day here while endless (and often identical) stacks are unfolded and displayed before you. Some of the most interesting are the Berber rugs from the High Atlas – bright, geometric designs that look very different after being laid out on the roof and bleached by the sun. The dark, often black, backgrounds usually signify rugs from the Glaoua country, up towards Telouet; the reddish-backed carpets are from Chichaoua, a small village on the way to Essaouira, and are also pretty common. There is usually a small **auction** in the *criée* at around 4pm – an interesting sight with the auctioneers wandering around the square shouting out the latest bids, but it's not the best place to buy a rug – it's devoted mainly to heavy, brown woollen *djellabas*.

AROUND THE KISSARIAS

Cutting back to **Souk el Kebir**, which by now has taken over from the Smarine, you emerge at the **kissarias**, the covered markets at the heart of the *souks*. The goods here, apart from the numerous and sometimes imaginative *couvertures* (blankets), aren't especially interesting; the *kissarias* traditionally sell the more expensive products, which today means a sad predominance of Western designs and imports.

Off to their right, at the bottom end of the *kissarias*, is **Souk des Bijoutiers**, a modest jewellers' lane, which is much less varied than the one established in the Mellah (see "The Lower Medina") by Jewish craftsmen. At the top end is a convoluted web of alleys that comprise the **Souk Cherratin**, essentially a leather workers' *souk* (with dozens of purse makers and sandal cobblers), though it's interspersed with smaller alleys and *souks* of carpenters, sieve makers and even a few tourist shops. If you bear left through this area and then turn right, you should arrive at the open space in front of the Mosque Ben Youssef; the *medersa* (see the section below) is off to its right.

THE DYERS' SOUK AND A LOOP BACK TO THE DJEMAA

Had you earlier taken the left fork along **Souk el Attarin** – the spice and perfume *souk* – you would have come out on the other side of the **kissarias** and the long lane of the **Souk des Babouches** (slipper makers). The main attraction in this area, and by far the most colourful sight in the city, is the *souk* of the dyers, or **Teinturiers**. To reach it, turn left a couple of steps before you come to Souk des Babouches. Working your way down this lane (which comes out in a square by the Mouassin Mosque), look to your left and you'll see the entrance to the *souk* about halfway down – its lanes rhythmically flash with bright skeins of wool, hung from above. If you have trouble finding it, just follow the first tour group you see, or ask one of the kids to lead you.

There is a reasonably straightforward alternative route back to Djemaa el Fna from here, following the main street down to the **Mouassin Mosque** (which is almost entirely concealed from public view, built at an angle to the square beside it) and then turning left on to Rue Mouassin. As you approach the mosque, the street widens very slightly opposite an elaborate triple-bayed **fountain**. Built in the mid-sixteenth century by the prolific Saadian builder, Abdallah el-Ghalib, this is one of many such fountains in Marrakesh with a basin for humans set next to two larger troughs for animals; its installation was a pious act, directly sanctioned by the Koran in its charitable provision of water for men and beasts.

Below the Mouassin Mosque is an area of coppersmiths, **Souk des Forgerons**. Above it sprawls the main section of **carpenters'** workshops – with their beautiful smell of cedar – and beyond them a small *souk* for **oils** (**Souk des Huivres**) and the **Souk Haddadine** of blacksmiths and metal-workers – whose sounds you'll hear long before arriving.

The Ben Youssef Medersa

One of the largest buildings in the Medina, and preceded by a rare open space, the **Ben Youssef Mosque** is quite easy to locate. Its **Medersa** – the old school annexe for students taking courses in the mosque – stands off a side street just to the east, distinguishable by a series of small, grilled windows. The entrance porch is a short way down the side street, covering the whole lane at this point. Recently restored, it is open from 8am to noon and 2.30 to 5.45pm, except on Mondays and Friday mornings; admission is the standard 10dh.

Like most of the Fes *medersas* (see p.159 for a description of their development and function), the Ben Youssef was a Merenid foundation, established by Sultan Abou el Hassan in the fourteenth century. It was, however, almost completely rebuilt under the Saadians, and it is this dynasty's intricate, Andalusian-influenced art that has left its mark. As with the slightly later Saadian Tombs, no surface is left undecorated, and the overall quality of its craftsmanship, whether in carved wood, stuccowork or *zellij*, is startling. That this was possible in sixteenth-century Marrakesh, after a period in which the city was reduced to near ruin and the country to tribal anarchy, is remarkable. Revealingly, parts have exact parallels in the Alhambra Palace in Granada, and it seems likely that Muslim Spanish architects were employed in its construction.

Inside the *medersa*, you reach the main court by means of a long outer **corridor** (an unusual feature in a *medersa*, though fairly common in palace architecture) and a small entry **vestibule**. To the side of this are stairs to **student cells**, arranged around smaller internal courtyards on the upper floors, an **ablutions hall** and **latrine**. At the corner of the vestibule is a marble **basin**, rectangular in shape and decorated along one side with what seem to be heraldic eagles and griffins; an inscription amid the floral decorations records its origin in tenth-century Córdoba, then the centre of the western Muslim world. The Ommayad caliphs, for whom it was constructed, had few reservations about representational art. What is surprising is that it was brought over to Morocco by the Almoravid sultan Ali Ben Youssef and, placed in his mosque, was left untouched by the Almohads before finally being moved to the *medersa* in the course of the Saadian rebuilding.

The **central courtyard**, weathered almost flat on its most exposed side, is unusualy large. Along two sides run wide, sturdy, columned arcades, which were probably used to supplement the space for teaching in the neighbouring mosque. Above them are some of the windows of the **dormitory quarters**, from which you can get an interesting perspective – and attempt to fathom how over eight hundred students were once housed in the building.

At its far end, the court opens on to a **prayer hall,** where the decoration, mellowed on the outside with the city's familiar pink tone, is at its best preserved and most elaborate. Notable here, as in the court's cedar carving, is a predominance of pinecone and palm motifs; around the *mihrab* (the horseshoe-arched prayer niche) they've been applied so as to give the frieze a highly three-dimensional appearance. This is rare in Moorish stuccowork, though the inscriptions themselves, picked out in the curling, vegetative arabesques, are from familiar Koranic texts. The most common, as in all Moroccan stucco and *zellij* decoration, is the ceremonial *bismillah* invocation: "In the name of Allah, the Compassionate, the Merciful . . . ".

The Almoravid Koubba

After the *medersa* or the *souks*, the **Almoravid Koubba** is easy to pass by – a small, two-storey kiosk, which at first seems little more than a grey dome and a handful of variously shaped doors and windows. Look closer, though, and you will begin to understand its significance and even fascination. For this, the only intact Almoravid building, is at the root of all Moroccan architecture. The motifs you've just seen in the *medersa* – the pinecones, palms and acanthus leaves – were all carved here for the first time. The windows on each of the different sides became the classic shapes of Almohad and Merenid design – as did the *merlons*, the Christmas tree-like battlements; the complex "ribs" on the outside of the dome; and the dome's interior support, a sophisticated device of a square and star-shaped octagon, which is itself repeated at each of its corners. Once you see all this, you're only a step away from the eulogies of Islamic art historians who sense in this building, which was probably a small ablutions annexe to the original Ben Youssef Mosque, a powerful and novel expression of form.

Excavated only in 1952 – having been covered over amid the many rebuildings of the Ben Youssef *medersa* – the *koubba* lies just to the south of the present (mainly nineteenth-century) mosque. It is mostly below today's ground level, though standing with your back to the mosque you can make out the top of its dome behind the long, low brick wall. There is an entrance gate down a few steps, opposite the Ben Youssef mosque, where a *gardien* will emerge to escort you around – and may also show you the huge, old water conduits nearby, which brought water from the Atlas; if this is closed, you can get almost as good a view from the roof of a very ancient (but still active) *hammam* down to the right. Either way, you'll be expected to tip.

The tanneries and northern gates

The main *souks* – and the tourist route – stop abruptly at the Ben Youssef *medersa*. Above them, in all directions, you'll find yourself in the ordinary **residential quarters** of the Medina. There are few particular "sights" to be found here, but if you've got the time, there's an interest of its own in following the crowds, and a relief in getting away from the central shopping district of Marrakesh, where you are expected to come in, look around and buy.

Probably the most interesting targets are **Bab Debbagh** and **Souk el Khemis**. From Ben Youssef you can reach these quite easily: it's about a fifteen-minute walk to the first, another fifteen to twenty minutes around the ramparts to the second. As you pass the entrance porch to the *medersa,* you'll quickly reach a fork in the side street. To the left, a covered passageway leads around behind the mosque to join Rue Amesfah (see below). Head instead to your right, and then keep going as straight as possible until you emerge at the ramparts by Bab Debbagh; on the way you'll cross a small square and intersection, **Place el Moukef**, where a busy and sizeable lane goes off to the left – a more direct approach to Bab el Khemis.

BAB DEBBAGH AND THE TANNERIES

Bab Debbagh is supposedly Almoravid in design, though over the years it must have been almost totally rebuilt. Passing through the gate, you become aware of its very real defensive purpose: three internal rooms are placed in such a manner as to force anyone attempting to storm it to make several turns. To the left of the first chamber, there's a stairway that (for a small fee) you can use to climb up to the roof.

Looking down, you have an excellent view over the **tanneries**, built out here at the edge of the city for access to water (the summer-dry Oued Issil runs just outside the walls) and for the obvious reason of the smell. If you want to take a closer look at the processes, come in the morning, when the cooperatives are at work. Any of the kids standing around will take you in.

BAB EL KHEMIS

Following the road from Bab Debbagh, outside the ramparts, is the simplest approach to **Bab el Khemis** (Gate of the Thursday Market) another reconstructed Almoravid gate, built at an angle in the walls. The **Thursday market** now seems to take place more or less daily, around 400m to the north, above a cemetery and *marabout's* tomb. It is really a local produce market, though odd handicraft items do occasionally surface.

North of the Ben Youssef Mosque

The area immediately north of the **Ben Youssef Mosque** is cut by two main streets: Rue Assouel (which leads up to Bab el Khemis) and Rue Bab Taghzout, which runs up to the gate of the same name and to the Zaouia of Sidi Bel Abbes. These were, with Bab Doukkala, the principal approaches to the city until the present century and along them you find many of the old **fondouks** used for storage and lodging by merchants visiting the *souks.*

One of these *fondouks* is sited just south of the mosque and a whole series can be found along Rue Amesfah – the continuation of Baroudienne – to the north and west. Most are still used in some commercial capacity, as workshops or warehouses, and the doors to their courtyards often stand open. Some date from Saadian times and have fine details of wood carving or stuccowork. If you are interested, nobody seems to mind if you wander in.

THE ZAOUIA OF SIDI BEL ABBES

Rue Amesfah runs for around 150m north of the intersection with Rue Baroudienne before reaching the junction of Rue Assouel (to the east) and **Rue Bab Taghzout** (to the west). Following Rue Bab Taghzout, you pass another *fondouk*, opposite a small recessed fountain known as **Chrob ou Chouf** ("drink and admire"), and, around 500m further down, the old city gate of **Bab Taghzout**. This marked the limits of the original Almoravid Medina, and continued to do so into the eighteenth century, when Sultan Mohammed Abdallah extended the walls to enclose the quarter and the **Zaouia of Sidi Bel Abbes**.

Sidi Bel Abbes, a twelfth-century *marabout* and a prolific performer of miracles, is the most important of Marrakesh's seven saints, and his **zaouia**, a kind of monastic cult centre, has traditionally wielded very great influence and power, often at odds with that of the sultan and providing a refuge for political dissidents. The present buildings, which are strictly forbidden to non-Muslims, date largely from a reconstruction by Moulay Ismail – an act that was probably inspired more by political manipulation than piety. You can see something of the complex and its activities from outside the official boundary – do not, however, try to pass through the long central corridor. The *zaouia* still owns much of the quarter to the north and continues its educational and charitable work, distributing food each evening to the blind.

There is a smaller, though again significant, **zaouia** dedicated to **Sidi Slimane**, a Saadian *marabout,* a couple of blocks to the southwest.

West to Bab Doukkala: the Dar el Glaoui

A third alternative from Ben Youssef is to head west **towards Bab Doukkala.** This route, once you've found your way down through Souk Haddadine to **Rue Bab Doukkala,** is a sizeable thoroughfare and very straightforward to follow.

Midway, you pass the **Dar el Glaoui**, the old palace of the pasha of Marrakesh and a place of legendary exoticism throughout the first half of this century. El Glaoui, cruel and magnificent in equal measure, was the last of the great southern tribal leaders, an active and shrewd supporter of French rule and a personal friend of Winston Churchill. He was also one of the most spectacular partygivers around – in an age where rivals were not lacking. At the extraordinary *difas* held at Dar el Glaoui, "Nothing", as Gavin Maxwell wrote, "was impossible" – hashish and opium were freely available for the Europeans and Americans to experiment with, and "to his guests T'hami gave, literally, whatever they wanted, whether it might be a diamond ring, a present of money in gold, or a Berber girl or boy from the High Atlas".

Not surprisingly, there has been little enthusiasm for showing off the palace since El Glaoui's death in 1956, an event that led to a mob looting the palace, destroying its fittings and even the cars in the garages, and then lynching whoever of the pasha's henchmen they could find. However, a quarter of a century on, passions have burnt out and there are said to be plans to open it as a museum of some sort. You might ask at the tourist office in Gueliz – by all accounts, what survives of the palace's combination of traditional Moroccan architecture and 1920s chic is unique and pretty wonderful.

The Lower Medina: the palaces, Saadian Tombs and Mellah

Staying in Marrakesh even for a few days, you begin to sense the different appearance and life of its various Medina quarters, and nowhere more so than in the shift from north to south, from the area above Djemaa el Fna to the area below it. At the base here (a kind of stem to the mushroom shape of the city walls) is **Dar el Makhzen**, the royal palace. To its west stretches the old inner citadel of the **Kasbah**; to the east, the **Mellah**, once the largest Jewish ghetto in Morocco; while rambling above it are a series of mansions and palaces built for the nineteenth-century elite.

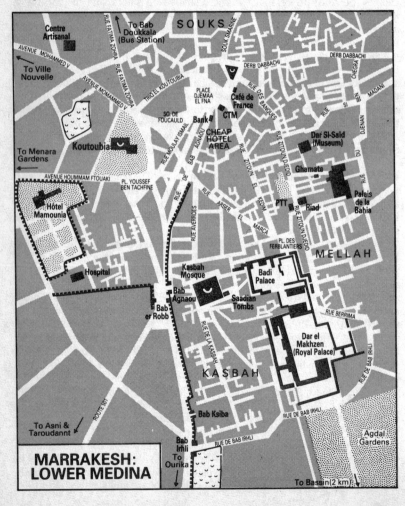

MARRAKESH: LOWER MEDINA

All in all, it's an interesting area to wander around, though you inevitably spend time trying to figure out the sudden and apparently arbitrary appearance of ramparts and enclosures. And there are two obvious focal points, not to be missed: the **Saadian Tombs**, preserved in the shadow of the Kasbah mosque, and **El Badi**, the ruined palace of Ahmed el Mansour.

The Saadian Tombs

Sealed up by Moulay Ismail after he had destroyed the adjoining Badi Palace, the **Saadian Tombs** lay half-ruined and half-forgotten at the beginning of this century. In 1917, however, they were rediscovered on a French aerial map and a passageway was built to give access from the side of the Kasbah mosque. Restored, they are today the city's main "sight" – overlavish, maybe, in their exhaustive decoration, but dazzling nonetheless. Friday mornings excepted, they are open daily from around 9am to noon and 2 to 6pm; go either early or late, if possible. As a national monument, admission is the usual 10dh; there is no longer, however, a compulsory guided tour – you are left to look around on your own or even just to sit and gaze. A quiet, high-walled enclosure, shaded with shrubs and palms and dotted with bright *zellij*-covered tombs, it seems as much a pleasure garden as a cemetery.

Some form of burial ground behind the royal palace probably predated the Saadian period, though the earliest of the tombs here dates from 1557, and all the principal structures were built by Sultan Ahmed el Mansour. This makes them virtual contemporaries of the Ben Youssef Medersa – with which there are obvious parallels – and allows a revealing insight into just how rich and extravagant the El Badi must once have been. Their escape from Moulay Ismail's systematic plundering was probably due to superstition – Ismail had to content himself with blocking all but an obscure entrance from the Kasbah mosque. Despite this, a few prominent *Marrakchis* continued to be buried in the mausoleums; the last, in 1792, was the "mad sultan", Moulay Yazid, whose 22-month reign was probably the most violent, vicious and sadistic in the nation's history.

THE MAUSOLEUMS

There are two main **mausoleums** in the enclosure. The finest is on the left as you come in – a beautiful group of three rooms, built to house El Mansour's own tomb and completed within his lifetime. Continuing around from the courtyard entrance, the first hall is a **prayer oratory**, a room probably not intended for burial, though now almost littered with the thin marble stones of Saadian princes. It is here that Moulay Yazid was laid out, perhaps in purposeful obscurity, certainly in ironic contrast to the cursive inscription around the band of black and white *zellij*: "And the works of peace they have accomplished", it reads amid the interlocking circles, "will make them enter the holy gardens".

Architecturally, the most important feature of this mausoleum is the *mihrab*, its pointed horseshoe arch supported by an incredibly delicate arrangement of columns. Opposite this is another elaborate arch, leading to the domed **central chamber** and **El Mansour's tomb**, which you can glimpse through the next door in the court. The tomb, slightly larger than those surrounding it, lies right in the middle, flanked on either side by those of the sultan's sons and successors. The room itself is spectacular, faint light filtering on to the tombs from an interior lantern in a tremendous vaulted roof, the *zellij* full of colour and motion and the undefined richness of a third chamber almost hidden from view. Throughout, there are echoes of the Alhambra in Granada, from which its style is clearly derived; oddly, though, it was completed nearly two centuries later and, except in detail and exuberance, seems hardly to show any development.

The **other mausoleum**, older and less impressive, was built by Ahmed in place of an existing pavilion above the tombs of his mother, Lalla Messaouda, and of Mohammed esh Sheikh, the founder of the Saadian dynasty. It is again a series of three rooms, though two are hardly more than loggias. Lalla's tomb is the niche below the dome in the outer chamber. Mohammed esh Sheikh is buried in the inner one – or at least his body is, since he was murdered in the Atlas by Turkish mercenaries, who salted his head and took it back for public display on the walls in Istanbul.

Outside, **around the garden and courtyard**, are scattered the tombs of over a hundred more Saadian princes and members of the royal household. Like the privileged sixty-six given space within the mausoleums, their gravestones are brilliantly tiled and often elaborately inscribed. The most usual inscription reads quite simply:

There is no God but God.
Muhammad is God's envoy.
Praise Be to God.
The occupant of this tomb died on . . . .

But there are others – epitaphs and extracts from the Koran – that seem to express the turbulence of the age to a greater degree, which, with Ahmed's death in 1603, was to disintegrate into nearly seventy years of constant civil war. "Every soul shall know death", reads one tombstone; "Death will find you wherever you are, even in fortified towers", another. And, carved in gypsum on the walls, there is a poem:

O mausoleum, built out of mercy, thou whose
walls are the shadow of heaven.
The breath of asceticism is wafted from thy tombs
like a fragrance.
Through thy death
the light of faith has been dimmed,
the seven spheres are fraught with darkness
and the columns of glory
broken with pain.

ACCESS
Getting to the Saadian Tombs, the simplest route from Djemaa el Fna is to follow **Rue Bab Agnaou** outside the ramparts. At its end you come to a small square flanked by two gates. Directly ahead is **Bab er Robb** – outside of which the *grands taxis* and private-line buses leave for Ourika and other local destinations. To the left, somewhat battered and eroded, is the city's only survivng Almohad gateway, **Bab Agnaou** (Gate of the Gnaoua [the

blacks]). This is an impressive structure, smaller than the monumental gates of Rabat, but sharing much of their force and apparent simplicity. Notice how the semicircular frieze above its arch creates a strong, three-dimensional effect without any actual depth of carving. At the time of its construction, it was the only stone building in Marrakesh apart from the Koutoubia Minaret.

Passing through the gate, the **Kasbah mosque** is in front of you: its minaret looks gaudy and modern but is, in fact, contemporary with both the Koutoubia and Hassan towers – it was restored to its exact original state in the 1960s. The narrow passageway to the Saadian Tombs is well signposted, at the near righthand corner of the mosque.

El Badi Palace

To reach the ruins of the **El Badi Palace** – which seems originally to have sprawled across the whole area east of the Kasbah mosque – you have to backtrack slightly from the Saadian Tombs. At Bab Agnaou, follow the ramparts up again, this time taking the road just inside them, until you come to a reasonably sized street on your right (just before the walls temporarily give out). Turn into this street, keep more or less straight, and in about 550m, you'll emerge at **Place des Ferblantiers** – a major intersection. On the south side of the *place* is a gate known as **Bab Berrima**, which opens on to a long rectangular enclosure, flanked on either side by walls; go through it, and on your right you'll come to the Badi's entrance. Hours are generally 9am to noon and 2.30 to 5.30pm; admission, once again, is 3dh; a guided tour is touted but far from essential.

AHMED EL MANSOUR

Though substantially in ruins, and reduced throughout to its red *pisé* walls, enough remains of **El Badi** to suggest that its name – "The Incomparable" – was not entirely immodest. It took Moulay Ismail over ten years of systematic work to strip the palace of everything movable or of value, and even so, there's a lingering sense of luxury and grandeur. The scale, with its sunken gardens and vast, ninety-metre-long pool, is certainly unrivalled, and the odd traces of *zellij* and plaster still left evoke a decor that was probably as rich as that of the Saadian Tombs.

The palace was begun shortly after Ahmed el Mansour's accession, its initial finance came from the enormous ransom paid out by the Portuguese after the Battle of the Three Kings at Ksar el Kebir. Fought in the summer of 1578, this was one of the most disastrous battles in Christian medieval history; ostensibly in support of a rival Saadian claimant, but to all intents a Portuguese crusade, it was led by King Sebastião, and supported by almost his entire nobility. Few escaped death or Moorish capture. Sebastião himself was killed, as were both the Saadian claimant and the ruling sultan.

As a result, Ahmed – dubbed *El Mansour* (The Victorious) – came to the throne, undisputed and commanding immediate wealth. He reigned for twenty-five years, trading in sugar and slaves with Britain, Spain and Italy; seizing the gold route across the Sahara with the capture of Timbuktu, which earned him the additional epithet *El Dhahibi* (The Golden); and maintaining peace in Morocco through a loose confederation of tribes. It was the most prosperous era in the country's history since the Almohads – a cultural and political renaissance reflected in the coining of a new title, the Shereefian Empire, the country's official name until Independence in 1956.

THE INCOMPARABLE PALACE

What you see today is essentially the ceremonial part of **the palace complex**, planned on a grand scale for the reception of ambassadors, and not meant for everyday living. It seems likely that El Mansour and the multiple members of his court each had private palaces – smaller, though built to a similar ground plan – to the west and south, covering much of the area occupied today by the Dar el Makhzen, the present Royal Palace.

The **entrance** in current use was probably not the main approach. Going through, you find yourself at the side of a **mosque**, like everything else within this complex, of enormous height. To the rear extends the great **central court**, over 130m long and nearly as wide, and constructed on a substructure of vaults in order to allow the circulation of water through the pools and gardens. When the pools are filled – as during the June folklore festival which takes place here – they are an incredibly majestic sight, especially the main one, with an island that was originally surmounted by an elaborate double fountain.

On each side of the pools were summer pavilions, traces of which survive. The most prominent is at the far end, a monumental hall that was used by the sultan on occasions of state and known as the **Koubba el Hamsiniya** (The Fifty Pavilion), for the number of its columns. Strangely enough, their size and splendor were documented by an observer far removed from the Arab chroniclers who extolled their beauty. The French philosopher Montaigne, while travelling through Italy, saw craftsmen preparing the columns – "each of an extreme height . . . for the king of Fes and Barbary".

South of the courtyard are ruins of the palace **stables,** and beyond them, leading towards the intriguing walls of the present royal palace, a series of **dungeons**, used into the present century as a state prison. You can explore part of these and could easily spend a whole afternoon wandering around the various inner courts above, with their fragments of marble and *zellij* and their water conduits for the fountains and *hammams*. Like the Saadian Tombs, the Badi inspired contemporary poets, and there is an account, too, by the chronicler El Ifrani, of its construction:

> *El Mansour made workmen come from all the different countries . . . . He paid for the marble sent from Italy in sugar, pound for pound awarded his workers very generously . . . and paid attention even to the entertainment of their children, so that the artisans might devote themselves entirely to their work without being distracted by any other preoccupation.*

If this is even half true, there could be no greater contrast with the next great Moroccan builder, and dismantler of the palace, Moulay Ismail, whose workmen were instead beaten up, starved and abused, and then buried in the walls where they fell. But sixteenth-century crèches aside, the most enduring account of the palace concerns its state opening, a fabulous occasion attended by ambassadors from several European powers and by all the sheikhs and *caids* of the kingdom. Surveying the effect, Ahmed turned to his court jester for an opinion on the new palace. "Sidi", the man replied, "this will make a magnificent ruin".

The Mellah

It was in 1558 – five years before Ahmed's accession – that the city's **Mellah**, the separate Jewish quarter, was created. There is no exact record of why this was done at this particular time. Possibly it was the result of a pogrom, with the sultan moving the Jews to his protected Kasbah – and they, in turn, forming a useful buffer zone (and scapegoat) between his palace and the populace in times of social unrest. But, as likely as not, it was simply brought about to make taxation easier. The Jews of Marrakesh were an important financial resource – they controlled most of the Saadian sugar trade, and comprised practically all of the city's bankers, metalworkers, jewellers and tailors. In the sixteenth century, at least, their quarter was almost a town in itself, supervised by rabbis, and with its own *souks,* gardens, fountains and synagogues.

The present Mellah, much smaller in extent, is now almost entirely Muslim – most of the *Marrakchi* Jews left long ago for Casablanca (where some 6000 still live) or emigrated to France or Israel. The few who remain, outwardly distinguishable only by the men's small black skullcaps, are mostly poor or old or both. Their quarter, however, is immediately distinct: its houses are taller than elsewhere, the streets are more enclosed, and even the shop cubicles are smaller. Until the Protectorate, Jews were not permitted to own land or property – nor even to ride or walk, except barefoot – outside the Mellah; a situation that was greatly exploited by their landlords, who resisted all attempts to expand the walls. Today its air of neglect and poverty – since this is not a prized neighbourhood in which to live – is probably less than at any time during the past three centuries.

AROUND THE QUARTER

The main entrance, in what is still a largely walled district, is at **Place des Ferblantiers**. This square, formerly called Place du Mellah, was itself part of the old Jewish *souk,* and an archway (to your right, standing at Bab Berrima) leads into it. Near the upper end is a **jewellers' souk**, one of the traditional Jewish trades now more or less taken over by Muslim craftsmen; further down are some good spice and textile *souks*. Right at the centre – and situated very much as the goal of a maze – is a small square with a fountain in the middle, **Place Souweka**. You will almost certainly find yourself back here if you wander around for a short while and manage to avoid the blind alleys.

To the east, some 200m away, is the old Jewish **cemetery**, the *Mihaara*. Closer by (and you'll need to enlist a guide to find them) are a number of **synagogues** (*s'noga*). Even when they were in active use, many were as much private houses as they were temples – " . . . serving also as places in which to eat, sleep and to kill chickens" according to Budgett Meakin – and most of them today remain lived in. One of the larger ones, attached to a kind of hostel financed by American Jews, can usually be visited, as (depending on who your guide knows) can a couple of other ones.

North of the Mellah: Palais El Bahia

Heading north from the Mellah – back towards Djemaa el Fna – there are three direct and fairly simple routes. To the left of Place des Ferblantiers, **Avenue Hoummam el Ftouaki** will bring you out by the Koutoubia. Above the *place*, two parallel streets, **Rue Zitoun el Kedim** and **Zitoun el Djedid** lead up to the Djemaa itself.

El Kedim is basically a shopping street, lined with grocers, barbershops, and at the upper end, a couple of *hammams* (open all day; one each for men and women). El Djedid is more residential, and it is here that you find the concentration of **palaces and mansions** built in those strange, closing decades of the last century, and the first few years of our own, when the sultans Moulay Hassan and Moulay Abd el Aziz held court in the city.

By far the most ambitious and costly of these was the **Palais El Bahia**, residence of the grand vizier, Si Ahmed Ben Moussa. Shrewd, wilful and cruel, as was the tradition of his age, Bou Ahmed (as he was better known) was a black slave who rose to hold massive power in the Shereefian kingdom and, for the last six years of his life, exercised virtually autocratic control. He was first chamberlain to Moulay Hassan, whose death while returning home from a *harka* he was able to conceal until the proclamation of Abd el Aziz in Rabat (see "Writers on Morocco", in *Contexts*, for the dramatic account). Under Abd el Aziz (who was just twelve when he acceded to the throne), Bou Ahmed usurped the position of vizier from the ill-fated Jamai brothers (see Fes), and then proceeded to rule.

He began building the Bahia in 1894, later enlarging it by acquiring the surrounding land and property. He died in 1900. The name of the building means "The Effulgence" or "Brilliance", but after the **guided tour** around various sections of the rambling palace courts and apartments you might feel this to be a somewhat tall claim. There is reasonable craftsmanship in the main **reception halls**, and a pleasant arrangement of rooms in the **harem quarter,** but for the most part it is all fabulously vulgar and hasn't aged too well. Perhaps this is the main reason for a visit: you come away realising just how much mastery and sophistication went into the Saadian *medersa* and tombs, and how corrupted and dull these traditions had become.

But there is also a certain pathos to the empty, echoing chambers – and the inevitable passing of Bou Ahmed's influence and glory. Walter Harris, who knew the vizier, described his demise and the clearing of his palace in *Morocco That Was*, published just twenty years after the events, by which time Bou Ahmed's name had already become "only a memory of the past":

> *For several days as the Vizier lay expiring, guards were stationed outside his palace waiting in silence for the end. And then one morning the wail of the women within the house told that death had come. Every gateway of the great building was seized, and no one was allowed to enter or come out, while within there was pandemonium. His slaves pillaged wherever they could lay their hands. His women fought and stole to get possesion of the jewels. Safes were broken open, documents and title-deeds were extracted, precious stones were torn from their settings, the more easily to be concealed, and even murder took place . . . . A few days later nothing remained but the great building – all the rest had disappeared into space. His family were driven out to starvation and ruin, and his vast properties passed into the possession of the State. It was the custom of the country.*

ACCESS

For some years during the Protectorate, the palace was used to house the resident-general, and it is still called into use when the royal family is in the city. This is usually from January through March, at which times there is no public admission. Its normal **opening hours** are daily (except Tuesday) from 9am to noon and 2.30 to 5.30pm; 10dh admission.

Finding your way to the palace is easy enough: from Rue Zitoun follow the signs to *Palais Gharnata*, keeping straight when they suddenly direct you to the right under an arch. The **Gharnata**, and the nearby **Riad**, "palaces" are among a number of mansions in this part of the city that have been converted into "Tourist Spectacle" restaurants. All of them are expensive – and the shows hideously inauthentic – but it's worth looking into one or two of them during the day, just to see the turn-of-the-century decor.

Dar Si Said Museum

Also worth your while on this route is the **Dar Si Said**, a smaller version of the Bahia, built by a brother of Bou Ahmed. The brother, something of a simpleton, nonetheless gained the post of royal chamberlain.

The palace is today a **Museum of Moroccan Arts**, particularly strong on its collections of southern **Berber jewellery and weapons** – large, boldly designed objects of great beauty. There are also fine displays of eighteenth- and nineteenth-century **wood carving** from the Glaoui Kasbahs, **modern Berber rugs** and a curious group of traditional **wedding chairs** – once widely used for carrying the bride, veiled and hidden, to her new home – and **fairground swings,** used at *moussems* until the 1940s.

There's pleasure, too, in the palace itself, with its beautiful pooled court-yards, cool and scented with lemon trees, palms and flowers. Dar Si Said is just a block to the west of Rue Zitoun el Djedid (turn right opposite a mosque, around halfway down); summer admission hours are 9am–noon & 4–7pm (winter 9am–noon & 2.30–6pm), closed Tuesday; 10dh admission.

The Gardens

With summer temperatures of 90 to 100°F – and peaks well above that – it seems best to devote at least the middle of a Marrakesh day to total inactivity. If you want to do this in style, it means finding your way to a garden. There are two – **Agdal** and **Menara** – designed for just this purpose. Each begins near the edge of the Medina, rambles through acres of orchards and olive groves, and has, near its centre, an immense, lake-size pool of water. This is all – they are not flower gardens, but, cool and completely still, they seem both satisfying and luxurious, and in perfect contrast to the close city streets. Other, smaller gardens of note include that of the **Hôtel Mamounia**, and the **Jardin Majorelle**, created by the French nineteenth-century painter.

With the exception of the Hôtel Mamounia, you will want **transport** to get to any of these gardens – either a *petit taxi* or *calèche*. If you are considering a *calèche* trip at any stage, the Agdal or Menara are as perfect destinations as any. Alternatively, to take in both gardens and tour the ramparts and palmery, you could hire a **bike** or *grand taxi* for the day (see p.255).

Jardin Agdal

The **Agdal** is a confusingly large expanse – some three kilometres in extent and with half a dozen smaller irrigation pools in addition to its *grand bassin*. Beginning just south of the Mellah and Royal Palace, it is watered by an incredible system of wells and underground channels that go as far as the base of the Atlas in the Ourika Valley and that date, in part, from the earliest founding of the city.

Over the centuries, the channels have often fallen into disrepair and the gardens have been abandoned, but the present nineteenth-century layout probably differs little from any of its predecessors. It is surrounded by walls, with gates at each of the near corners, while inside, the orange, fig, lemon, apricot and pomegranate orchards are divided into square, irrigated plots by an endless series of raised walkways and broad avenues of olive trees.

If you walk out here, the perimeter is around 4km from Djemaa el Fna – but it's a further 2km of unsignposted paths before you reach the main series of pools at its heart. The largest one is the **Sahraj el Hana** (Tank of Health), which was probably dug by the Almohads and is flanked by a ramshackle old *menzeh*, or summer pavilion, where the last few precolonial sultans held picnics and boating parties. You can climb up on its roof for a fabulous view over the park and across to the Koutoubia and Atlas, and if the caretaker's around, you'll be shown the steam-powered launch which capsized in 1873, bringing Sultan Sidi Mohammed to his death – or, as his epitaph rather more elegantly put it, he "departed this life, in a water tank, in the hope of something better to come".

These days, probably the most dangerous thing you could do here would be to swim in the algae-ridden waters, though the kids do it and it does look unbelievably tempting. It's perhaps better just to pick up some food beforehand – and perhaps a bottle of wine from the Gueliz – and spread out a picnic in local fashion on the paved, shaded pathway around the water's edge.

ACCESS

To get to the Agdal, take the road outside the ramparts below Bab Agnaou/ Bab er Robb, and then turn left as you are about to leave the city at Bab Irhli; this route will take you through a *mechouar* (parade ground) by the royal palace and to the corner gate of the garden. The garden is often closed during the winter months (November to January) when the king is in residence in Marrakesh.

Jardin Menara

The **Menara** is in a similar vein to the Agdal, though it has only a single tank and, being much closer to the city, is much more visited. If you just want to gaze upon one of these still sheets of water, then come out here; it's a lot easier to get to than the Agdal (and a cheaper ride, too).

Like the Agdal, the Menara was restored and its pavilions rebuilt by Sultan Abd er Rahman (1822–59). The famous poolside *menzeh* (5dh admission) is said to have replaced an original Saadian structure.

The garden couldn't be simpler to find: just follow Av. de la Menara from Bab Djedid, by the *Hôtel Mamounia*.

The Palmery and Jardin Majorelle

The best section of the **palmery** is signposted ("Route de Palmeraie"), around 2km out on Av. El Jadida, after the intersection with Av. Yacoub el Mansour. It is impressive as a first experience of southern landscape, though perhaps not a great priority if you are planning to cross the Atlas to the desert oases of the Drâa or Dades.

On the way, however, you can stop and take a look at the subtropical **Jardin Majorelle**, or *Bou Saf Saf* as it's now officially known. This small, meticulously planned botanical garden was created in the 1920s by the minor French painter, Louis Majorelle, and is now owned by Yves St Laurent. It is open daily for visits (8am–5pm; 10dh).

A sobering contrast to this luxuriance, as you pass **Bab Doukkala** en route, is the shantytown just outside the walls above the bus station – a quarter with its own industry, scrap and general goods *souks,* located in the city's old leper colony. Even in the early years of the protectorate, lepers from here used to beg at the gates of the Medina, which they were forbidden to enter.

The Hôtel Mamounia

Finally – and much closer – you might consider spending an hour or two looking around the gardens of the famed **Hôtel Mamounia**. Walled from the outside world, yet only five minutes' walk from the Djemaa, these were once royal grounds, laid out by the Saadians with a succession of pavilions. Today they're slightly Europeanised in style, but have retained the traditional elements of shrubs and walkways. For the cost of a drink or some tea on the terrace – the latter quite reasonably priced – you can sit down and admire the surroundings. Be prepared, though, to resist the swimming pool, since it is strictly reserved for residents.

If you ask at the desk, and the staff aren't too busy, someone may be prepared to give you a quick tour of the old part of the hotel – where the **Winston Churchill suite** is preserved as visited by its namesake. There are editions of Churchill's books on the shelves, a truly sultan-like bed (and smaller sleeping quarters for his manservant) and photographs of him painting in the gardens. Churchill was a frequent visitor to Marrakesh from the 1930s to the 1950s, and the Mamounia, so it is said, was his favourite hotel in the world. Even though it's been rebuilt and enlarged since his day, it's not hard to understand the lasting appeal.

Gueliz

As stressed earlier, it's distinctly preferable to stay in or near the Medina, rather than out in the Ville Nouvelle – the French-created **Gueliz** quarter. However, Gueliz is not completely without charms. In addition to the various restaurants, cafés and bars, detailed overpage, an evening in the new town offers the opportunity to start up conversations with Moroccans other than hustlers. There are, also, a number of exceptional **antique crafts shops**, where for a not too inflated price, you can secure some original, elegant objects – spired scent bottles, velvet-covered wooden water flasks, wooden Koranic tablets and the like.

Eating, drinking and nightlife

As with hotels, food options in Marrakesh break down less rigidly than usual between Gueliz and the Medina. Gueliz, naturally enough, is where you'll find French-style cafés and restaurants – and virtually all of the city's bars. In the Medina, however, in addition to the spectacle of the Djemaa el Fna foodstalls, there's a fair range of inexpensive café-restaurants, plus a number of upmarket options where you can dine out on Moroccan cuisine in some style.

Djemaa el Fna foodstalls

You might decide against eating at one of them – as even most of the hustlers caution – but at some stage you should at least wander down the makeshift lane of **food stalls** near the top of **Djemaa el Fna**. They tend to specialise in a few main dishes (though with often a larger range on display), and it's worth watching the crowds for a while to check out what is best to eat where.

If you do decide to throw caution to the winds – probably safer in winter than summer – take a seat on one of the benches, ask the price of a plate of food and order all you like; if you want to wash it down with a soft drink or some mineral water, the owners will send a boy off to get it for you. (Opinions differ widely on the health risks of these stalls: a lot of travellers eat there regularly and with no ill effect; others are convinced that the stalls acounted for three days laid out with upset stomachs.)

Inexpensive Medina café-restaurants

No more expensive and generally healthier are some of the **café-restaurants** on the side of the Djemaa. These include:

Chez Chegrouni, an unsigned place with a small terrace next to the Café Montréal (about 10m past the Café de France in the direction of the souks). Excellent *kefta* and *brochettes*, a fine chicken and lemon *tajine*, *harira*, salad and fresh yoghurt, and all at very low prices.

Café el Fath, at the north end of Djemaa el Fna. Good value set meals.

Other good possibilities are to be found just off the Djemaa el Fna in **Rue Bani Marin**, the street running between Rue Moulay Ismail and Rue de Bab Agnaou; many of these stay open late. *Mik Mak*, next to the *Hôtel Ali* on Place Foucauld is an excellent patisserie, good for tea or breakfast.

More expensive Medina restaurants

For a variation on the usual fare, or (at the bottom of this list) a quest for the ultimate Moroccoan gastronomic experience, pick from:

Restaurant Argana, Place Djemaa el Fna. Possibly the best Djemaa el Fna vantage point – and it's worth queueing for a table for this reason alone. Regular French-Moroccan food at modest prices. Sited opposite the *Banque de Maroc/Hôtel CTM*.

Hôtel Ali, Place de Foucauld. Justifiably popular restaurant, with reliable Moroccan set menus (40–60dh), friendly service and resident musician.

Hôtel-Restaurant Foucauld, Place de Foucauld. Quality can be patchy, but on good days the *Foucauld* is worth the prices (about 100dh a head) for its palace-type salon, pleasantly low-key musicians and massive portions of *pastilla*, soups, pâté and vegetables.

Grand Hôtel Tazi, Rue Bab Agnaou. The *Foucauld*'s sister hotel, the *Tazi*, just down the road, has a couple of restaurants, too – one on the roof in summer – and similar prices and menus. It's also good for breakfast and has the nearest **bar** to the Djemaa el Fna.

Restaurant Iceberg, Rue Bab Agnaou (between the *Foucauld* and the *Tazi*). Solid, French cuisine. Quality usually a bit higher than the *Foucauld* or *Tazi* and similar prices.

Le Restaurant Marrakechi, 52 Rue des Banques, Place Djemaa el Fna (on the corner of the road just north of the *Café de France*). A sumptuous new restaurant high up above the Djemaa. Imperial but intimate decor, impeccable service and indescribably delicious *pastilla*. Around 150–180dh a head for a 3- to 5-course, blowout meal.

Restaurant Relais Al Baraka, Djemaa el Fna, by the Commisariat (☎423.41). Expensive French-Moroccan restaurant in a fountain court; around 250dh a head. No credit cards.

La Maison Arabe, 5 Derb Ferrane, opposite the Bab Doukala mosque (☎226.04). Reputedly Morocco's finest restaurant; highly exclusive, with compulsory booking, and not much change from 300dh a head.

Le Restaurant Marocain, in the Hôtel Mamounia. The *Maison Arabe*'s rival. Similar priced.

Like Fes, Marrakesh also has several restaurants in converted **palaces**. However, virtually all are geared towards package groups, with kitsch belly-dancing entertainment laid on. Unless you've heard otherwise, ignore.

Gueliz restaurants

Although Gueliz is not so picturesque a setting for a meal, it would be a mistake to dismiss it entirely as modern and French. It is, after all, the city's main centre and has restaurants at all budgets.

Café Chaabia, Bd. Moulay Rachid; **Café de l'Union**, Rue Ibn Aicha (at the end of Av. Yacoub el Mansour/beginning of Bd. Zerktouni). Two of the cheapest Gueliz café-restaurants. the former is very close to the youth hostel and campsite.

Café Toubkal, 153 Rue el Beqal. Another very cheap, very reasonable café-restaurant.

Café La Mama, Rue Souraya (opposite the *Hôtel Palmeraie*). Open twenty-four hours a day, seven days a week, for plain, simply prepared food.

Hôtel Oasis, 50 Av. Mohammed V. Good value four-course meals around 40dh. Licensed.

Le Petit Poucet, 56 Av. Mohammed V. Stylish, old established French restaurant. Pricey.

Restaurant Chinois, 134 Av. Mohammed V; **La Trattoria**, Rue Mohammed Beqal; **La Pizza**, 63 Av. Mohammed V. For those in need of a break from French-Moroccan food: Chinese and Italian options, as the names suggest.

The **food market**, in the arcade off the middle of Av. Mohammed V, is convenient place for stocking up on supplies before heading off to the Atlas.

Bars

The only bars in easy reach of the **Medina** are in the hotels *Tazi*, *Foucauld* (on the roof) and *Yasmine*, or for those on expense accounts, the *Mamounia*. See hotel listings for addresses.

In **Gueliz**, there's more variety, and you are more likely to have Moroccans for company – though be aware that (outside of the hotels) most of the bars are very much male preserves. The liveliest places are generally:

La Renaissance (by the hotel of the same name), Av. Mohammed V. Long established café-bar with a rooftop terrasse. Closes around 10–10.30pm.

Le Petit Poucet, 56 Av. Mohammed V. Old rival to the *Renaissance*.

Bar-Café Oasis, 50 Av. Mohammed V. Good value for beer and snacks.

Les Ambassadeurs; **Le Regent**; **Les Negociants**. Av. Mohammed V, nos. 6, 34 and 108.

Fiarée; **Bagatelle**. At 33 and 101 Rue Yougouslavie.

Café Oued el Had, 100 Av. Casablanca (a *petit taxi* ride): An alternative option, open to 2am. This is in fact a complex of three bars – the best of them upstairs.

There is a cheap store for **buying wine** in Gueliz, on Av. Mohammed V. Following the road out of town, it is about 100m past the Avis car rental, on the left; a large selection of wine is stocked in a room at the back of the shop.

Music, discos and casinos
Entertainment and **nightlife** in the Medina revolve around Djemaa el Fna and its cafés. Sometimes, though, there might be a **music group** playing in an enclosure behind the Koutoubia on Av. Mohammed. Gueliz also has half a dozen or so **discos**. These include the *Pub Laurent*, on Rue Ibn Aicha, and *L'Atlas* and *Le Flash* on Av. Mohammed V.

And lastly, in case you get an urge to lose money more easily than on the Djemaa el Fna, there are two **casinos**: one in Hivernage, by the *Hôtel Es Saadi*, the other in the *Hôtel Mamounia*. Both are open from 8pm; they are not exclusive, but you need to dress up a bit (no jeans or T-shirts)

The Marrakesh Festival, *moussems* and local markets

The annual two-week **Folklore Festival**, held in the Badi Palace around the end of May/beginning of June, is almost worth planning your trip to Morocco around. Despite its touristy-sounding name, it is in fact a series of authentic and unusual performances, with groups of musicians and dancers coming in from all over the country. A typical programme will span the whole range of Moroccan music – from the Gnaoua drummers and the panpipers of Jajouka, to Berber *ahouaches* from the Atlas and southern oases, to classical Andalusian music from Fes. The shows are held each evening from around 9pm to midnight (tickets are 50dh); before they start, towards sunset, there is a **fantasia** at Bab el Djedid – a spectacle by any standard, with dozens of Berber horsemen firing their guns in the air at full gallop.

Outside Marrakesh
Outside Marrakesh, local **moussems** include: Setti Fatma (Ourika; August; see p.289), Sidi Bouatmane (Amizmiz; September) and Moulay Brahim (near Asni; held over the Mouloud; see p.296).

Worthwhile **weekly markets** in the area around the city include: Amizmiz (Tuesday; see p.291), Tamasloht (on the road to Amizmiz; Tuesday), Asni (the Toubkal trailhead; Saturday; see p.295) and Aït Ourir (on the road to Ouarzazate; Monday).

Listings

American Express c/o *Voyages Schwarz*, Rue Mauritania (off Av. Mohammed V: second left after Place de la Liberté if you're coming from the Medina). Business hours Mon–Fri 9am–12.30pm and 3–4.30pm, but stays open until 7pm for mail.

Banks As in other Moroccan cities, the *BMCE* is the best bet for exchange – accepting VISA/Mastercard, travellers' cheques and most currencies. It has branches in both the Medina (Place Foucauld) and Gueliz (144 Bd. Mohammed V), open from 8am to 8pm everyday. *Crédit du Maroc, Banque Populaire* and the *SGMB* all have branches on Rue Bab Agnaou – just off Djemaa el Fna – and in Gueliz.

Car Repairs The garage beside the *Hôtel Tazi* in Rue Bab Agnaou (☎223.39) fixes Renaults – and should be able to direct you elsewhere for spare parts of the makes they don't stock. *Ourika* at 66 Av. Mohammed V, Gueliz (☎301.55) deals with Fiats. Car parts are available in Gueliz from the *Centre Europén de l'Automobile* (18 Bd. Moulay Rachid; ☎315.30) and *Union Pièces Autos* (18 Bd. Mansour Eddahbi; ☎317.90)

Chemists There are several along Av. Mohammed V, including a good one just off Place de la Liberté, which has a doctor on call.

Dentist Dr. E. Gailleres, 112 Av. Mohammed V (opposite the ONMT office), is recommended; he speaks some English.

Doctor Dr. Perez, 169 Av. Mohammed V (☎310.30) is English speaking and reliable. Also see "Chemists", above.

Ferry tickets *Comanav Voyages,* 149 Av. Mohammed V (☎302.65). Accept cash only.

Golf The 18-hole *Royal Golf* is sited 4km out from the centre on the P31 (Tizi n'Tichka) road.

Newspapers *The International Herald Tribune, Time, Newsweek,* etc., plus occasional British newspapers, are available from the newsstands along Av. Mohammed V in Gueliz and in the fancy hotels – notably the *Mamounia.*

Post Office The main *PTT*, which receives all **Poste Restante** mail, is on Place 16 Novembre, midway down Av. Mohammed V; service hours are Mon–Sat 8am–2pm. The **telephone** section, with its own entrance, stays open until 9pm, and operators will (eventually) place a call for you. The Medina *PTT* in Place Djemaa el Fna stays open until 7pm; here you can phone direct, though it takes as long as in Gueliz.

Swimming Pools There's a large, very popular municipal pool on Rue Abou el Abbes Sebti – the first main road to the left off Av. Mohammed V as you walk past the Koutoubia towards Gueliz. Alternatives are to walk into one of the 4* or 5* hotels and salve your conscience by having a drink or a meal.

Tourist Offices Both the ONMT and *Syndicat d'Initiative* are on Av. Mohammed V – the first is in Place Abd el Moumen Benali, the second is a little way up towards the Medina, at no. 170. Both open daily 8.30am–noon and 3–6pm; the S.I. is closed Saturday afternoons and Sundays.

LEAVING MARRAKESH

Long distance buses
Buses to all long distance destinations leave from the main terminus at **Bab Doukkala**. Buy tickets in advance for the more popular destinations such as Fes, Essaouira, and El Jadida, or you could find yourself waiting for the second or third bus that's leaving. And be sure to turn up at least half an hour early if you're heading for **Taroudannt** over the Tizi n'Test route (the *SATAS* bus currently leaves at 5am), or for **Zagora** (7am; arrives 4.30pm). *CTM* buses cover the Tizi n'Tichka route to Ouarzazate at 5.30am and 5.30pm. *SATAS* have the best services to Agadir.

Bear in mind, that *CTM* and all the private companies have their own individual ticket windows – choices can be more extensive than at first appears.

Local buses
The **local exceptions** are buses to **Ourika**, **Asni** (the trailhead for Djebel Toubkal), and **Moulay Brahim**, which leave from just outside Bab er Robb. Some buses also run to Asni from the Bab Doukkala bus station, from 10am–7pm.

LEAVING MARRAKESH (CONT)

Grands taxis

Grands taxis can also be useful for getting to Ourika or to Asni – negotiate for these by Bab er Robb (about 15dh a place to Asni). Taxis run less frequently to other destinations but you could try asking some of the drivers at the stands in Djemaa el Fna and by Bab er Raha (between Av. Mohammed V and Bab Doukkala). Essaouira and Agadir are both possible (around 50dh and 70dh a place, respectively).

Train

Flying aside, trains are the quickest and most comfortable way of getting to Casa and Rabat. If you're heading back to Tangier it's possible to do the trip in one, most easily by booking (in advance) a *couchette* on the night train (depart 7.40pm, arrive Tangier 5.50am in theory, around 7am in practise; ordinary seats on this train are not recommended).

The train company, *ONCF*, also run **express buses**, leaving from the train station, to Agadir (12.58pm, 10.37pm), and Laayoune (10.37pm). There may also be shared taxis leaving the station at these times, a place to Agadir costing just 60dh.

Flights

Royal Air Maroc operates domestic flights to Casa (with onward connections to Tangier and Fes), and to Ouarzazate (taking just 25–30 minutes). They are currently rebuilding their office and have a temporary stall in the basement of the *Hôtel Atlas Asni* in Gueliz. International tickets should be reconfirmed there.

The **airport** is 5km out, off Av. de Menara (see p.258).

Hitching

As always, the campsite can be a good place to arrange lifts, or find people to share the cost of hiring a car or buying petrol. There are always people setting out for Ouarzazate and the southern Kasbah/oasis routes.

Car Hire

Marrakesh is the city where you're most likely to want to hire a car – and rates here are generally the most competitive after Casablanca. One of the cheapest places to arrange hire is at *Menara Tours* (59 Bd. Mansour el Eddabhi), who deal with a number of agencies. Alternatively, call around the individual companies, which include:

Concorde Cars, 154 Av. Mohammed V. Excellent reports on efficiency and helpfulness. They don't have offices elsewhere in Morocco but you can pay a premium to deposit the car in another city.

Atis Car, 76 bis Av. Abdelkrim el Khattabi. Also recommended.

LVS, 41 Rue Yougoslavie (☎332.14).

Budget Cars, 213 Bd. Mohammed V (☎334.24).

Europ.Car, 189 Bd. Mohammed V (☎303.68).

Sud Cars, 213 Bd. Mohammed V (☎309.97).

Transcar, 10 Bd. Zerktouni (☎316.47).

Tourist Cars, 64 Bd. Zerktouni (☎315.30).

Hertz, 154 Bd. Mohammed V (☎346.80).

THE HIGH ATLAS

The **High Atlas**, the greatest mountain range of North Africa, is for many travellers the most beautiful and intriguing part of Morocco. A historical and physical barrier between the northern plains and the pre-Sahara, its Berber populated valleys, Kasbahs and villages feel – and are – very remote from the country's mainstream or urban life.

Until recent decades, the mountain dwellers' isolation was virtually complete. When the French began their "pacification" in the 1920s, the Atlas way of life was essentially feudal, based upon the control of the three main passes – the *tizis* n'Tichka, n'Test and Imi n'Tanaout – by "clan" families, "the Lords of the Atlas". Even after the French negotiated the cooperation of these warrior chiefs, it was not until 1933 – twenty-one years after the establishment of the Protectorate – that they were able to subdue them and conquer their tribal lands. Today, the region is under official government control through a system of local *caids,* but in many villages the role of the state is still largely irrelevant – the Atlas Berbers are not taxed and nor do they receive any national benefits or services.

Atlas Berbers

If you go hiking in the Atlas – or even just stop for a day or two in one of the villages along the Test or Tichka passes – you soon become aware of the mountains' highly distinct culture and traditions. The longest established inhabitants of Morocco, the Atlas Berbers never adopted a totally orthodox version of Islam (see *Contexts*) and the Arabic **language** has, even today, made little impression on their indigenous Tachelhaït dialects. Their **music** and the *ahouache* dances (in which women and men join together in broad circles) are unique, as is the village **architecture**, with stone or clay houses tiered on the rocky slopes, craggy fortified **agadirs** (collective granaries), and **kasbahs**, which continued to serve as feudal castles of sorts for the community's defence right into the present century.

Berber **women** in the Atlas are unveiled and have a much higher profile than their rural counterparts in the plains and the north. They perform virtually all the heavy labour – working in the fields, herding and grazing cattle and goats and carrying vast loads of brushwood and provisions. Whether they have any greater status or power within the family and village, however, is questionable. The men, who often seem totally inactive by day, retain the "important" tasks of buying and selling goods and the evening/night-time irrigation of the crops.

As an outsider in the mountains, you'll be constantly surprised by the friendliness and openness of the Berbers, and by their amazing capacity for languages – there's scarcely a village where you won't find someone who speaks French or English, or both. The only areas where you may feel exploited – and pestered by kids – are the main trekking circuits around Djebel Toubkal, where tourism has become an all important source of income. Even the hustling, however, is gentler than in the cities – and, given the harshness of life up here, its presence is hardly surprising.

Out of Marrakesh: Ourika, Oukaïmeden and Amizmiz

If you spend a few days in any of the cheap Marrakesh hotels you're bound to hear about **Ourika,** a long and beautiful valley where young *Marrakchis* ride out on their mopeds to escape the city heat and lie around beside the streams and waterfalls. It is not a particularly dramatic "sight", nor – except for the ski resort of Oukaïmeden – is it on the mainstream tourist circuit. But for a day or two's summer break, it's pretty much ideal.

During the winter, beware that the valley's steep sides means that the sun leaves early, and nights can be very cool. The valley is subject, too, to **flash floods** – which were particularly severe in 1987 and 1989, washing away dozens of houses, bridges, fields and roads. The effects are still to be seen, with many of the smaller trails now hardly defined; the roads, though, have been more or less patched up.

Getting there

Access by public transport is simple. **Grands taxis, buses** and a fast **minibus** service leave Marrakesh's Bab er Robb regularly through the morning, from around 6am–noon, returning in the late afternoon/early evening.

The best place to head for is **Setti Fatma**, at the end of the road (67km from Marrakesh); the trip takes a little under two hours (more by bus) and taxi fares work out at about 20–25dh one way. Keep in mind that some of the Ourika taxis only run as far as **Dar Caid Ouriki** (33km) or **Arhbalou** (50km), and unless it's market day (Monday at Setti Fatma, when rides are easy), wait until you get one going the whole way or at least to **Asgaour** (63km), the last village before Setti Fatma. Returning to Marrakesh, you might have to walk up to Asgaour to pick up a bus or taxi.

The Valley: Setti Fatma

The road through the Ourika Valley is reliable enough in summer. In spring, however, you should expect to have some trouble from flooding towards the end of the valley; the road is often impassable at IRHEF, where a tributary of the Ourika regularly washes away the bridge/ford. If you camp in winter or early spring, be very aware of the possibility of flash floods and always pitch your tent on high ground, avoiding any spot where water can lie or that might become a course for the torrents when they fall.

Dar Caid Ouriki and Arhbalou

The valley really begins at **DAR CAID OURIKI** (33km from Marrakesh), a small roadside village with a mosque and *zaouia* set in the rocks to the left, as well as ruins of an old kaidal Kasbah. Ourika's main **market** takes place here on Mondays but unfortunately it has become an excursion offered by many of the package hotels in Marrakesh – and is now not really worth the time.

Beyond the village, scattered at intervals over the next 40km, are a series of tiny hamlets, interspersed by a few summer homes and the occasional hotel or café-restaurant. The one sizeable settlement is **ARHBALOU** (43km from Marrakesh), where most of the local people on the bus or in taxis will get off. The village has a new "palace-restaurant", *Le Lion d'Ourika* (☎453.22), which has plans to open as a hotel, as well as basic rooms to let in the village; good walking in the surrounding hills; and the possibility of some serious hiking in Djebel Yagour (see below). A road west into the mountains leads to the hiking trailhead and ski resort of Oukaïmeden (see overpage).

Moving on south **towards Setti Fatma**, there is an **antiques/crafts shop**, *Le Musée d'Arhbalou*, 4km south of Arhbalou, which often has interesting stock, and a further 2km on is the *Hôtel Amnougar* (☎453.28), which has very pleasant **rooms** at 3* prices.

Setti Fatma

SETTI FATMA is the most compelling Ourika destination. A little over a kilometre before you arrive, the road comes to an end and taxis drop off their passengers beside a stream of clear, icy water – which runs across the track even in August. The village, with its odd patches of grassy terrace, feels like a real oasis as you arrive from the dry plains around Marrakesh.

In the rocky foothills above the village are a series of six (at times, seven) **waterfalls**. The first couple are a not too strenuous clamber over the rocks, and there's a café in summer at the nearest; the higher ones are a bit trickier, but they are said to be the haunt of monkeys. From the falls, you can double back to Setti Fatma via the village's twin, ZAOUIA MOHAMMED, a few hundred metres further down the valley.

Setti Fatma has several **accommodation** options. The *Hôtel Azro* has rooms overlooking the river (cold in winter!); the *Café Azagza* lets out a few rooms; the *Café Atlas*, at the north end of the village, has roof space; or you can ask around for a bed in a village house. A second hotel, *La Chaumière*, is 2km back towards Arhbala – once quite chic, now run down and a bit squalid (and closed in winter). The best meals in the village are at the *Azro*.

The village hosts one of the main Atlas **mousseums**, which takes place for four days around the middle of August; it's as much a fair and market as it is a religious festival and well worth trying to coincide with.

Hiking from Setti Fatma

Ourika cuts right into the **High Atlas**, whose peaks begin to dominate as soon as you leave Marrakesh. At Setti Fatma they rise on three sides to 3658m: a startling backdrop which, to the southwest, takes in the main **hiking/climbing zone of Toubkal**. The usual approach to this is from Asni – described in the following pages – but it is possible to set out from Setti Fatma, or from Oukaïmeden (see overpage).

If you are thinking of approaching Toubkal from Setti Fatma, the best route is to **hike via Timichi to Oukaïmeden** and take the trail from there to Tachedirt (see overpage). The two-to-three-day trek direct to Tachedirt is a lot easier in the opposite direction – and is so described on p.302.

If you're feeling ambitious, you could alternatively head up **into Djebel Yagour**, with its numerous prehistoric rock carvings; explore the Djebel Tougledn (4064m; involving a night's camp); try a longer excursion to

Miltsen, via Ambougi and Turcht; or cut **through the Zat Valley** to emerge just beneath **Taddert on the Tizi n'Tichka**. This latter route takes three days to hike – carry all food for the journey. The trailhead is a few kilometres north of Setti Fatma.

For all of these trips, a **guide** would be useful. It's possible to hire mules and a guide in Setti Fatma: ask at the *Café Azagza* for Houssein Izahan.

Oukaïmeden

The village and ski centre of **OUKAÏMEDEN** is a much easier hiking base from which to set out towards Toubkal – and a good target in its own right, even if you don't have anything that ambitious in mind. "Ouka", as it's known, is reached via a good modern road which veers off from Ourika just before Arhbalou. There are regular **grands taxis** going up from Marrakesh in the winter for the skiers; at other times, you might have to charter a taxi for *la course*. The resort has a 5dh entrance fee.

Accommodation
Finding a place to stay is easy. There are numerous **hotels**, including the excellent *Chalet-Hôtel Chez Juju* (also known as the *Hôtel de l'Angour*, ☎05), which has rooms and dormitory accommodation, as well as solid French food and a bar. An alternative for hikers is the *Club Alpine Chalet*. Though this is officially for *CAF* members only, it is generally open to others of similar mind – at least for a night. It is well equipped, with a bar and restaurant, and the manager and fellow hikers are good sources of hiking information.

Rock carvings
Even if you don't stay at the chalet, you might still want to drop in and check the *CAF* diagram describing the whereabouts of the many **prehistoric rock carvings** cut into the sides of the mountain and plateau. Some of the drawings, depicting animals, weapons and geometric designs, are within a twenty-minute walk from the chalet. Hiring a guide is useful.

Skiing
Ouka has the best skiing in Morocco – on the slopes of Djebel Oukaïmeden – and up until the war it could boast the highest ski lift in the world, which remains impressive at 3273m. It gives access to good *piste* and *off-piste* skiing, too, with several nursery and intermediate runs on the lower slopes.

Snowfall and snow cover can be erratic, but February to April is fairly reliable. Slopes are icy early and wet by afternoon, but not having to queue in the mornings lets you get in plenty of sport. Equipment can be hired from a shop next to *Chez Juju* and lessons are available from local instructors. Several other summits are accessible for ski-mountaineering sorties from here as well, and cross-country enthusiasts often ski across to Tachedirt.

Hiking to Tachedirt
For **hikers**, the trails from Oukaïmeden are strictly summer only: routes can be heavily snow-covered even fairly late in spring. However, weather

conditions allowing, the **trail to Tachedirt** (and from there to Imlil) is pretty clear and easygoing.

It begins a short distance beyond the *teleski* (ski lift), veering off to the right of the dirt road that continues for a while beyond this point. The *col,* or pass, is reached in about two hours; on the descent, the trail divides in two, either of which will lead you down into Tachedirt.

For details of the route described from the Toubkal direction, see below.

Amizmiz

An easy day trip from Marrakesh, **AMIZMIZ**, to the west of the Tizi n'Test, is the site of a long-established **Tuesday souk**. One of the largest Berber markets south of the Atlas, this attracts few tourists and is an event worth catching. It takes place in the morning, finishing around midday.

The town in itself is interesting in a modest sort of way, its clusters of distinct quarters – including a *zaouia,* Kasbah and former *mellah* – separated by a small ravine. There are regular **bus** and **grand taxi** connections to Marrakesh (both operate from Bab er Robb); taxis are recommended, taking about 1hr (as opposed to 2–3hr on the bus). **Accommodation** is available at the basic (but licensed) *Hôtel du France.*

Amizmiz is another possible entrance to, or exit from, the High Atlas. There is a trail leading in about 7hr to **Ouirgane** (see "Tizi n'Test").

Toubkal National Park

Hiking in the Atlas is one of the best possible experiences in Morocco, and in summer, at least, it's accessible for anyone reasonably fit. The mule tracks around the mountain valleys are well contoured and kept in excellent condition, the main ridges of the range are usually quite broad, and there's a surprising density of villages and refuge huts. The villages look amazing, their houses stacked one on top of another in apparently organic growth from the rocks. And, corny as it might sound before you arrive, absolutely nothing rivals the costumes of the Berber women, which seem to be routinely composed of ten or twenty different and brilliant-coloured strips of material.

Possible treks

The **Toubkal National Park**, a more or less roadless area enclosing the Atlas's tallest peaks, is the goal of 95 percent of people who hike in Morocco. It's easy to get to from Marrakesh, with Asni, the "first base", just two hours by bus or, simpler, by *grand taxi*: both from Bab er Robb, and is reasonably well charted. It has not, however, been turned into an African version of the Alps: walking even fairly short distances, you feel very much a visitor in a rigidly individual world.

Djebel Toubkal, the highest peak in North Africa, is walkable right up to the summit; if you're pushed for time, you could hike it, and be back in Marrakesh, in three days. Further away, and much less visited, is the high plateau of **Lac d'Ifni**, while infinite variations on **longer treks** could lead you into the mountains for a week, two weeks, or more. For anyone really short on time, or who feels unable to tackle an ascent of Toubkal, it's possible to get a genuine taste of the mountains by exploring the beautiful valley between **Imlil and Aremd**, or between **Asni and Tachedirt**. The former is a just feasible day trip from Asni.

Equipment and experience

Unless you're undertaking a particularly long or ambitious hike – or are here in **winter conditions** (see "Hiking Practicalities" below) – you don't need any special equipment, nor will you need to do any actual climbing. The main physical problems are the high altitudes (from 3000–3700m throughout the Toubkal region), the midday heat and the tiring process of walking over long sections of loose *scree* – the mass of small volcanic chippings and stones which cover much of the mountains' surface.

HIKING PRACTICALITIES

Seasons Toubkal is usually under snow from November until mid-June. If you have some experience of winter hiking and conditions, it is feasible to hike the low-level routes, and Djebel Toubkal itself, at these times of the year, though you will need to use crampons (sometimes available for hire in Imlil or Aremd), and for Toubkal you may need to wait around a couple of days for clear weather. For beginners, hiking is better limited to late spring/summer. And only those with winter climbing experience should try anything more ambitious than Toubkal, or going much beyond hut level, from November to May; ice axe, crampons, good rain gear and winter competence are required, as several fatalities have recently shown. Full rivers and flash floods in February–March can pose additional problems to the snow.

Guides and Hire of Mules Guides can be engaged at Imlil and at a number of the larger villages in Toubkal; mules, too, can be hired, usually in association with a guide or porter. Rates are around 120–150dh a day for a guide, 70dh for a mule. One mule can usually be shared among several people – and if you're setting out from Imlil, say, for Lac d'Ifni, Lepiney or Neltner, it can be a worthwhile investment. Two extras are to be added to the price – a fee to the supervisor in Imlil and a tip to the porter at the end. Guides aren't necessary for the trek up Toubkal (which is a fairly clear and very well-trodden trail) but can be invaluable for a group trying more ambitious routes. Note that guides are very reluctant – and reasonably so – to work during the month of **Ramadan** (see *Basics*).

Hiking Books There are almost limitless Atlas hiking routes, only a mere selection of which are detailed in these pages. For further information ask the guides at Imlil, or invest in the Atlas Mountain hiking guides by Robin Collomb (West Col), Karl Smith (Cicerone Press) and Michael Peyron (West Col); you may well find one or other of these books on sale at Imlil. If you're reading this in advance, Hamish Brown's *Great Walking Adventure* (Oxford Illustrated Press) has an extensive chapter written for those visiting the Toubkal area, and an appendix on the splendid day-long walk from Oukaïmeden to Asni.

Accommodation At most Atlas villages, it is possible to arrange a room in a local house. At some of the villages on more established routes, there are regular homes to which you'll find yourself directed for the night. A preparedness to camp, however, is essential if you are doing anything remotely ambitious.

Asni and around

The end of the line for the Toubkal bus and Marrakesh *grands taxis*, **ASNI** is really little more than a roadside village and marketplace – and a spot many hikers pass straight through to get up into the mountains. If you're in a hurry, this is good reasoning, though it's no disaster if you have to stay overnight.

The village can feel a bit overcommercialised on arrival, as you are greeted with offers of meals and jewellery. But this hawking doesn't last for long, and between buses the village drifts back to its usual farming existence. Its big event – and the most interesting time to be here before heading on to Toubkal – is the **Saturday souk,** when the whole enclosure behind the row of shop cubicles is filled with produce and livestock stalls, an occasional storyteller and a pretty bizarre assembly of Berber barbers. An advantage of arriving on a Saturday morning (or Friday night) is that you can stock up

Altitude Toubkal is 4167m above sea level and much of the surrounding region is above 3000m, so it's possible that you might get altitude sickness and/or headaches. Aspirins can help, but just sucking on a sweet or swallowing often is as good as anything. If you experience more than slight breathlessness and really feel like vomiting, go down straight away.

Water There is *Giardia* bacteria in many of the streams and rivers downriver from human habitation – including Imlil. Purification tablets are advisable, as, of course, is boiling the water.

Clothes Even in the summer months you'll need a warm sweater or jacket and preferably a windbreaker, but tents at this time aren't necessary if you have a good sleeping bag and bivibag/groundsheet. Hiking boots are ideal – you can get by with a decent pair of trainers or jogging shoes, but certainly not sandals. Some kind of hat is essential and sunglasses are helpful.

Other Things Worth Bringing You can buy food in Asni, Imlil and some of the other villages – or negotiate meals – though it gets increasingly expensive the higher and the more remote you get. Taking along a variety of canned food, plus tea or coffee, from Marrakesh is a good idea. A quart bottle of water is enough because you can refill it regularly; water purification tablets are worthwhile on longer trips, as are stomach pills and insect repellent. Children are constantly asking you for *cigarettes, bon-bons* and *cadeaux* – but it's perhaps better for everyone if you don't give in, and limit gifts to those who offer genuine assistance. A worthwhile contribution hikers can make to the local economy is to trade or give away some of your gear – always welcomed by the guides, who need it.

Maps Survey-type maps are tricky to obtain in Morocco, and if you can possibly get a map of Toubkal in advance, do so. The best is a French satellite map, "Jebel Toubkal, 1:100,000". Moroccan government-produced *IGN* survey maps of Toubkal (1: 50,000) and, covering a wider area, the 1: 100,000 Toubkal-Oukaïmeden (NH-29-XXIII-1), are sporadically available at Imlil, and can be consulted in some refuges.

Skiing The Toubkal Massif is popular with ski-mountaineering groups from February to April. Most of the *tizis* (cols), including Djebel Toubkal, can be ascended, and a *Haute Route* linking the huts is possible. The Neltner refuge can get pretty crowded at these times, and the Tachedirt refuge (or, for a serious approach in winter, Lepiney refuge) can make better bases.

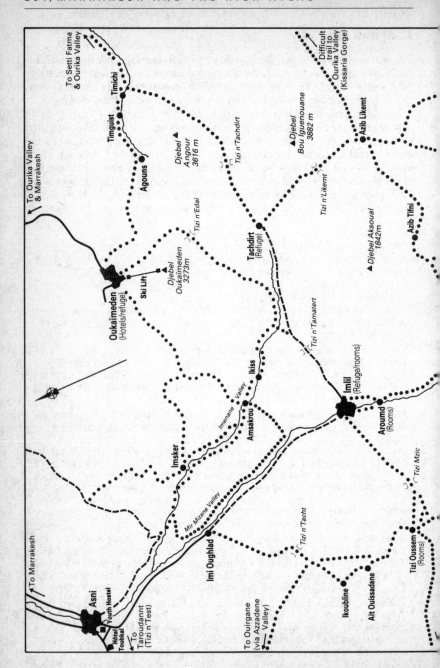

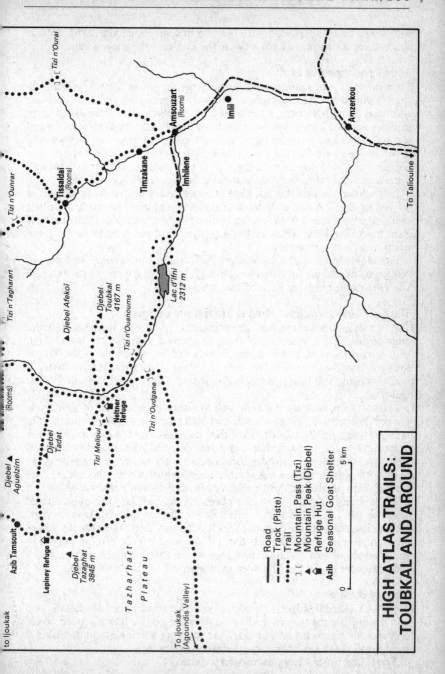

HIGH ATLAS TRAILS: TOUBKAL AND AROUND

Road
Track (Piste)
Trail
Mountain Pass (Tizi)
Mountain Peak (Djebel)
Refuge Hut
Azib   Seasonal Goat Shelter

0   5 km

Tizi n'Ourai
Amsouzart (Rooms)
Imili
Amzerkou
To Taliouine
Tissaldai (Rooms)
Timzakane
Imhilene
Tizi n'Ounrar
Lac d'Ifni 2312 m
Tizi n'Taght art
▲ *Djebel Afekoi*
▲ *Djebel Toubkal 4167 m*
Tizi n'Ouanoums
Tizi n'Oudgane
Neltner Refuge
Tizi Melloul
Djebel Aguelzim ▲
▲ *Djebel Tadat*
Azib Tamsoult
Lepiney Refuge
Djebel Tazaghat 3845 m
Tazharhart Plateau
To Ijoukak (Agoundis Valley)
to Ijoukak

with good, cheap supplies, before heading into the mountains. With time to spare, there are plenty of local walks in the fruit-growing areas around.

Accommodation and food
There are two accommodation options. At the far end of the village is a well-shaded **youth hostel** (*Auberge de Jeunesse*), open all year and to all comers, with slightly higher charges for non-IYHF members. There are no cooking facilities and you'll need your own sleeping bag, though blankets –not always scrupulously clean – can be hired; the location by the river can be very cold in winter. Be aware that the warden has given shelter to a madman in a cellar opposite the front door; he emerges from time to time, shouting abuse and occasionally throwing stones at hostellers, but has never hurt anyone.

Just beyond the hostel, a last taste of **hotel** luxury before the mountains is offered by the 3*A *Grand Hôtel du Toubkal* (no phone), complete with bar, swimming pool (filled from June to September) and excellent French meals. Both hostel and hotel will store **baggage** for you, if you want to carry a minimum load into the mountains.

For **meals**, most of the café-stalls will fix a *tajine* or *harira*. The offers of "couscous meals" are an alternative, though bargaining to get down to a halfway reasonable price can be a tedious business.

The Kik Plateau: walks to Moulay Brahim and Ouirgane
The forested slopes above Asni are dominated by a rocky scarp which is the edge of this hidden limestone plateau. In spring a walk up here is a delight, with a marvellous spread of alpine flowers and incomparable views. To get the best from the plateau, set off early in the day and carry water; six to eight hours' walking will bring you over the plateau and on to Moulay Brahim or Ouirgane.

Leaving Asni, walk up the Test road to where it swings out of sight (past the red conical hill). Just past a souvenir stall a mule track breaks off and can be seen rising up the hillside. Take this, then fork right to gain the first col. Turn right again, through fields, and you eventually join the plateau edge, which you can follow to **Moulay Brahim**; leave the crest to join a piste down to the left, which passes big marble quarries just before the village (see below). You can also cut down to Asni by leaving the route midway along.

An alternative day's hike on the plateau is to make for **Ouirgane**, further south on the Tizi n'Test road (see p.306). On the rise to the plateau keep on, forking left, to the col/village of TIZI OUADU and then follow the dip where a rough piste crosses. Take this down to the road at TIZI OUZLA and follow the road down, with slate mines apparent below. Turn off right to work through paths to join the Nfis river and thence follow this to Ouirgane.

Moulay Brahim
MOULAY BRAHIM is a lively village, just off the main Marrakesh-Asni road and dominating the gorges leading up from the plains. It is a popular weekend spot for Marrachis and an alternative base for a first night in the Atlas. It has a small **hotel**, several cafés and **taxis** to/from Asni.

The village hosts a large **moussem** in June.

From Asni to Tachedirt or Imlil

The routes towards Toubkal – to either Imlil or Tachedirt – are best hiked in the opposite(downhill) direction, and are described in the sections following. If you want to get acclimatised, you could taxi up to Imlil and walk back from there in the day.

Transport from Asni

Getting to Imlil is pretty straightforward, with pick-up vans (*camionettes*) and taxis shuttling back and forth along the 17km of road, along with larger lorries on Saturdays for the *souk*. The most regular departures from Asni are in the afternoon, from Imlil are in the morning. Both pick-ups and taxis normally wait until they fill their passenger quota, though the latter can be chartered; a place in a taxi is about 15dh, slightly less in a *camionette*.

Buses from Asni run to Marrakesh, Moulay Brahim or Ijoukak and – at around 6am – over the Tizi n'Test to Taroudannt (see p.304). A place in a **grand taxi** can be negotiated to Marrakesh (12dh), Moulay Brahim (3dh) or Ouirgane (8dh). Buses and taxis leave from the *souk* entrance area.

Imlil

The trip from Asni to **IMLIL** is a beautiful and a startling transition. Almost as soon as it leaves Asni, the road begins to climb, while below it the brilliant and fertile valley of the Oued Rhirhaia unfolds before you, and small villages crowd into the rocky slopes above. At Imlil the air feels quite different – silent and rarefied at 1740m – and paths and streams head off in all directions.

If you want to make an early start for the Neltner hut and the ascent of Toubkal, the village is a better trailhead than Asni.

Accommodation

Imlil comprises a small cluster of houses, along with many provisions shops, a prominent CAF refuge and several cafés. Most hikers choose to stay at the **CAF refuge**, which is open all year round and provides bunk beds, camping mattresses and blankets, as well as kitchen and washing facilities and luggage storage; rates are 20dh for a dormitory bed (15dh with IYHF card; 10dh with Alpine Club membership).

In addition, Imlil now has two **hotels**, the *Etoile de Toubkal* and the more basic *Hôtel-Café Soleil*, while several houses offer **rooms**. The guide Aït Idir Mohammed (contact at shop behind the concrete route indicator) has a fantastic view (and a toilet!) at his house in a village overlooking Imlil. Alternatively, you might decide to go on to Aremd rather than stay at Imlil; accommodation there can usually be arranged if you ask at the "Shopping Centre" in Imlil for Id Balaid Mohammed.

Hiking resources and guides

A definite first stop in Imlil should be the **"Shopping Centre"**, run by Lahcen Esquary, an experienced Atlas guide who speaks English well and has years of experience in organising hiking expeditions. Above the *Shopping Centre*, the *Ribat Tours* agency also organises activities. Both shop and agency sell maps and guides. Also helpful is Aziam Brahim, who owns the *Hôtel-Café Soleil*, and who works for part of the year for a French trekking company. Other sources of **information** in Imlil are the steady flow of hikers passing through and the *CAF* refuge, its noticeboard, book and *gardiens* (wardens).

Lahcen, Aziam and Aït Idir Mohammed, are the most experienced of the **qualified guides** listed on the noticeboard in the square, all of whom can arrange treks, ascents, mules, camping, guides, *gardiens* for your baggage and food. Standard prices are 100dh a day for a guide, 60dh a day for mules (allow one for every two walkers); rates displayed on the noticeboard are long out of date. Group rates, or rates for longer trips, are always negotiable with individual guides.

Walking back from Imlil to Asni

For a pleasant half-day walk from Imlil to Asni, walk back down the road, then, after about an hour's walk, shortly after the piste turns to tarmac, swap over to the old mule track on the east side of the valley. Take this path up thereafter to the col and along the trackless crest to the prow that looks to Asni and back to the hills. Descend from here and follow down along the east side of the valley to Asni.

Imlil to Neltner – and the ascent of Djebel Toubkal

Most hikers leaving Imlil are en route for the ascent of Djebel Toubkal – a walk rather than a climb, after the snows have cleared, but a serious business nonetheless (see box overpage). The route to the ascent, however, is fairly straightforward – and enjoyable in its own right, following the Mizane Valley to the village of **Aroumd** (4km from Imlil – 1hr–1hr 30mins) and thence through the hamlet of **Sidi Chamcharouch** to the **Neltner Refuge** (12km from Imlil – 5–6hr in all), at the foot of Toubkal.

If you start out late in the day, then Aroumd can be a useful first base. However, most people set out early to mid-morning from Imli to stay the night at Neltner, setting out at first light the next morning for Toubkal in order to get the clearest possible panorama from its heights.

Imlil to Aroumd

To **reach Aroumd from Imlil**, you basically follow the course of the Mizane river. On the west side (the right bank, coming from Imlil) there's a well-defined mule track that zigzags above the river for about 2km before dropping to the floor of the valley, just before a crossing point to Aroumd; over on the east bank, there's a much rougher path – around the same distance but slightly harder to follow.

AROUMD (or AROUND) is the largest village of the Mizane Valley – an extraordinary looking place, built on a spur of loose rock above the valley at 1840m (6040ft). The site resembles nothing so much as a landslide but it also commands one of the most fertile stretches of the Atlas. Terraced fields of corn, potatoes, onions, barley and various kinds of fruit line the valley sides and there is some grazing, too; the village streets are often blocked by goats or cattle – and permanently covered in animal excrement and flies.

This notwithstanding, Aroumd is very much on the hiking circuit. A British trekking company maintains a base in the village and there is a now a café and guesthouse by the river and quite a number of **rooms** rented out in the village houses. The local **organiser for guides and mules** is Brahim Aït el Kadi, who arranges treks for the British company. He rents out rooms (and will prepare meals) in his house, and can often loan crampons in winter.

Alternatively, it's possible to **camp** slightly upstream: you should ask permission first, and, as is usual, pay a small fee – a compensation for nonproduction of crops, since every possible bit of land in this valley is cultivated. There is as yet only one shop in Aroumd – despite a population of 500 – so if you lack the energy to arrange a meal, take along food from Asni or Imlil.

Aroumd to Neltner: Sidi Chamcharouch

From Aroumd, the **Neltner trail** follows the east (ie the Aroumd) side of the Mizane, climbing and zigzagging around the hard, grey rocks, high above the river. At intervals some of the larger rocks have been marked with red dots to reassure you that you're on the right track. If you have been following the main mule trail on the west side of the valley from Imlil to Aroumd, you can join the Neltner trail without going into Aroumd – it crosses over and merges with the section from Aroumd a short distance after you pass the village to your left.

The river is crossed once more, 1hr 30min to 2hr further down, just before you arrive at the village of **SIDI CHAMCHAROUCH**. Set beside a small waterfall, this is an anarchic cluster of houses, all built one into another. Its seasonal population of ten or twelve run softdrinks/grocery shops for tourist hikers and for Moroccan pilgrims, who come to the village's **marabout** shrine – sited across the gorge from the village and reached by a modern concrete bridge which non-Muslims are strictly forbidden to cross. The shrine is probably a survival of a very ancient nature cult – which in these parts are often thinly veiled in the trappings of Islam. (On the approach to the village you might have noticed a tree, sacred to local tradition, where the Berbers hang strips of cloth and make piles of stones.) **Camping** below the village, beside the stream, is possible. **Rooms** are also available.

Beyond Sidi Chamcharouch, the Neltner trail climbs steeply in zigzags and then traverses the flank of the valley well above the Mizane. (The water from the river is not safe to drink untreated until you get above the Neltner hut, though the smaller streams and springs by the path are said to be safe). The trail, however, is pretty clear the whole way to the **Neltner Refuge**, which, at 3207m, marks the spring snow line.

The Neltner Refuge

Even in mid-August it gets pretty cold up at the **Neltner Refuge** once the sun has disappeared behind the ridge. You will probably, therefore, want to take advantage of its shelter. The hut is open all year and charges 30dh per person for a bed (22.50dh with IYHF card; 10dh with Alpine Club membership). The *gardien* is usually prepared to cook meat or vegetable tajine for guests (about 25dh per person), though beware that the hut can be very busy – and crowded. It is badly in need of extension.

Another reason for staying at the refuge is that the area around is covered in rubbish (human waste, too), so if you plan on **camping near Neltner**, you'll want to go some way up towards the summit, where vegetation – and also rubbish – is correspondingly sparse.

CLIMBING TOUBKAL AND OTHER SUMMITS

Toubkal and the other major summits should always be treated as serious efforts. In winter they are only for properly equipped and experienced mountaineers and strictly out-of-bounds for walkers. Even in late spring, if the icy snow has lingered on, they may need ice axe and crampons to justify proceeding. There have been fatalities to inexperienced, ill-equipped walkers going out onto steep snow and slipping, so this is not an alarmist warning. If in doubt, turn back. There are trained guides at Imlil who can hire equipment and lead ascents; do not use casual "guides" encountered along the way, who will often not know the route themselves.

Climbing Toubkal

At Neltner you're almost bound to meet people who have just come down from **Djebel Toubkal** – and you should certainly take advantage of them (and/or the Neltner *gardien*) for a description of the routes and the current state of the South Cirque trail to the summit. The initial path from the refuge, especially, can be easy to miss.

THE SOUTH CIRQUE

The **South Cirque** (*Ikkibi Sud*) is the most popular and straightforward ascent and, depending on your fitness, should take between 2hr 30min and 3hr 30min hours (2–2hr 30min coming down). It is not a well defined route, with paths going off all over the place, but with reasonable instructions on the spot, it's easy enough to follow without a guide. More of a problem – and something you should be careful about at any time of the year – is finding the right track down. It is easy to find yourself in fields of loose scree.

The **trail** actually begins just below the Neltner hut, dropping down to cross the stream and then climbing over a short stretch of grass and rock to reach the first of Toubkal's innumerable fields of boulders and scree. These – often needing three steps to gain one – are the most tiring (and memorable) feature of the hike up, and gruelling for inexperienced walkers. The summit, a triangular plateau of stones marked by a tripod, is eventually reached after a lot of zigzagging through a gap in the ridge. It should be reiterated that in winter even this ascent is a snow climb; not for walkers.

THE NORTH AND SOUTHWEST CIRQUES

Robin Collomb, in his *Atlas Mountains* guide, recommends the **North Cirque** (*Ikkibi Nord*) as an alternative – though longer (4hr 30min) and more ambitious – ascent. It's a bad way down, however, vitually guaranteeing periods of sliding and scraping down the scree.

The **southwest/west cirque**, a third possible approach, is for experienced rock climbers only.

Lac d'Ifni: the route from Neltner

Lac d'Ifni is one of the largest mountain lakes in the Atlas – and the only one of any size in the Toubkal region. From Neltner it's about 4–5hrs hike, again involving long, tedious stretches over loose rock and scree, and with odd stretches of snow remaining into July. On the way back, the scree scrambling is even more pronounced. To make the trip worthwhile, take along enough food for a couple of days' camping; there are no facilities en route.

Neltner to Ifni

The **Ifni trail** begins immediately behind the Neltner hut, climbing up a rough, stony slope and then winding around to the head of the Mizane valley towards the imposing *tizi* (or col) of **Tizi n'Ouanoums**. The col is reached in about an hour and the path is reasonably easy to follow. There is just one vague division, a little before the ascent of the pass, where a path veers off to the right along the final stretch of the Mizane. The trail up the col itself is a good, gravel path, zigzagging continually until you reach the summit (3664m), a narrow platform between two shafts of rock.

The views from the summit here are superb, taking in the whole route that you've covered and, in the distance to the south, the hazy green outline of the lake. At this point the hard work seems over – but this is a totally false impression! The path down the valley to Lac d'Ifni is slow, steep progress, the scree slopes are apparently endless, and the lake often fades completely out of sight. It is, in fact, virtually enclosed by the mountains, and by what look like demolished hills – great heaps of rubble and boulders.

The only human habitations at **Lac d'Ifni** are a few shepherds' huts, and the only sound, that of water idly lapping on the shore. You can camp on vague, scrubby terraces, somewhat fly-ridden by day, or up at the huts. If you have some tackle (and, officially, a permit) you can also fish – there are apparently plentiful trout. Be warned, however, that the lake is exceptionally deep – 50m over much of its area – and some of the sides are a sheer drop.

On from Ifni: a loop to Imlil or Tachedirt

Most people return from Ifni to Neltner by the route they came but it's quite feasible to make a longer, anticlockwise, loop towards **Imlil** or **Tachedirt**.

From the lake, you can reach AMSOUZART (eat/sleep at Omar's house) in around three hours, then strike north to TISSALDAÏ (another 4hr; eat/sleep at Dilh Ahmed's) and then west to SIDI CHAMCHAROUCH (6hr minimum of strenuous hiking over Tizi n'Ounrar and Tizi n'Tagharat). Over this last stage, AZIB TIFNI, east of Tizi n'Tagharat is a possible overnight stop (*azib* is a goat shelter, usually, like here, with primitive huts).

Another alternative is to hike to AZIB TIFNI, then cross the first *tizi* and descend to AZIB LIKEMT, stay there overnight, then cross the high **Tizi n'Likemt to Tachedirt**. The country east of Azib Likemt is wild in the extreme (too hard even for mules!), so it is inadvisable to try and reach the Ourika Valley that way.

Note. All this area behind Toubkal needs to be treated as a proper expedition, and hiring a **local guide** is strongly recommended.

Tachedirt and beyond

Tachedirt (3000m), 8km east of Imlil, is an alternative and in many ways more attractive base for trekking expeditions. As at Imlil, there is a *CAF* refuge, and a fine range of local hikes and onward routes. But despite its comparatively easy access – a pleasant mule track up the valley over Tizi n'Tamatert (more direct than the recently blasted-out *piste*) – the village sees only a handful of the trekkers who make it up to Toubkal.

You can walk the **mulepath from Imlil** in three to four hours, or on Saturdays there's a Berber **lorry** (for the Asni *souk*) along the *piste*. There are as yet no shops in the village (though soft drinks are sold), so take along your own food. The **CAF refuge** (20dh a bed; cooking facilities and some supplies available through the *gardien*) is just above the trail on the lefthand side as you enter the village; it's kept locked, but the *gardien* should soon appear. He can arrange a guide and mules.

Tachedirt to Setti Fatma

This is one of the more obvious routes for anyone contemplating more than a daytrip into the hills. Taken at a reasonably human pace, the route can be accomplished in three days' walking from Tachedirt – two if you're fit. There is a well-defined trail all the way, used by locals (who take mules along the whole length), so no particular skills are demanded beyond general fitness. However, several sections are quite exposed – and there are points where a fall from the path would be fatal. You need a reasonable head for heights.

You'll probably want to carry some food supplies with you. However, meals are offered at the refuge at Timichi, so cooking gear and provisions are not essential. If you are carrying gear, you might want to hire mules at Tachedirt.

TACHEDIRT TO TIMICHI

Tachedirt to Timichi is a superb day's walk. The first three hours or so are spent climbing up to the col, at 3616m, and with ever more spectacular views. The character of the valley changes abruptly after the col, green terraced fields giving way to rough and craggy mountain slopes. The path down is one of the more exposed sections of the route. As you approach Timichi the valley again becomes more green and vegetated.

There are six villages in the valley and this can be a little confusing. Local children, however, will soon show you the correct path to **TIMICHI** and its **refuge**. The refuge is a welcoming place, with a very helpful *gardien*, who offers a tempting range of meals. If you arrive reasonably early in the day, you can make a loop around the hill, exploring all six valley villages, in around three to four hours.

TIMICHI TO SETTI FATMA

Timichi to Setti Fatma is another beautiful hike. The path becomes steadily wider and more used as you approach Setti Fatma, but it is clear enough along the whole course. At first you follow the river fairly closely but, at a very impressive village perched on a huge rock buttress, you climb upward, to about 1000 or 1500ft above the riverbed. There is little water available on the path for several miles, and potential campsites are limited to small, flat bivvying sites. The path is good but appears perched on the side of the extremely steep valley: care must be taken, as you would only bounce a few times before arriving at the river far below, if you fell. The path finally zigzags down into the Ourika valley about 2km north of Setti Fatma.

Tachedirt to Oukaïmeden
This is a fairly straightforward route – a three- to four-hour walk over a reasonable mule track by way of the 2960m Tizi n'Ou Addi; the Angour ridge lies off to the east along the first part of the trek. For Oukaïmeden, see p.290.

The Angour Ridge
Hiking along the ridge of Angour is pretty demanding, taking a full day from Tachedirt and (if the weather turns on you) demanding a night's bivouac.

From Tachedirt, the trail zigzags up the lefthand side of the **Imenane valley** up towards **Tizi n'Tachedirt** (which remains visible the whole way). At the col (a three-and-a-half-hour steep walk, taking you up to 3616m), a path climbs due north up a rough, grassy slope, to break through crags onto the sloping **plateau**, which can be followed to the **summit of Angour**. This plateau is an unusual feature on a peak with such dramatic cliffs. It is split by a valley. With care, experienced hikers can follow a ridge down from here to **Tizi n'Ou Addi** (to pick up the Oukaïmeden trail), or break away straight down to Tachedirt. A guide would be useful.

Tachedirt to Imlil via Tizi n'Aguensioual
Less ambitious, but still demanding a lot of care on the loose, steep scree paths, is an alternative route back from **Tachedirt to Imlil** by way of **Tizi n'Aguensioual**. This takes you first by a tricky-surfaced path to the hamlets of TINERHOURHINE (1hr) and IKISS (15min further down; soft drinks/ rooms). From Ikiss a good path (ask someone to point it out) leads up to the Aguensioual pass; over the other side, it's another stony scramble down to the village of AGUENSIOUAL, from where you can follow the road to Asni back up to Imlil.

Tachedirt to Asni
There is a long but straightforward trail from Tachedirt downvalley to Asni, taking around seven to nine hours. It's an enjoyable route, through a fine valley with no road or electricity – a good exit from the mountains, which is covered by few hikers.

If you are approaching from Imlil, there is a short cut to the trail at the Tizi n'Tamatert (1hr from Imlil), dropping down to the bottom of the valley at TINHOURINE. Beyond Tinhourine, the valley trail leads to IKISS and ARG, with a few possible campsites below the former, and many below the latter. There are rooms and soft drinks available at IKISS and AMSAKROUTE (or AMSEKROU; half an hour north of Ikiss).

Approximate **walking times**: Imlil/Tachedirt–Tinhourine (1hr); Tinhourine–Ikiss (40min); Ikiss–Arg (2hr); Arg–Imesker (1hr 30min–2hr); Imesker–Tansghart (1hr 30min); Tansghart–Asni (1hr).

West of Imlil: Tizi Oussem and Lepiney

The area west of Imlil and the Djebel Toubkal trail offers a good acclimatisation hike to **Tizi Oussem**, harder treks to the south to the **Lepiney refuge** (accessible also, from Neltner) and the possibility of one- or two-day hikes **out to Ouirgane or Ijoukak** on the Tizi n'Test road, or back to the Asni–Imlil road at **Tamadout**.

Tizi Oussem and on to Ouirgane

The village of **TIZI OUSSEM** is in the next valley west of Imlil and is reached in about four hours over the Tizi Mzic. The most interesting section is the path straight down from the col to the village; if you are heading for Lepiney, another path from the col follows around the hillside to Azib Tamsoult, and then to the gorge for the Lepiney hut.

The valley itself offers a long day's hike **down to Ouirgane** on the Tizi n'Test road. At its foot it becomes a road, but this wanders off to the right and you should abandon it in order to go left and, with luck, arrive at the *Au Sanglier Qui Fume* (see Ouirgane). Experienced walkers can make a two-day expedition to reach **Ijoukak**, with one camp/bivouac en route.

The route to Ouirgane keeps to the west side of the valley. Perhaps even more spectacular is to keep to the east side, crossing, eventually, the Tizi n'Tacht, angle down on a piste, then on by mule tracks to the Asni–Imlil road at **Tamadout**. This hike, in spring, is hard to equal, with green fields, blossoms and snow mountains beyond.

Lepiney and around

Some 6hr 30min to 7hr 30min from Imlil, the **Lepiney refuge** is essentially a rock-climbing base, above all for the barren cliffs of **Tazaghârt**, with its year-round snow. A porter or someone would have to go down to the village to get the hut *gardien*, Omar Abdallah, who can also rent you a room in the village. Details of a number of climbs are given in the Collomb guide; they require crampons and ice axes and are not to be undertaken lightly – there was a fatal accident here involving an organised trekking party in 1989.

Tizi Melloul (3–4hr from Lepiney) allows hiking access to Tazarghârt (3843m), an extraordinary plateau and fine vantage point. You can also cross Tizi Melloul and, with one camp or bivouac, walk **down the Agoundis Valley to Ijoukak**. This walk is described in *Travels* by Hamish Brown (Scotsmen Publications, 1986).

Tizi n'Test: Ijoukak, Ouirgane and Tin Mal

The **Tizi n'Test**, the road that extends beyond Asni to Taroudannt and Taliouine, is unbelievably impressive. Cutting right through the heart of the Atlas, it was blasted out of the mountains by the French in the first years of their "pacification" – the first modern route to link Marrakesh with the Souss plain and the desert, and an extraordinary feat of pioneer-spirit engineering. Until then, it had been considered impracticable without local protection and knowledge: an important pass for trade and for the control and subjugation of the south, but one that few sultans were able to make their own.

Through much of the last century – and the beginning of the twentieth – the pass was the personal fief of the **Goundafi** clan, whose huge Kasbahs still dominate many of the crags and strategic turns along the way. Much earlier it had served as the refuge and power base of the Almohads, and it was from the holy city of **Tin Mal**, up towards the col, that they launched their attack on the Almoravid dynasty. As remote and evocative a mountain stronghold as could be imagined, Tin Mal is an excursion well worth making for the chance to see the ruins of the twelfth-century mosque, a building close in spirit to the Koutoubia, and for once accessible to non-Muslims.

Practicalities

If you are setting out by **bus from Marrakesh,** you should have four choices, leaving at either 5am (sometimes 6am), 2pm, or 6pm. The 5am/6am bus is the only direct one to Taroudannt (7hr 30min), but the others go as far as Ijoukak (4hr); the 2pm bus stops there, and the 6pm one goes on to Taliouine (arriving, after a scary night descent, at around 1–2am). It's important to turn up at least half an hour early if you want tickets on the morning bus. If you're **coming from Asni**, you can pick up any of these buses a little over an hour after they leave Marrakesh.

For anyone **driving**, some experience of mountain roads is essential. The route is well contoured and paved, but between the col (the summit of the pass) and the intersection with the P32, the Taliouine–Taroudannt road, it is extremely narrow (one and half times a car's width) with almost continuous hairpin bends and blind corners. Since you can actually see for some distance ahead, this isn't as dangerous as it sounds – but you still need a lot of confidence and have to watch out for suicidal local drivers bearing down on you without any intention of stopping or slowing down. Bus and lorry drivers are, fortunately, more considerate. If you are driving a hire car, which is liable to overheat, try to avoid driving the route at midday in the summer months.

From November to the end of April, the pass is occasionally blocked with **snow**. When this occurs, a sign is put up on the roadside at the point where the Asni–Test road leaves Marrakesh and on the roadside past Tahanoute.

The road to the pass and beyond

Heading out on the dawn bus from Marrakesh, you have the least interesting part of the Taroudannt journey to catch up on lost sleep. The landscape over the first couple of hours – before you come to the village of Ouirgane and the beginning of the **Oued Nfis gorges** – is fairly monotonous.

Ouirgane and the Nfis Gorges

OUIRGANE is a tiny place, long touted by French guidebooks as a beautiful valley and *étape gastronomique*. In the early hours of an Atlas morning, coming from Marrakesh, this might not be much of an attraction, but if you have some money to spend after hiking around Toubkal, you could do a lot worse than come up here to lie around and recover.

There are two **hotels**, both with swimming pools. The big one, *Résidence la Roseraie* (☎04), is a grand 4*A place, with sauna, tennis and prices to match. It also offers horse riding: 250dh for a half-day, 3500dh for a week's package, including two nights at the hotel. A lot cheaper, and equally pleasant, is *Au Sanglier Qui Fume* ("the smoking wild boar"; ☎09). Run by the idiosyncratic Mme Thevenin, this has a series of cool chalet-type rooms, scattered around a garden. Its cooking is erratic, though you may strike a good day; avoid Tuesdays and Saturdays, when tour groups come out from Marrakesh. Mule hire for local treks can be arranged at the *Sanglier*.

From Ouirgane, a seven-hour walk by the **Nfis gorges** leads to **Amizmiz** (bus/taxis to Marrakesh: see p.291). A route can also be made to the **Tizi Ouzla** and the "lost world" of the **Kik plateau** – see Asni (p.293).

HIKES AROUND IJOUKAK

Ijoukak gives access to some of the most enjoyable hiking in the High Atlas – all much less developed than the main Toubkal area. Starting from the village, you can hike east up the **Agoundis valley towards Toubkal**, or west up the long **Ogdemt valley**. The region to the **west of the Tizi n'Test road** is wilder still; for details – in reverse – of the hike to Afensou and Imi n'Tanoute (on the Marrakesh–Agadir road), see the "Western High Atlas" section at the end of this chapter.

The **survey map** for the area (if you can get hold of it) is *Tizi n'Test* (1.100,000).

Agoundis Valley

East from Ijoukak winds the **Agoundis River valley**. It offers alternative access to Toubkal, but is seldom used. To reach the Neltner refuge below Toubkal would take two days of serious hiking. However, if "peak bagging" is not part of your plan, you could still enjoy a day's hike or an overnight trip up this way.

From Ijoukak walk back down the road towards Marrakesh until you cross the river (200m). A dirt road leads off to your right. A small sign there warns you not to fish for trout in the river. This road continues along the valley for about 10km. It's used by lorries hauling ore from the mines. If you're in a hurry, you could hitch a lift; otherwise, the walk is a pleasant one. There are several villages strung out along the valley making use of the year-round water to farm small patches in the river bottom and on the terraced hillsides.

About 2km down the road there is a small square hut below the road on the right. It's a water-powered **millstone** which is fascinating to watch if you happen to catch someone inside. Another 2km further and you'll pass an abandoned **rock crushing factory**, its huge tin and timber structure half falling down. Just beyond it is the village of **TAGHBART**.

The road splits after 8km, the right fork descending to the river, crossing and continuing on into the mountains to the south. Take the left fork (get off the lorry if you've hitched this far) and follow it as it curves around to the left, to the northeast. At the curve is another village, **EL MAKHZEN**. The road has now been extended a couple of kilometres to **TIJRHICHT**. Along this last section is an ingeniously constructed irrigation ditch hugging the cliffside beneath the road. Here the road ends and a mule trail begins. If you've hitched up here, it probably will have taken you no more than half an hour; on foot it's about two to three hours.

The **trail towards Neltner** begins to climb into a narrowing limestone gorge with the river a great distance below. Tiny Berber villages are perched on rocky outcrops every 2–3km. Good views in both directions. Toubkal finally appears, rising above the upper reaches of the valley.

Ijoukak

Moving on, the best base for a stay in the Tizi n'Test area is **IJOUKAK**. The village has a few basic shops and a couple of small **cafés**, both of which rent out rooms. The one nearest the bend in the road serves excellent *tajines*; it has no electricity – candles are provided when asked for – and there are no sheets, only blankets. It's also possible to camp, though the riverbed is pretty rocky. *Guide Collomb* indicates a *CAF*-supervised hut at Ijoukak, but it is actually the state forestry house and does not welcome guests.

Walking out from Ijoukak, you can easily explore Tin Mal and Talaat n'Yacoub (see overpage) or try some more prolonged **hiking in the Nfis and Agoundis valleys** – see below. The Agoundis can also be enjoyable just as a day's wandering, if you have nothing more ambitious in mind.

At **AÏT YOUB** (8km from the end of the road), you will have reached the last and highest cultivated areas (1900m). *Guide Collomb* estimates 3hr 30min to arrive this far, with the help of the occasional lift. Figure on six to eight hours' walking, depending on your fitness.

Neltner hut and Djebel Toubkal are another long day's hike from here. It's possible to hire a mule and a muleteer, who acts as a guide simply because he knows the way. However, this is not as straightforward and organised as in more frequented places like Imlil. This far into the mountains it is unlikely that you will find anyone who speaks English, but with simple French or Arabic phrases you should be understood.

If you wish to continue on foot alone, *Guide Collomb* is helpful from here. Keep in mind that snow can impede your crossing the pass until midsummer. In any case, you'll need to stay overnight in Aït Youb. Camping should be no problem. It's usually best to ask permission for politeness' sake. When you ask, be prepared for an offer of hospitality and a night's stay in the village. You're in no way imposing by accepting it, but it is understood in all but a few cases that you'll offer something in return when you leave. It will customarily be turned down at least once but usually accepted with persistence on your part.

Ougdemt Valley

West from Ijoukak and the Agoundis valley lies **the Ougdemt**, a long, pleasant valley filled with Berber villages surrounded by walnut groves.

A dirt road for lorries now stretches for several kilometres up the valley from **MZOUZITE** (3km beyond Tin Mal and 8km from Ijoukak). Beyond this, a trail continues winding up along the river to **ARG** at the head of the valley (6–7hr walking). From Arg you could go for **Djebel Erdouz** (3579m) to the north of Tizi n'Tighfist (2895m), or the higher **Djebel Igdat** to the south (3616m), by way of Tizi n'Oumslama. Both are fairly straightforward when following the mule paths to the passes and can be reached in five to six hours from Arg. Be sure to take your own water in summer as the lower elevations can be dry.

For the very adventurous, a further expedition could be undertaken **all the way to the Tichka plateau** – summer grazing pastures at the headwaters of the Nfis River – and across the other side to the Marrakesh–Agadir road. This would take at least six days from the Tizi n'Test road and require you to carry provisions (and water in summer) for several days at a time. For a detailed route description, see M. Peyron's *Great Atlas Traverse*. A brief summary of this trail, taken from the opposite direction, follows in the "Western High Atlas" section.

Idni and the Col du Tizi n'Test

Until the death of its *patronne*, Mme. Giplou, in 1985, the *Hôtel Alpina* made **IDNI**, just below the mountain pass, an even better place than Ijoukak in which to stop over. Sadly, the hotel seems shut for good now; a loss to the whole neighbourhood and to the buses, which used to break the journey here. Due to the *Alpina's* reputation, however, a number of travellers do still turn up in Idni (many, alas, guided by previous editions of this guide) and the *Café Igdet* across the road from the hotel has started renting out very basic rooms (with bed mats), as well as preparing hot meals and tea. It can get very cold up here at night (there's no electricity), but it's not a disastrous option.

The **Col du Tizi n'Test** (2100m) lies 18km south of Idni. There's a **café-restaurant**, the *Cassecroute*, just to the south of the pass, where you can normally get buses either to drop you off or pick you up. Walk back along the road a kilometre from here and you'll find a track leading straight up to the col – which itself is dark and restricted – towards a platform mounted by a TV relay station. The views down to the Souss Valley and back towards Toubkal can be stunning.

Over the col, the **descent towards Taroudannt/Taliouine** is hideously dramatic: a drop of some 1600m in little over 30km. Throughout, there are stark, fabulous vistas of the peaks, and occasionally, hundreds of feet below, a mountain valley and cluster of villages. Taroudannt is reached in around 2hr 30min to 3hr on the descent, Taliouine in a little more; coming up, needless to say, it all takes a good deal longer. For details on Taroudannt and Taliouine, see *Chapter Seven*.

Tin Mal Mosque

The **Tin Mal Mosque**, quite apart from its historic and architectural importance, is an extraordinarily beautiful ruin – isolated above a sudden flash of river valley, with stack upon stack of pink Atlas peaks towering beyond its roofless arches. It's an easy eight-kilometre walk from Ijoukak, passing en route the old Goundafi Kasbah in Talaat n' Yacoub (see overpage).

The mosque is set a little way above the modern village of TIN MAL (or IFOURIREN) and reached by wandering uphill, across the stream. A massive, square, Kasbah-like building, it is kept locked, but the *gardien* will soon spot you, open it up and let you look around undisturbed. It is currently being restored – and is used by the villagers for the Friday prayer – but can be visited at other times (a tip is expected by the *gardien*).

Some history

Tin Mal's site seems now so remote, and the land around here so unpromising, that it is difficult to imagine a town ever existing in this valley. In some form, though, it did. It was here that **Ibn Toumert** and his lieutenant, **Abd el Moumen**, preached to the Berber tribes and welded them into the **Almohad** (or "unitarian") movement; here that they set out on the campaigns which culminated in the conquest of all Morocco and of southern Spain; and here, too, a century and a half later, that they made their last stand against the incoming Merenid dynasty.

This history – so decisive in the development of the medieval Shereefian empire – is outlined in "The Historical Framework" in *Contexts*. More particular to Tin Mal are the circumstances of Ibn Toumert's arrival and the appeal of his puritan, reforming teaching to the local tribes.

Known to his followers as the *Mahdi* – "The Sinless One", whose coming is prophesied in the Koran – Toumert was himself born in the High Atlas, a member of the Berber-speaking Masmouda tribe, who held the desert-born Almoravids, the ruling dynasty, in traditional contempt. He was an accomplished theologian and studied throughout the centres of eastern Islam, a period in which he formulated the strict Almohad doctrines, based on the assertion of the unity of God and on a verse of the Koran in which Muhammad set out the role of religious reform: "to reprove what is disapproved and enjoy what is good". For Toumert, Almoravid Morocco contained much to disapprove of and, returning from the East with a small group of disciples, he began to preach against all manifestations of luxury – above all, wine and performance of music – and against women mixing in male society.

In 1121, Toumert and his group arrived in Marrakesh, the Almoravid capital, where they began to provoke the sultan. Ironically, this was not an easy task – Ali Ben Youssef, one of the most pious rulers in Moroccan history, accepted many of Toumert's charges and forgave his insults. It was only in 1124, when the reformer struck Ali's sister from her horse for riding unveiled (as was desert tradition), that the Almohads were finally banished from the city and took refuge in the mountain stronghold of Tin Mal.

From the beginning in this exiled residence, Ibn Toumert and Abd el Moumen set out to mould the Atlas Berbers into a religious and military force. They taught prayers in Arabic by giving each follower as his name a word from the Koran and then lining them all up to recite it. They also stressed the significance of the "second coming" and Toumert's role as *Mahdi*. But more significant, perhaps, was the savage military emphasis of the new order. Hesitant tribes were branded "hypocrites" and massacred – most notoriously in the Forty-Day Purge of the mountains – and within eight years none remained outside Almohad control. In the 1130s, after Ibn Toumert had died, Abd el Moumen began to attack and "convert" the plains. In 1145, he was able to take Fes and, in 1149, just twenty-five years after the march of exile, his armies entered and sacked Marrakesh.

The Mosque

The **Tin Mal Mosque** was built by Abd el Moumen around 1153–54, partly as a memorial and cult centre for Ibn Toumert and partly as his own family mausoleum. Obviously fortified, it probably served also as a section of the town's defences, since in the early period of Almohad rule, Tin Mal was entrusted with the state treasury.

Today, it is the only part of the fortifications – indeed, of the entire Almohad city – that you can make out with any clarity. The rest was sacked and largely destroyed in the Merenid conquest of 1276 – a curiously late event, since all of the main Moroccan cities had already been in the new dynasty's hands for some thirty years. That Tin Mal remained standing for that long, and that its mosque was maintained, says a lot about the power

Toumert's teaching must have continued to hold over the local Berbers. Even two centuries later the historian Ibn Khaldun found Koranic re. ders employed at the tombs, and when the French began the work of restoration in the 1930s they found the site littered with the shrines of *marabouts*.

Architecturally, Tin Mal presents a unique opportunity for non-Muslims to take a look at the interior of a traditional Almohad mosque. It is roofless, for the most part, and two of the corner pavilion towers have disappeared, but the *mihrab* (or prayer niche) and the complex pattern of internal arches are substantially intact.

The arrangement is in a classic Almohad design – the T-shaped plan with a central aisle leading towards the *mihrab* – and is virtually identical to that of the Koutoubia in Marrakesh, more or less its contemporary. The one element of eccentricity is in the placing of the **minaret** (which you can climb for a view of the general layout) over the *mihrab*: a weakness of engineering design that meant it could never have been much taller than it is today.

In terms of decoration, the most striking feature is the variety and intricacy of the **arches** – above all those leading in to the *mihrab*, which have been sculpted with a stalactite vaulting. In the **corner domes** and the **mihrab vault,** this technique is extended with impressive effect, despite their crumbling state. Elsewhere, and on the face of the *mihrab*, it is the slightly austere geometric patterns and familiar motifs (the palmette, rosette, etc.), of Almohad decorative gates that are predominant.

The Goundafi Kasbahs

The **Goundafi Kasbahs** don't really compare with Tin Mal – nor with the Glaoui Kasbah in Telouet (detailed in the following Tizi n'Tichka section). But, as so often in Morocco, they provide an extraordinary assertion of just how recent is the country's feudal past. Despite their medieval appearance, the buildings are all nineteenth- or even twentieth-century creations.

Talâat n'Yacoub
The most important of the Kasbahs is the former Goundafi stronghold and headquarters in the village of **TALÂAT N'YACOUB**. Coming from Ijoukak, this is reached off to the right of the main road, down a very French-looking, tree-lined country lane; it is 6km south of Ijoukak, 3km north of Tin Mal.

The **Kasbah**, decaying, partially ruined and probably pretty unsafe, lies at the far end of the village. Nobody seems to mind if you take a look inside, though you need to avoid the dogs near its entrance. The inner part of the palace-fortress, though blackened from a fire, is reasonably complete and retains traces of its decoration.

It is difficult to establish the exact facts with these old tribal Kasbahs, but it seems that it was constructed late in the nineteenth century for the next-to-last Goundafi chieftain. A feudal warrior in the old tradition, he was constantly at war with the sultan during the 1860s and 1870s, and a bitter rival of the neighbouring Glaoui clan. His son, Tayeb el Goundafi, also spent most of his life in tribal campaigning, though he finally threw in his lot with Sultan Moulay Hassan, and later with the French. At the turn of the century, he could still raise some 5000 armed tribesmen within a day or two's notice, but his power and fief eventually collapsed in 1924 – the result of El Glaoui's manoeuvring. The Kasbah here in Talâat must have already been in decay then; today, it seems no more linked to the village than any castle in Europe.

An interesting mountain **souk** takes place in the village on Wednesdays.

Tagoundaft

Another dramatic-looking Goundafi Kasbah is to be seen to the left of the road, a couple of kilometres south of Tin Mal. This one, **Tagoundaft**, is set on a hilltop, and is now privately owned. It is well preserved – as indeed it should be, having been constructed only in 1907.

Telouet and the Tizi n'Tichka

The **Tizi n'Tichka** – the direct route from Marrakesh to Ouarzazate – is less remote and less spectacular than the Test pass. As it is an important military (and tourist) approach to the south, the road is modern, well constructed and comparatively fast.

At Telouet, however, only a short distance off the modern highway, such mundane current roles are underpinned by an earlier political history, scarcely three decades old and unimaginably bizarre. For this pass and the mountains to the east of it were the stamping ground of the extraordinary Glaoui brothers, the greatest and the most ambitious of all the Berber tribal leaders. Their Kasbah-headquarters, a vast complex of buildings abandoned only in 1956, are a rewarding detour (44km from the main road).

For **hikers**, Telouet has an additional and powerful attraction, offering an alternative and superb approach to the south, following the old tribal **pass over the Atlas to Aït Benhaddou**.

Telouet: the Glaoui Kasbah

The **Glaoui Kasbah** at TELOUET is one of the most extraordinary sights of the Atlas – fast crumbling into the dark red earth, but visitable, and offering a peculiar glimpse of the style and melodrama of recent Moroccan political government and power.

The village holds a small **souk** on Thursdays and has a single café, which serves meals; there are no rooms available.

The Glaoui: some background

The extent and speed of **Madani** (1866–1918) and **T'Hami** (1879–1956) **el Glaoui's** rise to power is remarkable enough. In the mid-nineteenth century, their family were simply local clan leaders, controlling an important Atlas pass – a long-established trade route from Marrakesh to the Drâa and Dades valleys – but lacking influence outside of it. Their entrance into national politics began dramatically in 1893. In that year's terrible winter, **Sultan Moulay Hassan**, on returning from a disastrous *harka* (subjugation/burning raid) of the Tafilalt region, found himself at the mercy of the brothers for food, shelter and safe passage. With shrewd political judgment, they rode out to meet the sultan, feting him with every detail of protocol and, miraculously, producing enough food to feed the entire 3000-strong force for the duration of their stay.

The extravagance was well rewarded. By the time Moulay Hassan began his return to Marrakesh, he had given *caid*-ship of all the lands between the High Atlas and the Sahara to the Glaouis and, most important of all, saw fit to abandon vast amounts of the royal armoury (including the first cannon to be seen in the Atlas) in Telouet. By 1901, the brothers had eliminated all opposition in the region, and when **the French** arrived in Morocco in 1912, the Glaouis were able to dictate the form of government for virtually all the south, putting down the attempted nationalist rebellion of El Hiba, pledging loyalty throughout World War I, and having themselves appointed **pashas of Marrakesh**, with their family becoming *caids* in all the main Atlas and desert cities. The French were content to concur, arming them, as Gavin Maxwell wrote, "to rule as despots, [and] perpetuating the corruption and oppression that the Europeans had nominally come to purge".

The strange events of this age – and the legendary personal style of T'Hami el Glaoui – are beautifully evoked in Gavin Maxwell's *Lords of the Atlas*, the brooding romanticism of which almost compels a visit to Telouet:

> *At an altitude of more than 8,000 feet in the High Atlas, [the castle] and its scattered predecessors occupy the corner of a desert plateau, circled by the giant peaks of the Central Massif . . . . When in the spring the snows begin to thaw and the river below the castle, the Oued Mellah, becomes a torrent of ice-grey and white, the mountains reveal their fantastic colours, each distinct and contrasting with its neighbour. The hues are for the most part the range of colours to be found upon fan shells – reds, vivid pinks, violets, yellows, but among these are peaks of cold mineral green or of dull blue. Nearer at hand, where the Oued Mellah turns to flow though the Valley of Salt, a cluster of ghostly spires, hundreds of feet high and needle-pointed at their summits, cluster below the face of a precipice; vultures wheel and turn upon the air currents between them . . . .*
>
> *Even in this setting the castle does not seem insignificant. It is neither beautiful nor gracious, but its sheer size, as if in competition with the scale of the mountains, compels attention as much as the fact that its pretension somehow falls short of the ridiculous. The castle, or Kasbah, of Telouet is a tower of tragedy that leaves no room for laughter.*

And that's about how it is. If you've read the book, or if you've just picked up on the fascination, it's certainly a journey worth making, though it has to be said that there's little of aesthetic value, many of the rooms have fallen into complete ruin (restoration is "planned"), and without a car, it can be a tricky and time-consuming trip. Nevertheless, even after thirty years of decay, there's still vast drama in this weird and remote eyrie, and in the painted salon walls, often roofless and open to the wind.

The Kasbah

Once at Telouet, make your way to the second **Kasbah** on the hillside – beyond a desolate and total ruin which is all that remains of the original castle built by Madani and his father in the mid-nineteenth century. The castle-palace above is almost entirely T'Hami's creation, and it is here that the road stops, before massive double doors and a rubble-strewn courtyard.

Wait a while and you'll be joined by a caretaker-guide (tours 20dh per group), necessary in this case since the building is an unbelievable labyrinth of locked doors and connecting passages, which, so it is said, no single person ever completely knew their way around. Sadly, these days you're shown only the main halls and reception rooms. You can ask to see more – the harem, the kitchens, the cinema – but the usual reply is *"dangereux"*, and so it most likely is: if you climb up to the roof (this is generally allowed) you can look down upon some of the courts and chambers, the bright *zellij* and stucco enclosing great gaping holes in the stone and plaster.

The **reception rooms** – "the outward and visible signs of ultimate physical ambition", in Maxwell's phrase – at least give a sense of the quantity and style of the decoration, still in progress when the Glaouis died and the old regime came to a sudden halt. They have delicate iron window grilles and fine carved ceilings, though the overall result is once again the late nineteenth- and early twentieth-century combination of sensitive imitation of the past and out-and-out vulgarity. There is a tremendous scale of affectation, too, perfectly demonstrated by the use of green Salé tiles for the roof – usually reserved for mosques and royal palaces.

The really enduring impression, though, is the wonder of how and why it ever came to be built at all, since, wrote Gavin Maxwell :

> It was not a medieval survival, as are the few European castles still occupied by the descendants of feudal barons, but a deliberate recreation of the Middle Ages, with all their blatant extremes of beauty and ugliness, good and evil, elegance and violence, power and fear – by those who had full access to the inventions of contemporary science. No part of the Kasbah is more than a hundred years old; no part of its ruined predecessors goes back further than another fifty. Part of the castle is built of stone, distinguishing it sharply from the other Kasbahs that are made of pisé or sun-dried mud, for no matter to what heights of beauty or fantasy these might aspire, they are all, in the final analysis, soluble in water.

Getting to Telouet: Irherm, Taddert and Aït Ourir

Getting to Telouet is time consuming but not too hard. Take the bus along the Tizi n'Tichka to either Irherm (which has *grands taxis* out to Telouet) or to Taddert (which is a closer point to hitch – but has no transport). Getting back to the Tichka from Telouet should be less of a problem; there is usually a trickle of tourist traffic – and most people find it hard to turn down a lift. With your own transport you could easily set out from Marrakesh in the morning, take in Telouet and perhaps also the Kasbahs of Aït Benhaddou (see Ouarzazate), before reaching Ouarzazate in the early evening.

Irherm and Taddert

IRHERM, 10km beyond the Tichka mountain pass, has a small basic **hotel** and bar – a reasonable place to stay if you get stuck. **TADDERT**, however, on the Marrakesh side of the pass, is the more interesting overnight stop: a terraced roadside hamlet, with beautiful walks nearby and a good, cheap **auberge**, *Le Noyer*, run by an old French expatriate. One of the best walks is the half-hour to the village of TAMGUEMEMT, above a mountain stream.

Aït Ourir

An alternative stopping point, if you are following the Tichka north from Ouarzazate and don't want to carry on to Marrakesh, is **AÏT OURIR**, which has a pleasant, old-fashioned 2* hotel, *L'Hermitage* (☎04/2), with a bar, restaurant, swimming pool and garden.

Telouet to Aït Benhaddou

An alternative possibility, for hikers, is to continue **south beyond Telouet to Aït Benhaddou**. This is a great route, through some of the most beautiful and tranquil countryside in the High Atlas. Before the construction of the Tichka road, it was in fact the main pass over the Atlas. It was only the presence in the Telouet Kasbah of T'Hami's xenophobic and intransigent cousin, Hammou ("The Vulture") that caused the French to construct a road along the more difficult route to the west.

Anemiter

Today there is a *piste* southeast from Telouet as far as **ANEMITER**, a large village (much larger than Telouet), with a smaller Glaoui Kasbah and a welcoming **café-hotel**. This is run by one Elyazid Mohammed, who is a mountain guide and will take groups (or, at a price, individuals) on five-day **hiking tours** into the Atlas hereabouts. He speaks excellent French and a smattering of English.

South to Aït Benhaddou

South of Anemiter the trails and dirt roads take over for the 35km to Aït Benhaddou. The trail is just about negotiable – at least in summer – by sturdy vehicle – and a couple of correspondents have got through with few problems on mountain bikes (8 hours' leisurely ride from Anemiter to Aït Benhaddou). It is perhaps best of all for walkers, though, offering tranquility and unparalleled views of green valleys, a river that splashes down the whole course and remarkable turquoise scree slopes amid the high, parched hillsides.

Despite the absence of settlements on most of the maps, much of the **valley's northern reaches** are scattered liberally with communities, all making abundant use of the narrow but fertile valley plain. This unveils a wealth of dark red and crumbling **Kasbahs**, collections of homes grouped among patchworks of wheatfields and hay, terraced orchards, olive trees, date palms and figs – and everywhere children calling to each other from the fields, the river, or the roadside.

As you walk, all these are to be seen down below you in the valley. The main mule track clings to the valley side, alternately climbing and descending, but with a general downhill trend as you make your way south. Some 8km south of Anemiter you encounter the first of three **fords** (probably impassable for cars outside the summer months). Here the track forks: take the **lefthand trail** that mounts the hillside on the opposite bank of the river.

Moving towards Aït Benhaddou, the nature of the trail begins to change, as settlements become sparser and the track strays away from the river for some kilometres at a time. The countryside is dusty, the valley wider, and in summer dry and very hot. If you want to stay along the way, **TOURHAT** makes a good base – either for camping, or, as is likely to be offered, for a night in a village home. The village is about 6–7hr walking from Anemiter.

A few miles south of Tourhat, the trail takes you past **TAMDAGHT** (about 3hr), a scattered collection of buildings with a classic **Kasbah**. This was used as a setting for an *MGM* epic, and retains some of its authentic Hollywood decor, along with ancient and rickety storks' nests on the battlements.

From **Tamdaght to Aït Benhaddou** the road is again paved to AÏT BENHADDOU (see p.328), where there are cafés and a couple of hotels where you can pick up a taxi (or usually hitch a lift) on to Ouarzazate.

ATLAS PASSES EAST OF THE TIZI N'TICHKA

Some of the wildest *pistes* and countryside in the High Atlas are to be found east of the Tizi n'Tichka – dirt roads climbing up above KASBA TADLA and BENI MELLAL (see "Middle Atlas") to the high plateaus around IMILCHIL, eventually emerging in the fabulous gorges of the Drâa and Todrha.

These are really exciting – well off the standard routes of the country and taken, for the most part, by organised landrover expeditions. But, despite this, they are actually quite feasible for independent travel, and with the patience to fit in with the local market patterns, you can go all the way across by Berber or transit lorry. Details of some of these routes, and an account of what it's like to try them, can be found in the following chapter (see "Todra Gorge").

Marrakesh To Agadir: the Tizi Maachou and hiking in the the Western High Atlas

The direct route from **Marrakesh to Agadir** – the **Imi n'Tanoute**, or **Tizi Maachou**, pass – is, in itself, the least spectacular of the Atlas roads. If you are in a hurry to get south, however, it is a reasonably fast trip (4hr drive to Agadir) and when the Test and Tichka passes are closed through snow, it normally remains open. Convenience aside, **hikers** have the most reason for taking this road, for the access from Chichaoua, midway along the road, to the **Western High Atlas**.

Hiking in the Western High Atlas

Exploring this region of the Atlas, you move well away from the usual tourist routes, miles away from any organised refuge, and pass through Berber villages which see scarcely a tourist from one year to the next. You'll need to pack your own provisions, carry water supplies and be prepared to camp or possibly stay in a Berber village home if you get the invitation – as you almost certainly will. Sanitation is poor in the villages and it's not a bad idea to bring water purification tablets if you plan to take water from mountain streams – unless you're higher than all habitation. Eating and drinking in mountain village homes, though, is surprisingly safe as the food (mainly *tajines*) is cooked slowly and the drink is invariably mint tea.

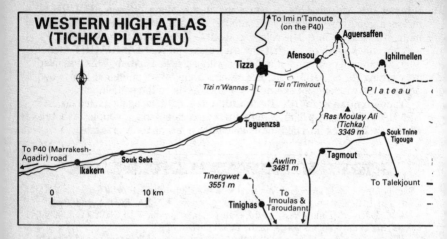

Getting into the mountains, there are approaches from both north and south: **Imi n'Tanoute** and **Tinesgadiouine**, on the main Marrakesh–Agadir bus route (north) and **Taroudannt–Ouled Behril** (south). From the north approaches, rides on trucks bound for mines or markets at trailheads have to be used; from the south, *camionettes* ply up daily to Imoulas, the Medlawa Valley, Tigouga, etc. Tali Abd el Aziz, who runs *Tigouga Adventures* in Taroudannt (see p.375), has full details on the southern approaches mentioned below.

The elusive *IGN* 1:100,000 maps for the area are *Tizi n'Test* and *Igli*.

Chichaoua and the pass

Leaving Marrakesh, the buses normally follow the Essaouira road (P10) as far as **CHICHAOUA**, a small village and administrative centre with several cafés and **hotels**. It is set at the entrance to the mountains, and is famed in a small way for its carpets. Brightly coloured and often using stylised animal forms, they are sold at the local **Centre Coopératif** and also at the **Thursday market**. The village is the most pleasant stop along the road to break your journey.

Beyond Chichaoua, the **road to Essaouira** continues efficiently across the drab Chiadma plains. SIDI MOKHTAR, 25km on from Chichaoua, has a **Wednesday souk** with an attractive array of carpets.

For Agadir, you begin a slow climb towards **IMI N'TANOUTE**, another administrative centre, with a **Monday souk**, and then cut through the last outlying peaks of the High Atlas. Imi n'Tanoute is of little interest, though if you need to stay before setting out on a hike (see below), there are **rooms** at a couple of the cafés, and provisions. In the hillside above the town, the phrase "Allah – Country – King" is laid out (in Arabic) in white painted stones, in letters over 50ft high.

The pass, **Tizi Maachou**, is at 1700m. Beyond it, there are occasional gorges and a handful of difficult paths up into the mountains. The buses usually take a

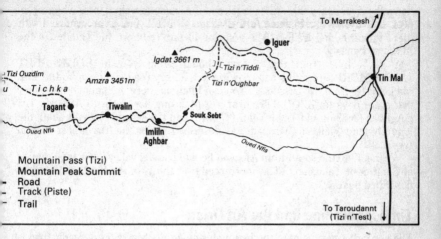

Mountain Pass (Tizi)
Mountain Peak Summit
Road
Track (Piste)
Trail

break at one of the villages on the way. If you are planning to hike into the Atlas from TIMESGADIOUINE, make sure you get dropped at the turnoff, 50km south of Imi n'Tanoute. Hiking aside, there's nowhere very compelling or interesting to stop along the main route.

Imi n'Tanoute to the Tizi n'Test

A dirt road leads up into the mountains from **Imi n'Tanoute to Afensou**. There's a Thursday market about 17km along the road, at SOUK EL KHEMIS, and so your best chance is to hitch up on a Wednesday with one of the lorries. This trip takes several hours, so don't arrive late in Imi n'Tanoute or you might get stranded. The road (possible for ordinary passenger cars) crosses the **Tizi n'Tabghourt** pass at 2666m, from where you have an excellent panorama of the entire area, which includes some peaks reaching 3350m.

At **AFENSOU** you are as close as you'll get by road to the centre of the Western High Atlas region. From here you can hike in either direction – east towards Ijoukak or west towards the Marrakesh–Agadir road at Timesgadiouine. Or perhaps just wander around the valleys and peaks at random. It's a somewhat complex system of intervening ridges, so you'll probably need the survey map.

Afensou to Ijoukak

To reach **Ijoukak** and the Tizi n'Test road, hike north from Afensou 4km up the Sembal River to AGUERSAFFEN. Here you turn east–southeast to follow the long **Gourioun River valley** to the **Tichka Plateau**, via the **Tizi 'n Asdim** pass (2842m), a trek requiring a whole day.

Cross the plateau – where you'll see shepherds, sheep and their shelters (*azib* on the map) in summer – following the **Nfis River** (see Ijoukak) as it winds through gorges which might force a detour occasionally. Continue east down the river valley through villages and the shade of walnut trees which reappear after the Tichka Plateau. At the village of IMLIL (not to be confused with the Toubkal hiking trailhead) is a shrine to Ibn Toumert, the founder of the Almohad dynasty.

A day's hike from the plateau should bring you to **SOUK SEBT TANAMMERT**. From this Saturday market, a lorry road climbs up to the Test road, not far from the pass itself. You can hitch out here or continue hiking for two more days to MZOUZITE, near Tin Mal: one day north to ARG via Tizi n'Aghbar (2653m) and Tizi n'Tiddi (2744m), and the second day east along the long Ogdemt Valley to Mzouzite, as described under the Tizi n'Test section (see p.304).

West and a little south from Afensou lie two parallel valleys which culminate at Souk Sebt Talmakent. The more scenic of the two, **Assif n'Aït Driss**, is described below.

Timesgadiouine and the Aït Driss

The second access point to the mountains along the Marrakesh–Agadir road is **TIMESGADIOUINE**, about 50km south of Imi n'Tanoute. ARGANA looks a more plausible point on the map, but the road is no longer used. A small sign around 15km north of Argana indicates Timesgadiouine: get off the bus here, where you'll see a dirt road, a small building and perhaps a few people who, like yourself, are waiting for lifts – nothing else signifies this as an entrance to the mountains. The actual village is 3–4km along the dirt road.

Souk Sebt

Your hitching destination is **SOUK SEBT TALMAKENT**. Lorries will be driving up on Friday afternoon for the Saturday *souk*, but others go up during the week to a mine above AFENSOU and they all pass through Souk Sebt. Be prepared for a wait and a long dusty ride. If you ride up on Friday afternoon, you can camp overnight. Basic food items can be bought here. There are no cafés and no rooms, although the government workers posted to this nowhere place might offer you a room in their offices.

The Aït Driss

The **Aït Driss River** winds its way just below Souk Sebt. It's a pretty valley that narrows to a gorge for a kilometre or two before spreading out and filling up with walnut trees and Berber villages. As you hike up, several other tributaries come down on your right from the main ridge. The two most conspicuous peaks, **Tinerghwet** (3551m) and **Awlim** (3482m) are the same two you can see from Taroudannt, which lies in the Souss plain on their far side. Turn up any of these tributaries for an interesting day's hike. For camping, you're better off in the Aït Driss valley, where the ground is flatter.

In August you'll see entire families out for the **walnut harvest**. The men climb high into the trees to beat the branches with long poles. Underneath, the women and children gather the nuts, staining their hands black for weeks from the outer shells. In this part of the Atlas, the women often wear their hair in pigtails that hang down the sides of their faces.

To the head of the Aït Driss
You can reach the **head of the Aït Driss** at TAMJLOCHT in a day's hiking
from Souk Sebt. From there a steep climb over the **Tizi n'Wannas** pass
(2367m) takes you to TIZZA, a small village at the head of the parallel valley,
the Warguiwn. Tizza is not a big market town nor does any road reach it, yet
somehow it merits a place on most Moroccan road maps.

From Tizza hike east up a small valley 2–3km, then climb up **Tizi
n'Timirout** (2280m) – which is not named on the survey map. There's a
dramatic view of the main ridge from this pass, its rugged peaks stretching to
the northeast. The most prominent one is Moulay Ali at 3349m. Afensou (see
above) awaits you after a long descent, from where you can hitch back out to
Souk Sebt or Imi n'Tanoute or continue on across to the Tizi n'Test road.

Southern approach to the Tichka Plateau

In the last few years the potential for mountain exploration in the Western
High Atlas has been realised by both local and international trekking companies. The previously mentioned *Tigouga Adventures*, based in Taroudannt,
can pass on information and/or organise everything for those wanting to visit
the "lost world" of the Tichka Plateau and the beautiful valleys leading up to
the heights, and the British trekking companies, *Waymark* and *Sherpa*, also
run spring treks in the region.

Going it your own way, *camionettes* from Taroudannt and Ouled Behril ply
up to **Imoulas**, **Tagmout** and **Souk Tnine Tigouga**, from whence mule
trails lead over the crests. The main routes are outlined below.

Imoulas
IMOULAS is the main town of the foothills, with a Sunday souk. From here
a *piste* extends for about 6km northwest to TINIGHAS, whence there is a
dramatic route through a gorge to high azibes and a hard ascent to **Djebel
Tinergwet** (3551m), the highest peak in the area.

East of Tinergwet extends the **"Ridge of a Thousand Peaks"**, with
Djebel Awlim (3481m) the next target for experienced walkers.

Tagmout
You can stay in a delightful old house at **TAGMOUT**, before following the
mule track north, up the stunning **Medlawa Valley**, to the Tichka Plateau.

Souk Tnine Tigouga
As the name suggests, **SOUK TNINE TIGOUGA** has a **Monday souk**, the
easiest time to get a lift up (or out of) here. Mule tracks north of the village
offer a more direct approach to the Tichka Plateau, and lead over to
Aguersaffen (see above).

travel details

Trains

Marrakesh–Casablanca (4 daily; currently at 1.20am, 7.25am, 9.00am and 5.27pm; 4hr).

Marrakesh–Fes/Meknes via Casablanca) (3 daily; 10hr 45min).

Marrakesh–Tangier (2 daily; currently 1.20am and 5.25pm; 15hr 30min).

Marrakesh–Safi (1 daily; 3hr 40min; but this is essentially a phosphate/freight train).

Buses

From Marrakesh Asni (8 daily; 1hr 30min); Taroudannt (2 at dawn; 8hr 30min); Taliouine (1; 7–8hr); Ouarzazate (4; 4–5hr)*; Zagora (2; 9–11hr)*; Agadir (1; 3hr 45min); Inezgane (4; 3hr 30min – change for Agadir); Essaouira (6; 3hr–4hr 30min); Safi (4; 3hr 30min); El Jadida (9; 3hr 30min); Casablanca (hourly; 4hr); Rabat (8 daily; 5hr 30min); Fes (3; 11hr; Beni Mellal (9; 3hr); Azrou (4; 5hr 30min) Demnate (4; 3hr).

The most comfortable is the 10am bus operated by Ligne du Zagora.

Grands Taxis

From Marrakesh Frequent and useful services to the Ourika Valley, Asni and Amizmiz; less frequent departures to Agadir (3hr); negotiable elsewhere, though no other standard runs.

Flights

From Marrakesh Daily (except Tuesdays) to Casablanca with connections on to Tangier. International flights via Tangier or Casablanca.

TELEPHONE CODE

MARRAKESH ☎04

CHAPTER SIX

THE GREAT SOUTHERN OASIS ROUTES

Immediately when you arrive in the Sahara, for the first or the tenth time, you notice the stillness. An incredible, absolute silence prevails outside the towns; and within, even in busy places like the markets, there is a hushed quality in the air, as if the quiet were a constant force which, resenting the intrusion of sound, minimizes and disperses it straightaway. Then there is the sky, compared to which all other skies seem faint-hearted efforts. Solid and luminous, it is always the focal point of the landscape. At sunset, the precise, curved shadow of the earth rises into it swiftly from the horizon, cutting it into light section and dark section. When all daylight has gone, and the space is thick with stars, it is still of an intense and burning blue, darkest directly overhead and paling toward the earth, so that the night never really grows dark.

Paul Bowles: *The Baptism of Solitude*

T he **Moroccan Pre-Sahara** begins as soon as you cross the Atlas to the south. It is not sand for the most part – more a wasteland of rock and scrub – but it is powerfully impressive. The quote from Paul Bowles may sound over the top, but staying at Figuig or Merzouga, or just stopping in the desert between towns, somehow has this effect. There is, too, an irresistible sense of wonder as you catch a first glimpse of the great river valleys – the **Drâa**, **Dades**, **Todra** and **Tafilalt**. Long belts of date palm oases, scattered with the fabulous mud architecture of kasbahs and fortified *ksour* villages, these are the old caravan routes that reached back to Marrakesh and Fes and out across the Sahara to Timbuktu, Niger and the Sudan. They are beautiful routes even today, tamed by modern roads and with the oases in decline – and if you're travelling in Morocco for any length of time, this is the part to head for. The simplest circuits – **Marrakesh–Zagora–Marrakesh**, or **Marrakesh–Tinerhir–Midelt** – can be covered in around five days; to do them any degree of justice, though, you need a lot longer.

The **southern oases** were long a mainstay of the precolonial economy. Their wealth, and the arrival of tribes from the desert, allowed three of the royal dynasties to rise to power, including, in the seventeenth century, the present ruling family of the Alaouites. By the nineteenth century, however, the advance of the Sahara and the uncertain upkeep of the water channels had led to a bare subsistence even in the most fertile strips. Under the

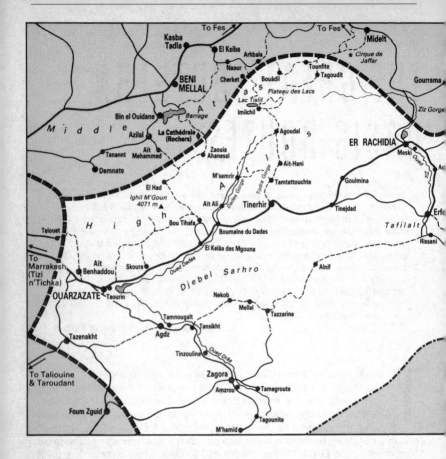

French, with the creation of modern industry in the north and the exploitation of phosphates and minerals, they became less and less significant, while the old caravan routes were dealt a final death blow by the closure of the Algerian border after independence. The pattern of the last two decades has been one of steady emigration to the northern cities.

Today, there are a few urban centres in the south – **Erfoud**, **Ouarzazate** and **Er Rachidia** are the largest – but these seem only to underline the end of an age. Although the date harvests in late October can still give employment to the *ksour* communities and tourism itself brings in a little money, the rest of the year sees only the modest production of a handful of crops – henna, some cereal grains, citrus fruits and roses (introduced by the French to produce *attar*, or rose-water, in the spring). To make the situation even more critical, in recent years the seasonal rains have failed, and perhaps as much as half the male population of the *ksour* now seeks work in the north for at least part of the year.

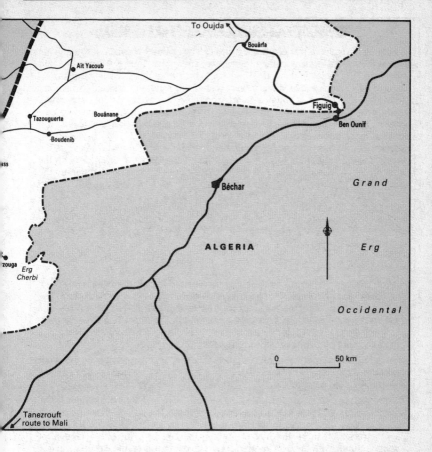

OUARZAZATE AND THE DRÂA

Ouarzazate – easily reached from Marrakesh (6hr by bus) or Taroudannt (6–7hr via Taliouine) – is the standard starting point for the south. East of the town stretches the Dades River, the "Valley of the Kasbahs", as the ONMT promotes it. South, on the other side of a tremendous ridge of the Anti-Atlas, begins **the Drâa** – 125km of date palm oases, eventually merging into the Sahara near the village of M'hamid.

Although it is possible to make a circuit along the *pistes* to Rissani or Foum Zguid, most travellers exploring the Drâa means going down to **Zagora** and then returning to Ouarzazate by the same route. If you're in a hurry, this might sound somewhat gratuitous, but it is a route that really shouldn't be missed, taking you well south of anywhere in the Tafilalt and flanked by an amazing series of turreted and cream-pink-coloured *ksour*.

SOUTHERN PRACTICALITIES

All the main routes in this chapter are covered by ordinary **local buses**, and often *grands taxis*, too. On many of the others, there are regular **Berber lorries** or **Land Rover taxis** (detailed in the text). The lorries cover a number of really adventurous desert *pistes* – such as the direct desert route from Zagora to Rissani – which are also practicable by car. If you plan to drive on these, however, or on the very rough roads over the Atlas behind the Dades or Todra gorges (which again can be covered by rides in Berber lorries), you'll need to be decently equipped and able to do basic mechanical repairs.

Travelling by **bus** in the desert, in summer, the only real disadvantage is the sheer physical exhaustion involved: most trips tend to begin at dawn to avoid the worst of the heat, and for the rest of the day it can be difficult to summon up the energy to do anything. If you **hire a car** you'll lose out by cutting yourself off from everyday life in the country, but you'll gain by being in the position to take in a lot more, with a lot less frustration, in a reasonably short period of time. There are a couple of hire outlets in Ouarzazate and one in Tinerhir; otherwise the nearest agencies are in Marrakesh and Agadir. Most allow you to complete a circuit and return the car to Marrakesh, Casablanca or Fes.

Some details

Petrol/car repairs Petrol stations can be found along all the main routes, but they're not exactly plentiful. Fill the tank whenever and wherever you have the opportunity; carry water in case of overheating; and, above all, be sure you've got a good spare tyre – punctures tend to be frequent on all southern roads. As throughout the country, however, local mechanics are excellent (in Er Rachidia, especially) and most minor problems can be quickly dealt with.

Rivers in the south are reputed to contain bilharzia, a parasite that can enter your system through the soles of your feet. Even when walking by streams in the oases, take care to avoid contact.

Temperatures can climb well above 120°F (50°C) in midsummer and you'll find the middle of the day is best spent being totally inactive. If you have the option, spring is by far the most enjoyable time to travel – particularly if you're heading for Zagora (reckoned to be the hottest town in the country), Rissani-Merzouga, or Figuig. Autumn, with the date harvests, is also good. In winter, the days remain hot, though it can get fairly cool at night, and further south into the desert, it can actually freeze. Some kind of hat or cap, and sunglasses, are pretty much essential.

Spring floods The Drâa, in particular, is subject to spring floods, as the snow melts in the Atlas and forges the river currents. Passes across the Atlas at this time, and even trips such as Ouarzazate to Aït Benhaddou, can be difficult or impossible.

These – **ksour** is the plural, **ksar** the singular – are to be found throughout the southern valleys and, to an extent, in the Atlas. They are essentially fortified tribal villages, massive but temporary structures, built in the absence of other available materials out of the mud-clay *pisé* of the riverbanks and lasting only as long as the seasonal rains allow. A unique and probably indigenous development of the Berber populations, they are often monumental in design and fabulously decorated, with bold geometric patterns incised or painted on the exterior walls and slanted towers.

The **kasbah**, in its southern form, is similar to the *ksar*, though instead of sheltering a mixed village community, it is traditionally the domain of a single family and its dependants. **Agadirs** and **tighremts**, also variants of the *ksar* structure, used to serve as a combination of tribal fortress and communal granary or storehouse in the villages.

Ouarzazate

At some stage, you're almost bound to spend a night in **OUARZAZATE** and it can be a useful base from which to visit the *ksour* and kasbahs of Aït Benhaddou or Skoura. It is not exactly compelling in itself, however. Like most of the new Saharan towns, it was created as a garrison and administrative centre by the French and remains pretty much the same today: a deliberate line of functional buildings, set along the main highway and lent an odd sort of permanence by the use of concrete in place of the *pisé* of the *ksour*.

What attraction it does have is due to the fact that it's a bit of a boomtown at present. The tourist industry has moved in with half a dozen luxury hotels, recognising Ouarzazate's marketability as a staging point for the "Saharan Adventure". And the town has had an additional boost from the attentions of Hollywood. The region first came to prominence in the film world nearly thirty years ago, when David Lean shot *Lawrence of Arabia* at nearby Aït Benhaddou (see below). In the last few years, scarcely a month has gone by without a director and crew in residence. There is even a permanent sound stage and processing plant – *Atlas Studios* – on the outskirts; it can normally be visited during working hours.

Orientation and practicalities

Orientation is simply a matter of getting your bearings along the highway and main road, **Av. Mohammed V**. The **CTM** bus station more or less marks the centre, with a **PTT** (with a direct-dialling international phone section; Mon–Sat 8.30am–noon & 2.30–6pm) alongside, and a **tourist office** across the road. **Private line buses** use a station a block to the west of the *CTM*; **grands taxis** operate out of the central Place Mouhadine; and, lastly, the **airport** is just 1km north of town. There are several **banks** on Av. Mohammed V.

Accommodation
Most of the **cheap (unclassified) hotels** are grouped in the centre, near the bus stations; pick from:

Hôtel Royal, 24 Av. Mohammed V (☎22.58). Recently modernised, with showers in each room.

Hôtel Es Salam, Av. Mohammed V – just across the road (no phone). Similar prices but rather less comfort.

Hôtel Atlas, 13 Rue du Marché (☎23.07). Another basic hotel on a street parallel to Av. Mohammed V, a block to the north.

Hôtel de la Vallée, 1km out from the centre on the Zagora road. New, friendly hotel, with clean (but tiny) rooms and a restaurant.

The **more upmarket** hotels are often full at peak periods (Christmas/ New Year and Easter) and booking at any time is advisable. Possibilities include:

Hôtel La Gazelle, Av. Mohammed V – 1km toward Taliouine (☎21.51). A comfortable, if slightly overpriced, place with a (generally full) swimming pool. *2*B.*

Hôtel Tichka Salam, Av. Mohammed V, midway between the centre of town and the Kasbah Taorirt (☎22.06). Very comfortable hotel with a reliable pool. *3*A.*

PLM Zat, Aït Ghief – up behind the town (☎25.21). Smaller and rather less pricey than the other new chain hotels. *4*A* .

The municipal **campsite** is 4km east of the centre, on the right of the Tinerhir road, a short way past the Kasbah Taorirt (see below). It has a tent restaurant (order meals in advance) and washing facilities (often pretty filthy); the swiming pool at the adjoining tourist complex is sometimes open to campers.

Food and drink

Café-restaurants are grouped around the bus station and along the nearby Rue du Marché; the *Es-Salaam*, on a side street opposite the *Pharmacie Centrale* (on Av. Mohammed V) is the best of these. A little bit pricier, but good, is the restaurant at the *Hôtel Royal*. If you want a **drink**, head for *Chez Dimitri*, a Foreign Legion era café-bar in the middle of Av. Mohammed V. It serves inexpensive *Flag* Specials and good pasta dishes and has definitively the best waiters' uniforms in the south.

For stocking up with your own supplies of **alcohol** – which becomes more and more sparse as you head south – the grocery across the street from *Chez Dimitri* sells discreet, newspaper-wrapped bottles of wine.

Transport on

There are regular **buses** to Marrakesh, Zagora (11am and noon on *CTM*; 3.30am and 7am on private lines) and east along the Dades. West, two daily buses (8am & 3.30pm) complete the marathon haul to Taliouine, Taroudannt and Inezgane (local connections to Agadir).

Grands taxis make regular runs along the Dades to Boumalne (15dh a place), where you can get connections on towards Tinerhir and Er Rachidia, and can be negotiated for Marrakesh or Zagora.

Car hire is available through *Hertz*, near the centre of town on Av. Mohammed V, and *Budget*, by the *Hôtel Gazelle*, 1km west on the road to Taliouine. **Flights** from Ouarzazate airport – to Casa, Marrakesh and Agadir – can be arranged at the *Pan Africa* agency at 55 Av. Mohammed V (☎22.03).

The town and around

Aside from the local Glaoui kasbah of **Taorirt**, and that of **Tifoultoutte** on the ring road outside town, Ouarzazate has little in the way of sights. If it's not too hot, a good walk is to the **Barrage El Mansour** (northeast of the town), quite a sight after heavy rains. If you follow the bank around to the east of the lake you come to the semi-ruined **Tamdaght Kasbah**, or "Kasbah des Cigoignes", with its storks nesting in the battlements.

There is little else in – or to – Ouarzazate, and really the most interesting option is to get out for the day, either to Aït Benhaddou (see below) or a little along the Dades to Skoura – a beautiful and rambling oasis (see p.336), easily accessible as a day trip using the Boumalne/Tinerhir buses.

Kasbah Taorirt

The **Kasbah Taorirt** (Mon–Fri 8.30am–noon & 3–6pm, Sat 8.30am–noon) stands to the right of Av. Mohammed V, at the east (Tinerhir direction) end of town. It's a dusty, twenty-minute walk from the bus station.

Although built by the Glaoui (see p.311 for background), the kasbah was never an actual residence of its chiefs. However, located at this strategic junction of the southern trading routes, it was always controlled by a close relative. In the 1930s, when the Glaoui were the undisputed masters of the south, it was perhaps the largest of all Moroccan kasbahs – an enormous family domain housing numerous sons and cousins of the dynasty, along with several hundred of their servants and labourers, builders and craftsmen, even semi-itinerant Jewish tailors and moneylenders.

Since then, and especially since being taken over by the government after independence, the kasbah has fallen into drastic decline. Parts of the structure have simply disappeared, washed away by heavy rains; others are completely unsafe; and it is only a small section of the original, a kind of village within the kasbah, that remains occupied today. That part is towards the rear of the rambling complex of rooms, courtyards and alleyways. What you are shown is just the main reception courtyard and a handful of principal rooms, very lavishly decorated but not especially significant or representative of the old order of things. With an eye, perhaps, to tourist demands, they have become known as "the harem".

Opposite the kasbah a *Centre Artesanal* is under construction. At present, the town's crafts co-op, the **Coopérative des Tisseuses** (Mon–Fri 8.30am–noon & 1–6pm, Sat 8.30am–noon) is located at the crossroads on the route out to Zagora. There is no true local craft tradition, but stone carving, pottery and the geometrically patterned, silky woollen carpets of the region's Ouzguita Berbers are all displayed and sold here.

If you're interested in **buying rugs or carpets**, you might also check the *Maison Berbère* back in town. One of a chain of three stores (others are at Tinerhir and Rissani), it offers good quality goods at very reasonable prices.

Tifoultoutte

Kasbah Tifoultoutte is nicely situated outside Ouarzazate, on the P31, which bypasses the town en route to Zagora. This was again a former Glaoui kasbah, though much smaller than Taorirt, and built (or at least rebuilt) only this century. In the 1960s, it was converted to a hotel for the cast of *Lawrence of Arabia*. Today it has been reduced to the role of "traditional-entertainment annexe" for the various hotel tour groups: all fabulously inauthentic banquets and German belly-dancing.

However, you can escape the tour groups by eating on the roof – and the kasbah is a fine if eccentric place to **stay the night**. The bedrooms are now very basic (no facilities) but the place has considerable atmosphere (☎28.13).

Aït Benhaddou

The first thing you hear from the guides on arrival at **AÏT BENHADDOU** is a list of its movie credits. This is a feature of much of the Moroccan south, where landscapes are routinely fantastic and cheap, exotic-looking extras are in plentiful supply; but, even so, the Benhaddou kasbahs have a definite edge over the competition. *Lawrence* was filmed here, of course, and for *Jesus of Nazareth*, the whole lower part of the village was rebuilt.

If this puts you off – and Aït Benhaddou is not really the place to catch a glimpse of fading kasbah life – don't dismiss it too easily. Piled upon a dark shaft of rock above a shallow, reed-strewn river, the village is one of the most spectacular in the Atlas and its kasbahs among the most elaborately decorated and best preserved. They are less fortified than is usually the case along the Drâa or the Dades, but, towered and crenellated, and with high, sheer walls of dark red *pisé*, they must have been near impregnable in this remote, hillside site.

As ever, it's impossible to determine how old the kasbahs are, though there seem to have been buildings here since at least the sixteenth century. The importance of the site, which commands the area for miles around, was its position on the route from Marrakesh through Telouet to Ouarzazate and the south: a significance that disappeared with the creation of the new French road over the Tichka pass, which has led to severe depopulation over the last thirty years. There are now only half a dozen families living in the kasbahs, earning a sparse living from the valley's agriculture and rather more from the steady trickle of tourists.

When you reach the village the road comes to an end at a café, where you'll likely be "adopted" by one of the village **guides** and led up through the incredibly confusing web of streets; in winter you have to wade across the river – usually only knee deep. If you ask, it should be possible to see the interior of one or two of the **kasbahs**. At the top of the hill are the ruins of a vast and imposing **agadir**.

Practicalities

The village has two new **auberges**, catering mainly for tour group lunches but offering basic meals in the evening, and accommodation. *La Kasbah* is poised on a terrace above the village; the tiny *Al Baraka* is on the road below.

Getting to Aït Benhaddou is simple enough by car. Leaving Ouarzazate on the P31 (Tichka) road, you turn right after 22km – along a rough, but signposted 9km road. Without a car, the best solution is to get together with others and charter a *grand taxi*. Otherwise, you're dependent on hitching along the turnoff road (which isn't easy) and, if you don't get a lift from fellow visitors, getting back by picking up one of the Ouarzazate buses (which may not be inclined to stop). As is often the case in the south, you may be able to negotiate a lift with other tourists: ask around in the evening at the Ouarzazate campsite or *Hôtel La Gazelle*.

If you're into **hiking**, or very rough driving, the jeep track beyond Aït Benhaddou continues to TAMDAGHT, and from there mule paths go up to the old pass to TELOUET (see pages 282–283).

South to Zagora: the Drâa oases

The road from **Ouarzazate to Zagora** is wide and well maintained, though it does seem to take its toll of tyres. As in the rest of the south, if you're driving make sure you have a good spare and the tools to change it with: there is regular traffic, but you can easily go half an hour to an hour without seeing or passing a thing. If you don't have transport, you might consider hiring a *grand taxi* for the day – or half-day – from Ouarzazate, stopping to explore some of the kasbahs en route; if you decide to do this, be very clear to the driver about your plans.

South to the oasis: the Tizi n'Tinififft

The route begins unpromisingly: the course of the Drâa lies initially some way to the east and the road runs across bleak, stony flatlands of semi-desert. However, at **AÏT SAOUN**, one of the few roadside villages along this stretch, a dramatic change takes place. Leaving the plains behind, the road climbs, twists and turns its way up into the mountains, before breaking through the scarp at the pass of **Tizi n'Tinififft** (1660m). From the summit of the pass there are fine views to the north, with the main Atlas Mountains framing the horizon.

The pass is just 4km beyond Aït Saoun. Beyond it the road swings down through a landscape of layered strata, until finally, some 20km from the pass, you catch a first glimpse of the valley and the oases – a thick line of palms reaching out into the haze – and the first sign of the Drâa kasbahs, rising as if from the land where the green gives way to desert.

Although Zagora is the ostensible goal of this trip along the Drâa, the valley is the real attraction. If you've got a car, try to resist the impulse to burn down to the desert, and take the opportunity to walk out to one or another of the *ksour* or kasbahs.

THE DRÂA KSOUR

Ksour line the route more or less continuously from Agdz to Zagora; most of the larger and older ones are grouped a little way from the road, up above the terraces of date palms. Few that are still in use can be more than a hundred years old, though you frequently see the ruins and walls of earlier *ksour* abandoned just a short distance from their modern counterparts.

Most are populated by **Berbers**, but there are also Arab villages here, and even a few scattered communities of **Jews**, still living in their *mellahs*. All of the southern valleys, too, have groups of **Haratin**, blacks descended from the Sudanese slaves brought into Morocco along these caravan routes. Inevitably, these populations have mixed to some extent – and the Jews here are almost certainly converted Berbers – though it is interesting to see just how distinct many of the *ksour* still appear, both in their architecture and customs. There is, for example, a great difference from one village to the next as regards women's costumes, above all in the wearing and extent of veils.

Visiting the region, bear in mind that all of the Drâa **ksour** and **kasbahs** tend to be further from the road than they look: it's possible to walk for several hours without reaching the edge of the oasis and the upper terraced levels.

Agdz

You descend into the valley at **AGDZ** (68km from Ouarzazate), a stopping point for many of the buses and a minor administrative centre for the region. If you stop here – in either direction – it is unlikely that you'll get a place on the Zagora/Ouarzazate bus; however, there are **grands taxis** from the village square. It is possible to stay, too. The village has a couple of basic, unclassified **hotels** and if you want a low-key introduction to the valley, you could do a lot worse than try them for a first night; the hotel on the corner, *Hôtel-Café du Drâa*, is good value. There is also a **campsite**, *La Palmeraie*.

From Agdz, there is access to a beautiful **palmery**, a short walk from where the bus stops; and if the river is low enough, you can get across (take care to avoid the bilharzia-infested water) to view a few **kasbahs** on the far side. If you're interested in the valley's handicrafts Agdz is also about the best place to see them: **carpet and pottery shops** line the road, and in the few minutes before the bus leaves, prices can drop surprisingly.

Tamnougalt and Timiderte

The *ksour* at **TAMNOUGALT** – off to the left of the road, about 4km past Agdz – are perhaps the most dramatic and extravagant of any in the Drâa. A wild cluster of buildings, each is fabulously decorated with pockmarked walls and tapering towers. The village was once the capital of the region, and its assembly of families (the *djemaa*) administered what was virtually an independent republic. It is populated by a Berber tribe, the Mezguita.

A further 8km south is the more palace-like Glaoui kasbah of **TIMIDERTE**, built by Brahim, the eldest son of the one time Pasha of Marrakesh, T'hami el Glaoui (see p.311).

Tinzouline

Another striking group of *ksour*, dominated by a beautiful and imposing kaid's kasbah, stands back from the road at **TINZOULINE**, 57km further on (30km north of Zagora). There is a large and very worthwhile **Monday souk** held here and, if you're travelling by bus, the village is one of the better places to break the journey for a while.

Zagora

ZAGORA at first sight seems unpromising: a single street with a group of modern administrative buildings and hotels. Two things, however, redeem it. The first is its location: this is the most productive stretch of the Drâa (indeed, of all the southern valleys) and you only have to walk a mile or so out of town to find yourself amid the palms and oasis cultivation. The second is its distinct air of unreality. Directly behind the town rises a bizarre Hollywood-sunset mountain, and at the end of the main street is a mock-serious roadsign to Timbuktu ("*52 jours*" – by camel – if the border was open).

The region's major festival is the **Moussem of Moulay Abdelkader Jilali**, celebrated over the Mouloud. This – and other national festivals such as the Fête de la Throne – are always entertaining here.

Orientation and transport

Though it can seem a bit hustley on arrival, and in summer the heat and dryness of the air are totally staggering, Zagora is a pretty easy place to get orientated – with the bus station, PTT, banks and most hotels along the central **Bd. Mohammed V**. Across the river is the adjoining palmery of **Amazrou**, on the edge of which there are also campsites and hotels.

Getting around – and exploring the Amazrou oasis or the kasbahs north of town – you might want to hire **bikes**, which are available (at negotiable hourly or daily rates) from the repair shop on Av. Hassan II. Leaving town, the most convenient departure is the *CTM* bus for Ouarzazate at 7am; there are two private line departures later in the day. For details of the more challenging routes east and west, see p.334.

Accommodation

Along the main street, Av. Mohammed V, are four **hotels** and a **campsite**:

Hôtel Café-Restaurant des Amis, on the left in the middle of town. The cheapest rooms in Zagora and in summer the hotel rents out (slightly cooler) space on its *terrasse*. No hot water. *Unclassified.*

Café-Hôtel Vallée du Drâa, next door to the above. Very welcoming and clean, and serving reasonable meals. *Formerly 1*A, now unclassified.*

Hôtel de la Palmeraie (☎8), at the far (south) end of the street. An enjoyable place, with a Berber tent out the back serving generous meals – and a lively bar. The hotel also runs tours into the desert "on the backs of camels, with nights under the stars or in tents, eating bread cooked by nomads on the sand" for a half-day, a day, or a week. *Unclassified, 2* prices.*

Hôtel La Tinsouline (☎22), at the near end of Av. Mohammed V. Zagora's "grand hotel", this has recently dropped a star – making it a pretty tempting option. Its **swimming pool** is open to non-residents for 30dh a day. Book if possible. *3*A.*

Camping Sindibad. Next to the *Hôtel Tinsouline*, so only five minutes' walk from the town centre. Pleasant café and an oasis setting between town and river.

A stay at Amazrou offers an attractive alternative to the hot, Mohammed V places, as well as proximity for exploring the **oasis**. To reach it, follow the signposts from town to the *Hôtel La Fibule*, which is located beyond the river, 2km from the centre of Zagora. On the sweep down to the river (and overlooking it) is the upmarket *Hôtel Club Rida* and beyond the river, on the left, the *Hôtel Kasbah-Asma*, built in pseudo-kasbah style. As you reach the river, a track to the right leads shortly to *Camping d'Amazrou*; a longer track to the right in 2km to the (signposted) *Camping Montagne*.

Hôtel-Restaurant La Fibule du Drâa (☎4). Set in gardens amid the palmery, this is a wonderful, small hotel. In the past it was a small restaurant with just a dozen bedrooms around a rooftop terrace. These remain as the "Hotel Kebir", each room with its own name and amazing decor – try the "Houria" for starters – and moderately priced at 85dh a double. Adjacent is the new "Hotel Ksar", built with the same *pisé* walls and wood throughout, with luxury rooms with en suite bathrooms (150dh a double). In summer there is also tented accommodation in the gardens. All guests have access to the **swimming pool**. The Moroccan **restaurant** is a bit pretentious but has reasonably priced set meals; it is patronised by tour groups at lunchtime but all is quiet again by around 3pm. Book ahead for rooms.

Camping d'Amazrou. Lowish prices and a good, grassy area for tents.

Camping Montagne. A beautiful site in the shadow of the sugarloaf Djebel Zagora mountain. Running water, cold drinks, meals to order, a swimming pool (quite often filled), and very friendly people in charge. Also camel rides to the Djebel Zagora.

Food

The best **place to eat** in Zagora is, as hinted above, *La Fibule* – under 50dh for a memorable meal. The restaurant at *La Tinsouline* is good, too, though more expensive. Cheapest food is at the hotels *Palmeraie* and *des Amis*, both of which are reasonable. For a **drink**, try the *Palmeraie* bar; the one at the *Tinsouline* is very overpriced.

TINFOU: AN ALTERNATIVE BASE

The **auberge** at **TINFOU**, 27km south of Zagora (see overpage), is one of the most enjoyable small hotels in Morocco. It is run by the artists Fatima Hassani and her husband Hassan el Farrouj, who produce intriguing naïve paintings and sculpture. The *auberge* itself is an ancient kasbah building, with a medieval room key system, art for sale on every inch of the wall, and a wonderfully ramshackle pool. At nights, you can move your mattress into the courtyard for the cool and the stars.

In addition, if further encouragement is needed, a **camel driver** is among the many permanent residents. He is a bit crazy, but don't be put off: a camel trip out with him to the sand dunes is a lot of fun.

Getting to Tinfou without your own vehicle, it's possible to charter a *grand taxi*, though even with haggling it'll be expensive – try to get a group together.

Amazrou and the Djebel Zagora

The closest village in the Zagora palmery, **Amazrou** is a wonderful place to spend the afternoon, wandering amid the shade of its gardens and *ksour*. It is, inevitably, wise to the ways of tourism (children try to drag you into their houses for tea), but the oasis life and cultivation are still fairly unaffected.

The **dates** here are some of the finest in Morocco and if you meet up with a guide, he'll probably explain a few of the infinite varieties: the sweet *boufeggou*, which will last for up to four years if stored properly; the small, black *bousthami*; and the light, olive-coloured *bouzekri*. (There is a date cooperative on the north side of Zagora, which can be visited for a taste of the varieties.)

The local sight, which any of the kids will lead you towards, is the old Jewish Kasbah, **La Kasbah des Juifs**. The Jewish community here were active in the silver jewellery trade – a craft continued by Muslim Berbers after their exodus. It's possible to visit some of the workshops.

Djebel Zagora

Across the valley from Zagora are two **mountains**. Djebel Zagora is strictly speaking the bulky one, with a military post on top, but the real eye-opener is the smaller, conical hill above *Camping La Montagne*. Watching the sunset from the slopes of the mountain is something of a tradition. Take the road out as for the *Hôtel La Fibule* (see previous page), then turn left almost at once at the river to follow the road/water conduit to *Camping La Montagne*. Here, swing right on the rough road which leads to the col between the two peaks. The road then bends back, rising across the hillside to make an elbow bend on a spur. This is the popular viewpoint – and just feasible by car. The views are startling: you look out across the palmery to further *ksour* and even a stretch of sand dunes to the south.

There are ruins a little downhill of an eleventh-century Almoravid fort, built as an outpost against the powerful rulers of Tafilalt. The road subsequently goes on to the military fort on the summit (entry forbidden) but the view gains little; from the spur a footpath runs across and down the hillside and can be followed back down to the road just opposite *La Fibule*.

On foot you can climb the mountain more directly on an old zigzag footpath up from near *La Fibule*.

M'hamid and Tamegroute

The Zagora oasis reaches some 30km south of the town, when the Drâa disappears for a while, to resurface in a final fertile belt* before the desert – **M'hamid el Ghouzlane** (Plain of the Gazelles). You can follow this route all the way down – the road is paved as far as M'hamid (90km from Zagora) – and with a car, it's an enticing option. It is no longer necessary to get authorisation or to take a guide, as it was in the past, since the region no longer has any military significance, with Polisario contained way to the south.

If you don't have a car, there are buses to both M'hamid and Tamegroute, though times (evening departure to Tamegroute) are a bit inconvenient. It's worth asking around at the campsites and hotels to get a lift; negotiating for a *grand taxi* tends to work out expensive unless you can find a group to share costs – and perhaps more trouble than it's worth. If you try, it's more economic to limit your sights to **Tamegroute** and its *zaouia*, and the **sand dunes** en route at Tinfou (see box opposite).

Note that there are no petrol stations in M'hamid or Tamegroute, or on the routes, so fill your tank in Zagora before setting out.

M'hamid

The route down to **M'HAMID** is the main attraction. The village itself is just a small administrative centre, with a not very memorable **Monday souk** (no sign of any Blue Men, as the tourist literature suggests). There are sand dunes about 4km away from the village – not an easy route to follow, so it's best to take a guide from the village. There is accommodation in the village.

En route, the village of **OULAD DRISS** is worth a stop, with a well-preserved *pisé* kasbah and mosque.

Tamegroute and Tinfou

Tamegroute is reached by a straightforward road down the **left bank of the Drâa**. Leave Zagora by the left fork and continue straight past the turnoff to the *djebel*; Tamegroute lies about 3km away from the edge of the oasis belt. The **dunes of Tinfou** (see box opposite for accommodation possibilities) rise to the left of the Tamegroute road, about 13km out of Zagora (7km south

---

*In the winter of 1988–89, freak rains swelled the Drâa, so that it filled the reservoir at Ouarzazate and ran its whole course to join the sea at Tan Tan.

of Tamegroute). The best formations in the region, they should be enough to satisfy most people's movie fantasies.

Tamegroute

TAMEGROUTE, 16km from Zagora, is an interesting and unusual village. It is essentially a group of *ksour* and kasbahs, wedged tightly together and divided by low, covered passageways. But at its heart is a very ancient and once highly prestigious **zaouia**. This, the base of the Naciri Brotherhood, exercised great influence over the Drâaoui tribes from the seventeenth century up until the last few decades. Its sheikhs (or holy leaders) were known as the "peacemakers of the desert" and it was they who settled disputes among the *ksour* and among the caravan traders converging on Zagora from the Sudan. They were missionaries, too, and even as late as the seventeenth and eighteenth centuries they sent envoys to preach to and convert the wilder tribes of the Rif, Middle Atlas and Anti-Atlas.

When you arrive in the village, you'll be "adopted" by a guide and taken off to see the **zaouia's outer sanctuary**, even today a refuge for the sick and the insane, and its **library** – once the richest in Morocco and still preserving a number of very early editions of the Koran printed on gazelle hide (closed at lunchtime; donation expected for the library).

The village also has a small *souk* of **potters' workshops** and a promising **Saturday souk**. There are a couple of restaurants and a pleasant small **hotel**, *Hôtel Said Naciri*, with an old section built like a palace and a very friendly family. It's just on the left of the main road as you arrive in the village.

On from Zagora: *pistes* east and west

Almost all travellers return from Zagora to Ouarzazate, the only route covered by bus and in some ways the most interesting, allowing you to continue along the Dades valley towards Boumalne and the Dades Gorge and and then Tinerhir and the Todra Gorge.

For the desert-minded, however, there are adventurous *piste* road alternatives **east to Rissani** or **west to Foum Zguid** (and beyond to Tata). The Rissani route is possible by Land Rover taxi, and the Foum Zguid route by lorry, if you coincide with the markets. With your own transport, you'll need a fair amount of confidence in desert driving and orientation skills over the uncertain and rough tracks.

Zagora to Rissani

The long route east from **Zagora to Rissani**, in the Tafilalt, is covered by **Land Rover** each Wednesday (and sometimes on Saturdays). Departure from Zagora is normally at some point between noon and 2pm, from the small permanent *souk* across the road from the *Hôtel Palmeraie*. Ask your hotel to try and reserve a seat for you (around 140dh) and/or arrive early in the day to book a place; take along food and water.

It's a rough ride but you should be dropped outside the hotel at Rissani (see p.352) in around nine to ten hours. Rissani's market takes place on Thursdays, and the Land Rover then makes the return trip (the Saturday departure returns on Sunday).

The route

The route is taken by some cars as well as lorries, though unless you have a really good sense of direction (and comprehensive spares and supplies), it might be wiser to drive back along the Drâa to **TANSIKHT** for the first part of the trip as far as Tazzarine: the unpaved road marked on the *Kummerley & Frey* map as being direct from Zagora to Tazzarine has partially disappeared and you have to negotiate a hard to follow track around by AÏT MENAD and AJMOU N'AÏT ALI OU HASSO. If in doubt, follow the telegraph poles. If you start at first light, it's possible to complete the journey in a (long) day.

Along the way, **TAZZARINE**, which sees an occasional bus or *grand taxi* from Tansikht, has a fairly large **café-hotel**, the *Bougaffer*. Travellers driving their own vehicles (and the occasional "expedition tour" group, in four-wheel drive lorries) tend to stop for a night either here or in **ALNIF** (67km further), a very small oasis with a café, where you can **camp** and get fresh water. Rissani is 100km beyond Alnif, along a fair track over flattish valleys framed by the mountains of the Djebel Ougnat.

West to Foum Zguid

West from Zagora the maps indicate a road **direct to Foum Zguid**: a route which extends beyond to Tata and from there on toward Tiznit or Taroudannt. After almost two decades of military restriction, this route has recently been opened to tourists; most hire cars should be able to withstand the road surface.

On market days (Sunday and Wednesday), a **lorry** leaves the marketplace in Zagora, again around noon to 2pm, arriving in Foum Zguid towards nightfall. Like the Rissani run, it's a bumpy, crowded ride and you should take along food and drink; a *place* is about 40dh. In **FOUM ZGUID**, you can pick up transport the following day to Tata (see Chapter Seven); there are also buses (Tues, Thurs & Sat) to Tazenakht (change for Taroudant/Agadir) and Ouarzazate. Foum has a Thursday *souk* and a café with **rooms**.

Agdz to the Taliouine road

Finally, and again to the west, there is a *piste* from **Agdz to Tazenakht**, on the road to Taliouine.

This dirt road is fairly practicable for cars (Renault 4s should be okay) but at times very difficult to follow – at least until you reach the paved section from the cobalt mines at ARHBAR to the S510 road to FOUM ZGUID. The main settlement en route is AÏT SMEGANE-N-EL GRARA, which has a café; the first available petrol is at **TAZENAKHT** (which has a **hotel** and some worthwhile carpet shops).

THE DADES AND TODRA

The **Dades**, rambling east from Ouarzazate, is the harshest and most desolate of the southern valleys. Along much of its length, the river is barely visible above ground, and the road and plain are hemmed in between the parallel ranges of the High Atlas and Anti-Atlas – broken, black-red volcanic rock and dismal limestone peaks. This makes the oases, when they appear, all the more astonishing, and there are two here – **Skoura** and **Tinerhir** – that are among the richest and most beautiful in the country. Each lies along the main bus route from Ouarzazate to Er Rachidia, offering an easy and excellent opportunity for a close look at a working oasis and, in Skoura, a startling range of kasbahs.

Impressive though these are, however, it is the two **gorges** that cut out from the valley **into the High Atlas** that really steal the show. The **Dades** itself forms the first gorge, carving up a final fertile strip of land behind Boumalne. The second – a classic, narrowing gorge of high walls of rock – is the **Todra**, which you can follow by car or transit lorry from Tinerhir right into the heart of the Atlas. If you're happy with the isolation and uncertainties of the **pistes beyond**, it is possible, too, to continue across the mountains – emerging finally in the Middle Atlas, near Beni Mellal on the road from Marrakesh to Fes. This needs a good four or five days if you're relying on local Berber lorries, and a certain craziness or wanderlust, but it's as exciting and rewarding a trip as you can make this side of the Sahara.

Skoura

The **Skoura Oasis** begins quite suddenly, a little over 30km out from Ouarzazate. It is an extraordinary sight even from the road, which for the most part follows along its edge – a very extensive, very dense palmery, with an incredibly confusing network of tracks winding across fords and through the trees to scattered groups of *ksour* and kasbahs.

Arriving by bus in **SKOURA** village – just a market square and a small group of administrative buildings – you'll probably want the services of a guide to explore some of the kasbahs, and possibly visit one or two that are still inhabited. If you plan to stay, there is now a basic **hotel**, the *Nakhil*, which enjoys a monopoly (haggle for rates) and has intermittent running water. Food is available at a couple of café-restaurants dotted about the oasis. There are **souks** on Monday and Thursday.

Kasbah Amerhidl

If you have a car, the best point to stop and explore is some 4km before you arrive at Skoura village proper (38km from Ouarzazate). Here, about 600m to the left of the road, is the kasbah of **Amerhidl**, the grandest and most extravagantly decorated in the oasis. As soon as you stop, you'll be surrounded by any number of boys, and you really have no option but to pay one to watch your car and another to be your guide.

Other kasbahs

Among the finest kasbahs elsewhere in Skoura are those of **Dan Aït Sidi el Mati**, **Dar Aït Haddou** and two former Glaoui residences, **Dar Toundout** and **Dar Lahsoune**. Most of these are, at least in part, nineteenth-century, though the majority of the Skoura and Dades kasbahs are much more modern. Dozens of the older fortifications were destroyed in a vicious tribal war in 1893, and many that survived were pulled down in the French "pacification" of the 1930s.

The kasbah walls in the Dades – higher and flatter than in the Drâa – often seem unscaleable, but in the course of a siege or war there were always other methods of conquest. A favourite means of attack in the 1890s, according to Walter Harris, who journeyed through the region in disguise, was to divert the water channels of the oasis around a kasbah and simply wait for its foundations to dissolve.

El Kelâa des Mgouna and Boumalne

Travelling through the Dades in spring, you'll find Skoura's fields delineated by the bloom of thousands of pink Persian roses – cultivated as hedgerows dividing the plots. At **EL KELÂA DES MGOUNA**, 50km east across another shaft of semi-desert plateau, there are still more, along with an immense kasbah-like **rose-water factory**, *Capp et Floral*, where the *attar* is distilled. Here, in late May (or sometimes early June), a **rose festival** is held to celebrate the new year's crops: a good time to visit, by all accounts, with villagers coming down from the mountains for the market, music and dancing.

The rest of the year, El Kelâa's single, rambling street is less impressive. There's a **Wednesday souk**, worth a break in the bus ride, but little else of interest beyond the site – above and back from the river – of the locked and deserted ruins of a **Glaoui Kasbah**, on a spur above it. The local shops are always full of *attar*, though, and the factory can be visited, too, for a look at (and an overpowering smell of) the distillation process.

The only **hotel** of any kind is the luxury 4*A *Les Roses du Dades* (☎18), next door to the kasbah: if you have a car and the money for a drink, it should be possible to stop here and use their pool. The hotel has a stable and runs one-day treks to visit a local kasbah and potteries (350dh including lunch). If you are interested in **hiking into the Atlas** from here, contact the **Bureau des Guides** opposite the *Café Rendezvous des Amis*. They run treks – from one to eight days – into the M'Goun Gorge, Djebel Sahro and southern High Atlas. Mules and accommodation are arranged.

Boumalne

Relying on public transport, it would perhaps be a better idea to head straight for Boumalne and the Dades gorge or, if you're strapped for time, Tinerhir.

BOUMALNE is attractively lined along both sides of a valley, another garrison town with an elongated market square and a "Grand Hôtel du Sud" – the 4*B *El Madayeq*, with a pool and a bar (☎31). In additon it offers a new

auberge, the *Hôtel-Restaurant Salam*, opposite the *Madayeq* and another basic hotel, the *Hôtel-Restaurant Vallée des Oiseaux* (☎38) by the petrol station. The *Café Atlas*, above the taxi stand, does excellent *tajine*, and there is a garage that mends punctures.

In addition to the town's regular **grands taxis** (arranged through a blue-coated *gardien*; 15dh a place to Tinerhir or Ouarzazate), there are unofficial Peugeot taxis and also transit vans and Berber lorries leaving intermittently from the market square. You can sometimes negotiate one of these (or maybe a Land Rover taxi) **up the Dades gorge**, the approach road to which veers off to the left a couple of kilometres before you reach the town. The trip as far as Msemrir (60km; 2hr) is a fairly standard local transport route and you should be able to get a place for around 20dh.

The Dades Gorge

The **Dades Gorge** – high cliffs of limestone and weirdly shaped erosions – begins almost as soon as you leave the P32 and head north of Boumalne on the road signposted "Mserhir". Most travellers cover the first 25km or so by car or taxi (see above), then turn back.

If you're equipped for an expedition route, however, or prepared to hitch (very sporadic) rides on local trucks, you can continue up **into (and across) the Atlas**, or **loop over to the Todra gorge**. Alternatively, a couple of days walking from Boumalne will take you over the most interesting section of the gorge, with plenty of mud architecture and fine landscapes to keep your interest, and a number of rooms, or infinite campsites, en route.

Into the gorge: to the bridge

For **the first 15–20km**, the gorge is pretty wide and the valley carved out of it is green and well populated. There are *ksour* and kasbahs clustered all along this stretch, many of them flanked now by more modern-looking houses, but usually retaining the decorative imagination of the traditional architecture.

Just 2km along the road from Boumalne, you pass an old **Glaoui Kasbah**, strategically sited as always to control all passage. Three kilometres further in, where the road turns more and more into a hairpin corniche, there is a dramatic group of **ksour** at AÏT ARBI, built against a fabulous volcanic twist of the rocks. These, like all the kasbahs of the Dades and the Todra, seem like natural extensions of their setting – tinged with the colour of the earth and fabulously varied, ranging from bleak lime-white to dark reds and greenish blacks.

The rocks in the valley around **TAMNALT**, just beyond Aït Arbi (15km from Boumalne), are known by the locals as the "Hills of Human Bodies", after their strange formations (which in fact look like feet). The village itself is a good place to stop, though you'll need to haggle to get a reasonable price for a **room** at the *Hôtel-Restaurant Kasbah*, whose management lays on "Berber Weddings" for tour groups. Cheaper, 2km south (towards Boulemane), is a friendly, unnamed **Café-Hôtel**, with doubles at 20dh.

The **bridge over the Dades**, where the road (already rough and unsurfaced *piste* for the last 12km) turns into a very poor, rocky and difficult track, is about a 45-minute (24km) drive from Boumalne at **AÏT OUDINAR**. There is an **auberge** here, the *Gorge du Dades*, where you can eat, rent a **room** and, if you're driving, ask about the state of the road beyond – with a hire car, you may decide to go no further. There is also a **campsite**. Within walking distance of the café is one of the most spectacular sections of the gorge. The hotel runs **mule trips** with a guide (100dh a day).

About 6km north of the bridge, there are several café-restaurants offering **rooms** at one of the most spectacular stretches of the gorge – a very narrow section, full of hairpin bends. At **AÏT HAMMOU**, 5km further on, there is also the basic (no electricity, outside toilet) *Café-Hôtel Taghea*, with numerous **rooms** and a terrace.

Msemrir and over the Atlas

The roads get worse beyond Aït Hammou, and in spring are likely to be impassable due to flooding. At other times of year, however, you can drive to Msemrir, and from there over the Atlas to Imilchil and Arhbala (see Chapter Three), or across to Tamtatouchte or Aït Hani (see map on p.342), where you can loop around to Tinerhir through the Todra.

It must be stressed, though, that these are really routes for lorries or Land Rovers. A Renault 4 *can* make it around to Todra between mid-June and late September, but it is a bit of a struggle. In either case, you'll need to be a confident driver (hairpin bends are routine) and an even more confident mechanic: hire cars are uninsured for trips like this, and anyway they're usually not in very good condition. Broken axles are not uncommon.

The loop to Todra

If you're really intent on **crossing between the Dades and Todra gorges**, you'll find it considerably easier to go in the other direction. Coming from the Dades it's a long, uphill trek, and the approximately one hundred kilometres of *piste* can easily take a full day. The approach to Agoudaz and Imilchil, too, is better from the Todra side.

There is a café with basic rooms in **MSEMRIR**. See the "Todra Gorge", following, for details beyond.

Tinerhir (Tineghir)

While **TINERHIR** again is pre-eminently a base – this time for the trip up into the **Todra gorge** – it is also a much more interesting town than the other administrative centres along this route. Only a couple of kilometres east of the modern section is the beginning of the **oasis** – really a world apart, with its groups of tribal *ksour* built at intervals into the rocky hills above. When passing through, don't be in too much of a hurry to catch the first lorry out to Todra or the next bus: this spot by itself offers rewarding exploration for the day, and, what's more, it's completely ignored by most tourists.

Practicalities

Arriving, things are again pretty straightforward. The **buses** stop at the arcaded Place Principal, and here you will also find all the other **facilities** – hotels, a couple of cafés, a post office, a **bank** and a **car hire** agency. There is a **Tuesday souk**. **Buses** and **grands taxis** make standard runs to Boumalne (change for Ouarzazate if you're going by taxi) and Er Rachidia.

Hotels

The best value of the cheap **hotels** is the unclassified *Oasis*, a good place to eat as well, and with cooler rooms than the *Salam*, over on the far side of the square. A third option, the *Hôtel Todra* (☎09), is officially 2*B, though apart from a spectacularly kitsch decor, it doesn't seem much different.

Once more, the only **swimming pool** belongs to the big luxury hotel, the 4*B *Hôtel Sargho* (☎01), left of the main road as you come in from Skoura/ Ouarzazate. The pool is open to non-residents for 20dh a day.

Beware that there is no **campsite** in the town; the "Camping" signposted near the centre is in fact 8km up the Todra gorge.

Food and carpets

For **food**, there are the usual café-restaurants around the central square; the hotels *Sargho* and *Todra* are the only places licensed to sell alcohol.

If you're interested in buying **rugs or carpets**, Tinerhir has another branch of the *Maison Berbère* (run by the same family as those in Zagora and Rissani), good for picking up quality merchandise.

Around the town and oasis

Dominating the town and with a tremendous view over the Todra is yet another **Glaoui Kasbah** – one of the grandest and most ornamental after Telouet and Ouarzazate, though now substantially in ruins.

To reach **the oasis**, walk out – or hitch a lift – along one of the tracks behind the town. When you arrive, it is possible to hire a mule (and a guide) in the main village, the former Jewish quarter, now essentially Berber, but still known as the **Mellah**. The finest of the kasbahs is that of **Aït Amitane** (a 6km walk), with its extraordinarily complex patterns incised on the walls. This is just one of many *ksour* and kasbahs here, however, and it's worth-while just to wander around.

The oasis follows the usual pattern in these valleys: date palms at the edge, terraces of olive, pomegranate, almond and fruit trees further in, with grain and vegetable crops planted beneath them. The **ksour** each originally controlled one section of the oasis, and there were frequent disputes over territory and, above all, over access to the mountain streams for each *ksour*'s network of water channels. Even in this century, the fortifications were built in earnest, and, as Walter Harris wrote (melodramatically, but probably with little exaggeration): "The whole life was one of warfare and gloom. Every tribe had its enemies, every family had its blood feuds, and every man his would-be murderer."

The Todra Gorge and a route over the Atlas

Whatever else you do in the south, at least spend a night at the **Todra Gorge**. You don't need your own transport, or any great expeditionary zeal, to get up there, and yet it seems totally remote from the routes through the main valleys – very still, very quiet and magnificent in the fading evening light.

The highest, narrowest, and most spectacular part of the gorge is only 15km from Tinerhir, and there are three small hotels at its mouth where you can get a room or sleep out on the terrace or roof. Beyond this point, the road turns into a *piste* and you're into true isolation: a route you can take all the way over the Atlas, if you can time your visit to fit in with the schedules of Berber lorries or, if driving yourself, you have considerable confidence and a very reliable and sturdy car.

From Tinerhir, the mouth of the gorge (where the *Hôtel El Mansour* is located) can be reached either by Peugeot **grand taxi** or **transit van**: both leave regularly through the day, the taxis from Place Principal, the van from near the bus station; both charge around 6dh a place to the gorge.

Into the gorge

En route to the gorge proper, the road climbs along a last, fertile shaft of land, narrowing at points to a ribbon of palms between the cliffs. There are more or less continuous villages, all of them the pink-grey colour of the local rock, and the ruins of kasbahs and *ksour* up above or on the other side.

To the right of the road, 9km from Tinerhir (and *past* the first signposted campsite), there is a freshwater pool, somewhat fancifully named "**The Source of the Sacred Fish**", flanking a particularly luxuriant palmery. It is a beautiful spot, with a small **café-hotel** opposite and a couple of **campsites** in the clearing – the *Camping Sacred Fish* has basic rooms, too. Anywhere else, a stay at these sites would merit a major recommendation – here, though, it seems almost churlish not to continue to the beginning of the gorge. And if the heat is not too much for you, there's a lot to be said for getting the lorry to let you off here and walking the final 6km.

The really enclosed section of **the gorge**, where the cliff walls rise sheer to 3000m on either side, runs for only a few hundred metres – its mouth a short walk from the group of hotels at the end of the surfaced road. The main attraction is lost unless you stay the night: the evening skies here are really incredible, and, if you're remotely interested in birdwatching, this is one of the best locations in the south. Possible sightings include pale crag martins, rock doves and grey wagtails and, higher up the gorge, Tristram's warblers, Bonelli's eagles and lanners.

The first **hotel** you see at the mouth of the "real" gorge, the *El Mansour*, is generally the cheapest: an attractively ramshackle place, with a pair of palm trees growing out through the roof, reasonable food and a choice of sleeping on the roof (easily the best option) or on couches downstairs. If you feel like having your own room, walk a couple of hundred metres around the corner to the *Hôtel des Roches* and *Yasmina*, both established in the 1930s. They're slightly fancier, with licensed restaurants catering for the half-dozen tour groups shuttled up each day, and mules hired for trips up the gorge. The *Yasmina* has the best food; the *Roches* the better rooms, and both, like the *El Mansour*, allow you to sleep out on the terrace for 10dh. All three of these hotels are very friendly and relaxed – a bit too hippy-like at times for some tastes – and all are very cold and damp in winter (no hot showers, either).

Over the Atlas

If you want to continue beyond the gorge to **Tamtatouchte**, and from there **across the High Atlas** to **Imilchil** and **Arhbala**, in the Middle Atlas, it is possible to do so by catching a succession of **Berber lorries**. Hire **cars** will have problems, though some French travellers seem to make it through in their Renaults and Citroëns. It is possible, too, to cover the route by **bike** – mountain models providing a distinct advantage. With your own transport, do not attempt the route outside the months of **June to September**.

Some practicalities

The arrival of ongoing **lorries** (*camions*) is inevitably hard to predict, though the people at the hotels usually have some idea of when the next ones will be going as far as Aït Hani. The most promising days to set out are generally **Wednesday** (for Aït Hani's *souk*) or **Friday** (for Imilchil's Saturday *souk*). But it is all a bit pot luck, and you should certainly be prepared for the odd day's wait in a village for a ride, or, better, to walk one or other of the stages of the route. Eventually, however, everyone seems to get across to **Arhbala** or **Naour**, where there is asphalt road again and regular buses down to El Ksiba and Kasba Tadla or Khenifra.

There is, of course, no **bank** between Tinerhir and Khenifra/Kasba Tadla. Don't underestimate the expense of buying **food** in the mountains (30–100 percent above normal rates), nor the prices charged for rides in the **Berber lorries**; as a very general guideline, reckon on about 15dh for every 50km.

The route

A personal account of the route, getting lifts from the lorries, is printed over-page. Everyone's experience (and exact route) is bound to differ a fair amount, but the pattern of travel should be pretty similar.

The first place to head for is **TAMTATOUCHTE** (17km from the hotels at the end of the gorge), quite a sizeable village, with several basic **hotels** and café-restaurants. The section of the route up to here from the gorge is the worst part – the track is little more than the stones of the river path. Beyond this point, the road improves considerably, though it is still unsurfaced and slow, difficult mountain driving. It's at Tamtatouchte that anyone intent on crossing over to the Dades gorge should turn off to the west, toward MSEMRIR; lifts are most unlikely, so it's basically an option for drivers.

Continuing north, into the High Atlas, you need to head towards **AÏT HANI**, another large village, almost the size of Tamtatouchte. It's just off the main route, and if you're driving you can keep going, turning after the town, rather than into it. On the outskirts as you approach from the south, there is a military post, café and store; there's no regular accommodation (but see the boxed account). This region is generally high and barren landscape – the locals travel amazing distances each day to collect wood for fuel.

After Aït Hani there is a stiff climb up to 2700m at **Tizi Tirherhouzine**, then down to **AGOUDAL**. This is a friendly village, and though there is no official hotel, you'll probably be offered a room. It is in a less harsh setting, too, better irrigated, and people seem more relaxed than at Aït Hani.

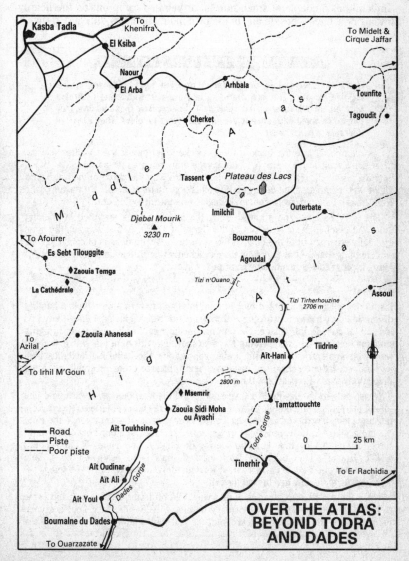

OVER THE ATLAS: BEYOND TODRA AND DADES

IMILCHIL is only 45km further on from Agoudal, on a fast road through a very fertile and highly populated region. A beautiful village, with a fine caidal kasbah, this is for most people the highlight of the route. It is famed for its **September moussem** – the so-called *Marriage Market of Aït Haddidou*. The *moussem*, once a genuine tribal function, is now considerably corrupted by tourism (Land Rover parties are shuttled up from Marrakesh for the day), but it's a lively, extravagant occasion all the same.

Imilchil has a couple of small **hotels**, or you can camp out on the nearby **Plateau des Lacs** – beside one of the twin mountain lakes, **Isli** and **Tislit**.

BOUZMOU AND BEYOND

Dan Richardson and Jill Denton set out from the *Hôtel El Mansour* with a Belgian traveller they met there; he had a useful smattering of Arabic phrases, they themselves had reasonable French. Both these factors, they felt, made some difference in the way they were received. They travelled the route in midsummer.

As we clambered into the back of the lorry the hotel owner tried to dissuade us. "You don't want to go there . . . This lorry's only going as far as Aït Hani – it's a horrible place . . . ". But after fourteen hours waiting on the porch of the hotel for a lift we weren't going to be deterred. Whatever was up there in the dry wastes of the High Atlas – the maps were enticingly vague – we meant to find out.

The lorry bumped and strained along the unpaved track, swathed in choking dust, and climbed steadily up out of the Gorge of Todra. As the sun fell, the stars gradually emerged until the bowl of the sky sparkled with dozens of constellations and shooting stars. After four hours, we reached a vast plateau and the gates of **Aït Hani**, incongruously manned by an armed soldier.

Aït Hani

Inside the village – a jumbled blur of mud huts and towers – there was a lengthy discussion on what to do with the *Nazarenes* (Christians). Finally, a man offered us his stable, outside the village. Despite our misgivings, he did us proud, bringing rugs for the floor and reappearing the next morning with mint tea, bread, and his wife, who was entranced by our foreign appearance. We found *her* looks fascinating, too – a tattooed chin, luminous eyes and a bizarre dress resembling a huge tinfoil doily shot with pale blue threads.

It was only in the daylight that we understood the previous day's warnings. The mountain, plateau and buildings were uniformly barren and colourless, except for a few tiny plots of withered vegetables. People peered at us from courtyards and from behind grilled windows, ignoring our tentative greetings, and our host of the night before led us to a low mud building bearing (in English) the name of "The Modern Coffee House". This title, we later learned, had been bestowed by a lone Englishman who had been marooned for four days in the village. We guess we were luckier – we only had to wait for two.

Once the sun was up, swarms of flies would lift off from piles of dung and come to crawl all over us. There was virtually nothing to see – the heat kept everyone indoors – and little to do but drink mint tea and gaze glumly at the decor of the

The next stage is a long slog to Arhbala through spectacular scenery, with steep drops off the road side, constant climbs and descents, and a slow move into forestation. This section has few settlements – nowhere the size of Imilchil – and locals are curious about travellers passing through. A paved road starts a few miles after **CHERKET**. At **ARHBALA** (see p.191), there is a very basic hotel near the marketplace (Wednesday *souk*), and a daily bus on to El Ksiba (see Chapter Three).

For more details – and an idea of what life is like up in the mountains and packed into the lorries – see the account below.

---

coffee house: sooty mud walls, pastel colours and a collage of sardine cans, postcards and Koranic inscriptions. The proprietor was a diminutive, dessicated ancient who vastly enjoyed our plight and told us that the next lorry out wasn't due "for some time, if Allah wills it", and in the meantime, wouldn't we like some food, which he could procure with great difficulty? Naturally, the price was astronomical, while the eggs smelt sulphurous and their yolks were flecked with blood. We couldn't really blame him, though, for in a village where there had been no rain for four *years*, where agriculture had almost collapsed and most of the young men had fled, we represented a veritable goldmine.

On to Bouzmou

When we eventually left Aït Hani, it was in a subdued state – obvious enough to the lorry driver, too, for he demanded an enormous price (40dh each to Imilchil) which, stupidly, we paid. A cardinal rule of this kind of travel is to pay only on arrival at your destination, as the Berbers do themselves, and it was all too predictable when, five hours later, the driver pulled into a village some 50km short of our destination and announced he was going no further.

Our protests were useless – the man shrugged, pretended to speak no French, and smirked at the other passengers. Then, inspired, the Belgian we were travelling with quoted a Koranic phrase equivalent to "by their deeds shall ye know them",* adding, for good measure, that the driver's behaviour was "not beautiful" (*hyrba*) in the sight of Allah. The effect was miraculous. The driver shrivelled with humiliation and returned half the money to us. In a more cheerful mood, we surveyed the village of Bouzmou, found an excellent teahouse on the roadside, and a cheerful lad to show us around.

Bouzmou was delightful: domed, honey-coloured houses, lofty trees, a gushing spring and a football match with fifty participants stirring up the dust in the *place*. Enchanting little girls with hennaed hair and huge earrings, torn between fear and the desire to touch us, scurried back and forth, clinging to each other and shrieking with laughter. The women were straightforward and curious to talk to us, a rarity in Morocco – even in the more "open" communities of Berber villages. Jill was swiftly "adopted", lent a shawl, and her eyebrows and cheeks hennaed. It was proposed that the women tattoo her as well, though the needle was like a cobbler's awl and caked with grime.

/ Continues overpage

---

* This phrase, which means, literally, "you can tell by the traces on his forehead how a man prays", can be rendered phonetically as: Si-ma-*hom*-fi-hi-*joo*-hi-*heem*.

Later, we were all directed to a small square where a rain dance was just beginning. Villagers formed circles around the dancers, beating tom-toms and uttering shrill cries. Once we were discovered, they demanded that we join in. Despite the clouds of dust, the noise and the heat, we gave a good ten-minute performance, hoping foolishly that the rain would fall and make us village heroes (it didn't).

Next morning – a Monday – nomads came in for the *souk* with their sheep herds roped neck to neck, to buy clothing, salt and tinware. Among the curiosities on sale were white rocks, which if burned "would reveal in the fire the face of your secret enemy", and smooth, sweet-smelling stones to be used as an "aftershave".

Bouzmou to Imilchil

We had to leave Bouzmou that afternoon, for our money was low and all the lorries were departing, laden with sheep and people. Our own – and we counted – held some thirty sheep on the upper deck, an unknown number on the lower, and 28 Berbers balanced on the rails and luggage racks.

In the scorching heat, at an average speed of 20km an hour, we spent the next six hours ascending tortuous roads, circumventing precipices, and seemed to *accelerate* as we approached blind corners. At every bend, the sheep bleated with fear and pissed and crapped over everyone's feet and luggage, while above them a Berber periodically unwrapped from the folds of his *djellabah* a hunk of fresh mutton, which he prodded appreciatively.

Tinerhir to Er Rachidia and Erfoud

Going **east from Tinerhir**, you can get buses or *grands taxis* along the **P32 to Er Rachidia**; the taxis involve changes at **Tinejdad** (buses and taxis leave from the east end of the town) and **Goulmina**.

Alternatively, a private line bus leaves Tinejdad (from the square used by the *grands taxis*, on the main road) daily at 9.30am along the minor **3451 road to Erfoud and Rissani**, arriving at Rissani about four hours later. To make the connection, it's best to get a *grand taxi* from Tinerhir to Tinejdad.

Er Rachidia via Goulmina

This is a straightforward and largely barren route, broken only by the oases of Tinejdad (see opposite) and Goulmina.

GOULMINA, a long, straggling palmery, is made up of some twenty or so scattered **ksour**. Without a car, though, you'll see little of it. If you're interested, ask directions along the complex network of tracks to the *ksour* known as **Gheris de Charis**; there is a small campsite here.

The modern one-road town beside the highway is about as drab as any in Morocco – the only sign of life is in the sentry boxes next to the "triumphal" entrance and exit arches. Buses leave from the street on the left of the eastern archway exit; taxis from further up this street.

Tinejdad to Erfoud

The alternative route – **direct to Erfoud** – is more interesting and, in parts, eerily impressive. It is covered by just the one daily bus, but any kind of trans-

At some point in the journey, we passed through **Imilchil**, and skirted one of the azure, salt-rimmed lakes on the **Plateau des Lacs**. We saw black nomad tents pegged in the wilderness, the occasional camel, and dozens of donkeys laden down with firewood from the distant forests. At a crossroads, around 15km from Arhbala, we got down from the sheep lorry and picked up another – this time comparatively luxurious with its freight of rough-cut stones.

Arhbala and out of the mountains

Arhbala, a small town surrounded by soft mountains and oak and cedar forests, seemed almost metropolitan with its semi-paved streets, electric lighting and double row of shops and cafés. There was no bus to Khenifra, where we hoped to change money, until 3am but, as is common in Morocco, we were "adopted" and taken home to be fed. The meal – couscous specially prepared in our honour – was delicious and our host and two older, male companions were hospitable. It left a sour taste, though, as the light bulb in the kitchen was brought out to give us extra light, leaving the man's wife and daughters (who had prepared the meal but not appeared) to crouch over the remains of the meal in the dark.

Around one o'clock, we left for the bus, crawled onto the seats and tried to sleep. Arguments blew around us, but the journey was straightforward and, after the mountains, routine and anticlimactic. At **Khenifra** we were back on the main road to Fes and all that civilisation had to offer: croissants, squat toilets and banks.

port along it is sparse: if you're driving, stock up on water, since any break-down could let you in for a long wait (probably half a day).

The road branches off from the main route to Rachidia at **TINEJDAD** and follows much of the course of this oasis – a lush strip populated by the Aït Atta tribe, traditional warriors of the south who used to control land and exact tribute as far afield as the Drâa. There are some impressive **kasbahs** – ask directions to the Asrir – and a single, basic **hotel-restaurant**, the *Tizgui*.

You leave the oasis at **MELLAB**, which has another fine **ksour**, and then on it's more or less continuous desert *hammada* until the beginning of the vast palmery of **EL DJORF** – the Tafilalt's largest *ksour* (6000 population) – on the approach to Erfoud. Beside the road, over much of this distance, the land is pockmarked by strange, volcanic-looking humps – actually man-made repair points for the underground **irrigation channels** that used to bring water to the Tafilalt almost 100km from the Todra and Ferkla rivers. Another curiosity that you notice here, and elsewhere along the oasis routes, are the bizarre Berber **cemeteries** walled off from the desert at the edge of the *ksour*. These consist of long fields of pointed stones thrust into the ground (but otherwise unidentified), a wholly practical measure to prevent jackals from unearthing bodies (and in so doing, blocking their entrance to paradise).

Although paved all the way to Erfoud, sections of this **road** are sometimes covered over with sand, the result of small, spiralling sandstorms that can suddenly blow across the region and, for twenty or thirty seconds, cut visibility to zero. In winter sections are sometimes washed away by flash floods, too. It's a simple enough road to drive, though, and shouldn't present too much of problem to follow.

ER RACHIDIA
AND THE TAFILALT

The great date-palm growing regions of the **Tafilalt** come as near as anywhere in Morocco to fulfilling Western fantasies about the Sahara. They do so by occupying the last desert stretches of the **Oued Ziz** valley: a route shot through with lush and amazingly cinematic scenes, from its beginnings at the *Source Bleu* (springwater pool) and oasis meeting point of **Meski**, to an eventual climax amid the rolling sand dunes of **Merzouga**. Along the way, once again, are an impressive succession of *ksour*, and an extraordinarily rich palmery – traditionally the most important territory this side of the Atlas.

As a terminus of the strategic caravan routes across the desert, Tafilalt has a **history** of giving rise to religious dissent and separatist movements. It formed an independent kingdom in the eighth and ninth centuries, and was at the centre of the Kharijisite heresy (a movement which used a Berber version of the Koran – orthodox Islam forbids any translation of God's direct Arabic revelation to Muhammad); later it was to become a stronghold of Shi'ite Muslims; and in the fifteenth century again emerged as a source of trouble, fostering the Marabout uprising that toppled the Saadian dynasty.

It is with the rise of Moualy er Rachid, however, and the establishment of the **Alaouite** (or, after their birthplace, *Filali*) dynasty that the region is most closely associated. Launched from a *zaouia* in Rissani, this is the dynasty which still holds power in Morocco, through Hassan II, the fourteenth sultan in the line. The Alaouites are also the source of the wealth and influence of many of the old kasbahs and *ksour*; from the time of Moulay Ismail, right through to this century, the sultans exiled princes and disenchanted relatives out here in the desert. The region was a major centre of resistance to the French, who were limited to their garrison at Erfoud until 1931.

Today, the Tafilalt is something of a backwater, with a population estimated at around 80,000 and declining, as the effects of drought and Bayoud disease* have taken hold on the palms. Most of the population are smallhold farmers, with thirty or so palms for each family, from which they could hope to produce around a thousand kilos of dates in a reasonable year. With the market price of dates around 10dh a kilo – but much less for those of inferior quality – there are no great fortunes to be made.

---

*Bayoud disease, first detected in the Drâa at the beginning of this century, attacks the roots of date palms. The disease, a kind of fungus, is spread from root to root – and possibly by transmission of spores (which jumps the fungus from one oasis to another). Palms die within a year of an attack, creating additional problems for the oasis by leaving a gap in the tight wedge of trees, which allows the winds to blow through.

It has been estimated that two thirds of the Moroccan oases are now infected with Bayoud. The disease cannot be treated economically – the most that farmers can do is to isolate trees by digging a ditch around them – and the only real hope seems to lie in the development of resistant species of palms. Moroccan and French scientists, in collaboration with the Total oil company, are at present working on new methods of propagation and cross breeding. A resistant species has already, in fact, been developed in France, but there's one problem: the dates taste awful . . .

Er Rachidia (Ksar es Souk)

ER RACHIDIA, established by the French as a regional capital (when it was known as *Ksar es Souk*, after their Foreign Legion fort), represents more than anywhere else the new face of the Moroccan south: a shift away from the old desert markets and trading routes, and, alongside it, increasing militarisation. During the Protectorate, this militarisation was directed against the tribal uncertainty of the region; since independence, the perceived threat has turned to the Polisario and to vague territorial claims from Algeria. Neither of these, however, have direct bearing on the town, which is basically an administrative centre and garrison for troops who might be needed elsewhere.

Unless you need to use the town's facilities – or await an early morning bus out – you're unlikely to want to stay. However, Er Rachidia has quite a relaxed, pleasant (and distinctly untouristed) feel, especially in the evenings, when the streets and cafés are packed out. The layout is pretty functional, with a sprawl of buildings lining the highway for some 3–4km before climaxing, inevitably, in a pretentious ceremonial arch. The one sight – worth the walk if you really have time to kill – is a large nineteenth-century **ksar**, visible from the bridge leading to Erfoud.

Orientation and transport

From the **bus station**, just about everything you might want to make use of is along the main street/highway, **Av. Mohammed V**, to your right. About 250m down is a **tourist office**, and opposite it the *Banque Populaire*. The **PTT** is down a side street behind the bank – turn left just before it. Note that Er Rachidia and Erfoud have the only **banks** in the Tafilalt – there's nowhere official to change money in either Meski or Rissani, and if you're going on to Figuig and Algeria you'll need to change travellers' cheques here. Er Rachidia is useful, too, if you want **car repairs** or spare parts: the *Elf* garage on the main square carries a large supply of standard parts and will order others efficiently from Fes.

Buses leave Er Rachidia at least four times a day for Erfoud/Rissani, and a similar number head north to Midelt and Fes or Meknes, via the dramatic Ziz Gorge (see p.190); note that the only bus to Figuig leaves at 5am, passing the turnoff for Meski about 25 minutes later. It is usually no problem to get a seat in a **grand taxi** to Erfoud or, if you gather together a group of people, to Meski. All of these leave from opposite the bus station.

Accommodation and food

For **cheap hotels**, cut up to the left of Av. Mohammed V after you pass the municipal market and you'll find yourself – in the square with the garage – facing a choice between the *Hôtel Mahraba* (also known as the *Hôtel Royal*), *Hôtel Les Oliveirs* and – distinctly preferable – the *Hôtel Renaissance* (19 Rue Moulay Youssef).

More upmarket alternatives include:

Hôtel Meski, Av. Moulay Ali Cherif (☎20.65); **Hôtel Oasis**, Rue Abou Abdellah (☎25.26). Both have pools and bars, hot showers and heating in winter. Respectively *2*B* and *2*A*.

Hôtel Rissani (☎21.86). Er Rachidia's "Grand Hotel" , with a more luxurious pool.

There is a **campsite**, 2km from the bus station, beside the road to Erfoud; this also has a pool, though not much in the way of security.

Eating is cheapest at the food stalls around the bus station; otherwise, there are quite a number of restaurants along Av. Mohammed V and in all the classified hotels. The *Hôtel Renaissance* also has a fair restaurant.

Meski: the Source Bleu

The small palm grove of **MESKI** centres on a natural springwater pool – the famous *source bleu*, created by the French Foreign Legion and long a post-card image of the south and favourite camping site for travellers. It's set in the shadows of a ruined *ksar* beside a riverbank, surrounded by wheat and barley fields, and in the past was a picturesque and enjoyable stop.

Recently, however, the **campsite** seems to have gone into terminal decline. The problem is partly one of overcrowding: Meski is firmly on the overland tour circuit and in the summer Er Rachidia's (male) youth arrive in force. But there are effects, too, from the drought that has struck over the last few years; showers no longer function and flies have become a major problem. The toilets, though, flushed by springwater, remain a bright spot.

The *source* is somewhat insignificantly signposted, to the right of the Erfoud road, 17km south of Er Rachidia. Coming by bus, ask to get out by the turnoff: from here it's only 400m down to the pool and campsite. **Going on** to Erfoud or back to Er Rachidia from Meski can be tricky, since most of the buses pass by full and don't stop. However, this is one of the easiest places around to hitch a lift and you should never be stranded for long.

South from Er Rachidia to Erfoud, Rissani and Merzouga

Make sure you travel this last section of **the Ziz** in daylight. It's one of the most pleasing of all the southern routes: a dry red belt of desert just beyond Meski, and then, suddenly, a drop into the valley and the great palmery and grain fields of central Tafilalt. Away from the road, **ksour** are almost continuous – glimpsed through the trees and the high walls enclosing gardens and plots of farming land.

If you want to stop and take a closer look, **AOUFOUSS**, midway to Erfoud, and the site of a **Thursday souk**, is perhaps the most accessible. **MAADID**, too, off to the left of the road as you approach Erfoud, is interesting – a really massive **ksour** and, like many in the Tafilalt (but few elsewhere in the south), with an entirely Arab population.

Erfoud

ERFOUD is another French-built administrative centre, with a rather desultory frontier-town atmosphere. Arriving from Er Rachidia, you get a first, powerful sense of proximity to the desert, with frequent sandblasts ripping through the streets. If you have the energy, climb up to **Borj Est**, the military hill-fort 3km across the river (leave by the back of the main square), and you can glimpse the sands to the south – if things are clear you can look back, too, right across the Tafilalt oasis to the beginnings of the Atlas. The fort itself is still used by the military.

Views apart, for most travellers Erfoud functions very much as a staging post for continuing on to Rissani and the sand dunes near Merzouga. It has a **bank** and a **PTT** in the centre of town by the intersection of the two main roads – Mohammed V and Moulay Ismail – and a marble factory, the *Marmar*, by the *Hôtel Salam*, which produces some interesting pieces with fossilised shells. Unless you have to wait until the bank opens, though, there's no great reason to stay – four **buses** a day go on to Rissani, as well as innumerable **grands taxis** (about 5dh a seat).

Accommodation and food

There are three cheap, unclassified **hotels** around Mohammed V/Moulay Ismail (walk down to the right as you come out of the bus station):

Hôtel-Bar Ziz, 3 Av. Mohammed V. The preferable choice, with a bar and good value meals.
Hôtel Les Palmeraies; **Hôtel-Restaurant de la Jeunesse**. Nothing much to distinguish these two fallbacks.

More upmarket hotels – all with bars and pools – are:

Hôtel Tafilalet, Av. Moulay Ismail, midway along Mohammed V (☎63.35). Good value deals on a room, dinner and breakfast. *3*B*.
Hôtel Sijilmassa (☎65.22). Dull, modern package hotel. *4*B*.
Hôtel Salam (☎66.65), on a hill on the outskirts. The old "Grand Hotel" and still keeping up standards. Good for a (not too pricey) restaurant meal. *4*A*.

The town's **campsite**, a ten-minute, signposted walk from the centre, is fairly basic; if you don't have a tent, you can rent a small, very inexpensive and totally unequipped **cabin** for the night. Don't expect its swimming pool to be filled – water is heavily rationed in Erfoud.

Moving on from Erfoud: routes to Merzouga

Continuing south from Erfoud, the most popular trip is to **the dunes at Merzouga, via Rissani** (see overpage). There are Land Rover tours from Erfoud along this route (offered by the *Hôtel Tafilalet*, among other places), or you can go by bus to Rissani and then on by lorry or Land Rover taxi to Merzouga. Alternatively, if you have the money or enough people to share expenses, it's possible to hire a Land Rover yourself in Erfoud (for around 1000dh per day).

Transport of your own would enable you to take the 57km **direct route from Erfoud to Merzouga**. This is surfaced for the first 16km only, but it is not too hard to follow the *piste*, which runs parallel to a line of telephone poles until you are within sight of the dunes, at which stage just take the piste, straight ahead of you, towards them. The drive takes a little over 45 minutes; en route (about 35km from Erfoud) there is a small café, with a gesture of a swimming pool.

The **route from Erfoud to Tinejdad** is detailed in reverse – see "Tinerhir to Erfoud" (p.346).

Rissani

RISSANI stands at the last visible point of the Ziz river; beyond it, steadily encroaching on the village and its ancient *ksour* ruins, begins the desert. The village, in an earlier incarnation, was the capital of Tafilalt and was for eleven centuries the final stop on the great caravan routes south. It was the site of the first Arab kingdom of the south – the semi-legendary **Sijilmassa**, founded in 707 – and, later, from the *zaouia* here (still an important national shrine), the Alaouite dynasty launched its bid for power, conquering first the oases of the south, then the vital Taza Gap, triumphing finally in Fes and Marrakesh.

The village and market

The **modern village** musters scarcely enough houses to merit the term. Most of the people live in a single large and decaying **ksour**, and, in addition to this, there is just one administrative street with a couple of **cafés**, a **bank**, a (men's) **hammam** and a **hotel**, the *Filalia*. If you plan to stay here rather than continue on to Merzouga, the best – and the cheapest – place to sleep is up on the hotel roof. The rooms themselves are invariably dirty, the water sulphurous. The cafés are not much better. A rare bright spot is the *Maison Berbère*, part of the chain of **rug and carpet** shops (see also Zagora and Tinerhir) and well worth an hour or two's browsing.

In fact, Rissani's only discernible life – the one time you might want to linger in the village – comes with the **market**, held three times a week (Sunday, Tuesday, Thursday), though even then it's a pretty quiet place compared to the old days when the caravans passed through. The caravans were still active into the 1890s, when the English journalist Walter Harris reported seeing thriving gold and slave auctions. Predictably enough, today's money making goods are all tourist-oriented, with inflated prices. However, there's often a good selection of local Berber jewellery – including the crude, almost iconographic designs of the desert Touaregs – and some of the basic products (dried fruits, farming implements and so on) are interestingly distinct from those of the richer north. Don't expect camels, though – apart from the caravans, these were never very common in Tafilalt, the Berbers preferring (as they still do) more economical mules.

Sijilmassa, the Zaouia and nearby Ksour

Rissani's older monuments are well into the process of erosion – both through crumbling material and the slow progress of the sands. **Sijilmassa**, whose ruins were clearly visible at the beginning of this century, has more or less vanished, though you can just about make out a few ruins along the course of the river a few minutes' walk to the west of the village. The various kasbahs and reminders of the Alaouite presence are also mostly in some stage of decay, but there is just enough remaining to warrant a battle with the morning heat.

The **ksar** that is still occupied by the Rissani market square is itself seventeenth-century in origin, though much restored since. From here you can cut across diagonally from the bus terminal towards another collection of *ksour*. The first you encounter, about 2–3km southeast, houses the **Zaouia of**

Moulay Ali Shereef, the original Alaouite stronghold and the mausoleum of the dynasty's founder. Many times rebuilt – the last following floods in 1955 – the shrine is forbidden to non-Muslims.

Beside it, dominating this group of buildings, is the nineteenth-century **Ksar d'Akbar**, an awesomely grandiose ruin which was once a palace exile, housing the unwanted members of the Alaouite family and the wives of the dead sultans. Most of the structure, which still bears considerable traces of its former decoration, dates from the beginning of the nineteenth century.

A third royal *ksar*, the **Oualad Abd el-Halim**, stands about 2km further down the road. Notable for its huge ramparts and the elaborate decorative effects of its blind arches and unplastered brick patterning, this is one of the few really impressive imperial buildings completed in this century. It was constructed around 1900 for Sultan Moulay Hassan's elder brother, whom he had appointed governor of the Tafilalt.

Getting to Merzouga

The trip from **Rissani to Merzouga** can be covered in a variety of ways. Simplest is if you have your own vehicle: the route is not that clear (sand often covers sections) but the destination, Merzouga's huge golden sand dune, the Erg Cherbi, is hard to mistake. Be wary, however, of high winds – you could easily get lost in a sandstorm – or recent rains, which would present problems to all but four-wheel drive vehicles.

Without your own car, you've a choice between **market day lorries**, laden to the hilt, which leave three times a week from the market square, or local Land Rover taxis (they park opposite the cafés where the buses arriving in town stop; most leave daily at around 4pm). The trip takes about two hours and costs 10dh a place by Land Rover taxi.

West from Rissani

Heading **west**, the 10am bus to Er Rachidia connects with the 1pm bus to Tinerhir (arriving around 4.30pm) and Ouarzazate.*Grands taxis* also run direct from Rissani to Tinerhir (45dh).

An alternative route out from Rissani is the **piste west to Zagora**. This is detailed in reverse on p.334. It's a possible route either with your own car, or if you can coincide with the market days, by a local Land Rover taxi. The taxi leaves every Thursday after the Rissani market, arriving in Zagora around ten hours later; a seat can be arranged through the hotel.

Merzouga

The attraction of **MERZOUGA** is **Erg Chebbi** (The Small *Erg*), Morocco's largest sand dune, 150m high at its tallest point, and stretching for some 15km or so into the haze, beyond the village. It is now very much part of the tourist circuit, but it would be foolish to let this put you off. Just getting out there from Rissani is an adventure in itself – blazing along the desert *piste* is for many travellers a highlight of travels in the south.

If you're in no hurry, it's good to stay a night at Merzouga, experiencing the isolation and silence of the desert. There are five **café-hotels** scattered around the village and below the dunes. The *Hôtel Merzouga*, at the foot of the dunes, is well run and does good dinners; it charges 50dh for a double room, 20dh a person for sleeping on its *terrasse*. Slightly cheaper alternatives include the *Café-Restaurant de Palmeraie* (signposted from Merzouga's triumphal arch), which offers couch space at 10dh a person, and the *Auberge Grand Dune*, a hostel-like place, basic but very friendly, with one large room divided by curtains. All of these are within easy walking distance of the village. If you've got a sleeping bag, bedding down on the dunes is perhaps the best option of all – and in summer, when even roofspace can be taken by mid-afternoon, it may be your only choice.

The area near Merzouga, incidentally, is used for the **North African Rally** every June to July, and it's the Erg Chebbi that appears in the famous Renault 5 advertisement, with the car driving down the dune. Rally-drivers' stickers on the Merzouga café windows add a rather surreal touch to the place. The Erg itself can be walked across in about an hour. Camel rides can also be arranged – contact the local camel driver, Hassan, at the *Auberge La Grand Dune* – for anything from a couple of hours to two or three days.

The lake
Birdwatchers may also find the area around Merzouga – and the route down from Rissani – of interest. Most winters a lake forms just to the west of the village. More unusual sightings, if you strike lucky, might include the desert sparrow, desert warbler, Egyptian nightjar and Arabian bustard. Numerous migrants should also be in evidence.

Back to Rissani
Getting back to Rissani, most of the Land Rover taxis leave around 7am; lorries at a similar time on the morning after a *souk*. At popular times of year it can sometimes be tricky to get a place in a Land Rover taxi and it may be worth trying to arrange a lift with fellow tourists. Note that in winter the mornings are extremely cold, so dress up warm if you're going on the lorry.

OUT EAST TO FIGUIG
AND THE ALGERIAN BORDER

The eight- to ten-hour desert journey from **Er Rachidia to Figuig** (pronounced F'geeg) is one of the most exhilarating and spectacular that you can make, certainly among those accessible to travellers without Land Rovers and proper expeditionary planning. It is startlingly isolated, almost throughout its 393km length, and physically extraordinary: the real outlands of Morocco, dominated by huge empty landscapes and blank red mountains.

What little there is in the way of human presence is a series of struggling mining villages and military outposts, ranging from the desolate, tiny mud hut-type constructions of MENGOUB to the prosperous administrative and garrison centre of **BOUARFA** – a friendly place, which has two basic hotels and where you'll probably have to change buses. The real focus of the region, though, is **Figuig** itself – a great medieval date palm oasis, in the bowl of the mountains and right on the border with Algeria.

If you want to continue on **into Algeria**, the border crossing here is open and functional. Staying in Morocco, you can head north from **Figuig to Oujda** (7hr by bus) and the Mediterranean coast.

The Figuig oasis

The southern oases are traditionally measured by the number of their palms, rather than in terms of area or population. **FIGUIG**, with something like 200,000 trees, has always been one of the largest – an importance further enhanced by its strategic border position. At least twice it has been lost – in the seventeenth-century wars, and again at the end of Moulay Ismail's reign – and as recently as 1975 there was fighting in the streets here between Moroccan and Algerian troops.

Orientation, hotels and food

The oasis has even less of an administrative town than usual, still basically consisting of its seven distinct *ksour* villages – which in the past feuded almost continuously over water and grazing rights.

Getting **orientated** is relatively simple. Everything lies on the road by which you enter the town. The *Hôtel Meliasse*, the first landmark, is on the right, above the Shell service station. The bus stops here – there is no bus terminal as such in Figuig – and then stops again outside the *Hôtel Sahara*, which has a *hammam* next door.

Beyond lie the various **shops and cafés**, selling a wide range of food. The *Café El Fath* will make an evening meal on request and delicious doughnuts are available from a stall nearby. A bank is to be found on the right of the road, then there is a double archway (police post on the left). If you go through the left arch, past the *Café Oasis* (meals again to order), you enter a garden part of town, which ends at the army barracks. The road turns left, then right, there is a short length of dual carriageway and then the **Hôtel Camping** is indicated through an arch. This has cheap (if not overclean) rooms, a **swimming pool** and superb views to the southern portion of the oasis. You camp in the garden, and meals, once again, can be cooked to order. It is definitely the preferable place to stay. The *Hôtel Meliasse* is very basic and has a mercenary manager who doesn't appear to employ any cleaners; the *Hôtel Sahara* is a little better – cleaner (despite a blind owner) and with balconies and a touch of sunlight in the rooms

Buses

The ticket office for **buses** north from Figuig is to be found by walking north from the *Hôtel Sahara* and turning left at the fountain/junction. The office is to the right, under the arcades.

The 6am departure goes direct to Oujda with a breakfast stop at Bouarfa. Heading for Er Rachidia, there are just two buses a day from Bouarfa (at 8am and 2pm); catch the 5am bus from Figuig if you want to avoid a long wait.

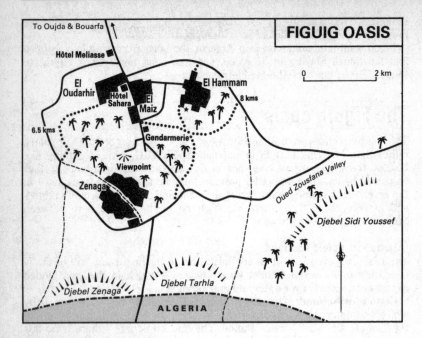

Exploring the ksour

Figuig's **ksour** are signposted off the main road and are spread out around the base of the hill – each enclosing its own palmery within high turreted walls. Although sporadically organised into a loose confederation, they were until this century fiercely independent – and their relations with each other were peppered with long and bitter blood feuds and, above all, disputes over the limited water supply. Their strange, archaic shape – with watchtowers rising above the snaking *feggaguir* (or irrigation channels) – evolved as much from this internal tension as from any need to protect themselves from the nomadic tribes of the desert. Likewise, within each of the *ksour*, the elaborate tunnel-like networks of alleys are deliberate (and successful) attempts to prevent any sudden or easy progress.

Your best chance of getting an overview of it all is to head for the **plat-forme**, poised above the *ksar* of Zenaga. The view from here spans a large part of the palmery and its pink-tinged *ksour*, and you can gaze at the weird, multicoloured layers of the enclosing mountains.

If you can find the energy – Figuig in summer feels a little like sitting inside a fan-heater – head down into **Zenaga**, the largest and richest of the seven villages. Going to your left, you should reach its centre, more developed than most in this area, with a couple of cubicle shops and a café in addition to a mosque. For a look at the other *ksour*, it is possible to loop to the right of the main administrative road, past El Maiz to El Hammam el Foukanni.

CROSSING INTO ALGERIA

Crossing into Algeria at Figuig is routine, with no restrictions on "pedestrian" passengers (as existed until recently at Oujda). However, there are a few formalities worth knowing before setting off.

First of all, before leaving the Figuig administrative centre, you must get your passport stamped at the **gendarmerie**. This must be done on the same day you cross the border – effectively ruling out an early start, since the police post opens at 8am (and closes at 3pm). Next, walk or hitch the 4km to the **border crossing** – a Beau Geste type of place with some palms and two tents – where you need to get more stamps on both the Moroccan and Algerian sides. There is also a customs check on the Algerian side – which can take a while if the officers decide to do a search; they may well, as they don't have a lot else to do. If you are driving, you will have to obtain (compulsory) insurance – currently 60 dinars for twenty days.

Beni Ounif

Finally, you can head for the Algerian frontier town of **BENI OUNIF**, another 3km. There are **banks** in Beni Ounif, and if you want to move on the same day it's vital to get into town early enough to change money. The banks (closed, as are all in Algeria, on Fridays and Saturdays) are in the area to the right of the main road. There is just one, rather basic, **hotel**.

Buses going north stop by the yellow taxi stand; at around 1.30pm, there's a departure to Saïda, which arrives in the evening (connections on from there to Algiers). There are also **trains** heading north, with early morning and evening departures.

El Maiz is the prettiest of the *ksour*, with small vaulted lanes and houses with broad verandas pointing south. In **El Hammam**, as the name suggests, there is a hot spring, used by the people for their ablutions. Anyone offering their services as a guide will take you to it. Back on the other side of the administrative road is the **Ksar El-Oudarhir**, which also has some natural springs (one hot, one salty), as well as terraces similar to the ones in El Maiz.

All of the *ksour* have exclusively Berber populations, though up until the 1950s and 1960s there was also a considerable Jewish population. Until the beginning of the twentieth century, Figuig was also the final Moroccan staging point on the overland journey to Mecca.

Figuig to Oujda

Unless you have a strange fascination for (very) small town life, there is really nowhere else on this eastern plateau between Figuig and Oujda which offers very much temptation. **TENDRARA** (Tuesday market) and **AÏT BENIMATHAR** both have basic café-hotels, if you decide to stay overnight. Aït Benimathar is the better choice – a quiet little **hot water oasis**, full of tortoises and snakes. Even if you don't want to stay, it's not a bad place to spend the middle of an afternoon, which you can do by taking the early morning bus from Figuig, then catching a later one for the final 50km to Oujda.

To the west of Bouarfa, the towns are all fairly bleak. If you're into *piste* driving, there are said to be troglodyte (cave) dwellings up in the hills behind BOUDENIB, towards GOUMARRA.

travel details

Buses

From Ouarzazate Marrakesh (4 daily; 6hr); Zagora (3; 5hr 30min)*; Tailiouine/Taroudannt (2; 3hr 30 min/5hr); Tinerhir (3; 5hr).

From Zagora Ouarzazate (4 daily; 4–5hr)*; Marrakesh (2 daily; 9–11hr)*.

From Tinerhir Er Rachidia (2 daily; 3hr); Ouarzazate (3; 5hr).

From Er Rachidia Erfoud/Rissani (4 daily; 1hr 30 min/3hr); Tinerhir (2; 3hr); Figuig (1 daily via Bouarfa, currently at 5am; 10hr); Midelt (5; 3hr 30 min); Fes (3; 8hr 30min); Meknes (1; 8hr).

From Erfoud Rissani (4 daily; 1hr 30min); Er Rachidia (4; 1hr 30min); Fes (daily; 11hr).

From Rissani Tinejdad/Goulmina (daily; 3hr 30 min/4hr).

From Figuig Oujda (4 daily; 7hr); Er Rachidia (via Bouarfa; 1 daily; 10hr).

The most comfortable bus on the Marrakesh–Ouarzazate–Zagora route is run by Ligne du Zagora.

Grands Taxis

From Ouarzazate Regularly to Zagora (3hr). Negotiable for Skoura (1hr) and Aït Benhaddou (1hr 45min, but expensive private trip).

From Zagora Regularly to Ouarzazate (3hr); lorries to Rissani (10hr) and Foum Zguid (8hr).

From Boumalne Land Rover taxi at least daily to Msemrir (3hr). Regular run to Tinerhir (50min).

From Tinerhir Regular runs to Boumalne (50 min) and Tinejdad (1hr; from there on to Er Rachidia).

From Er Rachidia Fairly frequent runs to Erfoud (along the route you can negotiate a ticket to Meski) and to Tinejdad (2hr).

From Erfoud Fairly frequent runs to Rissani (1hr 30min) and Erfoud (2hr). Land Rover trips direct to Merzouga (1hr; relatively expensive).

Trains

There is a night train from Bouarfa to Oujda (8hr), but this carries mainly freight, and is a distinctly eccentric alternative to the bus from Figuig.

TELEPHONE CODES	
ER RACHIDIA ☎057	OUARZAZATE ☎088

CHAPTER SEVEN

AGADIR, THE ANTI-ATLAS AND THE DEEP SOUTH

F lying to southern Morocco, your destination is most likely to be **Agadir** – built specifically as a resort following its destruction by an earthquake in 1960, and today something of a showpiece for the "new nation". It is unlikely, though, that you'll want to stay here for long. Agadir has been very carefully developed – its image is as a winter holiday spot for Europeans – and besides the beach and package tour hotels, there is not much life to be found. There certainly isn't anything at all Moroccan: this is tourism at its most irrelevant and bland, straining hard to avoid contact with any local culture.

Fortunately, little of this applies to the rest of **the coast**. Just north of Agadir is a series of small fishing villages and beaches, many of them still without electricity or running water. **Tarhazoute**, a popular hippy centre in the early 1970s, is the best known – though it is today a bit seedy, and not to everyone's taste. Inland from here, and part of the same mythology, is "Paradise Valley", a beautiful and exotic palm gorge which culminates in the seasonal waterfalls of **Immouzer des Ida Outanane**, a trip well worth making. To the south, the beaches are almost totally deserted in summer, ranging from solitary campsites at **Sidi Rbat** – one of Morocco's best locations for birdwatching – and **Sidi Moussa d'Aglou**, down to the old port of **Sidi Ifni** – only relinquished by Spain in 1969, and full of bizarrely grandiose Art Deco colonial architecture.

Inland, the two main towns of the **Anti-Atlas** – and for outsiders, its major attractions – are Taroudannt and Tafraoute, provincial and easy-going centres whose Chleuh Berber populations share the distinction of having together cornered the country's grocery trade. *Tafraoutis*, in particular, can be found throughout Morocco (as well as in Paris and Marseilles) running corner grocery stores, but eventually returning home to retire. The physical difference between the two towns could hardly be greater, though. **Taroudannt** has massive walls and is the modern (and traditional) capital of the fertile **Souss plain**; it's an animated city with good *souks* and hotels, and a natural place to stay on your way to Marrakesh or Ouarzazate. Further south, and reached by bus via Tiznit, **Tafraoute** is essentially a collection of villages built of stone, absurdly picturesque in a startling natural landscape of pink granite and strange, vast, rock formations. If you have time to visit only one place in the southwest, this should be it.

A more adventurous trip would take in the **Tata loop**, a little-travelled route across the southern Anti-Atlas to the pre-Sahara, comprising a string of

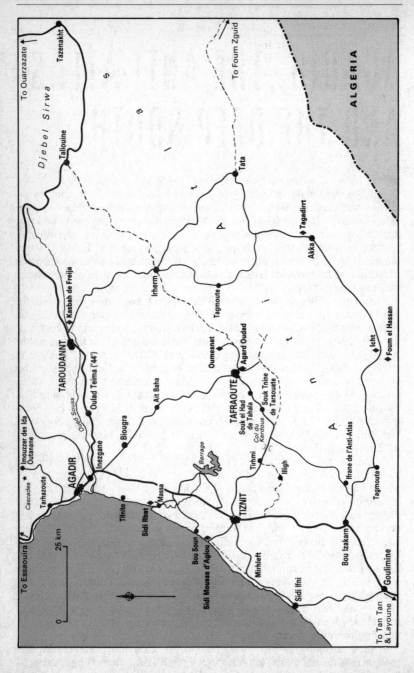

true desert oasis. The route is most easily covered from Tiznit, but it is feasible to do it east to west from Taroudannt. It's well off the usual (or even unusual) tourist trails and is highly recommended.

The **Deep South**, beyond Goulimine and down into the **Western Sahara**, has become more stable in recent years, as the Moroccan army has effectively contained its Polisario adversaries in the war over its "Saharan Provinces" – the former colonial zone of Spanish Sahara. There are now virtually no restrictions on travelling down the coast through Tan Tan and Laayoune as far south as Ad Dakhla, on (for the most part) a well-paved road. At present, however, you cannot continue from Ad Dakhla into Mauritania and the borders with Algeria remain closed.

For visitors, the Deep South's main appeal lies in the experience of travel in the desert, and in the great distances covered. **Goulimine**, the most accessible "desert town", is scarcely worth the trip for itself. Promoted for its camel market – the traditional meeting place of the "Blue Men" (Touareg tribesmen, whose faces are tinged blue by their masks and robes) – it is now more frequented by tourists than anyone else. But it is quite a ride all the same, and with your own vehicle you can explore several oasis nearby.

Going even further, you begin to need real commitment in order to travel to towns like **Tan Tan**, 125km further south, or **Laayoune**, reached after another 260km, both of which are essentially administrative centres. Again, however, you get a real taste of the desert, especially on the road between Tarfaya and Laayoune, with the dunes on one side, and the sands, dropping in sheer cliff to the ocean, on the other. Returning, if you don't fancy a repeat of the journey, there are flights from Ad Dakhla and Laayoune to Agadir, and from Laayoune (and Agadir) to the **Canary Islands**.

Agadir

Built up in organised sectors – one for tourist hotels, one for the port, and a third, some way out, for industry and local residents – **AGADIR** doesn't really lend itself to excitement or spontaneity. It does, admittedly, have a magnificent beach and it has avoided the high-rise architecture of its Spanish *costa* counterparts, but this is about as far as being positive will stretch. Unless you actually want a day or two's suspension from ordinary Moroccan life, it would be better to pass straight through. Rooms, in any case, can be a real problem to find at the height of the summer or winter/spring seasons.

If you are simply travelling through Agadir as a means of getting south, you might well prefer to stay in the town of **Inezgane** (see p.367), now almost a suburb of the city – 13km southwest.

Orientation, points of arrival and accommodation

The basic layout of Agadir is pretty straightforward. The **beach** and the **commercial zone** (centered around Place Hassan II and Av. Hassan II) are marked on the map overpage; the **port area** is to the north, below the old kasbah; and the **industrial zone** spreads south toward Inezgane.

Points of arrival

Agadir **airport** (☎311.06) is 4km out on the Inezgane road; there's an occasional bus to Place Salam (more regular ones if you walk 1km to the main road junction), or you can share a *grand taxi* (always available; about 50dh for up to six people). The *bureau de change* exchanges only cash currency.

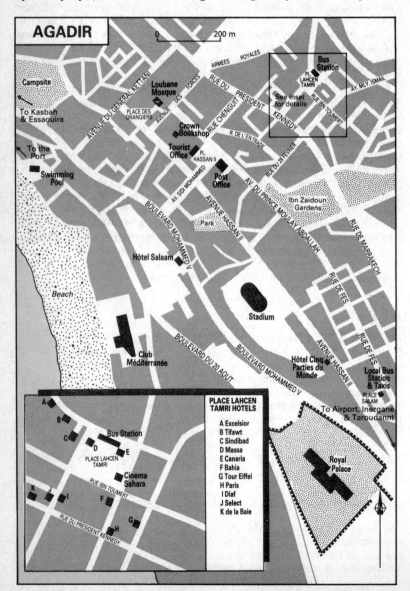

AGADIR

0   200 m

ARMEES ROYALES

Campsite

To Kasbah & Essaouira

To the Port

Swimming Pool

Beach

Loubane Mosque

PLACE DES ORANGIERS

Crown Bookshop

Tourist Office

PL. HASSAN II

Post Office

Hôtel Salaam

Club Méditerranée

Bus Station

PL. LAHCEN TAMRI

See inset for details

RUE DU PRESIDENT

RUE CHENGUIT

R. DE L'ENTRADE

AVENUE DU GENERAL KETTANI

AVENUE DES FORCES

AV. MLY. ISMAIL

RUE IBN TOUMERT

KENNEDY

RUE DU 29 FEVRIER

AV. SIDI MOHAMMED

AVENUE HASSAN II

AV. DU PRINCE MOULAY ABDALLAH

Ibn Zaidoun Gardens

Park

RUE DE MARRAKECH

Stadium

RUE DE FES

BOULEVARD MOHAMMED V

BOULEVARD DU 20 AOUT

BOULEVARD MOHAMMED V

AVENUE HASSAN II

RUE DE FES

Hôtel Cinq Parties du Monde

Local Bus Station & Taxis

PLACE SALAM

To Airport, Inezgane & Taroudannt

Royal Palace

A
B
C
D   E
PLACE LAHCEN TAMRI
Bus Station
K J I
F
G
H
Cinema Sahara
RUE IBN TOUMERT
RUE DU PRESIDENT KENNEDY

PLACE LAHCEN TAMRI HOTELS

A Excelsior
B Tifawt
C Sindibad
D Massa
E Canaria
F Bahia
G Tour Eiffel
H Paris
I Diaf
J Select
K de la Baie

The city is not yet on the rail line, though there are plans for connections to Marrakesh and south to Laayoune – routes which at present are covered by buses run by the rail company, *ONCF*, as well as *CTM* and other private lines. All buses that run direct to or from Agadir operate from the **Talborjt bus station** behind Place Lahcen Tamri (top centre-right on the map).

If you're coming in by **bus** from the south, however, you might actually be arriving in Inezgane. To get into Agadir from Inezgane, "city" buses #5 or #6 will drop you at the **Place Salam terminal** (bottom right on our map). **Grands taxis** do regular runs into Agadir, too – correct fare 3dh.

Getting around Agadir, you can hire mopeds and motorbikes near the *Hôtel Almohades*. For details of car hire, see the "Listings" on p.366, and for a rundown on some of the bus services out of the city, see p.367.

Hotels

Agadir has a vast number of hotels, tourist apartments and "holiday villages". Outside peak season, you can often get very good deals at some of the large, beachfront hotels (doubles at 4* hotels run at around £30–35 a night). At the more popular times, though – Christmas/New Year, Easter, July and August – it can be quite a battle finding anywhere at all that has space. The best bets at these times (and year-round if budget is your prime consideration) are likely to be the cheaper, independently run places – too small or too basic for the package tour groups – concentrated around and downhill from **Place Lahcen Tamri**, the area around the bus station, inset on our map.

PLACE LAHCEN TAMRI AREA

This quarter, known as Talborjt, is something of an "alternative Agadir", and frequented to an extent by young Moroccans on holiday. Good choices (keyed letters refer to the inset) include, in roughly ascending order of price:

Hôtel Massa (D), **Hôtel Canaria (E)**, both on Place Lahcen Tamri (no phones). No great claims to comfort or cleanliness, but generally the cheapest prices in Agadir. *Unclassified.*

Hôtel Select (J), Rue Allal Ben Abdallah. Another cheapie. *Unclassified.*

Hôtel Diaf (I), Rue Allal Ben Abdallah (☎231.79). Reliable budget choice – and the 1*B rating means that its prices are often lower than at the unclassified hotels. *1*B.*

Hôtel de la Baie (K), Rue Allal Ben Abdallah (☎230.14). Good value choice, with some balconied rooms. *1*B.*

Hôtel Excelsior (A), Rue Yacoub el Mansour (☎210.28). Reasonable rooms but, located amid a row of grill cafés, a bit noisy. *1*B.*

Hôtel Tifawt (B), Rue Yacoub el Mansour (☎243.75). Clean enough but don't count on the promised hot showers. *1*A.*

Hôtel El Bahia (F), Rue Mehdi Ibn Toumert (☎227.24). Unusually clean, tasteful and good value, located opposite the *Cinema Sahara*. Books up early in the day. *1*A.*

Hôtel de Paris (H), Av. Kennedy (☎22694). Sister hotel to the *Bahia*. Recently refurbished, with a pleasant courtyard set around a small fountain. *1*A.*

Hôtel Sindibad (C), Place Lahcen Tamri (☎234.77). Comfortable budget hotel that tends to be booked up by Germans; prices considerably higher than the above. *2*A.*

Hôtel Cinq Parties du Monde (L), Bd. Hassan II (☎225.45). Modern, clean rooms in tiled courtyard, plus a decent set-menu restaurant. *2*A.*

Hôtel Ayour, Rue de l'Entraide (☎249.76). Another new, medium-budget hotel – good for its class. A block north of Av. du Prince Moulay Abdallah. *2*A.*

BEACH AREA HOTELS

The **more upmarket hotels** are spread out on the avenues running back from the beach – Bd. du 20 Août, Bd. Mohammed V and Av. Hassan II. Worthwhile places (and one cheaper beachfront choice) include:

Hôtel Petit Suède, Bd Hassan II (☎228.79). Small hotel, 200m from the beach. *2*B*.

Hôtel Miramar, Bd. Mohammed V (☎226.73). Pleasant, small hotel above the harbour – one of the few that survived the earthquake. *3*A*.

Hôtel Club Salam (**M**), Bd. Mohammed V (☎221.20; or reserve through *Societé Salam* in Casablanca, ☎0/36.79.22). Very tasteful package hotel with a fine pool; labelled near the centre of our map. *4*A*.

Hôtel les Almohades, Quartier des Dunes (☎402.33). One of the best hotels in Agadir, sited at the edge of the beach – a big advantage – and reasonably priced for its class. *4*A*.

Campsite

The city's **campsite** (☎295.40) is fairly well located, within easy walking distance of the centre and beach, on Bd. Mohammed V. It is reasonably secure, and has a snack bar and other facilities. Prices are average to high.

Around the town

Even more than most resorts, Agadir's life revolves around its beach. If you're not into sunbathing, you won't want to stay long; if you're booked into a package holiday here, make as many independent excursions as possible – Immouzer, Taroudannt and Marrakesh are all in easy striking distance.

Along the beachfront

Few details are needed on the **beach** itself, which extends an impressive distance to the south of the town, is swept each morning and, being patrolled by mounted police, is almost devoid of hustlers. Along its course are a number of cafés which sell drinks and hire out sunbeds and umbrellas – the *Oasis Bar* is one of the nicest, very clean and with good service – and there's a municipal **swimming pool** at the north end if you don't care for the ocean. As a break from the sand, the **city park**, several hundred yards long and wide, offers the shade of eucalyptus trees. The **fishing port**, too, is worth a stroll. You can haggle for fish yourself, at very low prices, if you're doing your own cooking, or have it cooked for you at grills down by the entrance to the port. Most of these operate until 11pm in summer, 7pm in winter.

A little further afield, on the south side of town, Hassan II's **Palais Royale** is nearing completion. It cannot, of course, be visited, but you can get a good view of it from the river estuary. Built in an imaginative blend of traditional and modern forms, it is an exciting structure, even from outside the vast encircling walls. If you're interested in **birdwatching**, the estuary itself could be rewarding – constantly filled with flocks of sea birds.

The Kasbah – and some history

All that remains of old Agadir – the pre-earthquake town – is the **Kasbah** enclosure, on top of the hill to the north of the port. This is an eight-kilometre trip, worth making if you have transport, for a marvellous view of Agadir and the coast. The kasbah itself, however, is little more than a bare outline of walls and entrance arch – the latter with an inscription in Dutch recording that the Netherlands began trading here in 1746 (capitalising on the rich sugar plantations of the Souss plain).

It's not much, but it is one of the few reminders that the city has any past at all, so complete was the destruction of the 1960 earthquake. In fact, Agadir's history closely parallels that of the other Atlantic ports: colonised first by the Portuguese in the fifteenth century, then, recaptured by the Saadians in the sixteenth, carrying on its trading with intermittent prosperity – overshadowed, more often than not, by the activities of Mogador (Essaouira).

Abroad, up until its new tourist incarnation, Agadir's name was known mainly for a crisis in colonial squabblings in 1911. The Germans, protesting against French and British plans to carve up North Africa, sent a gunboat to Agadir, which let loose a few rounds across the bay. Like the Fashoda crisis in Egypt, the event very nearly sent the balloon up to launch World War I.

Eating and drinking

For an international resort, Agadir is something of a disappointment in the restaurant and nightlife stakes. Many of the package tourists seem to have meals included at their hotels and, though there are plenty of reasonable enough café restaurants, there is little that's very exciting. Nightlife, too, is on the tame side, with most bars and discos to be found in the large hotels.

As with hotels, the cheaper eateries are grouped around **Place Lahcen Tamri**, or streets running south from the square. At basic café-restaurants here, you can eat soup, *tajine* and salads, at pretty much regular Moroccan prices. For something a bit more fancy, you need to head towards the **beach**, or alternatively to *Les Pergolas* in Inezgane (see p.367).

Restaurants

Café-Restaurant Les Arcades, opposite *Hôtel de la Baie*; **Restaurant Sabir**, next to *Hôtel El Bahia*. Two of the better café-restaurants around Place Lahcen Tamri – see inset on map.

Mille et Une Nuits, next to *Hôtel Sindibad*, Place Lahcen Tamri. Classier *prix fixé* meals.

Café Taverner, Av. Hassan II. Reliable restaurant on a street worth menu browsing.

Pizzeria Annamunda, Av. Sidi Mohammed. Decent food and guitarists. The street runs between Place Hassan II and Bd. Mohammed V.

Le Tanalt, Place des Orangiers (off Av. Hassan II). French food and a reasonable *menu fixé*.

L'Etoile de Marrakech, Av. du Prince Moulay Abdallah, near the Ibn Zaidoun gardens. Generous portions of good French-Moroccan food.

Jour et Nuit, on the beachfront. Grill-café and **bar** open through the night.

Bars and nightlife

Corniche Restaurant Bar, close by the *Jour et Nuit* (see above) on the beachfront. A clear winner for night-time entertainment, hosting some excellent bands led by local musicians.

Disco Tan Tan, in the *Hôtel Almohades*. Perhaps the best of the hotel discos.

Bylbos Disco, in the *Hôtel Dunes d'Or*. This can be lively, too, though prices of admission and drinks are high.

Hôtel Atlas, **Hôtel Sahara**. Moroccan groups usually play (from around 8 to 11pm), prior to the discos, in these hotels.

Listings

Airlines *Royal Air Maroc* fly from Agadir to Laayoune and the Canary Islands, and to Tangier (via Casa). Their office is on Av. du General Kettani (☎321.45).

American Express c/o *Voyages Schwartz*, Bd. Hassan II; open Mon–Fri 9am–noon & 3–6pm; closed weekends.

Banks The *Banque Populaire* (Mon–Fri 8am–noon & 2.30–5pm, Sat & Sun 10am–noon) is the most helpful (they will guide you through the motions of opening an account if you decide to stay on in Morocco). *SGMB*, *Crédit du Maroc* and others can be found downtown, mainly along Av. des FAR. The *Hôtel Sahara* (Av. Mohammed V) exchanges currency at normal bank rates.

Books New and used English-language books are sold and exchanged at *The Crown English Bookshop* (50m along the balcony from the tourist office – see below). Run by an American, this takes pride to maintain background books on Morocco, including Paul Bowles' translations of contemporary writers, as well as dictionaries, phrasebooks and course books of Moroccan Arabic. English newspapers are also stocked.

Car hire If you're heading for the Anti-Atlas or cutting across to the south, Agadir offers the last facilities to speak of. Also, because it's very competitive, it's one of the cheapest places in the country to hire a car – and many of the hire companies will let you to return it in Marrakesh, Casablanca or Fes. *Golden Tours*, Bd. Mohammed V (☎84.03.62), is a useful agency, who can supply cars and also drivers if required at reasonable cost. Other companies worth shopping around include:

Leasing Cars, 107 Av. Hassan II (☎209.81); and at the airport.

LVS, 52 Av. Hassan II. Also has branches in Marrakesh and Casablanca.

Rent-a-Car, Av. Hassan II (☎237.50).

Afric Cars, Bd. Mohammed V (☎237.50).

Hertz-Maroc, Bungalow Marhaba, Av. Mohammed V (☎237.37).

Car repairs For Renaults try *Castano* (Av. El Moukaouama; ☎238.21); Citroëns, *Garage Citroën* (corner of Rue Bertholet/Rue Ampère); Fiats, *Auto-Hall* (Rue de la Foire; ☎224.86). And many others as well.

Consulates *Britain* , Rue des Administration Publiques (☎277.41).

Ferries For Tangier ferries, book at *COMANAV* (Place Mohammed V; ☎204.52).

Medical care *Hôpital Hassan II*, Route de Marrakesh (☎224.77). Most of the big hotels can also provide the addresses of English-speaking doctors.

Moped/Motorbike hire *MotoHire*, near the beach, on Bd. du 20 Août, hires out Yamaha 125s at about 150dh a day (lower rates for the week), well worth considering for trips to Immouzer and beyond. It also has cheaper mopeds, intended for local use but practical for shuttling to Banana Village and Tarhazoute (see "Around Agadir").

Post office The main *PTT* is right in the middle of town at the end of Av. Sidi Mohammed; hours are Mon–Fri 9am–noon & 3–6pm, Sat 9am–noon only; the efficient telephone section stays open 24hr.

Shopping If you want to buy your own booze, the cheapest spirits, beer and wine (and general provisions) are sold by the *Uniprix* shop at the corner of Av. Hassan II and Av. Sidi Mohammed. The *Uniprix* is also useful for checking prices of handicrafts, which it sells at fixed prices. If you buy anything elsewhere in Agadir – rugs, carpets, *babouches*, etc – you will have to do some very heavy bargaining indeed. Better by far, however, would be to visit the *souks* at Taroudannt (see p.373) for the day.

Tourist offices The ONMT is on the balcony level of Immeuble A, entered off Av. Sidi Mohammed along the raised walkway opposite the post office. There is a *Syndicat d'Initiative* on Av. Mohammed V (☎226.95).

LEAVING AGADIR

Buses

The railway company, **ONCF**, operates a number of **express bus** services – the most comfortable public transport out of the city. Departures are:

Marrakesh: 4.50am (arrive 8.50am); 2.26pm (arrive 6.26pm).

Goulimine/Tan Tan/Laayoune: 2.37am (arrive 6.02am/9.02am/1.52pm).

The best of the other services are those run by **CTM** and **SATAS**, though you will need to use other **private line** services for some more minor destinations. Among useful services are:

SATAS: Several direct buses daily to Marrakesh; useful departure to Tiznit at 5.30am, which would allow you to make a taxi connection to Tafraoute.

Immouzer Transport: Runs a bus to Immouzer, leaving daily at 2pm, arriving three hours later; it leaves around the corner from the Talborjt terminal.

Buses to all but local destinations run from the **Talborjt terminal** on Place Lahcen Tamri; local destinations (including Inezgane and Tarhazoute) run from the **Place Salam** terminal at the bottom end of Av. Hassan II. There are more frequent departures (at least on private line services) from **Inezgane** (see below).

Grands Taxis

Agadir's **grands taxis** do routine shuttles to Inezgane (3dh a place), from where you can make connections to Taroudannt, Taliouine, Tiznit, etc.

Flights

RAM have domestic **flights** to most destinations in Morocco, including Laayoune, though most others are routed through Casablanca. There are direct flights to Las Palmas in the Canaries. See "Arriving" for details of getting to the airport.

The ferry service to Las Palmas (Canary Islands) is no longer in operation.

Inezgane

Thirteen kilometres south and inland of Agadir, **INEZGANE** is a good place to stay on the night after arriving at (or before leaving) Agadir airport. The town is much more of a transport hub than Agadir, with buses and *grands taxis* going to most southern destinations, including regular departures to Taroudannt, Essaouira and Marrakesh. From Agadir you can reach Inezgane on the #5 or #6 bus (very frequent) or by *grand taxi* (3dh a place).

Perhaps more importantly, the town sees very few tourists and so has a completely unaffected feel to it. There should usually be room at the three or four **hotels** along the main street, right near the bus terminal, and some of the **restaurants** here are excellent, too. The best of all, worth a trip out from Agadir for some superb French cooking, is the *Hôtel Restaurant Les Pergolas*; it has pleasant rooms, too (☎307.05; 2*A).

Inezgane to Taroudannt

Inezgane to Taroudannt is a routine **grand taxi** route. There is a change of taxis midway at **OULAD TEIMA**, or "44" as it's known, which your first driver will arrange; costs are 8dh and 6dh for the two respective stages.

North of Agadir: Tarhazoute and Immouzer

Along the coast north of Agadir, tourist development rapidly begins to fade and the beach at **Tarhazoute** belongs to an entirely different world – one of Morocco's last vestiges of its hippy past from the 1960s and 1970s. Rather less of a throwback – and by far the best excursion in the Agadir region – is the aptly-named **"Paradise Valley"**, a beautiful palm-lined gorge, which runs inland near Tarhazoute and offers an approach into the mountains to the village of **Immouzer des Ida Outanane**, replete with waterfalls and a very wonderful small hotel.

Transport is pretty straightforward. From Agadir, city buses #12 and #14 run more or less on the hour up the coast to Tarhazoute. For Immouzer, there's a daily bus leaving Agadir at 2pm (from the street behind *Hôtel Sindibad* on Place Lahcen Tamri) which passes through the initial part of Paradise Valley; it returns each morning at 8am. Minibus taxis also make the trip to Immouzer for the Thursday market (book at any Agadir travel agent).

Tarhazoute

A cluster of compact, colour-washed houses, **TARHAZOUTE** (or TAGHAGANT, as it appears on some maps) is 18km north of Agadir. On either side of it – indeed, from way north of Cap Rhir down to Agadir – there's a great swathe of beach, interrupted here and there by headlands and for the most part deserted.

Whether you are able to enjoy all this, however, depends a lot on your tastes. Tarhazoute, like Essaouira/Diabat to the north, was Morocco's hippy resort *par excellence*, and things haven't changed all that much. The cafés here belt out rock music and local hustlers are a bit shocked if you're not interested in partaking of a little herbal indulgence to accompany the experience.

Accommodation and food

Until a couple of years ago, the village had no electricity, and it's still without running water – which, of course, is all part of the Tarhazoute "experience". **Accommodation** is mainly in private rooms, all pretty basic, and you're given buckets to fetch water from the spring beside the mosque. The rooms used to be very cheap but prices have gone up recently due to the increasing number of young and mostly affluent Moroccans who spend the summer here; expect to bargain for rates of 150–250dh a week. Note: there have been recent reports of the police forbidding rent of private rooms – though for how long (and how strictly) this will be enforced is uncertain.

The alternative to hiring a room is to camp out. There is an official **campsite** on the beach just south of the village, with a café and cold showers; it is packed in winter with elderly northern Europeans in camper vans. In summer, Moroccan families settle into an unofficial campsite, adjacent.

For **meals**, everyone seems to head toward the street filled with cafés at the edge of the village or to the excellent *Taoui-Fik* restaurant down by the campsite on the beach.

ARGAN TREES

One of the stranger sights of the Souss valley, around Agadir, are the spiny, knotted **argan trees** – often to be seen with goats clambering up their trunks. The trees, similar to the olive, are indigenous to the region. Their nuts are ready for harvest from late May onwards, depending on the height above sea level, and are often recovered from the goat dung. The oil from the nuts is sweet and rich, and is used in many Moroccan dishes and salads, or for dunking bread. It is quite a delicacy, and not easily extracted. One olive tree provides around five litres of olive oil, but it takes the nuts from thirty argan trees to make one litre of argan oil.

Anchor Point

Unofficial camping also takes place to the north of Tarhazoute at **"Anchor Point"**, towards Cap Rhir. This has become a popular destination for surfers and windsurfers – most of whom sleep out by the beach in camper vans.

Tamraht: "Banana Village"

The road from Agadir to Tarhazoute passes through the village of **TAMRAHT** (12km from Agadir), locally dubbed "**Banana Village**" after its thriving banana grove. All along the roadside stalls sell bunches of the fruit – at initially outrageous prices! In addition to bananas, the village has a couple of good café-restaurants and a **hammam** (women until 6pm; men afterwards), useful if you're staying in Tarhazoute.

In the centre of Banana Village, the road to Immouzer des Ida Outanane heads off into the hills. If you're without transport, it's usually fairly simple to hitch lifts, at least to the start of **"Paradise Valley"**.

"Paradise Valley"

You reach "Paradise Valley" after driving about 10km from Tarhant, as the road suddenly turns a bend into a deep, palm-lined gorge, with a river snaking along the base (although by June it's down to a trickle). Like Tarhazoute, the valley established a reputation in the 1960s and 1970s as a place to hang out, and there are still sporadic groups of hippy visitors in winter, as well as more "regular" travellers.

If you decide to **camp**, be aware of the possibility of flash floods (especially in spring) and pitch your tent well away from the riverbed. The best stretch of the valley starts just after the turnoff for Immouzer: get off the bus here (or park your car) and walk. It's possible to hire a mule to explore the valley's numerous Berber villages.

Immouzer des Ida Outanane

IMMOUZER DES IDA OUTANANE, 61km from Agadir, is a small village in a westerly outcrop of the Atlas mountains – a minor regional and market centre (of the Ida Outanane, as its full name suggests). It is a beautiful day excursion from Agadir – better still if you stay overnight, either camping out, or at the highly recommended *Hôtel des Cascades*.

If you're lucky, you will get a chance to see the **waterfalls** for which the village is renowned. These roll down from the hills 4km below the village: follow the road down through the main square and off to the left. The falls used to be spectacular in spring – when the waters nearly reach flood levels and almond blossoms are everywhere – but tight control of irrigation has reduced the cascade on most occasions to a trickle. The villagers now "turn on" the falls for special events only – and for their own, not tourists' benefit. They do, however, keep a natural **plunge pool** full. And there's a second waterfall, nearby, which is still allowed to flow its natural course: ask locals to direct you to "Le Deuxieme Cascade".

However, what is really appealing here is the overall feel of things. There's a small **village** just across the stream from the falls, and a **café** (*Café de Miel*) with basic food, near which you can camp out in the olive groves. The whole area is perfect for walkers. You can follow any of the paths with enjoyment – a good one, near the village, cuts up across the cliffs to the *Hôtel des Cascades* – or even trek off to the Marrakesh road (see below). In the village, there's a **souk** every Thursday. The local speciality is honey, and the bees are said to feed from wild marijuana and other herbs in the mountains.

The **Hôtel des Cascades** (☎16; book ahead if possible), on the edge of Immouzer (signposted from its main square) is a superb place to stay. Designated 3*B, it charges around 190dh for a double, but is open to bargaining on its "pension" rates. It is surrounded by gardens of vines, apple and olive trees, and hollyhocks, with a huge and placid panorama of the mountains rolling down to the coast. The food, too, is memorable and there's a swimming pool and tennis court, currently under repair.

A hike east from Immouzer

An old *piste* road breaks off from the Immouzer–Agadir road, 5km south of Immouzer, and leads to the Agadir–Marrakesh road (S511). The *Hôtel des Cascades* will run walkers to the end of the initial valley (or you could walk there the night before and sleep out on the pass beyond; carry water), from which the road winds up to cross a high limestone plateau. It then drops to circuit a huge hollow in the hills and descends to a (seasonal) river before climbing up to a pass through to the S511. It makes a varied and interesting full day's hike and you can catch a bus or taxi back from the S511 to Agadir.

South of Agadir: Massa and Sidi Rbat

South of Agadir, the **Massa lagoon** is possibly Morocco's most important **bird sites** (see "Wildlife" in *Contexts*). It attracts a mixture of resident birds and migrants, desert visitors and so on, and teems with flamingoes, avocets and ducks. The immediate area of the lagoon is a protected zone, closed to visitors, but you can get in some good birdwatching if you base yourself at nearby **Sidi Rbat**, itself an attractive place to stay, by a long, wild beach. The best **times to visit** are March to April or October to November.

Access

It is possible, though time-consuming, to get to Sidi Rbat by a combination of buses and walking. From Agadir, take the #5 or #3 bus to Inezgane (from the terminal at the corner of Bd. Hassan II and Av. Al Mougnouama), then a grand taxi to MASSA (10dh per person); from here, ask directions for the river (*oued*) and start walking. It's 5km to the campsite but you might just get a lift along the way.

On the retun journey, make all attempts to get a lift from Sidi Rbat, as few of the taxis stop in Massa on their way north to Agadir.

Sidi Rbat

A couple of kilometres north of the lagoon, along the coast road, **SIDI RBAT** comprises little more than a marabout's tomb (at the end of the track) and the **Complexe et Balnéaire Sidi R'bat**; there is no village.

The *Complexe* (☎ 94) stands out on its own beside the sea, reached along a track that skirts the lagoon. Around a shaded courtyard are arranged a tea-room and restaurant (dinner only) and some very pleasant and moderately priced cabins; you can also camp, for a small charge. **Note**: the future of this complex is uncertain, in the light of official plans for a zoo-like "nature park". Phone ahead if you are depending on a room.

The **beach** at Sidi Rbat can often be misty and overcast – even when Agadir is basking in the sun – but on a clear day, it's as good as anywhere else and the walks, at any rate, are enjoyable.

Tifnite

The stretch of coast immediately south of Agadir, and north of Massa, is virtually undeveloped, once you clear the sprawl at the edge of the city. It is accessible at a couple of points from the P30, but there is little to go out of the way for. **TIFNITE**, the name that appears most prominently on most maps, is a grim little collection of fishing huts, strange to come upon so close to "international" Agadir. It attracts a few camper-van travellers in summer.

Taroudannt

With its majestic, red-ochre circuit of walls, **TAROUDANNT** is one of the most elegant towns in Morocco and an excellent "first base" if you arrive in the country at Agadir. The walls, the *souks* and the stark, often heat-hazed backdrop of the High Atlas to the north, are the town's chief attractions – though none of them are powerful enough to bring in the Agadir tour groups in any great number. It is consequently a very friendly, laid-back sort of place and an easy point to get to grips with Moroccan city life. For hikers, the town also forms a useful base for heading into the Western High Atlas or on to the Djebel Sirwa to the east. And, for anyone into great road journeys, the town has a tempting location at the beginning of two superb road routes – north over the Tizi n'Test to Marrakesh (see p.304) and south to the oasis of Tata and Foum el Hassane (see p.378).

Taroudannt's position at the head of the fertile Souss valley has always given it a commercial and political importance – it was often the first major conquest of new imperial dynasties. It never became a "great city", however. Even the Saadians, who made Taroudannt their capital in the sixteenth century (and built most of its walls), moved on to Marrakesh. The town's present status, with a major market but a population of only around 30,000, is probably much as it always has been.

Orientation and hotels

On arrival, the town can seem highly confusing, with ramparts heading off for miles in every direction and large areas of open space. In fact, once you get your bearings, it's all remarkably clear. Within the walled "inner city" there are just two main squares – **Place Tamoklate** and **Place Assarag** – and the town's main street runs between them.

If you arrive by **bus**, *CTM* and *SATAS* services will deposit you at the Place Assarag, other lines at Place Tamoklate, from which *grands taxis* also operate. The **grands taxis** have regular runs to and from Inezgane, with a change of cars midway at Ouled Teima (see p.367), and can be negotiated for Taliouine or Marrakesh.

Getting around town, there are **petits taxis** (usually to be found in Place Tamoklate) and, with similar tariffs, a few **calèches** – horse-drawn cabs. You can also hire a bike from either the *Hôtel Salam* or one of the shops on the main street.

Hotels

Most of the cheaper **hotels** are grouped around Place Assarag, which, with its low arcaded front and its many cafés, is very much the centre of activity in Taroudannt. A couple of others are to be found in Place Assarag, while dotted around town are a few rather fancier places – including the old palace buildings of the *Salam*, a highly recommended splurge.

The options, in ascending order of price, include:

Hôtel Alouarda, Place Tamoklate. The cheapest and most basic of the hotels. *Unclassified.*

Hôtel de la Place, Place Tamoklate. A better choice if you can get one of the three rooms up on the roof terrace. *Unclassified.*

Hôtel Restaurant El Warda, Place Tamoklate. Front rooms have balconies over the square. Prices highly negotiable. *Unclassified.*

Hôtel Roudani, Place Tamoklate. A bit pricier but you get hot showers – and a fine rooftop terrace for breakfast. Recommended. *Unclassified.*

Hôtel Taroudannt, Place Assarag (☎24.16). A Taroudannt institution, this was run by a grand old French patronne up until her death in December 1988. It retains her influence (and amazing poster collection) and is well worth the money for its patio garden, cool air and bar. The meals (and pricey breakfasts) aren't recommended. *1*A.*

Hôtel Saadiens, Bordj El Mansour (☎25.89). A good modern hotel in the Medina, with a restaurant and small pool. *2*A.*

Hôtel Palais Salam (☎23.12). Located just inside the ramparts, in the kasbah quarter, this is a beautiful place, with its rooms either in the towers or garden pavilions. The *Salam* also has a small swimming pool (which, if you ask, may be open to non-residents in the summer). It gets packed out with tour groups at lunchtime but is otherwise a wonderful, quiet refuge. Cocktail bar, too. *4*A.*

There is a **hammam** next to the *Hôtel Taroudannt*, heading towards Bab Targhount; it is signposted only in Arabic – so you may need to ask. Men are admitted 9am to noon, women after noon.

Around the town

Taroudannt's twin attractions are its **ramparts** – best toured by bike – and its **souks**. The latter are not large by Moroccan city standards, but are varied and authentic and much of the work you find here is of outstanding quality.

On Thursdays and Sundays the town hosts a **regional souk**, which brings in Chleuh Berbers from the villages to sell farm produce and a few odd pieces of craftwork.

The central *souks*

The best approach to the *souks* is to follow the road in from beside the *Banque Marocaine* in Place Assarag (you'll probably come out again by the Place Tamoklate – it's that small an area). Look out especially, in this quarter, for the "antique" **jewellery** and striking limestone **sculptures**. The latter are similar to the ones found in the north at Chaouen and are an obvious oddity – often figurative in design and more African than Islamic. The jewellery comes mainly from the south (the town played its part in trans-Saharan trade) or was made by the many Jewish craftsmen who flourished here up to the 1960s. In April, the town is still host to a **handicrafts and folklore fair.**

The tanneries

The leather **tanneries**, as ever, are located some distance from the main *souks* – placed outside the town walls on account of their smell (leather is cured in cattle urine or pigeon droppings) and for the proximity to a ready supply of water. In comparison to Marrakesh, or particularly Fes, the ones here are small, but, sadly, they display a rare variety of skins for sale – not just those of the ubiquitous sheep and cows, but silver foxes, racoons and mountain cats as well. Many of these furs are illegal imports into Europe and we urge no participation in the process. If you want to visit the tanneries all the same, follow the continuation of the main street past the *Hôtel Taroudannt* to the ramparts; turn left there and, after 100m, take the first right – they're to your right, and give off such a stench that they'd be impossible to miss.

The walls – and out to the Gazelle d'Or

The town's various **walls and bastions** can hardly be ignored, and, outside the height of summer, they make an enjoyable circuit to explore. On your way around, take a good look at the old **kasbah quarter** around the *Hôtel Palais Salam*. Now a kind of ramshackle village within the town, this was once a winter palace complex for the Saadians and contains the ruins of a fortress built by Moulay Ismail.

Beyond the ramparts, signs direct the very well-heeled to the **Hôtel Gazelle d'Or** (☎2309), a former hunting lodge built by a French baron, and now the country's most exclusive hotel – patronised mainly by rich Brits. A mint tea on its terrace is just about affordable.

Eating and drinking

Basic but very inexpensive **café-restaurants** can be found along the street between the two main squares: you could pick from any one of these hole-in-the-wall stalls, most of which have just a couple of tables outside. Among places big enough to have a name, *Café-Restaurant Dallas*, opposite the *Hôtel Taroudannt*, is a friendly place and fine value, as is the *Tout va Bien*, above the pharmacy on Place Tamoklate; the best patisserie in town, incidentally, is in the far corner of this square.

For **more elaborate fare**, the *Hôtel Roudani* is pleasant and *Hôtel Saadiens* has a good Moroccan menu, served on a balcony. Alternatively, if you're prepared to pay fairly luxury prices, book in the morning for dinner at the Moroccan restaurant at the *Hôtel Palais Salam* (avoid lunches, which cater for tour groups). The *Salam* also has a **bar** and serves cocktails on the terrace; other bars are to be found at the hotels *Taroudannt* and *Saadiens*.

If you are stocking up with **supplies** for hiking, there's a grocer's shop, on the south side of the main street running between the two main squares, that sells just about everything.

BUSES FROM TAROUDANNT

Going on from Taroudannt by bus needs a little advance planning as regards routes and terminals. The most reliable services are those operated by *SATAS* and *CTM*, all of which leave from Place Assarag. *CTM* has an office in Place Assarag, *SATAS* has an unmarked one in Place Tamoklate.

SATAS departures include:

Tata Every Wednesday, Saturday and Sunday.

Casablanca Daily express via Agadir.

Tizi n'Test to Marrakesh This normally leaves from Place Assarag at 5am; however, it doesn't always run and it's essential to check times and buy tickets the night before. See p.304 or a description of the route. (Note: the other *SATAS* departures to Marrakesh are via Agadir.)

Buses to **Ouarzazate**, via **Taliouine** (see below), are run by other private lines and leave from Place Tamoklate.

Hiking around Taroudannt

The **Western High Atlas** – routes across which are covered on p.315–319 – are easily accessible from Taroudannt, the peaks of Tinergwet (3551m) and Awlim (3481m) on the **Tichka Plateau** looking temptingly close as you look out to the mountains from a roof terrace at dawn or dusk. The best time of year for a visit is from February to April.

If you are interested in **organising a hike**, contact *Tigouga Adventures* (☎085/30.98). They have an office at Immeuble Khiati, a new block by the Bab Targhount (ten minutes' walk from Place Assarag, following the road past the *Hôtel Taroudannt*) and can also be contacted through the *Hôtel Roudani*. The company is run by Tali Abdel Aziz and his assistant, Ali, and they take exclusively English-speaking groups to the Tichka Plateau and the beautiful valleys leading up to its heights.

Aziz provides real experience of Berber life on his treks, living and eating in local houses or camping on the plateau. Independent trekkers, however, can use his services to get established before going on to trek, climb or ski-tour. The company also arrange treks in the Djebel Sirwa (see section following).

Tigouga Adventures' postal address, if you want to arrange tours in advance, is BP132, Taroudannt. Alternatively, you can arrange to go on one of their treks through the British companies, *Waymark* and *Sherpa* (see *Basics*).

Taliouine and the Djebel Sirwa

Passing through a long stretch of scrubby *hammada*, the **P32 to Taliouine** lacks the drama of Tizi n'Test – the route most people take from Taroudannt. However, it is an efficient approach to the southern oasis, and the scenery livens up on the Taliouine–Ouarzazate section, changing gradually to semi-desert and offering views of the weirdly shaped mountains of the Anti-Atlas.

For hikers, once again, there are additional attractions. The **Djebel Sirwa** (or Siroua), north of Taliouine, is one of the finest mountain sections of the Anti-Atlas. It is scarcely less impressive than the more established High Atlas trekking areas, and a great deal less frequented.

Taliouine and the road to Ouarzazate

TALIOUINE lies at a pass, its land gathered into a bowl, with a scattering of buildings on or above the roadside. More village than town, it is dominated by a magnificent kasbah built by the Glaoui (see p.311).

Now largely in ruins, the **kasbah** is used mainly to house farm animals, but the best preserved section is still inhabited by a few families (as the TV antenna indicates) and you can look around the outside of it. The kasbah's decoration is very distinct from those further south: the walls are intricately patterned, the windows moulded with palm fronds (some still showing their original paint), and the towers (climb very much at your own risk) are built around squat, downward-tapering pillars.

With your own vehicle, you can set out from Taroudannt, visit the kasbah, and move on easily enough to Ouarzazate the same day. Relying on public transport, you should reckon on staying, which, in any case, is an attractive proposition. Few tourists do, despite the presence of two **hotels**: the expensive and luxurious *Grand Hôtel du Sud – Ibn Toumert* (☎30; 4*B), right next to the kasbah, and, on the main road below, the small *Auberge Souktana*.

The *Souktana* is moderately priced and very atmospheric, run by Jadid Ahmed and his French wife Michelle, with a swimming pool, great meals, and candles in the absence of electricity. In summer you can sleep out on their roof terrace or camp in the garden. At other times it's too cold, and since the hotel has just four rooms you should try to turn up early in the day. Travelling by bus, ask to be dropped at either the *Souktana* or the kasbah. If you arrive too late for a room at the *Souktana*, a café (the last building on the right as you enter from the west) rents out basic rooms. There is a **hammam** in the village; the *Souktana* will give you directions.

There is a Monday **souk** in Taliouine, held across the valley behind the kasbah and *Hôtel Ibn Toumert*.

Transport – and east to Ouarzazate

Buses and **grands taxis** are erratically timed, and many arrive and leave Taliouine full for Taroudannt or Ouarzazate. It pays, however, to go to the main bus stop – a bus can pass the *Souktana* full and then leave half empty from the stop. *Grands taxis* from Taliouine only go as far west as Oulad Behril (80km; change for Taroudannt) and as far east as Tazenakht (84km; change for Ouarzazate). For both buses and taxis, turn up early in the day to avoid standing about for hours in the heat. *Souk* days (Monday in Taliouine; Friday at Tazenakht; Thursday and Sunday at Taroudannt) are obviously better.

TAZENAKHT, at the junction of the Ouarzazate and Foum Zguid roads, has regular buses and *grands taxis* to Ouarzazate, plus buses to Foum Zguid (92km; see p.335) and also to Arhbar, from where you might be able to get a lift across to Agdz in the Drâa Valley (see p.330). **Rooms** and meals in the village are available at the unclassified *Hôtel Zenaga* (☎32), and, if you have time on your hands, there is a visitable carpet co-operative, which produces the bold geometric designs of the Ouzguita tribe.

The road beyond Tazenakht **to Ouarzazate** is unexciting, skirting well to the east of the Djebel Sirwa.

Into the Djebel Sirwa (Siroua)

The **Djebel Sirwa** (or Siroua, as it's often written) is an isolated volcanic peak, rising from a high area (3000m–plus, so take it easy!) to the south of the High Atlas. It offers as good trekking as you can find anywhere – rewarded by magnificent views, great hiking, a cliff village and dramatic gorges. It is highly recommended from winter into spring.

A week-long circuit, taking in Sirwa, is outlined on the map opposite, the numbers being the overnight halts. Mules to carry gear, as well as tent hire, can be arranged by Jadid Ahmed at the *Auberge Souktana* or by Aziz at *Tigouga Adventures* in Taroudannt. Mules would be a worthwhile investment to ensure enjoyment – and accurate navigation. Having Ahmed along, however, is the best guarantee of success; he is a great character, speaks fluent French and English and makes tasty *tajines*.

If you are going it alone, the relevant survey maps (1:100,000 *Taliwine* and 1:50,000 *Sirwa*) are hard to come by – try *Atlas Maps* (see p.15). Ahmed dispenses advice whether or not you hire his services.

The circuit

The initial day is a gentle valley ascent along a *piste* to **AKHEAMANE** where there are rooms and a kasbah. The *piste* actually reaches west of here as far as Atougha but, *souk* days apart, transport can be nil and the walk is a pleasant enough introduction.

Beyound Akhfamane the *piste* climbs over a pass to another valley at **TAMGOUT** and up it to **ATOUGHAL,** before contouring around into the upper valley, where you can stay at *azibs* (goat shelters) or bivouac.

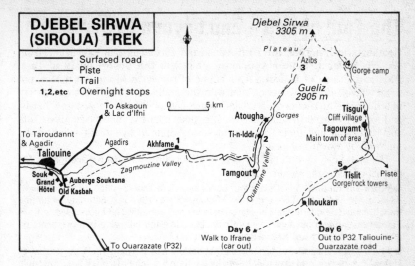

Djebel Sirwa (3304m) can be climbed from Atougha in 5 to 6 hours: a pull up from the southern cirque onto a plateau, crowned with rock towers; the nervous may want to be roped for one section of the final scramble. The subpeak of **Guiliz** is worth ascending, too, and a bivouac in the gorge below is recommended.

Beyond Guilez, keep to the lower paths to reach **TISGUI** and don't fail to visit the unique **cliff village** just outside: its houses, ranked like swallows' nests on a 1000ft precipice, are now used as grain stores. Continuing the circuit, past fields of saffron, you reach **TAGOUYEM**, the biggest village of the Sirwa area and connected by *piste* to the Taliouine road. Trails, however, leave it to pass through a couple of villages before reaching the river, which is followed to the extraordinary conglomerate features of the **Tislit gorges**. This natural sculpture park is amazing; you can camp or get rooms at the village.

On the last day, you can follow the valley to **IHOUKARN** and then to **IFRANE**, where it's possible to get a vehicle out; alternatively, a three-hour trek to the southeast leads to the Taliouine–Ouarzazate road, near its highest point, from where transport back to Taliouine is easier. Ahmed can arrange transport at either point to meet unaccompanied parties.

An approach to Djebel Toubkal

Intrepid hikers might consider an alternative approach from Taliouine to the Djebel Toubkal area (see p.291).

From **AOULOUZ** (Wednesday and Sunday *souks* and a café which rents rooms), between Taliouine and Taroudannt, there are fairly frequent shared taxis to **ASSARAG** (where you'll find rooms). A few hours' walk north from here takes you to **AMSOUZART**, where you can stay at Omar's (see p.301), and from there you can reach **Lac d'Ifni**. Both Ahmed at the *Souktana* in Taliouine and Aziz of *Tigouga Adventures* in Taroudannt have experience of organising parties to Lac d'Ifni and beyond.

The Tata circuit – and beyond

Heading **south across the Anti-Atlas** from Taroudannt, or east from Tiznit, you can travel by bus (or your own vehicle) to **the desert oasis of Tata, Aka**, and **Foum el Hassan**. This is one of the great Moroccan routes, not much travelled by foreigners, and with the feel, still, of a desert world very much apart. The scenery is wild and impressive, with occasional camel herds, and lonely, weatherbeaten villages. It is poor country, though; in 1988, Tata and its region had their first decent spring rains in five years – only to be followed by swarms of locusts.

The route can be covered **by bus** in either direction, from Taroudannt (as described) or from Agadir/Tiznit.

● **From Taroudannt** *SATAS* run four buses a week to Tata (8–10hr). Check days and times at the *SATAS* office: currently Monday, Wednesday and Saturday, returning from Tata to Taroudannt on Tuesday, Thursday and Sunday. The buses used to leave Taroudannt at 4am but now seem to run closer to 8am, following improvements on what used to be very bad *piste* between Igherm and Tata.

● **From Tiznit** Buses leave for Tata daily at 4.30am and at 11am. The 11am bus starts at Agadir, however, and may well be full by the time it reaches Tiznit. If it is, you could probably catch it at BOU IZAKARN (where it lets off some passengers), by taking a *grand taxi* there from Tiznit. On weekdays, the buses run through Ifrane de l'Anti-Atlas (see overleaf) to collect the mail.

Travelling by **car** is feasible – though, as with all these routes, take along essential spare parts (and extra petrol).

The circuit: Taroudannt to Tiznit

Leaving the P32 Taroudannt–Taliouine road at the 8km mark, the Tata road skirts through the edge of **FREIJA** (5km), a small oasis and village with a crumbling kasbah (now used as a farm building); the kasbah lies across the Souss, which in summer you can generally wade across. Another 12km on, you pass a turning to **TIOUTE**, a larger oasis with a local caid's kasbah that was once part of the Glaoui domain (see p.311).

Igherm

The road then begins to wind and climb into the stark Anti-Atlas mountains. At **IGHERM** (93km from Taroudannt) there's a **Wednesday souk**, where the bus will stop for a long break. The region is said to be known for its silver daggers and inlaid rifle butts, though more than likely you'll just find an assortment of hand-made copper pots and water urns. Igherm itself, now an administrative centre and with some new buildings to prove it, was a copper town for centuries, carrying on its long-distance trade with the Saharan caravans. After the *souk* is over, it settles back to being a very hot and sluggish town – not a place to get caught with no bus or lorry onwards. If you do find yourself stranded, there are **rooms** of a kind at the *Café de la Jeunesse* on the main street.

For the dedicated driver, *pistes* lead from here to **Tafraoute** and **Taliouine**, but both are in terrible condition.

Tleta n'Tagmoute

TLETA N'TAGMOUTE, 30km south of Igherm, is the most interesting village on the way to Tata. It springs out of the barren surroundings with a flash of life and disappears almost as suddenly a couple of bends down the road. There's a high, fortress-like **agadir**, with clusters of palm trees below it. The village itself seems to climb right up the hillside.

Beyond Tagmoute the road continues paved for about 6km, then it becomes dirt *piste* (not too difficult for passenger cars). This is a long, slow stretch, but is made enjoyable by the amazing contours of the mountains, which twirl and twist from pink to grey-green, the sharply defined bands of rock varying from horizontal to vertical. You eventually come out onto the Tata–Bou Izakarn road and must turn left for Tata (5km). The last 20km of this road is newly paved.

Tata Oasis

TATA is a large, rambling oasis: a place where – as in other southern oasis – you soon notice the desert influence of black turbans and the darker complexion of the people. The women, who dress in black throughout the Anti-Atlas, here wear colourful sari-like coverings.

Around the midway point of the long main street, you'll find two **hotels**, the *Sahara* and *Salam*. The latter, though a little dirty, is cheap and is located above a café that has a small kitchen – if you buy your own food, they will happily cook it for you for a few dirhams. There is also a 2*B hotel, the *Hôtel Renaissance* (96 Av. des FAR; ☎42), situated at the edge of town, on your left as you come in; they serve meals in the café-restaurant underneath. There's another (unnamed and unrecommended) hotel by the bus station. For anything else to eat, there's not much except for one small fried-fish stall. There is, however, a **bank** and a **post office**.

The **Tata oasis** is enticing – though frustrating in that its flatness means you can never get a true sense of its extent. In some parts of the oasis people live in separate houses, enclosed by private plots, in others there are clusters of dwellings with open, unwalled groves, criss-crossed by paths and irrigation ditches. Dates from the oasis here are sold at the **Thursday and Sunday souks** in Tata.

Buses from Tata run daily to Bou Izakarn and on to Tiznit and Agadir.

Akka, some rock carvings and Foum el Hassan

Continuing along the circuit towards Tiznit, you pass through another large oasis, **AKKA**, which has a couple of cafés (the *Tamdoult* has a few basic **rooms**) and a police checkpoint. It's said to have been one of the northern depots of the ancient caravan routes, but you wouldn't guess that by looking at it today. Some guidebooks speak of nearby prehistoric rock carvings (in the hills opposite Oum el Aoloine village); you would need a car and a lot of luck to find them.

However, there are more accessible **rock carvings** near Foum el Hassan. If you have a car, at 67km from Akka (23km before Foum), look out for a break in the wall of rocks running parallel to the road on your left (the south side). Walk through the break, turn left, and you'll find several carvings on the far side of this hill of rocks. Most are of antelopes or sheep-like animals, 15–30cm high, and dating roughly from 2000–500 BC.

There are more carvings in **FOUM EL HASSAN** itself. The bus will pull up near a large roundabout set in a wide open square. In the middle of the circle is a black concrete structure meant to resemble a nomad's tent, and in front of it are a couple of carved rocks; the irony is that there used to be many more of them, but now they're encased forever in tons of black concrete.

Foum is basically a military post on the edge of an oasis. Some fighting with Polisario took place here several years ago, but everything's quiet now; there is, however, passport control. If you need a **room**, the only possibility is at the café on the right-hand side of the square. Besides a couple of shops, there's very little else.

To see more **rock carvings**, in situ, head for the huge V in the mountains that rise up behind the town. A dirt road follows the valley and, after 4–5km, you should find some carvings. The best require a little climbing to get to, but they are reputedly the finest in Morocco. Pictures of elephants and rhinoceros have been discovered, dating back thousands of years to the time when the Sahara was full of lakes and swamps. You can hire a guide if you wish. **Camping** is possible here in the valley and preferable to staying in the town.

Amtoudi/Id Aïssa

West from Foum el Hassan, in addition to the daily Tiznit bus, you may find some extra traffic for hitching on Wednesday, Foum's **souk** day.

If you have transport, it's worth taking **an excursion to Amtoudi** (or Id Aïssa, as it appears on most maps), reached by turning right 55km from Foum el Hassan and about 18km before TARHJIJT. Without a car, Amtoudi is hard to reach: in Tarhjijt, a small oasis village, you might find a *grand taxi* willing to take you; alternatively, try hitching on a Monday, when there is a market at SOUK TNINE D'ADAÏ, on the way to Amtoudi. If you do hitch, be sure to have enough provisions, since Amtoudi has just one very small shop and a lunch-only restaurant for visiting tour groups from Agadir.

The sight that brings tour groups to **AMTOUDI** is its **agadir**, one of the most spectacular and best preserved in North Africa. *Agadirs* are collective, fortified storehouses, where grain, dates, gunpowder and other valuables were kept safe from marauding tribes. This one is built impressively on a pinnacle of rock. You can climb a long mule track and walk around in the site, providing the *gardien* is there. Unfortunately, you're unlikely to be alone, despite the remoteness of the site, as the *agadir* is firmly on an excursion route from Agadir (the city); you can avoid the midmorning rush of tourists easily enough, though. A walk up the palm-filled gorge (where yet another imposing but decaying *agadir* is perched on top of the cliff) will bring you, after about 3km, to a spring and waterfall. It is possible to **camp** near the riverbed.

Back on the main road, the oasis and village of **TARHJIJT** signals a return to regular communications: there are fairly routine *grands taxis* towards Tiznit, and a couple of roadside cafés. In **TIMOULAY**, 26km further, you should be able to pick up a *grand taxi* coming from Bou Izakarn and going to Ifrane de l'Anti-Atlas.

Ifrane de l'Anti-Atlas

One of the most beautiful oasis in the south, **IFRANE DE L'ANTI-ATLAS** is a small Berber town, with three surrounding *douar* (each with its own kasbah and endless walls) together with an administrative centre containing a pink, fort-like barracks.

The place is really out of the way and sees very few tourists – expect to be the object of attention and followed everywhere by kids. However, if you can handle the isolation, Ifrane is a great place to stay, offering beautiful walks among the *douar*, springs, and ingenious water channels. There is a small, clean **hotel**, the *Anti-Atlas*, and a few cafés, one of which, *Café de la Paix*, has very nice rooms on the roof, with a balcony view looking out across the valley and distant oasis. This café is perhaps also the best place to eat. A **Sunday souk** serves the surrounding villages and oasis.

Around the oasis: the Mellah

The oasis is the centre of one of the oldest settled regions in Morocco. It was also among the last places in the south to convert to Islam – there were still Jewish and Christian Berber communities here in the twelfth century.

Beyond the oasis and across the dry riverbed stand the ruins of the old Jewish quarter, the **Mellah**, which was supposedly settled in the sixth century BC by Jews fleeing persecution from King Nebuchadnezzar of Babylon. This particular history has yet to be substantiated, but it is certain that the Jewish community here goes back to pre-Islamic days. It endured up until the 1950s, when, as elsewhere in the south, there was a mass exodus to Israel and, to an extent, Morocco's northern cities, leaving the Mellah aban-

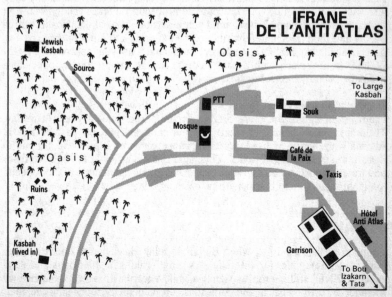

IFRANE DE L'ANTI ATLAS

Jewish Kasbah

Oasis

Source

To Large Kasbah

PTT

Souk

Mosque

Café de la Paix

Oasis

Taxis

Ruins

Kasbah (lived in)

Hôtel Anti Atlas

Garrison

To Bou Izakarn & Tata

doned. A Berber family has since moved into one of the inhabitable kasbahs, and a few of the other buildings remain partially intact; the rest is a mass of crumbling walls. Local people recall their former Jewish neighbours as "good people" who kept mainly to themselves.

Around the next bend in the stony riverbed, and up the hill on the right, lies the Jewish **cemetery**. Broken tombstones, inscribed in Hebrew, lie strewn about and it's said that relatives still come here to visit the graves and burn candles in memory of the deceased. The Muslim past of Ifrane is evident as well, with white-domed tombs of saints and marabouts dotting the surrounding countryside.

On to Bou Izakarn

From Ifrane, it's just 14km to **BOU IZAKARN**, another administrative centre and roadside town (several small **hotels**). Here, buses and *grands taxis* run routinely to Goulimine and Tiznit. Leaving from Bou Izakarn is also the best way to reach Tafraoute. (It is also possible – though unlikely to be easy – to get a ride on a lorry from Ifrane to Tafraoute.)

From Tata to Foum Zguid and Zagora

The route from **Tata to Foum Zguid** and, for the intrepid, beyond to **Zagora** is an even more remote journey than the "Tata loop", and strictly for the committed. At the time of writing, though, the route was open and could be travelled without a permit (a situation that could change at any time).

From Tata, there are occasional lorries travelling over the 150km of rough *piste* to Foum Zguid. This is a rocky ride, not really practicable with anything less than four-wheel drive. The route runs through a wide valley, following the course of a seasonal river, amid some extremely bleak landscape, which is now and then punctuated by the occasional oasis and *ksar*. There are passport controls at TISSINT (halfway) and again as you approach **FOUM ZGUID**, a tiny place with a café (rooms, but not much to eat) opposite a welcome palmery and some *ksour*.

Transport on from Foum Zguid

From Foum Zguid, there are *SATAS* **buses** three times a week (Tuesday, Thursday and Saturday at 7am) to Ouarzazate – and on to Marrakesh. Alternatively, a ride with a **lorry** along more very rough *piste* will get you to Zagora in seven or eight hours. This, again, is not suitable for light vehicles and the transport is a bit haphazard. The route also lacks most of the redeeming features of Tata to Foum, with no oasis or villages to break the tedium.

Tiznit

Founded as late as 1882, when Sultan Moulay Hassan was undertaking a *harka* – a subjugation or (literally) "burning" raid – in the Souss and Anti-Atlas, **TIZNIT** still seems to signal a shift towards a desert, frontier-town mentality. To the west in the Anti-Atlas, the Chleuh Berbers suffered their first true occupation only with the bitter French "pacification" of the 1930s, and the town itself was the base of El Hiba, who declared himself sultan at Tiznit in 1912 after learning of Moulay Hafid's surrender to the French with the Treaty of Fes. The so-called "Blue Sultan" – a name given due to his blue desert robes – El Hiba led a considerable force of Saharan Berbers to Marrakesh, which acknowledged his authority, before advancing on Fes in the spring of 1913. Here they were defeated but his resistance continued, first in Taroudannt, later further into the Anti-Atlas, until his death, near Tafraoute in 1919.

The town bears the stamp of its military history – huge *pisé* walls (over 5km in total), neat administrative streets, and a considerable garrison – but it's not such a bad staging point if (as is likely) you arrive here too late in the day to continue on to Tafraoute, Sidi Ifni or Tata. It is easily reached by bus from Agadir or *grand taxi* from Inezgane. And there is also an exhilarating beach nearby at Sidi Moussa, where the surf and the fierce Atlantic currents have warded off all but the most limited development.

Practicalities

Arriving from the south or north, **buses** or **grands taxis** will drop you in the **Mechouar** – the old parade ground, and now the main square – just inside the town walls.

It's here that you'll find most of the facilities (bank, post office, bus offices) and all of the **cheap hotels**, the best of which is the *Hôtel d'Atlas*, with a roof terrace overlooking the town. If that doesn't appeal to you, the *Hôtel Tiznit*, Rue de Tafoukt (☎24.11), is a classier – 3*A – alternative, with a swimming pool and nightclub, while out beyond the walls on Av. Hassan II, near the roundabout, is the 2*A *Hôtel de Paris* (☎28.65), with clean rooms and a good restaurant.

There are any number of **cafés** in and around the Mechouar, though things are slightly more animated (which isn't saying much) outside the main gates, on Av. Mohammed V.

The town

Tiznit is an important market centre and holds a large **Thursday souk** (out on the road to Tafraoute); otherwise, the promise of its walls turns out to be a little empty. There is, however, a certain fascination in realising just how recent it all is – a traditional walled town built only a century ago – and it's interesting to see how the builders simply enclosed a number of existing *ksour* within their new street grid.

Taking a brief loop through the town, start out at the **jewellery souk** (*Souk des Bijoutiers*), still an active crafts industry here despite the loss to Israel of the town's large number of Jewish craftsmen. The jewellers are at the end of the main *souk* area: leaving the Mechouar on the side near the main gates, turn right one block before you reach the walls.

Going in the other direction from the Mechouar – to the right at the far end of the square – Rue de l'Hôpital winds round (past the hospital, over a stream and up beside a cemetery) to the **Grand Mosque** and, next to it, the

Source Bleu de Lalla Tiznit. The mosque has an unusual minaret, punctuated by a series of waterspouts, or perches, said to be an aid to the dead in
climbing up to paradise – an architectural form more common well to the
south in Mali and Niger. The *source*, resplendent on old postcards of the
town, is dedicated to the town's patroness, Lalla, a saint and former prostitute
martyred on this spot (whereupon a spring miraculously appeared). In the
summer at least, it is now profoundly unflattering to her.

Following the street on from here, you reach the north gate, **Bab Targua**,
and the walls – take a right here and you can get up onto them, but it's a
somewhat mournful vantage point, looking out as it does over decaying olive
groves and an abandoned palmery.

Moving on from Tiznit

A few details about Tiznit's transport:

All the private line **buses** (three a day to Tafraoute – first and most direct
at 6.30am; two to Sidi Ifni; four or five down toward Goulimine) leave from
the Mechouar, as do the *SATAS* buses to Tata (at 4.30am and 7.30am)
described in the previous section. *CTM* buses generally run from a gate
called Bab Oulad Jarrar – 200m from the Mechouar, along the Agadir road
(and just off the roundabout and junction of the roads to Goulimine,
Tafraoute and Sidi Ifni).

Grands taxis toward Goulimine can be negotiated from outside the
Mechouar, or by the road just past the rotary. For Tafraoute, there are **Land
Rover taxis** (it isn't always possible to get a seat, and the last one leaves at
4pm; about 35dh a place) from a stop located between the new *Hôtel Tiznit*
and the Thursday marketplace on the Tafraoute road (again, about 50m past
the roundabout).

Sidi Moussa d'Aglou

To get out to the beach at **SIDI MOUSSA D'AGLOU**, you'll have to negotiate a *grand taxi* from just outside the Mechouar (towards Av. Mohammed
V). There is supposed to be a bus as well, but don't count on it. Hitching back
into Tiznit, however, isn't usually a problem.

The **beach**, 14km from Tiznit along a barren, scrub-lined road, is well
worth the effort – an isolated expanse of sand, with a wild, body-breaking
Atlantic surf (and with a dangerous undertow, too, so be careful). There's no
village as such at the beach itself, but walking around the headland to the
right (as you face the sea), you come to a tiny **troglodyte fishing village**, its
huts dug right into the rocks, surreal in its primitive austerity.

On a more practical level, there are a dozen or so ramshackle **cabins** to
rent at the *Motel d'Aglou*, just to the left of the road as you come down to the
beach, and, about 1500m further down (along a track away from the beach), a
campsite with a **café** and a handful of rooms. To the right of the road, still
under construction, is a new and larger campsite, though this seems a wildly
optimistic gesture. Except in the middle of summer and around Christmas
(when Moroccan families and migrant workers back from France come out
here to camp), you're likely to be the only people around.

Tafraoute

Approached by beautiful scenic roads through the Anti-Atlas – either from Tiznit (the best approach) or Agadir – **Tafraoute** is worth all the effort and time it takes to reach. The town and its circle of villages built of stone are situated on the strange, wind-eroded slopes of the **Ameln Valley**, shot through with pink and mauve-tinged bulbous fingers of granite, and enclosed by a jagged panorama of mountains – "like the badlands of South Dakota", as Paul Bowles put it, "writ on a grand scale".

The best time of all for a visit to Tafraoute is mid-February, in order to see the almond trees here in full blossom and enjoy the accompanying **Fête des Amandes**. At any time of the year, though, a couple of days spent wandering around the Ameln is a rewarding experience, both in terms of the extraordinary physical features of the land, and in the interest its unique social system holds (see box overpage).

The routes from Tiznit and Agadir

Both approaches to Tafraoute are rewarding, and you may well want to take advantage of this by coming in from Tiznit and leaving for Agadir, or vice versa. If you're doing just one, the Tiznit approach has a distinct edge, passing through a succession of gorges and a grand mountain valley.

Tiznit to Tafraoute

The road to Tafraoute from Tiznit passes a succession of oasis-like villages, almost all of them named after the *souk* that they are host to (see p.37 for explanation of the days). In winter and spring the road is sometimes crossed by streams but it is generally passable enough. The drive takes around four hours, but if you are driving, leave plenty of time to see (and navigate) the mountainous sections east of Tirhmi before dusk.

The last petrol before Tafraoute is at **TIRHMI** (44km from Tiznit), where the road begins its ascent of the **Col du Kerdous**. The *Hôtel Kerdous*, sited on the pass, has rooms and a pool. Beyond, you begin the descent into the Ameln Valley. **TIZOURHANE**, one of the larger villages, has a **café-hotel**, *La Victorie*, and other cafés along the way may rent rooms, too, if you ask.

Just before Tirhmi a road heads south into the Anti-Atlas to the **Zaouia of Sidi Ahmed ou Moussa** (11km), which for a while in the seventeenth century controlled its own local state, the Tazeroualt. The *zaouia*, these days, is most famous for its annual **moussem**, held over the second or third week of August. Sidi Ahmed is the patron of Morocco's acrobats – most of whom come from this region of Morocco – and they both attend and perform.

Agadir/Inezgane to Tafraoute

The bus service along this route has now resumed after being halted for a number of years. It runs to and from Inezgane (local connections with Agadir). The road is a bit drab between Agadir and Aït Baha, but the section from there on to Tafraoute is a very scenic mountain ride past a series of fortified villages

– **TIOULIT** is a particularly spectacular example. There is a confusing junction not far before you arrive at Tafraoute, with signs only in Arabic. Coming from Aït Baha, the road off to the left is to Irherm (a very rough *piste* once you pass the village of AÏT ABDALLAH), the right to Tafraoute.

AÏT BAHA, the largest village en route, is no great shakes: a characterless roadside halt with a small **hotel**, two cafés and very little shade. The buses generally stop here for a tea; the village hosts a **Wednesday souk**.

Tafraoute

TAFRAOUTE itself stands at the edge of a rambling palmery – quite unexpected after a rather barren approach over the last few kilometres from both Tiznit and Agadir. It is a small place, created as an administrative centre by the French; *Tafraoutis* generally prefer to stick to their villages or leave altogether.

Accommodation, food and other practicalities

The village has two modest unclassified **hotels** near the bus station, close to the main square. There's little to choose between them: many people choose to stay at the *Hôtel Redouane* (☎66; clean rooms, hot showers, very relaxed and a friendly family), and eat at the *Hôtel Tanger*. There used to be a third hotel in the town, the *Salem*, but this disappeared when its gas refrigerator exploded; it's currently being rebuilt and will probably charge 2* prices when it reopens. The only alternative to these is the mock-kasbah 4*B *Hôtel Les Amandiers* (☎8), ten minutes' walk up the hill above the centre of town.

Arriving on the Tiznit road, you will have passed signs advertising the town's **campsite**, a small and secure enclosure with good facilities; for those without transport, it can be worth a visit to arrange a lift.

The best **meals** are, predictably enough, at *Les Amandiers*. In the town proper, and more suited to limited budgets, choose between the hotels *Redouane* and *Tanger*, the *Café Atlas* and the *Restaurant l'Etoile du Sud*. The latter is a bit pretentious, with a tent done up for tourists and an embarrass-

---

AMELN VALLEY ECONOMICS

Among the Tafraouti villages, **emigration** to work in the grocery trade – all over Morocco and France – is a determining aspect of life. The men always return home to retire, however, building European-looking villas amid the rocks, and most of the younger ones manage to come back for a month's holiday each year – whether it be from Casablanca, Tangier or Paris.

But for much of the year, it is the women who run things in the valley, and the only men to be found are the old, the family-supported, or the affluent. It is a system that seems to work well enough: enormously industrious, and very community minded, the *Tafraoutis* have managed to maintain their villages in spite of adverse economic conditions, importing all their foodstuffs except for a little barley, the famed Tafraouti almonds and the bitter oil of the argan tree. Oddly enough, this way of life has exact parallels in Tunisia, with the people of Djerba; less surprisingly, both social structures developed through crisis and necessity. Between 1880 and 1882, this whole region was devastated by famine.

ing cabaret of music and belly-dancing, but the food can be worthwhile if you hit a good day. The only **bar** is at *Les Amandiers*.

Other facilities include a **hammam** (at the far end of town, in the direction of Tiznit: turn left where the bus stops); a **PTT** (8.30am–noon & 2–6.30pm); and two **banks**. The *Banque Populaire* is open only on Wednesdays for the town's **souk**, but there's an inconspicuous branch of the *BMCE* on the road behind the PTT, with standard opening hours. Phone calls can be made from the *Hôtel des Amandiers* when the PTT is closed; they charge 30 percent commission.

The Ameln Valley

You could spend days, if not weeks, wandering around the twenty-six villages of the **Ameln Valley**. Set against the backdrop of the rocks, they are all beautiful both from afar and close up – with springs, irrigation systems, brightly painted houses, and mosques. On no account, either, should you miss out on a walk to see the **painted rocks** – see box overpage.

Oumesnat and a northern circuit
OUMESNAT, 8km from Tafraoute town, is a good first objective. You can usually get a lift there, or take the occasional bus, since it's just off the road to Aït Baha and Agadir. Taxis can be hired, too.

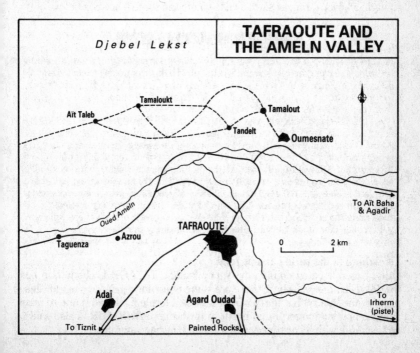

Like most Ameln settlements, the village emerges out of a startling green and purple rockscape, crouched against the rock walls of the valley, away from the arable land. It is accessible from the road only by crossing an intricate network of irrigation canals and allotments. The **houses**, perched on the rocks above, from a distance seem to have a solidity to them – sensible blocks of stone, often three storeys high, with parallel sets of windows. Close up, though, they are bizarre constructions, often built on top of older houses deserted when they became too small or decrepit. A few of the houses, their rooms jutting out over the cliffs, are held up by enormous stilts and have raised doorways entered by short (and retractable) ladders.

From Oumesnat, you can walk through or above a series of villages all the way to **AÏT TALEB**, a meandering hike taking three to four hours. In the summer, though, this might prove to be more than enough – you can usually hitch back to town. To extend the circuit, you could keep on going to **ADAÏ**, looping back to Tafraoute along the Tiznit road.

Agard Oudad

A shorter but equally rewarding walk is to head south to **AGARD OUDAD** (3km from Tafraoute), a dramatic-looking village built under a particularly bizarre outcrop of granite. Like many of the rocks in this region, this has been given a name. Most of the others are named for animals – people will point out their shapes to you – but this one is known (in good French-colonial tradition) as **Le Chapeau de Napoléon**. As if the rocks weren't weird enough, an even stranger sight awaits you to the south – see box below.

THE BLUE ROCKS

In 1984 a Belgian artist, **Jean Verame**, obtained permission from the Moroccan authorities to paint the rocks around Tafraoute. He had previously executed a similar project in Sinaï, so this was the development of a concept. Over the period since, the painted rocks have lost some of their sharpness of colour, but they remain weird and wonderful, and should on all accounts be seen.

To reach Vermae's canvas, you can ask anyone at Agard Oudad and a kid will be found to guide you to "Les Pierres Bleues". Alternatively, follow the road out to Agard Oudad until you reach the sign indicating the village. Here, turn on to a flat sandy *piste*, close to the base of the Chapeau de Napoléon (on your right). Follow this path for 4–5km, into a barren, flat land (a riverbed in winter), with rocky hills on either side. You pass a small house on your left, continue walking, and there they are – blue and red mountains, clusters of black and purple boulders, even some large technicolour rocks – all on a vast scale, and mesmerising in effect.

Verame stayed in Tafraoute at the *Hôtel Redouane* and the family there will show you a coffee-table book, detailing the project in its newly painted glory.

Elsewhere in the valley and beyond

Other possible excursions in the valley include **TAZAGHA**, about 2km past the *Hôtel Amandiers*, where there are some prehistoric paintings of gazelles – proof of the theory that the desert was once a fertile plain and home to many animals now no longer found north of the Sahara. **AHEMUR** is also said to be beautiful, with its own *source bleu* (natural springwater pool).

With a car, a beautiful day's outing would be to drive southeast towards **SOUK EL HAD ARFALLAH IRHIR** (Sunday *souk*), a route leading past a series of small oasis that produce all kinds of fruit. Just taking in a part of this route is worth your while – follow the road past Agard Oudad for about 15km, then bear left when the *piste* comes to an end.

Sidi Ifni

SIDI IFNI is not the most obvious of tourist spots – empty, prone to lingering sea mist and, all in all, extraordinarily wistful and melancholic. The town itself was relinquished by Spain only in 1969, after the Moroccan government closed off all landward access to the colonial enclave. The Spanish claim to Ifni dated from the Treaty of Tetouan (1860) – the culmination of Morocco's first military defeat by a European power in 200 years, and the start of its being carved up by the major colonial powers.

The old harbour, once a thriving duty-free zone, is now more or less abandoned, pending a redevelopment, and many of the old Spanish houses have been locked up and left to decay. However, if the mood takes you, the town can seem rather wonderful. Built in 1934, on a site above the top of a cliff, it is full of sweeping Art Deco lines and elaborate ironwork: all in all, a unique memorial to colonialism and surely the finest Art-Deco military town ever built. It is easily reached from Tiznit or Goulimine by **bus** or **grand taxi**.

Orientation and some Art -Deco sights

Entering Sidi Ifni, a road leads off right, down to the sea and a reasonable **beach**; straight ahead, you wind round to the two main streets and **Place Hassan II** – the street signs here only partially reflecting the change from its previous incarnation as the *Plaza de España*.

The *plaza* is the heart of the town and immediately sets a tone for the place. An Andalusian garden and tiled fountain, perfect for the evening *paseo*, flank its centre, while at one end stands a **Spanish consulate** – a building straight out of García Márquez, still open for business – and at the other, manically confused in its mixture of ideology and architecure, a **church** in Moorish–Art-Deco style. More fine Art Deco is to be seen in the post office, **CTT** in its Spanish form, and now severely underused; and in the monumental stairways, rambling down towards the port and beach.

Accommodation and practicalities

Following the steps below Place Hassan II, you emerge at the main classified **hotel**, the 1*A *Hôtel Aït Ba Hamram* (☎51.73). Along the way, near the bottom of the steps, is the cheaper and steadily decaying *Hôtel Suerte Loca* ("Crazy Luck"), every bit a small-town Spanish *fonda* with its *bodega*-style bar (now, alas, without alcohol) and ramshackle table-football game.

The **best places to stay**, however, are either the *Hôtel Beau Rivage* (on the hill above – follow the signs) or the *Hôtel Bellevue* (☎50.72, 1*A), just off Place Hassan II. The latter is an amazing building, with loads of 1930s neon lights on the walls and an occasionally functioning bar; it is welcoming, and good value. The *Beau Rivage* is also friendly and cheap – and about the only place you'll find a meal; it has a rather livelier **bar**, too.

On Sundays, Sidi Ifni is host to a huge **souk**, complete with storytellers and musicians. There are *Grands taxis* to Tiznit and Goulimine.

Mirhleft: the road from Tiznit

The route down the coast from **Tiznit to Sidi Ifni** passes, around the midway point, the roadside village of **MIRHLEFT**. There are four basic **hotels** here, much the best of which is the *Tafkout*, and a couple of cafés. They cater for the few groups of travellers who arrive here for a stay by the sea – most often in the winter months. The **beach**, a kilometre from the village, is a beautiful curve of sand, with crashing waves and strong currents (be careful). There are buses and *grands taxis* from Tiznit along this road.

Nearing Sidi Ifni, the road passes first through an extended Moroccan village, built across the valley from Ifni as a kind of rival garrison post. The old Spanish town begins at the base of the hill beyond. Stay on the bus!

Goulimine

GOULIMINE sounds prety exciting in the tourist brochures (and indeed in most other guidebooks): the "Gateway to the Sahara", with its nomadic "blue men" and traditional camel market.

The truth, sadly, is considerably more mundane. Though the scenery is indeed impressively bleak – liberal doses of it featured in both *Lawrence of Arabia* and *Mohammed, Messenger of God* – you're still a long way short of seeing any Saharan dunes, and the camel market itself is a rather depressing sham, maintained largely for the tour groups bused in from Agadir. Even the locals have begun to indulge in theatrical cons, bringing people out to see "genuine *hommes bleus*" in tents outside town

The one time that a visit to the town would be worthwhile in itself is if you can plan to coincide with one of Goulimine's annual **moussems** – when you really are likely to see Touareg nomads. It's difficult to get information about the exact dates of the *moussems* – they vary considerably from year to year – but, in general, there is usually one held in June at Asrir, 10km southeast of Goulimine; another, according to locals, takes place in August.

The route down from Tiznit: Bou Izakarn

The moussems apart, it is **the route down** to Goulimine that is the main attraction – it is best taken, at least in one direction, with a detour to Sidi Ifni (see above).

Travelling on the inland route, the only place of any size that you pass is the palmery and village of **BOU IZAKARN** (Friday *souk*), where the road to Ifrane and the Tata oasis (see p.378) heads off east into the Anti-Atlas. *Grands taxis* can be negotiated here for Ifrane de l'Anti-Atlas and Amtoudi (see p.380). There is also a basic **hotel**, the *Anti-Atlas* (☎41.34), on the Goulimine road, which does little to deserve its 2*B status.

Goulimine: practicalities

The phoney camel market aside, Goulimine is a fairly standard administrative town – drawn out and somewhat shapeless, though with a distinctly desert feel to it, and with a couple of small, fairly animated *souks*.

The main street, **Av. Mohammed V**, is flanked at its top end by **Place Bir Nazarene**, where there is a **bank**, a **post office** and (tucked in between this and the Grand Mosque) an excellent **hammam**. A five-minute walk down the hill takes you to the other – and livelier – square, **Place Hassan II**, the main commercial centre of the town and the best place to eat. If you arrive by **bus**, you'll be let off just below this square; coming by **grand taxi**, you'll probably get out at the Nazarene.

Accommodation is very limited and prices at most of the hotels are hiked up every Friday night as tourists come into town for the camel market. The unclassified hotels are particularly bad offenders in this respect, and for this reason – as well as the fact that the most basic hotels are too small and crowded to cope with the summer heat – you might decide it's worth paying the extra money for a room at the 2*B *Hôtel Salam* (Route de Tan Tan, near Place Nazare; ☎20.57). This is the town's finest, and maintains a small bar. On Saturdays, the hotel has performances of the Guedra dance.

Among the unclassified hotels, all on the Route de Tan Tan, or around the Place Bir Nazarene, *Hôtel l'Ere Nouvelle* and *Hôtel de la Jeunesse* are marginally the best. Alternatively, for terrace space (without any water), you could try the *Café Alag* in Place Hassan II. The **campsite** is not much of an option – stony, exposed, and a walk of about 1200m from Place Hassan II (follow the signs; it's just below the military garrison).

Several of the hotels put on shows of **Guedra dancing** on Friday and Saturday nights and Saturday lunchtimes. Much has been written about this traditional, seductive women's dance of the desert – performed, from a kneeling position (developed for the low tents) to a slow, repetitive rhythm. The shows, as you might imagine, are a bit of a travesty.

The "Camel Market"

The most enduring impression of a trip to Goulimine's **Saturday "camel market"** is of the lengths the local people have gone to in order to hide the fact that there hasn't been a real camel market here for years. What few camels you see have either been brought in just for show or to be sold off for meat. If you're curious (and having come here, why not?), the market is held about a kilometre outside the town on the road to Tan Tan; it starts around 6am and a couple of hours later the first tourist buses arrive from Agadir, which to be honest makes the whole thing a bit more interesting.

Abbainou

ABBAINOU, 15km northeast of Goulimine, is a relatively easy excursion, with *grands taxis* negotiable and affordable (from the main rank by the *souk*). It is a tiny oasis, with a *koubba* and several hot springs, channelled into two bath enclosures – divided according to sex – where you can soak the afternoon away. The women's enclosure is very welcoming.

If you want to **stay**, the *Hôtel-Camping Abaynou* is a pleasant alternative to a night in Goulimine. It has a licensed bar and restaurant.

Aït Boukha

To while away an afternoon, you might want to take a trip out from Goulimine to one of the oasis southeast of the town. The largest and most spectacular of these is at **AÏT BOUKHA**, 17km from Goulimine (the final 7km on a *piste* from Asrir, where the oasis becomes visible). To get there requires either your own transport or chartering a *grand taxi*.

An opulent-looking palmery, Boukha is a thriving agricultural community, little bothered by tourists or anything else. It has an especially lush strip along a canal, irrigated from the old riverbed and emerging from a flat expanse of sand; you might even see the odd herd of camels being grazed out here. To reach it, head for the thicket of palms about 2km behind the oasis (or pick up a guide on the way).

THE DEEP SOUTH AND WESTERN SAHARA

Few travellers venture south of Goulimine – and on the surface there is little enough to commend the trip. The towns – **Tan Tan**, **Tarfaya**, **Laayoune** – are modern administrative centres, with no great intrinsic interest. The route, however, across vast tracts of *hammada* – bleak, stony desert – is another matter. The odd line of dunes unfolds on the horizon to the east, the ocean parallels much of the road to the west, and there is no mistaking that you have reached the **Sahara** proper.

An additional point of interest, now that the war with Polisario seems to be on the wane, is the attention being lavished on the region by the Moroccan authorities. The **Western Sahara** (the old Spanish Saharan colony, reclaimed by Morocco with the 1967 Green March) begins just to the south of Tarfaya. **Laayoune**, never greatly regarded by the Spanish, has been transformed into a showcase capital for the new provinces; there are industrial plans, too, at **Tarfaya**; and, with an eye to the traditional nomadic dwellers, the Moroccan authorities have also been assisting in building up the local camel herds.

The region's economic importance was long thought to centre on the phosphate mines at **Boukra**, southeast of Laayoune. However, these have not been greatly productive in recent years and the deposits are not especially rich by the standards of the Plateau des Phosphates east of Casablanca. In the long term, the rich deep-water fishing grounds offshore are likely to prove a much higher earner. This potential is gradually being realised with the construction of a new port at Laayoune, together with industrial plant for fish storage and processing.

Note that throughout the former Spanish Saharan region, **Spanish** remains the dominant **second language**. Younger people and administrators, however, will generally speak good French.

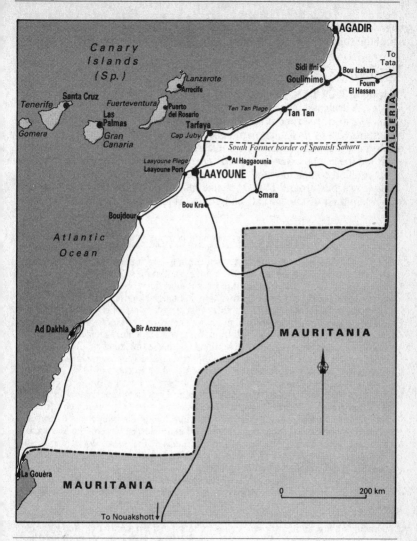

Goulimine to Tan Tan

The approach from **Goulimine to Tan Tan** runs along 125km of straight desert road, across a bleak area of *hammada*. By public transport, you have a choice of either a **grand taxi** (leaving Goulimine from out on the Tan Tan road, near the camel *souk*) or a **bus** (several daily, including express services from Agadir). There is no petrol station between Goulimine and Tan Tan.

There are no longer any military checkpoints north of Tan Tan, though when you arrive in town you'll have to stop at the local *gendarmerie* to fill in a questionnaire, stating the purpose of your visit. This is a good place to enquire about the state of roads and permits for trips south to Laayoune and beyond.

Tan Tan

Arriving at **TAN TAN**, you might find yourself wondering why you made the journey. A drab administrative centre, it survives in a low-key way through its status as a duty-free zone (the shops are full of radios and electric razors) and rather more so by its fishing port, which is responsible for a large percentage of Morocco's sardine exports. Its one claim to fame is that it was a departure point for the famous **Green March** (*La Marche Verte* – see box below), an event you find commemorated on postcards throughout the south.

The town has around 50,000 inhabitants, many of them former nomads, who retain their distinctive pale blue robes. This clothing is much in evidence

---

THE SAHARAN PROVINCES

Until 1987–88, any trip **south of Laayoune**, into the **former Spanish Sahara**, involved getting permission from the military authorities. The routes are today open quite routinely – indeed the Moroccan authorities are actively encouraging tourists to explore the region. There is a hotel complex under construction at Tan Tan Plage, and a French *Club Med* holiday village already established at Laayoune.

The politics of the area are a highly sensitive matter in Morocco: so much so, that all maps and guides of the country must have the territory included as part of the Moroccan kingdom. Some background to this is included in *Contexts*. The essential facts are that the old Spanish Southern Colonial Zone, sometimes referred to as the Western Sahara, was claimed and occupied by Morocco in 1976. The occupation was an enormously successful public relations exercise for King Hassan, who masterminded a **Green March** (*La Marche Verte*) into the territory by some 300,000 unarmed civilians. Territorial counterclaims, however, came almost immediately from Mauritania and from various groups among the indigenous Sahrawis. For the last decade, a war has raged on and off in the desert between the Moroccan army and authorities (who occupy and administer the entire former Spanish colony) and Algerian-backed Polisario guerrilla fighters, operating from bases around Tindouf, across the border in Algeria.

The war, which for a time affected areas within Morocco's "former" boundaries, has over the past few years largely been contained through the creation of an extraordinary "desert wall" (see *Contexts*), while in the meantime Polisario has increasingly turned to diplomacy to gather support. At present, there is only very sporadic fighting, around the wall, miles from any of the major routes. And with the rapprochement between Morocco and Algeria, there is genuine hope of a settlement. The UN is sponsoring talks about a long-discussed referendum amongst the population to choose between Moroccan or independent government. There seems little doubt, given the huge resources that the Moroccans have committed to their **Saharan Provinces**, that the territory will remain in the kingdom.

Given these somewhat uncertain factors, however, all travellers should check the most **up-to-date information** before attempting anything too ambitious in the region, and certainly before trying to take any road route into Mauritania (impossible at the time of writing). All the main road signs south of Agadir, however, now give the distances to Laayoune, Dakhla and even Dakar.

in the **souks** – the most animated part of a hot, sleepy town – as are a variety of *lithams*, strips of cotton that are wrapped around the head. The latter are a wise investment as sun protection if you are heading further south.

Hotels and transport

Many of Tan Tan's hotels are in permanent occupation by the military – reserved for troops (and their families) on leave from the Western Sahara. There are, however, five or six "open" **hotels** and several café-restaurants around the main square, **Place Laayoune**, and others nearby. The price differences are not great between one and another. The best, if they have space, are *Hôtel l'Etoile du Sahara*, 17 Rue El Fida (☎70.85), and *Hôtel Amgala* – both categorised 1*A – and the *Hôtel Dhakla* on Place Tan Tan. For a **meal**, try *Café-Restaurant Le Jardin* on Av. Mohammed V; the town has no bars.

Grands taxis can be arranged to Laayoune, as well as Goulimine and operate from Place Tan Tan; the **bus station** is about 200m down the main street, just off to the right.

Tan Tan Plage

TAN TAN PLAGE, 25km from town on the coastal route to Laayoune, has been earmarked for development as a resort. As yet, there is very little to see, even less to do, and nowhere to stay – but, if the weather hasn't brought in tons of seaweed, there's at least a chance to go swimming.

A four-star hotel, with tennis courts, swimming pool and conference centre, is **under construction**. Current facilities are limited to a pair of cafés.

A loop through Smara

Reports have come in of travellers making a loop **from Tan Tan along the new road to Smara**, returning by way of the P44 to Laayoune, and from there over to Tan Tan via Tarfaya – a circuit of some 1000km.

There are filling stations in Tan Tan, Smara and Laayoune – petrol, incidentally, is subsidised throughout the Western Sahara – so if you embark on the trip be sure to fill up, and to carry good supplies of water. Between Tan Tan and Smara there is just one roadside hamlet, ABBTIH, with no facilities.

Smara

SMARA itself is basically a military garrison town, with scant remains of an earlier past as the base of Ma el Ainin, the "Blue Sultan", who controlled the region at the turn of the last century. There are two small and basic **hotels**, the *Erraha* and *Sakia El Houria*, on the main street, and a scattering of cafés. The **road east from the town**, towards the Algerian town of TINDOUF (where the Polisario have their main base), is firmly closed.

West to Boukra . . . and on to Laayoune

West from Smara, heading to Laayoune, you pass through one of the more fertile strips of the Western Sahara, along the vague oasis strip of the Seguiat Al Hamra. There are occasional nomadic tents to be seen. The road eventually joins with that from Laayoune to Boukra, 20km northwest of the latter.

BOUKRA is not really worth the detour: a mining town with a large garrison. South of Boukra is a restricted military zone. It is unlikely, though just feasible, that you will be allowed to continue to GUELTA ZEMMOUR and beyond, into Mauritania.

Completing the loop **north to Laayoune**, the road from Boukra/Smara passes by the old Spanish fort of DCHIRA (out of bounds to all but the military) and the tiny oasis of LEMSEYED.

Tan Tan to Laayoune

The route between **Tan Tan Plage and Laayoune** is the most memorable stretch of the journey into the Deep South, cutting as it does between desert and ocean. The coast, somewhat defying expectations, is mainly cliff – the desert dropping directly away to the sea, with only the occasional stretch of beach.

En route from Tan Tan to Tarfaya there is little more than the single roadside settlement of **AKHFENIR** (about 150km south of Tan Tan) with its three cafés and petrol station. The stretch beyond this is accessible beach – with reputedly wonderful fishing.

Tarfaya

TARFAYA is a larger roadside settlement (population 7000) with a small fishing port and a prominent monument to the Green March. It may, however, be in line for greater things if an oil shale development, currently under consideration by Shell, goes ahead.

For the moment it's a quiet place, probably not far different from its years as a staging post for the *Aeropostale Service* – when aviators such as Antoine de St-Exupéry used to rest up on their way down to West Africa. The service is commemorated annually in October by a "Rallye Aérien", with small planes flying south from Toulouse to Dakar in Senegal; Tarfaya is a night's stop.

Oddly enough, the town was actually founded, at the end of the last century, by a British trader, and was originally known as Port Victoria. During the Spanish occupation, it was known as Villa Bens and served as very low-key capital for the "Southern Protectorate"; they abandoned it in 1958, leaving a church, barracks and a handful of villas. Today it has been passed over by Laayoune, and has just one (unsignposted and unclassified) **hotel**, located opposite the two cafés.

Khmiss Lagoon and south to Laayoune

If you've got an interest in birdlife, you might find the Tarfaya area rewarding. The nearby **Khmiss Lagoon** is an important migratory site, maintained as a **bird sanctuary**.

For most travellers, though, it is the sand desert south of Tarfaya, the **Erg Lakhbayta**, that is the most memorable feature. The drive on from here to Laayoune takes about an hour by car or *grand taxi*. South of Tarfaya you cross the old border of Spanish Sahara.

Laayoune

With a population of 100,000, **LAAYOUNE** (AL AYOUN) is the largest and the most interesting town of Western Sahara. Its development as a provincial capital is almost immediately obvious – and impressive, as you survey the new 30,000-seat stadium, complete with real grass, maintained for the area's handful of football teams. The city has the highest per capita government spending in Morocco and soldiers, billeted here for the conflict with Polisario, have been employed in many of the projects.

The population growth – from little more than a village when the Moroccans took over – has been aided by massive subsidies, which apply throughout the Western Sahara (petrol is half the price here as it is in the north) and by an agreement that settlers should initially pay no taxes. There is a mix of Sahrawis, many of them driven here by the drought of the last few years, and Moroccan immigrants from the north in search of work.

The town

Most of the new building is in the Upper Town; the old Spanish settlement, more dishevelled, lies down below, with its old and disused cathedral.

Most striking of the developments is the **Place du Mechouar**, beside the new Grand Mosque, with its exhibition hall devoted to photographs of the Green March. In addition to such public statements, though, there are a few pleasant corners, like the landscaped gardens of the **Colline des Oiseaux**, with their cages of exotic birds – complete with blinds to be drawn down over the cages in the event of sandstorms.

Accommodation

There are now three luxurious **hotels** in Laayoune, on most occasions pretty much empty. The *Hôtel Parador*, Rue Okba Ben Nafia (☎38.29), is the old Spanish state inn, and as good a place as any to hide away from the sun, if you can afford the prices. The more recently built *Hôtel Massira* (4*A) is on Av. dela Mecque (☎42.25); both are managed by the *Club Med*. A third 4* hotel, the *Hôtel Nagjir*, on Place Dchira (☎41.68), has the dubious distinction of being the only nightclub in Western Sahara.

On a more budget level, pick between the 2*A *Hôtel Residencia* on Rue Prince Moulay Abdallah (☎38.29) or the 1*A *Hôtel Marhaba* on Av. Hassan II. For **food**, there are various café-restaurants and more expensive meals in the flash hotels.

Other practicalities

On the practical front, Laayoune, rather incredibly, boasts an **ONMT** office (opposite the *Parador*), which can be a good source of information on the routes south from here; they can also arrange car hire (with or without driver). There are two **banks**: the *BMCE,* Rue Mohammed Zerktouni, and *Banque Populaire* , Av. Mohammed V.

RAM, on Place Bir Anzarene (☎224.077), operates flights from the town airport (a short taxi ride east) to Agadir, the Canary Islands and Ad Dakhla.

Laayoune Plage

LAAYOUNE PLAGE, 20km away, on the main road south, is a port for the region's phosphates, with a freight conveyor link to Boukra. It comprises a small village, a rather polluted beach and a lagoon with flamingoes.

South from Laayoune

Depending on the military situation, you might be able to obtain permission to continue **south of Laayoune** down to Ad Dakhla. There are no buses, but if you don't have a vehicle, it shouldn't be too hard to arrange a lift with a lorry. The road is reputedly quite good, though beware of occasional sand-drifts, and camels grazing by or on the road. The sea is guarded by cliffs for most of the way to Boujdor.

Lemsid and Boujdor

The first stop along the road is **LEMSID**, 110km from Laayoune, which, if you're not truly committed to travel for travel's sake, is perhaps the place to turn around. There is a small **café-shop** – and little else – that provides basic meals for the route's lorry drivers.

If you are determined, however, the route offers a brief stop at **BOUJDOR**, a fishing port, where you should expect to pass through a number of military checks. The landscape here is a little more mellow, with the village set by a lighthouse and fishing harbour. There is a petrol station and various cafés, though no official accommodation. South of the town stretches a long, long beach.

South to Dakhla

South again from Boujdor the road runs inland, rejoining the coast at the tiny settlement of SKAYMAT – less of an oasis than it looks on the map.

Finally, 322km from Laayoune, you reach the town of **AD DAKHLA**, on a long spit of land. This was a Spanish outpost, known as Villa Cisneros in the colonial days, when it served as a minor administrative centre for the Rio de Oro. It remains military in character, and once you have explained your presence, you should be prepared to mix largely with soldiers on leave. There are half a dozen basic **hotels**, cleanest of which is the *Hôtel Imlil* (in the centre of town), a couple of **hammams**, and even a **bar**, *Bar Juan*, with real beers.

Towards Mauritania

At present, the road **south of Ad Dakhla is closed** to all but military traffic. In theory, it might be possible to drive to LA GOUERA, the Moroccan frontier post with Mauritanian NOUADHIBOU.

travel details

Buses

From Agadir Essaouira (6 daily; 3hr 30min); Taroudannt (4; 2hr 30min); Tiznit (4; 2hr); Goulimine (2; 4hr 30min); Marrakesh (5; *SATAS/CTM* direct; 4hr); Tata (4am and 7am daily; 9hr); Casablanca (7.30pm; 5hr).

From Inezgane Marrakesh (4 daily; 3hr 30min); Goulimine (5; 4hr 30min); Taroudannt (4; 2hr); Taliouine/Ouarzazate (4; 3hr 30min/5hr).

From Taroudannt Marrakesh via Tizi n'Test (daily at 4am; 8hr 30min); Marrakesh, via Inezgane/Imi n'Tanoute (daily at 5am; 6hr); Taliouine/Ouarzazate (5 daily; 1hr 30min/3hr); Tata (3 a week; 8–10hr).

From Tiznit Tafraoute (4 daily; 3hr 30min–6hr 30min); Goulimine (6; 2hr 30min); Sidi Ifni (2; 2hr 30min); Tata (2; 7hr).

From Tafraoute Agadir (4 daily; 5hr); Tiznit (3; 3hr).

From Goulimine Tan Tan (3 daily; 3hr).

Grands Taxis

From Agadir Shuttle to Inezgane (15min; 2dh); regularly to Oulad Teima* (1hr; connection to Taroudannt).

From Inezgane Regularly to Oulad Teima* (40min; connection to Taroudannt) and Tiznit (1hr 30min).

From Oulad Teima* Regularly to Taroudannt (1hr).

From Taroudannt Linked service, with changes, to Ouled Behril, Aoulouz and Taliouine.

From Tiznit Land Rover taxis to Tafraoute (regular departures, not always easy to get on; they stop around 4pm; 2hr 30min). Regularly to Goulimine (2hr; sometimes with connection at Bou Izarkan).

From Goulimine Regularly to Tan Tan (2hr 30min).

*Oulad Teima is also known as Quarante-Quatre – "44" – as it is 44km from Agadir.

Ferries

From Agadir Weekly car/passenger ferry (Saturday 7pm) to Las Palmas, Canary Islands (arrives Sunday 5pm).

Flights

From Agadir Daily to Casablanca (and from there to Tangier, etc); several times a week to Tan Tan, Laayoune, and Las Palmas (Canary Islands); 3 times a week to Ad Dakhla. International flights to London, etc, though tickets are not especially cheap if you buy them at this end.

From Tan Tan Most days to Laayoune.

From Laayoune Most days to Las Palmas (Canary Islands), Tan Tan and Agadir.

From Ad Dhakla 3 times a week to Agadir.

TELEPHONE CODES

AGADIR ☎08	TAN TAN ☎087
GOULIMINE ☎087	TAROUDANNT ☎085
INEZGANE ☎08	TIZNIT ☎096
SIDI IFNI ☎087	

PART THREE

THE
CONTEXTS

THE HISTORICAL FRAMEWORK

Morocco's emergence as a "modern" nation-state is astonishingly recent, dating from the occupation of the country by the French and Spanish at the beginning of this century, and its subsequent Independence in 1956. Prior to this, it is best seen as a kind of patchwork of tribes, whose shifting alliances and sporadic bids for power defined both the government and its extent.

With a handful of exceptions, the country's ruling sultans controlled only the plains, the coastal ports and the regions around the imperial capitals of Fes, Marrakesh, Rabat and Meknes. These were known as *Bled el Makhzen* **– the governed lands, or, literally, "the Lands of the Storehouse". The rest of the Moroccan territories – the Rif, the three Atlas ranges and the outlying deserts – comprised** *Bled es Siba*, **"the Lands of the Dissidents". Populated almost exclusively by Berbers, the original (pre-Arab) inhabitants, they were rarely recognised as being anything more than under local tribal authority.**

The balance between government control and tribal Independence is one of the two enduring themes of Moroccan history. The other is the emergence, expansion and eventual replacement of the various **sultanate dynasties**. These at first seem dauntingly complicated – a succession of short-lived tribal movements and confusingly similar-named sultans – but there are actually just seven main groups.

The first of them, the **Idrissids**, became the model by founding the city of Fes towards the end of the eighth century and bringing a coalition of Berber and Arab forces under a central *makhzen* (government) authority. The last, the **Alaouites**, emerged in the mid-seventeenth century from the great palm oasis of Tafilalt and, continuing with the current king, Hassan II, still hold constitutional power. It is around these groups – together with the medieval dynasties of the **Almoravids, Almohads,** **Merenids, Wattasids** and **Saadians** – that the bulk of the following sections are organised.

PREHISTORY

The first inhabitants of the **Maghreb** – the Arab term for the countries of North Africa – probably occupied the **Sahara**, for thousands of years a great savannah fertile enough to support elephants, zebras and a whole range of other game and wildlife. Little is known about these ancestors of the human species, although it seems likely that there were groups of hunter-and-gatherer hominids here as early as 1,000,000 BC.

Around 15,000 BC there seem to have been **Paleolithic** settlements, and before the Sahara went into decline (from 3000 BC), primitive pastoral and agricultural systems had begun to develop. It is possible, too, to trace the arrival of two independent Stone-Age cultures in the Maghreb: the Neolithic **Capsian Man** (circa 10,000–5000 BC), probably emerging from Egypt, and slightly later, **Mouillian Man**. From these people, fair-skinned and speaking a remote "Libyan" language, stem the cave and rock drawings of the pre-Sahara and High Atlas, the earliest archaeological sites in Morocco.

PHOENICIANS AND CARTHAGINIANS

The recorded history of the area begins about 1100 BC with a series of trading settlements established by the **Phoenicians**. These were small, isolated colonies, usually built on defensible headlands around the coast, and there was probably little initial contact between them and the inhabitants of the interior, whom they knew as Libyans and Ethiopians – or collectively as *Barbaroi*, or **Berbers**.

As the emphasis shifted away from the Phoenicians themselves, and their African trading routes were taken over by the former colony of **Carthage** (modern Tunis), some of the ports grew into considerable cities, exporting grain and grapes, and minting their own coinage. On the "Moroccan" coast, the most important colonies were at Lixus (near Larache), Tingis (Tangier) and Chellah (near Rabat), but they spread as far east as Melilla; in the south a flourishing dye factory was also maintained on an island off Essaouira.

Officially, the Carthaginian empire collapsed with its defeat in the **Punic Wars** (196 BC) against Rome, but in these provincial outposts, life seems to have been little affected. If anything, the colonies grew in stature and prosperity, absorbing hundreds of Punic refugees after the Roman sacking of Carthage. It was a first sign of Morocco's intrinsic historic and geographic isolation in what was to become known as *Maghreb el-Aska* (The Land of the Farthest West). Even after the Romans had annexed and then abandoned the country, Punic was still widely spoken along the coast.

BERBER KINGDOMS AND ROMAN RULE

Prior to total Roman annexation, and the imposition of direct imperial rule in 24 AD, the "civilised" Moroccan territories for a while formed the **Berber kingdom of Mauretania**. This was probably little more than a confederation of local tribes, centred around Volubilis (near Meknes) and Tangier, but it gained a certain influence through alliance and occasional joint rule, with the adjoining Berber state of Numidia (essentially modern Algeria). The most important of the Berber rulers, and the only ones of which any substantial records survive, were **Juba II** (25 BC–23 AD) and his son **Ptolemy**. Both were heavily Romanised: Juba, an Algerian Berber by birth, was brought up and educated in Rome, where he married the daughter of Antony and Cleopatra. His reign, if limited in its extent, seems to have been orderly and prosperous, and under his son the pattern might well have continued. In 42 AD, however, Emperor Caligula summoned Ptolemy to an audience in Lyons and had him assassinated – so the story goes – for appearing in a more brilliant cloak than his own. Whatever the truth, and Rome may just have been eager for direct rule, it proved an inauspicious beginning.

ROMAN RULE

The early years of Rome's new imperial province were taken up with near constant **rebellions** – the first one alone needing three years and over 20,000 troops to subdue.

Perhaps discouraged by this unexpected resistance, the **Romans** never attempted to colonise Morocco-Mauretania beyond its old limits. The Rif and Atlas mountains were left unpenetrated, and, of the interior, it was only

Volubilis – already a city of sorts, and at the heart of the north's fertile vineyards and grain fields – that was in any way exploited. In this the Romans were establishing an enduring precedent: not just in their failure to subdue *Bled es Siba*, which also defied the later sultans, but also in their treatment of Morocco as a useful "corridor" to the greater agricultural wealth of Algeria, Tunisia and Spain.

When the Roman legions were withdrawn in 253 AD, and the **Vandals** took power in southern Spain, the latter were interested only in taking Tangier and Ceuta for use as staging posts en route to northern Tunisia. Similarly, the **Byzantine General Belisarius,** who defeated the Vandals and laid claim to the Maghreb for Justinian's Eastern Empire, did little more than replace the Ceuta garrison.

It was understandable, of course. Any attempt to control Morocco would need manpower far in excess of these armies, and the only overland route through the country – across the Taza gap – was scarcely practicable even in peacetime. Not until the tenth century, and the great northward expansion of the desert nomads, was Morocco to become a land worthy of substantial exploitation in its own right, and even then only through the unifying and evangelising impetus of Islam.

THE COMING OF ISLAM

The irruption of **Islam** into the world began in 622 AD, when the Prophet Muhammad moved with his followers from Mecca to Medina. Within thirty years they had reached the borders of India, to the east; were threatening Byzantine Constantinople, to the north; and had established themselves in the Maghreb at Kairouan in present-day Tunisia.

After this initial thrust, however, sweeping across the old provinces of the Roman world, the progress of the new religion was temporarily slowed. The Berbers of Algeria – mainly pagan but including communities of Christians and Jews – put up a strong and unusually unified resistance to Arab control. It was only in 680 that the governor of Kairouan, **Oqba Ibn Nafi,** made an initial foray into Morocco, taking in the process the last Byzantine stronghold at Ceuta.

What happened afterwards remains uncertain. There is a story, perhaps apocryphal, that Oqba embarked on a 5000-kilometre **march**

through Morocco, raiding and subjugating all in his path, and preaching Islam all the way to the west – the Atlantic Ocean. But whether this expedition had any real Islamising influence on the Moroccan Berbers is unlikely. Oqba left no garrison forces and was himself killed in Algeria on his return to Kairouan.

Islam may have taken root among some of the tribes. In the early part of the eighth century the new Arab governor of the West, **Moussa Ibn Nasr**, returned to Morocco and managed to establish Arab control (and carry out mass conversions to Islam) in both the northern plains and the pre-Sahara. Like the Romans and Byzantines before him, though, his main thrust was towards **Spain**. In 711, the first Muslim forces crossed over from Tangier to Tarifa and defeated the Visigoths in a single battle; within a decade the Moors had taken control of all but the remote Spanish mountains in northern Asturias; and their advance was only halted at the Pyrenees by the victory of Charles Martel at Poitiers in 732.

The bulk of this invading and occupying force were almost certainly **Berber converts** to Islam, and the sheer scale of their military success must have had enormous influence in turning Morocco itself into a largely Muslim nation. It was not at this stage, however, in any way an Arab one. The extent of the Islamic empire – from Persia to Morocco, and Ghana to Spain – was simply too great for Arab numbers. Early attempts to impose taxes on the Moroccan Berbers led to a rebellion and, once again outside the political mainstream, the Maghreb fragmented into a series of small, independent **principalities**.

THE IDRISSIDS (8TH–11TH CENTURIES)

This drift found an echo in the wider events of the Muslim world, which was undergoing its first – and most drastic – dissension, with the split into **Sunni** and **Shia** sects. In Damascus the Sunni Abbasid dynasty took power, the Shiites dispersing and seeking refuge both to the east and west.

One of them, arriving in Morocco around 787, was **Moulay Idriss**, an evidently charismatic leader and a direct descendant (great-grandson, in fact) of the Prophet Muhammad. He seems to have been adopted almost at once by the citizens of Volubilis – then still a vaguely

Romanised city – and by the Aouraba Berber tribe. He was to survive for three more years, before being poisoned by order of the Sunni caliph, but in this time he managed to set up the infrastructure of an essentially Arab court and kingdom – the basis of what was to become the Moroccan nation. Its most important feature, enduring to the present with Hassan II, was his being recognised as *Imam*. To the Moroccans this meant that he was both spiritual and political leader, "Commander of the Faithful" in every aspect of their lives.

Despite the brevity of Moulay Idriss's reign, and his sudden death in 791 or 792, his successors, the **Idrissids**, were to become the first recognisable Moroccan dynasty. Moulay Idriss himself left a son, born posthumously to a Berber woman, and in 807, after a period of an apparently orderly regency, **Moulay Idriss II** was declared sultan and *imam*. He ruled for a little over twenty years – something of a golden age for the emerging Moroccan state, with the extension of a central, Arabised authority throughout the north and even to the oases beyond the Atlas.

Idriss's most important achievement, however, was the establishment (if perhaps not the foundation) of the city of **Fes**. Here, he set up the apparatus of court government, and here he also welcomed large contingents of Shiite **refugees**. Most prominent among these were groups from Córdoba and Kairouan, then the two great cities of western Islam. In incorporating them, Fes (and, by extension, Morocco) became increasingly Arabised, and was suddenly transformed into a major centre in its own right. The **Kairaouine University** was established, becoming one of the three most important in Islam (and far ahead of those in Europe); a strong crafts tradition took root; and Fes became a vital link in the trade between Spain and the East, and between the Maghreb and Africa south of the Sahara.

Fes was to remain the major Moroccan city, and the country's Arab spiritual heart, right up until the present century. The Idrissid state, however, fragmented again into **principalities**, most of which returned to their old isolation, until, at the turn of the tenth century, the context began to change. In al-Andalus – the Muslim territories of Spain – the Western Caliphate collapsed and itself splintered into small rival states. Meanwhiile in Tunisia, the well-established Fatimid dynasty moved their capital to Egypt, clashed with their nominated governors, the Zirids, and unleashed on them the hostile nomadic tribe of the Banu Hilal.

It was a move which was to have devastating effects on the Maghreb's entire lifestyle and ecological balance, as the **Hilali** nomads swept westwards, destroying all in their path, bringing to ruin the irrigation systems and devastating the agricultural lands with their goats and other flocks. The medieval Maghrebi historian, Ibn Khaldun, described their progress as being like a swarm of locusts: "the very earth seems to have changed its nature", he wrote, "all the lands that the Arabs have conquered in the last few centuries, civilisation and population have departed from them".

THE ALMORAVIDS (1062–1145)

Morocco was to some extent cushioned from the Hilali, and by the time they reached its southern oases (where they settled), the worst was probably over. But with the shattered social order of the Maghreb, and shifting power struggles in Spain, came an obvious vacuum of power.

It was this which created the opportunity for the two great Berber dynasties of the Middle Ages – the **Almoravids** and the **Almohads**. Both were to emerge from the south, and in each case their motivating force was religious, a purifying zeal to **reform** or destroy the decadent ways which had reached Morocco from the wealthy Andalusian Muslims of Spain. The two dynasties together lasted only a century and a half, but in this period Morocco was pre-eminent in all of western Islam, maintaining an empire that at its peak stretched right across the Maghreb to Libya, south to Senegal and Ghana and north into Spain. Subsequent history and achievements never matched up to this imperial dream, though even today its memories are part of the Moroccan concept of nation. "Greater Morocco", the nationalist goal of the late 1950s, sketched out areas that took in Mauritania, Algeria, Tunisia and Libya, while even the present war in the Sahara looks back to the reality of the medieval empires.

The **Almoravids**, the first of these dynasties, began as a reforming movement among the Sanhaja Berbers in what is now Mauritania. A nomadic desert tribe – similar to the Touaregs who occupy the area today – they had been converted to Islam in the ninth century, but perhaps only to nominal effect. The founders of the movement, a local sheikh who had returned from the pilgrimage to Mecca and a *fakir* from the Souss plain, found widespread abuse of orthodox practice. In particular, they preached against drinking palm wine, playing licentious music and taking more than four wives. It seemed like a message unlikely to captivate an already ascetic, tent-living people, but it rapidly took hold.

Founding a *ribat* – a kind of warrior monastery similar to the European Templar castles, and from which the movement takes its name – they soon gained a following and considerable military force. In 1054, they set out from the *ribat* to spread the message through a *jihad* (holy war), and within four years they had gained control of Ghana to the south. Turning towards Morocco, they established themselves in Marrakesh by 1062, and, under the leadership of **Youssef bin Tachfine**, went on to extend their rule throughout the north of Morocco and, to the east, as far as Algiers.

At no time before had any one leader exercised such strong control over these territories, uniting the tribes for the first time under a single religious doctrine – a simple, rigorous and puritanical form of Sunni orthodoxy. And so it remained, at least as long as the impetus of *jihad* was sustained. In 1085, Youssef undertook his first, and possibly reluctant, expedition to **Spain**, invited by the Muslim princes of **al-Andalus** after the fall of Toledo to the Christians. He crossed over the straits again in 1090, this time to take control of Spain himself. In this he was successful, and before his death in 1107, he had restored Muslim control to Valencia and other territories lost in the first wave of the Christian Reconquest.

The new Spanish territories had two decisive effects. The first was to reorient Moroccan culture towards the far more sophisticated and affluent Andalusian civilisation; the second to stretch the Almoravid forces too thin. Both were to contribute to the dynasty's decline. Youssef, disgusted by Andalusian decadence, had ruled largely from **Marrakesh**, leaving his governors in Seville and other cities. After his death, the Andalusians proved disinclined to accept these foreign overlords, while the Moroccans themselves became vulnerable to charges of being corrupt and departing from their puritan ideals.

Youssef's son **Ali** was, in fact, extraordinarily pious, but, unprepared for (and not interested in) ceaseless military activity, he was forced to use Christian mercenaries to maintain control. His reign, and that of the Almoravids, was effectively finished by the early 1140s, as a new movement, the Almohads, seized control of the main Moroccan cities one after another.

THE ALMOHADS (1145–1248)

Ironically, the **Almohads** shared much in common with their predecessors. Again, they were forged from the Berber tribes – this time in the High Atlas – and again, they based their bid for power on an intense puritanism. Their founder **Ibn Toumert**, attacked the Almoravids for allowing their women to ride horses (a tradition in the desert), for wearing extravagant clothes, and for being subject to what may have been Andalusian corruptions – the revived use of music and wine.

He also provoked a **theological crisis**, claiming that the Almoravids did not recognise the essential unitary and unknowable nature of God: the basis of Almohad belief, and the source of their name – the "unitarians". Banished from Marrakesh by Ali, Ibn Toumert set up a *ribat* in the Atlas at **Tin Mal**. Here he waged war on local tribes until they would accept his authority, and eventually revealed himself to them as the Mahdi – "the chosen one" and the final prophet promised in the Koran.

Charismatic and brutal in his methods, Toumert was aided by a shrewd assistant and brilliant military leader, **Abd el Moumen**, who took over the movement after his death and extended the radius of their raids. In 1145, he was strong enough to displace the Almoravids from Fes, and two years later he drove them from their stronghold in Marrakesh. With the two cities subdued, he was now effectively sultan.

Resistance subsided and once again a Moroccan dynasty moved **towards Spain** – this time finally secured by the third Almohad sultan, **Yacoub el Mansour** (The Victorious), who in 1195 defeated the Christians at Alarcos. El Mansour also pushed the frontiers of the empire east to Tripoli, and for the first time, there was one single rule across the entire Maghreb. With the ensuing wealth and prestige, he launched a new building programme – the first and most ambitious in Moroccan history – which included a new capital in Rabat and the magnificent gateways and minarets of Marrakesh and Seville.

Once more, however, imperial expansion precipitated disintegration. In 1212, Yacoub's successor, **Mohammed en Nasr**, attempted to drive the Spanish Christians as far back as the Pyrenees and met with decisive defeat at the battle of **Las Navas de Tolosa**. The balance was changing, and within four decades, only the Kingdom of Granada remained in Spanish Muslim hands. In the Maghreb, meanwhile, the eastern provinces had declared Independence from Almohad rule and Morocco itself was returning to the authority of local tribes. In 1248, one of these, the **Merenids** (or Beni Merin), took the northern capital of Fes and turned towards Marrakesh.

THE MERENIDS AND WATTASIDS (1248–1554)

This last (300-year) period of Berber rule in Morocco is very much a tailpiece to the Almoravid and Almohad empires – marked by increasing domestic **instability** and economic stagnation, and signalling also the beginning of Morocco's **isolation** from both the European and Muslim worlds. The Spanish territories were not regained, and Granada, the last Moorish city, fell to Ferdinand and Isabella in 1492. Portuguese sea power saw to it that foreign seaports were established on the Atlantic and Mediterranean coasts. To the east, the rest of the Maghreb fell under Turkish domination, as part of the Ottoman Empire.

In Morocco itself, the main development was a centralised administrative system – the **Makhzen** – which was maintained without tribal support by standing armies of Arab and Christian mercenaries. It is to this age that the real distinction of *Bled el Makhzen* and *Bled es Siba* belongs – the latter coming to mean everything outside the immediate vicinities of the imperial cities.

THE MERENIDS

Perhaps with this background it is not surprising that few of the twenty-one **Merenid sultans** – or their cousins and successors, the Wattasids – made any great impression. The early sultans were occupied mainly with Spain, at first in trying to regain a foothold on the coast, later with shoring up the Kingdom of Granada. There were minor successes in the fourteenth century under the "Black Sultan", **Abou el Hassan**, who for a time occupied Tunis, but he was to die before being able to launch a planned major invasion of al-Andalus, and his son, **Abou Inan**, himself fell victim to the power struggles within the mercenary army.

The thirteenth and fourteenth centuries, however, did leave a considerable **legacy of building**, perhaps in defiance of the lack of political progress (and certainly a product of the move towards government by forced taxation). In 1279, the garrison town of Fes el Djedid was established, to be followed by a series of brilliantly endowed colleges, or *medersas*, which are among the finest surviving Moorish monuments. Culture, too, saw a final flourishing. The historians Ibn Khaldun and Leo Africanus and the travelling chronicler Ibn Battuta all studied in Fes under Merenid patronage.

THE WATTASIDS

The **Wattasids**, who usurped Merenid power in 1465, had ruled in effect for 45 years previously as a line of hereditary viziers. They maintained a semblance of control for a little under a century, though the extent of the *Makhzen* lands was by now minimal.

The Portuguese had annexed and colonised the seaports of Tetouan, Ceuta, Tangier, Asilah, Agadir and Safi, while large tracts of the interior lay in the hands of religious warrior brotherhoods, or *marabouts*, on whose alliances the sultans had increasingly to depend.

THE SAADIANS AND CIVIL WAR (1554–1669)

The rise and fall of the **Saadians** was in some respects an abridged version of all of the dynasties that had come before them. They were the most important of the *marabouts* to emerge in the early years of the sixteenth century, rising to power on the strength of their religious positions (they were *Shereefs* – descendants of the Prophet), climaxing in a single, particularly distinguished reign, and declining amid a chaos of political assassinations, bitter factional strife and, in the end, civil war.

As the first Arab dynasty since the Idrissids, they mark the end (to date) of Moroccan Berber rule, though this was probably less significant at the time than the fact that theirs was a government with no tribal basis. The *Makhzen* had to be even further extended than under the Merenids, and Turkish guards – a new point of intrigue – were added to the imperial armies.

Slower to establish themselves than the preceding dynasties, the Saadians began by setting up a small principality in the **Souss**, where they established their first capital in Taroudannt. Normally, this would have formed a regular part of *Bled el Makhzen*, but the absence of government in the south allowed them to extend their power to **Marrakesh** around 1520, with the Wattasids for a time retaining Fes and ruling the north.

In the following decades the Saadians made breakthroughs along the coast, capturing Agadir in 1540 and driving the Portuguese from Safi and Essaouira. When the Wattasids fell into bankruptcy and invited the Turks into Fes, the Saadians were ready to consolidate their power. This proved harder, and more confusing, than anyone might have expected. **Mohammed esh Sheikh**, the first Saadian sultan to control both the southern and northern kingdoms, was himself soon using Turkish troops, and was, in fact, assassinated by a group of them in 1557. His death unleashed an incredibly convoluted sequence of factional murder and power politics, which was only resolved, somewhat fortuitously, by a battle with the Portuguese twenty years later.

THE BATTLE OF THE THREE KINGS

This event, **The Battle of the Three Kings**, was essentially a Portuguese crusade, led by the youthful King Sebastião on the nominal behalf of a deposed Saadian king against his uncle and rival. At the end of the day, all three were to perish on the battlefield, the Portuguese having suffered a crushing defeat, and a little-known Saadian prince emerged as the sole acknowledged ruler of Morocco.

His name was **Ahmed "el Mansour"** (The Victorious, following this momentous victory), and he was easily the most impressive sultan of the dynasty. Not only did he begin his reign clear of the intrigue and rivalry that had dogged his predecessors, but he was immensely wealthy as well. Portuguese ransoms paid for the remnants of their nobility after the battle had been enormous, causing Portugal to go bankrupt – the country, with its remaining Moroccan enclaves, then passed under the control of Habsburg Spain.

Breaking with tradition, Ahmed himself became actively involved in European politics, generally supporting the Protestant north against the Spanish and encouraging Dutch and British trade. Within Morocco he was able to maintain a reasonable level of order and peace, and diverted criticism of his use of Turkish troops (and his own Turkish-educated ways) by embarking on an **invasion of Timbuktu** and the south. This secured control of the Saharan salt mines and the gold and slave routes from Senegal, each sources of phenomenal wealth, which won him the additional epithet of *El Dhahabi* (The Golden One). It also reduced his need to tax Moroccans, which made him a popular man.

CIVIL WAR

Ahmed's death in 1603 caused abrupt and lasting chaos. He left three sons, none of whom could gain authority, and, split by **civil war**, the country once again broke into a number of principalities. A succession of **Saadian rulers** retained power in the Souss and in Marrakesh (where their tombs remain testimony to the opulence and turbulence of the age); another *marabout* force, the **Djila**, gained control of Fes; while around Salé and Rabat arose the bizarre **Republic of the Bou Regreg**.

The Bou Regreg depended almost entirely on **piracy**, a new development in Morocco, though well-established along the Mediterranean coasts of Algeria and Tunisia. Its practitioners were the last Moors to be expelled from Spain – mainly from Granada and Badajoz – and they conducted a looting war against primarily Spanish shipping. For a time they met with astounding success, raiding as far away as the Irish coast, dealing in arms with the British and the French, and even accrediting foreign consuls.

MOULAY ISMAIL AND THE EARLY ALAOUITES (1665–1822)

Like the Saadians, the **Alaouites** were *Shereefs*; first establishing themselves as religious leaders – this time in Rissani in the **Tafilalt**. The struggle to establish their power also followed a similar pattern, spreading first to Taza and Fes and finally, under Sultan **Moulay Rashid**, reaching Marrakesh in 1669. Rashid, however, was unable to enjoy the fruits of his labour, since he was assassinated in a particularly bloody palace coup in 1672. It was only with Moulay Ismail, the ablest of his rival sons, that an Alaouite leader gained real control over the country.

MOULAY ISMAIL

The reign of **Moulay Ismail**, perhaps the most notorious in all of Morocco's history, stretched over 55 years (1672–1727) and was to be the country's last stab at imperial glory. In Morocco, where his shrine in Meknes is still an object of pilgrimage, he is remembered as a great and just, if unusually ruthless, ruler; to contemporary Europeans – and in subsequent historical accounts – he is noted more for his extravagant cruelty. His rule certainly was tyrannical, with arbitrary killings and an appalling treatment of his slaves, but perhaps it was not much worse than that of the European nations of the day. The seventeenth century was the age of the witch trials in Protestant Europe, and of the Catholic Inquisition.

Nevertheless, Moulay Ismail stands out among the Alaouites because of the grandness of the scale on which he acted. At **Meknes**, which he made his new imperial capital, he garrisoned a permanent army of some 140,000 black troops, a legendary guard he had built up personally through slaving expeditions in Mauretania and the south, as well as by starting a human breeding programme. The army kept order throughout the kingdom – Morocco is today still littered with their Kasbahs – and were able to raise taxes as required. The Bou Regreg pirates, too (the so-called Sallee Rovers), were brought under the control of the state, along with their increasingly lucrative revenues.

With all this, Ismail was able to build a palace in Meknes that was the rival of its contemporary, Versailles, and he negotiated on equal terms with the **Europeans**. Indeed, it was probably the reputation he established for Morocco that allowed the country to remain free for another century and a half before the European colonial powers began carving it up.

SIDI MOHAMMED AND MOULAY SLIMANE

Like all the great, long-reigning Moroccan sultans, Moulay Ismail left innumerable sons and a terminal dispute for the throne, with the powerful standing army supporting and dropping heirs at will.

Remarkably, a capable ruler did emerge fairly soon – Sultan **Sidi Mohammed** – and for a while it appeared that the Shereefian empire was moving back into the mainstream of European and world events. Mohammed retook El Jadida from the Portuguese, founded the port of Essaouira, traded and conducted treaties with the Europeans, and even recognised the **United States of America** – one of the first rulers to do so.

At his death in 1790, however, the state collapsed into civil war, the two capitals of Fes and Marrakesh in turn promoting claimants to the throne. When this period drew to some kind of a close, with **Moulay Slimane** (1792–1822) asserting his authority in both cities, there was little left to govern. The army had dispersed; the *Bled es Siba* reasserted its old limits; and in Europe, with the ending of the Napoleonic wars, Britain, France, Spain and Germany were all looking to establish themselves in Africa.

Moualy Slimane's rule was increasingly isolated from the new realities outside Morocco. An intensely orthodox Muslim, he concentrated the efforts of government on eliminating the power and influence of the Sufi brotherhoods – a power he underestimated. In 1818 the Berber tribes loyal to the Derakaoui brotherhood rebelled and, temporarily, captured the Sultan. Subsequently, the sultans had no choice but to govern with the cooperation of local sheiks and brotherhood leaders.

Even more serious, at least in its long-term effects, was Moulay Slimane's attitude towards **Europe**, and in particular to Napoleonic France. Exports were banned; European consuls banished to Tangier; and contacts which might have helped maintain Moroccan Independence were lost.

MOULAY HASSAN AND EUROPEAN DOMINATION

Once started, the European domination of Moroccan affairs took an inevitable course – with an outdated, medieval form of government, virtual bankruptcy and armies press-ganged from the tribes to secure taxes, there was little that could be done to resist it.

The first pressures came from the **French**, who defeated the Ottomans in 1830 and occupied Algiers. Called to defend his fellow Muslims, Sultan **Abd er Rahman** (1822–59) mustered a force but was severely defeated at Isly. In the following reign of **Mohammed III** (1859–73), **Spanish** aspirations were also established with the occupation of Tetouan – regained by the Moroccans only after the offer to pay the Spanish massive indemnities and provide them with an Atlantic port (which Spain later claimed in Sidi Ifni).

MOULAY HASSAN

Outright occupation and colonisation were by the end of the nineteenth century proving more difficult to justify, but both the French and the Spanish had learned to use every opportunity to step in and "protect" their own nationals. Complaints by Moulay Hassan, the last pre-Colonial sultan to have any real power, actually led to a debate on this issue at the 1880 **Madrid Conference**, but the effect was only to regularise the practice on a wider scale, beginning with the setting up of an "international administration" in Tangier.

Moulay Hassan could, in other circumstances, have proved an effective and possibly inspired sultan. Acceding to the throne in 1873, he embarked on an ambitious series of modernising **reforms**, including attempts to stabilise the currency by minting the *rial* in Paris, to bring in more rational forms of taxation, and to retrain the army under the instruction of Turkish and Egyptian officers. The times, however, were against him. He found the social and monetary reforms obstructed by foreign merchants and local *caids*, while the European powers forced him to abandon the plans for other Muslim states' involvement in the army.

He played off the Europeans as best he could, employing a British military chief of staff, Caid MacClean, a French military mission and German arms manufacturers. On the frontiers, he built kasbahs to strengthen the defences at Tiznit, Saïdia and Selouane. But the government had few modern means of raising money to pay for these developments. Moulay Hassan was thrown back on the traditional means of taxation, the *harka*, setting out across the country to subdue the tribes and to collect tribute. In 1894, returning across the Atlas on just such a campaign, he died.

THE LAST SULTANS

The last years of Independence under Moulay Hassan's sons, Moulay Abd el Aziz and Moulay Hafid, were increasingly dominated by Europe.

The reign of **Abd el Aziz** (1894–1907), in particular, signalled an end to the possibilities of a modern, independent state raised by his reforming father. The sultan was just a boy of ten at his accession, but for the first six years of his rule the country was kept in at least a semblance of order by his father's vizier, Bou Ahmed. In 1900, however, Bou Ahmed died, and Abd el Aziz was left to govern alone – surrounded by an assembly of Europeans, preying on the remaining wealth of the court.

The first years of Morocco's twentieth-century history were marked by a return to the old ways. In the Atlas mountains, the tribal chiefs established ever-increasing powers, outside the government domain. In the Rif, a pretender to the throne, **Bou Hamra**, led a five-year revolt, coming close to taking control of Fes and the northern seat of government.

European manipulation during this period was remorselessly cynical. In 1904, the French negotiated agreements on "spheres of influence" with the British (who were to hold Egypt and Cyprus), and with the Italians (who got Tripolitana, or Libya). The following year saw the German Kaiser Wilhelm visiting Tangier and swearing to protect Morocco's integrity, but he was later bought off with the chance to "develop" the Congo. France and Spain, meanwhile, had reached a secret arrangement on how they were going to divide Morocco and were simply waiting for the critical moment.

In 1907, the French moved troops into **Oujda**, on the Algerian border, and, after a mob attack on French construction workers, into Casablanca. Abd el Aziz was eventually deposed by his brother, Moulay Hafid (1907–12), in a last attempt to resist the European advance. His reign began with a coalition with the principal Atlas chieftain, Madani el Glaoui, and intentions to take military action against

the French. The new sultan, however, was at first preoccupied with putting down the revolt of Bou Hamra – whom he succeeded in capturing in 1909. By this time the moment for defence against European entrenchment, if indeed it had ever been possible, had passed. Claiming to protect their nationals – this time in the mineral mines of the Rif – the Spanish brought over 90,000 men to garrison their established port in Melilla. Colonial occupation, in effect, had begun.

THE TREATY OF FES

Finally, in 1910, the two strands of Moroccan dissidence and European aggression came together. Moulay Hafid was driven into the hands of the French by the appearance of a new pretender in Meknes – one of a number during that period – and, with Berber tribesmen under the walls of his capital in Fes, was forced to accept their terms.

These were ratified and signed as the **Treaty of Fes** in 1912, and gave the French the right to defend Morocco, represent it abroad and conquer the *Bled es Siba*. A similar document was also signed by the Spanish, who were to take control of a strip of territory along the northern coast, with its capital in Tetouan and another thinner strip of land in the south, running eastwards from Tarfaya. In between, with the exception of a small Spanish enclave in Sidi Ifni, was to be French Morocco. A separate agreement gave Spain colonial rights to the Sahara, stretching south from Tarfaya to the borders of French Mauritania. The arbitrary way in which these boundaries were drawn was to have a profound effect on modern Moroccan history. When Moroccan nationalists laid claim to the Sahara in the 1950s – and to large stretches of Mauritania, Algeria and even Mali – they based their case on the obvious artificiality of colonial divisions.

THE FRENCH AND SPANISH PROTECTORATES (1912–56)

The fates of **Spanish and French Morocco** under colonial rule were to be very different. When **France** signed its Protectorate agreement with the sultan in 1912, its sense of **colonial mission** was running high. The colonial lobby in France argued that the colonies were vital not only as markets for French goods and as symbols of France's greatness, but also because they fulfilled France's *"mission civilisatrice"* – to bring the benefits of French culture and language to all corners of the globe.

There may have been Spaniards who had similar conceptions of their role in North Africa, but reality was very different. **Spain** showed no interest in developing the Sahara until the 1960s; in the north the Spanish saw themselves as conquerors, more than colonists. Its government there, described by one contemporary as a mixture of "battlefield, tavern and brothel", did much to provoke the Rif rebellions of the 1920s.

LYAUTEY AND "PACIFICATION"

France's first resident general in Morocco was **General Hubert Lyautey**, often held up as the ideal of French colonialism with his stated policy: "Do not offend a single tradition, do not change a single habit". Lyautey recommended respect for the terms of the Protectorate agreement, which placed strict limits on French interference in Moroccan affairs. He recognised the existence of a functioning Moroccan bureaucracy based on the sultan's court with which the French could cooperate – a hierarchy of officials, with diplomatic representation abroad, and with its own social institutions.

But there were other forces at work: French soldiers were busy unifying the country, ending tribal rebellion; in their wake came a system of roads and railways that opened the country to further colonial exploitation. For the first time in Moroccan history, the central government exerted permanent control over the mountain regions. The "**pacification**" of the country brought a flood of French settlers and administrators.

In France these developments were presented as echoing the history of the opening up of the American Wild West. Innumerable articles celebrated "the transformation taking place, the stupendous development of Casablanca port, the birth of new towns, the construction of roads and dams . . . The image of the virgin lands in Morocco is contrasted often with metropolitan France, wrapped up in its history and its routines. . . ".

Naturally, the interests of the natives were submerged in this rapid economic development, and the restrictions of the Protectorate agreement were increasingly ignored.

SPAIN AND THE REVOLT IN THE RIF

The early history of the **Spanish zone** was strikingly different. Before 1920 Spanish influence outside the main cities of Ceuta, Melilla and Tetouan was minimal. When the Spanish tried to extend their control into the Rif mountains of the interior, they ran into the fiercely independent Berber tribes of the region.

Normally, the various tribes remained divided, but faced with the Spanish troops they united under the leadership of **Abd el-Krim**, later to become a hero of the Moroccan nationalists. In the summer of 1921, he inflicted a series of crushing defeats on the Spanish army, culminating in the massacre of at least 13,000 soldiers at Anual. The scale of the defeat, at the hands of tribal fighters armed only with rifles, outraged the Spanish public and worried the French, who had their own Berber tribes to deal with in the Atlas mountains. As the war began to spread into the French zone, the two colonial powers combined to crush the rebellion. It took a combined force of around 360,000 colonial troops to do so.

It was the last of the great tribal rebellions. Abd el-Krim had fought for an independent **Rifian state**. An educated man, he had seen the potential wealth that could result from exploiting the mineral deposits of the Rif. After the rebellion was crushed, the route to Moroccan Independence changed from armed revolt to the evolving middle-class resistance to the colonial rulers.

NATIONALISM AND INDEPENDENCE

The French had hoped that by educating a middle-class elite they would find native allies in the task of binding Morocco permanently to France. It had the opposite effect. The educated classes of Rabat and Fes were the first to demand reforms from the French that would give greater rights to the Moroccans. When the government failed to respond, the demand for reforms escalated into demands for total independence.

Religion also played an important part in the development of a nationalist movement. France's first inkling of the depth of nationalist feeling came in 1930, when the colonial government tried to bring in a **Berber dahir** – a law setting up a separate legal system for the Berber areas. This was an obvious breach of the Protectorate agreement, which prevented the French from changing the Islamic nature of government. Popular agitation forced the French to back down.

It was a classic attempt to "divide and rule", and as the nationalists gained strength, the French resorted more and more to threatening to "unleash" the Berber hill tribes against the Arab city dwellers. They hoped that by spreading Christianity and setting up French schools in Berber areas, the tribes would become more "Europeanised", and, as such, useful allies against the Muslim Arabs.

Before World War II, the nationalists were weak and their demands aimed at reforming the existing system, not independence. After riots in 1937, the government was able to round up the entire executive committee of the small nationalist party. In 1943, the party took the name of **Istiqlal** (Independence); the call for complete separation from France grew more insistent. The loyal performance of Moroccan troops during the war had raised hopes of a fairer treatment for nationalist demands, but France continued to ignore Istiqlal, exiling its leaders and banning its publications. But during the postwar period, it was at last developing into a mass party – growing from 10,000 members in 1947 to 100,000 by 1951.

The developments of the 1950s, culminating in Moroccan Independence in 1956, bear a striking resemblance to the events in Algeria and Tunisia. The French first underestimated the strength of these Independence movements, tried then to resist them, and finally had to concede defeat. In Algeria and Tunisia, the Independence parties gained power and consolidated their positions once the French had left. In Morocco, on the other hand, Istiqlal was never uncontested after 1956 and the party soon began to fragment – becoming by the 1970s a marginal force in politics.

The decline and fall of Istiqlal was due mainly to the astute way in which Sultan (later King) **Mohammed V,** associated himself with the Independence movement. Despite threats from the French government, Mohammed became more and more outspoken in his support for independence, paralysing government operations by refusing to sign legislation. Serious rioting in 1951 persuaded the French to act: after a period of house arrest, the sultan was sent into exile in 1953.

This only increased his popularity. After a brief attempt to rule in alliance with **Thami el-Glaoui**, the Berber pasha of Marrakesh who saw the sultan's absence as an opportunity to expand his power base in the south, the French capitulated in 1955, allowing the sultan to return.

The government in Paris could see no way out of the spiralling violence of the nationalist guerillas and the counterviolence of the French settlers. Also, perhaps equally significant, they could not sustain a simultaneous defence of the three North African colonies – and economic interests dictated that they concentrate on holding Algeria. Finally, in 1956, Morocco was given full **Independence** by France and Spain.

On independence, Sultan Mohammed V changed his title to that of king – reflecting a move towards a modern constitutional monarchy.

MOHAMMED V

Unlike his ancestors the sultans, **Mohammed V** had inherited a united country with a well-developed industrial sector, an extensive system of irrigation and a network of roads and railways. But years of French administration had left little legacy of trained Moroccan administrators. Nor was there an obvious party base or bureaucracy for the king to operate within.

In 1956, Istiqlal party members held key posts in the first **government**. The regime instituted a series of reforms across the range of social issues. Schools and universities were created, a level of regional government was introduced and ambitious public works schemes launched. There were moves, also, against European "decadence", with a wholesale clean-up of Tangier, and against the unorthodox religious brotherhoods – both long-time targets of the Istiqlal.

Mohammed V, as leader of the Muslim faith in Morocco and the figurehead of independence, controlled huge support and influence in Morocco as a whole. In government, however, he did not perceive the Istiqlal as natural allies. The king bided his time, building links with the army – with the help of Crown Prince Hassan as commander-in-chief – and with the police.

Mohammed's influence upon the army would prove a decisive factor in the Moroccan state withstanding a series of **rebellions** against its authority. The most serious of these were in the Rif, in 1958–59, but there were challenges, too, in the Middle Atlas and Sahara. The king's standing and the army's efficiency stood the test. Crown Prince Hassan, meanwhile, as the army commander, helped to deflect internal pressures into renewed nationalism. The army began a quasi-siege in the south, exerting pressure on the Spanish to give up their claims to the port of Sidi Ifni.

In party politics, Mohammed's principal act was to lend his support to the **Mouvement Populaire** (MP), a moderate party set up to represent the Berbers, and for the king a useful counterweight to Istiqlal. In 1959, the strategy paid its first dividend. Istiqlal was seriously weakened by a split which hived off the more left-wing members into a separate party, the **Union Nationale des Forces Populaires** (UNFP) under Mehdi Ben Barka. There had always been a certain tension within Istiqlal between the moderates and those favouring a more radical policy, in association with the unions.

MODERN MOROCCO: HASSAN II (1961–)

The death of Mohammed V in 1961 led to the accession of **King Hassan II**, the current ruling monarch. Today, some thirty yearson, his reign represents perhaps the longest period of stability – albeit with a few uncertain periods – in the country's history.

In many respects the nation's **development since Independence** has been remarkable. The French had built an administrative capital in Rabat and a relatively sophisticated infrastructure in Casablanca and other economically useful zones, but most other regions were left without adequate roads, health and education facilities or other trappings of a modernising state. In the kingdom's northern and southern extremities, the Spanish colonial rule left even less on which the new state could base its policy of creating viable development. On Independence, there were scarcely any doctors or graduates in the Spanish zones.

Despite the poverty still apparent in so much of the country, it should be remembered that in less than three decades much has been done to bring the whole kingdom into the twentieth century. It is an achievement in the face of a huge **population explosion** which means there are now more than 24 million Moroccans. They form a predominantly youthful population and clamouring for the sort of jobs and education their parents and grandparents were routinely deprived.

VALUES AND TRADITIONAL ROLES

While the quest for modernisation has been one theme running through post-Independence Morocco, **traditional values** – as they are perceived by the Palace – are another important factor in understanding the contemporary kingdom.

In many respects Hassan is a very modern monarch, regularly pictured playing golf, horse-riding with Ronald Reagan or meeting fellow heads of state. As a power politician he has few peers. But he is also careful to maintain his status as a traditional ruler – one of the very few left in the Afro-Arab world. When in his flowing robes at a state occasion or religious festival, Hassan is the *Amir al-Muminin* (Commander of the Faithful), Morocco's **religious leader** as well as its temporal ruler.

This role is of great political significance as it adds to Hassan's prestige in the country and gives his monarchy the sort of deep-rooted legitimacy so lacking in other developing countries. Presiding over a complex system of traditional loyalties, ethnic and regional divisions, Hassan has used traditions based in the days of the Sultanate to underpin his modern monarchy – and so far it has served him well.

This is one reason why the Palace remains at the centre of the Moroccan political universe and why one word from the king carries more weight than all the debates in a parliamentary session, the decisions of his most powerful ministers or even international opinion.

Critics say that for the system to evolve Hassan must genuinely devolve power. Through the promotion of local authorities (*collectivités locales*) and a new strata of regionally based *associations* a form of devolution is underway. Hassan has even talked of dividing the country along federal lines, taking the German *laender* as a model. But it remains to be seen whether the king will ever give up genuine power and, barring a major upheaval, it may have to wait until Hassan finally departs the scene for a more effective, broad-based democracy to develop.

CONSTITUTION AND ELECTIONS

Even before independence, in a 1955 speech, Mohammed V had promised to set up "democratic institutions resulting from the holding of free elections". The country's first **constitution** was not ready until after his death, however. It was only in 1962, under Hassan II, that it was put to, and approved by, a popular referendum.

The constitution was drafted in such a way as to favour the pro-monarchy parties of the centre. In the **1963 elections** that followed, Mouvement Populaire was absorbed into a special alliance, the FDIC (*Front pour la Défense des Institutions Constitutionelles*), on a ticket giving total support to the king's policy. The FDIC, accordingly, won a majority of seats, though with a strong showing still by the Istiqlal, whose powerbase was (and remains) in Fes and the agricultural belt of the north, and by the UNFP, who held much support in the Souss and in Casablanca.

There followed regional elections, in which the FDIC won much more conclusive support – amid allegations of vote fixing. The socialist UNFP became increasingly radical and outspoken against the government, and in particular against the king, looking for inspiration to the republican models of Egypt and neighbouring Algeria. In 1963, a plot against Hassan's life was "discovered", leading to the arrest of UNFP leaders and the exile of **Ben Barka**. In one of the most notorious episodes of modern Moroccan (and French) history, Ben Barka's assassination in Paris highlighted the high risks opposition could entail. The UNFP was itself to split in subsequent years, with a large element going on to form the USFP (*Union Nationale des Forces Socialistes*), led by Abderrahim Bouabid, and still the largest left-wing opposition party.

After student riots in Casablanca in 1965, Hassan declared a **state of emergency** and took over the government directly. The relative ease with which Hassan was able to rule without democratic institutions underlined the weakness of the parties. The Istiqlal was never able to recover from the 1959 split, and as an opposition party its power dwindled even further. The UNFP and the unions were weakened by the arrests of their leaders and by internal divisions over policy. Despite the increasingly strident attacks on what it called a "feudal" and "paternalistic" regime, the UNFP never managed to develop a coherent platform from which it could oppose the king and build real popular support.

The weakness of the parties was further revealed in 1970, when Hassan announced a **new constitution**, to bring an end to emergency rule. Its terms gave the king greater control over parliament than in 1962. As a sign more of their weakness in the face of royal power than of any new-found unity, the UNFP and Istiqlal came together in a "national front" to oppose it.

The events of 1971–72, however, were to show the real nature of the threat to the monarchy. In July 1971, a group of soldiers led by an army general broke into the royal palace in Skhirat in an attempt to stage a **coup**; more than 100 people were killed, but in the confusion Hassan escaped. The following year another attempt was launched, as the king's private jet was attacked by fighters of the Moroccan air force. Again, he had a very narrow escape – his pilot was able to convince the attacking aircraft by radio that the king had already died. The former interior minister, General Oufkir, seems to have been behind the 1972 coup attempt and it was followed by a major shake-up in the armed forces. Oufkir died soon after; his family remain imprisoned despite promises that they would be released.

THE GREEN MARCH AND SAHARAN WAR

The king's real problem was to give a sense of destiny to the country, especially to the increasingly disillusioned Moroccan youth, for whom employment opportunities had conspicuously failed to appear. The game of the political parties had proved sterile. What Hassan needed was a cause similar to the struggle for Independence that had brought such prestige to his father.

That cause was provided in 1975, when the Spanish finally decided to pull out of their colony in the **Western Sahara**. In the 1950s Istiqlal had laid claim to the Sahara, as well as parts of Mauritania, Algeria and Mali, as part of its quest for a "greater Morocco". By 1975, Hassan had patched up the border dispute with Algeria and recognised the independent government in Mauritania; it turned out this was only a prelude to a more realistic design – Moroccan control of the Western Sahara.

The discovery of **phosphate reserves** in the Sahara during the 1960s brought about Spain's first real attempt to develop its Saharan colony. Before then it had been content merely to garrison the small coastal forts in Dakhla (then known as Villa Cisneros) and La Guera, with occasional forays into the interior to pacify the tribes. With increased investment in the region during the 1960s, the nomads began to settle in the newly created towns along the coast, particularly the new capital in Laayoune. As education became more widespread, the Spanish were confronted with the same problem the French had faced in Morocco thirty years earlier – the **rise of nationalism**.

Pressure began to mount on General Franco's government to decolonise one of the last colonies in Africa. In 1966, he promised the UN that Spain would hold a referendum "as soon as the country was ready for it". Economic interests kept Spain from fulfilling its promise, and in 1969 work began on opening the phosphate mines in Bou Craa. Meanwhile, the Saharans began to press the case for independence themselves. In 1973, they formed the *Frente Popular para la Liberación de Saguia el-Hamra y Rio de Oro*, or **Polisario**, which began guerrilla operations against the Spanish. Polisario gained in strength as Spain began to signal it would pull out of the Sahara and as the threat to Saharan independence from Morocco and Mauritania grew more obvious.

Spanish withdrawal in 1975 coincided with General Franco's final illness. King Hassan timed his move perfectly, sending some 350,000 Moroccan civilians southward on the "Green March" – *La Marche Verte* – to the Sahara. Spain could either go to war with Morocco by attacking the advancing Moroccans or take the easy way out and withdraw without holding the promised referendum. Hassan's bluff worked and in November 1975 a secret agreement was reached in Madrid to divide the Spanish Sahara between Morocco and Mauritania as soon as Spanish troops withdrew.

The popular unrest of the 1960s and the coup attempts of 1971–72 were forgotten under a wave of patriotism. Without shedding any blood, Morocco had "recaptured" part of its former empire. But the king had underestimated the native Sahrawis' determination to

fight for an independent Sahara, their Saharan Arab Democratic Republic (SADR). Nearly 40,000 of them fled the Moroccan advance, taking refuge in Mauritania and Algeria.

In an unprecedented move, Algeria ceded an area of its territory in the desolate *Hamada* region southeast of **Tindouf** to Polisario. Sahrawi refugees – and almost certainly some other displaced Sahelian nomads – settled in camps run by Polisario. According to the best estimates there were about 165,000 people living in five tented and increasingly unhygienic camps by 1989. Polisario, however, had managed to set up schools and hospitals in these most unpromising circumstances – winning many friends abroad in the process, much to Morocco's displeasure.

The camps also formed a base for the movement's government-in-exile, the SADR, and a launch pad a for a classic guerrilla campaign against Morocco and Mauritania, until Sahrawi pressure proved too much for Nouakchott and it withdrew from its alliance with Morocco in 1979. By the early 1980s Polisario had succeeded in closing the territory's mines and had pinned the Moroccan *Forces Armées Royales* (FAR) into an area around the capital, Laayoune, and Dakla in the south.

The early success of Polisario's campaign said much for the Sahrawi's prowess as desert guerrilla fighters – a fact Morocco's FAR battle-hardened officers now willingly concede, even if the intensely nationalist local press does not. It was equally due to the high level of military support offered by Algeria, which used Polisario as a stick with which to beat Morocco, its perceived rival for regional dominance.

ECONOMIC AND SOCIAL PROBLEMS

At home, the attention and budget demanded by the Saharan war compounded the problems of the economy. By 1981, an estimated 60 percent of the population were living below the poverty level, unemployment ran at approximately 20 percent (40 percent among the young) and perhaps 20 percent of the urban population lived in shantytowns, or *bidonvilles*.

Official figures for **unemployment** and even gross domestic product (GDP) are often very approximate. The young "student" operating as a guide in Fes or Marrakesh may well not appear in national employment figures. The shopkeeper he leads you to could also be in the informal economy, outside the tax net and compass of official data. And despite sometimes strenuous efforts to modernise and rationalise economic behaviour in the 1970s and 1980s, the "**informal sector**" remains enormous – perhaps equal in size to GDP.

Informal economic activity and the family network (for many still the only effective system of social services they know) disguise the real socio-economic position, which bears little relation to the official figures. They have also acted as a safety-valve for an increasingly hard-pressed population. The informal economy also finances some of Morocco's richest citizens, whose huge wealth – reflected in the opulent villas, discreetly hidden in the most upmarket quarters of major cities – may also not appear in official data.

Throughout much of the 1980s, the government, preoccupied by the war, seemed to neglect these pressing **social problems**; indeed, an austerity campaign to please its international creditors, including a wage freeze and a cut in subsidies for basic foodstuffs, appeared to increase the problems even more for the poor. In June 1981 the socialists of the UNFP mounted a challenge by organising a one-day **protest strike**, with sad and dramatic effects. In Casablanca, the demonstrations led to a running battle with the police and at least 100 deaths. Demonstrators were brought to trial and given stiff sentences, as were UNFP leader Abderrahim Bouabid and fourteen socialist members of parliament.

Local **elections** were held in June 1983, and appeared to be a resounding royalist victory, providing the government with a mandate to continue with its austerity measures. But the opposition parties, including Istiqlal, complained of electoral fraud, and the failure to proceed with parliamentary elections in October showed that all was not well. Using Article 19 of the constitution, Hassan assumed all executive and legislative power, **governing by decree** in the absence of an elected government. He managed to coax support from the parliamentary parties, including the socialists, by handing out ministerial posts to them, but kept the real power firmly in his own hands.

It was a brave move on his part. The government was facing bankruptcy and if the IMF was to reschedule Morocco's massive debts, the **austerity campaign** would have to become even harsher. Hassan announced a 12.5 percent cut in government expenditure and massive cuts in subsidies, and then stood alone to face the backlash.

Demonstrations against the cuts began in Marrakesh in early January 1984, and within a week had spread north to Nador and Al Hoceima. Later, **riots** broke out in Oudja and Tetouan. Clashes with the authorities were inevitable, and by the end of the month between 100 and 600 people had died. Hassan announced on television that further cuts in subsidies would be postponed, but at the same time he condemned extremists on the left and right as being the instigators of the riots and promised the restoration of order. A massive campaign of arrests followed. Over 700 rioters were put in prison and, over the following months, sentenced to long prison terms.

THE IMF AND EC

Despite the pessimistic assessments of many analysts, the 1984 bread riots were not repeated later in the decade and the 1980s will be remembered as a period of relative social peace, economic hard times and consolidations in the Western Sahara after several years of setbacks. In 1985 Hassan went to the polls once more and was rewarded with the re-election of a centrist-royalist coalition. After six months of suspension, **democratic government** had been restored.

Following the mid-1980s economic crisis – which was compounded by a build-up of international debt, contracted in the over-optimistic mood of the previous decade when Morocco hoped that rising phosphate prices (which then did not hold) would do for it what rising oil prices did for the OPEC states – relations with the **IMF** and the World Bank have been a constant factor in Moroccan life. The struggle to mobilise sufficient funds to finance essential imports and schemes in priority sectors like agriculture, power and water is ever present. Without international support, achieving sustainable economic growth might prove impossible – although Moroccans also place much store in their native entrepreneurial talents. In sectors ranging from vehicle assembly to marketing, Morocco has developed domestic industries to a relatively high level.

Substantial international support remains essential, however, and Morocco is dependent on financial assistance from its allies in Europe and the Gulf (whose rulers have been generous in their efforts to maintain a fellow Arab monarch in power).* This has forced Morocco to depart from its nineteenth-century image as "the China of the west" and seek closer ties with a wide range of countries. The need for solid economic relationships has been reflected in Hassan's so far unsuccessful application for Morocco to join the **European Community**.

In line with wider world trends, the IMF, World Bank and bilateral supporters have prompted moves towards liberalising the economy in the period since Morocco's first rescheduling in 1984. In 1989 Hassan called for all non-strategic public companies and holdings to be privatised. A **privatisation** minister was subsequently appointed, but like many other policies, privatisation has taken longer to put into effect than its supporters had hoped – and is unlikely to have radical consequences for several years.

Meanwhile, with the king firmly nailing his colours to the mast of economic liberalisation, new efforts were made to encourage foreign investment, in technologically advanced manufacturing industries as well as **textiles** and **tourism**. With 1992 and Europe's single market approaching, it is hoped that multinationals and smaller investors will bring new capital and jobs to the kingdom by setting up plants to serve the EC market from an attractive southern Mediterranean base. **Tangier** is to have a new **free zone** and others could follow. The success of such policies is seen as essential if Morocco is to meet the basic demands for work and better living conditions from its fast-growing population.

INTO THE 1990s: OPPOSITION DEMANDS

There are signs that as the 1990s opened, the opposition which had been quiet through much of the 1980s was preparing to reassert itself. In May 1990, parliament awoke from its slumbers and debated the first ever motion of censure

*At the time of writing, the Gulf crisis over Iraq's occupation of Kuwait is under way. Significantly, King Hassan has committed Moroccan troops to the defence of Saudi Arabia – the only Arab country, other than Egypt, to do so.

against a Moroccan government. The motion, criticising the government's economic management, failed, but pointed to changing attitudes.

Such changes, though, cannot be judged by parliamentary elections until the end of 1991 at the earliest. In late 1989 Hassan asked the people to vote for a postponement of elections for two years so as to allow a peace settlement in the Sahara to be achieved. They duly did so, with a massive majority, but according to some observers this may represent the last time the so-called **"Saharan consensus"** will work. As the conflict with Polisario draws to a close, it is clear that economic and social issues – and demands – will become even more pressing on the king's agenda.

If the opposition is to play a more significant role it faces substantial problems. The majority of younger Moroccans have little time for the **established parties** and trade unions, now led, for the most part, by old men. Abderrahim Bouabid still heads the **USFP**; veteran communist (and royalist) Ali Yata continues to lead the **PPS** (Parti du Progrès et du Socialisme); and ex-foreign affairs minister M'Hamed Boucetta remains at the helm of **Istiqlal**. Furthermore, the disappointing performance of Morocco's parliamentarians poses major questions over the future of the existing system.

As the experience of the 1984 rioters – many of whom are still in prison – shows, those who oppose from outside the existing channels can expect severe problems. In some respects Morocco is in advance of changes in other developing countries, with the development of a sometimes critical press and a system which has allowed many former political opponents and prisoners to be reintegrated into daily life and hold responsible jobs. Former student radicals, who may have been imprisoned and even tortured, now hold positions of responsibility in the local press, universities and even government departments.

However, for those who remain outside the system, life is extremely difficult. Criticism of the kingdom's **human rights** record is widespread and has led to direct conflict with organisations like Amnesty International. Human rights remain a highly sensitive issue, despite some advances. Groups like Amnesty have either chosen to target Morocco for campaigns intended to undermine the state – according to Hassan's most vocal supporters –

or provide essential support for oppressed opponents, depending on which side of a very polarised debate one takes.

While leftists made the running in the first three decades of independence, **radical Islam** may pose the greatest threat in the 1990s – especially given Hassan's status as Al-Amir Al-Muminin, which is directly threatened by the Islamists. The largest group, *Al-Adl Wal-Ihsaan* (Justice & Benevolence), is led by the often imprisoned Abdessalam Yassine, who would now be considered a moderate by Middle East standards. *Al-Adl Wal-Ihssan* members are no strangers to arrest and prison for charges including belonging to an illegal organisation. In the past there have been incidents involving very small, violent groups, notably Abdelkarim Mottai's Islamic Youth Society. But these are few and far between and their influence should not be overstated.

The victory of an Islamist party, the *Front Islamique du Salut* (FIS), in Algeria's first open elections – local polls held in June 1990 – underlined the potency of the mix of Islam and politics. The month before the FIS's win in Algeria, some 2000 Moroccan Islamists marched through Rabat in an unprecedented protest which could point to bigger things to come. But the local Islamic movement remains fragmented and well-controlled. Apparently, it can count on much less support in universities, the countryside and even big cities than the FIS and other North African fundamentalists. Thus, although radical Islam could pose a threat to the system, it is unlikely to take the form of events in Algeria or elsewhere. At least for now, the monarchy seems secure – albeit in a fast-changing political environment

NORTH AFRICAN UNITY MOVES

In August 1984 King Hassan made the surprise announcement of a **"Treaty of Union" with Libya**. To the outside world, it seemed a bizarre act for Morocco to associate itself with Colonel Gaddafi, the arch enemy of the United States – which had for a decade been providing aid and military assistance to Morocco.

But Hassan had correctly judged the mood of his people and, in a referendum, the treaty was endorsed almost unanimously. Moroccans were more than happy to show their appreciation for a leading role in moves towards **Maghreb unity**.

The Libyan union reflected an idea deeply rooted in Maghreb history, which gained considerable ground in the late 1980s as North African governments looked for new ways of developing their economies and, above all, new evidence to persuade their youthful populations that development was still achievable in a region which risks becoming marginalised in a rapidly changing world. Some kind of **economic co-operation and unity in North Africa** also became a vital concept, as Spain and Portugal entered the European Community, and the traditional North African economic ties – with France long the major trading partner – came under threat.

In June 1988, a **Maghreb Summit** was held in Algiers. Hassan attended with a Moroccan delegation – his first visit to Algeria for two decades – and there was an immediate result in the resumption of full diplomatic ties between Morocco and Algeria, and the opening of the Oujda–Maghnia border to all traffic.

A SAHARAN SETTLEMENT?

The summit, and resumption of relations, have also promoted hopes for a negotiated **settlement to the dispute in the Sahara**. With riots of their own at home in October 1988, which included an attack on Polisario's office in Algiers, the Algerian government has shown signs of wanting to pull out from the conflict. In any case, over the decade, Morocco had gradually been winning the war. Beginning in 1981, the FAR have built a series of heavily defended **desert walls** that exclude the Polisario from successively larger areas of the desert; by 1985, the phosphate mines were back in use and by 1987, the sixth wall had effectively blocked off Polisario from Mauritania and left only 15 percent of the land area outside Moroccan control. Meanwhile the government was making concerted attempts to win the approval of the Saharan residents, injecting vast sums into creating a model city and capital in **Laayoune**.

Under United Nations auspices, a **cease-fire** was agreed in the spring of 1989. Although it has been somewhat sporadically observed, there has subsequently been no major military conflict. And, under UN auspices, negotiations continue for a **referendum** to be held among the Sahrawis to determine their future state. King Hassan has met with a Polisario deputation in Marrakesh, and has promised that if the Sahrawis vote for independence, Morocco will be the first nation to open an embassy in Laayoune. Such talk reflects a new confidence in the situation, and a conviction, seemingly shared among all parties, that the conflict has burned itself out.

UMA

Running parallel to these developments was the wider rapprochement in the Maghreb. This culminated, in February 1989, at a meeting of the Algerian, Libyan, Mauritanian, Moroccan and Tunisian leaders in Marrakesh to form the long-awaited regional grouping, the **Arab Maghreb Union** – known by its evocative acronym *UMA*, from the French *Union de Maghreb Arabe* – but sounding like the Arabic word *'umma*, or community.

One of the main consequences of the UMA's formation has been an **opening of borders**, to the benefit of travellers, but especially for the millions of North Africans who now go either to shop for scarce goods in neighbouring countries (stimulating the *tradenda* black market throughout the region) or to visit family and friends. Colonisation and the drawing of boundaries divided many thousands of families; rather like the situation in postwar Europe, Maghrebis have often had to struggle to be reunited with their families. If the UMA does nothing else it will have brought North Africans together.

The UMA has raised high hopes – many of which have yet to be achieved. But by bringing countries together and providing forums to discuss economic, political and social co-operation it has radically improved the often troubled relations between North African states. Even so, some major problems remain to resolve, not least the intractable Saharan dispute. However, by mid-1990, with the UN Secretary General, Javier Perez de Cuellar turning his attention to finally organising a referendum acceptable to all sides, a solution seemed nearer than ever before.

After the war the government will have to offer the population higher living standards and greater opportunities than during the past decade when the Saharan consensus meant a large part of the population making sacrifices for the national good. At least the budgetary strains imposed by the Saharan campaign will be eased, pumping more resources into areas where they are needed. But much will depend on how the Saharan issue is resolved as to the direction Morocco takes in the next decade. And as many young Moroccans will say, much remains to be done to make life a little easier than it is at present.

CHRONOLOGY

10,000–5000 BC	**Capsian** and **Mouillian Man** spread across the Maghreb Neolithic cultures	**Rock carvings** in Oukaïmeden, Foum el Hassan and other less accessible sites
1100 BC	**Phoenician** settlements	Bronze Age. First trading port in **Lixus** (near Larache)
500 BC	**Carthaginians** take over Phoenician settlements and greatly expand them	Remains in Lixus, and in Rabat Archaeological Museum
146 BC	Fall of Carthage at end of the Third Punic War; Roman influence spreads into **Berber kingdoms** of Mauretania-Numidia	Bust of Juba II (Rabat)
27 BC	Direct **Roman** rule under Emperor Caligula	**Volubilis** developed as provincial capital; other minor sites in Lixus and Tangier. Mosaics in Tetouan and Rabat museums
253 AD	Roman legions withdrawn	
429	**Vandals** pass through	
535	**Byzantines** occupy Ceuta	

ISLAM

622	Muhammad and followers move from Mecca to Medina and start spread of Islam	
ca. 705	**Moussa Ibn Nasr** establishes Arab rule in north and pre-Sahara, and in 711 leads Berber invasion of Spain	

IDRISSID DYNASTY (788–923)

788	**Moulay Idriss** establishes first Moroccan Arab dynasty	Founding of Moulay Idriss and Fes
807	Moulay Idriss II (807–836)	**Fes** developed with Kairouan and Andalusian refugee quarters, and establishment of Kairaouine Mosque
10th–11th c.	Hilali tribes wreak havoc on Maghrebi infrastructure	

ALMORAVID DYNASTY (1062–1145)

1062	**Youssef bin Tachfine** establishes capital in Marrakesh; first great Berber dynasty	**Koubba** in Marrakesh is only surviving monument, except for walls and possibly a minaret in Tit (near El Jadida)
1090	Almoravid invasion of **Spain**	

ALMOHAD DYNASTY (1147–1248)

1120s	**Ibn Toumert** sets up a *ribat* in Tin Mal in the High Atlas	Ruined mosque of Tin Mal
1145–1147	**Abd el Moumen** takes first Fes and then Marrakesh	Extensive building of walls, gates and **minarets**, including the Koutoubia in Marrakesh
1195	**Yacoub el Mansour** (1184–99) extends rule to Spain, and east to Tripoli	New capital begun in **Rabat**: Hassan Tower, Oudaia Gate
1212	Defeat in Spain at Las Navas de Tolosa	

MERENID DYNASTY (1248–1465)

1250s	**Abou Youssef Yacoub** (1258–86) establishes effective power	*Zaouia* and mausoleum in **Chellah** (Rabat); new city (El Djedid) built in **Fes**
1330s–50s	**Abou el Hassan** (1331–51) and **Abou Inan** (1351–58), two of the most successful Merenids, extend rule briefly to Tunis	**Medersas** in Fes (Bou Inania, Attarin, etc.), Meknes and Salé
1415	**Portuguese** begin attacks on Moroccan coast, taking Ceuta and later other cities	**Portuguese** cistern in El Jadida; walls and remains in Azzemour, Asilah, and Safi

WATTASID DYNASTY (1465–1554)

1465	Wattasids – Merenid viziers – usurp power	**Chaouen** built and **Tetouan** founded again by refugees
1492	Fall of **Granada**, last Muslim kingdom in Spain; Jewish and Muslim refugees settle in Morocco over next 100 years or so	
15th–16th c.	**Marabouts** establish *zaouias*, controlling parts of the country	

SAADIAN DYNASTY (1554–1669)

1550s	**Mohammed esh Sheikh** (d. 1557) founds dynasty in Marrakesh	**Saadian Tombs** and Ben Youssef *medersa* (Marrakesh); pavilion extensions to Kairaouine Mosque (Fes)
1578	Battle of Three Kings leads to accession of **Ahmed el Mansour** (1578–1603), who goes on to conquer Timbuktu and the gold and slave routes to the south	**El Badi** palace (Marrakesh)
1627	Pirate **Republic of Bou Regreg** set up by Andalusian refugees	**Rabat** Medina

ALAOUITE DYNASTY (1669–)

1672–1727	**Moulay Ismail** imposes the Alaouite dynasty on Morocco	New imperial capital in **Meknes** (Ismail's mausoleum, etc.); **Kasbahs** and **forts** built; **palaces** in Tangier and Rabat
18th c.	**Sidi Mohammed** (1757–90)	Ismail and his successors rebuild **grand mosques**, etc., especially in **Marrakesh,** where many later Alaouites make their capital – many of the city's **pavilions** and **gardens** date from the early eighteenth century
	Moulay Suleiman (1792–1822)	Final burst of **palace** building – El Badi (Marrakesh), Palais Jamai (Fes)
1912	**Treaty of Fes** brings into being French and Spanish **"Protectorates" (1912–56)**	European **Villes Nouvelles** built outside the Moroccan Medinas; **"Mauresque"** architecture developed for administrative buildings (best in Casa, Rabat, Tetouan and Sidi Ifni]
1921–27	Riffian revolt under Abd el Krim	
1920s–1956	**T'Hami el Glaoui** becomes Pasha of Marrakesh and rules south for French	**Glaoui palaces** in Telouet and Marrakesh; **Kasbah** fortresses throughout the south
1943	Nationalist **Istiqlal** party formed in Fes	
1956	**Independence**	
1961	Accession of **Hassan II**	New royal **palaces** in all major cities – most recently and spectacularly in Agadir
1975	**Green March into Western Sahara**	
1989–90	North African unity moves	**Hassan II Mosque** in Casablanca

ISLAM IN MOROCCO

It's difficult to get any grasp of Morocco, and even more so of Moroccan history, without first knowing something of Islam. What follows is a very basic background: some theory, some history and an idea of Morocco's place in the modern Islamic world. For more depth on each of these subjects, see the book listings in the section that follows.

BEGINNINGS: PRACTICE AND BELIEF

Islam was a new religion born of the wreckage of the Greco-Roman world around the south of the Mediterranean. Its founder, a merchant named **Muhammad*** from the wealthy city of Mecca (now in Saudi Arabia), was chosen as God's Prophet: in about 609 AD, he began to hear divine messages which he transcribed directly into the **Koran**, Islam's Bible. This was the same God worshipped by Jews and Christians — Jesus is one of the minor prophets in Islam — but Muslims claim He had been misunderstood by both earlier religions.

The distinctive feature of this new faith was directness — a reaction to the increasing complexity of established religions and an obvious attraction. In Islam there is no intermediary between man and God in the form of an institutionalised priesthood or complicated liturgy; and worship, in the form of prayer, is a direct and personal communication with God. Believers face five essential requirements, the so-called **"Pillars of faith"**: prayer five times daily; the pilgrimage (*hadj*) to Mecca; the Ramadan fast; a religious levy; and, most fundamental of all, the acceptance that "There is no God but God and Muhammad is His Prophet".

---

*"Muhammad" is the standard spelling today of the Prophet's name — and a more accurate transcription from the Arabic. In Morocco there is some cause for confusion in that the name of the former king, *Mohammed* V, is still spelled that way on maps and street signs and in most Western histories.

THE PILLARS OF FAITH

The Pillars of Faith are still central to Muslim life, articulating and informing daily existence. Ritual **prayers** are the most visible. Bearing in mind that the Islamic day begins at sunset, the five daily times are sunset, after dark, dawn, noon and afternoon. Prayers can be performed anywhere, but preferably in a mosque, or in Arabic, a *djemaa*. In the past, and even today in some places, a *muezzin* would climb his minaret each time and summon the faithful.

Nowadays, the call is likely to be less frequent, and prerecorded; even so, this most distinctive of Islamic sounds has a beauty all its own, especially when neighbouring *muezzins* are audible simultaneously. Their message is simplicity itself: "God is most great (*Allah Akhbar*). I testify that there is no God but Allah. I testify that Muhammad is His Prophet. Come to prayer, come to security. God is great". Another phrase is added in the morning: "Prayer is better than sleep".

Prayers are preceded by ritual washing and are spoken with the feet bare. Facing Mecca (the direction indicated in a mosque by the *mihrab*), the worshipper recites the Fatina, the first chapter of the Koran: "Praise be to God, Lord of the worlds, the Compassionate, the Merciful, King of the Day of Judgment. Thee do we worship and Thine aid do we seek. Guide us on the straight path, the path of those on whom Thou hast bestowed Thy Grace, not the path of those who incur Thine anger nor of those who go astray". The same words are then repeated twice in the prostrate position, with some interjections of *Allah Akhbar*. It is a highly ritualised procedure, the prostrate position symbolic of the worshipper's role as servant (Islam literally means "obedience"), and the sight of thousands of people going through the same motions simultaneously in a mosque is a powerful one. On Islam's holy day, Friday, all believers are expected to attend prayers in their local grand mosque. Here the whole community comes together in worship led by an *imam*, who may also deliver the *khutba*, or sermon.

Ramadan is the name of the ninth month in the lunar Islamic calendar, the month in which the Koran was revealed to Muhammad. For the whole of the month, believers must obey a rigorous fast (the custom was originally modelled on Jewish and Christian practice), forsaking all forms of consumption between sunrise and sundown; this includes food, drink, cigarettes and any form of sexual contact. Only a few categories of people are exempted: travellers, children, pregnant women and warriors engaged in a *jihad*, or holy war. Given the climates in which many Muslims live, the fast is a formidable undertaking, but in practice it becomes a time of intense celebration.

The pilgrimage, or **hadj**, to Mecca is an annual event, with millions flocking to Muhammad's birthplace from all over the world. Here they go through several days of rituals, the central one being a sevenfold circumambulation of the Kaba, before kissing a black stone set in its wall. Islam requires that all believers go on a *hadj* as often as is practically possible, but for the poor it may well be a once-in-a-lifetime occasion, and is sometimes replaced by a series of visits to lesser, local shrines – in Morocco, for instance, to Fes and Moulay Idriss.

Based on these central articles, the new Islamic faith proved to be inspirational. Muhammad's own Arab nation was soon converted, and the Arabs then proceeded to carry their religion far and wide in an extraordinarily rapid territorial expansion. Many peoples of the Middle East and North Africa, who for centuries had only grudgingly accepted Roman paganism or Christianity, embraced Islam almost immediately.

DEVELOPMENT IN MOROCCO

Islam made a particularly spectacular arrival in Morocco. **Oqba Ibn Nafi**, the crusading general who had already expelled the Byzantines from Tunisia, marked his subjugation of the far west by riding fully armed into the waves of the Atlantic. "O God", he is said to have exclaimed, "I call you to witness that there is no ford here. If there was, I would cross it".

This compulsory appreciation of Morocco's remoteness was prophetic in a way, because over the succeeding centuries Moroccan Islam was to acquire and retain a highly distinctive character. Where mainstream Islamic history is concerned, its development has been relatively straightforward – it was virtually untouched, for instance, by the Sunni-Shia conflict that

split the Muslim world – but the country's unusual geographical and social circumstances have conspired to tip the balance away from official orthodoxy.

Orthodoxy, by its very nature, has to be an urban-based tradition. Learned men – lawyers, Koranic scholars and others – could only congregate in the cities where, gathered together and known collectively as the *ulema*, they regulated the faith. In Islam, this included both law and education. Teaching was at first based entirely in the mosques; later, it was conducted through a system of colleges, or *medersas*, in which students would live while studying at the often adjoining mosque. In most parts of the Islamic world, this very learned and sophisticated urban hierarchy was dominant. But Morocco also developed a powerful tradition of **popular religion**, first manifested in the eighth-century Kharijite rebellion – which effectively divided the country into separate Berber kingdoms – and endures to this day in the mountains and countryside.

MARABOUTS

There are three main strands of this popular religion, all of them deriving from the worship of saints. Everywhere in Morocco, as well as elsewhere in North Africa, the countryside is dotted with small domed **marabouts**: the tombs of holy men, which became centres of worship and pilgrimage. This elevation of individuals goes against strict Islamic teaching, but probably derives from the Berbers' pre-Islamic tendency to focus worship around individual holy men. At its simplest, local level, these saint cults attracted the loyalty of the Moroccan villages and the more remote regions.

More prosperous cults would also endow educational institutions attached to the *marabout*, known as **zaouias**, which provided an alternative to the official education given in urban *medersas*. These inevitably posed a threat to the authority of the urban hierarchy, and as rural cults extended their influence, some became so popular that they endowed their saints with genealogies traced back to the Prophet. The title accorded to these men and their descendents was *shereef*, and many grew into strong political forces. The classic example in Morocco is the tomb of Moulay Idriss, in the eighth century just a local *marabout*, but eventually, as the base of the Idrissid clan, a centre of enormous influence that reached far beyond its rural origins.

Loyalty to a particular family – religiously sanctified, but essentially political – was at the centre of the shereefian movements. In the third strand of popular devotion, the focus was more narrowly religious. Again, the origins lay in small, localised cults of individuals, but these were individuals worshipped for their magical and mystical powers. Taken up and developed by subsequent followers, their rituals became the focal point of **brotherhoods** of initiates.

THE AISSAOUA

Perhaps the most famous Moroccan brotherhood is that of Sidi Mohammed Bin Aissa. Born in Souss in the fifteenth century, he travelled in northern Morocco before settling down as a teacher in Meknes and founding a *zaouia*. His powers of mystical healing became famous there, and he provoked enough official suspicion to be exiled briefly to the desert – where he again revealed his exceptional powers by proving himself immune to scorpions, snakes, live flames and other hostile manifestations. His followers tried to achieve the same state of grace. Six hundred were said to have attained perfection – and during the saint's lifetime, *zaouias* devoted to his teachings were founded in Figuig and elsewhere in the Maghreb.

Bound by its practice of a common source of ritual, the Aissaoua brotherhood made itself notorious with displays of eating scorpions, walking on hot coals, and other ecstatic customs designed to bring union with God. It was perhaps the most flamboyant of these brotherhoods, but most at any rate used some kind of dancing or music, and indeed continued to do so well into this century. The more extreme and fanatical of these rites are now outlawed, though the attainment of trance is still an important part of the *moussems*, or festivals, of the various confraternities.

TOWARD CRISIS

With all its different forms, Islam permeated every aspect of the country's pre-twentieth-century life. Unlike Christianity, at least Protestant Christianity, which to some extent has accepted the separation of church and state, Islam sees no such distinction. **Civil law** was provided by the *sharia*, the religious law contained in the Koran, and **intellectual life** by the *msids* (Koranic primary schools where the 6200 verses were learned by heart) and by the great medieval mosque universities, of which the Kairaouine in Fes (together with the Zitoura in Tunis and the Al Azhar in Cairo) was the most important in the Arab world.

The religious basis of Arab study and intellectual life did not prevent its scholars and scientists from producing work that was hundreds of years ahead of contemporary "Dark Age" Europe. The remains of a monumental water clock in Fes and the work of the historian Ibn Khaldun, are just two Moroccan examples. Arab work in developing and transmitting Greco-Roman culture was also vital to the whole development of the European Renaissance. By this time, however, the Islamic world – and isolated Morocco in particular – was beginning to move away from the West. The crusades had been one enduring influence towards division. Another was the Islamic authorities themselves, increasingly suspicious (like the Western church) of any challenge and actively discouraging of innovation. At first it did not matter in political terms that Islamic culture became static. But by the end of the eighteenth century, Europe was ready to take advantage. Napoleon's expedition to Egypt in 1798 marked the beginning of a century in which virtually every Islamic country came under the control of a **European power**.

Islam cannot, of course, be held solely responsible for the Muslim world's material decline. But because it influences every part of its believers' lives, and because East-West rivalry had always been viewed in primarily religious terms, the nineteenth and twentieth centuries saw something of a **crisis in religious confidence**. Why had Islam's former power now passed to infidel foreigners?

REACTIONS

Reactions and answers veered between two extremes. There were those who felt that Islam should try to incorporate some of the West's materialism; on the other side, there were movements holding that Islam should turn its back on the West, purify itself of all corrupt additions and thus rediscover its former power. While they were colonies of European powers, however, Muslim nations had little chance of putting any such ideas into effective practice. These could only emerge in the form of cooperation with, or rebellion against, the ruling power. But the postwar era of **decolonisation**, and the simultaneous acquisition through oil of relative economic independence, brought the Islamic world suddenly face to face with the question of its own spiritual identity. How should it deal with Western values and influence, now that it could afford – both politically and economically – almost total rejection? A return to the totality of Islam – **fundamentalism** – is a conscious choice of one consistent spiritual identity, one that is deeply embedded in the consciousness of a culture already unusually aware of tradition. It is also a rejection of the West and its colonial and exploitative values. Traditional Islam, at least in some interpretations, offers a positivist brand of freedom that is clearly opposed to the negative freedoms of Western materialism. The most vehement Islamic fundamentalists are not passive reactionaries thinking of the past, but young radicals – often students – eager to assert their new-found independence. Islam has in a sense become the "anti-imperialist" religion – think, for example, of the Black Muslim movement in America – and there is frequent confusion and even conflict between secular, left-wing ideals and more purely religious ones.

MODERN MOROCCO

There are two basic reasons why only a few Islamic countries have embraced a rigidly traditional or fundamentalist stance. The first is an ethical one: however undesirable Western materialism may appear, the rejection of all Western values involves rejecting also what the West sees as the "benefits" of development. Perhaps it is begging the question in strictly Islamic terms to say that the emancipation of women, for example, is a "benefit". But the leaders of many countries feel that such steps are both desirable and reconcilable with a more liberal brand of Islam, which will retain its place in the national identity. The other argument against militant Islam is a more pragmatic, economic one. Morocco is only one of many countries which would suffer severe economic hardship if they cut themselves off from the West: they have to tread a narrow line that allows them to maintain good relations both with the West and with the Islamic world.

ISLAM AND THE STATE

In Morocco today, Islam is the official state religion, and King Hassan's secular status is interwoven with his role as "Commander of the Faithful". Internationally, too, he plays a leading role. Meetings of the Islamic Conference Organisation are frequently held in Morocco and, in one of the most unlikely exchanges, students from Tashkent in the USSR have come to study at Fes University. For all these indications of Islamic solidarity, though, **state policy** remains distinctly moderate – sometimes in the face of extremist pressure.

RURAL RELIGION

Not surprisingly, all of this has had more effect on urban than on rural life – a difference accentuated by the gap between them that has always existed in Morocco. Polarisation in religious attitudes is far greater in the **cities**, where there is inevitably tension between those for and against secularisation. Islamic fundamentalism offers a convenient scapegoat to many Western-oriented governments in the Muslim world, but if its actual strength is sometimes open to doubt, its existence is probably not.

Away from the cities, religious attitudes have changed less over the past two generations. Religious brotherhoods such as the Aïssaoua have declined since the beginning of the century, when they were still very powerful, and the influence of mystics generally has fallen. As the official histories put it, popular credulity in Morocco provided an ideal setting for charlatans as well as saviours, and much of this has now passed. All the same, the rhythms of **rural life** still revolve around local *marabouts*, and the annual *moussems*, or festivals-cum-pilgrimages, are still vital and impressive displays.

WILDLIFE

Few countries in the Mediterranean region can match the variety and quality of the wildlife habitats to be found in Morocco. Whether you are an expert botanist, a dedicated birdwatcher or simply a visitor with an interest in a totally different environment, the wildlife experience of your travels should be extremely rewarding.

HABITATS

There are three main **vegetation zones** which can be distinguished as you travel through the country.

● The most northerly and westerly zone – the **Mediterranean** and **northern Atlantic coastal strips** – is typical of the European Med region, encompassing semi-arid pastoral lands of olive groves and cultivated fields.

● Further inland lie the barren **Rif mountains** (the home of *kif* or marijuana plants) and the more fertile **Middle Atlas range**, where the montane flora is dominated by cedar forest which, despite its reduction in more recent times, provides a unique mosaic of forest and grassland. The **High Atlas**, beyond, is more arid but has its own montane flora.

● Finally, there is the most southerly zone of the desert fringe or **Sahel**, a harsh environment characterised by pebbly *hammada*,

tussock grass, the occasional acacia tree and a number of sand dunes, or *ergs*.

These zones provide a wide variety of **habitat types**, from coastal cliffs, sand dunes and estuarine marshlands to subalpine forests and grasslands, to the semi-arid and true desert areas of the South. The **climate** is similarly diverse, being warm and humid along the coastal zones, relatively cooler at altitude within the Atlas ranges and distinctly hotter and drier south of the High Atlas, where midday temperatures often exceed 40°C during the summer months. Not surprisingly, the plant and animal life in Morocco is accordingly parochial, species distributions being closely related to the habitat and climate types to which they are specifically adapted.

Many of these habitats are currently under threat from land reclamation, tourist development and the inevitable process of **desertification**, and the resulting habitat loss is endangering the existence of several of the more sensitive species of plants and animals to be found in Morocco. Human persecution of wildlife, however, is limited, as the tribes are largely disarmed and hunting is more the preserve of French tourists.

On the positive side, the *International Committee for Bird Preservation* (I.C.B.P.) and the *Eaux de Forêt* of the Moroccan Agriculture Ministry have been involved in the designation of protected status to several **wetland sites** along the Atlantic coast; at Merdja Zerga and Lac de Sidi Bourhaba, education centres have been set up with resident wardens and interpretive materials. The government has also done some good work on the problems of erosion and desertification and has implemented extensive and impressive schemes of **aforestation and reclamation**.

BIRDS

In addition to a unique range of **resident bird species**, distributed throughout the country on the basis of vegetation and climatic zonation, the periods of late March/April and September/October provide the additional sight of vast **bird migrations**.

Large numbers of birds which have overwintered south of the Sahara migrate northwards in the spring to breed in Europe, completing their return passage through

Morocco in the autumn. Similarly, some of the more familiar northern European species choose Morocco for their overwintering grounds to avoid the harshness of our winter clime. These movements can form a dramatic spectacle in the skies, dense flocks of birds moving in procession through bottleneck areas such as Tangier and Ceuta where sea crossings are at their shortest.

RESIDENT SPECIES

The **resident species** can be subdivided on the basis of their preferred habitat type:

● **Coastal/marine species**. These include the familiar moorhen and less-familiar **crested coot**, an incongruous bird which, when breeding, resembles its northern European relation but with an additional pair of bright red knobs on either side of its white facial shield. Other species include the diminutive **little ringed plover** and **rock dove**.

● **South of the High Atlas**. Amongst these are some of the true desert specialities, such as the **sandgrouse** (spotted, crowned, pin-tailed and black-bellied varieties), **stone curlew**, **cream-coloured courser** and **Houbara bustard** – the latter standing over two feet in height. Other well represented groups include **wheatears** (4 varieties), **larks** (7 varieties) and **finches**, **buntings**, **warblers**, **corvids** (crow family), **jays**, **magpies**, **choughs** and **ravens**, **tits** (primarily blue, great and coal) and **owls** (barn, eagle, tawny and little). Although many of these species can be found in northern Europe, subtle variations in colour and pattern can be misleading and a closer look is often worthwhile.

Raptors (birds of prey) provide a mouth-watering roll call of resident species, including **red-** and **black-shouldered kite**, **long-legged buzzard**, **Bonelli's**, **golden and tawny eagles**, **Barbary**, **lanner and pere-grine falcons** and more familiar **kestrel**.

MIGRANT SPECIES

Migrant species can be subdivided into three categories: summer visitors, winter visitors and passage migrants.

● **Summer visitors**. The number of species visiting Morocco during the summer months may be low but includes some particularly interesting varieties. Amongst the **marine/coastal types** are the **manx shearwater**, **Eleonora's falcon** and **bald ibis** – in one of its few remaining breeding colonies in the world.

The **mountain species** include the small **Egyptian vulture** and several of the **Hirundines** (swallows and martins) and their close relatives, the **swifts**, such as **little swift**, **red-rumped swallow** and the more familiar **house martin**.

A particularly colourful addition at this time of year in the **Sahel regions** is the **blue-cheeked bee-eater**, a vibrant blend of red, yellow, blue and green, unmistakeable if seen close up.

● **Winter visitors.** The list of winter visitors is more extensive but composed primarily of the marine or coastal/estuarine varieties. The most common of the truly marine (*pelagic*) flocks include **cory's shearwater**, **storm petrel**, **gannet**, **razorbill** and **puffin**. These are often found congregated on the sea surface, along with any combination of **skuas** (great, arctic and pomarine varieties), **terns** (predominantly sandwich) and **gulls** (including black-headed, mediterranean, little, herring and the rarer Audouin's) flying overhead.

A variety of coastal/estuarine species also arrive during this period, forming large mixed flocks of **grebes** (great-crested, little and black-necked), **avocet**, **cattle egret**, **spoon-bill**, **greater flamingo**, and wildfowl such as **shelduck**, **wigeon**, **teal**, **pintail**, **shoveler**, **tufted duck**, **pochard** and **coot**.

Migrant **birds of prey** during the winter months include the **common buzzard** (actually a rarity in Morocco), **dashing merlin** and both **marsh** and **hen harriers**.

● **Passage Migrants**. There are many birds which simply pass through Morocco en route to other areas, and are thus known as passage migrants. Well-represented groups include **petrels** (5 varieties) and **terns** (6 varieties) along coastal areas, and **herons** (4 varieties), **bitterns**, **cranes**, **white and black stork** and **crake** (spotted, little, Baillon's and corncrake) in the marshland/estuarine habitats.

Further inland, flocks of multicoloured **roller**, **bee-eater** and **hoopoe** mix with various **larks**, **wagtails** and **warblers** (13 varieties), forming large "windfall" flocks when climatic conditions worsen abruptly. Individual species of note include the aptly-named

black-winged stilt, an elegant black and white wader, with long, vibrant red legs, often found amongst the disused saltpans; and the nocturnal **nightjars** (both common and red-necked), which are most easily seen by the reflection of their eyes in the headlamps of passing cars.

Birds of prey can also form dense passage flocks, often mixed and including large numbers of **black kite**, **short-toed eagle** and **honey buzzard**. Over open water spaces, the majestic **osprey** may be seen demonstrating its mastery of the art of fishing.

● **"Vagrant" Species**. Finally, Morocco has its share of occasional or "vagrant" species, so classified on the unusual or rare nature of their appearances. These include such exotic varieties as **glossy ibis**, **pale-chanting goshawk**, **arabian bustard** and **lappet-faced vulture**. Inevitably, they provide few, if any, opportunities for viewing.

FLORA

In the light of its climatic harshness and unreliable rains, the flora of Morocco is remarkably diverse. Plant species have adapted strategies to cope with the Moroccan climate, becoming either specifically adapted to one particular part of the environment (a habitat type), or evolving multiple structural and/or biochemical means of surviving the more demanding seasons. Others have adopted the proverbial "ostrich" philosophy of burying their heads (or rather their seeds in this case) in the sand and waiting for climatic conditions to become favourable – often an extremely patient process!

The type of flowers that you see will obviously depend entirely on where and when you decide to visit. Some parts of the country have very short flowering seasons because of high temperatures or lack of available water, but generally the best times of year for flowering plants are either just before or just after the main temperature extremes of the North African summer.

The best time to visit is **spring** (late March to mid-May), when most flowers are in bloom. Typical spring flowers include purple **barbary nut iris**, deep blue **germander** and the aromatic **claret thyme**, all of which frequent the slopes of the Atlas ranges. Amongst the

woodland flora at this time of year are the red **pheasant's eye**, pink **virburnum**, violet **calamint** and purple **campanula**, which form a resplendent carpet beneath the cedar forests. By late spring, huge tracts of the High Atlas slopes are aglow with the golden hues of **broom** and secluded amongst the lowland cereal crops, splashes of magenta reveal the presence of **wild gladioli**.

By **midsummer** the climate is at its most extreme and the main concern of plants is to avoid desiccation in the hot, arid conditions. Two areas of exception to these conditions are the **Atlantic coastal zones**, where sea mists produce a slightly more humid environment, and the upper reaches of the **Atlas ranges** which remain cool and moist at altitude throughout the year. Spring comes later in these loftier places and one can find many of the more familiar garden rock plants, such as the **saxifrages** and **anemones** in flower well into late July and August.

Once the hottest part of the summer is past (September onwards), then a second, **autumn** bloom begins with later varieties such as **cyclamens** and **autumn crocus**.

HABITAT VARIETIES

The range of plants you are likely to encounter is similarly influenced by specific habitats:

● **Seashores**. These include a variety of sand-tolerant species, with their adaptations for coping with water-loss, such as **sea holly** and **sea stocks**. The dune areas contrast starkly with the Salicornia-dominated salt marshes – monotonous landscapes broken only by the occasional dead **tamarisk** tree.

● **Arable land.** Often dominated by cereal crops – particularly in the more humid Atlantic and Mediterranean coastal belts – or **olive and eucalyptus groves**, which extend over large areas. The general lack of use of herbicides allows the co-existence of many **"wild flowers"**, especially in the fallow hay meadows which are ablaze with the colours of **wild poppy**, **ox-eye daisy**, **muscali** (borage) and various yellow composites.

● **Lowland Hills.** These form a fascinating mosaic of dense, shrubby species, known as *maquis*, lower-lying, more grazed areas, known as *garigue*, and more open areas with abundant aromatic herbs and shrubs.

Maquis vegetation is dominated by **cistaceae** (rockroses) and **euphorbia**, such as **argan**. The lower-lying *garique* is more typically composed of aromatic herbs such as **rosemary, thyme** and **golden milfoil**. Amongst these shrubs, within the more open areas, you may find an abundance of other species such as **anemones, grape hyacinths** and **orchids**.

The orchids are particularly outstanding, including several of the *Ophrys* group, who use the strategy of insect imitation to entice pollination and as such have an intricate arrangement of flowers.

● **Mountain slopes**. Flowering later in the year, the slopes of the **Atlas ranges** are dominated by the blue-mauve **pitch trefoil** and golden drifts of **broom**. As you travel south through the Middle Atlas, the verdant **ash, oak, atlantic cedar** and **juniper forest** dominates the landscape. Watered by the depressions that sweep across from the Atlantic, these slopes form a luxurious spectacle, ablaze with colour in spring.

Amongst the glades beneath the **giant cedars** of the Middle Atlas, a unique flora may be found, dominated by the vibrant **pink peony**. Other plants which form this spectacular carpet include **geranium, anchusa, pink verburnum, saffron mulleins, mauve cupidanes, violet calamint, purple campanula,** the diminutive **scarlet dianthus** and a wealth of **golden composites** and **orchids**.

Further south, the **Toubkal National Park** boasts its own varieties and spring bloom; the thyme and thorny caper are interspersed with the blue-mauve **pit trefoil, pink convulvulus,** the silver-blue and pinks of everlasting flowers of **cupidane** and **phagnalon** and golden spreads of **broom**. At the highest altitudes, the limestone Atlas slopes form a bleak environment, either covered by winter snows or scorched by the summer sun. However, some species are capable of surviving even under these conditions, the most conspicuous of these being the widespread purple tussocks of the **hedgehog broom**.

● **Steppeland**. South of the Atlas, temperatures rise sharply and the effect on flora is dramatic; the extensive cedar forests and their multicoloured carpets are replaced by sparse grass plains where the horizon is broken only by the occasional stunted **holm oak, juniper**

or **acacia**. Commonly known as wattle trees, the acacia were introduced into North Africa from Australia and their large yellow flowers add a welcome splash of colour to this barren landscape. One of the few crop plants grown in this area is the **date palm**, which is particularly resistant to drought. The steppeland is characterised by the presence of **esparto grass**, which exudes toxins to prevent the growth of competing species. These halfa grass plains are only broken by the flowering of **broom** in May. Within rocky outcrops, this spring bloom can become a mini-explosion of colour, blending the hues of **cistus** and **chrysanthemum** with the pink of **rockrose**, yellow of **milfoil** and mauve of **rosemary**.

● **Desert Fringe (*hammada*)**. Even the desert areas provide short-lived blooms of colour during the infrequent spring showers; dwarf varieties such as pink **asphodels**, yellow **daisies** and mauve **statice** thrive briefly whilst conditions are favourable. Under the flat stones of the *hammada*, colonies of **lichens** and microscopic algae eke out an existance; their shade-tolerance and ability to obtain sufficient water from the occasional condensation which takes place under these stones allows them to survive in this harshest of environs. No matter how inhospitable the environment or extreme the climate appear, somewhere, and somehow, there are plants surviving – if you take time to look for them.

AMPHIBIANS

There are very few remaining amphibians in Morocco – relics of a bygone, more fertile era, now restricted to scarce watery havens. They are more obvious by sound than sight, forming a resonant chorus during the night and early morning. One of the more common varieties is the **green frog**, typically immersed up to its eyes in water, releasing the odd giveaway croak. Another widespread individual, most abundant in the regions around Marrakesh, is the **western marsh frog**.

The toads are represented by the **Berber toad**, another nocturnal baritone, and the **Mauritanian toad** whose large size and characteristic yellow and brown-spotted colouration make it quite unmistakeable.

Some Moroccan amphibians are capable of survival at surprisingly **high altitudes**. The

painted frog is a common participant in the chorus that emanates from the *oueds* (river-beds) of the High Atlas, whilst the wide-ranging whistle of the North African race of the **green toad**, famed for its ability to change its colour with the surrounding environment, can be heard at altitudes in excess of 2000m.

REPTILES

Reptiles are far more widespread in their distribution than their amphibious cousins. Their range extends from the Mediterranean coastal strip – where the few remaining **tortoises** (sadly depleted through "craft items" sold to the tourist trade) are to be seen – to the *hammada* itself.

The forested slopes of the Middle Atlas are frequented by the **blue and green eyed lizard** and the **chameleon**; the former uses its size and agility to capture its prey, whereas the latter relies on the more subtle strategy of colour co-ordination, stealth and a quicksilver tongue.

Several species have adapted to the specific environment of the stony **walls** that form the towns and villages. The **Spanish wall lizard** is a common basker on domestic walls, as is the **Moorish gecko**.

Further south, the drier, scrub-covered slopes form an ideal habitat for two of Morocco's largest **snakes**. The **horseshoe snake** (which can exceed 2m in length) and **Montpelier snake** hunt by day, feeding on birds and rats. Also found in this harsh environment are the **Atlas agama** and **fringe-toed lizard**.

Finally, there are the **desert "specialists"**, such as the **Algerian sand lizard** and **Berber skink**. The skinks make a fascinating spectacle; commonly known as "sand fish", they inhabit the *ergs* and appear to "swim" through the sand, where their yellow-brown colouration provides the perfect camouflage. Of numerous species of lizard that live in the *hammada*, the more obvious include the many colours and varieties of the **spiny-tailed lizard** (*dhub* in Arabic), an omnivore feeding on a mixed diet of insects, fruit and young shoots. The one really poisonous species is the **horned viper**, only half a metre in length, which spends the days buried just below the surface of the sand and feeds by night on jerboas and lizards.

MAMMALS

Larger animal life in Morocco is dominated by the large nomadic herds of goats, sheep and camel which use the most inaccessible and barren patches of wilderness as seasonal grazing areas.

One of the most impressive of the wild mammals, however, is the **Barbary ape** – in fact not a true ape but a Macaque monkey. These frequent the cedar forests south of Azrou in the Middle Atlas and can be seen on the ground foraging for food in the glades. Other inhabitants of the cedar forest include **wild boar** and **red fox**.

A speciality of the Oued Souss, outside Agadir, is the **common otter**; this is now a rare species in Morocco and can only be seen with considerable patience and some fortune.

The majority of the smaller mammals in Morocco live south of the Atlas ranges in the *hammada*, where the ever present problem of water conservation plays a major role in the lifestyle of its inhabitants. Larger herbivores include the **Edmi gazelle** and the smaller, and rarer, **Addax antelope,** which graze the thorn bushes and dried grasses to obtain their moisture.

Many of the desert varieties reduce the problems of body temperature regulation by adopting a nocturnal lifestyle. Typical exponents of this strategy are the **desert hedge-hog** and numerous small rodents such as the **jerboa**. A common predator of the jerboa is the **fennec fox**, whose characteristic large ears are used for both directional hearing (invaluable as a nocturnal hunter) and heat radiation to aid body cooling.

INSECTS

Insect life is widespread throughout Morocco, its variety of form occupying unique, overlapping roles.

BUTTERFLIES

Most colourful are the butterflies, of which over a hundred species have been recorded, predominantly in the Middle and High Atlas ranges. The most obvious, which can be seen from April onwards, are generally the largest and most colourful, such as the brilliant sulphur **Cleopatra**, **large tortoiseshell** and **cardinal**. Located on the grassy slopes within the ranges are less conspicuous varieties: the **hermit**, **Spanish marbled white**, **fritillaries**, **graylings**, **hairstreaks** and **blues** – such as the small **larquin's** and **false baton**.

Later in the year, from about June onwards, the glades and woodland edges of the Middle Atlas cedar forests provide the perfect habitat for **dark green fritillaries**, while in the higher flowery fields, at altitudes of up to 2000m, **knapweed fritillaries**, **large grizzled** and **Barbary skippers** abound. Particularly attractive is the **Amanda's blue**, found at altitudes in excess of 600m through till midsummer if nectar remains available.

On the rocky slopes of Toubkal National Park, south of Marrakesh, the **Morrocan copper butterfly** may be seen flitting through the thyme. In the higher Atlas gorges (1700m or more), the **desert orange tip** is more prevalent, being found on its larval food plant, the thorny caper.

OTHER INSECTS

Other common groups include **grasshoppers**, **crickets** and **locusts**. In the High Atlas, **praying mantis** may be seen, such as **eremiaphila**, whose brown colouration provides excellent camouflage.

Beetles are another common group, though they tend to avoid the heat of the day, remaining in their burrows and emerging at night to feed. The **darkling beetles** are particularly abundant and voracious scavengers.

Finally there are **arachnids**, of which there are three major groups in Morocco – scorpions, spiders and camel spiders. **Scorpions** are nocturnal, hiding under suitable covered depressions during the day such as rocks and boulders (or rucksacks and shoes!). Some of the six or so species which may be found in Morocco are poisonous but most are harmless and unlikely to sting unless provoked. The **camel spiders** (or wind-scorpions) are unique. They lack a poisonous tail but possess huge jaws with which they catch their main source of prey, scorpions.

Spiders are rare in Morocco, only being found in large numbers within the Atlas ranges. Here, it is possible to see several small species of **tarantula** (not the hairy South American variety!) and the white **orb-web spider** *Argiope lobata*, whose colouration acts as a disruptive pattern against pale backgrounds.

NORTH–SOUTH: MAIN SITES OF INTEREST

MEDITERRANEAN COASTLINE

Morocco's Med runs from the Spanish enclave of Ceuta east to the Algerian border at Marsa Ben Mehidi and includes both freshwater and saline sites.

● **NADOR** (see p.111) makes a convenient centre from which to explore – not an exciting place, but with accommodation and access to good local sites.

● Just east of Nador one of the most accessible sites can be found at **KARIET ARKMANE** (daily bus; see p.112). Passing through the village, with its single mosque (and minaret) on your left-hand side, a path leads out past the salt pans and pumping station (right-hand side) to an **extensive area of salt marsh**.

The area is covered by the fleshy-stemmed **marsh glasswort** or *salicornia*: a characteristic "salt plant" or *halophyte*, it can survive the saline conditions through the use of glands which excrete the salt. The **insect life** of the salt marsh is abundant, including damselflies, brightly-coloured grasshoppers and various ants and sand spiders. The **birds** are even more impressive, with reasonable views of black-winged stilt, greater flamingo, coot, great-crested grebe and various gulls and terns wheeling overhead.

● Further along the coast, on the same bus route, lies the popular beach resort of **RAS-EL-MAR** (see p.112). Beyond the summer sprawl of tents, lean-tos and sunshades, miles of unspoilt **dunes** run virtually undisturbed to the Algerian border.

A gentle stroll along this system demonstrates the means by which plants invade sand dunes: this sequential colonisation is known as **"succession"** – one plant community gradually ceding to the next as a result of its own alteration of the environment. Typical early colonisers are marram grass and sea couch, which are eventually ousted by sea holly and sea spurge and finally by large, "woodier" species such as pistacihu, juniper and cistus *sp*. Whole sequences can be seen occurring over time along the beach.

The area attracts a variety of interesting **sea birds** as well, including two internationally rare species: **Audouin's gull** (thought to breed on the adjacent offshore Chafarinas Islands) and **slender-billed curlew**. Other more familiar birds include dunlin, Kentish plover and oystercatcher.

● Even further along the coast (and requiring personal transport) is the freshwater lagoon system which marks the mouth of the **OUED MOULOUYA**. The lagoons here are separated from the sea by a remarkable series of sand spits, no more than 50m across. The lagoons attract a variety of anglers (some human!) and the **birdlife** in particular is outstanding.

Secluded amongst the reedbeds, it is possible to locate grey heron, white stork and little egret whilst the water's surface is constantly patrolled by the ever-alert black terns and kingfishers. Other varieties which you should manage to spot, wading in the shallows, are redshank, spotted redshank (in summer) and black-tailed godwit.

THE RIF MOUNTAINS

The most northerly of the Atlas ranges, the Rif is easily accessed from Taza, although personal transport – a car or a preparedness for committed hiking – is really a necessity for proper exploration.

● The most rewarding site (and well away from the rather dodgy *kif*-growing areas of the range) is the **DJEBEL TAZZEKA NATIONAL PARK** (1980m), just south of Taza where the Rif merges with the Middle Atlas. The Tazzeka's slopes are covered in cork oak, the prime commercial crop of this area, interspersed with areas of mixed woodland containing holm oak, the pink-flowered cistus and the more familiar bracken. Woodland glades are frequented by a myriad of **butterflies** from late May/early June onwards; common varieties include knapweed, ark green fritillaries and Barbary skippers.

The forest floor also provides an ideal habitat for **birds** such as the multicoloured hoopoe, with its diagnostic crest, and the trees abound with the calls of wood pigeon, nuthatch, short-toed treecreeper and various titmice.

The roadside telegraph lines also provide attractive hunting perches for such brightly-coloured inhabitants as rollers and shrikes, both woodchat and great grey, who swoop on passing insects and lizards with almost gluttonous frequency.

ATLANTIC COAST: NORTH

The northern section of the Atlantic coast offers two of the few designated wildlife sites to be found in Morocco: Lac de Sidi Bourhaba and Medrja Zerga, both of which have recently achieved protected status. Further south, Oualidia is also a superb habitat.

● **MERDJA ZERGA** (or MERDJA LERGA) is a large wetland area adjacent to the coastal town of MOULAY BOUSSELHAM (see p.76). The surrounding areas are lined by dwarf palm and the giant succulent agave, and the open barren spaces are used by the large nomadic herds of sheep, cattle and goats as seasonal grazing areas.

The large area of the site offers a wide diversity of habitats and thus guarantees good **bird** numbers at all times of year but does reduce accessibility, so that views are often distant and indistinct. The site has large numbers of waders including little ringed plover, black-winged stilt and black-tailed godwit, but it is the **gulls and terns** that roost on the central islands which are worthy of the closest inspection, as amongst the flocks of lesser black-backed gull and black tern, it is possible to find rarer species such as **Caspian tern**. Sunset is a time for vigilance as the site also boasts several pairs of North African **marsh owl** which hunt over the adjacent grassland after dusk.

● **LAC DE SIDI BOURHABA** lies further south near Mehdiya Plage (see p.200), about 25km north of Rabat. It is a large freshwater lake, divided by a central causeway, with an *Centre d' Education* on the eastern bank and excellent camping facilities. The best viewing points lie on the causeway, where the ever-present damselflies and dragonflies provide a spectacular display of flight and colour. Marsh frogs and Berber toad make their vocal contribution from the sanctuary of the northern reedbeds.

The **birds** of Sidi Bourhaba are particularly outstanding; the **reedbeds** throng with the calls of flitting reed and melodious warbler and the open stretches of water hold good numbers of crested coot (in spring) and marbled teal (in autumn and winter). It is, however, for its **birds of prey** that the site is best known. Circling almost constantly overhead are marsh harriers, with their characteristic low quartering flight, and these are joined on occasion by the smaller and whiter black-shouldered kite with its diagnostic black shoulders (and red eyes if you get close enough!). This is another sunset site for African marsh owl.

● **OUALIDIA** (see p.239) is a tiny, coastal resort, with a delightful mix of ragged, rocky coast, sands, lagoon, marshes and salt pans. This variety of habitat can bring in vast numbers of flamingoes, avocets, stilts, godwits and many small waders, besides numerous countryside species. Golden oriole and hoopoe are recorded.

ATLANTIC COAST: ESSAOUIRA

● **ESSAOUIRA** (see p.242) is perhaps Morocco's most attractive coastal town – and it offers a dramatic and unique wildlife spectacle at sunset. Walking south from the town, the beach soon degenerates into a dune system with a sparse covering of marram grass, and after about two kilometres' walk the half-submerged remains of an old royal pavilion provide an excellent viewing platform for the offshore Ile de Mogador. Root around in the sand, too, and you're almost certain to come across dung beetles about their business.

The nearby river course (*oued*) has many **waders** and **egrets** and occasional rarities such as gull-billed tern and Mediterranean gull. However, it is the walk back to the town which provides views of one of Morocco's most dramatic birds – **Eleanora's falcon**.

Walking back in the half-light, it is possible to see as many as two or three dozen of these magnificent birds, gliding in low over the sea from their only non-Mediterranean breeding site on Ile de Mogador, to hawk for insects at dusk. The falcons are summer visitors to Morocco, staying between May and October before making the long return journey south to Madagascar for the winter.

ATLANTIC COAST: AGADIR

● The resort city of **AGADIR** (see p.361) offers two sites of wildlife interest, one literally on its doorstep at Oued Souss.

● **OUED SOUSS** lies 14km south of Agadir, 2km from the P8 road to Tiznit, signposted to "*Hotel Pyramid/Hotel Hacienda*" and lying adjacent to the Royal Palace. The northern banks of the river have good views of a variety of waders and wildfowl including greater flamingo, spoonbill, ruddy shelduck, avocet,

greenshank and curlew. The surrounding **scrubby banks** also have large numbers of migrant warblers and Barbary partridge.

● Less accessible but superbly rewarding for the more intrepid is the protected reserve of **OUED MASSA** (see p.370), near the chalet-campsite *complexe* of Sidi Rabat. The track from Massa crosses 8–9km of very sandy trails which can be problematic but the journey and the *complexe* are well worth the effort. The *complexe* offers its own wildlife highlights – a local population of Mauritanian toad in the shower block at night and a café terrace from which the more fortunate can observe overhead flocks of bald ibis. Beyond, it is a short walk to the large **inland lagoon**.

The habitat mix over this designated reserve is as good as any in Morocco; the **sandbars** are visited in the early morning by flocks of sandgrouse (black-bellied and spotted varieties); the ponds and **reedbed** margins conceal various waders such as black-tailed godwit, turnstone, dunlin, snipe and little crake; the deeper open waters provide feeding grounds for greater flamingo, spoonbill, white stork and black-winged stilt, and overhead the skies are patrolled by marsh harrier and osprey.

The surrounding **scrubby areas** hold black-headed bush shrike and a variety of nocturnal mammals such as Egyptian mongoose, cape hare and jackal.

THE LOWLANDS AND THE CITIES

Even the larger cities in Morocco have a wildlife interest which should not be overlooked – despite the myriad of alternative attractions.

● **FES**. The evening roost at Fes (see p.144) makes a spectacular sight. The performance begins with the frenzied activities of the resident starlings (including spotless starlings) but these are soon eclipsed by the overhead passage of dozens of little egret, gracefully returning to their roost sites in the Middle Atlas and environs. The skies soon appear to swarm with the appearance of literally thousands of alpine swift, wheeling on crescent-shaped wings in search of insects. To complete the spectacle, it is worth casting an eye along the rooftop silhouette as the light begins to fade. With a little perseverance it is possible to locate the characteristic body profiles of **white stork** on their rooftop nests along the perimeter walls which line Fes el Djedid.

● **MARRAKESH** (see p.253.) A respite from the tourist hustle can be achieved by retreating to the peaceful haven of one of the city's many gardens, such as the **Jardin Marjorelle**. Despite its proximity to the Medina (a mere ten-minute taxi ride), the Marjorelle has an amazing feeling of tranquillity, an atmosphere enhanced by the verdant groves of bamboo, dwarf palm amd agave, and the various lily-covered pools provide essential drinking and bathing water for the resident turtle doves and house buntings. The lasting sound of the gardens, however, is the constant chatter of the common bulbuls, flitting amongst the upper leaves of the date palms.

SOUTH OF AZROU: CEDAR FORESTS

● The **cedar forests** which lie to the south of **AZROU** (see p.184) are a unique habitat in Morocco, whose verdant atmosphere contrasts starkly with the surrounding aridity and barrenness of the Middle Atlas range. The cedars, mixed with ash, oak and juniper, provide shelter for a vibrant carpet; pink peonies, scarlet dianthus, blue germander, golden compositae and a variety of orchids combine to form a spectacular floral display. This habitat makes an ideal haven for numerous animals, including the green-eyed lizard and chameleon. A host of **butterflies** also frequent the glades from April onwards – among them the brilliant sulphur cleopatra, large tortoiseshell and cardinal.

One of the wildlife highlights of a visit to Morocco must be a glimpse of the infamous **Barbary apes**. The troupes can be found feeding along the forest margins but are reasonably shy and any excessive intrusion is likely to be met with a retreat to the lofty sanctuary of the treetops. The **birdlife** of the cedar forests is almost as exhilarating; possibilities include the two species of Moroccan woodpecker, the pied and red great spotted and green and yellow Levaillant's varieties. Other overhead highlights include the splendid **booted eagle**, often seen soaring on outstretched wings in an attempt to evade the unwanted attentions of resident ravens.

● Further south in the forests lies the large lake of **AGUELMAME AZIGZA** (see p.187), secluded amongst the cedar trees. The wooded slopes throng with insect life, including the brilliant red and black grasshopper (*Eugaster spinulosus*) and the beautiful small Amanda's blue

butterfly. The forest provides nesting and feeding areas for a variety of woodland finches and titmice, including the elusive hawfinch with its diagnostic heavy bill, and the waters of the lake have large numbers of diving duck (mainly grebes and coot) and marbled teal during the harsher seasons of autumn and winter.

MIDDLE ATLAS FRESHWATER LAKES

● In the lowland plains to the south of Fes are a series of freshwater lakes. Closest and most easily accessible is **LAC DOUYIÈT** (about 20km out on the Meknes road). Douyiet retains shallow waters throughout the summer drought, although the surrounding asparagus and smilax vegetation looks distinctly spartan by the end of August. These waters provide one of the few reliable feeding grounds for **waders** and **wildfowl** at this time of year and act as a magnet for a variety of species. Where the water is deep enough, mixed flocks of ruddy shelduck, gadwall and cape shoveler can be seen dabbling for food. Around the lake edge, the waders take precedence – particularly abundant varieties being black-winged stilt, green sandpiper, redshank and **avocet** (one of Morocco's most elegant birds). The skies are frequently crossed by flocks of collared pratincole, whose darting flight is spectacular, and quartering overhead, one can often locate the characteristic form of **Montagu's harrier**, ever alert for any unsuspecting duck on the lake below.

● Further south lies **DAYET AAOUA** (8km south of Imouzzer on the Fes–Azrou road; see p.183). The lake has a good mosaic of habitat types and supports a wide variety of animals. Large numbers of green frog take refuge from the summer drought within the lake's protective shallows, and a multitude of dragonflies and damselflies patrol the water's surface in their resplendent red, blues and greens.

The Aaoua **birdlife** is similarly diverse; the deeper waters provide food for large flocks of grebes (great-crested, black-necked and little varieties) and the large numbers of coot are swelled in the spring with the addition of the magnificent **crested coot**, with its spectacular bright red knobs on either side of its white facial shield, when in breeding condition. The reedbeds provide cover for grey heron and cattle egret and ring out with the sound of hidden reed and fan-tailed warbler. The water's edge is constantly traced by passage grey and yellow wagtails and in the summer the skies are filled with migrating swallows and martins – the sand martin especially. This abundance of life proves an irresistible draw for resident and migrant birds of prey and Aaoua offers regular sightings of the acrobatic **red kite** circling overhead.

HIGH ATLAS PASSES

The mountain passes of the High Atlas offer outstanding hiking country and a unique flora and fauna to match.

● Particularly rewarding areas include the lofty reaches of the **TOUBKAL NATIONAL PARK** (see p.291), south of Marrakesh. For a brief exploration, **OUKAÏMEDEN** or **IMLIL** would make convenient centres, with a complete spectrum of walks available, suitable for even the most reluctant rambler.

The spring bloom on the lower Atlas slopes comprises aromatic thyme and thorny caper, interspersed with golden spreads of broom. Higher slopes are covered by more resilient species, such as the purple tussocks of hedgehog broom. The passes ring to the chorus of the painted frog and the North African race of the green toad during their spring breeding seasons, while some species of reptile have become adapted to the specific environment of the stony walls that form the towns and villages of the Atlas mountains, such as the **Moorish gecko**. **Butterflies** which brave these heights include the Moroccan copper and desert orange tip. Other inhabitants range from the almost-invisible praying mantis to the scampering ground squirrel and rare elephant shrew.

Birds to be found amongst the sparse vegetation include Moussier's redstart and the crimson-winged finch, which prefers the grassy slopes where it feeds in flocks; both birds are unique to North African mountains. The rocky outcrops provide shelter for both chough and alpine chough, the mountain rivers are frequented by dippers who swim underwater in their search for food. Overhead, darting Lanner falcon or flocks of brilliantly coloured bee-eater add to the feeling of abundance which permeates the slopes of the High Atlas. In the cultivated valleys look out for the red-backed stork and the magpie which, uniquely, has a sky-blue eye mark. Other High Atlas birds, as

the snow melts, include shore larks, rock bunting, alpine accentor, redstarts and black redstarts. The wet meadows produce a fantastic spread of hooped-petticoat daffodils, *romulea* and other bulbs.

● **THE TODRA GORGE** (see p.341), most easily reached from TINERHIR on the Ouarzazate–Er Rachidia road, also offers excellent walking and wildlife opportunities. The **riverbeds** house colonies of marsh frog and green toad and the rocky slopes provide shelter for small numbers of ground squirrel. The **scrubby areas** ring to the calls of common bulbul and the **rocky outcrops** provide occasional glimpses of black wheatear, blue rock thrush and rock dove. There are good numbers of pale crag martin wheeling overhead and soaring above the gorge crest and , it is also possible to observe the pair of **Bonelli's eagles** which nest in the gorge.

THE DESERT FRINGE

The **desert fringe** – or *hammada* – provides an austere environment, but the dry, sunny conditions are ideal for cold-blooded **reptiles** and are frequented by Montpelier snake, Atlas agama and fringe-toed lizard. The **grassy plains** provide food for small herds of Edmi gazelle and Addax antelope and shelter for a variety of specialist bird species such as cream-coloured courser, red-rumped wheatear and thick-billed lark. Predatory lanner falcon and long-legged buzzard patrol the skies and the rare and elusive **Houbara bustard** makes an occasional appearance.

● Particularly abundant and accessible areas of *hammada* extend south from **BOULMALNE** (see p.337) beyond the tracks that lead to Tagdilt.

THE SAND DESERT

The sandy (or "true") desert completes the habitat spectrum and provides yet another unique environment, with associated collection of flora and fauna. The inaccessibility of many sites adds to their intrigue and the intrepid explorer is well rewarded with sightings of some marvellous adaptations to these least hospitable living conditions.

Plant life is limited because of the intense scarcity of water; the only survivors include the lichens and algae which can take up sufficient water from the condensation of dew which forms on the undersurfaces of rocks and stones, although even the desert has an all-too-brief **spring bloom** when the rains do come – dominated by pink asphodels and mauve statice.

The desert is an ideal environment for **reptiles**, however, including the Algerian sand lizard and Berber skink, and typical **desert mammals** – more often located by their giveaway tracks in the morning sand than by nocturnal sightings – include the jerboa, desert hedgehog and Fennec fox. The **birdlife** of the sand desert is often centred around the watery havens offered by the **oases**, where specialist strategists such as fulvous babbler, blue-cheeked bee eater, the rare desert sparrow and even Arabian bustard may be found.

● **MERZOUGA** (see p.317) makes an excellent centre for the exploration of such sandy desert areas; the hotel accommodation is as unique and fascinating as the surrounding wildlife – highly recommended!

FIELD GUIDES

There are few books written specifically about Moroccan wildlife, but field guides covering Mediterranean Europe sometimes extend coverage to North Africa – and are in any case reasonably practicable for the area. Pete Raine's *Mediterranean Wildlife: The Rough Guide* (Harrap Columbus, £7.95) includes a detailed chapter on Morocco, as well as very readable rundowns of species.

MOROCCO SPECIFIC GUIDES
P and F Bergier *A Birdwatcher's Guide to Morocco* (Prion Press, 1990). Excellent practical guide.
Let's Look at Southern Morocco (*Ornitholidays*, c/o 1/3 Victoria Drive, Bognor Regis, Sussex). Useful briefing sheet published by the birdwatchers' holiday company.

GENERAL FIELD GUIDES

● **Plants**
Oleg Polunin and Anthony Huxley *Flowers of the Mediterranean* (OUP, £9.95). Covers the flowers of the whole region; invariably selective but good photographs and easily portable.

● **Birds**
Heinzel, Fitter and Parslow *The Birds of Britain and Europe with North Africa and the Middle East* (Collins, £7.95). One of the best standard works.
Foreign Birdwatching Reports and Information Service. A brilliant scheme, run by Steve Whitehouse (5 Stenway Close, Blasckpole, Worcester WR4 PXL; ☎0905/54541). Amateur birdwatchers send in reports of their foreign trips, which are then available for a nominal sum to everyone. Invaluable for serious birders – write off for a catalogue.

● **Butterflies**
Lionel Higgins and Norman Riley *A Field Guide to the Butterflies of Britain and Europe* (Collins, £8.95). The standard field guide, reliable and beautifully illustrated, but perhaps too detailed for casual naturalists.

● **Mammals**
Theodor Haltenorth and Helmut Diller *A Field Guide to the Mammals of Africa* (Collins, £9.95), of which the vast majority naturally refers to species found south of the Sahara.

BOOKSHOPS
Most booksellers stock field guides. If you have problems, *The Natural History Book Service* (2 Wills Road, Totnes, Devon; ☎0803/865913) has a comprehensive, efficient **mail order service**, and produces a mouthwatering catalogue.

SPANA

SPANA – the Society for the Protection of Animals in North Africa – is a fifty-year-old charity, whose core work involves providing welfare to working and domestic animals. They have centres in Tangier and Fes (the original "Animal Fondouk") and representatives elsewhere. Increasingly, they are also expanding their activities to education on wildlife issues – a recent venture was to publish a Moroccan bird identification book in Arabic, French and English. If you are interested in making contact (and, better still, a much-needed donation), they can be reached through the British Moroccan Society, 15 Buckingham Gate, London SW1E 6LB (☎071/828 0977).

MUSIC

Wherever you go in Morocco you are likely to hear music. It is the basic expression of the country's folk culture – indeed to many of the illiterate countrypeople it is the sole expression – and in its traditions it covers the whole history of the country. There are long and ancient pieces designed for participation by the entire communities of Berber villages; songs and instrumental music brought by the Arabs from the east and Andalusian Spain; and in more recent times, the struggle for independence, too, found celebration in song.

Although the most common musical phenomenon that you will hear is the *muezzin* calling the faithful to prayer, amplified from minarets, most Moroccan music is performed for the sake of entertainment rather than religion. At every weekly *souk*, or market, you will find a band playing in a patch of shade, or a stall blasting out cassettes they have on sale. In the evenings many cafés feature musicians, particularly during the long nights of Ramadan. Television also plays its part, with two weekly programmes devoted to music, and the radio stations, too, broadcast a variety of sounds.

BERBER MUSIC

Berber music is quite distinct from Arab influenced forms in its rhythms, tunings and sounds. It is an extremely ancient tradition, probably long predating even the arrival of Arabs in Morocco, and has been passed on orally from generation to generation. There are three main categories: village music, ritual music and the music of professional musicians.

Village music is always essentially a collective performance. Men and women of the entire village will assemble on festive occasions to dance and sing together. The best known dances are the **ahouach**, in the western High Atlas, and the **ahidus**, performed by Chleuh Berbers in the eastern High Atlas. In each, drums (*bendirs*) and flutes are the only instruments used. The dance begins with a chanted prayer, to which the dancers respond in chorus, the men and women gathered in a large ring in the open air, around the musicians. The *ahouach* is normally performed at night in the patio of the Kasbah; the dance is so complicated that the musicians meet to prepare for it in a group called a *laamt* set up specially for the purpose. In the *bumzdi*, a variation on the *ahouach*, one or more soloists perform a series of poetic improvisations.

Ritual music is rarely absent from any rites connected with the agricultural calendar – such as *moussems* (see *Basics*) – or major events in the life of individuals, such as marriage. It may also be called upon to help deal with *djinn*, or evil spirits, or to encourage rainfall. Flutes and drums are usually the sole instruments, along with much rhythmic hand-clapping, although a community may have engaged professional musicians for certain events.

The **professional musicians**, or *imdyazn*, of the Atlas mountains are itinerant, travelling during the summer, usually in groups of four. The leader of the group is called the *amydaz* or poet. He presents his poems, which are usually improvised and give news of national or world affairs, in the village square. The poet may be accompanied by one or two members of the group on drums and *rabab*, a single-string fiddle and by a fourth player, known as the *bou oughanim*. This latter is the reed player, throwing out melodies on a double clarinet, and also acts as the group's clown. *Imdyazn* are found in many weekly *souks* in the Atlas.

Chleuh professional musicians are known as *rwais*. A *rwai* worthy of the name will not only know all the music for any particular celebration, but also have its own repetoire of songs – again commenting on current events – and be able to improvise. A *rwai* is made up of a single-stringed *rabab*, one or two *lotars* and sometimes a *naquous*. Once the *lotar* has been tuned to the *rabab*, a piece begins with an improvisation on the *rabab* before the main tune, and quickens in pace as it builds towards an abrupt end. One of the most famous *rwai* performers is **Lhaj Aomar Ouahrouch**, who has made numerous records and cassettes.

ANDALOUS MUSIC

Morocco's classical music comes from the **Arab-Andalusian tradition** and is to be found, with variations, throughout the Maghreb. It is thought to have been invented, around a thousand years ago, in Córdoba, in then Moorish Spain, by an outstanding musician called Ziryab from Baghdad. He founded the classical suite called *nawba.*

The original 24 **nawba** were directly linked with the hours in the day; only four full and seven fragmentary *nawba* have been preserved in the Moroccan tradition. Complete *nawbat,* which can last several hours, are rarely performed in one sitting. Pieces are usually chosen according to the hour of the day or the circumstances. The movements are made up of poems, or *can'a,* set to music, with instrumental introductions. The lyrics usually deal with love, though they are sometimes religious, glorifying the Prophet and divine laws.

When the Arabs were driven out of Spain, which they had known as Al Andalus, the different musical schools were dispersed over the Maghreb. The Valencian school continued in Fes, the Granadan in Tetouan and Chaouen. All have to an extent been influenced by Berber folk music. In fact many groups in northern Morocco play both Andalous music and Berber folk. The three most important **orchestras** are that of Fes, led by Abdelkrim Rais; that of Tetouan, led by Abdesadak Chekara; and that of Rabat, led by Loukili; Chaouen has also produced many great Andalusian musicians.

Orchestras are made up of *rababs* (fiddles), *ouds* (eleven-string fretless lutes), *kamanjehs* (violins) of various pitches, *derbukas* (pottery drums), *tars* and sometimes a *kanum* (zither).

FASSI MUSIC

Modern *Fassi*, the music of Fes, is a mixture of Andalous music and *chaabi* (see overpage). It takes the melodies of Andalous music and puts them into popular song form. The leading exponent of this style is L'Hadj l'Hocine Toulali (or Toulali for short). He is also one of the leaders of the Andalous orchestra of Fes.

RELIGIOUS MUSIC

As well as the chants of the Koran, which are improvised on a uniform beat, the *adhan*, or call to prayer, and the songs about the life of the prophet Muhammad, there is a whole other range of prayers and ceremonies belonging to the Sufi **brotherhoods**, or *tarikas*, in which music is seen as a means of getting closer to Allah. These include the music used in processions to the tombs of saints during *moussems*.

The aim is for those present to reach a state of mystic ecstasy. In a private, nocturnal ceremony called the *hadra*, the Sufi brothers attain a trance by chanting the name of Allah (*dker*) or dancing in a ring holding hands. The songs and music are irregular in rhythm, quickening towards an abrupt end. Some brotherhoods play for alms in households that want to gain the favour of their patron saint.

GNAOUA

The **Gnaouas** are a religious brotherhood (see "Islam in Morocco") whose members are descendants of slaves brought from the Sudan by the Arabs. They have devotees all over Morocco, though the strongest concentrations are in the south, particularly in Marrakesh.

The brotherhood claim spiritual descent from Bilal, an Ethiopian who was the Prophet's first *muezzin.* Most Gnaoua ceremonies, or *deiceba,* are held to placate spirits, good and evil, which have inhabited a person or place. These rites have their origins in sub-Saharan Africa, and an African influence is evident in the music itself. The principal instrument, the *gimbri,* is a long-necked flute almost identical to instruments found in Mali, Senegal and elsewhere in West Africa, among the Wolof and Mandinka peoples. The other characteristic sound of Gnaoua music is the *garagab,* a pair of metal castanets, which beat out a trance-like rhythm.

Nowadays, Gnaoua music can be heard at festivals and in the entertainment squares in Marrakesh and elsewhere.

THE ARAB TRADITION

The effect of constant wars and changes of ruler has been to prevent **Middle Eastern Arab music** from having as strong an influence as might be expected. One kind of song with close Arab links is the classical *malhum,* which is accompanied on lute, *kamanjeh*, and percussion, always obeying the rules of the Eastern mode system, or *makam*.

The songs are classified according to the structure and metre of their verses, which are reflected in the music. One of the most famous contributors to this genre was the seventeenth-century poet Abdelaziz al Maghrawi. More recently, radio and television have brought *asri*, in which classical and popular, Eastern and European influences are mixed within the basic framework of the Middle Eastern *makam*, with plenty of instrumental improvisation thrown in for good measure.

The popular Arab music known as *sh'sha'abi* follows the same mode system but has a different verse structure. *L'aita*, a variation on this from the plains between the Casablanca coast and the High Atlas mountains, relies for its effect on the interplay of free singing over a rhythmic accompaniment. One star of all these genres is **Abdeslam Cherkaoui** of Fes, who has made several records.

CHAABI

Chaabi means "popular" and the music that takes this name started out as street music performed in the squares and *souks*. It can now be heard in cafés, at festivals and at weddings, especially in the summer. At its more basic level, it is played by itinerant musicians, who will turn up at a café (some cafés keep their own instruments for musicans) and play some songs. Songs are usually finished with a *leseb*, which is often twice the speed of the song itself and forms a background for syncopated clapping, shouting and dancing. Early evening during Ramadan is the best time to find music cafés of this kind in full swing.

During the 1970s a more sophisticated version of *chaabi* began to emerge, with groups setting themselves up in competition with the commercial Egyptian and Libyan music which dominated the market (and the radio) at the time. These groups were usually made up of two stringed instruments – a *sentir* (bass *guimbri*) and a lute – and a *bendir* and *darabuka* or *tan-tan* as percussion. As soon as they could afford to they updated their sound and image with the addition of congas, bouzoukis, banjos and even electric guitars. The *sentir* and *bendir*, however, remain indispensable.

Their music is a fusion of Arab, African and modern Western influences, combining Berber music with elements taken from the Arab *malhum* and Sufi rituals, Gnaoua rhythms and the image of European groups. Voices play an important part. The whole group sings, either in chorus or backing a lead soloist. The lyrics deal with both love and social issues, sometimes carrying messages which have got their authors into trouble with the authorities. Sometimes there are breaks for speeches.

The three most popular groups of this kind are Jil Jilala, Lem Chaheb and Nass el Ghiwane, all from Casablanca. **Jil Jilala** was formed in 1972 as part of a Sufi theatre group. Their music is based on a Milhun style, using poetry as a reference (and starting) point. More recently they have worked with Gnaoua rhythms. They use a *ghaita* and – rare in these lineups – some Western wind instruments. **Nass el Ghiwane**, the most politicised of the three (and frequently in trouble with the authorities), lays great emphasis on the words of its recitatives and anthems/verses and choruses. Its music again combines Sufi and Gnaoua influences.

Lem Chaheb is probably the Moroccan group best known abroad, through its work with the German group Dissidenten, two of whose members play and record with them. It has an excellent lead singer, and the substitution of an electric guitar and congas for the *sentir* and *tan-tan* has enabled it to develop its music further than other groups.

In the 1980s another generation of groups has emerged which combines traditional with modern influences, this time based in Marrakesh but again concentrating on Gnaoua rhythms. The most successful of these is **Muluk el Hwa**, a group of Berbers who used to play in the Djemaa el Fna square. The lineup is entirely acoustic: *bendir*, *tan-tan*, *sentir*, bouzouki, *karkabat* and hands.

Nass el Hal, formed in 1986, offers two shows, one using a traditional acoustic line-up with bouzouki and violin, the other with drum kit and electric guitar. Its repertoire includes peasant harvest and hunting dances, and religious dances.

Other groups with records to their name include **Izanzaren**, of the Casablanca school, and **Shuka**, who do everything from Andalousian to Gnaoua. Capitalising on the success of all these groups and the demand for cassettes, several *sentir* players have also made recordings, with percussion accompaniment. These include Hassan el Gnaoui, L'Gnaoui Mahmoud and company.

FUSION

Morocco is an ideal place for experiment with fusion of all kinds. Such disparate figures as Brian Jones, Robin Williamson and John Renbourn have been attracted by its rhythms, and in 1989 the Rolling Stones returned to record an album, using the **Pan Pipers of Jajouka** (whom Brian Jones had originally recorded).

The most successful group has been the Berlin-based **Dissidenten**. Before their collaboration with Lem Chaheb, they had also worked with Mohammed Zain, a star *nai* (flute) player from Tangier who belongs to a Sufi sect, and the Gnaoua *gimri* players Abdellah el Gourd, Abdelkader Zefzaf and Abdalla Haroch, producing several records. The remarkable *oud* player **Hassan Erraji** has been working in Britain, and recently Belgium, with his groups Belcikal and Arabesque Music.

The **Spaniards** have concentrated mainly on Arab-Andalousian music. There have been several notable collaborations between flamenco musicians and Andalousian orchestras, such as that of José Heredia Maya and Enrique Morente with the **Tetouan Orchestra**, and Juan Peña Lebrijano with the **Tangier Orchestra**. Muluk el Hwa has also done interesting work with the Spanish group Al Tall on the medieval Valencian music known as "Xarq Al Andalus".

RAÏ

Raï – the word means "opinion" – originated in the western Algerian region around the port of Oran, and in the last years of the 1980s it has been toppling the Egyptian and Libyan stars who once ruled the cassette stores.

It has traditional roots in Bedouin music, with its distinctive refrain (ha-ya-raï), but as a modern phenomenon has more in common with western music. The backing is now solidly electric, with rhythm guitars, synthesizers and usually a rock drum kit as well as traditional drums. Its lyrics reflect highly contemporary concerns – cars, sex, sometimes alcohol –

which have created some friction with the authorities. However, Moroccans have taken easily to the music and there are now up-and-coming Moroccan *raï* stars such as **Cheb Khader** and the mysterious **Chaba Zahouania**. The latter is said to be forbidden by her family from being photographed on her records.

Raï influence is also to be heard in the folk music of the **Oujda** area, the closest Moroccan town to Oran, in artists like **Rachid Briha** and **Hamid M'Rabati**.

Algerian *raï* stars who are popular in Morocco include Cheb Khaled, Cheb Mami and Chaba Fadhela. Cassettes of all these artists are available in the cities.

SEPHARDIC MUSIC

Moroccan Jews, many of whom have now emigrated to Israel, left an important legacy in the north of the country. Their songs and ballads are still in the medieval Spanish, spoken at the time of their expulsion from Spain five centuries ago.

Apart from the narrative ballads, these are mainly songs of courtly love, as well as lullabies and some on biblical themes. They are usually accompanied on a *tar*. The marriage ceremony has also been carefully preserved.

FOLK INSTRUMENTS

Folk instruments are very rudimentary and fairly easy to make, and this, combined with the fact that many music cafés keep their own, allows for a genuinely amateur development. Many of the instruments mentioned below are also to be found under the same or similar names (and with slight variations) in Algeria, Tunisia, Libya and even Egypt.

Morocco has a great many string and percussion instruments, mostly fairly basic in design. There are also a few **wind instruments**. The **Arab flute**, known by different tribes as the *nai*, *talawat*, *nira* or *gasba*, is made of a straight piece of cane open at both ends, with no mouthpiece and between five and seven holes, one at the back. It requires a great deal of skill to play it properly, by blowing at a slight angle. The **ghaita** or *rhita*, a type of oboe popular under various names throughout the Muslim world, is a conical pipe made of hard wood, ending in a bell often made of metal. Its double-reeded mouthpiece is encircled by a broad ring on which the player rests his lips in order to produce the circular breathing needed to obtain a continuous note. It has between seven and nine holes, one at the back. The **aghanin** is a double clarinet, identical to the Arab *arghoul*. It consists of two parallel pipes of wood or cane, each with a single-reed mouthpiece, five holes and a horn at the end for amplification. One pipe provides the tune while the other is used for adornments.

The most common **string instrument** is the **gimbri**. This is an African lute whose sound box is covered in front by a piece of hide. The rounded, fretless stem has two or three strings. The body of the smaller treble *gimbri* is pear-shaped, that of the bass *gimbri* (*hadjouj* or *sentir*) rectangular. The Gnaouas often put a resonator at the end of the stem to produce the buzz typical of Black African music. The **lotar** is another type of lute, used exclusively by the Chleuh Berbers. It has a circular body, also closed with a piece of skin, and three or four strings which are plucked with a plectrum.

The classic Arab lute, the **oud**, is used in classical orchestras and the traditional Arab orchestras known as *takhts*. Its pear-shaped body is covered by a piece of wood with two or three rosette-shaped openings. It has a short, fretless stem and six strings, five double and one single. The most popular string instruments played with a bow are the **kamanjeh** and the **rabab**. The former is an Iranian violin which was adopted by the Arabs. Its present Moroccan character owes a lot to the Western violin, though it is held vertically, supported on the knees. The *rabab* is a spike fiddle, rather like a viol. The bottom half of its long, curved body is covered in hide, the top in wood with a rosette-shaped opening. It has two strings.

The Chleuh Berbers use an archaic single-stringed *rabab* with a square stem and sound-box covered entirely in skin. Lastly, there is the **kanum**, a trapezoidal Arab zither with over seventy strings, grouped in threes and plucked with plectra attatched to the fingernails. It is used almost exclusively in classical music.

Rapid hand-clapping and the clashes of bells and cymbals are only part of the vast repertoire of Moroccan **percussion**. Like most Moroccan drums the **darbuka** is made of clay, shaped into a cylinder swelling out slightly at the top. The single skin is beaten with both hands. It is used in both folk and classical music. The **taarija**, a smaller version of the *darbuka*, is held in one hand and beaten with the other. Then there are treble and bass **tan-tan** bongos, and the Moorish **guedra**, a large drum which rests on the ground. There is also a round wooden drum with skins on both sides called a **tabl**, which is beaten with a stick on one side and by hand on the other. This is used only in folk music.

As for **tambourines**, the ever-popular **bendir** is round and wooden, 40 or 50cm across, with two strings stretched under its single skin to produce a buzzing sound. The **tar** is smaller, with two rings of metal discs around the frame and no strings under its skin. The **duff** is a double-sided tambourine, often square in shape, which has to be supported so that it can be beaten with both hands.

Only two percussion instruments are made of metal: **karkabat**, double castanets used by the Gnaouas, and the **nakous**, a small cymbal played with two rods.

WHERE TO BUY INSTRUMENTS

MEKNES

A musical instrument *souk* is under the archway connecting Souk Bezzarin and Rue des Sarraria, on the edge of the Medina – just past Bab el Djedid, if coming from Place el Hedim. Stalls are good value and there is much choice in a small area.

TETOUAN

A couple of good shops to browse and bargain in are to be found in and around the Rue Terrafin and Rue Ahmed Torres area.

FES

Both Talâa Kebira and Talâa Seghira, close to Bab Boujeloud, have stores at intervals. Nearby here, ask for Abdillah Alami in the Kasbah Boujeloud, who sells excellent hand-made drums.

AVERAGE PRICES

Oud (£35–70); *Ghaïta* (£10–18); *Naï* (£3–6); *Bendir* (£3–6); *Tara* (£3–6); *Hadjouj* (£30–50); *Darabouka* (£8–12); *Qasba* (£8–12); *Garageb* (£2–3); *Tan-Tan* (£5–15); *Gimbri* (£15–30).

CASSETTES AND RECORDS

In Morocco, **cassettes** of all kinds are readily available – folk, traditional, modern, and especially those made by the better known groups – Jil Jilala, Nass el Ghiwane, Lem Chaheb, Muluk el Hwa, Nass el Hal, etc. They cost around 14–17dh (£1–1.50) for a tape – which almost always lasts exactly 46 minutes!

Good choices to start a collection could include:

Nass el Ghiwane (La Voix el Maarif, LVEM 125).

Nass el Ghiwane: Chant d'Espoir (Nassana, EH1264).

Jil Jilala (Disques Gam, GB8788).

Orchestra Fisal (Fourkafane FM14).

Hamïd Zahir (Tichkophone, TCK548).

Records are much harder to find and better bought in Europe, though there they are limited to ethnic, folk and Andalous music, or fusion with European groups. In the listings below, those with an asterisk are highly recommended; those with two asterisks, you'd be cheating yourself not to enjoy . . .

GENERAL COMPILATIONS

Music of Morocco (Library of Congress). A rare but wonderful compilation by Paul Bowles – available in some record libraries.*

Music of Morocco (Folkways). Another Library of Congress Project, more easily available.

BERBER MUSIC

Maroc/1, Musique Tachelhit: Rais Lhaj Aomar Ouahrouch (Ocora).*

Maroc/2, Moyen Atlas, Musique Sacrée et Profane (Ocora).*

Orchestre de Fes, Maroc: Musique Classique Andalou-Maghrebine (Ocora).**

Maroc: Chants et Danses (Le Chant du Monde).

Berberes du Maroc, Ahwach (Le Chant du Monde).*

Maroc Eternel (Arion).

Hmaoui Abd El Hamid, La flûte orientale (Arion).**

The Rwais, Moroccan Berber Musicians from the High Atlas (Lyrichord).*

Songs and Rhythms of Marocco (Albatros).

Muluk el Hwa, Cançons de Jma-el-Fna (Di-fussió Mediterrania).

Master Musicians of Jajouka (Adelphi).

RELIGIOUS MUSIC

Morocco, Music of Islam & Sufism (BM).

ARABIC TRADITIONS

Abdeslam Cherkaoui, Morocco: Arabic Traditional Music (Unesco collection; Auvidis).*

Hassan Erraji, Moroccan Folk Song (ME).*

Arabic Songs And Dances (Request).

ANDALOUS MUSIC

Ustad Massano Tazi, Musique Classique Andalouse de Fes (Ocora; CD/cassette only).**

Chekara con la Orquesta de Tetuan (Ariola).*

ANDALOUS/FLAMENCO CROSSOVERS

José Heredia Maya y Orquesta Andalusi de Tetuan, Macama Jonda (Ariola).*

Juan Peña "El Lebrijano" and the Orquesta de Tanger, Encuentros (Globestyle).**

FUSION

Hassan Erraji and Arabesque , Nikriz (Sterns).*

Lem Chaheb with Dissidenten, La Chanson Populaire Marocaine (Club du Disque Arabe; CD only, containing their two best Moroccan cassettes),** *Sahara Electrik* (Globestyle),* *Arab Shadows* (Nuevos Medios, Madrid).

Kwaku Baah and Ganoua (Island).

SEPHARDIC MUSIC

Judeo-Español Songs from Morocco (Saga).

Sephardic Jews – Ballads, Wedding Songs, Songs, and Dances (Folkways).

MOROCCAN FICTIONS

Storytelling is an age-old Moroccan tradition – and an active one, as any visit to a weekly *souk* will reveal. The American novelist Paul Bowles, a resident in Tangier more or less since the war, became interested in such tales in the early 1950s and began tape recording and transcribing examples told by various Moroccan friends – Ahmed Yacoubi, Larbi Layachi, Abdeslam Boulaich and, in particular, Mohammed Mrabet, with whom he continues to collaborate.

Mrabet's work now amounts to a dozen collections of stories, novels and novellas. The piece included here is in some ways atypical – Mrabet's interests are rooted more in his experience of city life – but it shows his showmanship and masterful handling of a deeply traditional theme of Moroccan storytelling, the casting of spells. Abdeslam Boulaich, better known as a painter, reveals a similar interest in folk humour. Mohammed Chourki, by contrast, is a more literary figure, with a novel and books on Tennessee Williams and Jean Genet to his name. Alone among the three authors here, he wrote his text (in Classical Arabic), with Bowles translating from an oral reading in Maghrebi.

For details of books by these various authors, see the bibliography on p.463.

MOHAMMED MRABET: THE LUTE

A young man named Omar got onto his mare one day and rode over his father's land for many miles, looking for the right place to build a small house of his own. He came to a hill between the forest and the olive groves. This is the spot, he said. Here I can play my lute all day.

Little by little he built a cottage, bringing the materials from his father's house, and doing all the work himself. When it was done he furnished it with everything he needed for the pleasant life he intended to lead. His most important possession was his lute, which he had trained so that when anyone was coming it sounded its strings in warning. Then Omar would look into the opening under the strings and watch the person as he approached.

Outside the house he built an arbor of canes where he could lie back and drink his tea. And he would sit out there in the shade of the arbor with the green trees all around him, smoking kif and drinking tea. At length he would take down his lute and begin to play.

Farther down the valley lived two sisters whose father and mother had died, leaving them alone in a big house. The younger sister was still only a girl, and there was a handsome village lad with whom she was friendly. The older sister, who desired the boy for herself, caught sight of him talking to the girl under a tree. Later she questioned her.

Who was that you were talking to?

The boy from the village.

What did he say to you?

The girl smiled and looked very happy. He said beautiful words and wonderful things. Because I love him and he loves me.

What? cried the woman. And you're not ashamed to say such a thing?

Why should I be? We're going to be married.

The older sister jumped up and rushed out. She began to burn powders and to chant, and it was not long before she burst into the room with a scream and flung a handful of black powder over the girl. At that instant her sister no longer stood in front of her – only a camel, which she chained outside.

A few days later the village boy came to see the younger sister. The woman greeted him from the doorway and invited him into the house. He sat down and looked around, and then through the window he saw the camel.

Why have you got that camel chained to the ground with its legs tied together? he asked her.

She's a bad animal, the woman said. I have to keep her chained up so she won't get into trouble.

Let the poor thing loose so it can graze, he told her. It has no life at all this way. Unfasten the chain and untie the ropes.

No, no. I can't do that.

The boy waited a moment. Then he said: The girl who lives here. Where is she?

That girl? She's getting married tomorrow.

What? he cried. But she was going to marry me!

No. She never mentioned anything about that to me, she told him. Anyway, that's the way it is.

Then she laughed. And what about me? Don't you like me?

Yes, he said. Of course I like you.

Why don't you and I get married, then?

The boy looked at her, and then he looked out at the camel. All right, he said at length. I'll marry you. But only if you set that camel free.

Without saying anything the woman went outside and undid the chain and ropes, and the camel walked away. Then she came in and said she would see him that evening.

As the boy went along the path to the village he came upon the camel waiting for him. He was horrified to hear it speak with the voice of the girl.

Don't trust my sister, it said. You see what she's done to me. I'm the one you were going to marry. Go as far away from here as you can, and stay away. I've got to try and get back my body somehow.

Then the camel walked away, and the boy was too downcast to call after it. He left the village the same afternoon.

One day not long afterward as Omar lay under his arbor on a mat drinking tea, the cords of his lute suddenly sounded. When he peered inside it he saw a camel. He watched it come nearer, and then he hung up the lute and went out into the orchard. The camel walked straight to him and said: Good afternoon.

Omar was startled. You can speak?

I said good afternoon. Yes, I can speak.

I've never seen a talking camel, he said.

But I'm not a camel. That's the trouble. And she told him what her sister had done to her. Then she said: I have a favor to ask of you. Let me stay here with you for a while.

Omar looked thoughtfully at the animal, and said: Ouakha. You can stay with me.

The camel lay down beside the arbor, and Omar began to play the lute. It was the hour when the birds sang and flew from tree to tree. When the birds became quiet, he glanced at the camel and saw that tears were falling from its eyes. He put the lute aside.

The next day as Omar sat in the arbor talking with the camel, he heard the strings of the lute. When he looked inside, he saw a woman walking through the wilderness, over the rocks and between the trees. He watched for a while, but she did not come any closer. Finally she disappeared. He sat down.

Tell me, he said to the camel. What was your sister doing at the moment you felt yourself becoming a camel?

The camel thought for a while. Then it said: She sprinkled some powder over my head, and she had a piece of green cloth in her hand. I saw her fold it three times and then throw it on top of a chest.

I have a friend who might be able to help, Omar told her. He often comes by around this hour.

As they sat there a large crow came flying over the trees, and alighted on the ground beside the arbor. After they had greeted each other, Omar said: You're an expert thief, aren't you?

The crow was embarrassed. It's true I've stolen things. But all that is in the past.

Omar smiled. Good, he said. But you've still got to steal one more time. Do you know Tchar Flanflani?

Yes.

You've got to get into that big house there and look around until you find a green cloth. Don't unfold it. Bring it to me.

Ouakha, said the crow, and it flew off.

They did not have to wait long for it to return, carrying the green cloth in its claws. As Omar took the cloth in his hands and let it unfold, instead of a camel lying on the ground beside the arbor, it was a girl.

He stared at her first in amazement and then with delight, for she was beautiful. Then she jumped up and threw her arms around him, and he embraced her. Together they went into the house.

The following day when the sister looked to see if the green cloth was safe in its place, she did not find it. She searched for it inside the house and out, but without success. As Omar and the girl sat in the shade of the arbor, the strings of the lute began to vibrate. He peered into it and saw the woman walking in the forest.

Here, he said to the girl. Look in here and see if you know who that is.

She looked inside the lute and drew back. It's my sister! she whispered. She's looking for me.

Omar hung up the lute and walked out to the orchard to meet the woman. When he came up to her she looked at him and said: Who are you?

That's what I want to ask you, he said. Who are you and where have you come from and what do you want here? This is my land you're on, and the edge of it is a long way from here.

I'm looking for a camel, she said. A camel I've lost.

I have your camel, he told her.

What! Where is it? What have you done with it?

It's over there, he said, pointing to the arbor where the girl stood. And she came out and walked toward them.

The woman looked at Omar. You won't win! she cried. Then she turned and went back the way she had come.

A few days after this, Omar put the girl onto the mare and rode with her to his father's house, where they celebrated their marriage with a wedding feast that lasted for three days. Then the married couple rode back to the little house. The two were very happy together, and the days passed swiftly.

But one moonlit night as they lay asleep in bed, the lute hanging on the wall twanged its strings. Omar sprang up and put his eye to the hole. A woman dressed all in white walked in the brilliant moonlight. He pulled the lute down and played softly for a while. The next time he looked in, a dense white cloud had formed around the figure of the woman in the orchard, and the cloud was so thick that she could not move one way or the other. Omar hung the lute on the wall and got back into bed.

What was it?

It was your sister. She's down there in the orchard now, dressed all in white. I've got her shut in. She can't go forward or backward.

Let her go! the girl begged him. We mustn't be cruel to her. I can't bear to think of her suffering.

Omar paid no attention to her pleas, but turned over and went to sleep. In the morning after he had bathed and had his breakfast, he sat down under the arbor, smoked a few pipes of kif, and said to the girl: Come here and look.

Inside the lute she saw the swirling cloud among the olive trees. Omar took the lute and played on it for a moment. Then he handed it back, and she looked again. The cloud had disappeared, and the woman stood there shouting up at them from the orchard.

I'll be back! she screamed.

Another night as they slept, the lute again sounded a warning, and Omar seized it and put his eye to the hole. Seeing the woman, he played a loud fast melody for a while. When he peered in the next time, he saw that once again a cloud had formed around the woman, but this time it had risen high into the air with her, where it remained, as still as a rock. He got into bed and said nothing about it.

But the next morning when the girl looked outside she called to Omar. There's something hanging in the air above the orchard!

It's your sister, he said.

Forgive her this time, and she'll never come back to bother us any more, his wife said, and she went on pleading with him.

Your sister will never change, Omar told her. She ought not to be pardoned and turned loose to do harm in the world.

But the girl sobbed and begged him to let her sister down, and finally he got up and plucked on the lute. The cloud slowly settled onto the ground and blew away. This time the woman did not stay to say anything, but ran off as soon as she felt the earth beneath her feet.

When she got back to her house, she shut herself in and fasted for four days. At the end of this time she had a vision of two trees whose trunks stood very close one to the other. She forced herself between them and knew that something great had happened. When she turned, she saw eight strings of gut stretched from a crosspiece between the tree trunks, and she knew that this was the way to get into Omar's house without alerting the lute. From then on she spent all her time preparing the strips of gut and the other things she would need when she found the two trees. When she had everything ready, she began to go regularly to the forest below the little house, in search of the place she had seen in her vision. She found it one night. It was in a dense part of the woods, just below the house. Quickly she squeezed in between the two tree trunks.

The moment she had pushed through, a wall formed around her body and over her head, so that she was encased in a shell of rock between the two trees. The lute by Omar's bed made a loud sound as though it had been hurled to the floor, and then it began to play a strange, halting melody, a thing Omar had never heard it do before. He waited until it had stopped, and then he took it down and looked into it.

Your sister! he cried. There's nothing I can do! She's dying. The lute did it by itself. I didn't touch it.

The girl seized the lute and held it close to her face. Beyond the strings she saw the two trees and the boulder between them. And then through the casing of the stone she saw her sister's face. Her mouth was open and her eyes rolled from side to side as she gasped

Then the wall of stone around her body became smoke and blew away through the trees, and she fell forward onto the ground.

The next morning Omar and his wife went to the spot and found her body lying there between the two arar trees.

We must bury her, said the girl.

Not on my land, Omar told her. On her own land, if you like, but not here.

And each afternoon when he sat with his wife under the arbor playing the lute, the crow came and sat with them, and listened.

1977.

ABDESLAM BOULAICH: *THREE HEKAYAS*

Cowardice

A Moslem, a Jew, and a Christian were sitting in a cafe talking about Heaven. They agreed that it was a difficult place to get into, but each one thought he would have a better chance than the others.

You have to have the right clothes, the Christian told them. I always wear a jacket and a tie.

Let's go and see, said the other two.

They started out, and when they got close to Heaven, the Moslem and the Jew stopped walking, and the Christian kept going until he reached the door of Heaven.

Our Lord Solomon, who guards the door, said to him: Where are you going?

Inside, the Nazarene answered.

Who are you?

My name is John.

Stand back, said Our Lord Solomon.

Then the Jew and the Moslem spoke together. The Moslem said: He didn't get in. But we will.

I'll go first, said the Jew.

That's right. You go, the Moslem told him.

So the Jew walked up to the door of Heaven. And Our Lord Solomon said to him: Where are you going?

Inside.

Who are you?

Yaqoub, said the Jew.

Stand back!

The Moslem saw this and said to himself: That's that. Neither one of them got in. Now I'll try.

He walked until he got to the door of Heaven. Then he pulled the hood of his djellaba down over his face. And Our Lord Solomon said to him: Where are you going?

Inside.

Who are you? Our Lord Solomon asked him.

I am the Prophet Mohammed, he said. And he went in. The Jew was watching. He said to himself: If he can get in there, so can I.

And he took a sack and filled it with sticks of wood and slung it over his shoulder. Then he walked up to the door.

Where are you going? asked Our Lord Solomon.

The Jew stuck his foot in the door.

Who are you?

The Prophet Mohammed's manservant, he said. And the Jew went in.

The Christian had been watching. He was afraid to try to get in by lying, and so he went back to his country and told everyone that Heaven did not exist.

Stupidity

In a small mountain village lived a man who could not talk very well because he had no roof to his mouth. When it came time for him to marry, his family chose him a girl who had the same trouble. But since the man had never seen her, nor had the girl seen him, neither one knew how the other one spoke.

The day of the wedding, the man went into the girl's room. The servant brought in the taifor with a pot of couscous on it, and then she went home, leaving the front door unlatched.

The man sat with his hands folded in front of him, and so did the girl. Each one was looking at the other, waiting for the other to speak. She was waiting for the man to say: Eat. And he was waiting for her to say: Eat. He was afraid to speak for fear she would hear his voice and not be able to love him. And the girl was afraid he would hear hers and not want her for a wife. Each one looked at the other, and the door of the house was unlatched.

A beggar was passing through the street, crying: For the love of Allah, a little bread! And no one paid him any attention. When he came to the house of the bridegroom he saw the door ajar, and he pushed it open and walked in. He went through the courtyard and came to the room where the two were sitting. Then he saw the man and the girl looking at one another, with the food in front of them on the taifor, and neither one saying anything. The bridegroom saw the beggar standing there. He wanted to tell him to get out. But he would not speak, and so he shook his head up and down at him. But the beggar thought he meant: Go on and eat. He sat down and began to eat the couscous, and he went on eating until there was only a little left. Then he ate the meat, and when he had finished, he took the bone and hung it around the man's neck on a string, because he thought the man was simple-minded. And he went out.

A dog was running through the street. When it came to the house of the bridegroom it caught the smell of food coming through the open door, and it went into the courtyard. It·ran to the door of the room where they were sitting, and went in. The man and the girl sat still and said nothing. The dog put its feet up on the taifor and licked up the rest of the couscous. It was still hungry. Then it saw the bone that hung around the bridegroom's neck, and it seized it between its jaws and tried to run. The man fell over onto the floor, and the dog dragged him to the door. The dog kept pulling, and the man's head hit the wall.

Then the man cried out: Help me untie the string!

The girl heard his words, and she was no longer afraid to speak.

The beggar was right! she said. I can't live with such a man!

But you speak the same way! he cried.

I'm the only one who wouldn't have minded that, she told him. And she went out of the house, and left the man on the floor with the dog pulling at the bone.

Greed

A sickly man who lived in the city married a girl from the country. He was never very hungry, but the girl was healthy and ate a great deal. One day the man went to the market and bought many vegetables and four cow's feet. When he took the food home to his wife, he told her: Make me a stew so I can have it when I come home for lunch.

Yes, she said.

But wait for me, he said. Don't eat anything until I get back.

I won't, she said.

When he had gone she made the stew. And then she waited. He ought to be here soon, she said to herself. He'll be here any minute.

After he had finished working, the man went to a café and began to play cards. He stayed there in the café a long time, and his wife went on waiting. Soon she was very hungry. She took one of the cow's feet out of the stew and ate it. And she said to herself: It doesn't matter. When he comes I'll make up something to tell him.

The man came home and sat down. Where's the stew? he said. You haven't eaten anything, have you?

Not yet, she told him. She brought the stew and began to ladle it out. Then the man noticed that there were only three feet in the pot. He began to shout: And the other foot? Where is it?

I haven't got it, she said. You brought three and I cooked three. I hate cow's feet anyway.

The man was very unhappy. Do you want to kill me? he cried. Bring me the other foot, or I may die right here.

Die, if that's what you want, she told him. Why are you waiting?

The man rolled over onto the floor and began to moan.

Get up! said his wife. But he only told her to fetch the fqih and make him wash him so he could be buried.

When she came in with the fqih, the girl said to her husband again: Get up off the floor!

Have you got the cow's foot? he asked her.

The fqih began to wash him.

Get up! she said. Don't you want to have your burial clothes put on you?

Have you brought the cow's foot?

She did not answer. The people came in and dressed the man in his kfin, ready to be buried. And then they laid him on the litter.

You're off to the cemetery, his wife told him.

They carried him through the doorway into the street.

Where's the cow's foot? he cried. His wife shut the door.

The people walked through the streets carrying him on the litter. When they passed in front of the market, the butcher saw the procession. Who's that who has died? he asked. They told him.

And to think that only this morning he was here in my shop, the poor man, and he bought four cow's feet!

When the dead man heard this, he sat up on his litter. How many did you say? he called to the butcher.

Four!

Ah, you see? he said. And my wife told me I'd bought only three.

No. It was four, said the butcher.

The man lay down again. And the men carrying him were talking and did not notice anything. They went on their way to the cemetery. When they got there they lifted him off the litter and started to lower him into the ground. But at that moment he sat up again.

Wait! he told the fqih. I've got three cow's feet at home that I still haven't eaten. It's not good to be hungry when you arrive in Heaven. I'm going to run back and eat them now. If I do get to Heaven then, at least I'll have some food inside me.

The people let go of him, and he ran home. When he went into the house his wife said: You came back? You're still alive?

Give me the three cow's feet, he told her. She gave them to him. He ate one. But then he was no longer hungry, and his wife ate the other two.

1961

MOHAMMED CHOUKRI: THE PROPHET'S SLIPPERS

More pleasure and fantasy. More money, more ways of getting hold of it. I was tired of enjoying myself, and yet I was not satisfied. Fatin walked toward me, white as snow in the blood-red light of the bar. She took one of my notebooks, looked at it, and grinned.

She muttered something unintelligible and moved away again, disappearing among those who were kicking the air. It was three o'clock in the morning, and I was bored and nervous. Om Kalsoum was singing: "Sleep never made life seem too long, nor long waiting shortened life."

A black man appeared, white on black. He took one of my books and began to read aloud: "This total liberty has its tragic and pessimistic side." He put it down. "What's that book about?" he demanded.

"It's about a man who doesn't understand this world," I said. "He hurts himself and everybody who comes near him."

He nodded, lifted his glass, and drank. When he had finished, he said: "You're crazy."

I saw Fatin writing in a notebook. Meanwhile I smoked, drank, and thought about the matter of the slippers. The lights went off. Women cried out. When they came on again,

both men and women murmured. I bought another drink for Khemou, and she gave me a kiss that left a sweet taste in my mouth. Her brown tongue tickled. She was eating chocolate, and her laugh was red in the light from the bar. Khemou walked off and Fatin came up to me. She handed me a slip of blue paper. On it she had written: *Rachid. What do you know about love? You spend more time writing about love than you do making love. The one who has never studied love enjoys it more than the one who knows all about it. Love is not a science. Love is feeling, feeling, feeling.*

Miriam Makeba went into "Malaysia." She has a white voice. I began to write on the same piece of blue paper. *Fatin, you are my red bed, and I'm your black blanket. I'm beginning to see it that way.*

I looked around for Fatin. Her mouth was a wound in her face, and a foreign sailor was sucking on it. She had her right arm around him and was pouring her drink onto the floor with her left hand. Khemou came by and offered me her lips, like a mulberry. I bought her another drink. I was so pleased with the effect of her kiss that I began to think once more about selling the slippers. How much ought I to ask for them? A million francs, the Englishman ought to pay, if he wants the Prophet's slippers. He's an idiot in any case, or he couldn't be taken in by such a tale. But how can I tell just how stupid he is? It was he who first brought it up, the black-market story.

Fatin appeared, black, blonde, white. I handed her the slip of blue paper. She looked at me and smiled. I was thinking that girls like her only made trouble. Her little mouth now looked like a scar that had healed. I thought of the Indian poet Mirzah Asad Allah Ghalef:

For those who are thirsty
I am the dry lip.

She wants a kind of love that will make her unhappy. What I like about her is that she still believes the world ought to be changed.

Khemou and Latifa began to scream at each other like two cats fighting, while Miriam Makeba's white voice continued to sing. Khemou pulled Latifa's black hair, knocked her down, and kicked her face. Latifa screamed and the blood ran from her nose. The colors all came together in my head. Leaving the blue paper with me, Fatin ran to separate the two. I read on it: *You're right. I serve them my flesh, but I don't feel it when they eat me.*

Vigon is singing in his white voice. "Outside the Window." Vigon is singing, and I think of the almond trees in flower, and of snow, which I love.

Khemou and Latifa came out of the rest room. They had made up, like two little girls. They began to laugh and dance as if nothing had happened. I sat there smoking, while in my imagination I attacked each man in the bar whose face I didn't like. A kick for this one. a slap in the face for that one, a punch in the jaw for that one over there. Watching myself do as I pleased with them put me into a better frame of mind.

Tomorrow I'll sell the slippers. Fatin came past again, and I asked her why Khemou and Latifa had been quarreling. She said it was because Khemou had told the man Latifa was drinking with that she had tuberculosis.

Is it true? I asked her.

Yes, she said. But she says she's cured now.

The Englishman and I were at my house, eating couscous. He turned to me and said: "This is the best couscous I've ever tasted."

From time to time he looked toward the corner where my grandmother sat, her head bent over. I told him the couscous had been sent from Mecca. "My aunt sends a lot of it each month."

He looked at me with amazement. "It's fantastic!"

So that he would get the idea, I added: "Everything in the house was brought from Mecca. Even that incense burning is sent each month."

We finished the couscous and started on another dish of meat baked with raisins and hot spices. "It's called *mrozeya*," I told him.

He muttered a few words, and then said: "Ah, nice. Very nice." My grandmother's head was still bent over. I saw that the Englishman was looking at her, sitting there in her white robes. The incense and the silence in the room made her seem more impressive. She was playing her part very well. Our demure little servant brought the tea in a silver teapot. She too was dressed in immaculate white, and she too kept her face hidden. Her fingers were painted with elaborate designs in henna, and her black hair shone above her enormous earrings. She made no false moves. She greeted the Englishman without smiling, as I had instructed her to do. It became her to look grave. I had never seen her so pretty.

The mint tea with ambergris in it seemed to please the Englishman. "Do you like the tea?" I asked him.

"Oh, yes! It's very good!"

There was silence for a while. I thought: The time has come to rub Aladdin's lamp. I got up and went to whisper in my grandmother's ear. I did not even form words; I merely made sounds. She nodded her head slowly, without looking up. Then I lifted the white cushion and removed the piece of gold-embroidered green silk that covered it.

The Englishman looked at the slippers, made colorless by age. His hand slowly advanced to touch the leather. Then he glanced at me, and understood that I did not want him to touch them.

"My God! They're marvelous!"

I covered the slippers as I stood there, in order to let him observe them through the veil of green silk. Slowly and with great care I turned and put the cushion back into its place, as if I were applying a bandage to an injury. He glanced at me, and then stared for a long time in the direction of the slippers. Understanding that it was time to leave, he stood up.

We were sitting at the Café Central. For the third time since we had left the house, he said: "Then it's impossible?"

"A thing like that is so difficult," I said. "I wouldn't know how to do it. It was hard enough to get her to let you even look at them. You can be sure you're the only Christian ever to have seen them. And no other is going to, either."

"I understand," he said. "But perhaps we can come to an agreement."

"I understand too. But what can I do? Those slippers are my grandmother's very life. If she should find them missing, she might lose her mind, or have a heart attack. I'm very fond of her, naturally, and I respect her feelings about the slippers."

"I'll give you time to think about it," he said. "But try and persuade her."

"Yes. But when you think of how hard it was to get her to allow you to look at them, you can see how much harder it would be to persuade her."

"Do what you can," he said.

I said I would, but that I thought it was out of the question. Then I said: "Listen. I have an idea. But only on one condition."

"What's that?"

I hesitated for an instant.

"Tell me. Perhaps we can find a way."

"You'd have to leave Tangier the minute you got the slippers."

"That would be all right," he said, understanding. "It's an excellent tactic."

"And I'd have to get out of Tangier myself and stay somewhere else. And I couldn't come back as long as my grandmother was still alive."

"No."

"I couldn't stay on here once they were gone."

"I quite understand."

"It's those slippers that keep her alive, you might say."

"Yes, yes. How much do you want for them?"

I stared at him, and my voice said: "A million francs."

"Oh!" he cried. "No! That's very high!"

"But you'll have something extremely rare. No museum has anything like them. And I'll regret what I've done for the rest of my life."

"I know, I know. But that's a great deal of money. I'll give you half a million. I can't pay any

more than that."

"You'd have to pay more than that," I told him.

"No, no. I can't. I haven't got it."

"You give me your address, and I'll write you from wherever I go, and you can send me the rest later."

We looked at each other for a few seconds. In my mind I was thinking: Go on, say the word, Mister Stewart.

"Very well," he finally said.

Wonderful, Mister Stewart, I thought.

"Where shall we meet tomorrow?" I asked him.

He reflected for a moment, and said: "I'll wait for you in the lobby at the Hotel Minzah."

"No," I said. "Outside the hotel. In the street. And you must have your ticket with you, so you can leave the minute I give you the slippers."

"Of course."

"What time will that be?"

While he hesitated I was thinking: Come on, Mister Stewart. Make up your mind.

"At three o'clock in the afternoon."

I got up, shook hands with him, and said: "Keep it to yourself."

"I shan't breathe a word."

"It's not only my grandmother who's going to be upset, but everybody who knows she has the slippers."

I walked away. A moment later I turned and saw him leaving the café.

I found him waiting for me in front of the hotel. He seemed nervous, and he looked wide-eyed at the bag I was carrying. I saw that he had a packet in his hand. Half a million, I thought. More pleasure, more time to think of other such tricks later. The colors in the bar.

I motioned to him to follow me, and stopped walking only when we were a good distance from the entrance to the hotel. We stood facing one another, and shook hands. He looked down at my bag, and I glanced at the packet he held in his hand.

I opened the bag, and he touched the slippers for a second. Then he took it out of my hands, and I took the packet from him. Pointing to a parked car, he said: "There's the car that's going to take me to the airport."

I thought to myself: And tonight I'll be at the Messalina Bar.

I sat down in the corner the same as

always. I smoked, drank, and bought kisses without haggling over their price. I'm fed up with pleasure. Fed up, but not satisfied. One woman is not enough.

"Khemou's in the hospital," Fatin told me. "And Latifa's at the police station. She got drunk and hit Khemou on the head with a bottle."

I asked Fatin who the girls were who were sitting in the corner opposite me. She said they were both from Dar el Beida. She picked up one of my notebooks and walked away with it. I waved at the younger of the two. She spoke for a while with her friend. And I drank and smoked and waited for the first kiss of a girl I had never yet touched.

She got up and came over, and I saw the small face relax. Her mouth was like a strawberry. She began to sip the drink I bought her. Her lips shone. Her mouth opened inside mine. A strawberry soaked in gin and tonic. Eve eating mulberries. Adam approaches her, but she puts the last berry into her mouth before he can get to her. Then he seizes the last berry from between her teeth. The mulberry showed Eve how to kiss. Adam knows all the names of things, but Eve had to teach him how to kiss.

Two men had begun to fight over one of the girls. The shorter of the two lost his balance. The other kicked until someone seized him from behind.

Fatin put a piece of blue paper in front of me. I was drinking, smoking, and eating mulberries from the new small mouth. I read what was written on the piece of blue paper. *I'm not the same person I was yesterday. I know it but I can't say it clearly. You must try and understand me.*

The new face held up her empty glass. I looked again at the mulberries. The barman was busy drawing squares on a small piece of white paper. "Give her another drink," I told him. The friend who had been sitting with her came over. "Give her a drink too," I said.

I thought: More mulberries and human flesh. More tricks and money. I began to write on Fatin's slip of blue paper: *I must not try to understand you.*

1973

All stories © Paul Bowles and reprinted by permission; first published in *Five Eyes* (Black Sparrow Press, Santa Barbara, California, 1979).

WRITERS ON MOROCCO

As any glimpse at the book listings following will show, there's also a long tradition of British and American writing on Morocco. The pieces that follow – from Budgett Meakin, Walter Harris, Elias Canetti and Paul Bowles – represent the best of the genre and much of its range.

BUDGETT MEAKIN: IN MOORISH GUISE

To those who have not themselves experienced what the attempt to see an eastern country in native guise entails, a few stray notes of what it has been my lot to encounter in seeking for knowledge in this style, will no doubt be of interest. Such an undertaking, like every other style of adventure, has both its advantages and disadvantages. To the student of the people the former are immense, and if he can put up with whatever comes, he will be well repaid for all the trials by the way. In no other manner can a European mix with any freedom with the natives of this country. When once he has discarded the outward distinguishing features of what they consider a hostile infidelity, and has as far as possible adopted their dress and their mode of life, he has spanned one of the great gulfs which have hitherto yawned between them.

Squatted on the floor, one of a circle round a low table on which is a steaming dish into which each plunges his fist in search of dainty morsels, the once distant Moor thaws to an astonishing extent, becoming really friendly and communicative, in a manner totally impossible towards the starchy European who sits uneasily on a chair, conversing with his host at ease on the floor. And when the third cup of tea syrup comes, and each lolls contentedly on the cushions, there is manifested a brotherly feeling not unknown in Western circles under analogous circumstances, here fortunately without a suggestion of anything stronger than "gunpowder".

Yes, this style of thing decidedly has its delights – of which the above must not be taken as the most elevating specimen and many are the pleasant memories which come

before me as I mentally review my life "as a Moor". In doing so I seem to be again transported to another world, to live another life, as was my continual feeling at the time. Everything around me was so different, my very actions and thoughts so complete a change from what they were under civilisation, that when the courier brought the periodical budget of letters and papers I felt as one in a dream, even my mother tongue sounding strange after not having heard it so long.

Often I have had to "put up" in strange quarters; sometimes without any quarters at all. I have slept in the mansions of Moorish merchants, and rolled up in my cloak in the street. I have occupied the guest chambers of country governors and sheikhs, and I have passed the night on the wheat in a granary, wondering whether fleas or grains were more numerous. I have been accommodated in the house of a Jewish Rabbi, making a somewhat similar observation and I have been the guest of a Jewish Consular Agent of a Foreign Power, where the awful stench from the drains was not exceeded by that of the worst hovel I ever entered. I have even succeeded in wooing Morpheus out on the sea-shore, under the lea of a rock, and I have found the debris by the side of a straw rick an excellent couch till it came on to rain. Yet again, I have been one of half a dozen on the floor of a windowless and doorless summer-house in the middle of the rainy season. The tent of the wandering Arab has afforded me shelter, along with calves and chickens and legions of fleas, and I have actually passed the night in a village mosque.

When I set out on my travels in Moorish guise, it was with no thought of penetrating spots so venerated by the Moors that all non-Muslims are excluded, but the idea grew upon me as I journeyed, and the Moors themselves were the cause. This is how it came about. Having become acquainted to some extent with the language and customs of the people during a residence of several years among them as a European, when I travelled – with the view of rendering myself less conspicuous, and mixing more easily with the natives – I adopted their dress and followed their style of life, making, however, no attempt to conceal my nationality. After a while I found that when I went where I was not known, all took me for a Moor till they heard my speech, and recognised the foreign accent and the blunders which no native could make. My Moorish friends would often remark that were it not for this I could enter mosques and saint-houses with impunity.

For convenience' sake I had instructed the one faithful attendant who accompanied me to call me by a Muslim name resembling my own, and I afterwards added a corruption of my surname which sounded well, and soon began to seem quite natural. This prevented the attention of the bystanders being arrested when I was addressed by my man, who was careful also always to refer to me as "Seyyid", Master, a term never applied to Europeans or Jews.

Having got so far, a plan occurred to me to account for my way of speaking. I had seen a lad from Manchester, born there of an English mother, but the son of a Moor, who knew not a word of Arabic when sent to Morocco by his father. Why could I not pass as such a one, who had not yet perfected himself in the Arabic tongue? Happy thought! Was I not born in Europe, and educated there? Of course I was, and here was the whole affair complete. I remember, too, that on one or two occasions I had had quite a difficulty to persuade natives that I was *not* similarly situated to this lad. On the first occasion I was taken by surprise, as one among a party of English people, the only one dressed in Moorish costume, which I thought under those circumstances would deceive no one. When asked whence I came, I replied "England", and was then asked, "Is there a mosque there?" I answered that I was not aware that there was one, but that I knew a project had been set on foot to build one near London. Other questions followed, as to my family and what my father's occupation was, till I was astonished at the enquiry, "Has your father been to Mekka yet?"

"Why, no", I answered, as it dawned upon me what had been my interrogator's idea – "he's not a Muslim!"

"Don't say that!" said the man.

"But we are not", I reiterated, "we are Christians".

It was not as difficult to persuade him that I was not at least a convert to Christianity from Islam, as I should have thought it would have been to persuade him that I was a Muslim. Bearing this in mind, I had no doubt that by simply telling the strict truth about myself, and allowing them to draw their own conclusions, I should generally pass for the son of a Moorish merchant settled in England, and thus it proved. Once, during a day's ride in Moorish dress, I counted the number of people who saluted by the way, and was gratified to find that although on a European saddle this suggested to the thoughtful that my mother must have been a European, and I heard one or two ask my man whether she was a legal wife or a slave! In conversation, however, I was proud and grateful to proclaim myself a Christian and an Englishman. My native dress meant after all no more than European dress does on an Oriental in England: it brought me in touch with the Moors, and it enabled me to pass among them unobserved.

Another striking instance of this occurred in Fez, where, before entering any house, I paid an unintentional visit to the very shrine I wished to see. Outside the gates I had stopped to change my costume, and passing in apart from my faithful Mohammed, after a stroll to about the centre of the city, I asked at a shop the way to a certain house. The owner called a lad who knew the neighbourhood, to whom I explained what I wanted, and off we started. In a few minutes I paused on the threshold of a finely ornamented building, different from any other I had seen. All unsuspicious, I enquired what it was, and learned that we were in a street as sacred as a mosque, and that my guide was taking me a short cut through the sanctuary of Mulai Idrees!

Some days later, lantern and slippers in one hand, and rosary in the other, I entered with the crowd for sunset prayers. Perspiring freely within, but outwardly with the calmest appearance I could muster, I spread my prayer-cloth and went through the motions prescribed by law, making my observations in the pauses, and concluding by a guarded survey of the place. I need hardly say that I breathed with a feeling of relief when I found myself in the pure air again, and felt better after I had had my supper and sat down to commit my notes to paper. In the Karûeeïn I once caught a suspicious stare at my glasses, so, pausing, I returned the stare with a contemptuous indignation that made my critic slink off abashed. There was nothing to do but to "face it out".

From *The Land of the Moors: A Comprehensive Description*, by Budgett Meakin (London, 1901).

WALTER HARRIS: *THE DEATH OF A SULTAN*

In 1893 Mulai Hassen determined to visit the desert regions of Morocco, including far-off Tafilet, the great oasis from which his dynasty had originally sprung, and where, before becoming the ruling branch of the royal family, they had resided ever since their founder, the great-grandson of the Prophet, had settled there, an exile from the East.

Leaving Fez in the summer, the Sultan proceeded south, crossing the Atlas above Kasba-el-Maghzen, and descended to the upper waters of the Wad Ziz. An expedition such as this would have required a system of organisation far in excess of the capabilities of the Moors, great though their resources were. Food was lacking; the desert regions could provide little. The water was bad, the heat very great. Every kind of delay, including rebellion and the consequent punishment of the tribes, hampered the Sultan's movements; and it was only toward winter that he arrived in Tafilet with a fever-stricken army and greatly diminished transport.

Mulai Hassen returned from Tafilet a dying man. The internal complaint from which he was suffering had become acute from the hardships he had undergone, and he was unable to obtain the rest that his state of health required, nor would he place himself under a régime. For a few months he remained in the southern capital, and in the late spring 1894 set out to suppress a rebellion that had broken out in the Tadla region.

While camping in the enemy country he died. Now, the death of the Sultan under such circumstances was fraught with danger to the State. He was an absolute monarch, and with his disappearance all authority and government lapsed until his successor should have taken up the reigns. Again, the expedition was in hostile country, and any inkling of the Sultan's death would have brought the tribes down to pillage and loot the Imperial camp. As long as the Sultan lived, and was present with his expedition, his prestige was sufficient to prevent an attack of the tribes, though even this was not unknown on one or two occasions, and to hold his forces together as a sort of concrete body. But his death, if known, would have meant speedy disorganisation, nor could the troops themselves be trusted not to seize this opportunity to murder and loot.

It was therefore necessary that the Sultan's demise should be kept an absolute secret. He had died in the recesses of his tents, themselves enclosed in a great canvas wall, inside which, except on very special occasions, no one was permitted to penetrate. The knowledge of his death was therefore limited to the personal slaves and to his Chamberlain, Bou Ahmed.

Orders were given that the Sultan would start on his journey at dawn, and before daylight the State palanquin was carried into the Imperial enclosure, the corpse laid within it, and its doors closed and the curtains drawn. At the first pale break of dawn the palanquin was brought out, supported by sturdy mules. Bugles were blown, the band played, and the bowing courtiers and officials poured forth their stentorian cry, "May God protect the life of our Lord". The procession formed up, and, led by flying banners, the dead Sultan set out on his march.

A great distance was covered that day. Only once did the procession stop, when the palanquin was carried into a tent by the roadside, that the Sultan might breakfast. Food was borne in and out; tea, with all the paraphernalia of its brewing, was served: but none but the slaves who knew the secret were permitted to enter. The Chamberlain remained with the corpse, and when a certain time had passed, he emerged to state that His Majesty was rested and had breakfasted, and would proceed on his journey – and once more the procession moved on. Another long march was made to where the great camp was pitched for the night.

The Sultan was tired, the Chamberlain said. He would not come out of his enclosure to transact business as usual in the "Diwan" tent, where he granted audiences. Documents were taken in to the royal quarters by the Chamberlain himself, and, when necessary, they emerged bearing the seal of State, and verbal replies were given to a host of questions.

Then another day of forced marches, for the expedition was still in dangerous country; but Mulai Hassen's death could no longer be concealed. It was summer, and the state of the Sultan's body told its own secret.

Bou Ahmed announced that His Majesty had died two days before, and that by this time his young son, Mulai Abdul Aziz, chosen and nominated by his father, had been proclaimed at Rabat, whither the fleetest of runners had been sent with the news immediately after the death had occurred.

It was a *fait accompli*. The army was now free of the danger of being attacked by the tribes; and the knowledge that the new Sultan was already reigning, and that tranquillity existed elsewhere, deterred the troops from any excesses. Many took the occasion of a certain disorganisation to desert, but so customary was this practice that it attracted little or no attention.

Two days later the body of the dead Sultan, now in a terrible state of decomposition, arrived at Rabat. It must have been a gruesome procession from the description his son Mulai Abdul Aziz gave me: the hurried arrival of the swaying palanquin bearing its terrible burden, five days dead in the great heat of summer; the escort, who had bound scarves over their faces – but even this precaution could not keep them from constant sickness – and even the mules that bore the palanquin seemed affected by the horrible atmosphere, and tried from time to time to break loose.

No corpse is, by tradition, allowed to enter through the gates into a Moorish city, and even in the case of the Sovereign no exception was màde. A hole was excavated in the town wall, through which the procession passed direct into the precincts of the palace, where the burial took place. Immediately after, the wall was restored.

From *Morocco That Was*, by Walter Harris (1921). Reprinted in a paperback edition by Eland Books.

ELIAS CANETTI: *THE UNSEEN*

At twilight I went to the great square in the middle of the city, and what I sought there were not its colour and bustle, those I was familiar with, I sought a small, brown bundle on the ground consisting not even of a voice but of a single sound. This was a deep, long-drawn-out, buzzing "e-e-e-e-e-e-e-e". It did not diminish, it did not increase, it just went on and on; beneath all the thousands of calls and cries in the square it was always audible. It was the most unchanging sound in the Djemaa el Fna, remaining the same all evening and from evening to evening.

While still a long way off I was already listening for it. A restlessness drove me there that I cannot satisfactorily explain. I would have gone to the square in any case, there was so much there to attract me; nor did I ever doubt I would find it each time, with all that went with it. Only for this voice, reduced to a single sound, did I feel something akin to fear. It was at the very edge of the living; the life that engendered it consisted of nothing but that sound. Listening greedily, anxiously, I invariably reached a point in my walk, in exactly the same place, where I suddenly became aware of it like the buzzing of an insect: "e-e-e-e-e-e-e-e".

I felt a mysterious calm spread through my body, and whereas my steps had been hesitant and uncertain hitherto I now, all of a sudden, made determinedly for the sound. I knew where it came from. I knew the small, brown bundle on the ground, of which I had never seen anything more than a piece of dark, coarse cloth. I had never seen the mouth from which the "e-e-e-e-e" issued; nor the eye; nor the cheek; nor any part of the face. I could not have said whether it was the face of a blind man or whether it could see. The brown, soiled cloth was pulled right down over the head like a hood, concealing everything. The creature – as it must have been – squatted on the ground, its back arched under the material. There was not much of the creature there, it seemed slight and feeble, that was all one could conjecture. I had no idea how tall it was because I had never seen it standing. What there was of it on the ground kept so low that one would have stumbled over it quite unsuspectingly, had the sound ever stopped. I never saw it come, I never saw it go; I do not know whether it was brought and put down there or whether it walked there by itself.

The place it had chosen was by no means sheltered. It was the most open part of the square and there was an incessant coming and going on all sides of the little brown heap. On busy evenings it disappeared completely behind people's legs, and although I knew exactly where it was and could always hear the voice I had difficulty in finding it. But then the people dispersed, and it was still in its place when all around it, far and wide, the square was empty. Then it lay there in the darkness like an old and very dirty garment that someone had wanted to get rid of and had surreptitiously dropped in the midst of all the people where no one would notice. Now, however, the people had dispersed and only the bundle lay there. I never waited until it got up or was fetched. I slunk away in the darkness with a choking feeling of helplessness and pride.

The helplessness was in regard to myself. I sensed that I would never do anything to discover the bundle's secret. I had a dread of its shape; and since I could give it no other I left it lying there on the ground. When I was getting close I took care not to bump into it, as if I might hurt or endanger it. It was there every evening, and every evening my heart stood still when I first distinguished the sound, and it stood still again when I caught sight of the bundle. How it got there and how it got away again were matters more sacred to me than my own movements. I never spied on it and I do not know where it disappeared to for the rest of the night and the following day. It was something apart, and perhaps it saw itself as such. I was sometimes tempted to touch the brown hood very lightly with one finger – the creature was bound to notice, and perhaps it had a second sound with which it would have responded. But this temptation always succumbed swiftly to my helplessness.

I have said that another feeling choked me as I slunk away: pride. I was proud of the bundle because it was alive. What it thought to itself as it breathed down there, far below other people, I shall never know. The meaning of its call remained as obscure to me as its whole existence: but it was alive, and every day at the same time, there it was. I never saw it pick up the coins that people threw it; they did not throw many, there were never more than two or three coins lying there. Perhaps it had no arms with which to reach for the coins. Perhaps it had no tongue with which to form the "*l*" of "Allah" and to it the name of God was abbreviated to "e-e-e-e-e". But it was alive, and with a diligence and persistence that were unparalleled it uttered its one sound, uttered it hour after hour, until it was the only sound in the whole enormous square, the sound that outlived all others.

From *The Voices of Marrakesh*, by Elias Canetti (Marion Boyars, London, 1978); first published in German in 1967.

PAUL BOWLES: POINTS IN TIME, X

The country of the Anjra is almost devoid of paved roads. It is a region of high jagged mountains and wooded valleys, and does not contain a town of any size. During the rainy season there are landslides. Then, until the government sends men to repair the damage, the roads cannot be used. All this is very much on the minds of the people who live in the Anjra, particularly when they are waiting for the highways to be rebuilt so that lorries can move again between the villages. Four or five soldiers had been sent several months earlier to repair the potholes along the road between Ksar es Seghir and Melloussa. Their tent was beside the road, near a curve in the river.

A peasant named Hattash, whose village lay a few miles up the valley, constantly passed by the place on his way to and from Ksar es Seghir. Hattash had no fixed work of any sort, but he kept very busy looking for a chance to pick up a little money one way or another in the market and the cafés. He was the kind of man who prided himself on his cleverness in swindling foreigners, by which he meant men from outside the Anjra. Since his friends shared his dislike of outsiders, they found his exploits amusing, although they were careful to have no dealings with him.

Over the months Hattash had become friendly with the soldiers living in the tent, often stopping to smoke a pipe of kif with them, perhaps squatting down to play a few games of ronda. Thus, when one day the soldiers decided to give a party, it was natural that they should mention it to Hattash, who knew everyone for miles around, and therefore might be able to help them. The soldiers came from the south, and their isolation there by the river kept them from meeting anyone who did not regularly pass their tent.

I can get you whatever you want, Hattash told them. The hens, the vegetables, oil, spices, salad, whatever.

Fine. And we want some girls or boys, they added.

Don't worry about that. You'll have plenty to choose from. What you don't want you can send back.

They discussed the cost of the party for an hour or so, after which the soldiers handed Hattash twenty-five thousand francs. He set off, ostensibly for the market.

Instead of going there, he went to the house of a nearby farmer and bought five of his best hens, with the understanding that if the person for whom he was buying them should not want them, he could return the hens and get his money back.

Soon Hattash was outside the soldiers' tent with the hens. How are they? he said. The men squeezed them and examined them, and pronounced them excellent. Good, said Hattash. I'll take them home now and cook them.

He went back to the farmer with the hens and told him that the buyer had refused them. The farmer shrugged and gave Hattash his money.

This seemed to be the moment to leave Ksar es Seghir, Hattash decided. He stopped at a café and invited everyone there to the soldiers' tent that evening, telling them there would be food, wine and girls. Then he bought bread, cheese and fruit, and began to walk along the trails that would lead him over the mountains to Khemiss dl Anjra.

With the twenty-five thousand francs he was able to live for several weeks there in Khemmiss el Anjra. When he had come to the end of them, he began to think of leaving.

In the market one morning he met Hadj Abdallah, a rich farmer from Farsioua, which was a village only a few miles from his own. Hadj Abdallah, a burly, truculent man, always had eyed Hattash with distrust.

Ah, Hattash! What are you doing up here? It's a while since I've seen you.

And you? said Hattash.

Me? I'm on my way to Tetuan. I'm leaving my mule here and taking the bus.

That's where I'm going, said Hattash.

Well, see you in Tetuan, said Hadj Abdallah, and he turned, unhitched his mule, and rode off.

Khemiss dl Anjra is a very small town, so that it was not difficult for Hattash to follow along at some distance, and see the house where Hadj Abdallah tethered his mule and into which he then disappeared. He walked to the bus station and sat under a tree.

An hour or so later, when the bus was filling up with people, Hadj Abdallah arrived and bought his ticket. Hattash approached him.

Can you lend me a thousand francs? I haven't got enough to buy the ticket.

Hadj Abdallah looked at him. No. I can't, he said. Why don't you stay here? And he went and got into the bus.

Hattash, his eyes very narrow, sat down again under the tree. When the bus had left, and the cloud of smoke and dust had drifted off over the meadows, he walked back to the house where the Hadj had left his mule. She still stood there, so he quietly unhitched her, got astride her, and rode her in the direction of Mgas Tleta. He was still smarting under Hadj Abdallah's insult, and he vowed to give him as much trouble as he could.

Mgas Tleta was a small tchar. He took the mule to the fondaq and left it in charge of the guardian. Being ravenously hungry, he searched in his clothing for a coin or two to buy a piece of bread, and found nothing.

In the road outside the fondaq he caught sight of a peasant carrying a loaf in the hood of his djellaba. Unable to take his eyes from the bread, he walked towards the man and greeted him. Then he asked him if he had work, and was not surprised when the man answered no. He went on, still looking at the bread: If you want to earn a thousand francs, you can take my mule to Mdiq. My father's waiting for her and he'll pay you. Just ask for Si Mohammed Tsuli. Everybody in Mdiq knows him. He always has a lot of men working for him. He'll give you work there too if you want it.

The peasant's eyes lit up. He agreed immediately.

Hattash sighed. It's a long time since I've seen good country bread like that, he said, pointing at the loaf that emerged from the hood of the djellaba. The man took it out and handed it to him. Here. Take it.

In return Hattash presented him with the receipt for the mule. You'll have to pay a hundred francs to get her out of the fondaq, he told him. My father will give it back to you.

That's all right. The man was eager to start out for Mdiq.

Si Mohammed Tsuli. Don't forget.

No, no! Bslemah.

Hattash, well satisfied, watched the man ride off. Then he sat down on a rock and ate the whole loaf of bread. He had no intention of returning home to risk meeting the soldiers or Hadj Abdallah, so he decided to hide himself for a while in Tetuan, where he had friends.

When the peasant arrived at Mdiq the following day, he found that no one could tell him where Si Mohammed Tsuli lived. He wandered back and forth through every street in the town, searching and enquiring. When evening came, he went to the gendarmerie and asked if he might leave the mule there. But they questioned him and accused him of having stolen the animal. His story was ridiculous, they said, and they locked him into a cell.

Not many days later Hadj Abdallah, having finished his business in Tetuan, went back to Khemiss dl Anjra to get his mule and ride her home. When he heard that she had disappeared directly after he had taken the bus, he remembered Hattash, and was certain that he was the culprit. The theft had to be reported in Tetuan, and much against his will he returned there.

Your mule is in Mdiq, the police told him.

Hadj Abdallah took another bus up to Mdiq.

Papers, said the gendarmes. Proof of ownership.

The Hadj had no documents of that sort.

They told him to go to Tetouan and apply for the forms.

During the days while he waited for the papers to be drawn up, signed and stamped, Hadj Abdallah grew constantly angrier. He went twice a day to talk with the police. I know who took her! he would shout. I know the son of a whore.

If you ever catch sight of him, hold on to him, they told him. We'll take care of him.

Although Tetuan is a big place with many crowded quarters, the unlikely occurred. In a narrow passageway near the Souq el Fouqi late one evening Hadj Abdallah and Hattash came face to face.

The surprise was so great that Hattash remained frozen to the spot, merely staring into Hadj Abdallah's eyes. Then he heard a grunt of rage, and felt himself seized by the other man's strong arm.

Police! Police! roared Hadj Abdallah. Hattash squirmed, but was unable to free himself.

One policeman arrived, and then another. Hadj Abdallah did not release his grip of Hattash for an instant while he delivered his denunciation. Then with an oath he struck his prisoner, knocking him flat on the sidewalk. Hattash lay there in the dark without moving.

Why did you do that? the policemen cried. Now you're the one who's going to be in trouble.

Hadj Abdallah was already frightened. I know. I ought not to have hit him.

It's very bad, said one policeman, bending over Hattash, who lay completely still. You see, there's blood coming out of his head.

A small crowd was collecting in the passageway.

There were only a few drops of blood, but the policeman had seen Hattash open one eye and had heard him whisper: Listen.

He bent over still further, so that his ear was close to Hattash's lips.

He's got money, Hattash whispered.

The policeman rose and went over to Hadj Abdallah. We'll have to call an ambulance, he said, and you'll have to come to the police station. You had no right to hit him.

At that moment Hattash began to groan.

He's alive, at least! cried Hadj Abdallah. Hamdul'lah!

Then the policemen began to speak with him in low tones, advising him to settle the affair immediately by paying cash to the injured man.

Hadj Abdallah was willing. How much do you think? he whispered.

It's a bad cut he has on his head, the same policeman said, going back to Hattash. Come and look.

Hadj Abdallah remained where he was, and Hattash groaned as the man bent over him again. Then he murmured: Twenty thousand. Five for each of you.

When the policeman rejoined Hadj Abdallah, he told him the amount. You're lucky to be out of it.

Hadj Abdallah gave the money to the policeman, who took it over to Hattash and prodded him. Can you hear me? he shouted.

Ouakha, groaned Hattash.

Here. Take this. He held out the banknotes in such a way that Hadj Abdallah and the crowd watching could see them clearly. Hattash stretched up his hand and took them, slipping them into his pocket.

Hadj Abdallah glared at the crowd and pushed his way through, eager to get away from the spot.

After he had gone, Hattash slowly sat up and rubbed his head. The onlookers still stood there watching. This bothered the two policemen, who were intent on getting their share of the money. The recent disclosures of corruption, however, had made the public all too attentive at such moments. The crowd was waiting to see them speak to Hattash or, if he should move, follow him.

Hattash saw the situation and understood. He rose to his feet and quickly walked up the alley.

The policemen looked at each other, waited for a few seconds, and then began to saunter casually in the same direction. Once they were out of sight of the group of onlookers they hurried along, flashing their lights up each alley in their search. But Hattash knew the quarter as well as they, and got safely to the house of his friends.

He decided, however, that with the two policemen on the lookout for him, Tetuan was no longer the right place for him, and that his own tchar in the Anjra would be preferable.

Once he was back there, he made discreet enquiries about the state of the road to Ksar es Seghir. The repairs were finished, his neighbours told him, and the soldiers had been sent to some other part of the country.

From *Points in Time,* by Paul Bowles (Peter Owen, London, 1982).

ONWARD FROM MOROCCO

Going on overland from Morocco there are two basic options. The most obvious is to take in something of **Spain** and, if you've developed any interest in Moorish art, to visit the three great Andalusian cities of the south – **Granada**, **Córdoba** and **Sevilla**. Each of these boast superb Islamic monuments, which, to be honest are more spectacular than any in Morocco. Granada has the fabulous fifteenth-century Alhambra palace, home of the last Moorish rulers in al-Andalus; Córdoba has a tenth-century mosque, now the city's cathedral; and Seville has one of Yacoub el Mansour's magnificent Almohad towers, again adapted to Christian use as the local bell tower, or Giralda. For all of this – and a great deal more – *The Rough Guide to Spain* (Harrap-Columbus, £6.95) has the requisite details.

The second option, and one that is considerably more ambitious, is to travel **"the Maghreb Circuit"** east from Morocco into **Algeria** and **Tunisia**, where, if you still have the time and energy, you could cross over by ferry to Italy and either loop back to northern Europe (Italian trains are cheap) or take another ferry on from Bari or Brindisi to Greece. Don't be put off by the distances involved in any of this, nor by travellers' tales of Algerian bureaucracy at the border (though these are true enough); it's an exciting, feasible and immensely satisfying trip, and there's an added fascination in that all of this region – from Spain and Morocco up as far as Sicily – comprised the western Arab empire in the early Middle Ages.

Mosques, incidentally, may be visited freely in Algeria and, to an extent, in Tunisia.

ALGERIA

Algeria is much less well known in the West than either Morocco or Tunisia and it has always been the most adventurous part of North Africa to travel through. This it remains – above all in its mind-boggling desert routes.

Algerians themselves are extremely hospitable, and there is none of the hustling that you find in Morocco. If you can speak French, you will be able to communicate with ease – the language of colonial years (150 years here, as opposed to just 50 in Morocco) endures, along with many facets of French culture. Indeed, all European travellers are initially assumed to be French. It tends to be an advantage if you can make it clear that you're not.

Red Tape

Visas are essential for all Europeans (except Scandinavians, Spanish and Swiss) and for North Americans and Australasians. Technically, they should be obtained in your home country – a good idea if you are organised – although it is usually possible to obtain one, within the day, at the Algerian consulate in Rabat (see Rabat "Listings"), or (a much longer process) in Oujda.

While in Algeria you are required to change 1000 dinars (about £70) into Algerian currency at the official rate; you may be asked to do so at the border. This restriction is no longer waived for students, and money cannot be changed back again. The black market is widely used, and if you're staying longer than your officially changed 1000 dinars will last, you will find rates offered up to three times better. The best currency for black market exchange is French francs. However, beware of losing track of what you've declared on your C.D. form and what you have in your pocket.

Borders

There are two **borders** open between Morocco and Algeria – at OUJDA and, 300km to the south, at the desert oasis of FIGUIG. The former used to be closed to "pedestrian traffic" but it is now routinely open, following the improvement in Moroccan–Algerian relations after the 1988 Maghreb Summit.

Routes

The fastest route through Algeria cuts across the big **northern cities** of ORAN, ALGIERS and CONSTANTINE. This is not in itself the most interesting part of the country, though the mountain scenery is often spectacular.

Making relatively short detours the rewards are greater. TIMGAD, almost completely preserved, is one of the most extraordinary Roman towns anywhere; any one of the roads between BATNA and the immense oasis of BISKRA will take you through dramatic canyons; the TURQUOISE COAST, west of Algiers, is a long series of mountainous and isolated coves; and in the mountains by the Moroccan border,

TLEMCEN's Islamic architecture is among the most important and beautiful in North Africa.

If you have time to spare, though, even as little as a week, try to take in at least something of **the south**. The sheer size of the desert regions here is hard to grasp: TAMANRASSET, near the Niger border, for instance, is further from Algiers than London is. Closer, and easily accessible from the north, there are also some of the most spectacular Saharan dunes – stretching between EL OUED, the so-called "City of a Thousand Domes", and the fantastic architecture of GHARDAIA.

Going through the deep south really does feel more like travel than tourism and time and energy are needed to explore the desert *pistes*. The two really compelling attractions are both mountain ranges: the HOGGAR, rising over 3000m to the north of Tamanrasset, and the TASSILI, some way to the east, with its exceptional prehistoric cave paintings.

Guidebooks

The trip across the Algerian Sahara to West Africa is covered in detail in the *Rough Guide to West Africa* (Harrap Columbus, £9.95). Simon and Jan Glen's *Sahara Handbook* (Lascelles, £18.95) is also useful for the practicalities of taking a car across the desert. The only guides to Algeria itself are in French: try a combination of the *Guide Bleu: Algerie* and, for budget practicalities, the *Guide du Routard: Algerie-Tunisie* (both published by Hachette).

TUNISIA

Crossing from Algeria to Tunisia is normally straightforward, though the number of border posts open varies according to the state of relations between the two countries (which are currently good). The most regular posts are in the north at ANNABA-BABOUCH and SOUK AHRAS-GHARDIMAO (the train crossing), but at the time of this writing you can cross in the south, too, at EL OUED-HAZOUA.

Much more Westernised than either Morocco or Algeria, Tunisia is recognisably Mediterranean in character and a relaxed place to end up after some desert travelling. Its best-known attractions are the long white-sand **beaches** and easy-going resorts, and in a North African context these are perhaps its greatest novelty. But there is considerably more to the country than this – not least its highly individual **desert architecture**, and the Maghreb's most important **Roman sites** – and the accessibility of everything (you can comfortably travel its length in a couple of days) makes it a satisfying place to visit and get to know.

Red Tape

North Americans, Australasians and Benelux nationals need a **visa** to visit Tunisia. This can be obtained in a couple of hours from the Tunisian Consulate in Rabat (see Rabat "Listings"). Other Europeans need no visa.

On to Sicily or beyond

Continuing on from Tunisia, there are regular, year-round **ferries** to the Sicilian ports of PALERMO and TRAPANI, and links from there to Naples, Genoa, Sardinia and Malta. Apart from the last two weeks of August (when all ferries from Tunis are packed with returning migrant workers) it is usually possible to get tickets on these; if you have a car, however, it's essential to make your bookings in advance for travel between July and September.

Guidebook

For a full treatment of the country, *The Rough Guide to Tunisia* (Harrap-Columbus, £5.95) seems an obvious choice.

THE CANARY ISLANDS

A last alternative, onward from Morocco, is to head for the **CANARY ISLANDS**, just a few miles offshore from the disputed territory of the former Spanish Sahara. There is a weekly car and passenger ferry from Agadir to Las Palmas (see Agadir "Practicalities") between September and May. Alternatively, you can fly to Las Palmas from Agadir or Laayoune.

BOOKS

Books designated o/p are out of print, but still worth tracking down second-hand or in libraries.

GENERAL/TRAVEL

Paul Bowles, *Points in Time* (Peter Owen, £4.50), *Their Heads Are Green & Their Hands Are Blue* (Abacus, £3.99). Novelist, poet and composer Paul Bowles has lived in Tangier most of his life and more or less singlehandedly brought translations of local writers (see "Moroccan Fictions" on p.444) to Western attention. *Points* is a remarkable series of tales and short pieces inspired by episodes and sources from earliest times to the present day; the final piece is excerpted in the "Writers on Morocco" section. *Heads* includes a couple of travel essays on Morocco and a terrific piece on the psychology of desert travel. Bowles's autobiography, *Without Stopping* (Papermac, £7.95) is also of interest for its Moroccan episodes, as is his more recent *Two Years Beside the Strait: A Tangier Journal, 1988–89* (Peter Owen, £5.95).

Peter Mayne, *A Year in Marrakesh* (Eland Books, £4.95). Mayne went to Marrakesh in the early 1950s, found a house in an ordinary district of the Medina, and tried to live like a Moroccan. He couldn't, but wrote an unusually perceptive account explaining why.

Elias Canetti, *The Voices of Marrakesh* (Marion Boyars, £5.95). Impressions of Marrakesh in the last years of French rule, by the Nobel prize-winning author. The atmosphere of many pieces still holds – see the excerpt printed under "Writers on Morocco".

OLDER ACCOUNTS

Walter Harris, *Morocco That Was* (1921; reprinted by Eland Books, £4.95). Harris, *Times* correspondent in Tangier from the 1890s until his death in 1933, saw the country at probably the strangest ever stage in its history – the last years of "Old Morocco" in its feudal isolation and the first of French occupation. *Morocco That Was* is a masterpiece – alternately sharp, melodramatic and very funny. It incorporates, to some extent, the anecdotes in his earlier *Land of an African Sultan* (1889, o/p) and *Tafilet* (1895, o/p).

Edmondo de Amicis, *Morocco: Its People and Places* (1882, reprinted by Darf Publishers, London, £22). More intrepid journeying in the Harris mould – illustrated with copious line drawings.

R. B. Cunninghame Graham, *Mogreb el Acksa: A Journey in Morocco* (1912; reprinted by Marlboro Press, US, $10.95). And yet more adventuring and anecdotes in a book that wears its age better than most. George Bernard Shaw and Joseph Conrad were contemporary admirers.

Budgett Meakin, *The Land of the Moors* (1900; reprinted by Darf Publishers, London, £35), *The Moors: A Comprehensive Description* (1902, o/p). These wonderful encyclopaedic volumes were the first really detailed books on Morocco and Moroccan life. Many of Meakin's "Comprehensive Descriptions" remain accurate and the sheer breadth of his knowledge – from "Berber Feuds" to "Specimen Recipes" and musical notations of "Calls to Prayer" – is fascinating in itself. Highly recommended library browsing.

Leo Africanus, *History and Description of Africa* (no recent edition but available in major libraries). Written in the mid-sixteenth century, this was the book Meakin himself followed, "astounded at the confirmation [of its accuracy] received from natives of remote and almost inaccessible districts". Leo, who was Moroccan by birth, was captured as a young man by Christian pirates. He subsequently converted and lived in Italy; the book was suggested to him by the Pope, and so there's more than a hint of propaganda about some of the accounts. (See also Amin Malouf, under "Fiction".)

OF LESSER INTEREST

Wyndham Lewis, *Journey into Barbary* (1932; reprinted by Black Sparrow Press, US, $12.50). Terrific drawings and an obscure, eccentric and very rambling text.

Edith Wharton, *In Morocco* (1920; reprinted by Century, 1983, o/p). The American novelist dedicated her book to General Lyautey, Consul General of the Protectorate, whose modernising efforts she greatly admired. By no means a classic, it is nonetheless worth reading for glimpses of harem life in the early part of the century.

Nina Epton, *Saints and Sorcerers* (Cassell, 1958, o/p). Highly readable travelogue, concentrating on folk customs and religious sects and confraternities.

Rom Landau, *Morocco: Marrakesh, Fez, Rabat* (Elek Books, 1967, o/p). Landau has written numerous books on Morocco, none of them very inspiring. This one's redeeming feature is an excellent series of photographs – including rare pictures of mosque interiors.

HISTORY

Neville Barbour, *Morocco* (Thames & Hudson, 1965, o/p). A lucid, straightforward account of Morocco from the Phoenicians to "the present day" (1965).

Ibn Khaldun, *The Muqaddimah: An Introduction to History* (Routledge, £10.99). Edited translation of the greatest work of the fourteenth-century Moorish scholar – a fascinating mix of history, sociology and anthropology, centuries ahead of its time.

Roger Le Tourneau, *Fez in the Age of the Marinides* (University of Oklahoma Press, US, $8.95). Interesting if slightly specialist study of the Merenid capital of Morocco. Tourneau's *The Almohad Movement* (Princeton University Press, 1981, o/p) is also worth looking out for in libraries.

Douglas Porch, *The Conquest of Morocco* (Papermac, £7.95). Accessible and fascinating account of the extraordinary manoeuvrings and characters of Morocco's turn-of-the-century history.

David Woolman, *Rebels in the Rif* (Stanford University Press, US, $25). Academic but very readable study of the Riffian war in the 1920s and of the tribes' uprising against the Moroccan government in 1956.

Gavin Maxwell, *Lords of the Atlas* (1966, Century reprint 1983, o/p). Drawing heavily on Walter Harris' accounts of the Moorish court (see above), this is the story of the extraordinary Glaoui family – literally the "Lords" of the High Atlas, where they exercised almost complete control from the turn of the nineteenth century right through to Moroccan independence in 1956. Not an attractive tale but a compelling one, and again superbly written. (Note: This book is officially banned from sale in Morocco, due to its view of historical events.)

Tony Hodges, *Western Sahara: the Roots of a Desert War* (Croom Helm, 1983, o/p). The former Spanish colony of Western Sahara-Rio d'Oro is the most contentious issue of modern Moroccan politics: this is the latest, fullest and most interesting book on the subject.

NORTH AFRICA/ARAB WORLD

J.M Abun-Nasr, *History of the Maghreb in the Islamic Period* (Cambridge University Press, 1971, o/p). Morocco in the wider context of North Africa by a distinguished Arab historian.

R. Oliver and J. D. Fage, *A History of Africa* (Penguin, £5.99). Morocco within the context of its continent.

Peter Mansfield, *The Arabs* (Penguin, 1973, o/p). Best general introduction to the Arab world, from its beginnings through to the 1970s. Short final sections deal with each individual country.

ANTHROPOLOGY

Fatima Mernissi, *Beyond the Veil: Male-Female Dynamics in Modern Muslim Society* (Al Saqi Books, £4.95). Seminal book by a feminist Moroccan sociologist from the Mohammed V University in Rabat.

Fatima Mernissi, *Doing Daily Battle: Interviews with Moroccan Women* (The Women's Press, £5.95). Eleven women – carpet weavers, rural and factory workers, teachers – talk about all aspects of their lives, from work and housing to marriage. A fascinating insight into a resolutely private world.

Elizabeth Fernea, *A Street in Marrakesh* (Doubleday, US, o/p). Highly readable account of a woman anthropologist's period of study and experiences in Marrakesh.

Elizabeth Fernea and Basima Q. Bezirgan, *Middle Eastern Muslim Women Speak Out* (University of Texas Press, US, $13.95). Straightforward and accessible social anthropology, including interesting transcriptions of Berber women's songs from the High Atlas.

Ernest Gellner and Charles Micaud (eds.), *Arabs and Berbers* (Duckworth, 1973, o/p). Authoritative collection of anthropological articles on Berbers and tribalism in Morocco. Interesting, if read on a rather selective basis.

Ernest Gellner, *Saints of the Atlas* (University of Chicago Press US, $20). The bulk of this book is an in-depth study of a group of *zaouia*-villages in the High Atlas, but there are excellent introductory chapters on Morocco's recent past and the concept and origins of Berbers.

Kevin Dwyer, *Moroccan Dialogues: Anthropology in Question* (Waveland Press, US, $9.95). Fascinating series of recorded conversations with a farmer from a village near Taroudannt, ranging through attitudes to women, religion and village life to popular Moroccan perceptions of the Jews, the French and even the hippies. Well worth a look.

Vincent Crapanzano, *Tuhami: Portrait of a Moroccan* (University of Chicago Press, US, £7.25). Tuhami is an illiterate Moroccan tile-maker in Meknes: this study is an interesting, if at times slightly impenetrable, mix of ethnography and psychology.

David Seddon, *Moroccan Peasants: A Century of Change in the Eastern Rif* (William Dawson, £18). Covers similar ground to David Woolman (see "History"), though with a more strictly anthropological approach.

Bernard Lewis, *The Jews of Islam* (Routledge, 1987, o/p). Morocco had over 30,000 Jews until the mass emigrations to Israel in the 1940s and 1950s. Lewis discusses their position (which was perhaps the most oppressed within the Arab world) and their political and cultural contributions. Disappointingly, he doesn't attempt to cover the period of emigration itself.

Shlomo Deshen, *The Mellah Society: Jewish Community Life in Sherifian Morocco* (University of Chicago Press, US, £9.50). Academic study of economic activity and political organisation in the *mellahs* prior to the French Protectorate.

Edward Westermarck, *Ritual and Belief in Morocco* (1926); *Wit and Wisdom in Morocco* (1930). *Ritual* is a seminal work on Morocco and remains a fascinating storehouse of social and anthropological detail. *Wit* is entirely a collection of Moroccan proverbs – wild, humorous and gripping. Both are well worth the effort to track down in libraries

ISLAM

The Koran (numerous editions). The Word of God as handed down to the Prophet is the basis of all Islam, so essential reading for anyone interested. If you can find it, the Oxford University Press edition (currently o/p) is the clearest and liveliest translation.

S. H. Nasr, *Ideas and Realities of Islam* (Allen & Unwin, £4.95). Probably the clearest and most useful general introduction.

Maxime Rodinson, *Muhammad* (Penguin, £5.99). Challenging account of the Prophet's life and the immediate impact of his ideology.

ART/ARCHITECTURE

Richard Parker, *A Practical Guide to Islamic Monuments in Morocco* (Baraka Press, Charlottesville, Virginia, US). Exactly what it claims to be – very helpful and well informed, with introductory sections on architectural forms and motifs, and craft traditions. Available at the *American Bookstore* in Rabat.

Titus Burckhardt, *Fes: City of Islam* (Islamic Texts Society, o/p); *Moorish Culture in Spain* (Allen & Unwin, o/p). Burckhardt's *Spain* is a superb study of architecture, history, Islamic city-design and the mystical significance of its art – and as such it's entirely relevant to medieval Morocco. *Fes* (if you can find it) is worth dipping into; if only for the photos, as the conceptual approach and respect for tradition can be a bit hard going.

Michael Brett, *The Moors* (Orbis, o/p). A beautifully illustrated survey of the Moorish Empire, extremely well thought out and with an understanding text.

David Talbot Rice, *Islamic Art* (Thames & Hudson, £5.95). Clear, interesting and well-illustrated survey – though only two chapters directly concern Morocco.

Andre Paccard, *Traditional Islamic Craft in Moroccan Architecture* (Editions Atelier,

France, 2 vols; £140). French coffee-table tome beyond all possible rival. The text is forgettable, but it is massively illustrated and – uniquely – includes photographs of Moroccan Royal Palaces currently in use: this alone makes it worth a look.

Jean Besanceon, *Costumes of Morocco* (KPI, £50). Lavish prints, drawn in the 1930s and 1940s when they were still current. Most are now museum pieces.

FOOD

Robert Carrier, *Taste of Morocco* (Arrow, £7.99); **Paula Wolfert**, *Good Food from Morocco* (John Murray, £9.95). Mouthwatering recipes from the largely domestic canon of Moroccan food. Wolfert's book, originally published in the 1960s, has a more rural emphasis than Carrier's tour of the grand kitchens.

PHOTOGRAPHS

Owen Logan, *Al Maghrib: Photographs from Morocco* (Polygon, £6.95). Superb black and white portrait studies in a beautifully produced monograph that includes three stories by Paul Bowles (see "Fiction", below).

Shirley Kay, *Morocco* (Quartet, 1984, o/p). Glossy and well written picture book introduction to the country.

MOROCCAN FICTION

TRANSLATIONS BY PAUL BOWLES

Mohammed Mrabet, *Love with a Few Hairs* (City Lights, US, $6.95); *The Boy Who Set the Fire & Other Stories* (City Lights, US, $6.95); *The Lemon* (Peter Owen, £10.95; City Lights, US, $6.95); *M'Hashish* (City Lights, US, $3.95); *The Chest* (Tombouctou, US, $7.95); *Marriage With Papers* (Tombouctou, US; UK distrib. Airlift Books, £5.95); *The Big Mirror* (Black Sparrow Press, US); *Harmless Poisons, Blameless Sins* (Black Sparrow Press, US; UK distrib. Airlift Books, £8.50); *The Beach Café and The Voice* (Black Sparrow Press, US; UK distrib. Airlift Books, £3.95); *Look and Move On: An Autobiography* (Peter Owen, £12,95).

Mohammed Choukri, *For Bread Alone: An Autobiography* (City Lights, US, $6.95). Choukri is also author of two brief anecdotal biogra-

phies – *Jean Genet in Tangier* (Ecco Press, US, 1974, o/p) and *Tennesee Williams in Tangier* (Cadmus Editions, US, 1979, o/p), also translated by Bowles.

Larbi Layachi, *A Life Full of Holes* (published under the name Driss ben Hamed Charhadi; Grove Press, US, $3.50). See also "Other Moroccan Fiction", below.

Five Eyes, stories by **Mohammed Mrabet**, **Larbi Layachi**, **Mohammed Choukri**, **Ahmed Yacoubi** and **Abdesiam Boulaich** (Black Sparrow Press, US, o/p).

All of the above are taped and translated from the Moghrebi by **Paul Bowles**. It is hard to generalise about them, except to say that they are for the most part "tales" (even the autobiographies, which seem little different from the fiction), share a common fixation with intrigue and unexpected twists in the narrative, and are often punctuated by episodes of extreme violence. None have particular characterisation, though this hardly seems relevant since they have such a strong, vigorous narrative style – brilliantly matched by Bowles's sharp, economic language.

The **Mrabet** stories – *The Beach Cafe* is perhaps his best – are often kif-inspired, and this gives them a slightly paranoid quality, as Mrabet himself explained: "Give me twenty or thirty pipes . . . and an empty room can fill up with wonderful things, or terrible things. And the stories come from these things."

For a taste of the stories, see "Moroccan Fictions" on p.444–452.

OTHER MOROCCAN FICTION

Tahar Ben Jelloun, *The Sand Child* (Quarter, £11.95). Ben Jelloun, resident in Paris, is Morocco's most acclaimed writer – and in the case of this novel, which won the French Prix Goncourt, the reputation is just. An unusually "fictional" tale, its subject, the Sand Child, is a girl whose father brought her up as a boy. Quartet also publish another Ben Jelloun novel, *Sacred Night* (£12.95).

Larbi Layachi, *Yesterday and Today* (Black Sparrow Press, US, $8.50), *The Jealous Lover* (Tombouctou, US, $7.50). The former is a kind of sequel to *Life Full of Holes* (see above), describing in semi-fictionalised form Layachi's time with Paul and Jane Bowles; the latter is more of a novel and rather less successful.

Abdelhak Serhane, *Messaouda* (Carcanet, £8.95). Adventurous, semi-autobiographical novel about growing up in Azrou during the 1950s. The narrator's development parallels that of his country; his attempts to free himself from the patriarchy and authoritarianism of his father are used as an allegory for the struggle against French colonialism and its aftermath.

Driss Chraibi, *Heirs to the Past* (Heinemann African Writers Series, £3.45). Again concerned with the crisis of Moroccans' postcolonial identity, and again semi-autobiographical as the author-narrator (who has lived in France since the war) returns to Morocco for the funeral of his father. Also available – though in rather over-literal and unspirited translation – are two further novels, *The Butts* and *Mother Comes of Age* (Three Continents Press/Forest Books, both £7.95).

Brick Ousaïd, *Mountains Forgotten by God* (Three Continents Press/Forest Books, £6.95). Autobiographical narrative of an Atlas Berber family, which gives an impressive sense of the harshness of mountain life. As the author describes it, it is "not an exercise in literary style [but] a cry from the bottom of my heart, of despair and revolt".

Margot Badran and Miriam Cooke (eds), *Opening the Gates: A Century of Arab Feminist Writing* (Virago, £16.99). Includes three Moroccan pieces, including a traditional women's tale, recounted by the Moroccan feminist, Fatima Mernissi.

WESTERN FICTION

PAUL BOWLES

NOVELS: *The Sheltering Sky* (Granada, £3.99); *Let It Come Down* (Arrow, £2.95); *The Spider's House* (Arena, £3.95). (A fourth novel, *Up Above the World*, is set in Latin America.) STORIES: *Collected Stories of Paul Bowles 1939–76* (Black Sparrow Press, US; UK distrib. Airlift Books, £8.95) gathers together work from numerous, earlier editions. Post-1976 collections include *Midnight Mass* (Peter Owen, £11.95), *Call at Corazón* (Peter Owen, £11.95) and *Unwelcome Words* (Tombouctou, US; UK distrib. Airlift Books, £4.95).

Bowles stands out as the most interesting and the most prolific writer using North African themes – and with Bertolucci's filming of *The Sheltering Sky* looks set, at last, to regain recognition (the novel was a best seller on publication in 1955). Many of his stories are similar in vein to those of Mohammed Mrabet (see above), employing the same sparse forms, bizarre twists and interjections of violence. The novels are something different, exploring both Morocco (or, in *The Sheltering Sky*, Algeria) and the ways in which Europeans and Americans react to and are affected by it.

If you read nothing else on the country, at least get hold of **The Spider's House** – one of the best political novels ever written, its backdrop the traditional daily life of Fes, its theme the conflicts and transformation at the last stages of the French occupation of the country.

OTHER FICTION SET IN MOROCCO

Amin Malouf, *Leo the African* (Quartet, £12.95). Superb historical novel, recreating the life of Leo Africanus, the fifteenth-century Moorish geographer, in Granada and Fes and on his later travels.

Arturo Barea, *The Forging of a Rebel* (Flamingo reprint in 3 volumes, 1988, o/p). Spanish autobiographical trilogy dealing with events of the 1930s. The second volume, *The Track*, concerns the war and colonisation of the Rif, the Spanish entry into Chaouen and life in Tetouan.

Richard Hughes, *In the Lap of Atlas* (Chatto, 1976, o/p). Traditional Moroccan stories – cunning, humorous and ironical – reworked by the author of *A High Wind In Jamaica*. Also includes a narrative of Hughes' visit to Telouet and the Atlas in 1928.

Leonora Peets, *Women of Marrakesh* (C.Hurst, £12.95). Stories of domestic life in the city from the 1930s to 1970 by a long-term Estonian resident.

Elisa Chimenti, *Tales and Legends of Morocco* (Astor-Honor, US, $10.95). Travelling in the 1930s and 1940s with her father, personal physician to Sultan Moulay Hassan, Chimenti learned many of these simple, fable-like tales from Berber tribesmen whose guest she was.

Jane Kramer, *Honor to the Bride Like the Pigeon that Guards its Grain Under the Clove Tree* (Farrar, Straus & Giroux, US, 1970, o/p). Fictional narrative based on the true story of a Berber woman's kidnap in Meknes.

Jane Bowles, *Everything is Nice – Collected Stories* (Virago, 1989). The title story is a perfect evocation of Moroccan life, rendered in the author's unique and idiosyncratic style. Jane Bowles was resident in Morocco on and off, with Paul Bowles, from the 1940s until her tragic death in 1973. Millicent Dillon's biography, *A Little Original Sin: the Life of Jane Bowles* (Virago, £10.95), includes some fascinating material.

William Bayer, *Tangier* (Dutton, US, 1971, o/p). Thinly disguised potboiler set amid the Tangier expat life of the 1960s.

Anthony Burgess, *Earthly Powers* (Penguin, £5.99), *Enderby Anthology* (Penguin, £5.99).

Sporadic scenes in 1950s-decadent Tangier.

Brion Gysin, *The Process* (Paladin, £3.95). Beat novel by ex-Tangier resident and friend of William Burroughs. Fun, if a little caught in its (zany 1960s) age.

Robin Maugham, *The Wrong People* (Gay Men's Press, £4.95). Gay classic, set in Tangier.

Elspeth Davie (ed.), *Original Prints Volume II* (Polygon, £4.95). New writing by Scottish women – includes an excellent account of a Moroccan wedding ("Jamila's Wedding") by Gillean Somerville.

SPECIALIST BOOKSHOPS

For the books detailed in this section (and also for the hiking guides detailed on p.000, the following bookshops are well worth a ring:

Stanfords 12–14 Long Acre, Covent Garden, London WC2E 9LP (☎071 836 1321). The world's oldest established map and guidebook suppliers; they also stock history and general books.

Daunt's Books for Travellers, 83 Marylebone High St, London W1M 4AL (☎071 224 2295). A shop that aims to stock all books related to travel – from guides to local literature. Wonderful concept and a beautiful place to browse. Includes a small second hand selection.

The Travellers' Bookshop, 25 Cecil Court, London WC2 (%071/836 9132). Impressive selection of modern and antiquarian books.

Dillons, 82 Gower Street, London WC1 6EQ (☎071 636 1577). Includes substantial Africa section and a fine selection of fauna and flora

field guides to the region in the natural history section.

Africa Centre, 38 King Street, Covent Garden, London WC2 (☎071 836 1973). A unique resource centre, library and excellent bookshop

The Maghreb Bookshop, 45 Burton St, London WC1 (☎071/388 1840). Small bookshop supplying new, rare and out of print books on all aspects of North Africa. Run by the highly knowledgeable Mohammed Ben Madani (from Sidi Ifni), who will search for books if requested.

Madani also published ***The Maghreb Review***, a quarterly journal in French and English covering social, political and anthropoligcal issues, and with full reviews of all books relating to North Africa.

LANGUAGE

Very few people who come to Morocco learn to speak a word of Arabic, let alone anything of the country's three individual Berber dialects. This is a pity – you'll be treated in a very different way if you make even a small effort to master basic phrases – though not really surprising. Moroccans are superb linguists: much of the country is bilingual in French, and anyone who has significant dealings with tourists will know some English and maybe half a dozen other languages, too.

If you can speak **French,** you'll be able to get by almost anywhere you care to go; it is worth refreshing your knowledge before coming – and, if you're not too confident, bringing a good English–French phrasebook. **Spanish** is also useful, and widely understood in the old Spanish colonial zones around Tetouan and the Rif, and in the Deep South.

MOROCCAN ARABIC

Moroccan Arabic, the country's "official" language, is substantially different from "classical" Arabic, or from the modern Arabic spoken in Egypt and the Gulf States. If you speak any form of Arabic, however, you will be able to make yourself understood. Egyptian Arabic, in particular, is familiar to most Moroccans, through soap operas on TV, and many will adapt their speech accordingly.

Pronunciation

There are no silent letters – you pronounce everything that's written. Letters and syllables in italics should be stressed.
Here are some keys to follow in pronouncing:

kh	like the "ch" in Scottish lo*ch*		ay	as in "say"
gh	like the French "r" (a slight gargling sound)		q	like "k" but further back in throat
ai	as in "eye"		j	like "s" in pleasure

Basics

Yes	*Naham, Ee*yeh		(Very) good	Mizee*yen* (b*zef*)
No	La		Bad	*Me*shee mizee*yen*
Please	Min*fad*lik/ *A*fek		Today	Ly*oom*/ lee*oom*
Thank you	*Shok*ran/ Baraka*lay*fik		Tomorrow	*Gh*edda
(polite response – *Ble*jmeel)				

Greetings and Farewells

Hello	La *bes*		What's yours?	S*mee*tik?
(informal, to one person)			See you later.	N'*shoo*fik min bad
Hello	Sal*am* Wa*lay*koom		. . . God willing	. . In*shall*ah
(formal, to a group; response – Wa*lay*koom sal*am*)			(response to "In*shall*ah" is In*shall*ah)	
Good morning	Sbah l'*khir*		Good night	*Lee*la sa*iee*da
Good afternoon	Msa l'*khir*		Good-bye	B*sle*mah
My name is	Ismee. . .		Bon voyage	Treq sa*lama*

Directions, Travelling, and Accommodation

Where is . . . ?	Fayn kayn . . . ?	Here, there	Hnna, Temma
. . . a (good) hotel?	. . . O*tel* (mizee*yen*)	When is the bus/train?	Waq*tash* l'kar/tren?
. . . a campsite?	. . . Moo*khaiy*em	First/last/next	Loo*wel*/L'*akher*/Lee minbad
. . . a restaurant?	. . . Restaurant	Write it (please).	Ktib ha (*Afek*)
. . . a bank?	. . . Bank	Do you have a room?	Wesh *and*ik wahid beet?
. . . the bus station?	. . . *Ma*hatat d'lkee*ran*	Can I see it?	Wesh yimkin nshoof?
. . . the train station?	. . . *Ma*hatat d'ltren	Is there. . . ?	Wesh kayn . . . ?
. . . a toilet?	. . . Vaysay/ W.C.	. . . a (hot) shower?	. . . Doosh (skhoon)
Straight	Nee*sham*/ tol	. . . a window?	. . . Serjem
(To the) left, right	(Al) Leeser, Lee*min*	. . . a key?	. . . Saroot
Near, far	Qreeb, Baieed	Can we camp here?	Wesh yimkin n*khai*moo
Junction	Rompwa		hanna

Buying and Numbers

How much (is that)?	Bsh *hal* (hadeek)	I want something. . .	Bgheet shi*haja* . . .
This isn't good	Hadee *mesh*ee mizee*yen*	. . . else	. . . okhra
Too expensive	Gha*lee* b*zef*	. . . better than this	. . . khir min hadee
. . . (for me)	(a*li*ya)	. . . like this	. . . b*hal* hadee
Still too expensive	Mazal gha*lee* b*zef*	(but)	(walakeen)
Do you have. . . ?	wesh *and*ik. . . ?	. . . larger, smaller	. . . kbee*ra*, sgjee*ra*
Okay	*Wa*kha	. . . cheaper	. . . r*khay*sa

1	wahed	12	etnach	50	khamsin
2	tnin (Classical)	13	tlatach	60	settin
	joob (everyday)	14	arbatach	70	seba'in
3	tlata	15	khamstach	80	tmanin
4	arba	16	settach	90	tsa'in
5	khamsa	17	sebatach	100	mia
6	setta	18	tmentach	200	mitin
7	seba	19	tsatach	300	tlata mia
8	tmenia	20	achrin	400	arba mia
9	tse'ud	21	wahed u achrin	1000	alef
10	achra	30	tlatin		
11	hadach	40	arbain		

Reactions, etc.

I've seen it already.	Shift ha badas	Help!	Ateqq/ Ow*nee*!
I don't want any.	Mabgheet *shee*	How do you say?	Keef t*koolo*?
I don't understand.	Mat*hem*sh	Excuse me	*Smeh* lee
Do you understand?	Wesh f*hem*tee?	Sorry, I apologise	As*if*
Get lost!	Seer!	Never mind, so it goes	*Maa*lesh
Everything's fine.	*Kool*shee mizee*yen*	No problem	Mush mush*killah*
Let's go!	Ha*la*!	Respect yourself	*Ih*tarim n*af*sak
Watch out!	An*dak*/ *Ba*lek!	(a term of admonition)	
I've lost . . .	Msha leeya . . .	Calm down	*Ta*wil *ba*lak
. . . passport	. . . passeport	(literally, "lengthen your	
. . . ticket	. . . *bee*yay/ warqa	mind")	
. . . key	. . . sa*root*	You honour us	Too-shah-rif-na
. . . baggage	. . . bag*gai/ho*wayj	Patience is a virtue	As-*sobr*min Allah

BERBER WORDS AND PHRASES IN TASHELHAÏT

There are three **Berber dialects** which encompass roughly geographical areas. They are known by several names, of which these are the most common:

Riffi – The Rif Mountains and Northern Morocco
Zaian, Tamazight – The Middle Atlas and Central Morocco
Tashelhaït, Soussi, Chleuh – The High and Anti Atlas and the South

As the most popular Berber areas for visitors are the High Atlas and South, the following is a very brief guide to **Tashelhaït words and phrases.**

Basics

Yes, no	Eyeh, Oho	Today	Zig sbah
Thank you, please	Barakalaufik	Tomorrow	Ghasad
Good	Eefulkee/Eeshwa	Yesterday	Eegdam
Bad	Khaib	Excuse me	Semhee
		Berbers	Shleuh

Greetings and Farewells (All Arabic greetings understood)

Hello	La bes darik (man)	See you later	Akrawes dah inshallah
(response – *la bes*)	La bes darim (woman)	Goodbye	Akayaoon Arbee
How are you?	Meneek antgeet?	Say hello to your	Sellum flfamilenik
(response – *la bes lmamdulah*)		family	

Directions and Names on Maps

Where is. . . ?	Mani heela . . . ?	I want to go to . . .	Reeh . . .
. . . the road to . . .	. . . aghares s . . .	(literally, "I want")	
. . . the village . . .	. . . doowar . . .	**On survey maps you'll find these names:**	
. . . the river . . .	. . . aseet . . .	Mountain	Adrar, Jbel
. . . the mountain . . .	. . . adrar . . .	River	Assif, Oued
. . . the pass . . .	. . . tizee . . .	Pass (of)	Tizi (n.)
. . . your house	. . . teegimeenik	Shepherd's hut	Azib
Is it far/close?	Ees yagoog/eeqareb?	Hill, small mountain	Aourir
Straight	Neeshan	Ravine	Talat
To the right/left	Fofaseenik/fozelmad	Rock	Azrou
Where are you going?	Manee treet? (s.)	("n" between words indicates the	
	Manee drem? (pl.)	possessive, "of")	

Buying and Numbers

1	yen	21	Ashreent d yen d mrawet	A lot/little	Bzef/eemeek
2	seen	22	Ashreent d seen d mrawet	Do you have . . . ?	Ees daroon . . . ?
3	krad	30	Ashreent d mrawet	Is there . . . ?	Ees eela . . . ?
4	koz	40	Snet id ashreent	. . . food	. . . teeremt
5	smoos	50	Snet id ashreent d mrawet	. . . a mule	. . . aserdon
6	sddes	100	Smoost id ashreent/meeya	. . . a place to sleep	. . . kra lblast
7	sa				mahengwen
8	tem	How much is it?	Minshk aysker?	. . . water	. . . amen
9	tza	No good	oor eefulkee		
10	mrawet	Too expensive	Eeghula bzef	**Imperatives you may hear**	
11	yen d mrawet	Come down a	Nuqs emeek	Sit	Gawer, Skoos
12	seen d mrawet	little (in price)		Drink	Soo
20	Ashreent	Give me . . .	Feeyee . . .	Eat	Shta
		I want . . .	Reeh . . .	Here	Omz
		Big/Small	Mqorn/Eemzee	(when handing something to someone)	

FRENCH ESSENTIALS

Basics and Greetings

Yes/no	Oui/non	Could you?	Pourriez-vous?
Hello, good day	Bonjour	Why?	Pourquoi?
Sorry, excuse me	Pardon	What?	Quoi?
How are you?	Ça va?	Open	Ouvert
Goodbye	Au revoir	Closed	Fermé
Please	S'il vous plaît	Go away!	Va-t-en
Thank you	Merci	Stop messing me about!	Arrête de m'emmerder!
I/you	Je/tu	No confidence!	Pas de confiance!

Directions

Where is the road for . . . ?	Quelle est la route pour . . . ?	Far	Loin
Where is . . . ?	Où est . . . ?	When?	Quand?
Do you have . . . ?	Avez vous . . . ?	At what time?	A quelle heure?
. . . a room?	. . . une chambre?	Write it down, please	Ecrivez-le, s'il vous plaît
Here, there	Ici, la	Now	Maintenant
Right	A droite	Later	Plus tard
Left	A gauche	Never	Jamais
Straight on	Tout droit	Today	Aujourd'hui
Near	Proche, près	Tomorrow	Demain
		Yesterday	Hier

Things

Bus	Car, autobus	Key	Clef
Bus station	Gare routière	Roof	Terrasse
Railway	Chemin de fer	Passport	Passeport
Airport	Aeroport	Exchange	Change
Railway station	Gare	Post office	Poste
Ferry	Ferry	Stamps	Timbres
Lorry	Camion	Left luggage	Consigne
Ticket (return)	Billet (de retour)	Visa	Visa
Bank	Banque	Money	Argent

Buying

How much/many?	Combien?	Like this/that	Comme ceci/cela
How much does that cost?	Combien ça coute?	What is it?	Qu'est-ce que c'est?
Too expensive	Trop cher	Enough	Assez
More/less	Plus/moin	Big	Grand
Cheap	Bon marché	Little	Petit

ARABIC NUMERALS

١	1	١٠	10	١٩	19	٨٠	80
٢	2	١١	11	٢٠	20	٩٠	90
٣	3	١٢	12	٢١	21	١٠٠	100
٤	4	١٣	13	٢٢	22	٢٠٠	200
٥	5	١٤	14	٣٠	30	٣٠٠	300
٦	6	١٥	15	٤٠	40	٤٠٠	400
٧	7	١٦	16	٥٠	50	١٠٠٠	1000
٨	8	١٧	17	٦٠	60		
٩	9	١٨	18	٧٠	70		

ARABIC/BERBER PHRASEBOOKS AND LEARNING MATERIALS

Arabic Phrasebooks

Lamzoudi, *Guide de Conversation* (Editions El-Atlassi, Casablanca). French–Moroccan Arabic. Not very functional, but the only widely available Moroccan Arabic phrasebook.

(There is no English–Moroccan Arabic phrasebook).

Arabic Coursebooks

Ernest T. Abdel Massih, *An Introduction to Moroccan Arabic* ($18; 3 accompanying tapes, $20); *Advanced Moroccan Arabic* ($15; 4 tapes $32). Both published by University of Michigan Press.

Richard S. Harris and Mohammed Abn Tald, *Basic Course in Moroccan Arabic* (Georgetown Univ. Press, 1980).

Berber Coursebooks

Ernest T. Abdel Massih, *A Course in Spoken Tamazightt: Berber Dialects of the Middle Atlas* ($15; 7 tapes $49); *A Reference Grammar of Tamazight, Plus An Introduction to the Berber Language* ($15). University of Michigan Press.

Arabic Lessons in Morocco

Contact the *American Language Centre* (head office: 1 Place de la Fraternité, Casablanca).

University of Michigan Publications.

For **books** write to The Publications Secretary, Centre for Near Eastern and North African Studies, 144 Lane Hall, University of Michigan, Ann Arbor, Michigan 48109. For **tapes** write to: Michigan Media Resource Centre (Tape Duplication Service), University of Michigan, 400 S. Fourth Street, Ann Arbor, Michigan 48103.

Bookshops

The following bookshops usually have language reference material:

Librairie des Colonnes, Bd. Pasteur, Tangier.

American Language Centre Bookstore, Bd. Moulay Youssef, Casablanca.

American Bookstore, Rue Tanja, Rabat.

Crown English Bookstore, Av. Sidi Mohammed, Agadir.

GLOSSARY OF MOROCCAN TERMS

ADHAN the call to prayer

AGADIR fortified granary

AGDAL garden or park containing a pool

AGUELMANE lake

AÏN spring

AÏT tribe (literally, "sons of"); also BENI

ALAOUITE ruling Moroccan dynasty from the seventeenth century to the present king, Hassan II

ALMOHAD the greatest of the medieval dynasties, ruled Morocco (and much of Spain) from ca.1147 until the rise to power of the Merenids ca.1224

ALMORAVIDS dynasty that preceded the Almohads, from ca. 1060 to ca. 1147

ANDALOUS Muslim Spain (a territory that centred on modern Andalucía)

ARABESQUE geometrical decoration or calligraphy

ASIF river that flows throughout the year

BAB gate

BABOUCHES slippers (usually yellow)

BALI (or **QDIM**) old

BARAKA sancity or blessing, obtained through saints or *marabouts*

BARBARY European term for North Africa in the sixteenth–nineteenth centuries

BENI tribe (as Aït)

BERBERS native inhabitants of Morocco, and still the majority of the population

BLED countryside, or, literally "land"; **BLED ES MAKHZEN** – governed lands; **BLED ES SIBA** – land outside government control

BORDJ fort

CAID district administrator; **CADI** is an Islamic judge

CHLEUH southern Berber from the High or Anti-Atlas or plains

COL mountain pass (French)

DAR house or palace; **DAR EL MAKHZEN**, royal palace

DAYA, DEYET lake

DJEBEL mountain; hence **DJEBALI**, someone from the mountains; the **DJEBALA** are the main tribe of the Western Rif

DJEDID, JDID new

DJELLABA wool or cotton hooded outer garment

DJEMAA, JAMAA mosque, or Friday (the main day of worship)

DJINN nature spirits (genies)

ERG sand dune

FAKIR, FKIH Koranic schoolteacher or lawyer, or just an educated man

FANTASIA display of horsemanship performed at larger festivals or *moussems*

FASSI inhabitant of Fes

FILALI alternative name for the Alaouite dynasty – from the southern Tafilalt region

FOKKARA underground irrigation canal

FONDOUK inn and storehouse, known as a *caravanserai* in the eastern part of the Arab world

GANDOURA man's cotton garment (male equivalent of a kaftan)

GHARB coastal plain between Larache and Kenitra

GNAOUA Moroccan black person, originally from Guinea; also a sect, or brotherhood, which plays drum-based trance music

HABBOUS religious foundation or bequest of property for religious charities

HADJ pilgrimage to Mecca

HAMMADA stony desert of the sub-Sahara

HAMMAM Turkish-style steam bath

HARKA "burning" raid undertaken by sultans in order to raise taxes and assert authority

IDRISSID first Arab dynasty of Morocco – named after its founder, Moulay Idriss

IMAM prayer leader and elder of mosque

ISTIQLAL nationalist party founded during the struggle for independence

JOUTIA flea market

KASBAH palace centre and/or fortress of an Arab town; also a feudal family castle in the south. Like the Spanish *alcazar*

KIF hashish, cannabis

KOUBBA dome; small *marabout* tomb

KSAR, KSOUR (pl.) village or tribal stronghold in the south

LALLA "madam"

LITHAM veil

MAGHREB "West" in Arabic, used for Morocco and the North African countries

MAKHZEN government

MARABOUT holy man, and by extension his place of burial. These tombs, usually white-washed domes, play an important (and unortho-dox) role in the religion of country Berber areas.

MECHOUAR assembly place, court of judgment

MEDINA literally, "city", now used for the original Arab part of any Moroccan town. The Kasbah is usually a quarter of the Medina.

MELLAH Jewish quarter

MEDERSA student residence and, in part, a teaching annexe, for the old mosque universities

MERENIDS dynasty from eastern plains who ruled from the thirteenth to fifteenth centuries

MIHRAB niche indicating the direction of Mecca (and for prayer)

MINARET tower attached to a mosque, used for call to prayer

MINZAH pavilion in a (usually palace) garden

MOULAY descendant of the Prophet Muhammad, a claim and title adopted by most Moroccan sultans

MOULOUD festival and birthday of the Prophet

MOUSSEM pilgrimage-festival

MSALLA prayer area

MUEZZIN, MUEDDIN singer who calls the faithful to prayer

NAZARENE, NSRANI Christian

OUED river; also **ASRIR**

PISÉ mud and rubble building material

PISTE rough road

PROTECTORATE period of French and Spanish colonial occupation (1912–56)

QAHOUAJI café patron

RAMADAN month of fasting

RAS source

RAS EL MA water source

RIBAT monastic fortress

SAADIAN southern dynasty from Drâa valley, who ruled Morocco during the fifteenth century

SEBGHA lake or lagoon

SEGUIA irrigation canal

SHEIKH leader of religious brotherhood

SHEREEF descendant of the Prophet

SIDI, SI respectful title used for any man, like "Sir" or "Mister"

SOUK market, or market quarter

SUFI religious mystic; philosophy behind most of the religious brotherhoods

TABIA mud building material, as *pisé*

TIGHREMT similar to an *agadir* – fortified Berber home and storage place

TOUAREG nomadic Berber tribesmen of the disputed Western Sahara, fancifully known as "Blue Men" because of the blue dye of their cloaks (which gives a slight tinge to their skin)

TIZI mountain pass; as COL in French

WATTASID fifteenth-century dynasty who replaced their cousins, the Merenids

ZAOUIA sanctuary established around a *marabout*'s tomb; seminary-type base for religious brotherhood

ZELLIJ geometrical mosaic tilework

INDEX

MAP INDEX

HELP US UPDATE

This third edition of *The Rough Guide to Morocco* has been extensively revised (and expanded) from its previous incarnations – but . . . facts are not the easiest available commodity in Morocco, hotels and restaurants open and close, standards rise and fall, roads get washed away, buses change their terminals, all with chaotic frequency.

If you find changes (or errors), places we've overrated or underpraised, things we've missed, or covered but which no longer exist, then please write and tell us. Letters about obscure routes through the mountains and desert are as interesting as the low-down on your favourite bar, hotel or restaurant. This edition owes an enormous debt to previous readers and users.

We'll acknowledge all information used in the next edition and will send a **free copy**, or any other *Rough Guide* if you prefer, for the most useful (and legible!) letters. Send them along to:

Mark Ellingham, Rough Guides, 149 Kennington Lane, London SE11 4EZ.

MEDITERRANEAN WILDLIFE

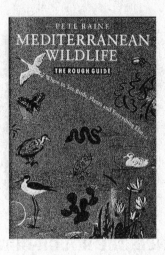

MEDITERRANEAN WILDLIFE: THE ROUGH GUIDE
is an essential companion for anyone interested in the
birds, plants and animals of the Med region. It features
country-by-country site guides – including chapters on
Morocco and Tunisia – along with practical details on how
to get to the sites and where to stay nearby. Introductory
sections provide a keynote guide to the species, while
"Contexts" pieces pull together some of the environmental
issues for the Med in the 1990s.

Written and researched by Pete Raine, with a team of
international wildlife contributors. Illustrated throughout
with line drawings by Tessa Lovat-Smith.

Published by Harrap Columbus, price £7.95.

WEST AFRICA

THE ROUGH GUIDE

ROUGH GUIDES' BIGGEST EVER PRODUCTION!

WEST AFRICA: THE ROUGH GUIDE is the result of three years' painstaking research: over 1000 pages of hard, practical information covering the trans-Saharan routes through Algeria and no less than seventeen West African nations.

Countries covered: Algeria (trans-Saharan routes); Niger; Mali; Mauritania; Senegal; The Gambia; Cape Verde Islands; Guinea-Bissau; Guinea; Sierra Leone; Liberia; Côte d'Ivoire; Burkina Faso; Ghana; Togo; Benin; Nigeria; Cameroon.

Written and researched by Richard Trillo and Jim Hudgens

Published by Harrap Columbus, price £9.95.

THE MOROCCO SPECIALISTS

• Fly/drive arrangements to Tangier, Casablanca, Fes, Marrakesh, Ouarzazate, Agadir and Laayoune. You can fly to one place and return from another. Cars arranged to fit in with your itinerary.

• Personalised itineraries using hotels from Tangier to Laayoune, Fes to Erfoud in hotels known to us ranging from 3-star to 5-star luxury choices.

• Sports and special interest. Golf – Tennis – Riding in the Atlas mountains – Shooting – Painting – Archaeology – Birdwatching – Walking – Special Garden tours with a chance to meet the people choosing to live in Morocco.

CLM
4a William Street
London SW1X 9HL
Tel: 071-235 2110

CLM consultants have lived for many years in Morocco and know the country intimately.

Please ask for our full colour brochure

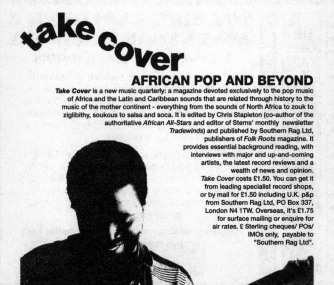

take cover

AFRICAN POP AND BEYOND

Take Cover is a new music quarterly: a magazine devoted exclusively to the pop music of Africa and the Latin and Caribbean sounds that are related through history to the music of the mother continent - everything from the sounds of North Africa to zouk to ziglibithy, soukous to salsa and soca. It is edited by Chris Stapleton (co-author of the authoritative *African All-Stars* and editor of Sterns' monthly newsletter *Tradewinds*) and published by Southern Rag Ltd, publishers of *Folk Roots* magazine. It provides essential background reading, with interviews with major and up-and-coming artists, the latest record reviews and a wealth of news and opinion.
Take Cover costs £1.50. You can get it from leading specialist record shops, or by mail for £1.50 including U.K. p&p from Southern Rag Ltd, PO Box 337, London N4 1TW. Overseas, it's £1.75 for surface mailing or enquire for air rates. £ Sterling cheques/ POs/ IMOs only, payable to "Southern Rag Ltd".

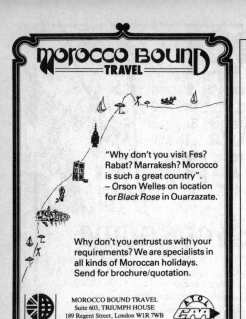